this major 'state of the art' survey, a highly distinguished team of contributors dresses the complex and crucial role of finance in European history during the riod 1880–1960. Throughout the volume a comparative, global perspective is d in the analysis of a problem that may in fact be perceived at four levels. rstly, the economic: what was the weight of the financial sector in a given economy? Secondly, the social: what was the specific position of the financial elites in society? Thirdly, the political: what was the impact of financial interests in politics? And finally, the international: the establishment and gradual erosion of Europe's position as the 'world's banker'.

Six European countries (the UK, France, Germany, Belgium, Sweden and Switzerland) are singled out for particular attention, and the rise of extra-European centres of financial power (notably USA and Japan) considered in an extended concluding section. Both subjects and authors are truly international, and *Finance and financiers in European history* will make a substantial contribution to an area of economic activity that is returning forcefully to the historical agenda.

This book is published as part of the joint publishing agreement established in 1977 between the Fondation de la Maison des Sciences de l'Homme and the Press Syndicate of the University of Cambridge. Titles published under this arrangement may appear in any European language or, in the case of volumes of collected essays, in several languages.

New books will appear either as individual titles or in one of the series which the Maison des Sciences de l'Homme and the Cambridge University Press have jointly agreed to publish. All books published jointly by the Maison des Sciences de l'Homme and the Cambridge University Press will be distributed by the Press throughout the world.

Cet ouvrage est publié dans le cadre de l'accord de co-édition passé en 1977 entre la Fondation de la Maison des Sciences de l'Homme et le Press Syndicate de l'Université de Cambridge. Toutes les langues européennes sont admises pour les titres couverts par cet accord, et les ouvrages collectifs peuvent paraître en plusieurs langues.

Les ouvrages paraissent soit isolément, soit dans l'une des séries que la Maison des Sciences d l'Homme et Cambridge University Press ont convenu de publier ensemble. La distribution dans le monde entier des titres ainsi publiés conjointement par les deux établissements est assurée par Cambridge University Press.

FINANCE AND FINANCIERS IN EUROPEAN HISTORY, 1880–1960

edited by
YOUSSEF CASSIS
Department of History and Centre for European Law Studies, University of Geneva

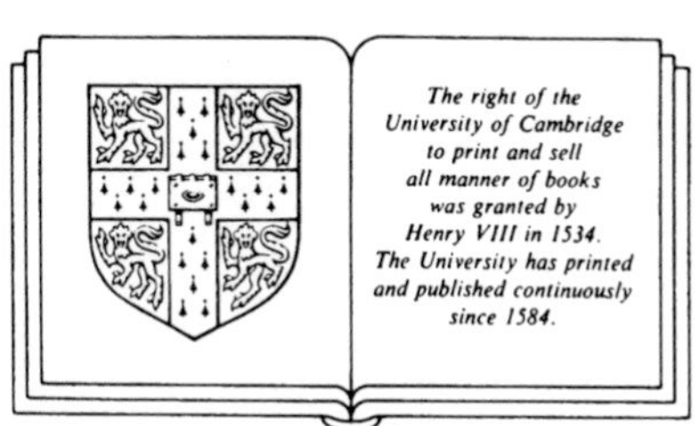

CAMBRIDGE UNIVERSITY PRESS
Cambridge
New York   Port Chester
Melbourne   Sydney
EDITIONS DE
LA MAISON DES SCIENCES DE L'HOMME
Paris

PUBLISHED BY THE PRESS SYNDICATE OF THE UNIVERSITY OF CAMBRIDGE
The Pitt Building, Trumpington Street, Cambridge, United Kingdom
and Editions de la Maison des Sciences de l'Homme
54 Boulevard Raspail, 75270 Paris Cedex 06

CAMBRIDGE UNIVERSITY PRESS
The Edinburgh Building, Cambridge CB2 2RU, UK
40 West 20th Street, New York NY 10011–4211, USA
477 Williamstown Road, Port Melbourne, VIC 3207, Australia
Ruiz de Alarcón 13, 28014 Madrid, Spain
Dock House, The Waterfront, Cape Town 8001, South Africa

http://www.cambridge.org

First published 1992
First paperback edition 2002

A catalogue record for this book is available from the British Library

Library of Congress Cataloguing in Publication data
Finance and Financiers in European history 1880–1980 / edited by
Y. Cassis.
p. cm.
ISBN 0 521 40024 4
1. Banks and banking – Europe – History – 19th century. 2. Banks and banking – Europe – History – 20th century. 3. Capitalists and Financiers – Europe – History – 19th century. 4. Capitalists and Financiers – Europe – History – 20th century. 5. Finance – Europe – History – 19th century. 6. Finance – Europe – History – 20th century.
I. Cassis, Youssef.
HG2974.F56 1991
332'.094–dc20 90-19525 CIP

ISBN 0 521 40024 4 hardback
ISBN 2 7351 0403 6 hardback (France only)
ISBN 0 521 89373 9 paperback

CONTENTS

FIGURES

TABLES

PREFACE

This book is the result of a conference held in October 1989 in Geneva, Switzerland. The conference was entirely financed and administratively organized by the Centre d'Etudes Juridiques Européennes of the University of Geneva.

I should like to thank the Centre d'Etudes Juridiques Européennes, and in particular its director, Professor Gérard Hertig, not only for his generosity, but also for his open-mindedness. As indicated by its title, the Centre d'Etudes Juridiques Européennes is concerned primarily with Law studies; and although financial law is high on its agenda, this is far and away from financial history. It is I believe an extremely rare example of true interdisciplinary spirit to finance a conference on behalf of another – much poorer – discipline, which must be emphasized and, hopefully, followed. I should also like to thank Patricia Christen, secretary of the Centre, whose commitment and expertise smoothed away all difficulties in the running of the conference and the preparation of this volume.

Youssef Cassis

1 Introduction: the weight of finance in European societies

Y. CASSIS

The object of this book is to attempt an evaluation of the role of finance in European history from the late nineteenth to the mid twentieth century. It is innovative in the field of financial history by adopting simultaneously a global approach and a comparative approach.

By 'global approach' one means that European finance cannot be understood only at the economic level but should also be considered at the social and political levels as well as in the general context of international politics and economics. Thus this book analyses the position of the financial sector in the economies of six European countries by considering various indicators ranging from the share of the sector in the GNP or the workforce to its contribution to economic growth and the effects of state regulation. It then turns to the position of financial elites in society, discussing to what extent financial elites form a distinct business and social elite, an 'aristocratic bourgeoisie', enjoying a special social status. The weight of financial interests in the shaping of government policies, in particular economic policies, is also examined, which in turn requires paying attention to such themes as financial lobbying, the possible conflicts of interests between banking and industry, or the role of the central bank. But European finance cannot be considered independently from the rest of the world. Although the well-worked theme of finance and imperialism[1] is not directly addressed in this book the impact of the rise of extra-European financial centres is discussed, in the first place New York, but also the background to the rise of Tokyo and more recently such centres as Hongkong, Singapore, Bahrein or Sydney. The advantages of such a global, multiple approach are widely acknowledged. However, although it has been practised by individual scholars, it still remains rarely attempted, especially when more than one or two countries are involved.

As for the 'comparative' perspective it has produced important contributions which had added a great deal to our knowledge of the subject. One thinks in particular of the work of Rondo Cameron and his collaborators, published some twenty years ago,[2] to which Sidney Pollard and Dieter Ziegler come back in more detail in the following chapter.

Combining the global and the comparative perspectives is no easy task if one wants to avoid the trap of either treating each country globally but separately or limiting the comparison to a single level of analysis. It is not only a question of detecting the interactions and *correspondences* between the economic, social and political levels, but also the discrepancies, the differing rhythms of evolution for each level and for each country. The way suggested here in order to integrate the economic, social and political levels in a comparative perspective is through a broad measure of the weight of finance in the economies and societies concerned – a measure which can be taken at any of these levels. In one country, finance can weigh very heavily at the economic level but comparatively lightly at the social one. Different combinations could be found for other countries or change over time. An example of such a difference of appreciation is given in chapter 19 by Kathleen Burk about the concept of 'financial power': does it mean, in a strictly economic sense, abundance of private money, or should this concept be used only if these funds can be directed according to government policy?

An estimate of the weight of finance poses a series of problems. The objective is obviously not to quantify all the variables in order to obtain a statistical presentation of the weight of finance in each country. There has been some important quantitative comparative analysis of the development of banking and finance, in particular the work of Raymond Goldsmith on the relationship between the growth of financial intermediation and the modernization of the economy.[3] Some of the data considered here are quantitative, but some others are highly qualitative and lend themselves with difficulty to any positive evaluation. The more so as some of these qualitative data are often part of controversial historical debates: for example the City and the performance of the British economy,[4] the role of the banks in German industrialization,[5] the feudalization of the German bourgeoisie[6] or France's economic backwardness.[7] Any global evaluation and comparison will therefore have to remain tentative and provisional. A qualitative approach, despite its limitations, appears especially desirable when comparing countries of broadly similar social structure and degree of development.

A certain number of criteria can nevertheless be defined in order to estimate the weight of finance. Nine criteria have been retained here: four at the economic level, two at the social level and three at the political level.

Financial institutions

A first possible measure of the weight of finance is given by the size of the largest financial institutions, in comparison, for example, with the size of the largest industrial concerns. In chapter 5, Richard Tilly points out that the three largest German companies in 1913, by capital, were banks, and banks made up seventeen of the top twenty-five. This phenomenon can be observed in most European countries. In France, the three largest companies in 1913 were also banks, and the gap separating them from the largest industrial companies was wider than in Germany.[8] The largest companies were also banks in Belgium and Switzerland. The reverse was true for Britain, and this could seem surprising in view of the predominant position of British finance in the world economy. But the British banks worked with a much smaller capital than their continental counterparts; if measured by total assets, the English, French and German largest banks were roughly of the same size at the eve of the First World War. In addition, it would be misleading to compare only banks, as Britain had a much more developed capital market than France and Germany. The situation changed in the interwar period. Banks were outdistanced by industrial companies in Germany whereas the gap narrowed in both France and Britain, meaning as far as the banks' position was concerned a relative weakening in France and a relative strengthening in Britain. Despite these differences, Harold James interestingly points out in his comments on part I that in all European countries the long-term development of the great banks was interrupted in the 1930s.

Economic share

Another quantitative estimate of the economic weight of finance can be attempted through its share of the working population and of the national income. Data are not readily available on these items, particularly for the earlier periods. On the basis of the chapters by Cottrell, Gueslin and Cassis and Tanner, some indicative comparisons can be made between Britain, France and Switzerland in the interwar years. In 1931, 2.2 per cent of the working population in Britain was employed in the financial sector, as against 1.5 in Switzerland and 0.8 in France. It should be pointed out that in both Britain and Switzerland the figures include insurance and other financial services. In Switzerland, this percentage was roughly equal to that of the workforce employed in the chemical industry, whereas in Britain it was larger than a number of industrial branches, including textiles, iron and steel and chemicals. Finance also contributed more to the GDP in Britain than in a country which must have topped the

European league, Switzerland; it was 5.6 per cent for Britain in 1931 as against 3.3 per cent for Switzerland in 1929, and again 5.6 per cent for Britain in 1938 as against 2.3 per cent for Switzerland in 1939. The two indicators, size of the financial institutions and share of workforce and national income, therefore do not necessarily move in the same direction. In some countries, banks as companies could be of paramount importance, for example Germany before 1914, whereas in other countries, such as Britain, the size of the sector as a whole is a more determinant factor. The answer to the question as to which of the two indicators has more weight must be found in the role played by the financial sector in economic development.

Economic influence

An estimate of the weight of finance in terms of economic influence can only be made in a qualitative way. Economic influence refers here to the role played by finance at the micro- and macro-economic levels. At the micro-economic level, it is the extent to which financial institutions can exert a control over other companies or influence their policy, either through an interest held in these companies or through other forms of representation. At the macro-economic level, it is the question of the contribution of banks to economic development.

The general trend which emerges in the cases of larger European countries is an emphasis on the limits of banking influence. Distinctions should of course be made between the pre-war and post-war periods, which has already been underlined in connection with the growth of the financial institutions. French, and especially German banks, lost ground after the First World War as shown by André Gueslin and Gerald Feldman respectively in chapters 4 and 13. However, even for Imperial Germany, Richard Tilly stresses the persistence of the role of the private banks and of the publicly owned banks, such as the savings banks, as well as the crucial role played by self-financing in the supply of funds to German industry. Philip Cottrell points out the separation between domestic banking and the City of London until the 1920s. André Gueslin underlines the slow growth of banking deposits in France even before 1913, and the fact that the flow of savings went mostly outside banking. In the smaller countries, by contrast, there appears to be a greater degree of banking intervention from the 1880s on. For Switzerland, Cassis and Tanner suggest that the real level of banking concentration in the 1930s and 1940s might be underestimated in the official figures and notice the wide network of influence exercised by the big banks during that period. Ginette Kurgan points out the increased number of universal banks and finance companies in Belgium, which reveals closer links between banks and industry, as well as the dominance of the banking sector by the Société Générale. Larsson and Lindgren reveal the devices used by the Swedish commercial banks to circumvent the law forbidding them to own shares of industrial companies. This general trend appears to be dominant despite the set-back of the 1930s.

It remains difficult to ascertain whether these diverging trends are the result of the emphasis put by the authors or whether they reflect a significant difference in the degree of economic influence. It is not inconceivable that banks had a greater influence in the economies of the smaller European countries, if only because of their relative size. The most striking case is that of the Société Générale de Belgique, which became in 1930 the largest bank in Europe, including the British banks. The recent literature on the relationships between banks and industry in Germany tends to underline the independence of the large industrial concerns, not only as a result of the war and inflation, but in fact since the beginning of the twentieth century.[9] Were these industrial firms more independent of the banks than their Belgian, Swiss or Swedish counterparts? Or have the debates and resulting investigations gone further in Germany and therefore produced more balanced views? The answer depends on further research being undertaken about the poor relatives of comparative analysis: the smaller European countries.

As to the role of banking in economic development, the generally accepted view is that banks played a more positive role in Germany than in Britain and France from the 1880s on, that is with the emergence of the 'new' industries of the second industrial revolution. This view is in all probability correct, and in his comparative remarks on Britain and Germany, Richard Tilly attributes the greater flexibility shown by the German capital market concerning the issue of equity capital as well as the greater efficiency of the German portfolio investment to the differences in the relationships between banks and industry, in particular the better access to information by banks and shareholders.[10] However, although the amalgamation movement which gathered pace in England in the late nineteenth century resulted in a limitation of the banks' commitment to industry, one should not forget the change which occurred in the 1920s; the British banks became more involved in industrial finance[11] at a time when many German industrial companies were able to emancipate themselves from the banks.[12] In France, the disengagement of the big banks from industrial finance from the 1880s was compensated by the activities of the larger regional banks which were particularly close to their industrial customers in the economically most dynamic regions: the north and the east.[13]

This raises the question of the adaptability of a banking system to a particular stage of economic development. Was the English banking system well suited for the financial needs of the first industrial revolution but much less so for the greater requirements of the second one, to which the German banking system responded more adequately? Looking back at the role of the banks in earlier stages of industrialization, Pollard and Ziegler make an important methodological as well as theoretical point regarding comparative analysis. Rather than comparing the banking systems of a number of countries, each at their own stage of industrialization, account should be taken of the stage of the world economy in which each take-off took place, which required that the industrializing country set up a banking system different from that of its predecessor, and in turn that the predecessor adapted its system to new demands. Another important factor in the role of banking in industrial development is the stability of the banking system, and this forms another part of the weight of finance. The English banking system is usually considered as superior to the German one in that respect, although some authors would argue that the German system was in no way unstable before 1914.[14] However, the banking crisis of 1931 provoked a change in opinion concerning the respective merits of the British and German systems.

International finance

Part of the weight of the financial sector in the economy is also made up of international financial activities. A first measure of this weight can be taken through the position of a country in world finance. One indicator of this position is the export of capital. As is well known, and despite some controversies surrounding the estimate of capital exported,[15] Britain was by far the largest exporter of capital before 1914, followed by France, Germany and the United States.[16] On a per capita basis, however, some authors have argued that Switzerland was ahead of Britain in 1913, with smaller European countries such as Belgium and Holland not very far behind.[17] The situation again changed in the interwar period, with the United States challenging Britain, France falling far behind the two Anglo-Saxon countries and Germany becoming a debtor nation. The smaller European countries, however, maintained their position at the top of the league.[18] Another indicator is the presence in the country of a major financial centre. This approach in terms of a hierarchy of financial centres is very finely used by Geoffrey Jones to analyse the rise of such centres in Asia, the Middle East and Australia, although it is not done systematically in the papers covering the European countries. Here again, London has maintained an almost uninterrupted supremacy for over a century, while Paris and Berlin remained major centres, Berlin being however replaced by Frankfurt after the Second World War.[19] Despite its role in international finance, Switzerland did not produce a centre of major international significance before the 1960s, contrary to Belgium and Holland. Another point to be noticed is that, apart from New York, whose rise and growing competition with London is analysed in chapter 19 by Kathleen Burk, and the very recent rise of Tokyo, the emergence of extra-European financial centres hardly affected the position of the leading European centres. However, as Mira Wilkins makes clear in her comments on part V, whatever the role of European financial centres, Britain's – and more particularly London's – pre-eminence appears overwhelming.

From our perspective on the weight of finance, the position in world finance must be considered in terms of its effects, positive or negative, on the domestic economy. A strong international position can add to the weight of finance by its contribution to the balance of payments or by leading to the growth of the financial institutions. But capital exports have also been considered to be harmful to the domestic economy, while the requirements of a leading position to international finance might run contrary to those of domestic trade and industry. These contradictions were most acute in Britain, and to a certain extent also in Switzerland, after the First World War. In France, on the contrary, despite the occasional politically driven attempts to see Paris supplant London as the leading European financial centre, these contradictions did not exist, probably because France was not prepared, or was not in a position, to support all the effects of holding such a position.[20]

Is there any correspondence between economic power and social status? Before considering this question, it is necessary to start with a definition of the financial elite. Where should the line be drawn between elite and non-elite? If only the directors and senior managers of the major joint-stock banks and the partners of the most influential private banks are to be considered, then we are dealing with a very limited number of people, in particular in the smaller European countries: in Switzerland, three or four joint-stock banks and half-a-dozen private banks; in Belgium, it seems that the financial elite consisted, besides a few private bankers, of the directors of the Société Générale. Even in the larger countries, the financial elite is much less numerous than the industrial one. The financial elite could also be described as a wealth elite, see Dolores Augustine on Germany in chapter 9; this criterion also results in having a narrowly defined elite, with a strong representation of private bankers. Martin Daunton proposes in chapter 7 a wider definition of the British financial elite, including segments of the City of London which have hardly been investigated so far, such as members of the London Stock Exchange and of Lloyd's of London as well as commodity brokers and other types of brokers and merchants. Considering that many of these activities were much less developed in other financial centres, this would mean that the financial elite was significantly more numerous in England than in the other European countries. Although this could seem normal given the position of London as the financial centre of the world for much of the period under review, one should not neglect the fact that many of these activities were performed by salaried executives in continental Europe. It appears therefore necessary to establish a hierarchy within this wider financial elite and isolate a financial aristocracy from the rest.

Professional status

A first measure of the weight of finance at the socio-professional level can be taken by considering the professional status of partners in private banks, and of directors and managers of joint-stock banks, which could be compared with the status given to similar positions in other professions. Until 1914, the emergence of giant financial institutions did not fundamentally alter the internal hierarchy of the banking world. In all the countries considered, the financial elite remained dominated by the private bankers, although to varying degrees. Political and social *notables* formed a significant proportion of the financial elite in the continental countries; in Germany, executives of the joint-stock banks were more prominent than in the other countries, especially Britain.[21] The notion of a distinctive financial elite becomes more problematic with the decline of the private banks. Could the characteristics of the private bankers, as described for example by Walter Bagehot in the case of the London private bankers,[22] still be found in the senior executives of the joint-stock banks and therefore justify setting them apart from the rest of the business community? With the exception of England, where the City has retained up to this day a higher social status than industry, this does not seem to be the case.

Social status

The strong influence of the banks in the German economy does not seem to be reflected in the position of bankers in German society. Conversely in Britain, where banks were less involved in the domestic economy, bankers enjoyed a higher social status and were more fully integrated into the upper classes. Dolores Augustine states that 'the image of bankers as the highest-status group within the business class is an optical illusion' and Harold James, while conceding in chapter 14 that the Berlin bankers formed a *Geldaristokratie*, also quotes a British commentator noticing that 'in the generation immediately preceding the war...leaders of outstanding ability were more often found in the ranks of industrialists than in those of bankers'. For the pre-1914 period, it is difficult to evaluate whether bankers enjoyed a lower social status than industrialists in Germany or whether the business elite as a whole, while being internally tightly knit, was less integrated into the upper classes than in Britain. The social status of the business elite improved in post-war Germany, but as Gerald Feldman clearly shows in chapter 13, bankers were distinctly dominated by industrialists. For the smaller countries, Switzerland, Belgium and Sweden, it is difficult at this stage to compare the social status of bankers with that of other socio-professional groups. Bankers appear to have belonged to the upper echelons of the social hierarchy together with other members of the business elite, but not to have weighed more heavily than in other groups. France was somewhat closer to Britain. The notion of 'Haute banque' and of 'aristocratie bourgeoise' after all originated in France where, as Alain Plessis shows in chapter 8, the financial elite retained a special and distinguished status. But Alain Plessis also shows that part of the French society felt for a long time a hostility to bankers, which was however more widespread among the lower-middle and rural classes than among the upper classes where bankers were fully integrated. Among the reasons for the similarities between Britain and France is the fact that London and Paris were older financial centres than Berlin, and this favoured the formation of dynasties of national, indeed international stature.

Political connections

Personal connections form an integral part of the political weight of finance. Individual bankers, or at least the most prominent of them, have always enjoyed a close relationship with political power, most often as advisers to politicians. This feature is common to all the countries considered and derives from the bankers' familiarity with technical financial matters. This 'knowledge' factor has been noticed by both Ewen Green in chapter 11 and Hubert Bonin in chapter 12, while Harold James in chapter 14 notes that bankers have a more global view of economic matters than industrialists. At this individual level, therefore, bankers enjoyed a closer relationship with political power than industrialists, although it was by no means exclusive. Although private bankers were able to retain a high degree of political influence, incommensurate with the size of their firms, senior officials of the joint-stock banks were increasingly consulted by governmental circles, even before 1914. This influence of the joint-stock banks was reinforced by the frequent tendency to invite senior civil servants and politicians to fill senior management positions, especially in France, but also in Germany and Belgium; less so in Britain and Switzerland.

Political pressure

Another common feature to all the countries considered is the lack of development of banking pressure groups compared with industrial ones. The case is made particularly clearly by Hubert Bonin about France and there are indications that the situation was similar elsewhere. Britain here appears to have been the exception. Its banking associations were founded earlier than, for example, those of Germany where the level of professional organization has always been very high. The Committee of the London Clearing Bankers went back to the early nineteenth century and the wider-reaching Central Association of Bankers was founded in 1895 as against 1901 for the Centralverband des deutschen Bank- und Bankiergewerbes.[23] In a country with relatively weak pressure groups the City of London was, as shown by Ewen Green, the most efficient and homogeneous lobbying group. Next was Switzerland, where the Bankers' Association (established in 1912) and banking interests generally were well organized, but they were apparently more strongly counterbalanced by industrial pressure groups than in Britain. Bankers had, therefore, other means of political intervention. One possible instrument in their hands was the central banks, although to varying degrees. Ewen Green and Hubert Bonin reach different conclusions in the cases of Britain and France. In the former case, the links between the Bank of England and the Treasury appear as a prime factor in the political influence of the City of London, whereas in the latter state power as well as internal cleavages seem to act as a check to the political influence of the Banque de France. In Switzerland the foundation of the National Bank in 1905 and the creation of a national currency undoubtedly suited the interests of the large banks; whereas in Belgium, as Ginette Kurgan interestingly points out, between 1918 and 1933, private bankers had an enormous influence and actually supplanted the National Bank in such issues as the negotiations over German reparations or the stabilization of the franc.

Political influence

Whatever their degree of organization, what kind of political influence were bankers able to exert? This can first be judged by their ability to defend their own interests, and a good comparative example is provided by their capacity to maintain their independence from state interference. British bankers were particularly successful in this respect as, until the nationalization of the Bank of England in 1946, the practice of self-regulation remained unimpaired. And, even after the nationalization of the Bank, the government's authority over the banking sector remained limited.[24] French bankers also enjoyed a similar absence of regulation until 1941, although state intervention in financial affairs had always been stronger than in England, as for example the Governor of the Banque de France was appointed by the state. In 1945–6, however, the position of the banking world, and of the business community in general was too weak to prevent the nationalization not only of the Banque de France but also of the commercial banks and insurance companies.[25] In the other countries, particularly in the 1930s, bankers had to face banking legislation. Swiss and Belgian bankers were rather successful in defending their position. In 1934 the Swiss banks managed to limit the control of the Banking Commission, and the introduction of banking secrecy was very much to their advantage.[26] The banking law of 1935 in Belgium increased state regulation but was inspired by bankers who managed to preserve their interest.[27] German bankers did not fare so well during the same period. In 1920–1, they were successful in their struggle against the establishment of an Economic Bank, thanks to the support of the Reichsbank and the Finance Ministry.[28] But after the banking crisis of 1931, they had to face hostility from the policy-makers; bank directors were massively purged and closer regulation and control of banking and accounting practices were introduced in 1931 and reinforced in 1934.[29] In Sweden, the operations of the commercial banks were subject to strong supervision from the late nineteenth century, culminating in the detailed regulations of the banking Acts of 1911 and 1934. However, as shown by Larsson and Lindgren, bankers were able to circumvent their main purpose.[30]

But to what extent beyond the defence of their own direct interests do the financial elite influence central political decisions with national or international repercussions? Such a capacity would obviously weigh very heavily on the side of the banking world. The answer to this question depends on two factors. Firstly, whether the financial world, in its relationship with the state power, constitutes the dominant partner. Secondly, whether financial interests are more capable than other economic interests of gaining effective political support. In the cases of France and Germany, where the historiographical tradition is mainly concerned with the first factor, both Hubert Bonin and Harold James conclude that the state ultimately held the dominant position. The discussion of the second factor is more common in English historiography and is developed by Ewen Green, who underlines the continued dominance of financial over industrial interests. The relative degree of political influence enjoyed by bankers and industrialists is less clear for France and Germany. Nevertheless, Gerald Feldman makes it clear that, in pre-war as in post-war Germany, industrial interests, and values, were dominant, and that bankers were prepared to follow the industrialist lead. In sum, it still appears that financial interests had more political weight in Britain than in the other European countries. Switzerland was probably the nearest case, and conflicts between financial and industrial interests occurred during the period under review.

As indicated at the beginning, the global and comparative approach proposed in this volume is not intended to produce statistical results or any classification of countries in terms of financial weight. A heavy weight of finance should not be seen as an objective to be reached, as it would not necessarily affect in a positive sense global economic and social developments. The controversial role of finance in British economic development bears witness to the fact, as does the recurring concern about the growth of financial services at the expense of the 'real economy' in the more developed countries. Nor can any ideal weight be determined. A weight can only be adequate to specific conditions, such as the financial history of a country, the development of its institutions, its place in the world economy, the role of the state, the position of its financial elites.

The combination of factors making up the weight of finance varied both from one country to another and over time. Among the various elements producing such combinations, two can be briefly outlined here: the position in international finance and the action of the state.

The weight of financial interests in British, and also in Swiss politics points to the importance of the international factor, as both countries, at different levels, were more fully integrated in the international financial system. The interaction between the economic, social and political levels is particularly visible when taking account of the international dimension. For example a dominant international financial position requires adjustments of the domestic banking system, as is best seen in pre-1914 Britain; whereas a change in the international position has effects on the performances of the banks, and in turn on the standing of the financial elite, as can be seen from the example of interwar Germany. The Anglo-American financial rivalry in the 1920s is a clear testimony to the value attached to a dominant international position, which both the banking and political authorities are prepared to defend even at a cost. The composition of the financial elite is also influenced by the international character of a financial centre because of the status derived from such a position and also in the sense that an international centre attracts foreigners who in turn help to renew this elite and add to the cosmopolitanism of the centre.

The interaction between the economic and political levels is immediate in the case of state intervention and regulation. For instance, the state can encourage banking involvement in industrial development, as in the case of the Prussian Seehandlung in the early nineteenth century;[31] or it can restrain the share of the banking sector, as in the case of France in the

1930s. The emergence and maintenance of international financial centres offer good examples of the role played by state regulation.[32] But the nature of state intervention and the type of relationships existing between the two partners can be influenced by the composition of the financial elites; they can be close to the political elite, as in Britain, or tend to form, together with the top politicians, civil servants and industrialists, a single elite group, as in the case of France in the last two or three decades.[33]

The notion of the weight of finance, and the analysis of its various determinants, should therefore serve as a tool for comparison whose objective is above all to separate the general from the specific.

Notes

1 Among the more recent publications on the subject, see P. J. Cain and A. G. Hopkins, 'Gentlemanly capitalism and British expansion overseas. I. The old colonial system, 1688–1850', *Economic History Review*, 2nd ser., 39, 4 (1986), 'II. New imperialism, 1850–1945', *Economic History Review*, 2nd ser., 40, 1 (1987), A. N. Porter and R. F. Holland (eds.), *Money, finance and empire, 1790–1960* (London, 1985); L. E. Davis and R. A. Huttenback, *Mammon and the pursuit of empire. The political economy of British imperialism 1860–1912* (Cambridge, 1987); J. Thobie, *La France impériale 1880–1914* (Paris, 1982); J. Bouvier and R. Girault, *L'impérialisme à la française, 1914–1960* (Paris, 1986); J. Marseille, *Empire colonial et capitalisme français. Histoire d'un divorce* (Paris, 1984).

2 R. Cameron, in collaboration with Olga Crisp, Hugh T. Patrick and Richard Tilly, *Banking in the early stages of industrialization: a study in comparative economic history* (New York, 1967); R. Cameron (ed.), *Banking and economic development* (New York, 1972).

3 R. W. Goldsmith, *Financial structure and development* (New Haven and London, 1969).

4 The literature is vast on the subject. See in particular P. L. Cottrell, *Industrial finance 1830–1914* (London, 1980), W. A. Thomas, *The finance of British industry, 1918–1976* (London, 1976), S. Pollard, 'Capital exports, 1870–1914: harmful or beneficial?', *Economic History Review*, 2nd ser., 38, 5 (1985), W. P. Kennedy, *Industrial structure, capital markets and the origins of the British economic decline* (Cambridge, 1987), G. Ingham, *Capitalism divided? The city and industry in British social development* (London, 1984). For a recent discussion of the problem, see Y. Cassis, 'British finance: success and controversy', in J. J. Van Helten and Y. Cassis (eds.), *Capitalism in a mature economy. Financial institutions, capital exports and British industry 1870–1939* (Aldershot, 1990).

5 See in particular J. Riesser, *The German great banks and their concentration* (Washington D.C., 1911), W. Feldenkirchen, 'The banks and the steel industry in the Ruhr, 1873–1914', *German yearbook on*

business history (1981), R. Rettig, *Das Investitions – und Finanzierungsverhalten deutscher Grossunternehmen 1880–1911* (Diss., Münster, 1978), R. Tilly, 'German banking, 1850–1914: development assistance to the strong', *Journal of European Economic History*, 15 (1986).

6 For a recent comparative discussion of the problem see J. Kocka (ed.), *Bürgertum im 19. Jarhhundert. Deutschland im europäischen Vergleich*, 3 volumes, Munich, 1989; see also H. Kaelble, 'Wie feudal waren die deutschen Unternehmer im Kaiserreich?', in R. Tilly (ed.), *Beiträge zur quantitativen vergleichenden Unternehmensgeschichte* (Stuttgart, 1985).

7 For a recent 'revisionist' discussion of the problem see P. Fridenson and A. Straus (eds.), *Le capitalisme français, 19e–20e siècle. Blocages et dynamismes d'une croissance* (Paris, 1987).

8 The nominal capital of the largest French bank, the Crédit Lyonnais, was Ł10 million in 1910, as against Ł2.4 million for the largest industrial company, Saint Gobain, whereas in Germany the Ł10 million nominal capital of the Deutsche Bank were almost matched by the Ł9 million of Krupp. In Britain, the capital of the largest industrial companies far exceeded that of the largest banks. With Ł17 million in 1907, Imperial Tobacco was by far the most highly capitalized industrial concern in Europe; with Ł3.85 million Lloyds Bank, the largest bank at that time, was far behind.

9 J. Kocka, 'Entrepreneurs and managers in German industrialization', in *Cambridge economic history of Europe*, vo. VII, part I (Cambridge, 1978).

10 Similar conclusions are reached by W. P. Kennedy, see his *Industrial structure* and 'Capital markets and industrial structure in the Victorian economy' in Van Helten and Cassis (eds.), *Capitalism in a mature economy*.

11 See S. Tolliday, *Business, banking and politics. The case of British Steel, 1918–1939* (Cambridge, Mass., 1987); D. Ross, 'The clearing banks and industry: new perspectives on the interwar years', in Van Helten and Cassis (eds.), *Capitalism in a mature economy* and D. Ross, forthcoming thesis on the subject; P. L. Cottrell, in this volume;

12 See Feldman and James in this volume.

13 See Gueslin in this volume.

14 For example Riesser, *German great banks*, pp. 555–9.

15 D. C. M. Platt, *Britain's investment overseas on the eve of the First World War* (London, 1986).

16 United Nations, *International capital movements during the interwar period* (New York, 1949).

17 P. Bairoch, 'L'économie suisse dans le contexte européen: 1913–1939', *Revue Suisse d'Histoire*, 34 (1984), pp. 479–82.

18 United Nations, *International capital movements*.

19 For a historical view of the hierarchy of financial centres, see H. C.

Reed, *The pre-eminence of international financial centers* (New York, 1981).

20 This was already one of the aims of the Péreire brothers in the 1850s. Attempts at displacing London are, however, mostly visible in 1931–2. Similar intentions lay behind the deregulation of the Paris financial market in the late 1980s.

21 On the prominent position of the private bankers in pre-1914 Europe, see J. Harris and P. Thane, 'British and European bankers 1880–1914: an aristocratic bourgeoisie?', in P. Thane, G. Crossick and R. Floud (eds.), *The power of the past. Essays for Eric Hobsbawm* (Cambridge, 1984).

22 W. Bagehot, *Lombard Street* (London, 1873), p. 270.

23 Y. Cassis, *Les banquiers de la City à l'époque Édouardienne, 1890–1914* (Geneva, 1984), pp. 327–30; W. Treue, 'Der Privatbankier an der Wende vom 19. zum 20. Jahrhundert', *Tradition*, 5 (1970), p. 231.

24 See Green in this volume.

25 See Bonin in this volume.

26 See Cassis and Tanner in this volume.

27 See Kurgan in this volume.

28 See Feldman in this volume.

29 See James in this volume.

30 See Larsson and Lindgren in this volume.

31 See Pollard and Ziegler in this volume.

32 See Jones in this volume.

33 See Plessis in this volume.

2 Banking and industrialization: Rondo Cameron twenty years on

SIDNEY POLLARD AND DIETER ZIEGLER

It is now just over twenty years since Rondo Cameron published, in 1967, his pioneering study on *Banking in the early stages of industrialization*[1] in which he set out to reassess the role of banking and of the financial intermediaries generally in the phase of the industrial revolution. The conclusion he reached was that their significance was greater than had up to then been allowed. A second volume of essays followed five years later.[2]

Not all financial intermediaries operating in the early stages could be properly called 'banks', but we shall, following Cameron's example, use this term as a shorthand for all the relevant institutions. We should emphasize also that we shall be concerned, as was he, with the early or breakthrough stages of industrialization, including what has come to be known as the 'take-off', which is a stage considerably earlier than is covered by most of the other chapters in this book. But we hope to be able to show that the discussion of the role of banking in the earlier phase has relevance to the wider discussion of the significance of banking in all phases of modern economic development.

In his introduction, Cameron described the stark contrast existing in the literature. There were those, 'the majority of economists who have dealt with this question', who assumed that financial intermediaries would appear as soon as they were needed – 'a case of demand creating its own supply'. At the other extreme, there were actual historical instances 'in which financial institutions constituted leading sectors in development: these institutions were "growth-inducing" through direct industrial promotion and finance'.[3] This might be called the 'strong' Cameron, and scarcely appears again in the two volumes. A rather weaker formulation describes financial service as a 'passive, permissive or facilitating agent' in contrast with the financial structure which 'affects the character and effectiveness of the (economic) system's functions': 'The way in which banks perform (their) functions in underdeveloped and developing economies may well determine the degree of success of the development effort', and 'the way the (banking) system is structured can either significantly hasten or retard development'.[4]

Most of the historical discussion in these volumes, as distinct from the programmatic introduction, does, in fact, operate within the weaker version of Cameron, the more or less gray rather than the black and white. There cannot be many historians, surely, who would maintain that the kind of financial structure which a country possessed made no difference at all to its rate of growth, or that, in particular, ill-considered intervention by government in monetary or financial matters could not retard potential development. But Cameron must have intended more than this, to grant banking a larger role in the comparative success or failure in a nation's path to industrialization than would commonly be allowed.

In the following, we shall begin with some theoretical considerations, and propose, instead of the criterion of a greater or lesser contribution of banking, measured quantitatively, an alternative approach, which stresses the different needs of individual countries for different types of banking and financial services. The next section will examine Cameron's leading example, Scotland compared with England, in the light of the research and writing in the past twenty years. Limitations of space forbid a similar re-examination of his other main comparison, Belgium and France. The following section will extend the debate to Ireland and Prussia, which failed to match the British industrialization in the phase to c. 1840, to be followed by a discussion of the role of the Prussian banking system in the mid nineteenth century. A concluding section will return to the issue of the different roles to be expected of a 'permissive' banking system, according to the needs and structure of the economy.

I

Our first problem is the very general one, of the use of history for the purpose of choosing between different theoretical approaches particularly as exemplified by the strong version of Cameron. Let us say that we found splendidly efficient banking systems together with successful industrialization, and inefficient banking systems together with lagging industrialization. This could not help us decide which theory is right: it might be that the successful economy had created its exceptionally useful banks, or that a good banking system had made a significant contribution to economic development. We have an association, but no indication of causality. However, if we found that there is no close correspondence between banks and economy, then both the old orthodoxy and Cameron would be wrong.

In practice, the issue is never so clear-cut. For most countries, a rather better banking system than the actual one might theoretically be conceivable, as might an inferior one, and the same goes for their growth rate. Detailed and specific research would be required to come to any plausible conclusion on causality, but precisely that was made impossible because of the limited space devoted to each country, and because of a similar grid of questions which had to be imposed on the authors.

A second problem concerns the way in which the contribution of the banks is measured in the Cameron volumes. The individual chapters show a common pattern. They indicate first, the provision of means of payment where metallic money was inadequate, and secondly, the provision of credit, short-, medium- and long-term, for industry and the necessary commerce and services. The money supply, together with 'bank' credit, provides the key. Although some qualitative issues are also discussed, such as the importance of the 'cash credit' system of the Scottish banks, the approach is quantitative, down to counting how many bank offices there are per thousand population. The more money and credit, the better apparently for growth and industrialization.

The trouble here is that 'there is no accepted and tried kit of concepts for measuring financial structure and thus distinguishing, clearly and quantitatively, changes in structure over time or differences in structure over countries or regions', quite apart from 'finding data for different dates and different countries that are sufficiently comprehensive, detailed and comparable to justify their application.'[5] Moreover, as Sydney Checkland noted in a lengthy, thoughtful review,[6] and as most contributors found in practice, the quantity of money and credit and their availability cannot be the sole criterion. There are others, and among the foremost of them must be the safety and stability of the system.

There are two types of stability that are relevant. The first is to be sought at the macro-level, namely stability of general prices and of the foreign exchanges. The latter would be guaranteed under a gold standard. This was stressed by some of Cameron's own contributors[7] and it would not be too much to say that in some of the later industrializing countries the need for stability, attained largely by introducing and keeping the gold standard, dominated financial policy.[8] In Britain, a stable currency had been achieved by the eighteenth century, largely thanks to a government which had learned to balance its books – very much in contrast to the French. This in turn, can be traced to a superior tax collection system, above all the excise which was 'administered by one of the most professional and efficient bureaucracies available to any Government in Europe'.[9] Coupled with a dependable debt servicing policy, this ensured an extraordinarily high credit rating for the British government, whose obligations gradually came to be treated as synonymous with absolute security. They became the foundation on which the British capital market, and particularly the London capital market, was built up: government paper was the 'basis...of the English money market...(It was) the basis of a pyramid of other loans within the business community',[10] state papers together with the shares of the Bank of England and of the East India Company being the most widespread means of long-term investment.

There is some debate on how far government borrowing in the numerous wars crowded out productive investment in the short-term. In the long run, it certainly stabilized interest rates and it reflected their tendency to fall during the century, while the Usury Laws, holding all other lending at 5 per cent may have provided some incentive for firms to plough back their surpluses into their own businesses.[11]

The other form of stability is that of banks and other institutions at the micro-level. The issue is of some importance for Cameron's own leading case study, in which the Scottish joint-stock banks are presented as being more stable than the typical English country bank. This will be discussed in the next section.

These considerations show that a mere quantitative comparison, of 'more or less', hardly does justice to the complexities of the role of banking in industrialization. There are several possible criteria, and they in turn, depend on the varying needs of economies at different stages of their industrialization, and occupying a different place in the sequence of European economic development. To this approach, pioneered some time ago by the late Jean Bouvier,[12] we return below.

II

One of Cameron's main examples, possibly his most significant, consists of the comparison of England and Scotland in the phase of the industrial revolution. England is said to have failed to create a financial structure equivalent to the Scots, and thus her economic growth stayed below the Scottish rate. Some of the details on which this view is based must be revised in the light of recent work.

One concerns the alleged inferiority of the credit per head provided in England. This is based on a traditional approach which may overlook some important sources. One was the attorneys, whose role in the provision of credit from the middle of the eighteenth century at least until the third decade of the nineteenth has been greatly underrated. In the two key industrialized areas, Lancashire and Yorkshire, the attorneys' role was, *inter alia*, to tap the private savings in their vicinity and transmit them to those seeking short-term and also long-term funds; being frequently quite rich, they would invest their own funds as well. What is important here is that, at a time when capital markets were still broken and localized, their intimate knowledge of the area and people allowed them to close gaps which otherwise would have remained unrecognized.

In this way they provided 'at least some capital for the region's "take-off" period after 1760';[13] but their contribution would not be included in the kind of overall statistics provided by Cameron.

Trade credit was a second major source of credit in the fast growing key industrial sectors. This was taken into account by Cameron, but probably its full significance was not recognized, nor could it be properly incorporated into the statistics. Thus Pat Hudson was able to show in her recent study on the West Riding the enormous contribution the credit supplied by the wool staples, among others, made in the eighteenth century, until the banks gradually took over these functions in the early years of the nineteenth.[14] Similar credit was also available in Lancashire.[15]

The provision of short-term accommodation by the English country banks, linked to their London correspondents mainly via the bill of exchange, to industry and commerce has always been acknowledged. The problem, it is sometimes alleged, lies in the failure of the system to provide long-term, investment credit. For that, industrialists had to rely on themselves and their families and friends.

We know that some long-term capital, particularly for mill buildings, could be raised on mortgage,[16] but much was also in fact supplied by the banks. It had long been recognized that rolling short-term credit, perpetually renewed, could be the equivalent of long-term capital, or could be used to free the firm's own resources for long-term investments, and loans not repaid could have the same effect. However, this contribution may have been underrated in the past. It was not only prominent enterprises like the Duke of Bridgewater's Canal, Matthew Boulton's Birmingham enterprise or Carron Company which could get, in effect, bankers' investment credit.[17] Since Cameron wrote, numerous other cases have come to light, with insurance companies as well as banks contributing,[18] to make aid of this kind less of an exception and more like a calculable possibility.

Lastly, the examples of bankers as industrialists themselves, either because they had begun as industrialists and had added a banking business, or because as bankers they had spread into industry, or had to take over a mill that had been transferred to them as security,[19] are more numerous than was once thought.

In view of this and other evidence, the notion that developments in the English industrial revolution were held up because of an actual overall shortage of capital can scarcely be upheld today. Seeing that only 10 per cent of British investment was absorbed by industry, Kindleberger thought it 'dubious that the industrial revolution (in Great Britain and Germany) had anything to do with capital markets at all'.[20] After all, iron masters and cotton spinners are widely known to have laid out their money on large estates, and the early railways were built with, apart from local resources, largely Lancashire capital where there must have been a lot to spare.[21] The real problem lay in the absence of a perfect capital market, in the fact that separate pools of capital did not necessarily find their way to where they were needed as M. M. Postan pointed out in a classic article many years ago. 'The overwhelming feature of the capital market in Yorkshire throughout the period 1750–1850', it has recently been confirmed, 'was its very local and highly personal nature'.[22] At the same time, Cameron's point that only the banks, and not any of the other named institutions, could create money, remains valid.

There is some recent research which has tended to support the Cameronian thesis of a less than optimal provision by the financial institutions in England. It is above all Stanley Chapman who thought that the Lancashire cotton industry between 1790 and 1850 'was serviced by a financial system whose members were characteristically inexperienced, insecure and unprepared to meet the unprecedented developments in industry and overseas markets', and in particular held back the growth of firms to optimum size after 1815: 'evidently', he judged, 'it was financial restraints, rather than modest aspirations, that set the limits to growth'.[23]

However, the detailed account on which this judgement is based is more differentiated. The largest firms, it appears, could get sufficient credit, even from London; only the smaller ones complained that they found it hard to raise capital – a not uncommon phenomenon. Up to c. 1815 profits were high enough in Lancashire to allow firms to grow by ploughing back their surpluses, and after c. 1828 there was an oversupply of joint-stock banking facilities in Manchester, as well as an expansion of the merchant banks, some with branches in Lancashire and Yorkshire, to finance overseas sales. Thus only the brief period in between may have been one of credit starvation.[24]

At the other extreme, there is a view which discounts the influence of banking on growth: 'The development of financial institutions was one of the later linkages generated by industrial expansion. The continued expansion of the cotton industry provided the motive power to sustain the development of joint-stock banking on a large scale.' In other words, 'the bankers were followers rather than leaders, reacting to changes in the economy rather than initiating them'. Much the same was said of Birmingham after 1765 where 'the establishment of professional banking... helped to increase the pace of development and demonstrates the vitality of local industry and trade without in itself initiating a new phase in industrial expansion'.[25]

Was Scotland better provided for than England? Did the banks there take the initiative and actually drive the economy forward noticeably faster than it would have gone with a different system, as we are told by Cameron?

The argument rests partly on the initial statement that Scotland had a higher growth rate than England in the period of industrialization. But since Scotland started from a much lower level, and since she possessed excellent resources of coal and iron, of fertile land, good harbour facilities and good educational foundations, it is not surprising that access to British and colonial markets and to British technology should have led to some catching up.[26] There is no need to look to banking for an explanation for this, especially since the Scots even by the end had a per capita income well below the English.

As for the banking, Cameron stressed the absence of the central bank's monopoly in Scotland and the prevalence of joint-stock banks, whether chartered or with unlimited liability, with more branches and more assets per head than their English counterparts. According to him, they were more able to help industry and commerce and did not share the 'pathological concern of the English banks for liquidity'. To this would have to be added the practical banking innovations, including the free issue of small denomination notes, the acceptance of small deposits and the payment of interest on deposits, all of which encouraged a larger proportion of the population to use the banking system, and the provision of 'cash credit' to customers. Checkland, against this, emphasized the similarities rather than the differences between the English and the Scottish systems, especially the countries' legal framework.[27]

Yet the Scottish banking system did not find unalloyed approbation even in its own country. 'Scotland was often short of capital...The country's banking system may have been a major cause of her economic growth but its resources were often strained and certainly contemporary Scotsmen were more aware of the system's deficiencies than of its advantage.' Though there was no legal monopoly of note issue as in England, the three chartered banks acted as a tight oligopoly. Too much of the banks' assets were in government stocks, businessmen could not count on getting credit freely, and many had to resort to mortgages, or to raising loans on their stocks. Since the public borrowed from the private banks, but these in turn got their funds from the chartered banks, the latter determined the quantity of credit, and the customer paid more. At least one observer thought that 'Scottish industry does not appear to have benefited from a greater degree of financial freedom than existed elsewhere'.[28]

Possibly the greatest benefit allegedly provided by the Scottish banking system was its stability. This was the major debating point in 1825, when some sixty English banks collapsed in the crisis as against only three minor ones in Scotland, and it lay at the core of the English demand for joint-stock banks in imitation of the Scots at that time. But the matter was not so simple. It must not be forgotten that it was precisely in Glasgow that the cotton firms in their rapid phase of expansion suffered from insecure credit conditions. Moreover, even in Scotland, one fifth of the provincial banking companies failed between 1747 and 1830. However, thanks to their better capital base and to the ability of the Edinburgh banks to act, in Munn's phrase, as the 'reserve of the system', the Scottish performance was substantially better than the English failure rate of one third.[29]

After 1830, when the English joint-stock banks had entered the scene, the stability of the Scottish banking system was no longer superior to that of the English. Apart from the fact that the English banks improved in terms of their micro-economic stability, the Scottish public banks were no longer able to perform their 'reserve' function. The alleged advantage of the Scottish system in not having a 'central bank' turned out to be a disadvantage. When any of the joint-stock banks, which were enormously large by contemporary standards, entered into a liquidity crisis, there was no institution in Scotland in a position to support them. The Union Bank survived the crisis of 1857 only because it had access to London, in particular the Bank of England as 'last resort' which rediscounted bills of an aggregate value of £2 million.[30]

The collapse of one of these giants, of the Western Bank in 1857 or of the City of Glasgow Bank in 1878, caused at least as much havoc as the bankruptcy of a whole host of English (private and joint-stock) country banks. Thus, just as in the case of the provision of means of payment and of credit, it is of limited value in an assessment of a banking system's relative stability simply to count the number of failed banks.

The most serious question mark against the thesis of Scottish banking superiority, however, derives from the fact that Scotland was not an independent country, and its economy not an independent economy. After the Scottish banks had set up a kind of exchange equalization fund in the third quarter of the eighteenth century to keep the exchanges with London stable,[31] and thus tied themselves to the London gold standard, they were the beneficiaries of the British monetary and fiscal stability. One cause of the generous credit facilities in Scotland lay in the low cash reserve kept by the Scottish bankers, in the knowledge that in times of trouble they could draw on London. Though not entitled to it, as were the Bank of England and the Bank of Ireland, the Scottish joint-stock banks followed the suspension of cash payments in 1797; of the Exchequer bills with which the government helped out the banks at the time, Scotland received one-fifth.[32] Thus, as in the case of Scottish economic progress in general, the causes of Scottish success are to be found at least as much south of the border as north of it.

III

An interesting parallel to the relationship Scotland–England (as also Belgium–France), in which the smaller northern partner registers the earlier onset of industrialization is furnished by Ireland (though the bulk of the country was altogether behind Great Britain). Here also it was the north, the Province of Ulster, and above all the city of Belfast, which industrialized first:

> The dramatic rise of Belfast as a major industrial city in the last century ran counter to the experience of Ireland as a whole.
>
> By the mid-century Belfast, with its mills, factories and expanding population, was clearly Ireland's only recognisable Victorian industrial city.[33]

Various causes for this success within the general industrial failure of Ireland have been proposed. They include religion, education, the agrarian system and the proximity to Scotland and to Lancashire. Against this, natural resources cannot be held responsible, since Ulster had none worth mentioning beyond those available to all Ireland, nor can the banking system.

Ireland in the eighteenth century had a fairly sophisticated banking structure, but it was centred, like almost all else, on Dublin, not Belfast, and it was geared to supporting commerce and the agrarian sector and not industry. An early banking venture, founded in 1786 to service the linen industry in Belfast, had collapsed, and by 1800 there was not a single bank in Belfast, though there were eleven in Ireland as a whole. The growing industrial activity led to the formation of three private banks in Ulster in 1808–9, and, by 1820, Ireland had a banking system 'broadly similar to what had emerged in England'[34] not least because the Bank of Ireland enjoyed a monopoly similar to that of the Bank of England. Its monopoly was whittled down at about the same pace as that of its London counterpart, and, by 1845, the system approximated that of Scotland. By then Ireland had nine joint-stock banks, no country banks and six private banks, beside the Bank of Ireland.

As for Belfast, the first joint-stock bank was opened there in 1824: the Northern Banking Co. with a nominal capital of £500,000. A branch of the Bank of Ireland followed in 1825, another joint-stock bank in 1826 and a third, combining earlier private banks, in 1827. The Ulster Bank followed in 1836.

Beside issuing notes, these banks accepted deposits, and provided credit by discounts, advances and cash credits as well as overdrafts. Prohibited by their statutes to engage in direct investment, they nevertheless managed to support railway building, among other activities, by a flexible interpretation of their functions as railways bankers. The banks, in other words, stood ready to support the process of Belfast's industrialization much by the same methods as in Great Britain. The banks were equally ready to provide credit also in those parts of Ireland where industrialization failed to take off. There was no problem in financing the Irish railway building, nor the needs of agriculture and commerce. 'Capital was readily forthcoming for the development of agricultural processing industries... and for the introduction of steam navigation in the Irish Sea.'[35]

These views are supported by modern Irish historiography. According to Cullen:

> Many contemporaries advocated the extension of banking on the grounds that banking services would promote economic development... In reality... Ireland did not suffer from a shortage of capital. There was, in fact, an abundance of capital... More was deposited in Irish banks than they could usefully lend.

And, to add Munn's judgement: 'The failure of Ireland to mature... was due to factors other than its banking system.'[36]

Only Joel Mokyr adds a note of disagreement. 'Many aspects of Ireland's stunted industrialization can be traced in one way or another to inadequate capital formation', he wrote. But then he qualified this:

> [this] does not mean that lack of capital *caused* the failure of Ireland to undergo an industrial revolution. It would be more accurate to say that the failure to accumulate capital and the industrial failure were by and large the same thing... capital accumulation was a mechanism through which deeper factors in the economy transmitted signals resulting either in successful industrialization or in late and slow industrialization.

There was, he admitted, no shortage of overhead capital for roads, canals or schools. Moreover, Ireland was not alone in lacking banks that would transfer long-term capital: 'almost nowhere did banks and similar organisations play a central role in the process of capital formation before 1850'.[37] This, too, is a long way from the Cameron thesis.

A second example of the limits of the growth inducing capacity of a banking system is furnished by the Prussian case in the second quarter of the nineteenth century. Contrary to Ireland, where a fairly well-developed banking system did not stimulate growth, the Prussian banking system was very much underdeveloped. The most important commercial centres in Germany such as Frankfurt/Main, Hamburg, Leipzig, Augsburg and Vienna, which had fairly large numbers of merchant banks, exchange banks and other types of private banks specializing in the financing of the various German states,[38] lay outside the Prussian border. The only place in Prussia with banks of more than local importance was Cologne and even there the first 'pure' banking concern appeared only in 1830.[39] The Berlin banks and the city's stock exchange were as yet of no importance.[40]

Banks in a position to finance industry, such as the country banks in England or the provincial banking companies in Scotland did not exist at all. From the 1820s, however, the Prussian government developed its formerly bankrupt state bank, the *Preußische Seehandlung*, into a sort of 'educational bank' for Prussian industrialists. If David Good's assumption is right that a 'moderately backward country' such as Prussia relied more heavily on qualitative support from the banking system (which lay somewhere in the 'entrepreneurial sphere') rather than on quantitative assistance (measured by an asset/GNP ratio),[41] the *Seehandlung* is an extremely good example. Already in 1794 its charter stated that the *Seehandlung* was 'permitted to undertake all sorts of commercial business without exception'.[42] After having overcome the disastrous effects of the Napoleonic War on the Prussian state finances, the *Seehandlung* began to act in this way: it granted credits (short-term and long-term), took part in the management of those enterprises which relied on the bank's injections of finance and finally it founded some new factories and took over others, many of which were nearly bankrupt. Although the intention of this policy lay in the direction of the Prussian eighteenth-century mercantilistic tradition in which the state acted as entrepreneur in order to become independent of imports,[43] the outcome was a strong modernizing effort. The bank was anxious to install the most modern machinery so that the factories could become models which could be inspected and copied by private industrialists.[44] In the early 1840s the *Seehandlung* was the largest single entrepreneur in Prussia, having an interest in the Prussian (mainly Silesian and Berlin region's) textile (flax and wool), grain milling, engineering and other industries.

Although the *Seehandlung* did not ignore the question of profitability, the enterprises in which it normally engaged either failed to become profitable at all, or only did so after the passage of years. This resulted in a serious lock-up of the bank's resources, so that it had to ask for Treasury and Prussian Bank loans in 1843 and 1848 respectively. Since this endangered its most important service for the government, i.e. the supply of short-term credit, and in the face of ever-increasing criticism from the liberal public, particularly from the Prussian industrialists and private bankers, the King ordered in 1845 that no new industrial establishments should be set up (or taken over) by the *Seehandlung*. A few years later it lost its relative independence and came under close Treasury supervision. Finally, its new (post-1848) liberal president began to liquidate its participations in order to avoid the threatening suspension of payments.[45]

Historians are still divided on the question whether to stress the modernizing efforts of the Prussian bureaucracy, including the actions of the *Seehandlung*,[46] or to emphasize the anti-liberal attitude of the *Seehandlung* in concert with the Royal Bank, which failed to make credit available to industry and commerce in general, but rather pumped its limited means into a few, partly inefficiently managed enterprises.[47] As far as this paper is concerned, there can be no doubt about the outcome. The

Seehandlung's idea of promoting industrial activities failed regardless of its intentions and/or the quality of its factory management, because the Prussian society as a whole was not as yet ripe for industrialization, so that the modern factories created by the *Seehandlung* remained isolated. Consequently, they could neither stand on their own feet nor provide the incentives hoped for to others. It is not without significance that the winding up of the 'educational bank' took place at the same time as the 'take-off' in Prussia began. Moreover, the industrialization was located in that part of the country (i.e. the western provinces) where the *Seehandlung* was almost never engaged.

Even after the industrialization process had begun, the Prussian case was a prototype of what Checkland called a banking system representing a 'state syndrome'. In contrast to the English and Scottish banking systems where the state merely attempted to control the 'great bursts of banking initiative',[48] the Prussian state, dominated as it was by a pre-modern, partly anti-industrialist class,[49] which had its own particular financial needs and a great concern for political and thus macro-economic stability, at first seriously hindered the development and adjustment of the banking system to the needs of an industrializing country. At the same time, the state had to intervene in order to sustain an essentially weak banking system by the creation of the Prussian Bank. This 'interaction of state and private initiative' (Checkland) turned out to be a success: the Prussian Bank developed relatively soon as a provider of means of payment and short-term credit as well as a transmitter of funds, thanks to its unique network of branches, and as 'lender of last resort'.[50]

The story of the development of Prussian banking to 1870 is well known[51] and need not to be repeated here. It developed in a direction totally different from the English and Scottish systems. By the mid nineteenth century the world economy had reached a new stage in its industrial development, which meant that newcomers had to supply financial services unknown to the pioneers. It is important to stress that it was not so much the stage of an individual country's industrialization that shaped the banking system but rather the stage of the world industrial economy. In the Prussian case, in which the railway formed the 'leading sector' of the economy and in which industry had a substantially more capital intensive structure than in the case of Britain in the eighteenth century, the banking system had to make more long-term finance available in order to become a 'permissive' factor. Under the given circumstances the Prussian 'mixed banking' turned out to be a necessary precondition for a successful adjustment of the banking system.

Yet in none of the three cases of successful industrialization, viz. England, Scotland and Prussia from about 1850, had the market simply called forth the banking it needed. In all of them, even in Scotland,[52] institutional factors had been important in shaping the banking system. These institutions had various objectives and motives for their intervention, often inconsistent with a policy of letting the market adjust banking to industrialization. And, even if the intention was positive to that aim, the outcome was not necessarily so. In the Prussian case, the early development of 'mixed banking' was not least due to state intervention designed specifically to achieve macro-economic stability, by the suppression of private note-issuing banks, such as were thought to have caused the crisis in England in the 1820s. The Prussian legislation was thus a more radical equivalent of the English banking reform Acts of 1826 and 1844. Contrary to England, however, where the circulation of metallic money was much higher and where the system was able to replace the suppressed banknote circulation by more advanced substitutes, Prussia was starved of means of payment. Culminating in the mid 1840s, the shortage of means of payment did in no way result in a greater stability. On the other hand, the suppression of note-issuing business forced many bankers to break new ground. Instead of adjusting their assets into the kind of structure of liabilities which prevented extensive long-term lending in Britain, they had to adjust their liabilities to fit the necessary asset structure, that is, they needed a large portion of proprietors' capital and reliable current account balances in order to engage in the remaining promising business of financing industry by short-term and long-term credits. Yet, despite their liability structure, these banks were still vulnerable to the effects of business recessions. The authorities, especially the new heads of Prussian Bank and *Seehandlung* after 1848, were well aware of these weaknesses, but, instead of teaching bankers 'sound banking' as the Bank of England had done by the mid nineteenth century,[53] the Prussian Bank emerged as a fairly effective 'lender of last resort' who was ready to make sacrifices in its earning capacity in order to preserve the stability of the banking system.[54]

The development of the 'mixed banking' structure in Prussia was thus neither the result of design by a far-sighted government nor created simply by market forces. Rather, it was the result of a mixture of chance, of unwitting government intervention and of the pressing demands of an expanding industrializing economy.

IV

A brief, cursory review of developments in a small number of countries cannot form an adequate basis of setting up generally valid theories. After all, Cameron used twelve countries and still we are not satisfied. But such a review, made on the basis of a great deal of recent work, may give us a few useful hints.

It was Cameron's great merit to bring the discussion of the role of banking in industrialization to the fore and to submit it to systematic consideration. As a result of his work, it became impossible to ignore that role and, having established that it existed, research could then turn to examine the question what that role was, and how to estimate it.

In retrospect, the quantitative tendency of the early Cameron studies, though necessary as an early stage to set some sort of perspective, has proved to be of limited value. The provision of means of payment and of credit can take many forms, not all of them easily encompassed in available statistical series. Nor is it always clear, against which turnover to measure the provision of credit; not all forms of economic activity are equally in need of money or credit.

A further merit of Cameron's work was the more critical attitude towards the actions of governments. Here, too, the context has turned out to be significant. At some time and in some places, positive action by government was required in some form; at others, the government did best which did least. It was not merely direct banking legislation, but also budget policy, the handling of state debts and state enterprises, and central bank policy, inasmuch as it was influenced by governments, which might turn out to be the elements which mattered.

Above all, the Cameronian concept of comparing banking systems of different countries during their individual 'early stages of industrialization' forgets that industrialization is a supra-national process. The 'take-off' periods of the national economies studied by Cameron and his colleagues took place at very different stages in the world's economic development. Their success, therefore, required very different preconditions, depending, beside the country's position in the world market, also on the development of the world economy. In turn, classifications of a banking system's 'permissiveness' demand definitions of what a banking system would be required to supply not only for each country but also for every stage of the world economy.

It is certainly true that the major financial requirements for industrialization are 'the accumulation of capital, the mobilization of capital and the efficient utilization of capital',[55] but no set of detailed rules can be drawn up without regard to the historical context. In theory, optimum efficiency in the use of capital is achieved when the banking system supplies smoothly all kinds of credit demands. In historical analysis, however, the requirements of a country for long-term capital in its 'take-off' phase, especially if it is endowed with much wealth in the hands of its entrepreneurs, cannot be compared with those of another, half a century later, and consequently forced to build up more capital-intensive industries, especially if it is much poorer to start with.[56]

Rather than comparing the 'take-offs' of different national economies, we might more usefully compare national economies at the same stage in the world's economic development. Thus a relevant comparison for the Prussian 'take-off' would be the English banking system of the railway age; a relevant comparison for the Italian 'take-off' would be the contemporaneous British or German banking systems during the so-called 'second industrial revolution'. We would then be aware that it is not only the latecomer who has to develop a permissive banking system, but that the industrialized national economies, too, have to adjust their banking systems to new demands.

In both cases, adjustment depends on very different factors, on available organizations and traditions, on the wealth of the country and on its industrial structure, and not least also on the actions of its government. It is the varieties of these adaptations, and the success with which they have been carried through, which offer the most hopeful topics for future research. The chapters presented in this book are certainly marked by an understanding of the value of this approach.

Notes

1 Rondo Cameron, *Banking in the early stages of industrialization* (New York, 1967).
2 Rondo Cameron (ed.), *Banking and economic development* (New York, 1972).
3 Cameron, *Early stages*, p. 1.
4 Cameron, *Early stages*, p. 1; Cameron, *Development*, pp. 8, 24. Also see his intervention in the debate after the paper by Jean Bouvier, 'Rapports entre systèmes bancaires et enterprises industrielles dans la croissance européenne au XIXe siècle', in Pierre Léon, François Crouzet, Richard Gascon (eds.), *L'industrialisation en Europe au XIXe siècle* (Paris, 1972), p. 138.
5 Raymond W. Goldsmith, *Financial structure and development* (New Haven, 1969), pp. x–xi. Also the contribution of R. M. Hartwell to the debate on Bouvier's paper cited in the preceding note, p. 139.
6 Sydney Checkland, 'Banking history and economic development: seven systems', *Scottish Journal of Political Economy*, 15 (1968), 146, 164–5.
7 E. G. Crisp, in *Early stages*, p. 236, Patrick, in *Early stages*, p. 253, Cohen, in *Development*, p. 84, Green, in *Development*, p. 201.
8 John R. Lampe, 'Varieties of unsuccessful industrialization: the Balkan states before 1914', *Journal of Economic History* (henceforth *J.Ec.H.*), 35 (1975), 74.
9 Patrick K. O'Brien, 'The political economy of British taxation, 1660–1815', *Economic History Review* (henceforth *Ec.H.R.*), 2nd ser., 41 (1988), 28. Also see Peter Mathias and Patrick O'Brien, 'Taxation in Britain and France, 1715–1810', *Journal of European Economic*

History (henceforth *J.E.Ec.H.*), 5 (1976), 601–50; P. M. G. Dickson, *The financial revolution in England: a study in the development of public credit 1688–1756* (London, 1967).

10 D. M. Joslin, 'London private bankers, 1720–1785', *Ec.H.R.*, 7 (1954–5), 185. Also A. H. John, 'Insurance investment and the London money market of the 18th century', *Economica*, 20 (1953), 138, 144–8.

11 Seymour Shapiro, *Capital in the cotton industry in the industrial revolution* (Ithaca, 1967), pp. 58, 65–7, 72, 147ff.; D. M. Joslin, 'London banker in wartime 1739–84', pp. 156–77, and L. S. Pressnell, 'The rate of interest in the eighteenth century', pp. 178–214, both in L. S. Pressnell (ed.), *Studies in the industrial revolution* (London, 1960).

12 Bouvier, as in note 4 above. The paper was also published in *Annales, E.S.C.*, 27 (1972), 46–70.

13 M. Miles, 'The money market in the early industrial revolution: the evidence from West Riding attorneys c. 1750–1800', *Business History* (henceforth *Bus.H.*), 23 (1981), 127; B. L. Anderson, 'The attorney and the early capital market in Lancashire', in François Crouzet (ed.), *Capital formation in the industrial revolution* (London, 1972), pp. 223–55; Pat Hudson, *The genesis of industrial capital. A study of the West Riding wool textile industry c. 1750–1850* (Cambridge, 1986), pp. 212f.

14 Hudson, *Genesis*. Also R. G. Wilson, *Gentlemen merchants. The merchant community in Leeds 1700–1830* (Manchester, 1972), pp. 154–7; and, more generally, Jacob M. Price, 'What did merchants do? Reflections on British overseas trade, 1660–1790', *J.Ec.H.*, 49 (1989), 278, 281.

15 Shapiro, *Capital*, pp. 15, 139–42; B. L. Anderson, 'Money and the structure of credit in the eighteenth century', *Bus. H.*, 12 (1970), 95–7.

16 Hudson, *Genesis*, pp. 76–7, 99; Peter Mathias, 'Capital, credit and enterprise in the industrial revolution', *J.E.Ec.H.*, 2 (1973), 125.

17 H. Malet, *The canal duke* (London, 1961); F. C. Mather, *After the canal duke* (Oxford, 1970); R. H. Campbell, 'The financing of Carron Company', *Bus. H.*, 1 (1958), 21–34, and his *Carron Company* (Edinburgh, 1961, pp. 124–31, 135–6; Joslin, 'Private bankers', p. 186; Eric Hopkins, 'Boulton before Watt: the earlier career reconsidered', *Midland history*, 9 (1984), 47; Sir Eric Roll, *An experiment in industrial organisation. Being a history of the firm of Boulton and Watt, 1775–1805* (London, 1968), p. 10.

18 Mathias, 'Capital', pp. 135–9; Hudson, *Genesis*, pp. 223–34; Hudson, 'The role of banks in the finance of the West Yorkshire wool textile industry, c. 1780–1850', *Business History Review*, 55 (1981), 379–402; P. L. Cottrell, *Industrial finance 1830–1914. The finance and organization of English manufacturing industry* (London, 1980), pp. 15, 19, 253; A. H. John, *The industrial development of South Wales, 1750–1850* (Cardiff, 1949), pp. 43–9; R. O. Roberts, 'The operations

of the Brecon old bank of Wilkins & Co. 1778–1890', *Bus.H.*, 1 (1958), 38, 43–7; Michael Atkinson and Colin Baber, *The growth and decline of the South Wales iron industry 1760–1880* (Cardiff, 1987), pp. 48–52.

19 W. F. Crick and J. E. Wadsworth, *A hundred years of joint-stock banking* (London, 1936), pp. 46–7ff.; McCord, *North east England*, pp. 59–60; Hudson, 'Role of banks'; Shapiro, *Capital*, p. 107; Cottell, *Finance*, pp. 14–5.

20 See the evidence cited by François Crouzet, Introduction to his *Capital formation*, pp. 37–43, 67–8; Quotation from C. P. Kindleberger, *A financial history of western Europe* (London, 1984), p. 193.

21 Shapiro, *Capital*, p. 151; E. L. Jones, 'Industrial capital and landed investment: the Arkwrights in Herefordshire, 1809–43', in E. L. Jones and G. E. Mingay, *Land, labour and population in the industrial revolution* (London, 1967), pp. 48–71.

22 M. M. Postan, 'Recent trends in the accumulation of capital', *Economic history review*, 6 (1935); Hudson, *Genesis*, p. 211; Pressnell, 'Rate of interest', p. 185; Mathias, 'Capital', p. 124; John G. Gurley and E. S. Shaw, 'Financial aspects of economic development', *American Economic Review*, 45 (1955), 515–38.

23 S. D. Chapman, 'Financial restraints on the growth of firms in the cotton industry, 1790–1850', *Ec.H.R.*, 32 (1979), 50, 65. Also see Joslin, 'Private bankers', 186.

24 Chapman, 'Financial restraints'.

25 Stuart Jones, 'The cotton industry and joint-stock banking in Manchester 1825–1850', *Bus.H.*, 20 (1978), 181–2; Eric Hopkins, *Birmingham: the first manufacturing town in the world 1760–1840* (London, 1989), p. 31.

26 Charles W. Munn, *The Scottish provincial banking companies 1747–1864* (Edinburgh, 1981), p. 230.

27 Checkland, 'Banking history', p. 154; Rondo Cameron, 'Banking and industrialization in Britain in the nineteenth century', in Anthony Slaven and Derek H. Aldcroft, (eds.), *Business, banking and urban history. Essays in honour of S. G. Checkland* (Edinburgh, 1982), pp. 102–11 and Cameron, *Early stages*, pp. 97–8.

28 Anderson, 'Attorney', p. 251; R. H. Campbell; *Scotland since 1707. The rise of an industrial society* (Oxford, 1971), esp. pp. 21, 72–3, 135–50.

29 C. H. Lee, 'Marketing organisation and policy in the cotton trade... 1795–1835', *Bus.H.*, 10 (1968), 91–4, 99; Munn, *Scottish*, p. 236.

30 Munn, *Scottish*, pp. 49, 87, 221; S. G. Checkland, *Scottish banking history, 1695–1973* (Glasgow, 1975), pp. 131, 407–9; Michael Collins, 'The business of banking: English bank balance sheets, 1840–80', *Bus.H.*, 26 (1984), 49; Norman McCord, *North east England. An*

economic and social history (London, 1979), pp. 60–3; N. Tamaki, *The life cycle of the Union Bank of Scotland 1830–1954* (Aberdeen, 1983), p. 71.

31 Maxwell Gaskin, *The Scottish banks. A modern survey* (London, 1965), p. 16; Checkland, 'Banking history', pp. 148–9 and Checkland, *Scottish banking*, p. 253; Munn, *Scottish*, pp. 29, 64; Campbell, *Scotland*, p. 139.

32 Checkland, *Scottish banking*, pp. 218, 233, 432; Munn, *Scottish*, p. 83; Edwin Cannan, *The paper pound of 1797–1821* (New York, 1968), pp. XVI, XX; Frank Whitson Fetter, *Development of British monetary orthodoxy 1797–1875* (Cambridge, Mass., 1965), p. 122.

33 Quotations from E. R. R. Green, 'Belfast entrepreneurship in the nineteenth century', in L. M. Cullen and P. Butel (eds.), *Négoce et industrie en France et Irlande aux XVIIIe et XIXe siècles* (Paris, 1980), p. 137; Gearóid O' Tuathaigh, *Ireland before the famine 1798–1848* (London, 1972), p. 127.

34 Charles W. Munn, 'The coming of joint-stock banking in Scotland and Ireland, c. 1820–1848', in T. Devine and David Dickson (eds.), *Ireland and Scotland 1600–1850* (Edinburgh, 1983), p. 205; also, in general, Philip Ollerenshaw, *Banking in nineteenth-century Ireland: the Belfast banks, 1825–1914* (Manchester, 1987); and Crick and Wadsworth, *Hundred years*, p. 351.

35 Peter M. Solar, 'Agricultural productivity and economic development in Ireland and Scotland in the early nineteenth century', in Devine and Dickson, *Ireland and Scotland*, pp. 81–2. Also Cormac O'Grada, *Ireland before and after the famine. Explorations in economic history, 1800–1925* (Manchester, 1988), pp. 27–9; J. Lee, 'Merchants and enterprise: the case of the early Irish railways 1830–1855', in Cullen and Butel (eds.), *Negoce*, pp. 148–58; L. M. Cullen and T. C. Smouth (eds.), *Comparative aspects of Scottish and Irish economic and social history 1600–1900* (Edinburgh, 1977), editors' Introduction.

36 L. M. Cullen, *An economic history of Ireland since 1660* (London, 1987), p. 129; Munn, 'Joint-stock banking', p. 215.

37 Joel Mokyr, *Why Ireland starved* (London, 1983), pp. 177, 181–2, 185.

38 H. Pohl, 'Das deutsche Bankwesen (1806–1848)', in *Deutsche Bankengeschichte* (vol. 2, Frankfurt/Main, 1982), pp. 22–42; H. Pohl, *Entstehung und Entwicklung des Universalbanksystems* (Frankfurt/Main, 1986), pp. 17–23; P. Schwartz, *Die Entwicklungstendenzen im deutschen Privatbankiergewerbe* (Strasbourg, 1915), pp. 12–23.

39 R. Tilly, *Financial institutions and industrialization in the Rhineland, 1815–1870* (Madison, 1966), p. 53; P. Coym, *Unternehmensfinanzierung im frühen 19. Jahrhundert – dargestellt am Beispiel der Rheinprovinz und Westfalen* (Diss. Hamburg, 1971), p. 80; K. van Eyll, 'Kölner Banken im 19. Jahrhundert und ihr Influß auf die Industrialisierung in der Rheinprovinz', *Mitteilungen der Industrie- und Handelskammer*

Köln (73), p. 252; K. van Eyll, 'Die Kölner Wirtschaft 1800–1870', in H. Kellenbenz (ed.), *Zwei Jahrtausende Kölner Wirtschaft* (vol. 2 Cologne, 1975), p. 232; W. Feldenkirchen, 'Kölner Banken und die Entwicklung des Ruhrgebiets', *Zeitschrift für Unternehmensgeschichte*, 27 (1982), p. 85.

40 H. Pohl, *Bankwesen*, pp. 19, 40; Schwartz, *Privatbankiergewerbe*, p. 18.

41 D. Good, 'Backwardness and the role of banking in the nineteenth century European industrialization', *J.Ec.H.*, 33 (1973), 850.

42 Quotation from H. Pohl, *Bankwesen*, p. 49.

43 W. Radtke, *Die Preußische Seehandlung zwischen Staat und Wirtschaft in der Frühphase der Industrialisierung* (Berlin, 1981), p. 87.

44 Examples are given in C. von Rother, *Die Verhältnisse des Königlichen Seehandlungsinstituts und dessen Geschäftsführung und industrielle Unternehmungen* (Berlin, 1845); W. Lexis, 'Seehandlung', *Handwörterbuch der Staatswissenschaften*, vol. 7 (3rd edn 1911), p. 407; Radtke, *Seehandlung*, pp. 129–244; K. Fuchs, 'Neue Beiträge zur Bedeutung der königlichen Seehandlung für die schlesische Spinnstoff- und Metallindustrie', *Tradition* (1966), 57–69; W. O. Henderson, *The state and the industrial revolution in Prussia 1740–1870* (London, 1967), pp. 131–8; I. Mieck, *Preußische Gewerbepolitik in Berlin 1806–1844* (Berlin, 1965), pp. 171–200.

45 H. von Poschinger, *Banwesen und Bankpolitik in Preußen*, vol. 2 (Berlin, 1878), pp. 58–60; H. Pohl, *Bankwesen*, p. 51; Radtke, *Seehandlung*, pp. 345–57; Fuchs, 'Beiträge', p. 68f.; O. Büsch, *Industrialisierung und Gewerbe im Raum Berlin/Brandenburg 1800–1850* (Berlin, 1971), pp. 30f.; Mieck, *Gewerbepolitik*, pp. 201–6.

46 Henderson, *State*, pp. 145–7, 190f.; Mieck praised the Prussian 'Gewerbeförderungspolitik', but was more critical about the Seehandlung. See Mieck, *Gewerbepolitik*, p. 206.

47 Tilly, *Rhineland*, pp. 14, 67; Radtke, *Seehandlung*, pp. 75, 81–3, 372f.

48 Checkland, 'Banking history', p. 154.

49 The most recent account of the 'dualism' in the Prussian pre-1848 political system is in H.-U. Wehler, *Deutsche Gesellschaftsgeschichte*, vol. 2 (Munich, 1987), pp. 145–61.

50 Twenty years ago Richard Tilly was rather critical of the Prussian Bank's role (see Tilly, in *Early stages*, pp. 167–9 and Tilly, *Rhineland*, pp. 36–42). In more recent articles, however, the Prussian Bank is seen in a more favourable light. See Tilly, 'German banking 1850–1914: development assistance for the strong', *J.E.Ec.H.*, 51 (1986), 122f. and 'Banking institutions in historical and comparative perspective: Germany, Great Britain and the United States in the nineteenth and early twentieth century', *Journal of Institutional and Theoretical Economics*, 145 (1989), 193f.

51 See Tilly's account in *Early stages*. There have been no substantially

new developments in German banking historiography in the 1970s and 1980s, and some major problems still remain open.

52 Checkland, 'Banking history', pp. 148–51.

53 Th. Hankey, *The principles of banking* (London, 1867), pp. 20f.; D. Ziegler, *Das Korsett der 'Alten Dame': Die Geschäftspolitik der Bank of England 1860–1913* (Diss. Florence, 1988), ch. 8, pp. 311–24.

54 In the crisis year of 1857, for example, the Bank sold investments worth 14m. Taler (out of a total of about 15.5m. Taler) bearing an aggregate loss of about 95,000 Taler. *Verwaltungsbericht der Preußischen Bank* von 1857, App. 'Bilanz' and 'Gewinnberechnung'; a more general account is given in C. Schauer, *Die Preußische Bank* (Halle, 1912), p. 97.

55 Cameron, *Early stages*, p. 292.

56 More recently, Cameron has stated that the English banking system 'facilitated growth' while the Scottish system 'promoted industrial growth ... by making advances on plant and equipment and other non-liquid securities' (Cameron, 'Banking', pp. 105f.). Munn saw a similarity between the Scottish system of the 'take-off' period and the German banks in the second half of the nineteenth century: C. W. Munn, 'Scottish provincial banking companies: an assessment', *Bus.H.*, 23 (1981), 28.

I FINANCIAL SECTOR AND ECONOMY

3 The domestic commercial banks and the City of London, 1870–1939[1]

P. L. COTTRELL

The 'City' is a useful synonym for the phrase: the British financial sector. Accordingly it is frequently employed, but inevitably with various shades of meaning, along the lines that 'words mean what I say that they mean ...'[2] This ambiguity has substantial implications because the growth of the financial sector has been characterized by both specialization of function and until the 1880s differentiated spatial development. As with the financial sector in its totality, the 'City' was (and still is) made up of many different parts – not only banking and finance, but also insurance, shipping and commodity markets. While spatially compact, these components were (and are) nonetheless functionally segmented, being integrated only to varying degrees. The result was the persistence of parallel markets both within the 'City' and beyond at regional and local levels. These gradually coalesced to varying and growing degrees; in the case of domestic commercial banking, initially through expensive correspondent and agency relationships between provincial and London banks.

In this chapter there is only space to review one particular point – when did domestic commercial banking become a full component of the 'City' and what were some of the effects of this combining? The point arises from functional specialization within the financial sector. This division of labour led to, for instance, the consequent absence in the UK, until relatively recently, of metropolitan-based 'universal banking', in marked contrast to its development from the 1850s in some European countries. Rather, within England, before the 1880s, there were almost two separate financial sectors, consisting on the one hand of the 'City', largely looking outwards to the rest of the world, reflecting Britain's dominant position in the global economy, and on the other country banking, a product of regional economic transformation. These two components came to be fused from the 1880s but that alloying took nearly four decades. This continuing division may have delayed full financial maturity of the economy until the opening decades of the twentieth century.

This chapter will proceed by first examining, albeit briefly, the timing of the internationalization of the 'City' and subsequent changes in its world role, before turning to glance at broad quantitative assessments regarding the size of the overall financial sector and the timing of its maturity. Thereafter it will entirely concentrate upon the institutional development of the English domestic commercial banks, reviewing when they made contact with the 'City' and contrasting their organizational structures with comparable banks in Scotland and Ireland. It then analyses the post-1880 amalgamation movement which did produce a centralized domestic banking system in England by the early 1920s. Lastly the implications of the attainment of financial maturity for industrial lending by the domestic commercial banks will be considered, together with an overview of their subsequent relationships with industry until 1939.

It is difficult to date precisely the emergence of London as a global financial market. The proto-'City' was a provider of international credit from the 1780s and, in peacetime, became a market for international capital from the 1820s. Nonetheless the provision of credit remained its dominant global function until the mid 1850s, as British capital exports were relatively low during the second quarter of the nineteenth century. Although capital exports increased substantially over the mid century, during this period London had a rival in Paris. But in the early 1870s Paris's position was diminished by the Franco–Prussian war and its effects, whereas the subsequent weakness of the French balance of payments until the 1890s constrained Gallic international lending. Consequently London only reigned supreme over international financial transactions – the provision of both credit and capital – from the early 1870s. As such it was the node of the multilateral system of payments behind world trade and international financial transactions during the classic period of the gold standard.

London retained its key world position during the *fin-de-siecle* period, despite the resumption of French overseas lending and the growing international importance of German financial institutions. Britain exported substantial amounts of capital during the Edwardian period, with the result that British overseas holdings in August 1914 amounted to between £2.5 billion and £4 billion.[3]

The First World War had a substantial impact upon London. However, just as the volume of Britain's pre-war international financial dealings are difficult to measure, so too are the effects of the First World War upon them. Consequently there are varying estimates of the net change in Britain's international financial position between 1914 and 1919. War financing involved the sale of about £550m. privately owned foreign investments, but against this had to be set new investment abroad, probably some £250m. This would indicate a net sale of £300m. – say 10 per cent of overseas holdings – to which a further 4–5 per cent has to be added for assets lost in enemy countries and confiscated in Russia.[4] Further, by 1924, there was an external deficit on the government account of £25m., whereas probably in 1913 the position had been of rough balance. Moreover, it is likely that London's short-term international creditor position was also not regained after 1918. In 1913 the 'City's' short-term overseas lending had probably totalled £350m.,[5] but the net balance is difficult to establish and may have been considerably less than some estimates.[6] Overall it is highly probable that the war reduced London's gross or net short-term creditor position by £250–300m.

Much greater than the effect on the invisibles was the consequences of the widening visible trade deficit, a result not only directly of the war but also of long-term structural changes accelerated by the war. By 1924 the trade deficit had substantially increased to £355m. Although the positive balance on invisibles had grown (in terms of current prices, from £399m. to £410m. between 1913 and 1924), the sharp deterioration in the visible balance resulted in a much reduced positive balance on the overall current account – £73m. in 1924 as opposed to £205m. in 1913.[7]

Despite these substantial changes, the 'City' attempted to regain its pre-war international position as a major, if not the key, financial market. Competition for this global function now came from New York, the First World War having transformed the US into a major international creditor.[8] Trans-Atlantic rivalry was one constraining factor; another was the continuation of wartime controls over the export of capital. Such official supervision was an entirely new procedure for the 'City', although with some foundation in the consultations between the Bank of England and the issuing houses immediately prior to the war. By 1924 all general restrictions had been lifted and the aim of official policy switched from assisting domestic reconstruction to sustaining the foreign exchanges. 'The old full freedom of the market' was finally restored in November 1925 but the authorities retained a watching brief and found the 2 per cent Stamp Duty on bearer bonds not only a useful check on foreign issues but a welcome source of revenue.[9]

Actually foreign lending by the 'City' was at its post-war maximum during the period of formal controls. Overseas flotations averaged £130m. per annum during the first half of the 1920s, accounting for 60 per cent of all new issues, as opposed to £104m. per annum between 1925 and 1931. After 1925 domestic new issues made up more than 50 per cent of new capital flotations annually, the only exception being 1931. After 1931 foreign lending came almost to an end through an informal ban imposed by City institutions.[10]

While the 'City' tried to regain its international role, its particular

Table 3.1 *Employment by the financial sector, Britain, 1871–1931*
(thousands)

	(i) Insurance, banking and finance	(ii) Total working population	(iii) i/ii × 100 %
1871	40	14,050	0.3
1881	70	15,060	0.5
1891	110	16,660	0.7
1901	150	18,680	0.8
1911	230	20,390	1.1
1921	334	17,908	1.8
1931	410	18,665	2.2

Source: C. H. Feinstein, *National income, expenditure and output of the United Kingdom 1855–1965* (Cambridge, 1972), T59 and T60.

institutions did become more domestically orientated, especially, and perhaps ironically, after Britain's ill-fated return to the gold standard in 1925. Further, by the early 1930s, the financial sector in total – insurance, banking and finance – had become a significant component of the British economy, responsible for about 5.6 per cent of GDP at factor cost in 1931.[11]

Actually it was only by the 1920s that the British financial sector was finally fully integrated, with in particular the major domestic banks – now the 'Big Five' – becoming fully fledged 'City' institutions. The primary purpose of the rest of this paper is to trace that process of integration. But, before undertaking this, one other theme, already alluded to – the weight of the financial sector within the economy – will be briefly addressed.

London's post-1870 dominance within world finance was one factor amongst many behind the growing importance of insurance, banking and finance in the late nineteenth-century economy. The contribution of services to national income is notoriously difficult to measure, especially with historical estimates. Nonetheless all the evidence points in the same direction. Employment in insurance, banking and finance rose substantially from 1871, so that by 1931 this sector accounted for 2.2 per cent of total employment (see table 3.1). Employment in financial services by 1931 was greater than the labour forces of a number of manufacturing industries. However, service industries are usually labour intensive, particularly in the case of finance before the advent of the mechanization of book-keeping. Nonetheless, whereas employment in finance increased by 575 per cent between 1871 and 1911, real output of this sector grew by

Table 3.2 *Output at constant factor cost, Britain,* 1871–1931 (1913 = 100)

	Insurance, banking and finance	Distribution and other services	GDP
1871	11.1	45.5	47.4
1881	20.0	55.0	56.2
1891	31.1	66.4	67.3
1901	53.3	80.1	80.8
1911	91.1	94.5	93.8
1921	79.8	93.8	93.7
1931	92.2	96.2	102.3

Source: C. H. Feinstein, *National income, expenditure and output of the United Kingdom 1855–1965* (Cambridge, 1972), T8, T53.

Table 3.3 *An approximate of FIR for Britain, 1880–1938*

1880	0.9
1900	0.9
1913	1.0
1929	1.3
1938	1.6

Source: Calculations based on the estimates of assets of financial institutions and GNP undertaken by Goldsmith (see note 13).

820 per cent, as opposed to 207 per cent for all services and 197.89 per cent for GDP at factor cost (see table 3.2) That same relative growth with respect to GDP is not evident in the interwar period; the real output of services as a whole stagnated, whereas financial output fell sharply during the early 1920s. However during the interwar years the particular contribution of financial services to GDP becomes more clearly marked statistically, accounting for 3.3 per cent in 1921 and 5.6 per cent in both 1931 and 1938.[12]

The relative steadiness of the contribution of finance to GDP by the 1930s is a possible pointer to financial maturity for the British economy, in terms of the culmination of various trends, both domestic and international, underway since the 1830s. This may seem a surprising conclusion to make at this particular juncture, even allowing for its still tentative nature, but it will receive a further foundation in later sections. At this point, limited support comes from examining an approximate of Goldsmith's financial interrelations ratio (FIR) – the ratio of financial assets to national wealth.[13] Generally this ratio rises with the modernization of an economy as a result of the growth of financial intermediation, but with an upper bound of the order of 1 to 1.5. In Britain's case this was reached, in terms of the ratio of financial assets to GNP, in the 1930s (see table 3.3). Certainly the British economy was hovering on the verge of financial maturity from the 1880s, allowing for the nature of the estimates deployed, but a marked feature is the rise of the British FIR during the interwar period. The developing and unfolding hypothesis is that the British financial sector was not full grown and integrated until the interwar period. In particular it was only from the 1920s that the domestic commercial banks became fully 'City' institutions, while the traditional organs of the 'City' began to add a domestic role to their, by then, long-standing international functions.

The relative lateness of British financial maturity, with respect to domestic commercial banking, is underscored by an examination of a range of criteria – size, links with the metropolitan market and organizational structure.

Only by 1909 were the total assets of three of the leading English commercial banks – Lloyds, the Westminster and the Midland – on a par with comparable European financial institutions such as the Deutsche Bank and the Crédit Lyonnais.[14] This is surprising, since during the nineteenth century the UK was the wealthiest European economy, in terms of real GNP per capita, and one of its fortes was banking – domestic as well as international. Moreover, the adjective 'English' is being used here advisedly and with purpose. The domestic banking systems of England and Wales, Scotland, and Ireland were separate organizational entities until the early 1920s, the product of different legal systems and different paths of modern historical development. The Midland acquired the Belfast Banking Company as an affiliate in 1918/19,[15] concluding similar arrangements with the Clydesdale in 1919 and the North of Scotland Bank in 1924. Affiliation was required because of the Treasury Agreement of 1918 regarding bank amalgamations. This pattern of association was quickly followed by Lloyds, Barclays Bank and, finally, by the Westminster, with respect to the Ulster Bank, in 1924.[16]

These affiliations did not give Irish and Scottish banks a London/metropolitan presence as some had already established that fifty years earlier, beginning with the National Bank of Scotland in 1864. These developments coincided with the opening of London offices by European banks – the Crédit Lyonnais in 1871 and the Deutsche Bank in 1873. The inception of these metropolitan links both further internationalized the 'City' and were an acknowledgement of London being the key financial centre. However three of the English progenitors of the 'Big Five' of the

1920s did not come to London in a formal organizational sense until a decade or two later, beginning with Lloyds in 1884.[17] Generally it was not until these English banks formally and institutionally entered the 'City' that their shares were quoted on the London Stock Exchange, as with the Midland in 1891. A London office, ultimately to be the head office, did have growing attractions, such as earning an extra £20,000 on London balances, as one Scottish banker informed Howard Lloyd,[18] but these advantages did not outweigh the banks' provincial roots and clienteles until the 1880s and 1890s.

The continuing reliance of major English provincial banks on expensive correspondent and agency relationships with the London financial markets was one point of contrast with the Scottish banking system between the 1860s and the 1890s. Another was their large numbers. Whereas there were only twelve Scottish banks in 1871 (falling to nine by 1911) and nine Irish banks throughout the late nineteenth century, there were 363 English banks in 1871 of which 117 were joint stock. The number of English joint-stock banks did not reach a maximum until 1880 – 128[19] – and even in the early 1890s there were still over 150 independent English banks. As during the 1830s, when English joint-stock country banking emerged, so in the closing decades of the nineteenth century its constituent units continued to be predominantly small and parochial, or at best regional banks. In 1871 the average ratio of offices to an English provincial bank was but 6.4 and this ratio had increased to only sixteen two decades later. Until the turn of the century the Irish and Scottish centralized banking systems, with London connections, had a greater number of branches, relative to population, than the whole of the segmented English banking system – private and joint-stock, London, London and provincial, and provincial[20] (see table 3.4).

In contrast to the centralized Scottish and Irish banking systems with wide branch networks, until 1901 the English commercial banking system continued to be composed of three major parts – the London banks (of which the joint-stock were the most important), the London and provincial joint-stock banks, and the provincial joint-stock banks (table 3.5).

In terms of share of total deposits, the provincial joint-stock banks were on a par with the whole of London banking – private, joint-stock and 'ephemeral' – until the 1890s and controlled the largest proportion of bank offices. It was out of this group that two of the progenitors of the 'Big Five' arose – Lloyds and the Midland. With respect to two other 'cores' of the 'Big Five' – the Westminster had its origins as the first London joint-stock bank, whereas the promoters of the National Provincial had toyed with being London-based at the time of the bank's inception in the 1830s, but chose to pursue provincial note-issuing until

Table 3.4 *Scottish and Irish bank offices relative to the UK domestic banking system and UK population, 1871–1921*

	Scottish and Irish bank offices Total UK bank offices %	Scottish and Irish population Total UK population %
1871	42.3	27.8
1881	38.8	25.4
1891	32.5	23.0
1901	26.6	21.5
1911	24.1	20.2
1921	22.7	19.6

Sources: Calculated from F. Capie and A. Webber, *A monetary history of the United Kingdom, 1870–1982* (1985), appendix III, pp. 576–8 and B. R. Mitchell with P. Deane, *Abstract of British Historical Statistics* (Cambridge, 1971), p. 6–7.

Table 3.5 *The English and Welsh banking system, 1871–1921*
(in terms of % of total number of English and Welsh banking offices and % of total English and Welsh banking deposits)

	London banks		London and provincial joint-stock banks		Provincial joint-stock banks	
	Branches %	Deposits %	Branches %	Deposits %	Branches %	Deposits %
1871	5.5	33.4	24.9	11.25	37.7	30.2
1881	5.4	31.7	26.4	19.0	43.5	31.3
1891	4.7	26.3	36.3	30.1	41.25	29.9
1901	3.2	19.3	47.4	55.7	35.2	27.0
1911	0.5	6.9	73.6	71.9	24.1	19.3
1921	0.4	5.0	87.7	84.8	11.8	9.8

Sources: Calculated from F. Capie and A. Webber, *A monetary history of the United Kingdom, 1870–1982* (1985), p. 432 and appendix III, pp. 567–8.

the 1860s. Consequently England's centralized domestic commercial banking system was to a substantial degree the product of 'provincials coming to town' and that journey was not made until the final two decades of the nineteenth century.

The persistent division of English nineteenth-century commercial banking into three main parts arose from legislation and the regional nature of industrialization. Joint-stock banks could not be established in

London until 1833 and then only as deposit banks, not note-issuers, in deference to the monopoly of the Bank of England. Legal constraints made a long-lasting impression; when the London and County Bank, formed in 1836, pursued a policy of opening suburban and provincial branches in the 1860s, nearly all were within the sixty-five mile radius of London – the Bank of England's post-1826 monopoly area.[21]

This monopoly had been questioned in Joplin's campaign of the 1820s and early 1830s to introduce joint-stock banking on the Scottish model south of the border. The 1826 edition of his *Essay* had included a prospectus for a London bank and again in 1833 he had argued for a metropolitan base for a national joint-stock bank.[22] But Joplin's fellow promoters decided that their National Provincial would be a provincial note-issuer with only an administrative London base. The bank's management maintained this stance until the mid 1860s, despite the declining importance of notes in England after 1839.[23]

However, unlike nearly all[24] other early English provincial joint-stock banks, the National Provincial began with a large branch network – 39 in 1836[25] – and, with the London and County, had more than 100 offices in the 1870s and 1880s. That select club had expanded to twelve by 1899 – Lloyds joining it in 1890, the Midland in 1893, and Barclays in 1896. The London and Westminster did not reach this level of branches until 1909, by when this group of substantial multi-branch banks numbered nineteen.[26]

The high incidence of failure amongst early joint-stock banks led to the imposition of severe legislative restrictions on further bank formation in 1844, which remained in force until 1857.[27] With the general liberalization of company law between 1855 and 1862, there was a substantial boom in the creation of new domestic joint-stock limited banks during the upswings of the mid 1860s and the early 1870s.[28] Amongst these there were seven new London banks, out of which only three had any longevity,[29] and seven London and provincial formations. Three of the latter nearly became progenitors of the English centralized banking structure of the 1920s – the Capital and Counties of 1878, the London and Provincial Bank of 1864, and Parr's Bank, formed in 1865 – but all eventually fell victim to the amalgamation movement.

A centralized banking system in England did develop from the late 1870s as a result of mergers – the amalgamation movement. For Britain as a whole between 1870 and 1921, 370 banks disappeared and there were 264 banking mergers, of which half consisted of the acquisition of private banks by joint-stock. This latter activity peaked in 1891, but did not lead *pari passu* to concentration within English banking. The five largest English banks held about a quarter of total English bank deposits throughout the period 1870 to 1890 and in 1891 this group consisted of the National Provincial, the London and County, Lloyds, the Capital and Counties, and the London and South Western. The share of deposits held by the largest five banks, a group which changed in composition, only rose substantially from 1910 – to 80 per cent by 1920. The effect of mergers upon concentration was initially offset by the growth of smaller banks, with the share of total deposits held by the sixth to tenth largest banks increasing from 7.8 per cent to 21.7 per cent between 1870 and 1910. But over the next decade the share of deposits held by this group fell back to 16.6 per cent.

Capie and Rodrik-Bali[30] have suggested that the lack of a direct and immediate relationship between mergers and concentration was due to internal growth, but it is evident that the sixth to tenth largest banks also grew by merger. Further, they find no relationship between the timing of banking mergers and general economic conditions. This may be valid for the post-1900 period, but, in the late nineteenth century, peaks in their series for bank disappearances and banking mergers – 1878 and 1891 – coincide with the failure of the City of Glasgow Bank[31] and the Baring crisis.[32]

Two Birmingham joint-stock banks – the Midland and Lloyds – grew rapidly in the 1880s and 1890s from their provincial roots to become major national institutions as a result of both merger and internal expansion. These two banks established in the 1890s the strategy of competition through size. However neither initially had a foundation in a large branch network, yet by 1913 the Midland had 846 branches and Lloyds 673. Branches were the source of deposit growth and mergers were a cheap way of acquiring them.

The Midland did not begin to buy banks beyond its immediate locality until 1889. A major question for its management was whether to enter the metropolis and the attractions were now great. Its local competitor – Lloyds – had already taken that step and, besides matching it, there were the advantages stemming from membership of the London Clearing House (which it had been a *sine qua non* of Lloyd's acquisition of a London bank), the apparent relatively 'underbanked' nature of the metropolitan area and the opportunity of diversifying the 'proto-Midland's' assets – in particular a shift away from large industrial accounts linked to its Birmingham directors. Further the bank would obtain for its clientele direct connections with the services of the 'City'. Immediately after the Baring crisis, it acquired the Central Bank of London, but at the same time the bank also moved into the north-west. Although now an emerging nationwide bank, the management of the 'proto-Midland' still regarded Birmingham as the bank's centre. That perspective changed during the 1890s for a number of reasons.

After the Baring crisis, the shares of 'London and provincial' banks appreciated whereas those of 'London' banks fell. The shares of the Midland and Lloyds rose between 1891 and 1893 but not to the same degree as either the London and County or the London and South Western. Other factors pushed in the same direction. The mid 1890s were marked by low interest rates, leading to a search for economies of scale, particularly removing the costs of expensive London agency arrangements. This was coupled with attempts to increase business and sustain deposit growth, especially against the competition of savings institutions. One strategy was to open new branches, possibly in every major urban centre, and this was pursued. But, as the Midland had found from the late 1880s, new branches were expensive and amalgamation was a better route for growth. Holden, the bank's general manager from 1897, decided to reinforce the bank's links with London and in 1898 the City Bank was acquired. The product was the London, City and Midland, a major London and provincial bank; its deposits at £31.9m. placed it fourth after Lloyds (£37.7m.), the London and County (£43.5m.) and the National Provincial (£49.3m.).

From 1898 the Midland began a deliberate programme of national expansion but by acquiring deposits cheaper than through opening new branches. The targets in this growth by amalgamation were multi-branch country banks in regions where the Midland's representation was thin, which were under-capitalized, yet relatively 'solvent', and had a large number of shareholders. However other banks responded, with a major change in the size-based competitive structure of the industry resulting from the London and Westminster merging with the London and County in 1909 to form the London, County and Westminster with aggregate deposits of £72m. as opposed to the Midland's £70m. and Lloyds' £76m. Their responses were delayed until 1914 when Lloyds acquired the Wilts. and Dorset Bank and the Midland took over the Metropolitan Bank, increasing its deposits to £125m., so making it the largest bank in the UK.

The First World War did not stop this process and in February 1918 it became public knowledge that the National Provincial was to amalgamate with the Union of London and Smith's Bank and, similarly, the London, County and Westminster Bank was to merge with Parr's. As in 1909, the other banks reacted but now far more rapidly; Lloyds fused with the Capital and Counties, and Barclays with the London, Provincial and South and Western Bank. The Midland's response was to re-open negotiations with the London Joint Stock Bank, forming the London Joint City and Midland Bank, with deposits of £350m. and 1,300 offices, the then biggest joint-stock commercial bank in the world.

The 1918 Treasury Agreement put an end to major domestic bank amalgamations for the next half century, thus perhaps ossifying the structure of English commercial banking. The 'Big Five' in the 1920s competed by opening further branches, led by the National Provincial which expanded its network by 58 per cent from 820 to 1,308. However the two biggest banks by 1929 in terms of width of branching were the Midland (2,044) and Barclays (2,042), whilst the Westminster hardly joined in the fray, only increasing its number of branches by 5 per cent to 1,050.[33]

Not all accepted the growing domination of big banks which linked the metropolis and the provinces. Between 1891 and 1920, 42 new banks were formed in England and Wales but none made a major mark. In the provinces the City of Birmingham Bank, deliberately formed in 1897 as an anti-amalgamation bank, was within three years acquired by the Midland. Only in the north-west did some existing banks retain their independence, while three further new banks were promoted in the region.[34]

However, these independent Lancashire banks ran into difficulties in the mid 1920s which led Montagu Norman, who believed in the policy behind the Treasury Agreement of 1918, to attempt to form a sixth big bank. The negotiations proved difficult and the only immediate outcome was the merger in December 1927 of the Bank of Liverpool and Martins with the Lancashire and Yorkshire Bank to form 'Martins Bank'. Continuing difficulties over cotton accounts led in 1930 to the Royal Bank of Scotland taking over Williams Deacon's, which although it had its head office in Manchester was a member of the London Clearing House. Norman acted as midwife in this transaction but never succeeded in producing his Big Sixth. The only other domestic merger of consequence was that between the Manchester and County Bank and the District Bank in 1935.[35]

While the major English provincial banks only established London offices from the mid 1880s, they had had links with the City from their inception in the 1830s. During this decade, through the thickening of correspondent relationships between provincial and metropolitan banks and the emergence of the discount houses, the London money market became the centre of the domestic credit system. From the 1870s 'City' metropolitan institutions looked increasingly to the provincies for financial resources. As a result the Midland, for instance, began to place money at call with London discount houses from 1871, and London stockbrokers from 1881. Accordingly in December 1889, before the Midland had a London office, 6.1 per cent of its total assets consisted of lending at call to London.[36] Some country banks had been placing short-term funds with London stockbrokers since the mid 1820s.[37]

Falling yields on Consols from the early 1880s led to other changes in bank assets – both provincial and London. With Goschen's conversion of the National Debt, the Midland became more concerned with its investment earnings. This led to the buying of overseas securities so that by the late 1880s Indian railways and colonial stocks comprised 46 per cent of the Midland's investments. In 1908 merely 29 per cent of the Midland's investments consisted of domestic paper and the strategy for its portfolio was aggressively directed to maximizing earnings.[38] The acquisition of overseas securities for investment induced some London joint-stock banks to underwrite foreign issues, as it was a cheaper way of acquiring such paper, and ultimately to act as issuing houses. The normally conservative London and Westminster was a leader in this field. From 1870 the London Joint Stock was associated with German issues, whereas, arising from personal connections, Parr's, a London and provincial bank, undertook issues for China and Japan. In 1909 the Midland, now a national bank with London headquarters, undertook a Russian railway issue and its management were interested in other Russian ventures.[39]

In addition to coalescing with the international capital exporting activities of the City, the domestic banks, both London and provincial, entered into the provision of international credit. Such international acceptance business undertaken by London joint-stock banks had grown from the late 1860s,[40] whereas the Midland largely entered this field in 1898 through its absorption of the City Bank, the London correspondent for forty overseas banks. In 1902 the Midland established a Foreign Bank Department, by 1908 it had 132 overseas correspondent links and in 1918, 850, in part arising from its recent merger with the London Joint Stock.[41]

Other members of the emerging 'Big Five' went further and established overseas branches. In 1911 Lloyds purchased Armstrong & Co. of Paris and turned it into Lloyds Bank (France). The aim was to provide a service for British expatriates and this also motivated the Westminster to establish a Paris subsidiary in 1913. The First World War acted as a further spur. The major domestic commercial banks followed the troops abroad whereas the European market place was less crowded following the expulsion of German banks from Allied territory. This migration was encouraged by both the Authorities, with the establishment of the British Trade Corporation and the British Italian Corporation, and welcoming invitations. In 1917 the National Provincial took a 50 per cent share in Lloyds (France) by when it had branches in five French cities. Immediately after the war this bank opened branches in Belgium, Germany and Switzerland and in 1921 established further French branches. The Westminster Foreign Bank moved into Spain in 1917 and Belgium in 1918. In 1918, as a result of its merger with the London and South Western Bank, Barclays acquired Cox & Co. (France) Ltd. This became Barclays Bank (Overseas) in 1922 and was reformed again in 1926 as

Barclays Bank (France) by when Barclays also had a 50 per cent holding in the Banque de Commerce, Antwerp.

The overseas expansion of the major English commercial banks was unduly rapid and as early as 1919 an internal report of the Westminster was highly critical of what it regarded as an ill-planned development. In this case there had been a lack of a well-informed guiding hand from the London head office, resulting in expensive purchases and large overseas staffs. All the banks began to close some of their European branches from the early 1920s. The Lloyds and National Provincial Foreign did try to make a business in a now openly hostile overseas environment by cultivating British expatriates, which called for further branches at fashionable spas and resorts – 'banking on the riviera' as Geoffrey Jones has called it. This did not rebuild profits which had peaked in the early 1920s and so the 'riveria branches' were also closed. There was an attempt from 1927 to switch to local commercial clients, but with mixed success. With first the German *Stillstand* and then the franc crisis, the 1930s were years of bad debts for the overseas offshoots of the 'Big Five'. It had been a precocious development and, until the 1960s, the Midland's strategy of not competing with European banks in their own domestic markets proved to be more sound. Even in the 1930s acting as a London correspondent for foreign banks was more profitable – during this decade of moratoria and exchange control the net profits of the Midland's Overseas Branch in Threadneedle Street were equivalent to 23.1 per cent of the bank's published profits.[42]

The expansion of four of the 'Big Five' into Europe from the 1910s was followed in the 1920s by Lloyds and Barclays acquiring controlling stakes in 'Anglo-International' banks. In 1923 Lloyds purchased the London and River Plate Bank and the London and Brazilian Bank to form the Bank of London and South America. This was not welcomed by Governor Montagu Norman who did not wish to see domestic and international banking becoming closely intertwined, largely because of the threat to the stability of the former arising from the latter. Nonetheless Barclays developed controlling interests in the Colonial Bank, the Anglo-Egyptian Bank and the National Bank of South Africa, rationalized in 1925 with the formation of Barclays Bank (Dominion, Colonial and Overseas). Norman reacted with a policy of both closing the Bank of England accounts of overseas banks controlled by, or affiliated to, English commercial banks and discriminating against their acceptances. This did not stop Lloyds from taking over the Egyptian offices of the Bank of British West Africa. Norman's policy ended in stalemate. The banks had to accept the inconveniences and higher costs that the policy caused but did not divest themselves of their international entanglements; instead they made repeated appeals through the late 1920s and the 1930s for a change in policy, which only came after the outbreak of war.[43]

Did the transformation of English commercial banking during the forty years after 1880 have any affect upon their lending policies, especially with regard to manufacturing enterprises? Such a question needs a point of departure – namely what were the lending policies of English country banks during the development of Britain as a mature industrial economy? This initial point has usually been met by the presentation of a simple stereotype which maintains that from the industrial revolution English banks were overwhelmingly providers of credit and eschewed medium- and long-term lending to industry. This soldiers on despite the increasing accumulation of evidence for both the classic industrial revolution period and the mid nineteenth century that banks in industrial areas did lend on medium- and long-term to industrial customers, sometimes to the peril of the bank.[44]

Until the 1880s English country banks were products of the localities and regions that they served; customers and shareholders were frequently the same people. The banks' constituencies both owned the banks and did business with them. Directors and managers knew their customers well and with prudence and local knowledge were prepared to go beyond the bounds of short-term lending. The amalgamation movement broke those links, but there were other forces – growing professionalism and concern over liquidity and reserve levels – acting in the same direction. Further, by the last quarter of the nineteenth century, the nature and scope of industrial financial requirements, as a result of the growth of fixed capital, particularly the general adoption of steam power,[45] was increasingly beyond the limited capacities of local and regional country banks.

One major change in the nature of lending from the mid 1870s was the declining use of the domestic bill of exchange, leading in turn to a fall in bank discounting. Bill finance only remained important in but a few areas by the early 1890s. Consequently by 1896 bills merely accounted for 25 per cent of London bank advances and 21 per cent of provincial bank advances. The nature of bank accommodation therefore changed from the mid 1870s: in the provinces the overdraft replaced discounting; in the metropolis, loans. These assets were more remunerative than discounts, particularly loans, but they were more illiquid and could not be readily recycled, as bills had been by rediscounting on the London money market. This change in the nature of bank lending was linked with another general growing concern from the mid 1870s – liquidity – which was to persist thereafter.[46]

The heightened awareness amongst bankers regarding liquidity arose from the impact of banking failures and financial crisis – the crash of the City of Glasgow Bank in 1878 and the Baring crisis of 1890. The latter resulted in Goschen's call for banks to publish their balance sheets which added another twist to the concern over liquidity. Immediately after the City of Glasgow Bank failure, the Midland introduced more explicit controls over lending, requiring all overdrafts of more than £200 to be referred to the bank's directors.[47]

This growing stress on liquidity and reserve levels was a factor in the reduction of the 'overlent' nature of English country banks in industrial areas during the last quarter of the nineteenth century. The average ratio of advances plus discounts to deposits for banks in the midlands fell from c. 100 per cent in the early 1870s to c. 65 per cent by the mid 1890s. A similar fall occurred with respect to banks in the north-east, Lancashire and Yorkshire – from c. 96 per cent down to c. 75 per cent.[48]

Organizational changes, arising from the growth of branch networks in the 1880s, worked in the same direction. Branch expansion led to the employment of new staff, problems of managerial control and increased responsibilities for directors. The growth in banking staffs resulted in the greater development of professionalism marked by the formation of the Institute of Bankers in England and Wales in 1879, four years after a comparable body had been established in Scotland.[49] There had been practical textbooks for the conduct of banking since the 1830s, but now there were national examinations, which bank managements encouraged their staff to take. Warnings had always been given regarding the dangers of short-term accommodation 'drifting into dead loans', but from the mid 1870s, with the decline of discounting, there was greater attention to the nature of securities for loans, particularly the difficulties of real property proffered as collateral. In 1891 the *Banker's Magazine* pointed out that 'ships also share with mills, factories and stocks of goods two fatal objections, that they are not readily vendible and their value cannot always be approximately ascertained'. Schuster of the Union of London and Smith's Bank admitted in 1910 that the new security rules were more rigid; but he maintained that, with the conversion of partnerships into companies, concerns now had in the debenture a security which a banker was entitled to require for a loan.[50]

The amalgamation movement was a further factor encouraging standardization, towards being more passive and rigid, of banking practice regarding lending. In the case of the Midland, one of the reasons for its expansion through mergers was precisely an attempt to diversify its assets away from large industrial accounts arising from the personal interests and the connections of its Birmingham directors. Moreover, frequently its targets for absorption were country banks, such as the Cumberland Union,[51] which, although solvent, were nonetheless embarrassed by long-term sizeable commitments to a few local industrial concerns. Such banks could be bought relatively cheaply. More generally the amalgamation movement led to the creation of nationwide branch networks which multiplied the already growing problems of control from the emerging London head offices. In the late 1890s the Midland introduced standard regulations and procedures for the conduct of its branch managers. These once more stressed the problems of the evaluation of securities, but also detailed the handling of bad and doubtful debts. This was followed in 1900 by the introduction of a procedure requiring all overdrafts over £2,000 to be referred to the board for approval. Finally in 1906 the Midland established a London Committee of eight directors to review all advances in the range £2,000–£5,000.[52]

Whereas Cottrell in 1975 maintained that the growing bureaucratization of banking reduced the flexibility of branch managers in dealing with all customers,[53] the recent historians of the Midland have turned the evidence that he used against him. They point out that the lending limits that the Midland imposed on branch managers from 1900 were frequently higher than those that had been employed by the banks that it absorbed, as with the City Bank. Unfortunately still not enough is known about the change in bank/customer relationships from the 1880s to go beyond a few limited examples. Certainly the Midland was the most centralized of the banks in terms of managerial control before 1914 and Holmes and Green, with respect to the Midland, point to greater post-amalgamation problems for its industrial customers arising from the bank's growing policy of limiting the extent of its commitment to particular industrial sectors, the board being particularly adverse to colliery accounts. The main gain that they see arising from the amalgamation movement was the ability of large corporate customers to deal directly with the London board, so side-stepping the intermediary of the branch manager.[54]

Edwardian contemporary comment points to the amalgamation movement having a negative effect upon industrial finance. Joseph maintained that overdrafts were generally limited in size and that an industrial customer could not always rely on a request for such accommodation being treated favourably. He was on the customer's side, but his comments coincided with Schuster's attitude that banks should not be providers of working capital, only granters of temporary loans. Both do not contradict Lavington's prediction in 1914 that bank assets would change, as long loans made by absorbed banks were recovered by their new managements, who would then place the resources so released in 'advances both secured and more readily recoverable'.[55]

Lavington's expectation regarding the 1910s did not entirely come about; this was not due to the direct financial effects of the First World War, but rather the participation of the English commercial banks – both the 'Big Five' and the remaining independent concerns – in the hectic and highly speculative post-war restocking boom. Bank advances increased from £519m. in 1918 to £926m. in 1920, from 30 per cent of total assets to 42 per cent. A considerable proportion of this expansion went to finance the over-capitalization of the 'staple industries', especially cotton, steel and ship-building. Some thought that competition between the banks had been a factor in the mushroom boom, certainly as far as Lancashire was concerned: 'The mainspring of the Cotton Boom of 1920 was competition between various banks for the... accounts of cotton spinning mills. In those days loans of hundreds of thousands of pounds were readily granted by the competing banks to all and sundry to enable cotton mills to be purchased.'[56]

As such, bank/industry relationships of the early 1920s initially and ironically had the effect of perpetuating Britain's now increasingly outmoded industrial structure. They thereby augmented the problems of its transformation during the interwar period. Bankers together with industrialists and speculators were misled by the false dawn of the post-war boom.

It is still not clear whether bank accommodation to the staples in the early 1920s consisted of predominantly either short- or medium-term finance. The post-1920 problems of the staple industries resulted in it becoming in practice long-term finance. By 1924 14 per cent of private overdrafts, some £63m., consisted of financial facilities granted to heavy industry, £16m. to steel alone. In 1928 12.5 per cent of the Midland's overdrafts were to the cotton industry and 7.75 per cent to the steel industry. Some other members of the 'Big Five' were in a similar position – Lloyds with 7 per cent of its overdrafts to cotton and 3.4 per cent to steel, while in the case of the National Provincial 10 per cent of its overdrafts were committed to the steel industry.[57]

Such lending endangered the foundations of some banks – the still independent regional banks of Lancashire. By 1925 at least the Manchester and County, the District and the Lancashire and Yorkshire were facing difficulties arising primarily from the illiquid state of accommodation granted to the cotton industry. In particular the Manchester and County now needed 'support' which it defined as the 'ownership by a strong bank'. These banks could not agree over the proposed formation of a 'Lancashire Textile Corporation' but the Bank of England decided to assist in its establishment, although this rationalization body took about four years – from 1928 to 1931 – to come about. Williams Deacon's managed to survive outwardly over the mid 1920s by exhausting its hidden reserves but still in 1928 had £3.77m. outstanding to forty cotton companies. It was now a question for this bank of reducing its public reserves by £1m., which could have had wider implications for domestic banking in general. The Bank of England stepped in by guaranteeing these illiquid advances, the debtor firms were merged into the Lancashire Cotton Corporation, and William Deacon's was taken over by the Royal Bank of Scotland. With the world crisis William Deacon's incurred further cotton losses of £1m. in 1930 which were covered by the Royal Bank and the Bank of England, with the total contribution of the latter rising at one point to £4m.[58]

Illiquid loans and overdrafts led the banks to be involved in the rationalization of the staple industries. The Bank of England had been initially drawn in as a result of the problems of one of its private customers, the armaments producer Armstrong, Whitworth. Its difficulties were the first step in a process by which Norman came to be enmeshed not only in the problems of the cotton industry, but also of ship-building and steel and which culminated in the creation of Securities Management Trust and the Banker Industrial Development Company (BIDCo) – organizations for 'taking these questions out of the Governor's room'. The commercial banks, along with other institutions of the 'City' subscribed for 75 per cent of the capital of BIDCo. However its formation in 1930 was not to prove to be a new beginning in industrial finance, but instead a high watermark, following which the tide turned. BIDCo did undertake issues for the Lancashire Cotton Corporation and the parallel rationalizing body in ship-building in 1931, but thereafter during the rest of the 1930s only assisted in the creation of Stewart and Lloyd's new tube works at Corby. BIDCo's life was extended for a further five years in 1935 and it issued an invitation to industry for proposals for assistance. However during the so-called recovery of the 1930s existing major firms were largely able to look after themselves.[59]

Commercial bank loans to the staple industries actually fell substantially over the 1930s, from £63m. in 1929 to £40m. by 1936, with for instance the banks' commitment to the steel industry declining from £16m. and £3.5m. Up to the peak of the recovery in 1936/7 established companies generally obtained financial resources from either profits, in the time honoured fashion, or by new issues. Some of the major City merchant banks, such as Morgan Grenfell, Lazards and Higginson, had become involved with electrical companies in the 1920s, whereas Barings, Rothschilds, Schroeders and Hambros had begun to undertake more domestic issuing work in general. This was encouraged by Norman, but these houses would still only consider making large issues – the minimum being £0.2m. in the 1920s, but falling to £0.1m. in the 1930s. In all this the role of the commercial banks was largely passive as, with the cheap money policy of the 1930s, industrial firms found another way of financing – by selling government securities which the commercial banks bought. Accordingly the commercial banks played but an indirect role in financing industrial expansion in the 1930s through increasing their holdings of Gilts.[60]

One reason for the commercial banks' indirect role was that they continued to maintain their customary minimum interest rates after 1932, when cheap money was introduced, and so priced themselves out of the market. This stance received substantial criticism and led to a government-inspired investigation by the Bank of England. Minimal floors to bank charges did thereafter break up. This intervention by Norman was coupled with promptings, increasingly sharp, that the banks should have a greater involvement in long- and medium-term industrial lending, analogous to the arrangements behind the Agricultural Mortgage Corporation of 1928. In 1934 there were considerations in Threadneedle Street for an Industrial Mortgage Corporation but they reached no definite conclusion. Instead in 1936 the commercial banks did form, with the Bank of England, the Special Areas Reconstruction Association. This provided some limited financial assistance for the creation of new, small firms in depressed areas, where unemployment had increased, in part due to the actions of the rationalization bodies of the late 1920s. Larger and more purposeful bodies, designed to fill the 'Macmillan gaps' observed in the early 1930s, were not established by the commercial banks until 1945.[61]

However the commercial banks' stance was not totally passive in the 1930s. For instance, along with some insurance companies, they did lend to the steel industry in the late 1930s to allow the introduction of new technology and the manufacture of 'lighter' products. However, as with 1919–20, this lending once again gave rise to problems and prompted once more the intervention of the Bank of England. This occurred, for example, with the decision of Richard Thomas & Co. to erect a new integrated steel plant at Ebbw Vale. The programme was initially financed by both a debenture issue undertaken by Rothschilds and substantial borrowing from Lloyds, the company's bankers. Yet costs rose and Lloyds felt unable to increase the accommodation that it had granted. The situation was remedied by the Bank of England providing first, temporary assistance, eventually totalling £1.1m., and then arranging a banking syndicate which supplied £6m. through shares but predominantly debentures.

The retardation of British economic growth from the late nineteenth century has been explained in terms of the 'handicap' of the early start – problems stemming from Britain being the first industrial nation. These have been detected most clearly in the nature and scale of social infrastructure investment – the canal and railway systems. However they may also be evident in the emergence of the British financial sector, with the almost separate development of domestic commercial banking from the growth of the 'City' before the 1880s and 1890s. The subsequent fusion was not fully accomplished until the 1920s and it largely consisted of provincial banks becoming 'City' institutions, rather than London banks reaching out to the provinces and so encompassing the whole of the economy. There is evidence that industrial lending may have been a victim of the amalgamation movement, but it was also affected by the banks' continuing concern from the late nineteenth century with liquidity. Industrial lending was a threat to liquidity. It had caused the failure of country banks in the nineteenth century, it enfeebled them and made them prey to being absorbed after 1880, and in the 1920s these lessons were reinforced, particularly in Lancashire, by the financial results of the post-war boom.

Notes and references

The place of publication is London, unless otherwise indicated.

1 I am grateful to my colleague D. M. Williams, to members of the symposium, and to the editor for comments on earlier versions of this paper.

2 '"When *I* use a word" Humpty Dumpty said in a rather scornful tone, "it means just what I choose it to mean – neither more nor less".' Lewis Carroll, *Through the looking-glass*, chapter VI.

3 There is now a major debate over the volume of British capital exports, especially after 1870; see D. C. M. Platt, *Britain's investment on the eve of the First World War. The use and abuse of numbers* (1986); S. Pollard, 'Capital exports, 1870–1914: harmful or beneficial?', *Economic History Review*, 2nd ser., 38 (1985); C. Feinstein, 'Britain's overseas investments in 1913', *Economic History Review*, 2nd ser., 43 (1990).

4 See W. A. Ashworth, *An economic history of England 1870–1939* (1960), pp. 287–8.

5 Committee on Finance and Industry [Macmillan Committee], *Minutes of evidence* (1931), q. 1273.

6 A. I. Bloomfield, *Short-term capital movements under the pre-1914 gold standard*, Princeton Studies in International Finance, 11, p. 71ff and P. H. Lindert, *Key currencies and gold, 1900–1913*, Princeton Studies in International Finance, 24, 56–7.

7 D. E. Moggridge, *British monetary policy 1924–1931* (Cambridge, 1972), table 2, p. 30.

8 See C. P. Parrini, *Heir to Empire. United States economic diplomacy 1916–1923* (Pittsburgh, 1969); M. J. Hogan, *Informal entente. The private structure of co-operation in Anglo-American diplomacy 1918–1928* (1977); R. W. D. Boyce, *British capitalism at the crossroads, 1919–1932: a study in politics, economics and international relations* (Cambridge, 1987).

9 Moggridge, *British monetary policy*, pp. 201–19 and J. M. Atkin, 'Official regulation of British overseas investment, 1914–1931', *Economic History Review*, 2nd ser., 23 (1970).

10 See S. Diaper, 'Merchant banking in the inter-war period. The case of Kleinwort Sons & Co.', *Business History*, 28 (1986) and A. T. K.

Grant, *A study of the capital market in Britain from 1919–1936* (2nd edn., 1967).

11 C. H. Feinstein, *National income, expenditure and output of the United Kingdom 1855–1965* (Cambridge, 1972), table T9.

12 Feinstein, *National income*, table 9, TT26–7.

13 See R. W. Goldsmith, *The determinants of financial structure* (Paris, 1966) and *Financial structure and development* (New Haven and London, 1969).

14 A point made by Y. Cassis, although in a different context, in 'Management and strategy in the English joint stock banks 1890–1914', *Business History*, 27 (1985), 301.

15 See N. Simpson, *The Belfast Bank 1827–1970* (Belfast, 1975), pp. 217–29.

16 See for instance A. R. Holmes and Edwin Green, *Midland 150 years of banking business* (1986), pp. 157–63.

17 The precise dating of the beginnings of Lloyds as a London and provincial bank is difficult, but here the formal merger of Lloyds Banking Co. Ltd with Barnetts, Hoare's, Hanbury & Lloyd, and Bosanquet Salt & Co. in 1884 is regarded as the inception rather than the incorporation of Lloyds Banking Co. Ltd in 1865, the criterion apparently used by F. Capie and A. Webber, *A monetary history of the United Kingdom, 1870–1982* (1985) p. 550. See also R. S. Sayers, *Lloyds Bank in the history of English banking* (Oxford, 1957).

18 Sayers, *Lloyds*, p. 247.

19 S. Nishimura, *The decline of inland bills of exchange in the London money market 1855–1913* (Cambridge, 1971), pp. 80–1; Capie and Webber, *Monetary history*, appendix III, pp. 576–8.

20 The figures are drawn from the herculian work of Capie and Webber, *Monetary history*, but they, through their allocation of banks to the different groups, may as a result have down played to a degree the overall importance of the provincial joint-stock banks before the 1890s. This is because Capie and Webber include the Alliance (1862) as a London bank, when it was a London and provincial bank – its full title being the Alliance of London and Liverpool. Further, under this head they place the London Banking Association which was not a domestic commercial bank at all but a private investment bank involving London merchant bankers and the Parisian 'haute banque' (see P. L. Cottrell, 'Investment banking in England, 1856–1882,' Ph.D thesis, University of Hull, 1974, pp. 622–3). Most seriously, and as has already been commented upon above, they place Lloyds as a London and provincial bank in 1865 rather than in 1884 when it opened its own London office.

21 W. F. Crick and J. E. Wadsworth, *A hundred years of joint stock banking* (3rd edn, 1958), p. 37 fn (i).

22 T. Joplin, *An essay on the general principles and present practice of banking in England and Scotland*...(1827) and *The advantages of the*

proposed National Bank of England, both to the public and its proprietory (1833), extracts from both reprinted in B. L. Anderson and P. L. Cottrell, *Money and banking in England. The development of the banking system 1694–1914* (Newton Abbot, 1974).

23 See H. Withers, *National Provincial Bank 1833 to 1933* (1933).

24 The major other exceptions are Welsh banks – the Glamorganshire Banking Company, the Monmouthshire and Glamorganshire Banking Company and the North and South Wales Bank. See P. L. Cottrell, 'Banking and finance', in J. Langton and R. J. Morris (eds.), *Atlas of industrializing Britain 1780–1914* (1986), p. 151.

25 See the evidence of D. Robertson, general manager of the National Provincial, to the *S. C. on Joint Stock Banks* (1836), reprinted in Anderson and Cottrell, *Money and banking*, pp. 287–94.

26 Nishimura, *Decline of inland bills*, pp. 84–5.

27 K. S. Toft, 'A mid-nineteenth century attempt at banking control', *Revue internationale d'histoire de la banque*, 14 (1972).

28 B. L. Anderson and P. L. Cottrell, 'Another Victorian capital market: a study of banking and bank investors on Merseyside', *Economic History Review*, 2nd series, 28 (1975) and P. L. Cottrell, 'Credit, morals and sunspots: the financial boom of the 1860s and trade cycle theory', in P. L. Cottrell and D. E. Moggridge (eds.), *Money and power. Essays in honour of L. S. Pressnell* (1988).

29 The Central Bank of London (1863–1891), the Imperial Bank (1862–1893) and the West London Commercial Bank (1866–1887).

30 F. Capie and G. Rodrik-Bali, 'Concentration in British banking 1870–1920', *Business History*, 24 (1982).

31 M. Collins, 'The banking crisis of 1878', *Economic History Review*, 2nd ser., 42 (1989).

32 L. S. Pressnell, 'Gold reserves, banking reserves, and the Baring crisis of 1890', in C. R. Whittlesey and J. S. G. Wilson (eds.), *Essays in money and banking in honour of R. S. Sayers* (Oxford, 1968).

33 The above paragraphs are drawn from Holmes and Green, *Midland 150 years*, pp. 74–80, 85, 92–105, 121–9, 169.

34 On the Mercantile Bank and the Palatine Bank, see G. Chandler, *Four centuries of banking*, II, *The northern constituent banks* (1968), pp. 462–83, 501–15.

35 R. S. Sayers *The Bank of England 1891–1944* I (Cambridge, 1976), pp. 253–9. See also Chandler, *Northern constituent banks*, pp. 580–8; and Anon., *Williams Deacon's 1771–1970* (Manchester, 1970), pp. 157–60.

36 Holmes and Green *Midland 150 years*, p. 81.

37 Sayers, *Lloyds*, pp. 183–5, 38.

38 Holmes and Green, *Midland 150 years*, p. 141.

39 C. A. E. Goodhart, *The business of banking 1891–1914* (1972), pp. 134–6; Holmes and Green, *Midland 150 years*, pp. 135–40.

40 *The Economist* (1869), 116.

41 Holmes and Green, *Midland 150 years*, pp. 132, 166.

42 The above paragraphs are drawn from G. Jones, 'Lombard Street on the Riviera: the British clearing banks and Europe 1900–1960', *Business History*, 24 (1982).
43 Sayers, *Bank of England*, pp. 243–8.
44 See R. E. Cameron, 'England, 1750–1844', in Cameron (ed.), *Banking in the early stages of industrialisation* (1967); P. Mathias, 'Credit, capital and enterprise in the industrial revolution', *Journal of European Economic History*, 2 (1973); M. Collins and P. Hudson, 'Provincial bank lending: Yorkshire and Merseyside, 1826–1860', *Bulletin of Economic Research* (1979); P. L. Cottrell, *Industrial finance 1830–1914* (1980), pp. 210–28.
45 A. E. Musson, 'Industrial motive power in the United Kingdom, 1800–70', *Economic History Review*, 2nd ser., 29 (1976).
46 'How do our banks employ their money', *The Bankers' Magazine* (1880), 903–5; 'Business in the United Kingdom – its progress and prospects', *The Bankers' Magazine* (1884), 238; J. Dick, 'Banking statistics of the U.K. in 1896', *Journal of the Institute of Bankers*, 27 (1897), 197; Sayers, *Bank of England*, pp. 21–2; Goodhart, *Business of banking*, pp. 125, 130–3, 143–6, 151.
47 Holmes and Green, *Midland 150 years*, p. 63.
48 Nishimura, *Decline of inland bills*, pp. 106–8.
49 Holmes and Green, *Midland 150 years*, pp. 64–8.
50 Cottrell, *Industrial finance*, p. 238.
51 Holmes and Green, *Midland 150 years*, p. 105; Cottrell, *Industrial finance*, pp. 223–8.
52 Holmes and Green, *Midland 150 years*, pp. 108–13.
53 Cottrell, *Industrial finance*, pp. 237–9.
54 Holmes and Green, *Midland 150 years*, pp. 115, 117.
55 L. Joseph, *Industrial finance. A comparison between home and foreign developments* (1911), p. 9; F. Lavington, *The English capital market* (1921), p. 145; National Monetary Commission, *Interviews on the banking and currency systems of England*... (Washington, D.C., 1910). Interview with Sir Felix Schuster, pp. 47–8.
56 S. S. Hammersley, *The Times* (29 December 1928) quoted in Sayers, *Bank of England*, p. 320, fn 1.
57 S. Tolliday, *Business, banking and politics. The case of British Steel, 1918–1939* (1987), p. 178.
58 Sayers, *Bank of England*, pp. 319–20.
59 Sayers, *Bank of England*, pp. 323–7, 546–551.
60 Tolliday, *Business, banking and politics*, p. 184.
61 Sayers, *Bank of England*, pp. 557–9.

4 Banks and state in France from the 1880s to the 1930s: the impossible advance of the banks

ANDRÉ GUESLIN

The crisis of the 1880s brought to an end the preliminary phase of banking development in France: it consolidated the position of the great credit institutions and generated a policy of management rationalization which was coupled in due course with an 'industrial disengagement'. It inaugurated the 'golden age' of a finance-market economy. The crisis of the 1930s marked the end of this period.[1] Using modern economic concepts with care, I mean by this that, throughout the period, banking credit remained more or less limited and the financing of the economy came about through the accumulation of savings: primarily as companies directly used parts of their cash flow, but also by the transfer of domestic savings via the financial market.

Between the 1880s and the 1930s the state's influence was consolidated. Not that the preceding period was one of unadulterated liberalism; but, even before 1914, the germs of state intervention, very apparent after the First World War, were already perceptible. On the other hand, the war abruptly shattered the homogeneity of the period through the abandonment of the gold standard. And this was not without its consequences not only in the monetary, but also in the financial sphere.

The financial history of this half-century was still, I believe, dominated by the inability of the French private banks (unlike the banks of neighbouring countries with similar economic systems) to dominate financial channels. In other words, the increase in economic activity following the upsurge of the 1840s to 1860s might have brought about a rise in the power of banks as intermediaries. It never happened. I shall now attempt to demonstrate the truth of this and explain the reasons.

Table 4.1 *Composition of the French money supply (M1) from 1880 to 1913 (in percentages)*

	Coin	Fiduciary issues	Bank deposits
1880	65.7	17.2	17.2
1885	63.4	20.9	15.7
1895	51.7	23.8	24.5
1913	34.7	21.0	44.3

Source: Saint-Marc, *Histoire monétaire.*

The monetary approach: difficulties in stimulating the growth of banking money

The strength of conservatism in monetary matters

The money supply (M1: coinage, fiduciary issues, bank deposits) doubled between 1880 and 1913, representing a mean annual growth of 2.2 per cent in a period which was economically non-homogeneous, with a depression lasting until 1895 followed by an expansionist phase. The liquidity ratio, i.e. the ratio of M1 to GNP, rose from around 0.5 to 0.75.[2] France changed from a largely sub-monetary economy to a highly monetary one reflecting its 'economic take-off'.

The growth in the banks' most typical monetary resource, bank deposits, accounts for more than 87 per cent of the overall growth in the money supply. The number of cheques subject to stamp duty rose from about 5.5 million in 1881 to over 16.1 million in 1913, and the number of open accounts on the books of the Crédit Lyonnais alone rose from about 126,000 in 1890 to 667,000 in 1913. Since the creation of the major banks at the beginning of the second half of the nineteenth century, and in spite of the 1880s crisis which reduced the absolute value of bank deposits, the banking network had been expanding, though it was still a long way behind that of neighbouring countries such as the UK. The number of outlets of the Crédit Lyonnais, the Société Générale and the Comptoir d'Escompte, which made up between a third and a half of the banking outlets at the end of our period, rose from 195 in 1880 to 1,519 in 1912.[3]

Nonetheless, in 1913 bank deposits still did not represent the largest proportion of the money supply. Fiduciary issues, supplied in abundance by the Banque de France as a set-off, more than held their own. But Maurice Lévy-Leboyer is also right to point out the role of monetary substitutes (bills of exchange in the hands of companies outside the banking system) alongside the orthodox instruments. In 1913 these bills might well have been worth as much as the fiduciary issues.[4] The result was a seepage out of the banking channels, which however remains difficult to evaluate in the absence of any clear picture of the function of those bills. Nevertheless, we may emphasize that it supplies one explanation for the limitations of banks as intermediaries.

Both in the UK and in the United States, bank deposits represented about 88 per cent of the money supply (M1) at this time. The slow spread of bank deposits is explained by the economic structures of France and by the importance of the rural areas. Coin was traditionally scanty in the countryside, and up to the 1870s payment in kind was very common. Coins circulated only when annual rents were paid at Martinmass (11 November). It was only with the ending of rural isolation that monetary circulation began to force out the traditional payments in kind.[5] Then the banknote slowly usurped the place of coin. But there was considerable mental resistance. On the eve of the First World War, various departmental monetary surveys showed a connection between the spread of fiduciary issues and the level of development.[6] The bankruptcies of the eighteenth and nineteenth centuries were still present in people's minds, even if the Franco-Prussian War of 1870 had finally consolidated the position of the banknote. Finally, it must be pointed out that the banks' policy was more inclined towards the promotion of earnings from savings than towards deposit accounts.[7] All this explains the slow spread of the deposit account, which requires a certain economic education.

The question could be approached through a study of inheritances. The spread of deposits is closely connected with development and standards of living. Thus, in the sample of Parisian estates analysed by Adeline Daumard, the proportion of deposit accounts rose from 0.4 per cent in 1820 to 1.7 per cent in 1847, and finally to 4.5 per cent in 1911.[8] Similarly, the proportion of deposits was larger in very large estates (4.9 per cent in 1911) than in small or medium ones (3.3–3.4 per cent).[9] Claude Mesliand's analyses of the Vaucluse region reveal, in spite of the fact that it was a region open to speculative agriculture, that there were virtually no bank accounts in peasant inheritances in the year 1900 and only 2 per cent in 1910.[10]

The hazardous growth of banking money (1913–38)

Bank deposits, which were rising rapidly in 1913, did not keep up with inflation during the war. Although their nominal value doubled between 1913 and 1920, their real value actually halved. In general, inflation reduced the liquidity ratio (M1/GNP) from 0.72 to 0.44 between 1913 and 1921 as the speed of circulation increased. However, M1 diminished in volume more slowly than bank deposits alone. This was due to the growth in fiduciary issues in the wake of their counterparts, Treasury bonds, and especially advances from the Banque de France. This explains why, in

Table 4.2 *Composition of the French money supply (M1) from 1913 to 1938 (in percentages)*

	Coin	Fiduciary issues	Bank deposits, inc.:	PCCs	(b) Cooperative banks
1913	34.7	21.0	44.3	—	0.0
1920	1.5	56.7	42.5	0.4	0.1
1929	0.5	43.1	56.3	1.5	2.1
1932	0.8	45.4	53.8	1.3	2.5
1935	1.9	54.2	44.0	1.5	3.1
1938	1.5	49.5	49.0	2.0	5.5

Notes: PCCs Postal cheque centres.
Cooperative banks include Crédit Agricole and popular banks.
Source: Saint-Marc, *Histoire monétaire*; bank archives.

terms of relative values, the growth in the proportion of bank deposits, which was characteristic of the whole process, was interrupted by the war.

In the 1920s the relative growth in bank deposits was able to resume thanks to the regained dynamism of the banks. From 1925, bank deposits made up the largest part of M1; however, it was not until 1927 that the volume seen in 1913 was surpassed. The upsurge of 1927 is clearly to be linked with the Poincaré stabilization, which, by reversing the direction of speculation, allowed an influx of foreign capital. This real growth lasted up to the high point of 1932 (1931 in nominal values). Once again it is tempting to explain the reversal of the situation by the flight of speculative capital following the devaluation of the pound. However, in terms of relative values the high point was reached at the end of 1929 or the beginning of 1930. The highest nominal value of deposits in commercial banks alone probably occurred in June 1930.[11] It is well-known that the banks' earliest difficulties occurred relatively early in the development of the economic crisis in France: as early as November 1930 the Adam Bank of Boulogne crashed, causing panic in other provincial banks. The failure of the Banque Nationale de Crédit in September 1931 marked another stage in the crisis and aroused public distrust. Withdrawals connected with the bank's difficulties became less important after that, but a tendency to hoard banknotes becomes apparent. In 1938 the volume of bank deposits was only one-quarter greater than it had been in 1913. As a proportion of the GNP it shrank from about a third (32 per cent) to a quarter (25.2 per cent), while in the same period of time the proportion of notes rose from 15.2 per cent to 25.5 per cent. If we deduce the collection of postal cheques and the cooperative networks instituted by the state after 1918, we find that the relative proportion of money created by the commercial banks dropped from 44.3 per cent to 41.5 per cent between 1913 and 1938.

Thus the slow growth in bank deposits between 1913 and 1938 could be explained by a development in compensation procedures and a subsequent progress towards a final stage of monetarization.[12] In reality, the growth in the number of bills presented for compensation was relatively limited in view of the country's then state of development. Henri Laufenburger's statistics allow the calculation of a disparity with England of 1 to 2.2 in 1913 and of 1 to 3.8 in 1937.[13] More significant are the particular brakes put on the use of cheques: public payments only by postal transfer; substantial stamp duty on cheques up to 1938. Resistance to change and adaptation by the banks to the real state of the country explain the relatively low proportion of banking moneys on the eve of the Second World War.

The savings approach: a flow essentially outside the banks

It is traditional to emphasize the importance of savings in pre-1914 France. Guizot's exhortation is famous: 'Get rich – *enrichissez-vous* – by work and saving and you will become an elector.' Saving became a civic virtue. Socially speaking it was necessary in order to consolidate or constitute an inheritance and to pass it on to one's children. Finally, saving, in a society which had no effective system of social security, was a matter of simple foresight in case of unemployment, sickness or merely the advent of old age. However, contrary to all expectations, the level of gross private savings, outside the public sector, calculated on the basis of changes in inheritances, reached an average of 17 per cent of GDP between 1896 and 1913. Throughout the 1920s it remained stable at about 17 per cent, but in the 1930s it tended to rise, towards 19 per cent. But this was still much less than at the end of our period (22 per cent between 1958 and 1963).[14] However, these figures reflect both family and business savings (self-financing). Now, when we speak of a 'golden age' of saving in the period just before the First World War, we are of course speaking of domestic savings. We have no reliable statistics. However, to reverse the tendency we have just described, it would be necessary to show that the proportion of business savings within private savings had considerably increased. Now, the development of external sources of finance after the Second World War goes to show that it was in fact the contrary which must have happened. It will be observed that the ratio of domestic savings to the total resources in the *compte d'affectation* (a special account related to incomes in the French national account) was 10.8 per cent in 1938 as against about 12 per cent in the early 1960s. In fact, if savings were indeed the residue, as proposed by economic theory, this must, up to 1960, be the reflection of a country with a still rather low standard of living.

Table 4.3 *Stock-market capitalization and national income in France, 1913 and 1966 (in billions of francs)*

	1913	1966
National income (1)	41.8*	398.5
Stock-market capitalization (2)	116	167
(2)/(1)	277.5%	41.9%

Notes: * Includes Alsace-Lorraine.

The difficulty of making these observations is obvious. Thus Bouvier, p. 168, gives an estimated proportion of 345% for 1913, which would imply a margin of error of about 25%. This raises the problem of determining the date and basis of stock-market capitalization and national income in the absence of a national accounting system.

Sources: INSEE; Sauvy, *Histoire économique*; Saint-Marc, *Histoire monétaire.*

The picture which many people have of the period preceding the First World War has been distorted by the apportionment of the savings concerned. Their movement was marked by a very distinct diminishing of real estates in favour of financial savings. Secondly, savings made use of a symbolical channel, that is to say, the stock market.

The banks' role in the collection of financial savings

Between 1880 and 1913 stock-market capitalization (on the Paris Bourse) doubled, from 60 to 116 billion gold francs, representing a mean annual growth of 2 per cent. With current and deposit accounts, the ratio in 1913 was at least 1 to 6. In 1913, stock-market capitalization was 2.8 times higher than national income as estimated by Alfred Sauvy. And that is really the great difference made by the '*Trente glorieuses*' (1948–75) even if the rise in prices just before the war did help to accentuate the disparity.

In terms of gross issues related to gross internal production, the ratio went from 4 per cent in 1896 to 9.2 per cent in 1913. This was a much higher level than that seen after the Second World War (2 to 3.7 per cent).[15] As regards the structure of inheritances, this 'golden age' is particularly revealing. Thus, Adeline Daumard's calculations show that the proportion of stocks and shares in Parisian estates rose from 16.6 per cent in 1847 to 51.4 per cent in 1911.[16] It would be interesting to be able to interpret this structure in terms of age of the deceased, because the variation decreases with age. Consequently, our perception of the changing behaviour of economic agents is probably biased by the advanced age of the persons concerned. Claude Mesliand's analysis of

Table 4.4 *Elements in the composition of Parisian inheritances, 1847–1911 (in percentages)*

	1847	1911
Real estates	44.7	31.1
Debts, bills	21.5	4.9
Transferable assets	16.6	51.4
Total	82.8	87.4

Source: Daumard, *Fortunes françaises.*

peasant inheritances in the Vaucluse shows a broadly similar development, but with a time-lag which becomes apparent after the 1914–18 war. From 1900 to 1910, the proportion of estates including stock-market securities rose from 7 per cent to 10 per cent in number, meaning, at that time, more than 42 per cent in actual worth. Once again it is in the largest estates that the greatest penetration is found: 37 per cent in number, 59 per cent in actual worth.[17]

This represents a shift in the direction of long-term savings: the proportion of real estates can be estimated at about two-thirds of inheritances in 1851–5 and less than 44 per cent just before the war.[18] This is very apparent in the Paris sample if one focuses on the entries for houses, claims and transferable securities. Bearing in mind the importance of these three entries, we must conclude that the pattern of investments had altered. The direction of stock-market investments must be defined before we attempt a global analysis. It is difficult, without an exhaustive enquiry, to give an exact description of the structure of investments in transferable securities which would consider both the nature of the guarantee offered and the economic sector which issued them. They can, however, be approached by comparing variable-interest stock unguaranteed by the state (shares) with fixed-revenue stock or stock promoted by the state (debentures, *rentes*, foreign securities). M. Saint-Marc has calculated their market value from fiscal statistics and used a correcting factor to allow for non-taxable stocks. Between 1880 and 1895, the proportion of 'guaranteed savings' in the stock-market capitalization rose from 53.3 per cent to 63 per cent. But after 1895 there was a distinct setback, which became even faster after 1905: the proportion fell to less than 49 per cent in 1913. Certainly it must be borne in mind that under the 'share' entry we find railway stocks which were perceived almost as state securities. Regional variations can also be introduced. Thus in 1908–11, 'guaranteed savings' represented more than 75 per cent of the transferable securities in Parisian estates, whereas in Lyon the proportion did not reach 57 per cent. In any case, it is stocks which are involved and to perceive tendencies it is necessary to take account of fluctuations. Issues took fluctuations into account and, unlike stocks held by residents, they reflected the stock-market's investment capacity. But as a reflection of national behaviour patterns they are somewhat imprecise, since non-residents could also invest in France. In his study of state borrowings between 1878 and 1901, André Straus has concluded that Alfred Neymarck's estimate, according to which the proportion of foreign investment was 11 per cent in stocks in 1895, was certainly a ceiling as regards public issues.[19] However that may be, we must conclude that the general tendency of issues reflects national attitudes towards savings. In terms of issues on the French market, 'guaranteed savings' did not develop in any clearly discernible way: 84.5 per cent in 1892, 64.6 per cent in 1900 but 72.4 per cent in 1913.[20] This does indeed mask a change in absolute values. As a proportion of GDP, the importance of gross share issues in France was steadily growing: 0.9 per cent in 1896, 2 per cent in 1900 and 2.6 per cent in 1913.[21] Looking at the total, however, we may conclude that the most dynamic kind of saving, the one which had an element of risk and looked to the future, had great difficulty in establishing itself on the French stock market.

The other question brings us back to investment in foreign securities. Gross issues represented less than 2 per cent of GDP between 1895 and 1900 but 3.2 per cent in 1913. This was about a third of the issues on the French financial market. That level was never to be remotely approached at any time during the period under discussion. It must also be borne in mind that, on the eve of the 1914–18 war, international political crises limited the scope of the financial market. Statistics on stock-market capitalization are too vague to be reliable. And we are reduced to looking at inquiries into inheritances, despite the reluctance of older people to make changes in portfolio arbitrage. The proportion of foreign transferable securities in the total of private inheritances apparently rose from 8.8 per cent in 1890–5 to 14.1 per cent in 1910–14.[22] For 1908–11, Adeline Daumard values these investments, as a proportion of inheritances, at 19.1 per cent of the total value of estates, or 37 per cent of transferable securities. In Lyon the proportion was about the same, but was only 14.3 per cent of the value of the estate. In Bordeaux it was 10.5 per cent of the total inheritances but 42 per cent of the portfolio.

It is now time to analyse this turning towards financial assets in the prosperous France of 1895–1913. It has been attributed to the banks' policies, which were already coming under fire at the time, as in Lysis's famous pamphlet of 1906–7. The banks' policy of encouraging financial savings, and particularly foreign securities, has been sufficiently well analysed, and I shall not return to it here. To the banks it appeared to have a two-fold advantage. Firstly, a financial one: it consolidated their profits at a time of falling interest rates (up to the turn of the century). This brought in substantial commissions to some of the banks, notably the Société Générale and the Comptoir d'Escompte, not to mention provincial banks like the Société Nancéienne. On the other hand, the proportion of bond issues in the gross receipts of the Crédit Lyonnais was no higher than 10 to 15 per cent of the total at the turn of the century.[23] The second advantage of this policy was that it kept to the banks' rules of orthodoxy, which were hostile to any long-term use of their short-term liabilities ('transformation'). Under these conditions, and taking account of the limited use of commercial discounts, the Crédit Lyonnais resorted to encouraging its clients to buy stocks by arbitrage, using part of its deposits. Supply was an important factor in the choice of investments made by domestic savers.[24] And we must not lose sight of the actual supplier of transferable securities and of the fact that the banks, despite their ability to put pressure on investors, were first and foremost intermediaries. This brings us, as we consider the flow of financial savings, to the question of the policies of the 'suppliers' of financial instruments, i.e., essentially, private companies and public bodies. Thus, if banks in Lorraine, led by the Société Nancéienne, went in for a policy of collecting financial savings before 1914, it was on the request of the industrialists who sat on their board of directors.[25]

However, this policy won spontaneous approval, which alone made it practicable. In other words, domestic savers had a pre-existing attitude which inclined them to a certain type of investment. This is particularly clear if we look at long-term changes in investment preference throughout the nineteenth century. The shift in preferences from saving for real estates and *rentes*, then for debentures, and finally for foreign securities, bespeaks a time-lag in behaviour and attitudes rather than a complete change. First of all there was a demand for regular and sufficient returns rather than for substantial plus values. C. A. Michalet has shown an inverse proportion of the price of *rentes* to the stock held by domestic savers.[26] Then there was the search for security. Confidence in the state was something new at the end of the nineteenth century but it spread rapidly through all levels of society. Changing from one type of investment to another, bearing in mind the changes in their respective returns, was actually a way of continuing the traditional management of one's fortune. Finally, this was further extended by the essential part played by the rural market, which exacerbated types of behaviour which crystallized notably at the turn of the century. The opening up of the countryside accelerated the decline of hoarding, and investment on the stock market, guaranteed – or thought to be guaranteed – by the state, was the logical sequel. As for the returns on landed estates, they were endangered by the fall in agricultural incomes.

Therefore, state guarantees and anonymity encouraged people to redirect part of the yields of *rentes* into transferable securities rather than reinvesting in agriculture. Overall, the banks maintained an attitude towards saving grounded in notions of profitability and security by minimizing the inherent risks of foreign investments. For savers, investments before 1914 were not as irrational as has sometimes been maintained. Why invest in industrial securities which seemed to be less secure and gave no higher returns than bonds or foreign securities? Such was the situation in 1914 that a German analyst produced the following diagnosis: 'If they do not succeed in changing the attitudes of the higher classes of the population, then nothing will stop France from becoming a nation of rentiers. The organization of her banking system is well designed to produce such an outcome.'[27]

One exception must be pointed out, however: industrial Lorraine, where the two regional banks, the Société Nancéienne and the Banque Renauld, succeeded in creating a climate of confidence which allowed savings to be channelled into local industrial securities. But, unlike in Paris where savers no longer controlled the direction of their savings, in Lorraine savers probably had, rightly or wrongly, the feeling of being close to industrial activity. Similarly, from 1895 the growth of investment in shares, even if it did not endanger the preponderance of other investments in transferable securities, might have been obeying both the pro-arbitrage policies of the issuing companies and the encouragement of the banks during moments of international political crisis, and also the savers' own demand for returns and plus values. This hypothesis, that investments followed a certain logic, allows us to take a second look at the archaizing view of the French economy at the dawn of the twentieth century. In other words, savers' attitudes, bearing in mind the nature of the information at their disposal, were not as hidebound as has sometimes been claimed. And consequently, the banks' strategies had to take account of savers' preferences, since they could not always shape them.

We might then ask how savers adapted to monetary inflation, then to the economic slump of the interwar period. Inflation ate deep into the real value (capitalized interest) of rentes and bonds, and the crisis also affected shares. In this climate, the real value of shares shrank on average by 9 per cent between 1914 and 1939, that of rentes and bonds by 47 per cent.[28] This explains why, all other things being equal, stock-market capitalization diminished. In real terms it dropped 42 per cent between 1913 and 1937. This goes beyond a mere change in rates linked with the value of money. In proportion to the national income it had regressed considerably. Savings in transferable securities continued to increase, in nominal value but quite distinctly; new savers turned rather to short-term investments. Thus the ratio of stock-market capitalization to current and

Table 4.5 *Stock-market capitalization and national income in France, 1913, 1929 and 1937 (in billions of francs)*

	1913	1929	1937
National income (1)	41.8	334	304
Stock-market capitalization (2)	116	374	377
(2)/(1)	277.5%	111.9%	124.0%

Source: As for table 3.

deposit accounts fell from 6.2 to 2.1 between 1913 and 1937. And if amongst deposits we single out those of the savings banks which were comparable to investments in transferable securities, the ratio dropped from 20 to 6.2. In terms of gross issues of transferable securities in proportion to GDP, it can be calculated that the big break occurred in the early thirties. Up till then it was possible to find rates similar to those seen in 1913: 9.6 per cent in 1930 as against 9.2 per cent in 1913. With the economic crisis the rates fell sharply, and in the years up to the war never went above 3 per cent.[29]

Nonetheless, economic agents still tended to prefer financial assets, as they had at the start of our period. This is clearly shown by an analysis of inheritances. While there was a slight diminution in value compared with 1913, linked with the drop in rates of return, there was a clear increase in numbers. In 1913 only one estate in twenty had included shares; between 1934 and 1949 it was one in seven or eight. Similarly, in fixed-income securities the ratio rose from 1:14 in 1913 to 1:6 or 1:5 in 1934–49.[30] Claude Mesliand's calculations, based exclusively on peasant inheritances in the Vaucluse, show that while in 1910 one estate in ten included transferable securities, the proportion went up to nearly one in three (29 per cent) in 1938. This is not far removed from the rates of ownership of passbooks from the Caisse d'Epargne (savings bank). Naturally, the proportion was over 50 per cent in the more substantial estates. Overall we can talk about a wide diffusion of transferable securities among the public.

We might be tempted to go back on our initial hypothesis – of the rationality of economic agents – if we consider the vast capital losses in real terms and the consistently negative average real interest rates (except between 1928 and 1931, and then only for shares). Several explanations are possible. The first is a certain conservatism, or more precisely, a time-lag in adapting to the new monetary deal. It is also true that financial intermediaries, now solidly established in the countryside, went on propagating these securities at a time when other investment opportunities

Table 4.6 *Composition of deposits in France, 1891–1913 (in millions of contemporary francs)*

	1891	1913
Private:		
Bank deposits*	2055	9550
Public and state:		
Banque de France deposits	400	575
Caisses d'Epargne deposits	3,559	5,829
Other deposits, Caisses des Dépôts	829 (1890)	2,623
Crédit Agricole	—	4

Note: *Bank publishing a balance sheet.
Source: Crédit Lyonnais; Journal Officiel.

appeared to be limited. Working within legislation unfavourable to property owners, investments in real estate seemed unprofitable (rents were pegged, market values stagnant). The buying power of owners of real property was cut by a third to 50 per cent, in spite of a fillip at the end of the twenties.[31] We can thus understand why the proportion of real estate in inheritances declined up to 1930 (from 43.6 per cent in 1910 to 39.4 per cent in 1928). It rose slightly after that (40.6 per cent in 1934), while the proportion of transferable securities dropped (33.4 per cent to 30 per cent between 1928 and 1934).[32] The shift to short-term investments (see below) could not but be limited by the atmosphere of crisis in the banks and by the exceedingly negative real interest rates.

The other explanation relates to the relative security offered by some transferable investments at a time of economic crisis. A gathering momentum raised the proportion of foreign securities in inheritances from 6.5 per cent to 9.5 per cent between 1908 and 1934, but in 1949 it dropped to 2.7 per cent, reflecting the loss of confidence during the thirties. The proportion of gross issues of foreign securities in the GDP, which had reached 3.2 per cent in 1913, slumped – with occasional exceptions – to less than 1 per cent in the interwar period. It must be said that, with regard to foreign-security portfolios set up before 1914, the expression 'rentiers' euthanasia' is entirely justified: of the 40 billion gold francs existing in 1913, less than 10 billion remained in the 1920s.[33] In this situation the market was once again stabilized by the dissemination of state securities. However, there was a real 'scissors' effect between company share issues and issues from public bodies and the state. Between 1919 and 1923, state issues made up nearly 60 per cent of the total. After the Poincaré stabilization of 1926, private issues regained the advantage with a maximum net issue of over 15 billion in 1930. But between 1933 and 1938, net company share issues were always below 4 billion francs per year, while state issues were nearly, or clearly, over 10 billions (more than 60 per cent of the total in 1933–5 and in 1937–8).[34] The banks, which were then losing fat commissions on private issues, talked about a 'crowding-out effect'. The failure of the public loan of December 1935 might have been the result of exhaustion in a market which had been heavily played by the state. But it must be remembered that some private issues were not quoted on the stock market and thus do not appear in the statistics. Besides the effect of the state demand for capital, which created a supply, there may also have been an attempt on the part of the public to protect itself. This would explain *a contrario* the slight and temporary resurgence of public channels in moments of political crisis after 1935.

All in all, the development of financial markets rested on the association of three or four kinds of partnerships with different attitudes: businesses and state on the issuing side, savers and financial intermediaries. And the banks' capacity to exercise a guiding hand may have been exaggerated...

The rise in the power of public channels for deposit collection

The favourite kind of saving before 1914 was financial investment, but it did nothing to swell the banks' resources, since they acted purely as intermediaries. It was their capital, reserves and especially deposits, which maintained the banks' finances. It is hard to measure the ebb and flow of liquid and short-term savings, because balance sheets often lumped current accounts together with deposit accounts. Certainly deposit accounts were on average more liquid than savings accounts with the savings banks. However that may be, our object here is to compare the ability of the public sphere to collect with that of the private sphere. But the banking statistics available for this period are very incomplete. In particular, they concern only those banks which published their balance sheets. We have no evidence of a whole area of small businesses which must have had some effect on the overall state of deposits. Taking account of those limits, we can estimate the collection of deposits for France between 1891 and 1913, with the results given in table 4.6.

Owing to statistical uncertainties, it would be vain to attempt to give an exact total before 1913. In 1891 public channels were well ahead in the collection of liquidities, in a proportion of two to one. The imbalance sprang from the run which was triggered by the banking crisis of the early 1880s. It is known that the absolute value of demand deposits dropped from 1.9 billion to 1.7 billion francs between 1880 and 1885,[35] while deposits in savings banks rose from 1.2 billion to 2.3 billion in spite of tensions in 1882–3. But, in 1913, the banks caught up with the public channels and even overtook them slightly. They seemed much more resilient.[36] Nonetheless, this early prominence of public channels does raise a question. Looking at the Banque de France, the proportion was modest and represented accounts belonging to privileged clients of provincial branches. The assets of the Caisse des Dépôts et Consignations (without the deposits of the Caisses d'Epargne) mainly consisted of investments linked to the creation during and after the Second Empire of a state-run system of social security: funds for old-age pensions (1850), for accident and life assurance (1868), for private pensions and for other mutual societies. The sphere of action of these institutions was still very limited. The infrequency of deposit accounts in French society and the accumulation of reserve funds increased their importance.

Still more intriguing is the importance of funds held by the savings banks (Caisses d'Epargne), since it reflects an aspect of social behaviour. These institutions, created by private enterprise in the first third of the nineteenth century, had after some mid-century difficulties resumed their expansion to the point where in 1881 there appeared, alongside the private network which was strictly supervised by the state, a network of postal savings banks – Caisses d'Epargne Postale. Undoubtedly the use of post offices succeeded better than the banks in covering the potential market without excessive costs, as is attested by a special commission of the Parliament in 1891: 'In some small places where there is no banking house, the Caisse d'Epargne absorbs all the floating capital; in some larger cities, the Caisse d'Epargne has become the deposit bank for small businesses.'[37] The financial mechanism whereby the moneys deposited at the savings banks could be recycled at the Caisse des dépôts et Consignations made it possible to invest them in rentes and to give considerably higher interest than the banks did: in 1913, on the average, the banks were paying 1.5 per cent on deposit accounts and the Caisses d'Epargne 2.75 per cent. Finally, at a time when people on the whole had little understanding of how banks worked, it was the state guarantee which fuelled this dynamism. The drawback was the ceiling on the amount which could be invested. If the growth in the early 1880s can be partly explained by the doubling of the ceiling in 1881, from 1,000 francs to 2,000, one might also expect the contrary: that the lowering of the ceiling to 1,500 francs in 1895 contributed to the relative decline. In this connection, even in the nineteenth century it could be said that the banking and financial market was 'managed'. The state's policy with regard to the Caisses d'Epargne came to depend more and more on its financial needs.[38] Nevertheless, the Caisses continued their advance at a rate of 1.9 per cent per year. Above all, their passbooks began to penetrate throughout French society. In 1880 there were fewer than 4 million passbook holders (10.6 per cent of the population); in 1913 there was 15.1 million (31.1 per cent of the population). Averaged over the 12 million

French households existing in 1913, this means that some homes had more than one passbook!

The study of inheritances throws still more light on the frequency of passbook ownership. In value, the proportion of capital deposited in the Caisses d'Epargne remained modest. In 1903 it was less than 2 per cent of estates.[39] But the existence of a ceiling greatly reduces the significance of this figure. Mesliand's study of peasant inheritances in the Vaucluse shows that in 1900 21 per cent of estates included a passbook; in 1910, the proportion had reached a third, in spite of the traditional cheating on the declaration. And nearly one in two of the larger estates (on the author's criteria, those worth between 20,000 and 60,000 francs) included a passbook. It must also be remembered that the rules of inheritance excluded the youngest generations. We can therefore conclude that ownership of a passbook from a Caisse d'Epargne was advancing very rapidly on the eve of the First World War.

The changes in the total collection of deposits in the interwar years are still very hard to determine. We have three estimates. Henri Laufenburger seems to be using the combined results of all the banks publishing a balance sheet. On the other hand, the League of Nations and J. P. Patat and M. Lutfalla, make use of correcting factors based on the results of the biggest deposit banks. The League of Nations' estimate assumes that the collection of the six biggest deposit banks consistently represented 80 per cent of total deposits. This means that Laufenburger's results for some years are undercut by a third. Patat and Lutfalla's estimate is based on sliding correcting factors related to global censuses available for some years.[40] It is much more reliable, and overall supplies a corrective to Henri Laufenburger's more detailed observations.

The statistics for deposits clearly show the monetary, or quasi-monetary, character of bank deposits, unlike those of the Caisse d'Epargne which normally were less liquid. They closely echo the effects of inflation. Consequently, the change, already noted, in favour of bank deposits went on until 1930. We must add that the banks were very vigorous whereas the Caisses d'Epargne may have suffered from the political uncertainties of wartime. The creation and promotion of public or quasi-public institutions in the post-war period had not yet made itself felt.

The turning point was rather the economic crisis. More than the ensuing period, it was the crisis of the 1930s which established state domination of the channels for collection of deposits. It can be shown that at this period it was the Caisse des Dépôts, which was managing over 100 billion francs just before the war, which enjoyed the highest relative growth. Part of the deposits represented social insurance funds, which were expanding rapidly at this time. But the vigour came especially from the Caisses d'Epargne, as table 4.8 shows.

Table 4.7 *Composition of deposits in France, 1913–1937* (*in millions of contemporary francs*)

	1913	1920	1930	1937
Private:				
Bank deposits*	9,550	30,480	89,530	67,443
Public:				
Banque de France deposits	575	3,300	12,600	16,548
Caisse d'Epargne deposits	5,829	8,100	38,763	61,638
Caisse des Dépôts	2,623	3,461	11,678	28,664
CCP	—	300	2,000	3,413
Crédit Agricole	4	27	999	1,297
Popular banks	?	?	1,135	1,102
Public total	9,031	15,188	67,175	112,662

Note: * Banks publishing a balance sheet.
Sources: for 1913 and 1937, Laufenburger, *Enquête* and Journal Officiel.

Table 4.8 *Index of nominal growth of deposits in the six French big banks and the Caisses d'Epargne* (*1913 100*)

	Commercial bank deposits	Caisses d'Epargne
1913	100	100
1921	332	165
1926	615	269
1929	904	459
1930	894	665
1931	750	873
1932	754	982
1935	555	1,039
1937	654	1,053

Sources: after Patat and Lutfalla, *Histoire économique*, pp. 244–62; Journal Officiel.

In the 1920s the banks' importance increased dramatically. Bank accounts, which had appeared in one inheritance out of every thirty in 1908, figured in one out of every eleven in 1934.[41] After 1926, the banks' superiority was further reinforced by the influx of external floating capital. But between 1929 and 1931, the Caisses d'Epargne once again caught up with the banks in terms of relative growth. This must partly be due to the policy of the state towards the Caisses, which were collecting an important resource: their interest rates became more and more favourable. In 1913 the average interest rates of the banks and the Caisses were 1.5 per cent and 2.75 per cent respectively. But from 1919 to January 1927 they were very close (between 3 per cent and 4 per cent). However, from 1927 the banks' rates dropped steadily to 1 per cent in January 1931, while the Caisses' rate remained at 3.5 per cent. The latter also offered other advantages, such as exemption from new direct taxes and the conversion, without commission, of state bonds. Moreover, the ceiling on passbooks was raised. Thus, in March 1931 it was raised to 20,000 francs (6,000 times the hourly wage of a provincial workman), far above the 1,500 francs of 1913 and even the 7,500 francs of April 1925. And, to the great disadvantage of the banks, the Caisses tended more and more to receive the trading capital of small and medium-sized industrial and commercial firms.[42] It was the political situation – the Popular Front, followed by international tension – rather than the economic crisis which put a brake on the upsurge of the Caisses d'Epargne from 1936. But by that time passbooks had become part of everyday life. Between 1920 and 1935 their number rose from 15.5 million to 20 million. This means that, on average, every other Frenchman owned a passbook from a Caisse d'Epargne. In his study of private fortunes in France, based on inheritances, Paul Cornut notes that passbooks were part of one inheritance in five in 1908, and one in four in 1934.[43] The outstanding value of passbooks, one-third higher than that of bank accounts in 1908, surpassed it therefore by 120 per cent! In the peasant inheritances of the Vaucluse, passbooks figured in four estates out of ten in 1930, and in almost one in two of the medium and large estates.[44]

The economic crisis, with its bankruptcies and general panic, caused the destruction and transfer of deposits, especially between 1932 and 1935. Some withdrawals went to swell inactive cash hoards of gold and banknotes, especially 1,000-franc notes. The medium-term connection between withdrawal of deposits and banknotes in circulation is hard to prove, but there are striking examples of the reverse movement: in February–March 1934, while the deposits in the four big banks dropped by 2.5 billion, the number of notes in circulation rose by 3.4 billion.[45] As regards transfers, it is known that the banking crisis first affected average-sized institutions, allowing the bigger organizations to consolidate their hold. This was particularly true of the CIC which, by taking over the Société Nancéienne, got hold of the latter's clientele, and also that of the Banque Renauld which had ceased operations. But some withdrawals swelled the issues of public or quasi-public bodies, especially in 1933,[46] or went into personal accounts with the Banque de France: over 26,000 accounts were opened in 1931, as against 7,800 in 1930. Finally, the tendency to withdraw also affected foreign capital (cf. above).

For the banks, the history of the crisis of the 1930s was the history of a rise followed by an abrupt fall. To all appearances, while they channelled investment in transferable values, between 1895 and 1930 they had built up a collection of services of their own which backed their direct role as intermediaries. By upsetting the equilibrium of banking activities, the 1930s assured the domination of state channels. It is clear that this had a serious effect on banks as sources of finance.

The approach in terms of business finance: a limited function for the banks

We are short of statistics right up to 1945. Moreover, overall statistics omit, by definition, contributions in kind and private issues not addressed to the public. For all these reasons any interpretation must necessarily be tentative. If we approach the problem in terms of the finance supplied by the banks we must bear in mind the exceptional nature of the period, which was characterized both by the economic context of the financial markets and by the impact of specialized state channels. In terms of demand, we must not underestimate the distrust of credit among owners of small and medium businesses.

Between 1880 and 1913, the total credit granted by banks to non-banking agents grew from 1 billion francs to 13.4 billion.[47] As a proportion of GDP it grew from 7 per cent to over 40 per cent (it was about 60 per cent on the threshold of the 1980s). The financial orthodoxy of the period, together with the expansion of the networks, encouraged short-term credit (principally discounts), i.e. the financing of circulating capital, even if some repeated renewals of overdrafts or advances on stocks were actually masking a financing of fixed capital. In 1909 it was estimated that the French deposit banks had invested 54 per cent of their productive capital (capital, reserves and deposits) in bills of exchange, as against 28 per cent for the six biggest German banks.[48] It must be said that the regulations of the Banque de France, based on a single rate and the obtaining of three signatures, created a sort of captive market for the deposit banks, which was not the case in England or Germany. However, the Banque de France had been taking account of this since 1869 by admitting as the third signature a deposit of stocks, then especially, at the end of the century, a simple endorsement. It is nonetheless true that the creation of fiduciary money and bank deposits drew strength from this expansion in the private bills of exchange held by the big credit companies. Note, however, with Alain Plessis that, if the Banque de France's portfolio was overtaken by that of the four principal banks, it still steadily represented, between 1884 and 1913, from 9 to 13 per cent of all the bills of exchange in circulation owing to discounts by local banks and direct discounts.[49]

But the main problem, in studying a country which is past the first stage of economic development, is the financing of investments. On this essential point, some controversy has arisen over the function of the banks. It is well known that the tensions of the 1880s led big deposit banks into an 'industrial disengagement' which is reflected in the drop in their portfolios. As for the commercial banks, they were more selective in their direction and their foreign operations remained integral to them. Before 1913, investment still mainly came from self-financing. But historians rarely venture to give figures, for lack of sufficient information.[50] G. F. Teneul's estimates, based on a simplified capital account of the nation, produce a rate of self-financing of 65 per cent in 1900–13, which seems to me to be the minimum possible. However, M. Lévy-Leboyer maintains that the rate dropped to 40–5 per cent in 1910, probably because he used a sample of very big businesses which, even before 1914, were turning to the financial market and to bank credit.[51] In any case, even if there were some exceptions, most investment on the eve of the First World War did come from undistributed profits.

But sources of external finance were changing. Beside studies of businesses, which still tend to be too narrow, we can approach this change via study of inheritances. In the first phase of industrialization two important sources of finance were in decline. Thus, in Parisian inheritances, the proportion of assorted debts fell from 20.2 per cent to 4.9 per cent; that of capital from dormant partners remained extremely low, falling from 2.6 per cent to 2.4 per cent.[52] 'In France, there are no dormant partners, or at least, fewer than elsewhere,' as a contemporary analyst remarked. A new stage in the development was reached when the market in transferable securities became capable of allowing an extension of investment. In which case it might be the direction of that market which explains the importance of self-financing.

Leroy-Beaulieu, the great *fin-de-siècle* liberal economist, was highly critical of the flight of savings from productive channels: 'The State, which neither farms, nor produces goods, nor sells them, has forced on these [savings] banks the obligation to put all their assets into buying rentes or into current accounts with the Treasury.'[53] The other quasi-public channels, such as the Crédit Agricole, were still at the embryonic stage (it was worth less than 100 million francs), or, like the Crédit Foncier, were devoted to the financing of the market in real estates. As for investment in foreign securities, Lysis's strictures have already been mentioned. The big banks were also stigmatized for their insufficient attempts to help new businesses, or small- or medium-sized ones.

Without wishing to cast serious doubt on these analyses, it is possible to reconsider them. The savings collected through public and quasi-public channels were not wholly unproductive. They could have contributed to spending on infrastructure and equipment with likely leading effects. Deposit banks not only financed the national debt, but also advanced funds to local municipalities and public enterprise. In 1913, this amounted to 1.2 billion francs, to which must be added 800 million in assorted securities, mainly railway-company bonds. The detailed analyses of M. Lévy-Leboyer and F. Bourguignon have further shown that businesses may have been running into difficulties in procuring investment just at the time when capital exports were slowing down (1869–89).[54]

It may also be that too much attention has been paid to the policies of the big banks. Certainly they accounted for between half and two-thirds of total banking activity. But they were, by definition, strongly inclined towards investment in the public domain. They were the tip of the iceberg; beneath them, and not to be neglected, were the provincial banks. The League of Nations has numbered these banks at 600 (1,000 outlets), with a total capital of 1.6 billion francs in 1913, when the capital of the ten biggest French banks was no greater than 1.1 billion.[55] No doubt they suffered considerably from competition from the larger institutions, and the regional banks at least were in grave difficulties. But it should not be forgotten that the industrial regions underpinning the French economy – the north and east – and even new industrial regions such as the Isere, had a banking system geared to their needs. In 1904, the banks of the Meurthe-et-Moselle region showed a productivity of 2.8 billion, as against only 900 million for the agencies of the big banks.[56] And their success is attributable to an innovation which was described as follows by an inspector of the Banque de France's branch in Nancy:

> Backed by three banks of the first rank, the Lorraine region is continuing its vigorous industrial expansion, an expansion which the extensive support of the Banque de France has advanced by ten years. At the time of writing, the portfolio of the Nancy branch is the largest in the entire province. Most of it is in the form of capital from dormant partners. The immobility generally exhibited by such capital is much attenuated, here in Nancy, thanks to the method used here to encourage new businesses. The share capital is never taken up in its entirety: the initial organization is done with capital loaned by the bankers and supplied by the local branch, but as soon as the business has proved itself and can go public, bonds are issued and the overdraft is paid off. Thus the bankers' capital is tied up only for a relatively short period.[57]

So rapid was the growth that, in 1913, the total balance-sheet of the Société Nancéienne was equivalent to 10 per cent of that of the Crédit Lyonnais. The banks of Lorraine – the Nancéienne, and also the Banque Renauld – were at that time maintaining a genuine regional financial market based on the issue of securities by heavy industry. Michel Lescure's study of the Société Marseillaise de Crédit leads to the same conclusion. Where the local economy was buoyant, the regional banks

Table 4.9 *Changes in estimated ratio of private assets to loans and advances by the six French big deposit banks*

1913	1921	1925	1929	1937
1.48	1.79	1.37	1.39	1.63

Source: League of Nations. The total of private assets in portfolio has been recalculated on the basid of Teneul's estimates in percentages: *Financement*, p. 208.

answered to its needs, and indeed were a 'key element in regional growth'.[58]

Finally between 1890 and 1913 we may note a change of outlook in the financial market. G. F. Teneul's calculations show that the net contribution of financial savings to the financing of businesses in metropolitan France rose from 325 million francs in 1890 to 750 million in 1900 and 1,500 million in 1913.[59] This could still be ascribed to international crises which forced savings back on to the home market. But there was also a new buoyancy in the French economy and the pressure of need. Nonetheless, the intervention of the banks remained on a small scale.

Between the wars, the growing needs of the state had a direct effect on the financing of businesses. Studies by Marcel Malissen[60] show the rise in the rate of self-financing (from 40 per cent to 50 per cent). The role of the banks as sources of credit is a general problem. It was this period which saw the birth of specialized private banks such as the UBR (CIC group), UCINA, a subsidiary of the Crédit Lyonnais and the Comptoir d'Escompte, and CALIF (Société Générale group), through the perfecting of a rediscounting procedure for medium-term assets on the part of the Caisse des Dépôts. In fact, these operations remained embryonic, with a maximum of 2 per cent of bank credits in 1931. The 'loans and advances' entry on the balance sheets of the banks, even when dealing with short-term credits, often represented the financing of investments. Hubert Bonin notes that the BNC was financing investments with the help of overdrafts.[61] The 'loans and advances' entries of the six big deposit banks had plummeted because of wartime inflation. However, between 1930 and 1935 they regained their 1913 level before entering on another regression consequent on the erosion of monetary values in 1936–8. But between discounts and advances, the banks' strategy scarcely changed from what it had been pre-war, as is shown in table 4.9.

The total value of bank credit has been quite convincingly estimated by M. Saint-Marc. As a proportion of the national income as estimated by A. Sauvy, it can be seen that these credits dropped from 32 per cent in 1913 to less than 20 per cent in the 1920s (maximum 29 per cent in 1929), to less than 18 per cent at the end of our period. Thus, the banks' contribution was less than it had been before 1914, and their disengagement, at this time of crisis, raises grave questions.

The decrease in intervention by the banks was a consequence of the ever-increasing demands made on them by the state. This in turn was connected with the war, and beyond that, with the birth of the welfare state. State debts, which represented 10 per cent of GDP before 1914, rose to 20 per cent at the end of the war, a level which was reached again during the crisis after having fallen back to 14 per cent in 1929. The banks then got into the habit of including in their portfolios a substantial proportion of public bonds (Treasury bills issued during the war): over 60 per cent in 1920–4, less than 50 per cent thereafter (only 25 per cent in 1929–31 and 1937–8). Consequently, the level of self-financing rose during the large public issues of the early 1920s and in 1937–8. An apparent exception is 1933–5, when state issues were numerous, but the level of self-financing by companies was low in relative terms (20–25 per cent) because of the drop in cash-flow. They called for financial savings, but it was in order to finance 'investments' (calculated on the base of undistributed profits and transferable issues) which were in free fall (on average, about 10 billion as against over 20 billion at the beginning of the decade). Thus, the actual volume of bank intervention had declined.

It is in times of crisis that the 'eviction crowding-out effect' comes into play, especially between discounts and public assets. Thus, the statistics of the four big deposit banks (Lyonnais, Générale, CIC, Comptoir National d'Escompte) show that in 1932, when commercial securities fell by more than a billion francs, the total value of public assets rose by 3 billion.[62] The League of Nations analyst once again points out that in 1934 the commercial portfolio contracted to the benefit of the Banque de France (rediscount or direct discount), while the portfolio of Treasury bills remained constant. It was only from 1936 onwards that the banks became visibly uneasy. Certainly this disengagement can be explained by their distrust of the economic and financial policies, as well as the National Defence policy, led by the Popular Front.[63] Total short-term credit to business then regained its 1931 level (over 50 billion) but remained distinctly inferior to that of 1929–30 (63 billion).

This picture must certainly be nuanced. The fall in credit to the economy, which in 1930 amounted to over half the counterpart of the money in circulation, but to less than a third in 1934, cannot be explained simply by shifts of a few billion francs in the banks' portfolios. We have seen that other asset entries were also on the decline. In fact, the banks' crisis management reflected both the fall in their own resources and a search for financial security. At the same time, the importance of the banks was diminishing due to the encouragement of public channels: the

Table 4.10 *Financing of French business: rise of the public and semi-public organizations (in millions of francs)*

	Commercial banks (1)	Deposit bank (2)	Crédit Agricole (3)	Crédit National (4)	(5) (2)+(3)+(4)	(5)/(1)
1913	13,400	—	79	—	79	—
1920	26,000	582	189	31	802	3.1%
1929	70,000	2,779	1,873	527	5,179	7.4%
1931	56,000	7,765	2,906	800	11,471	20.5%
1935	50,000	14,535	3,112	997	18,644	37.3%
1938	60,000	16,455	5,691	1,181	23,327	38.9%

Source: Saint-Marc, *Histoire économique*: R. Priouret, *La Caisse des dépôts et consignations* (1966); Teneul, *Financement*; Journal Officiel.

Crédit National and the popular banks were rejuvenated and required to reinvigorate the small- and medium-sized business sector; the Crédit Agricole was restructured as a national state institution in 1920. In more prosperous times, even if the state 'protected' and favoured its own institutions, there seemed to be room for a balanced financial duality. But the crisis consolidated the rise of the state as the banks lost substance and as the public or quasi-public sector appeared to 'hold up'. It is useful to compare the credit of the commercial banks and the business investments of three of the most important public or quasi-public institutions, the Caisse des Dépôts, the Crédit Agricole and the Crédit National (see table 4.10).

Of course, in order to estimate the industrial role of the commercial banks we should have to assess the value of the industrial securities they owned. The nature of our sources makes this almost impossible. However, it can reasonably be thought that the volume of industrial securities owned by the banks tended to diminish throughout the period under examination. Thus, relatively speaking, the interwar period shows a certain retreat by the banks which is made still clearer by comparison with other countries.

The 'weight' of the French banks: towards a comparative analysis

Within an economy of financial markets and taking account of public and quasi-public channels, the 'internal weight' of the banks remained limited throughout our period.

Looking at the banking population in the broadest sense of the term, including collectors and other bank messengers, the number of employees

Table 4.11 *Estimate of the number of inhabitants per bank and banking agency at the end of* 1929

	Inhabitants per bank	Inhabitants per permanent agency
USA	5,000	4,500
Switzerland	21,000	6,500
France	70,000	7,300[a]
Belgium	90,000	6,000
Germany	135,000	30,000
Scotland	611,000	3,000
England and Wales	1,193,000	4,000

Note: [a] The League of Nations gives a bracket for France of 8 to 13,000 depending on whether one counts all the agencies or only the permanent ones. Comparing with Laufenburger's sources on the total number of outlets, which must have shrunk somewhat during the crisis, we can see a decrease. I have therefore rectified the League of Nation's evaluation on the basis of a comparison of the evaluation for the total number of agencies: this would give 7,300 instead of 13,000.
Source: League of Nations.

in the commercial banks, which was around 8,000 in 1866, rose to 32,000 in 1896, 121,000 at the census of 1921 and 160,000 at that of 1931. Within the working population, as far as this can be estimated, it amounted to 0.2 per cent in 1896, 0.6 per cent in 1921 and 0.8 per cent in 1931. Obviously it was still a minority occupation, utterly different from the importance it was to assume in the 1960s.

Another measure of the prominence of the banks is the number of outlets. According to Henri Laufenburger, there were probably 6,000 permanent and temporary outlets in 1913, and 9,366 in 1935: one per 6,600 of the population in 1913, one per 4,500 in 1935. The League of Nations has made some international comparisons based only on permanent outlets. Some of the results are reproduced in table 4.11.

For the penetration of the banks we can make a comparison with the Anglo-Saxon countries and with the Continent. It was Germany, not France as might be expected, which had the smallest banking network. This can probably be explained by the prevalence there of the savings banks, and above all the wide-ranging cooperative organizations (Raffleisenbank, Volksbank). The French banking network was of average size. This can also be explained by the large competing organizations: in 1938, against 9,057 banking outlets there were 10,200 for the main public and quasi-state institutions (ordinary savings banks,

Crédit Agricole, popular banks, Banque de France) and 16,800 post offices dispensing products of the Centres de Chèques Postaux and the Caisse Nationale d'Epargne.

It is true that the dissemination of banking outlets can be explained by the policy of promoting transferable securities. But the basis of the banks' intervention was the collection of deposits, which also partly reflected their policy on loans. The League of Nations has in fact given an evaluation for the same date; it poses the general problem of monetary comparisons which take account of exchange rates at any given time (table 4.12).

What comes out particularly clearly is the contrast between Switzerland and the Anglo-Saxon countries on the one hand, and the other countries on the Continent on the other. Estimates in francs for the end of 1937 reinforce this imbalance: 12,000 francs' worth of deposits per inhabitant in the United States, 10,100 francs in England, 1,700 francs in France.[64] The situation in France seems to be comparable with that in Belgium. The apparent 'backwardness' of France can be explained by the lesser importance there of bank deposits, the existence of channels for financial savings, the competition of the savings banks (which does not, however, seem to have been greater than in neighbouring countries), and by the probable existence of hoarding, reflecting the still essentially rural nature of the country.

Before the Second World War, French private banks were subject to numerous restrictions, mostly connected with the behaviour of economic agents and the level of development of the country. The economy of capital markets limited the banks' intervention, but still more it was the rules and customs of financial orthodoxy which worked against making a long-term use of short-term liabilities. Another brake was the absence of a reliable inter-bank organization. There was no real money market before 1938. The statutes of the Banque de France effectively prevented it from operating on the open market. As its branches were in competition with the big, widely distributed commercial banks, the latter avoided any rediscounting with the former. The existence of bilateral relations between banks could not compensate for the absence of an inter-bank market. It is this lack of internal organization in the banking sector which accounts for the impact of the crisis, which consolidated the intervention of the state, which had begun even before the First World War. No doubt we must take into account the absence of co-ordination in the public and quasi-public banking sector, and even the restriction on open competition was not enough to produce what could be called a real duality in the banking world. The development of the debt-based economy after 1945 was at first to benefit the public and quasi-public channels, reinforced still

Table 4.12 *Estimate of bank assets and the collection of deposits in dollars per inhabitant at the end of 1929*

<table>
<tr><th></th><th>Assets
(1)</th><th>Deposits
(2)</th><th>Deposits with other networks
(3)</th><th>Total deposits
(4)</th></tr>
<tr><td>Switzerland</td><td>800</td><td>580</td><td>134</td><td>714</td></tr>
<tr><td>USA</td><td>495</td><td>351</td><td>87</td><td>438</td></tr>
<tr><td>Scotland</td><td>310</td><td>250</td><td rowspan="2">53[a]</td><td rowspan="2">292</td></tr>
<tr><td>England and Wales</td><td>279</td><td>238</td></tr>
<tr><td>Belgium</td><td>131</td><td>102</td><td>30</td><td>132</td></tr>
<tr><td>Germany</td><td>99</td><td>62</td><td>60</td><td>122</td></tr>
<tr><td>France</td><td>71</td><td>60–99[b]</td><td>90–129</td><td></td></tr>
</table>

Notes: [a] Discount agencies and savings banks.
[b] The League of Nations bases its estimates on the 75 per cent ratio of the collection of the six big deposit banks to the total collection by all banks. All the direct estimates show that this ratio was distinctly too high for 1929. I have corrected it on the basis of Laufenburger's direct estimates: this changes 60 dollars per inhabitant to 99.
[c] Savings banks only.
Source: League of Nations.

further by the post-war political environment and the development of the welfare state. It was only after 1966, and not without difficulty, that the commercial banks of France were really able to flourish.

Notes

1 This chapter owes a great deal to the pioneering work of J. Bouvier. The author also expresses his thanks to Patrick Verley (University of Paris I), who kindly read and commented on this paper; the final responsibility rests with the author.

2 M. Saint-Marc, *Histoire monétaire de la France 1800–1980* (Paris, 1983), pp. 74–5.

3 J. Bouvier, in F. Braudel and E. Labrousse (eds.), *Histoire économique et sociale de la France, années 1880–1914* (Paris, 1979), p. 171; H. Laufenburger, *Enquête sur les changements de structure du crédit et de la banque. Les banques françaises*, vol. I (1940), p. 25.

4 M. Lévy-Leboyer and F. Bourguignon, *L'économie française au XIXe siècle. Analyse macro-économique* (Paris, 1985), pp. 309–11.

5 E. Weber, *La fin des terroirs. La modernisation de la France rurale 1870–1914* (1976–83), pp. 59–70.

6 Figures from Y. Nakagawa, 'La circulation monétaire dans les départements français des années 1870 à 1914', *thèse 3ème cycle* (unpublished), University of Paris I (1981), fol. 90.

7 See above, pp. 68–75.
8 Enquiry directed by A. Daumard and published as *Les fortunes françaises au XIXe siècle* (Paris/The Hague, 1973), p. 166.
9 Ibid., p. 241.
10 C. Mesliand, 'La fortune paysanne dans le Vaucluse (1900–1938)', *Annales ESC*, no. 1 (January/February 1967), 115.
11 J.-P. Patat and M. Lutfalla, *Histoire monétaire de la France au XXe siècle* (Paris, 1986), p. 254.
12 According to Saint-Marc's estimates (*Histoire monétaire*, pp. 81–2), the rate of turnover of bank deposits probably rose from 1.6 in 1913 to 5.2 in 1938 after reaching a high of 12 in 1924.
13 Laufenburger, *Enquête*, vol. I, p. 203.
14 Rates calculated by J. J. Carré, P. Dubois and E. Malinvaud, *La croissance française. Un essai d'analyse économique causale de l'après-guerre* (Paris, 1972), p. 365.
15 Rates calculated by Carré, Dubois and Malinvaud, *Croissance française*, p. 422.
16 Daumard, *Fortunes françaises*, pp. 232–5.
17 Mesliand, 'Fortune paysanne', pp. 115 and 123.
18 C. A. Michalet, *Les placements des épargnants français de 1815 à nos jours* (Paris, 1968), p. 101.
19 A. Straus, 'Trésor public et marché financier. Les emprunts d'Etat par souscription publique (1878–1901)', *Revue Historique*, 541 (January/March 1982), 75.
20 Statistique Générale de la France.
21 Rates calculated by Carré, Dubois and Malinvaud, *Croissance française*, p. 422.
22 Michalet, *Placements*, pp. 120ff.
23 See the analysis by J. C. Billoret, 'Système bancaire et dynamique économique dans un pays à monnaie stable, France 1816–1914', *thèse Sciences Economiques*, (Nancy 1969), fols. 399–404. Using commissions on public borrowing, Straus ('Trésor public et marché financier', p. 91), gives estimates of around 0.1 per cent, but raises the question of hidden commissions, notably in connection with exchange. It is also certain that the largest commissions were on private or foreign issues.
24 Michalet, *Placements*, passim.
25 From a study still in progress.
26 Michalet, *Placements*, p. 159.
27 E. Kaufmann, *La Banque en France* (*considérée principalement au point de vue des trois grandes banques de dépôts*) (1914), cited in Billoret, *Système bancaire*.
28 A. Sauvy, *Histoire économique de la France entre les deux guerres* (Paris, 1965–7), vol. II, p. 279.
29 Rates calculated by Carré, Dubois and Malinvaud, *Croissance française*, pp. 365, 422.

30 P. Cornut, 'Contribution à la recherche de la répartition de la fortune privée en France et dans chaque département au cours de la première moitié du XXe siècle', *thèse Droit* (1963), fol. 48.
31 A. Hirsch, 'Le logement', in Sauvy, *Histoire économique*, vol. III, p. 101.
32 Michalet, *Placements*, p. 240.
33 Sauvy, *Histoire économique*, vol. II, p. 270.
34 Ibid., p. 282; A. Straus, 'Le financement des dépenses publiques dans l'entre-deux-guerres', *Le capitalisme français 19e–20e siècle. Blocages et dynamismes d'une croissance* (Paris, 1987), p. 102.
35 Saint-Marc, *Histoire monétaire*, p. 33.
36 H. Bonin, in 'Les banques françaises de la seconde industrialisation', *Revue Historique*, 543 (July/September 1982), 208, defends the contrary thesis, but conditionally and giving no figures. In fact, in the absence of detailed statistics it is best to conclude that the two poles remained in balance.
37 Cited in H. Darrès, 'Concurrence des Caisses d'Epargne et des Banques de dépôts', *thèse Droit* (1933), fols. 32–3.
38 This is particularly clear in the 1881 legislation which answers a need to finance the floating debt.
39 Figures by R. Pupin, corrected by Lévy-Leboyer and Bourguignon, *Economie française*, p. 90.
40 Patat and Lutfalla, *Histoire monétaire*, pp. 239–40.
41 Cornut, 'Répartition de la fortune', fol. 48.
42 Laufenburger, *Enquête*, pp. 78, 169.
43 Cornut, 'Répartition de la fortune', fol. 48.
44 Mesliand, 'Fortune paysanne', p. 121.
45 A calculation for the period 1928–34 of the correlation between fiduciary issues and bank deposits (monthly values) yielded no decisive results in spite of some negative signs. See League of Nations, *Les banques commerciales 1925–34* (Geneva, 1935), pp. 50–1.
46 League of Nations, *Les banques commerciales 1925–1933* (Geneva, 1934), p. 132.
47 After estimates by Saint-Marc, *Histoire monétaire*, pp. 62–5.
48 Kaufmann, *La Banque en France*, p. 275.
49 A. Plessis, 'Les concours de la Banque de France à l'économie (1842–1914)', *Etats, Fiscalités, Economies*, Actes du Cinquième Congrès de l'Association Française des Historiens Economistes, 16–18 June 1983, Publications de la Sorbonne, pp. 169–80.
50 As an illustration the excellent work of M. Hau may be consulted: 'L'industrialisation de l'Alsace (1803–1939', *thèse d'Etat* (Strasbourg, 1987), fols. 338–43; or that of J. M. Moine, 'Les Barons du Fer. Les maîtres de forges en Lorraine du milieu de 19e siècle aux années 1930. Histoire sociale d'un patronat siderurgique', *thèse Histoire*, (Nancy II, 1987) fols. 353–8.
51 G. F. Teneul, *Le financement des entreprises en France depuis la fin du*

XIXe siècle à nos jours (Paris, 1961), p. 102; Lévy-Leboyer and Bourguignon, *Economie française*, p. 95.

52 Daumard, *Fortunes françaises*, p. 235.

53 P. Leroy-Beaulieu, *Traité théorique et pratique d'économie politique*, vol. IV (Paris, 1896), p. 396.

54 Lévy-Leboyer and Bourguignon, *Economie française*, pp. 84–5.

55 League of Nations, *Les Banques commerciales 1913–1929* (Geneva, 1931), p. 153.

56 Kaufmann, *La Banque en France*, p. 381.

57 *Archives de la Banque de France*, 'Rapport concernant la vérification de la succursale de la Banque de France à Nancy par M. Sevène', 1912.

58 M. Lescure, 'Banques régionales et croissance économique au XIXe siècle: l'exemple de la Société Marseillaise de Crédit', *Banque et Investissement en Mediterranée*, Chambre de Commerce de Marseille (1985), p. 113.

59 Teneul, *Financement des entreprises*, p. 84.

60 M. Malissen, 'Contribution à l'étude de l'autofinancement des sociétés en France et aux Etats-Unis', *doctorat Droit* (Grenoble, 1952), fol. 109.

61 Bonin, 'Les banques françaises', pp. 216–17.

62 League of Nations, *Les banques commerciales 1925–1933*, p. 132.

63 R. Frankenstein, 'Le prix du réarmement français (1935–1939)', *thèse Histoire* (Paris, 1982), fols. 100, 141–3, 244.

64 Laufenburger, *Enquête*, p. 187.

5 An overview on the role of the large German banks up to 1914

RICHARD TILLY

To discuss the role of banks and bankers in nineteenth-century Germany is to hallow one of that country's historiographical traditions. For the topic is an evergreen, as old as the German consciousness of industrial development as a national achievement itself. Entrepreneurs, and especially bankers, contributed to the literature from the start, but financial journalists, academic economists and even politicians spoke out as well. To point to the fact that many of these writers were engaged in special interest, pleading rather than attempting to write banking history as it 'really was', may be logically fallacious as criticism, but nevertheless relevant. That standard work on Germany's large banks, by Jacob Riesser (*The German Great Banks and their Concentration*)[1], was a response to public criticism of those banks and their power for evil by a director of one of the largest banks, the Bank für Handel und Industrie zu Darmstadt. He argued for a minimum of government regulation on the grounds that the banks 'naturally' operated in the public national interest without compulsion – an important part of his argument built on the belief that competition among banks remained intense, despite growing concentration at the top. About the same time (1909) Rudolf Hilferding's study, *Finanz-Kapital*[2] appeared, covering some of the same ground as Riesser but focusing on the considerable degree of monopoly power he believed the banks to have over industry and integrating that phenomenon into a revision of Marxist theory (as part of the concept, 'Organized Capitalism'). More on this question below.

A consensus

Since that golden age of pre-1914 work the great banks have continued to attract the attention of scholars, though interest in the pre-1914 developments has become increasingly academic, a matter for economic historians. This is not the place for a full review, but a brief sketch of the literature's consensus may be appropriate. That consensus embraces five main points. First, there is general agreement about the striking prominence of the large, joint-stock 'mixed' banks, particularly from an international comparative perspective. In 1913 Germany's three largest enterprises (by capital) were joint-stock banks, as were seventeen of the top twenty five. That relative bank position was equalled in no other industrial country at this time. Moreover, taking account of inter-bank share ownership and pooling agreements would place the share of total bank assets controlled by the top five Berlin banks at over 40 per cent.[3]

Second, despite some dissent, the historical literature generally attributes to the banks a positive and significant contribution to Germany's economic development in the nineteenth century. This contribution consisted in the financing of risky investments, particularly in heavy industry, and included entrepreneurial feats such as the formation of new enterprises, the implementation of mergers and the organization of cartels.[4] I have argued elsewhere that recent work suggests that the German institutional arrangements for capital market finance of risky industrial investments were significantly more effective in the 1870–1913 period than those of Great Britain at this same time.[5]

Third, there is more dissent but on balance a clear preference in the literature for the view that these 'great' banks and their executives exercised considerable power in German economic life, power indicated by the large number of banks they took over and the resultant increase in their share of total bank deposits, by the large number of directorships they occupied in German business corporations, by their well-known ability to control strategic decisions through the institution of proxy voting in shareholders' meetings, by the close links between leading bankers and the political elite of the German Kaiserreich, and by a number of well-documented concrete cases of enterprise decision-making in which conflicts resolved themselves in favour of intervening banks.[6] This is related to the first point about financing risky investments, for such power reflected banker access to information which could lower their *ex ante* risk assessment.

Fourth, in spite of quantum differences between joint-stock banks and private bankers, most historians would accept the theses of the pioneer role of the latter in creating the former and of the continuity linking both. 'Universal banking', that is perhaps most significant, was developed by private bankers as early as the 1830s and 1840s – in association with the organization and financing of the railroads. And the joint-stock banks themselves were developed by the private bankers to assist in those organizational and financial tasks.[7]

Fifth, the literature agrees that, by concentrating on the financing of small numbers of relatively large-scale projects and established enterprises, the 'great banks' neglected large segments of the country's financial business: agricultural credit, housing, small business (especially new business enterprises), small savings, denote fields left to the municipal savings banks, the credit cooperatives, local small private bankers – so far as these fields attracted financial intermediaries at all. After all, then, as later, most industrial investment was self-financed.[8] It was only in the 1890s that the large credit banks, spurred by the expansion of the savings banks and the credit cooperatives, began to utilize their branch systems to attract small savings and finance smaller business.[9] The relatively elite character of their business operations, in fact, explains much of their willingness to engage in fairly risky investment finance and also the low cash reserves they maintained.

Quantitative dimensions

These last observations call attention to some of the quantitative dimensions of German banking. References to equity capital have already been made. In that respect the large joint-stock banks had no equals. Looking at table 5.1, however, one notes the relatively great importance of areas those banks did not serve: the areas serviced by the savings banks, credit cooperatives, mortgage banks and so on. Note also the continued prominence of the private bankers as late as 1880. That strengthens our fourth 'consensus' point above in the sense that private bankers continued to play an important role long after the joint-stock banks had established themselves. Finally, note that these figures do *not* capture the influence of self-financing, indisputably German industry's principal source of funds in the 1850–1914 period. An idea of how important this might have been can be derived from a comparison of total financial assets and estimated total wealth with estimated value of assets held by financial institutions. This is in table 5.2.

Assets held by financial institutions grow not only absolutely but relatively to total financial assets. Still, the gain is not huge and the value of financial assets held outside the specialized financial sector remains large. To some extent, to be sure, the willingness of private wealth-holders to take assets into their portfolios will have depended upon the efforts and guarantees given by those specialized institutions. That is clearly true for the 'securitization' of corporate finance. More on this theme below.

It has by now become commonplace to point out the important role played by the state in shaping the development of banking institutions. Nevertheless, the point merits emphasis. In the German case, the connections between government regulation of note-issue and the development of 'mixed' or universal banking is of special significance. In

Table 5.1 *Assets of German financial institutions, 1860–1913* (*in billions of marks*)

	1860	1880	1900
Banks of issue	0.95	1.57	2.57
Credit banks	0.39	1.35	6.69
Private banks	1.50	2.50	3.50
Saving banks	0.51	2.78	9.45
Credit cooperatives	0.01	0.59	1.68
Mortgage banks	0.09	1.85	7.50
Public land and mortgage institutions	0.68	1.76	4.05
Life insurance companies	0.07	0.44	2.42
Other insurance companies	—	0.35	0.83
Social insurance	—	—	0.87
Other	—	—	—
Total	4.25	13.5	40.5

Source: R. Tilly, 'Verkehrs- und Nachrichtenwesen, Handel, Geld-Kredit- und Versicherungswesen 1850–1914', in W. Zorn (ed.), *Handbuch der deutschen Wirtschaftsgeschichte* (*Stuttgart*, 1976), *p*. 591.

Table 5.2 *Assets in Germany, 1875–1913* (*billions of marks*)

	1875	1895	1913
1 Total financial assets	44	98	252
of financial institutions	11	29	83
2 Land	54	52	97
3 Other real domestic assets	81	104	265
4 Other assets	7	14	25
5 Total assets	186	268	639

Source: R. Goldsmith, Comparative national balance sheets. *A study of twenty countries, 1688–1978* (Chicago and London, 1985), appendix A, pp. 221–6.

most German states and in Prussia, by far the most important state, the issue of banknotes was recognized as a kind of money creation having a 'public good' character and one offering the possibility of seignorage gains. This recognition in governing circles ruled out delegation of note-issuing rights to private banks. With the founding of the Prussian Bank in 1846 the monopoly of issue by a government institution was all but settled. For by the 1860s that bank's note circulation had already become the principal form of cash other than coin, while its growing system of branches and the rediscounting and clearing facilities they offered were making it the center of Prussia's payments system. In 1875, when the

Reichsbank took over the Prussian Bank's facilities, the system of government monopoly of issue was extended to all of Germany.

The significance of this development lies in the fact that banks of issue must maintain convertibility and to secure this, must maintain relatively liquid portfolios. Banks which were denied the right of issue, would necessarily pursue less liquid lines of business. Thus the typical German joint-stock banks could develop 'mixed' banking, a combination of short-term credit and deposit business with investment banking activities. Thus a division of labour between government and private (joint-stock) banking institutions emerged: the former dominated the payments and short-term credit business, the latter commercial and investment banking. Moreover, the former proved increasingly willing to serve as rediscounter of bills and lender of last resort in times of illiquidity. This made the private institutions all the more willing to engage in risky investment banking activities, for, if difficulties arose, they could look to the Reichsbank for help. By the end of the nineteenth century, that is, universal banks could build their business operations – at least in part – on the Reichsbank's liquidity guarantee.[10]

Contributions to industrialization

One of the most difficult questions to answer concerns how banks contributed to economic growth and industrialization. Quite a few scholars have stressed the role of banks in providing current account advances to industrial customers on a liberal, flexible basis.[11] In some notable cases industrial firms ran up considerable deficits on current accounts and were financing long-term investment with more or less revolving bank credits; and in a number of such cases, when the time seemed ripe, those firms and their bankers then turned to the capital market for refunding by issuing equity shares or bonds.

But though the pattern seems clear enough, systematic empirical proof is largely *ad hoc*, based on assorted examples (or samples), the representativeness of which is uncertain. For this reason a few attempts at more systematic interpretation deserve mention. The first concerns E. Eistert's 1970 study.[12] He focuses on an estimate of annual current account business turnover (on the debit side of the banks' ledgers) which is then compared with an indicator of aggregate business activity, in this case bill of exchange volume and, also, net national product. According to Eistert's interpretation of the 'credit availability' thesis, if the volume of annual bank advances grows more rapidly over time than indicators of business volume, then bank credit was not a limiting factor on growth. Since Eistert's empirical results show just that, he concludes that the banks contributed positively to growth in the sense of posing no bottle-neck. I have discussed the naivety of this test elsewhere and must leave further adjudication of the question to the reader.[13]

The validity of tests juxtaposing annual series of bank credit volume and net national product can be questioned, obviously, and for that reason the study of Neuburger and Stokes which goes beyond that test is worth mentioning here.[14] These authors constructed a model using Eistert's bank credit series but containing two further modifications: first, the inclusion of other macro-economic variables explaining economic growth: the capital stock, the labour supply and a time trend reflecting autonomous technical progress; and second, the notion that bank credit could be highly concentrated in certain sectors of the economy (e.g. heavy industry) at the expense of an undersupply to other branches and with the result of a misallocation of resources. This is consonant with the belief – frequently found in the literature – that the large German credit banks did favour large, heavy industrial enterprises in their allocation of their credit. Their regressions on the relevant time series data, in fact, show the ratio of current account advances to total bank credits (CA/MB) to have contributed *negatively* to growth. The higher the share of current advances in overall bank activities, the lower the rate of growth. Given the shaky data base and the absence of direct information on sectoral allocation of bank credit, the test is questionable. Nevertheless, it does draw attention to the difficulty of constructing systematic tests of the bank-industrialization relationship and also to the possible relevance of market imperfections. That is something.

Investment banking in comparative perspective

A problem of the Eistert and the Neuburger and Stokes' analyses was that they did not have or use data on allocation of bank credits to different sectors or branches of economy. One way to estimate that allocation is to mobilize the data on new issues of domestic securities, available for the 1883–1913 period. It is possible to use these data as an index of the distribution of banks' current account advances. These data appear in table 5.3. With a little imagination and the help of some heroic assumptions, they can be seen as individual investments in portfolios, with the sectorial growth rates of output representing yields (and expected yields) and the variance around those yields the associated risk (and expected risk). The new issue shares obviously represent the portfolio shares and determine the overall portfolio yield. Note that two-thirds of the credits were funnelled into just four rapidly growing sectors (excluding finance). But the test of efficiency of intermediation by banks is in the distance between the overall (bank-intermediated) portfolio and the theoretical optimum – the 'efficient portfolio frontier'. This latter is

Table 5.3 *Assumed asset yields and asset shares in bank portfolio, Germany, 1880–1913* (*in* %)

	Assumed			Share in portfolio	
Branch	Nr.	Yield	Risk	Including sector 12	Excluding sector 12
Mining	1	4.13	4.41	5.30	6.80
Quarrying	2	4.30	8.58	1.20	1.50
Metals	3	5.65	7.64	15.80	20.40
Engineering	4	6.01	6.34	10.50	13.50
Chemicals	5	5.98	3.85	4.80	6.20
Textiles	6	2.52	8.11	2.10	2.70
Wood and leather	7	3.62	7.75	2.20	2.90
Food and drink	8	2.81	3.91	3.20	4.20
Ultilities	9	9.80	10.37	16.60	21.40
Construction	10	4.22	7.17	2.50	3.20
Transportation	11	5.63	3.19	10.40	13.40
Trade, finance and insurance	12	3.50	2.27	23.80	
Miscellaneous	13	2.73	2.33	2.20	2.90
Portfolio yield				5.51	5.96
Standard deviation				3.09	

Source: Richard Tilly, 'German banking, 1850–1914: development assistance to the strong', in *Journal of European Economic History*, 15 (1986).

generated by an algorithm described among other places in the Kennedy and Britton paper cited above.[15]

How well did the German bankers do? In this connection the already cited work of William Kennedy on British portfolios for the same period is relevant, for it allows a direct, if rough, comparison with the German realized portfolio. Two rough measures are available. First, following the German approach, one may estimate a collective portfolio for Britain on the basis of new capital issues in the London market, 1880–1913. This can be linked to the sectoral growth rates as discussed above and a mean yield and variance calculated. The result (in table 5.4) is unfavourable to Britain in the sense that the portfolio's ratio of yield variance to mean is higher than the German estimate but also in the sense that it lies relatively further away from the efficient portfolio frontier (as calculated by Kennedy) than the German one. The British 'capital market' portfolio lies, given its variance, more than 100 per cent below the corresponding yield on the frontier (about $5.33–2.45/2.45 = 1.17$), whereas the German bank portfolio lies about 25 per cent below the frontier at the relevant point ($6.78–5.51/5.51 = 0.23$). Second, Kennedy's estimates of a large number

Table 5.4 *Assumed asset yields and asset shares in British capital market portfolio, 1882–1913* (in %)*

Branch	Assumed yield	Assumed risk	Share in portfolio
1 Mining	2.31	7.28	3.33[1]
2 Quarrying	2.31	7.28	2.00[2]
3 Metals	2.55	9.05	1.43[1]
4 Chemicals	3.63	8.71	4.31
5 Engineering	3.00	9.84	10.60
6 Textiles	1.52	9.33	4.82
7 Food and drink	1.38	4.36	20.71
8 Gas, electricity and water	4.86	3.89	5.16
9 Paper	5.04	10.78	1.76
10 Transport and communications	2.74	2.44	26.60[3]
11 Distribution	2.16	4.00	1.28
12 GDF	2.00	2.64	18.00[4]
13 Portfolio	2.45	8.20	100.00

Notes: *Actually covers years 1882–1905, 1907 and 1910–12.
[1] Data on new issues of mining and metal production enterprises were merged as originally collected. Here they are assigned to coal and iron and steel as in the 1907 production census: 3:1.
[2] As in (1) with 1907 weight 13/126 for coal mining.
[3] Includes 'docks and shipping'.
[4] Category 'other' in 'capital created' statistics of IMM.
Source: R. Tilly, 'Zur Finanzierung des Wirtschaftswachstums in Deutschland und Großbritannien, 1880–1913', in Ernst Helmstädter (ed.), *Die Bedingungen des Wirtschaftswachstums in Vergangenheit und Zukunft, Gedenkschrift für Walter G. Hoffmann* (Tübingen, 1984).

of Scottish portfolios suggest that movement to the efficient frontier could have produced a gain in yield for a given level of risk of about 40 per cent – once again, well above the German figure.[16] In short, to the extent that the data are comparable, the results tend to confirm historiographical judgements about the role of German banks as efficient organizers of the financing of industrial growth and also concerning the inefficiencies of the British capital market in the same period.[17]

Industrial finance

Source problems and limitations of available archival materials have spurred research into the industrial side of the banking–industry nexus. A number of interesting studies have emerged in recent years.[18] These studies have source problems of their own, especially insofar as they build on the experience of unusually long-lived enterprises or on published information. Nevertheless, some of the findings are worth reporting. Table 5.5 summarizes some of the relevant information (based on published sources). It uses the methodology of balance sheet differences which defines:

$$\begin{aligned} \text{Total finance as} = \quad & \text{Retained profits} && (1)\\ & +\text{Depreciation charges} && (2)\\ & +\Delta\ \text{Reserves} && (3)\\ & +\Delta\ \text{Share capital} && (4)\\ & +\Delta\ \text{Debt} && (5)\\ & -\Delta\ \text{Liabilities} && (6) \end{aligned}$$

and

$$\text{Internal finance as} = (1)+(2)+(3)+(6)$$
$$\text{External finance as} = \text{Total finance} - ((1)+(2)+(3))$$

and

$$\text{Self-finance as} = (1)+(3)$$

The basic findings are:

1 The dominance of internal finance is clear. But the growing importance of external finance over time is also evident.
2 One sees the clear positive connection between the business cycle position and external finance. This followed mainly from equity capital increases which yielded particularly large investments to reserves in 'good times' when premia on newly issued shares could be realized.
3 There is a significant difference between changes in the level of long-term debt and other forms of capital with respect to timing, only implied in table 5.5 but worth commenting on. In recessions, hardly less long-term debt (capital) was raised than in prosperity phases. A contingency table yields the following picture for fifty enterprises and thirty-one years (see table 5.6).

This was related to different capital costs with interest rate considerations weighing more heavily in recessions and share prices more heavily in prosperity.

Here, too, the analysis can be given a comparative perspective by drawing on the British experience. Of interest is the relationship between capital market conditions on the one hand, and the equity–debt relationship on the other. A remarkable contrast in the capital market concerns the share of equity capital in total issues in the 1880–1913 period. Table 5.7 reveals the difference.[19] Note, however, that the German market showed much more flexibility. When the stockprice:dividend ratio was high (and the realized rate of return – stemming from capital gains –

Table 5.5 *Indicators of enterprise growth and sources of finance, Germany 1880–1911*

(a) Indicator	Total growth (m. marks)[a]	Share in years of Recession[b]	Share in years of Prosperity[c]
Fixed investment	16.9		
Working capital[d]	9.8		
Equity capital	12.7		
Debt	11.8		
Internal finance %	55	64	45
External finance %	45	36	55
Self finance %	14	16	12

(b) Distribution of enterprises by degree of internal finance

		1880–95	1896–1911
Number of enterprises with internal finance of:			
Less than 50%	4	7	
50 to 75%	23	33	
More than 75%	23	10	

Notes: [a] Average of sample of fifty enterprises.
[b] 1881–87, 1891–95, 1902–3 and 1908–10.
[c] 1888–90, 1896–1901, 1904–7 and 1911.
[d] Including inventories.
Source: R. Rettig, 'Das Investitions und Finanzierungsverhalten deutscher Großunternehmer, 1880 bis 1911' (Diss. Univ. Münster 1978).

Table 5.6 *Average changes in long-term debt of German enterprises, 1880–1911*

Position of business cycle	Average changes in long-term debt: Above average	Average changes in long-term debt: Below average
+	6	13
–	7	5
	13	18

Table 5.7 *Rate of return on ordinary shares, bond rate and share of issues of ordinary shares in total industrial issues, London and Berlin, 1883–1912* (*in* %)

	Berlin			*London*		
	Shares %	*Rate of return on shares*	Bond rate	Shares %	Rate of return on shares	Bond rate
1883–6	50	12.74	3.82	61	7.16	2.99
1887–9	80	19.67	3.63	56	11.24	2.95
1890–3	38	−5.50	3.70	72	2.47	2.84
1894–1900	76	11.66	3.48	47	7.32	2.58
1901–3	51	7.43	3.57			
1904–6	76	9.34	3.60	22[a]	6.73[a]	2.81[a]
1907–8	64	−1.34	3.80			
1909–12	70	7.91	3.80	19	6.44	1.84

Notes: [a] 1904–5.
Source: Own calculations for tables 5.2 and 5.3, in R. Tilly, 'Zur Finanzierung des Wirtschaftswachstums in Deutschland und Großbritannien, 1880–1913', in Ernst Helmstädter (ed.), *Die Bedingungen des Wirtschaftswachstums in Vergangenheit und Zukunft, Gedenkschrift für Walther G. Hoffmann* (Tübingen, 1984).

high), equity issues clearly predominated; but with low stockprices and relatively low interest, fixed interest debentures gained significantly. This kind of response was hardly evident in the British market. The difference deserves comment.

In general, the significance of the national differences lies in the fact that in Germany industrial enterprises in search of capital were able to transfer a larger share of their financial risks on to the investors than was possible in Britain. Industrial enterprises came through 'hard times' more easily if their liabilities were not dominated by fixed interest claims. But there are two ways of looking at this difference. One view stresses investor preferences. Faced with investor preferences favouring fixed interest securities, as were characteristic in Britain, industrial enterprises were likely to respond by behaving cautiously, spending less, having less recourse to the capital market than was warranted in the German case, where industrial shares dominated. This could explain why Berlin overtook London in the issue of industrial securities after 1900 (on a 20 marks to one pound basis of comparison). There is another interpretation, however. It stresses the interest of industrial entrepreneurs in maintaining control over 'their' enterprises. Issuing mainly preference shares and debentures was a way of financing growth without facing a loss of control to 'outside' shareholders. This nexus is fairly well documented – for

British as well as German enterprises.[20] For German enterprises as a whole the use of ordinary shares as a financial vehicle was, as already noted, much more prominent than in Britain, and German listed enterprises which grew very slowly tended to be relatively reluctant to issue shares. But why the national differences? The answer, I suggest, lies in the relationship between banks and industrial enterprise, in a variant of Hilferding's *Finance Capitalism*: thanks to the development of company law in Germany since the 1880s and to Stock Exchange practice, banks and shareholders generally were well informed as to the financial status of most listed industrial companies; and banks were also by virtue of their ability to dominate shareholder meetings and appoint directors, in a position to influence policy, to break down the resistance of enterprise management to issue new shares, not least of all because they were so frequently able to offer attractive issue terms.[21] In Britain, at least prior to 1900, insiders organizing new enterprises or enlarging existing ones had a distinct information advantage over the general investor, but, as Kennedy has recently argued, this could only be exploited for very limited times and at the long-run expense of not being able to fashion a permanent market for industrial securities calling for more than a minimum of risk bearing.[22] Thus the two interpretations merge into one: British investor preferences in favour of fixed-interest securities reflected the paucity of information and relatively weak financial controls on the operations of company founders and insiders. Cottrell suggests, in addition, that in terms of yields 'outside' holders of ordinary shares did not do as well, on the average, as holders of preference shares and debentures, at least in the 1870–1914 period.[23]

The question of external enterprise growth and merger activity also warrants consideration here. For German industry in the Kaiserreich period, external growth and mergers appear to have been closely associated with buoyant capital market conditions and growth of equity capital. The emergence of large enterprises, and also market concentration, derived in considerable measure from such external growth and mergers.[24] Financial conditions, that is, were important factors shaping the timing and structure of German industrial growth. And in Germany, 'financial conditions' mean, at least as far as supply is concerned, 'the banks'.

Foreign business

In turning to this chapter on German banking activity one must bear in mind the distinction between short- and long-term financial needs. Banks served both; but they had more autonomy with respect to the latter, with which our discussion begins.

The private bankers and joint-stock banks became significant intermediaries of foreign portfolio investments in the 1870s. Their interests grew with special force in the 1870s. For one thing, the financial crash of 1873 and ensuing depression, in and of themselves, enhanced the attractiveness of foreign investment to German bankers and capitalists by virtue of the destruction of domestic investment opportunities with which they were associated. In addition, the Prussian government's purchase of the extensive private railway network beginning in the late seventies increased the domestic supply of funds in search of higher (if riskier) returns on portfolio investment than domestic, non-railway securities offered.

In the wake of these changes, German bankers and banks appear to have ridden a first and substantial wave of foreign investment running through the decade of the 1880s. It involved a wide range of government and railroad investments in Eastern Europe (above all, Imperial Russia) and South America. It also included some important banks in South America and China. This first wave received a setback in 1887 when Bismarck, on foreign policy grounds, banned Russian bonds from the list of securities eligible as collateral for Reichsbank credit; but it really broke in the early 1890s, when a number of foreign governments, above all Argentina (the Baring Crisis), but also Portugal and Greece, temporarily ceased servicing their debts. A smaller wave recurred in the mid 1890s (to 1898), once again including Eastern Europe and South America as recipients of new capital, but this time also marked by a penetration of Italian banking and industry. Thereafter, foreign investment played only a relatively minor role in German capital issues, rising to a substantial sum in but one year – 1905 – the result of an unusual coincidence of heavy foreign demands, including those of both participants in the Russo–Japanese War of 1904–5.

Taken as a whole, the story is one in which certain phases of especially pronounced foreign engagements occur, as already mentioned, but in which the amount of foreign business in general tends to reflect the amount of *total* business, i.e. foreign issues depend to a significant extent on the buoyancy of the domestic capital market rather than on changes in opportunities abroad. Of course, foreign portfolio investment differed from its domestic counterpart in that fixed-interest securities dominated the former; moreover, German banks also implemented projects involving large amounts of *direct* foreign investment and not necessarily having the same temporal pattern as portfolio investment. But it is most unlikely that these would change the chronological pattern indicated, could they be quantified.[25]

The simplest and in my opinion the most plausible explanation of German foreign portfolio investment lies in their expected profitability.

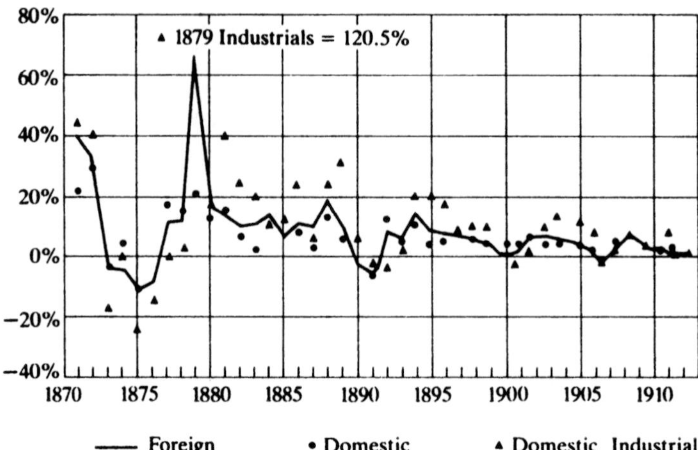

Figure 5.1 Mean realized returns on traded securities, Germany 1880–1911 (in 1913 prices and weighted by amounts outstanding in 1900). *Source*: Author's calculations.

Using information on the prices and yields of domestic and foreign securities traded on German Stock Exchanges it is possible to estimate the rates of return German investors realized over the period 1870 to 1913. The estimates are summarized in figure 5.1 and table 5.7.

If one follows the 'mean-variance' model of portfolio theory here one may interpret the long-run trend of return as expected yields and fluctuations of returns around that trend as expected risks. This leads to the following conclusions. On the one hand, foreign securities yielded – and promised – a significantly higher rate of return and higher risks than did comparable domestic ones. On the other hand, those returns and risks were lower than investments in domestic equities (shares) generated. This seeming ambivalence may well have represented the closing of a gap in the German capital market, i.e. the satisfaction of a certain investor preference (for just that combination of risks and returns which foreign securities embodied). Certainly contemporary observers said as much. In the terminology of modern portfolio theory, these securities contributed to improved diversification of German financial portfolios. Note a double long-run tendency of the security returns: the tendency for the yields and 'risks' of foreign securities to decline; and the accompanying convergence of yields and risks among the different security groups. This supports the notion that expected returns can explain German foreign portfolio investment pretty well, and also that their realization was not achieved at the expense of foregone domestic investments, at least not in the dimensions some contemporaries believed.[26]

Objections to this type of long-run interpretation can be raised, but this

Table 5.8 *Mean and variance of realized returns, securities traded on Berlin Stock Exchange, 1870–1913*

Security type	(1) Arithmetic mean, nominal	(2) Arithmetic 1913 prices	Covariances for (1)	Covariances for (2)
1 Prussian state consols	0.039372	0.047435	0.000675	0.000997
2 Municipal bonds	0.030305	0.036577	0.000340	0.000551
3 Mortgage bank debentures	0.042405	0.051331	0.000251	0.000390
4 Industrial I				
Shares	0.100253	0.125015	0.034175	0.051363
Bonds	0.032803	0.037668	0.000181	0.000273
5 Industrial II				
Shares	0.111663	0.140537	0.111980	0.179457
Bonds	0.025803	0.028275	0.000262	0.000316
6 Industrial III				
Shares	0.096868	0.123390	0.041857	0.062924
Bonds	0.035487	0.041299	0.000446	0.000572
7 Banks (shares)	0.090776	0.108961	0.020170	0.028324
8 Foreign shares	0.088718	0.108203	0.020426	0.029630
9 Foreign railroad bonds				
Europe	0.059763	0.072469	0.002779	0.004310
USA	0.056093	0.068639	0.002404	0.004076
Other	0.055096	0.064054	0.001228	0.016618
10 Foreign government bonds				
Europe	0.056380	0.068461	0.001923	0.003134
other	0.055817	0.067397	0.011071	0.016618
11 Sample	0.075237[a]	0.092701[a]		

Notes: [a] Unweighted.
Industrial I: Mining and metallurgy, metal-working, transportation, electricity.
Industrial II: Textiles, food and beverages.
Industrial III: Chemicals, construction, other.
Source: Author's calculations.

is not the place to take them up.[27] Instead, we draw brief attention to the banks as intermediaries of short-term capital. A major task of intermediation was to finance German exports and imports and this involved foreign exchange transactions. Given the great weight of British foreign trade in the world economy as of 1870 it is not surprising to note the dominance of sterling as a world (key) currency, even for German export and import transactions. This relative weight correlated positively with the efficiency of Britain's financial headquarters, the London money market. It thus proved profitable for German bankers to intermediate via bill acceptances funds raised in London to German traders and their customers. This led German banks to establish branches in London, and these came to execute a significant share of the German banks' foreign business.[28] The funds raised, however, were not merely for trade finance but involved interest arbitrage movements as well. Given the ongoing thrust of the German industrial economy, its interest rates tended to remain above those of the London or Paris money markets in the period from, say, 1880 to 1913, and large sums of short-term capital flowed to Berlin and Hamburg. Indeed, in the early 1900s Germany may well have been the world's largest net debtor on short-term capital account. This may have aided German industrial growth in the period, although it also raised certain doubts in the minds of contemporaries about the risks of financial dependence upon the outside world.[29]

Competition in banking and industry

The literature on German banking has long recognized the critical role of competition as a determinant of bank power and influence. One of the reasons behind interest in joint-stock banks since the second quarter of the nineteenth century was the high rate of profits attributed to large private banking houses such as Rothschilds. For joint-stock banks such as the Credit Mobilier were presumed to justify themselves by competing those profits away and in the process, furthering industrial growth. Governments in search of cheaper loans and bankers desirous of entering the foreign loan business also found this line of argument congenial. The Austro-Hungarian governments, for example, welcomed penetration of the Rothschild syndicate by the Disconto-Gesellschaft in the 1860s for this reason. In the 1880s it was the group around Eugen Bontoux which brought new competition to that empire's loan business. In fact, some of the bad loans and debt crises which marked the 1870s or 1890s doubtless resulted from the growing competition of banks for the government loan business, for intense competition could generate a lowering of quality standards. Examples abound.[30]

Intense competition in German commercial banking since the 1880s led to concentration, first involving the demise of private bankers (frequently taken over by the joint-stock banks), then to interest associations or interlocking equity holdings among joint-stock banks. However, it is doubtful whether concentration weakened competition among banks more than it did in heavy industry. For one thing, improved communications and easier payments transfers via the Reichsbank network probably enhanced interregional competition among joint-stock banks. For

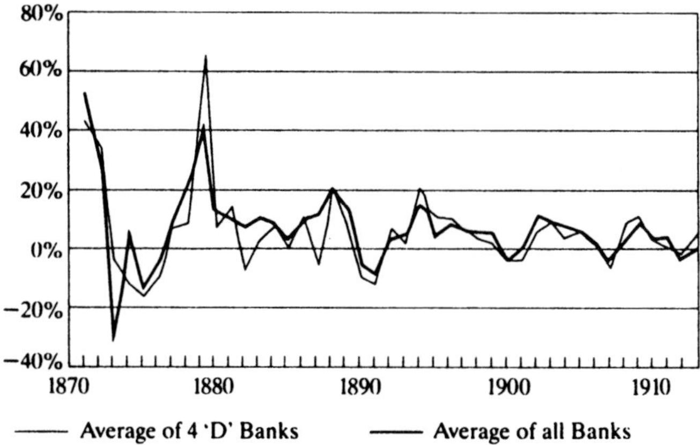

Figure 5.2 Realized rate of return on German bank shares, 1870–1913. *Source*: Author's calculations.

another, the growth of the public savings banks and credit cooperatives posed a further competitive threat, at least after the 1890s. Large banks possessed an advantage in the capital market *vis-à-vis* smaller ones and this advantage contributed something to concentration by take-overs.[31] However, in the banking business, capital was increasingly mobilized via deposits and here there were fewer economies of scale to be exploited. Attempts to brake competition were undertaken – e.g. in the formation of syndicates to float security issues, or in the Stempelvereinigung of Berlin banks coordinated by the Reichsbank since about 1908 – but they were apparently not too successful.[32] In heavy industry, in contrast, cartels and oligopolistic market sharing agreements may have been more successful. From the 1890s on, *large* industrial enterprise certainly, proved more and more able to exploit competition among the banks to improve their financing conditions. In fact, one has the distinct impression that the oft-discussed balance of power between large industrial enterprise and 'great banks' favoured the former from the 1890s on.[33] The number of industrial directorships held by bankers in this period, though often cited as a manifestation of banker power, may reflect only the interest of industrial enterprises in an institutionalization of bank competition. If we look at rates of profit and rates of return, finally, we note that banking generated lower returns than did industry over the period 1870–1913, with one plausible explanation being higher barriers to entry in industry. Figures 5.1 and 5.2 show the secularly falling returns and the narrowing of differences over the period.

In spite of concentration and enterprise giants, German commercial banking remained a competitive business before the First World War.

Conclusion

The foregoing has attempted to focus on the role of banks as instruments of economic development. Banks exist because they reap economies of scale in the production and distribution of information on returns and risks to financial investments in the economy; and they contribute to economic development, I believe, by providing investors with diversified opportunities and thus, directly or indirectly, enhancing the supply of capital to risky, innovative lines of activity. Under certain circumstances, which I see as given for Germany in the 1850–1914 period, large and powerful banks may be expected to fulfill the above-mentioned development function better than highly competitive financial markets.

This brings me to a second point. German banking development in the period observed here reflects institutional innovation in response to 'relative backwardness' and the large capital demands associated therewith. Innovation involves the development of hierarchies relative to markets (O. Williamson).[34] Finance is a matter of small-group negotiation rather than the reading of anonymous price signals, and it frequently reflects banker initiative. 'Universal banking' – the union of commercial and investment banking activities – had banks closely monitoring their customers' activities, sometimes controlling the latter, always treating the relationship as an ongoing (long-term) one. The bankers offered a wide range of services, including intermediation of foreign investments and finance for foreign trade. These close relations and comprehensive services permitted, in a large sense, the relatively full diversification of portfolios of German wealthholders across the assets of the economy, including in particular the finance of risky investments. Playing such a key role no doubt involved some concentration and economic power; related inefficiences also resulted from large-scale organization and banks' control of industry (viz. Neuburger and Stokes).[35] However, such inefficiencies were limited by (a) certain returns to control in the form of lower costs of risk diversification and by (b) continuing competition within the financial sector itself.

Notes

1 Berlin, 1910.
2 Berlin, 1909.
3 Richard Tilly, 'Banken und industrialisierung in Deutschland: Quantifizierungsversuche', in F. W. Henning (ed.), *Entwicklung und Aufgaben von Versicherungen und Banken in der Industrialisierung* (Berlin, 1980).
4 W. P. Kennedy and R. Britton, 'Portfolioverhalten und wirtschaftliche Entwicklung im späten 19. Jahrhundert. Ein Vergleich zwischen Großbritannien und Deutschland. Hypothesen und Spekulationen', in

Richard Tilly (ed.), *Beiträge zuz quantitativen und vergleichenden Unternehmensgeschichte* (Stuttgart, 1985); Richard Tilly, 'External growth and finance in the development of large-scale enterprise in Germany, 1880–1913', in *Journal of Economic History*, 42 (1982), 629–58; and Ulrich Wengenroth, *Unternehmensstrategien und technischer Fortschritt. Die deutsche und britische Stahlindustrie 1865–1895* (Göttingen, Zürich, 1986).

5 Kennedy and Britton, 'Portfolioverhalten'; and Richard Tilly, 'German banking, 1850–1914: development assistance to the strong', in *Journal of European Economic History*, 15 (1986), 113–52.

6 Otto Jeidels, *Das Verhältnis der deutschen Großbanken zur Industrie, mit bes. Berücksichtigung der Eisenindustrie* (Leipzig, 1905). Wilfried Feldenkirchen, 'The banks and the steel industry in the Ruhr. Developments in relations from 1873 to 1914', in *German yearbook on business history* (1981). Wengenroth, *Unternehmensstrategien und technischer Fortschritt*. P. C. Witt, *Die Finanzpolitik des Deutschen Reiches von 1903 bis 1913* (Lübeck und Hamburg, 1970). Even today the power of the largest German banks is viewed as an important factor in the economy. On this F. U. Pappi, P. Kappelhoff and C. Melbeck, 'Die Struktur der Unternehmensverflechtung in der Bundesrepublik', in *Kölner Zeitschrift für Soziologie und Sozialpsychologie* (KZSS), 39 (1987), 693–717.

7 Tilly, 'German banking'.

8 Rudi Rettig, 'Das Investitions – und Finanzierungsverhalten deutscher Großunternehmen, 1880–1911' (Dissertation, Univ. Münster, 1978); and Hans Pohl, 'Formen und Phasen der Industriefinanzierung bis zum 2. Weltkrieg', Bankhistorisches Archiv 9, Beiheft (Frankfurt/M., 1983).

9 Manfred Pohl, *Entstehung und Entwicklung des Universalbankensystems* (Frankfurt/M., 1986).

10 Tilly, 'German banking'.

11 Ekkehart Eistert, *Die Beeinflussung des Wirtschaftswachstums in Deutschland von 1883 bis 1913 durch das Bankensystem*, (Berlin, 1970). Jeidels, *Das Verhältnis der deutschen Großbanken zur Industrie*; and Riesser, *Die deutschen Großbanken*.

12 Cited in previous note.

13 Tilly, 'Banken und Industrialisierung' (note 3).

14 Hugh Neuburger, and Houston Stokes, 'German banks and German growth: an empirical view', in *Journal of Economic History*, September 1974.

15 Kennedy and Britton, 'Portfolioverhalten'; also Tilly, 'German banking'.

16 Ibid.

17 William P. Kennedy, 'Institutional response to economic growth: capital markets in Britain to 1914', in Leslie Hannah (ed.), *Management strategy and business development* (London, 1976).

18 Wilfried Feldenkirchen, *Die Eisen- und Stahlindustrie des Ruhrgebietes, 1879–1914* (Wiesbaden 1982); Feldenkirchen, 'The banks and the steel industry in the Ruhr'; Rettig, 'Das Investitions- und Finanzierungsverhalten'; Wengenroth, *Unternehmensstrategien und technischer Fortschritt*; and also Volker Wellhöner, *Großbanken und Großindustrie im Kaiserreich* (Göttingen, 1989).
19 More on this in Richard Tilly, 'Financing industrial enterprise, in Great Britain and Germany in the nineteenth century. Testing grounds for Marxist and Schumpeterian Theories?' in J. W. Drukker and H.-J. Wagner (eds.), *The economic law of motion of modern society. A. Marx, Keynes, Schumpeter centennial* (Cambridge, 1986).
20 Philip Cottrell, *Industrial finance, 1830–1914* (London and New York, 1980). pp. 166–7; Rettig, 'Das Investitions- und Finanzierungsverhalten deutscher Großunternehmen, 1880–1911' (Dissertation, Univ. Münster, 1978), 243–6; Feldenkirchen; 'The banks and the steel industry in the Ruhr', 440.
21 Tilly, 'German banking'.
22 Kennedy, 'Institutional response to economic growth'.
23 Cottrell, *Industrial finance*, p. 164; and Tilly, 'German banking', 230–2.
24 Tilly, 'Mergers, external growth and finance'.
25 On this whole question, Richard Tilly, 'Some comments on German foreign portfolio investment, 1870–1914'. Conference Paper, Campinas, Brazil, 1989.
26 More details on this in ibid.
27 Sidney Pollard, 'Capital exports, 1870–1914: harmful or beneficial?', *Economic History Review*, 2nd Ser., 338 (1987).
28 Manfred Pohl, '100 Jahre Deutsche Bank London Agency', *Beiträge zu Wirtschafts- und Währungsfragen und zur Bankgeschichte*, 10 (1973). Also Richard Tilly, chapter on Germany, in Rondo Cameron and V. Bovykin (eds.), *International banking and international finance* (New York, 1990).
29 Knut Borchardt, 'Währung und Wirtschaft', in Deutsche Bundesbank (ed.), *Währung und Wirtschaft in Deutschland 1876–1975* (Frankfurt/M., 1976).
30 See Tilly, 'Some comments'.
31 M. Pohl, *Konzentration im deutschen Bankwesen (1848–1980)*, (Frankfurt, 1982).
32 Knut Borchardt, 'Währung und Wirtschaft'.
33 Hilferding, *Finanzkapital*; and Wellhöner, *Großbanken und Großindustrie*.
34 O. Williamson, *Markets and hierarchies: analysis and antitrust implications* (New York, 1975).
35 Neuburger and Stokes, 'German banks and German growth'.

6 Banks and economic development: comments

HAROLD JAMES

In all the countries examined in the chapters presented above and in part IV, there have been long running, and often highly politicized, debates about the influence of banks. In the papers it is chiefly the economic impact of banks that provides the focus of attention: did the nature of the financial system accelerate or retard economic development? In the light of the political controversy about this issue, it is surprising that most economic historians have not been able to give any kind of confident answer. The conclusion of Raymond Goldsmith's path-breaking work is self-consciously agnostic:

> A Scotch verdit [not proven] seems to be the only conclusion that the insufficient data and analysis now available permit. One cannot well claim that a superiority in the German financial structure was responsible for, or even contributed to, a more rapid growth in the German economy as a whole compared to the British economy in the half-century before World War I.[1]

Two of the most popular criticisms of banks have been on the one hand that they denied credit to industry (as a result of excessive caution, or of a gentlemanly contempt for manufacture), and on the other that they diverted funds into excessive overseas lending. These points have been made for the British, Belgian, French, German, Swedish and Swiss cases. Accounts of the malaise vary from country to country: capital export is much more of a theme in the French, British and Swiss literature than it is in the German example. They raise very large and complicated issues about the way in which a whole society operates: Cassis and Tanner well describe how capital export is built into Switzerland's political and economic structures; and authors such as Cain and Hopkins have made similar points about Great Britain.[2]

Often the arguments presented in making these criticisms are superficial.

It is, for instance, of little help to describe individual cases of businessmen who could not obtain credit.[3] There is always an unsatisfied demand for credit by potentially risky undertakings; in making a historical verdict, what we need to do is to judge how appropriately financial institutions were able to assess and measure risk. Did banks attempt to gather information about risks, or did bankers just rely on a casual network of social acquaintances?

We cannot simply assert that banks should lend to anyone who can use money, or deny that some potential debtors represent bad risks. The same issues arise in considering foreign investment: such flows may generate not simply high rates of return but also create valuable new markets for domestic producers. We need to discover the respective risks and returns in foreign and domestic investments in judging the efficiency of the financial sector: a task well performed for the British case by Michael Edelstein.[4] But even when these questions have been answered we still know that the social overall risks and returns are not necessarily identical with the private ones.

The papers presented here offer some interesting ways of using new approaches to analyse the relationship between the financial sector and the rest of the economy.

1 Some use the Goldsmithian concept of increasing financial intermediation as a characteristic of the modern economy. At first such an approach may seem to emphasize the similarities across different national experiences; and to show how very different institutional structures produced a similar financial outcome.

Cottrell treats England in a Goldsmithian way; and Gueslin examines the quantity of bank and savings bank deposits relative to the money supply, and uses a comparison with England as a way of registering and describing financial modernization. Cassis and Tanner pick out chronological periods when bank assets grew quicker than GNP.

However, the long-run Goldsmithian analysis in fact turns out to offer historians who are interested in the analysis of the chronology of development, as well as of change in shorter time periods, a valuable tool. We can use long-run developments to detect breaks in a secular pattern of development.

The late nineteenth century saw the rise of large-scale commercial banking in all the countries discussed.

In Britain, a modern financial structure emerged in the 1880s in the aftermath of a merger movement, and as several large provincial banks (Barclays, Lloyds and the Midland) moved to London and the national market: Cottrell describes this development as 'the relative lateness of British financial maturity'. A national branch banking system in France developed with the expansion of the Crédit Lyonnais, the Société Générale and the Comptoir d'Escompte between 1880 and 1912. Tilly describes the German merger movement after the 1880s, in which the large Berlin banks built up branch systems in order to obtain a greater fund of deposits. In Sweden the corresponding national branch system developed slightly later, after 1900, with a dramatic merger movement after 1910. Cassis and Tanner see 1885 as the turning point in Switzerland, after which the major banks developed an important industrial business. Kurgan describes the development of the Belgian Société Générale into a universal bank as occurring after 1880, with several other banks rapidly following and imitating the strategy of the Société Générale.

This development was then roughly contemporaneous; it also coincided with the growth and development of overseas financing.

One of the most interesting turning points that emerges here in all the papers is the break in the secular trend associated with the world depression of the early 1930s. In each case, a quite dramatic shift *within* the financial sector is detected. The influence of large commercial banks fell off during the 1930s. Cottrell tells how in England and Wales lending to the staple industries fell off after 1930 (and then attributes the decline to the concern of banks in the crisis with liquidity, and to their high customary interest charges and fees which priced them out of the lending market). At the same time the deposit and lending activity of building societies increased with the housing boom. In the other countries – Belgium, France, Germany, Switzerland – there were banking crises in this decade. In France and Germany in the wake of the crises, savings bank deposits grew faster than those in commercial banks; in Switzerland similarly it was the cantonal banks which expanded rapidly in this decade, while the commercial banks suffered. Since commercial and savings banks have very different loan customers, such shifts may be expected to have altered the conditions for economic life.

The years between the 1880s and the 1930s thus emerge as a sort of golden age, the 'era of the great banks', within the broader framework of financial innovation and modernization.

2 What were the achievements of these great banks? Sometimes striking national differences become apparent in considering the relationship of banks and industry. The classic contrast remains that between England and Germany: as expounded by analysts such as Hilferding and Gerschenkron the relationship was much closer in Germany than in Britain, and Germany is usually considered to be the most striking example of bank induced industrialization.

While William Kennedy still claims that 'after 1878, no longer would banks become willingly involved in the long-term financing of industry...just as industry's demands were growing in response to advancing technological possibilities and foreign competition',[5] Cottrell shows that the neglect of British industry by banks is something of a myth. In the nineteenth century banks in industrial areas lent to industrial borrowers on long and medium term, although industrial credit declined at the end of the century as banks engaged in mergers partly in an attempt to gain liquidity and avoid being locked into a long-term relationship with local businesses. But, after the First World War, the large commercial banks again became involved in precisely such a relationship – though often to their cost.

Tilly's examination of sectoral growth rates in Britain and Germany shows on a national level a less efficient British portfolio. There was a pronounced sectoral misdistribution, with an over-concentration on transport, communications and food and drink, with relatively little investment flowing into newer developments such as metals, engineering or utilities (where the Germans achieved high rates of investment and of growth).

It is still not possible on the basis of quantitative correlations to determine whether these different investment patterns reflected the supply of capital or the demand for it. Perhaps the newer British capitalists demanded less investment resources? Or did investors' preferences dictate a more conservative pattern of investment? Or were the financial intermediaries at fault?

Gueslin tackles this sort of problem head-on in a revealing way. He is concerned to examine whether banks channelled the funds of their depositors in a certain direction – as was alleged at the beginning of the century by the critic Lysis. An alternative explanation would be that the investors themselves had a taste for conservative investments, and that the banks merely responded to this pre-existing taste. He finds that banks did indeed make high commission earnings that disposed them to push certain kinds of paper; on the other hand, there existed an investors' psychology (what Gueslin calls a 'culture') that made for a certain asset structure – a search for the security offered by railway and state paper.

Tilly's explanation of the superiority of the German market is of great interest in this regard.[6] The banks according to his argument supplied both their investors and their borrowers with information that allowed a better (more informed) choice of investment. This explains the more efficient German 'national portfolio'. In the German economy, banks supplied not just capital but also knowledge. They educated the economy. In the British securities market, information was limited and difficult to obtain; as providers of unsecured credit, German banks were by contrast in an excellent position to compare the position of different firms within an industry, and of different industries across the national economy.

Financiers' function as improvers of information flows was recognized by some perceptive contemporaries. As the famous Swedish banker Marcus Wallenberg Sr said (quoted by Lindgren): 'The experience that a managing director for a larger bank now accumulates is far more comprehensive than that which an individual industrialist can gain.'

Such an analysis allows us to develop a more precise picture of the development in the financial structure during the course of economic modernization: the contribution of bankers and other intermediaries should not be measured simply in terms of credit allocation but also by describing how they established communications by which knowledge could flow through national and international markets.

3 One additional theme that appears prominently in all of these papers is the effect of state action on financial systems. The state provides a legislative and regulatory framework: one reaction to banking problems such as those that arose in the 1900s or again in the early 1930s, was to extend regulation. This regulation directly affected the banks' asset structure. The separation in USA of commercial from investment banking in the Glass–Steagall Act of 1933 was also proposed in Germany (though the eventual control was more limited); but it was carried out under the 1935 Belgian banking reform. Swiss banks agreed to limit their capital exports voluntarily in return for a law on bank secrecy. Swedish banks were forbidden to hold industrial shares after 1938. In 1945 some French banks were nationalized – this was not simply a reaction to wartime politics, but also a delayed response to what were believed to be the problems of the depression era.

But the state also acts in other ways to influence financial behaviour and alter the structure of financial assets. Foreign policy may create an environment in which bank lending overseas becomes more attractive, since it serves a political and diplomatic purpose, and in consequence benefits from state protection. It is well known that before the First World War French and German banks were orchestrated by their governments in the service of imperialism.

The state is in addition a major borrower. The expansion of French government debt allowed French investors to satisfy their wish for secure and stable investments according to Gueslin's account. After the First World War, the size of the state debt increased and now offered much more security than foreign investments, whose share in French portfolios declined dramatically. Alterations in the terms on which the state financed itself have an immediate impact on the rest of the financial world: an interesting example given by Cottrell is the British conversion of the 1880s, which pulled down interest rates and made overseas investments more attractive. Another example is the conversion in the 1930s and the consequent era of cheap money which reduced the demand for bank credit as firms no longer held government stock as assets.

One feature of economic modernization widely commented on since Adolph Wagner is the so-called law of increasing state expenditure. If that expenditure cannot be financed through increased taxation because of resistance on the part of tax-payers, the state needs to borrow. Once the state's role as a borrower increases in importance, it can make matters easier by propaganda. The state is also an educator or a supplier of information. Such information may – as it did in the case of France – help to itensify the bias existing in the 'economic culture' in favour of secure state paper.

Taking a very broad perspective, both the state and the financial sector can be viewed as service activities. Both grow during the course of economic modernization. Both play an important role in supplying the information on which depends economic activity. But in many countries – especially where there is a strong centralizing and etatist tradition such as in France, less in Switzerland where power is more localized – the state has many advantages over the banks. As both a borrower and a regulator, it can bias the credit market in favour of its own requirements. This is the development that set an end to the 'era of the great banks'.

When we consider the question of the impact of banks on the rest of the economy, this context of state regulation and of state financial action also needs to be borne in mind. Banks are not just acting on their own in a neutral, antiseptic environment: they are part of a larger financial (and social) system, in which the state is a major actor, and which is subject to many economic and political influences.

Notes

1 R. M. Goldsmith, *Financial structure and development* (New Haven 1969), p. 407.
2 P. J. Cain and A. G. Hopkins, 'Gentlemanly capitalism and British expansion overseas', *Economic History Review* 40 (1987), 1–26.
3 See W. P. Kennedy, *Industrial structure, capital markets and the origins of British economic decline* (Cambridge 1987), pp. 139–41: Kennedy presents such material, although he sets it in a more far-ranging discussion.
4 M. Edelstein, *Overseas investment in the age of high imperialism: the United Kingdom 1850–1914* (London 1982).
5 Kennedy, *Industrial structure*, p. 122.
6 Kennedy also raises the critical question of the ability of a capital market to disseminate information uniformly: *Industrial structure*, pp. 110–12.

II FINANCIAL ELITES AND SOCIETY

elite. The long-established notion that the British landed class was peculiarly open to newcomers, and that this formed the basis for political and social stability, has been challenged by a number of historians who contend that, on the contrary, the level of entry was low at least until the 1880s and that landed society was more in the nature of a closed caste. Only then, it has been argued, did the decline in rents lead to an erosion in landed wealth, and a search for new means of survival at the apex of British society. One potential means which came to hand was fusion with the wealthy financial families of the City, who even before the 1880s had been the nearest rivals to the fortunes of the landed aristocracy.[5] Here, it is suggested by a number of scholars, was a social process which helps to explain the neglect of the interests of industry both by the City in investment decisions, and by the state in the formulation of policy. The literature on the social history of the City has therefore been dominated by the issue of the survival of aristocratic and landed values, rather than by questions which emerge from an attempt to understand its own internal dynamics and structure. The result has, arguably, been to misunderstand some of the crucial features of the social history of the City of London.

The picture which has emerged of the City of London in the period from 1880 to 1950 has stressed a number of characteristics which may best be understood in terms of the typology of elites proposed by Anthony Giddens.[6] An obvious distinction may be made between 'open' elites which have a high level of entry and turnover, and those which are 'closed' with a low level of entry and stability of membership. It is this simple dichotomy which has dominated the literature on the landed aristocracy. It is not without problems, for it is not self-evident what level of entry is necessary in order to create an 'open' elite. One historian's stability is another's change. Further, the channels by which newcomers enter the elite might be as important as the level of turnover. It might be quite feasible for a high degree of entry and turnover to make very little difference to the nature of an elite, for the channel of recruitment might operate in such a way that the entrants were virtually indistinguishable from existing members. A lower level of entry could create greater social change where the channel of recruitment allowed the selection of elite members from a wider background. It is therefore helpful to move beyond a simple division between the elite and the non-elite, and to think instead in terms of a division between elite, 'secondary stratum', and non-elite. The secondary stratum might itself be divided into the 'recruitment stratum' and the 'administrative apparatus'. The members of the 'administrative apparatus' were usually salaried officials who did not aspire to elite membership, although in some circumstances there might be an overlap with the 'recruitment stratum' which would, for example, allow an able manager to be promoted to a partnership or directorship of a business venture. In the case of the legal elite of England, to take one example, judges are drawn from the 'recruitment stratum' of barristers by a process of selection controlled by the Lord Chancellor. However high the level of entry on to the judicial bench, the character of the legal elite will not change so long as the barristers of the 'recruitment stratum' are themselves selected by a process which limits their social background. Solicitors, who have a wider social background, are – at least at present – excluded from the 'recruitment stratum' for judges. A change in the channel of recruitment might produce a similar level of turnover in the ranks of the judges but might have a more marked impact on their social background and attitudes. The precise nature of the 'recruitment stratum', and whether members of the 'administrative apparatus' supply entrants to the elite, are as important as the level of entry.

The nature of the channels of recruitment will influence the degree of social and moral integration of the elite. By moral integration is meant the extent to which common ideas and assumptions are accepted, and how far there is a solidarity of interests. Social integration refers to the degree of intermarriage or friendship amongst elite members. The two are normally connected, and Giddens proposes that elites should be defined according to their level of integration as well as the extent to which they are open or closed. The result is to produce a typology of four elite groups. The first is the 'uniform elite' which has closed recruitment and high integration. The relative closure of entry is likely to produce a coherent process of socialization as a result of common education and intermarriage. The second is the 'established elite' with closed recruitment and low integration, in which the elite is divided despite limited recruitment. The third is the 'solidary elite' with open recruitment and high integration. This would apply to a religious or political elite whose members are recruited from diverse backgrounds and yet have a common ideology which acts as a binding force. The fourth is an 'abstract elite' with open recruitment and low integration, which does not function as a social group. The application of this typology to the recent literature on the financial elite of the City of London would lead to the conclusion that it was a uniform elite with closed recruitment and high integration. This literature is outlined in the next section, before proceeding to suggest that reality might have been somewhat different.

I

The first detailed analysis of the financial elite of the City was undertaken by sociologists in the 1950s who challenged the common assumption that since the Second World War there had been a 'decomposition' of the ruling class, which was replaced by a more amorphous and pluralist collection of leadership groups.[7] An enquiry was undertaken by Lupton and Wilson into the links of education, kinship, club membership and so on between various groups giving evidence to the Bank Rate Tribunal of 1957. The City cohort was drawn from directors of the Bank of England, directors of the major clearing banks, directors of fourteen merchant banks and discount houses, and the directors of eight insurance companies. The results indicated a high level of integration, with a considerable role for custom, precedent and informality in relationships. For example, twelve of eighteen directors of the Bank of England had been educated at six leading public schools, forty-six of 107 directors of merchant banks and discount houses, seventy-one of 148 directors of clearing banks, and seventy of 149 directors of insurance companies. This similarity of background was confirmed by the construction of kin networks which linked the prominent figures giving evidence to the Tribunal. Family connections were dense and numerous, not only between members of City firms but also with landed society and the government. This may be illustrated from one particular web: C. F. Cobbold, the governor of the Bank of England was himself a member of the landed gentry; his relative, Lt.-Col. John Cobbold was married to the daughter of the Duke of Devonshire; and Col. Cobbold's sister married Charles Hambro, the merchant banker and director of the Bank of England. Another member of the Hambro family (Lt.-Col. H. E. Hambro) married the widow of the fifth earl of Cadogan, whose grandson married a daughter of Lt.-Col. Cobbold. Sir Everard Hambro married into the family of Montagu Norman, the governor of the Bank from 1920 to 1944. A cousin of Norman married the uncle of R. A. Butler, the Chancellor of the Exchequer, and a daughter of this marriage married Sir George Abell, a director of the Bank, whose brother-in-law married a Hambro. Another daughter of the Duke of Devonshire married Harold Macmillan, the Prime Minister – and so the connections ramified to incorporate the families of the Marquis of Salisbury, Lord Bicester of Morgan Grenfell and so on.[8] The rise of the meritocracy was, it appeared from such analyses, greatly exaggerated and the hold of an established elite of finance and the aristocracy was resilient.

The recent work by historians on the nature of the aristocracy and landed society has tended to suggest that the crucial turning-point in the emergence of such a pattern came in the 1880s. Although there are differences of emphasis, a composite picture may be drawn from the work of a number of historians, which would run as follows. Until the mid nineteenth century, the City of London experienced competitive openness, which gave way to closure in the latter part of the nineteenth century. The clearing banks became more concentrated, as the largest five firms in England and Wales increased their share of deposits from 25 per cent in

1870 to 43 per cent in 1910 and 80 per cent in 1920. The Bank of England achieved more power over money markets, and the major merchant banks increased their capitalization. The level of integration increased within the City. Merchant banks came to cooperate in the syndication of loans, which required a high degree of trust and integrity for success. Partners and directors of the major financial firms were associated together on the boards of such bodies as the Royal Exchange Assurance, London Assurance, the Merchants' Trust and, above all, the Bank of England. The Bank in particular has been seen as vital to the integration of the City, acting to maintain an exclusive social order based on informal social controls and mutual protection which guaranteed dynastic continuity and set limits to competition, so producing 'a community like social system' in which members of the financial elite 'co-operated with their competitors, who were also their cousins and friends in a self-perpetuating community of mutual regard'. Thus an integrated and closed elite emerged within the City by about 1900.[9]

This financial elite, so the argument continues, drew closer to the old elite of landed society up to the First World War. Successful members of the financial community acquired country houses, sent their sons to public schools (particularly Eton from 1870), and entered Society so that their daughters 'came out' and joined the aristocratic marriage market.[10] At the same time, the landed elite was ceasing to be so exclusive. The writings of both the Stones and Rubinstein have suggested that there was a low level of entry by new men of wealth into the ranks of landed society in the middle decades of the nineteenth century, so that the assumption that English landed society during the industrial revolution was peculiarly open is a myth. Indeed, they suggest that the landed elite was becoming more closed during the period of the industrial revolution and up to about 1880. The conclusion of Rubinstein's study of the wealthy is that 'the British landed aristocracy was increasingly becoming a caste-like and socially isolated group, distancing itself from, and distanced from, the newer business magnates, who found it nearly impossible in many cases to gain full acceptance into the inner circle of high landed society'. The ties between land and finance were, if anything, weakened because of the declining importance of government loans (which had been a major part of the function of the City during the wars of the eighteenth and early nineteenth centuries), and the reduction of the role of the state as a provider of privilege and favour which had tended to bring together aristocratic placemen, the Church, and the law with the beneficiaries of the East India Co. and the mercantilist system. Retrenchement and the reduction in the role of 'old corruption' acted to sever the ties between finance and the aristocrats, allowing them to go their own separate ways. Financiers turned towards foreign loans, where there was less need for the favour of the British government; and the landed aristocrats were able to make large sums out of their estates at least up to the breaking of prices in 1873.[11] This, so the argument runs, started to change from about 1880.

The rent rolls of many members of the landed aristocracy started to fall, which forced them to adjust in several ways. One was to change their attitudes to their landed estates. In the past, they were willing to exploit the potential of their estates by encouraging industrial or commercial developments, taking part in the provision of infrastructure such as docks and railways which would allow minerals to be extracted from their estates, or encouraging the development of towns and suburbs which would increase their income from urban ground rents. They were active and entrepreneurial, but in a particular way: the aim was to extract the maximum income from landed estates with the end that they might be conserved and protected. From about 1880, this started to change and the desire to maximize income could mean the abandonment of ancestral acres. This is very clear from the behaviour of the eighth Duke of Devonshire. When he inherited in 1891, the finances of the estate were not sound and the strategy followed by the seventh duke of investing in ventures such as ship-building and railways to increase income from the estate was abandoned. Instead, large amounts of land were sold and the surplus left after the payment of debts was invested in a wide portfolio of shares and bonds. By the First World War, about 30 per cent of the income of the Duke of Devonshire came from dividends.[12] A similar strategy was pursued by the second Earl of Leicester. The decennial net income from his landed estate at Holkham fell from £749,924 in 1870–9 to £356,310 in 1890–9; meanwhile, income from a wide range of shares unconnected with the estate increased from 0.6 per cent of net estate income in the 1860s to 48.9 per cent in the 1880s.[13] The Devonshires and the Leicesters were more involved in the world of the Stock Exchange and international finance, although very much at arms length, without necessarily leading to social fusion. In other cases, the relationship could be much closer. The second Earl of Verulam is a case in point. In the 1870s, he had an expenditure of about £20,000 a year and an income of about £17,000; by 1889, he had pared his expenditure to £15,000 but the income had fallen to £14,000. Only an unexpected legacy kept him afloat, and when the third earl inherited in 1895 he revived the family fortune through direct involvement in the City. By 1913, he was a director of thirteen companies which paid fees ranging from £50 to £500 a year, and by 1913 fees and dividends amounted to about a third of his income. The process of interconnection between aristocracy and City went further: Verulam's daughter married a nephew of Ernest Cassel, the *confidante* of the Prince of Wales and a major international financier, whose daughter married Mountbatten, a member of the Royal family and the last Viceroy of India.[14]

The result, it has been contended, was a recreation of the earlier links between aristocracy and financiers, on somewhat different terms. Whereas land had earlier been the dominant partner, in the later nineteenth century it was the City. The sons from the two elites met at public school and university, where they were taught a 'gentlemanly' ethos which was purged of feudal remnants. This is indicated by Casiss's sample of 413 partners or directors of London-based private banks, merchant banks, joint-stock banks, Anglo-foreign and colonial banks, and the Bank of England, who were active between 1890 and 1914. He found that 51 per cent were educated at a public school and Oxbridge; this figure rose to 67 per cent for directors of the Bank of England.[15] It was a capitalist ethic, but of a particular type which has been termed 'gentlemanly capitalism', formed by 'a formidable mix of the venerable and the old... The more an occupation or a source of income allowed for a life-style which was similar to that of the landed classes, the higher the prestige it carried and the greater the power it conferred.' There was a common ethos of leisure and country pursuits, distance from the contamination of industrial production and the need to control large numbers of workers. It was possible to gain entry into the ranks of society without needing to surrender active involvement in business, which was not possible for industrialists. Bankers had, so Cassis argues, a 'distinguished semi-amateur status', and 'gentleman capitalists' had 'relative immunity from the stresses of class conflict', which allowed them to appear as natural leaders.[16] It was also this reformed 'gentlemanly capitalism' which has been seen as the key to British imperialism. The beneficiaries of the empire were, claim Davis and Huttenback, the City of London and the landed elite which benefitted from the higher rate of return on imperial investments and positions in the official service. The costs of defending the empire, they argue, could not be passed onto the colonies and this meant that British defence expenditure and hence taxation was much higher than in other economically developed countries; these costs were borne by the working class and industrialists. On this argument, therefore, the empire involved a transfer payment between the 'gentlemanly capitalists' on the one hand and industrial capital and the working class on the other.[17]

A point of contention within this general interpretation is the significance of intermarriage between finance and land. Cassis found that, in his sample of 413 partners and directors of banks who were active between 1890 and 1914, 35 per cent of known marriages were with the daughters of aristocrats and landowners; many other marriages were with groups such as clergy and the forces which were traditionally associated with landed society. At the heart of the web of kinship, Cassis found a number of well-established banking families which he terms the 'banking aristocracy' of the Barings, Hambros, Grenfells, Glyns, Smiths who intermarried with each other and into the aristocracy. The Grenfells may be taken as an illustration. Charles Pascoe Grenfell (1790–1867) married the daughter of the Earl of Sefton, and his daughter married the banker George Carr Glyn of Glyn, Mills and Co. Charles William Grenfell (1832–61) married the granddaughter of the second Earl of Harewood; the daughter of the third Earl married Charles Henry Mills (1830–98). Charles Molyneux (1875–1915) married the daughter of Charles Henry Mills, and Arthur Morton Grenfell (1873–1958) married the daughter of the fourth Earl Grey. This Grenfell web was in turn connected with the web based on the Barings. The result of such patterns was, argues Cassis, to maintain the identity of banking families through a high degree of intermarriage, without dissolving into the aristocracy. The merger was not on the aristocracy's terms, and the outcome was 'the formation of a renewed elite which added the financial power of the City to the prestige of the old aristocracy'.[18]

The importance of intermarriages might be overstated, for Lisle-Williams has argued that it rested upon a relatively small number of families. It was, he claims, a secondary phenomenon rather than the primary cause of integration in the City.[19] What is agreed is that a high degree of integration *did* emerge within the City in the late nineteenth century, based on an ethos which was less the result of a one-way process of assimilation with the aristocracy, than of convergence. The City, argues Cassis, was marked by a high degree of economic specialization, yet he finds an underlying coherence of interest. The City was, he remarks, 'une et multiple', 'divisée en de multiples unités rigoureusement specialisées, mais parties d'un tout remarquablement homogène'.[20] It is also agreed that this 'increasingly integrated plutocracy' excluded industrialists before the First World War.[21]

This obviously leads on to the political consequences of such a social structure, for it is easy to conclude that industry was subordinated and sacrificed as a result of a merger of land and finance. This might amount to a conspiracy theory, in which the City asserted its hegemony over the state.[22] Cassis is more cautious than this, for he claims that bankers showed very little interest in general policy, which could safely be left to the professional politicians with whom they had so much in common.[23] Ingham stresses that policies which were in the interests of the City (by which he understands not only finance but also commerce) might be pursued for quite independent reasons, and he emphasizes that, far from being passive instruments, the Bank of England and Treasury had autonomous power. The pursuit of financial orthodoxy by the Bank and Treasury in order to sustain gold or sterling did (he believes) benefit the City and harm industry, but this could be as a result of the desire of the Treasury and the Bank to maintain power in their own domains of the state bureaucracy and the banking system. The Treasury, for example,

Table 7.1 *Economy, state and civil society relations*

Economy		State	Civil society	
City		Treasury	Clarendon public schools	
	Bank of England	Foreign Office		South
Land			Aristocracy	
		Dominant governing class		
		Industrial bourgeoisie		
Industry		Parliament	Provincial grammar schools/	North
Provincial Finance			Lesser public schools	

Source: Ingham, *Capitalism Divided?*, (Basingstoke, 1984) p. 151.

might wish to tackle separate issues such as inflation or the issue of loans; and in its concern to retain power over the spending departments of the government, an appeal to international financial confidence might be a useful weapon. It was not a simple case that the City was the dominant fraction of capital which determined policy, for, argues Ingham, the institutions of the state had their own independent existence. Interests of the City and the Treasury and Bank were separate but coincident. The policies which were pursued nevertheless allowed the City to survive, and to ride out the challenge of New York. The explanation, he suggests, was non-economic. In the United States, a powerful industrial bourgeoisie could block the development of policies which would have subordinated domestic to international monetary matters, whereas in Britain industry was not integrated into the dominant class, and had a low level of organization and solidarity. Although Ingham does not adopt a conspiracy theory, the outcome is the same: as economic decline began, the incompatibility between industrial and commercial/financial capital became obvious. The City, he believes, never depended upon domestic accumulation, so that financiers did not mobilize to modernize the productive base, and industry was starved of long-term capital.[24]

A common theme in the recent literature has therefore been the duality between industrial capitalism and the service economy of the south where 'gentlemanly capitalism' was dominant (of which Table 7.1 could be an illustration). Britain, it would seem, 'constitutes a unique case of one in which international commercial capitalism has been dominant, and has had a determinant impact on its class and institutional structure'.[25] This is not, as accounts such as Wiener's would have us belief, a simple gentry counter-revolution against an enterprise culture, an obeisance to the lure of the Arcadian myth,[26] for there was a major restructuring of landed society in the late nineteenth century as it fused with the elite of the City. Or such, at least, is the case which has been put forward and which is in danger of becoming a new orthodoxy in modern British history. The contention in the remainder of this chapter is that the extent to which the City was dominated by a 'uniform elite' has been exaggerated, and that it was neither so closed nor so integrated as most recent accounts would suggest.

II

What was the degree of closure in the elite of the City? This, of course, depends to a considerable extent upon the definition of the elite which is used. The focus of attention is very often upon a specific part of the financial community, the bankers. However, the extent to which bankers dominated a financial community varied between countries, which means that care must be taken in international comparisons. In some financial centres, the banks might themselves act as the key players upon the stock market, whereas in other centres (such as London) the members of the stock market were distinct from the banks, at least until 'big bang'. Although the level of closure of the banking elite might be similar in the two centres, this would obscure the existence in one centre of a separate elite which might produce a greater degree of openness. There might also be a different relationship between financiers and the ancillary services provided by lawyers and accountants. In some centres, lawyers and accountants might be salaried officers of the banks, and might form part of the 'recruitment stratum' of the banking elite. In other cases (such as London) they might be located in separate, specialist firms, such as Freshfields in law or Price Waterhouse in accountancy which did not form part of the 'recruitment stratum' for the financial elite. The definition of the financial elite or elites may effect the conclusions which are reached, and this is sometimes obscured by the use of the omnibus term 'City' without a clear specification of what exactly is included. The question should be posed is whether there was a single elite or a cluster of elites; and, if there was a cluster, when (if at all) did they draw together? Arguably, the City of London should be seen as a cluster of elites to a greater extent than other major financial centres.

Although directors of large insurance companies appear in Lupton and Wilson's study of the Bank Rate Tribunal of 1957, they are used by Lisle-

Williams only as one measure to indicate common interests among merchant banking families; he is accordingly not interested in directors drawn from other groups. Neither, of course, are they included by Cassis in his analysis of bankers, which has not prevented some commentators from extrapolating his figures to cover the whole of the City. Insurance should surely be included as part of the financial elite or elites of the City, but the issue then is, which sections of insurance? The large, joint-stock insurance companies such as the Royal Exchange and London Assurance tended to look to established names for their courts of directors, and turned (amongst others) to leading bankers and merchant bankers. There was also a strong element of family representation. Thus Pascoe Grenfell joined the court of the Royal Exchange Assurance in 1789, and served as governor from 1829 to 1838; he was followed on the court by Riversdale William Grenfell, who was in turn succeeded in 1871 by Charles Seymour Grenfell. Similarly, a member of the Lubbock family (another of Cassis's group of aristocratic bankers) served on the court from 1798 to 1914.[27] The problem here is the same as with the court of the Bank of England: existing members tended to elect men drawn from their immediate circle, and largely from established firms where partners had the time to devote to outside activities. The result might be to exclude some of the most thrusting and dynamic firms, which were not part of the clique or were too involved in business. The members of the clique might reflect past glories rather than present importance. The way in which the financial elite is defined, and interconnections measured, might therefore bias the result in favour of dynastic continuity and integration.

The large companies were not the whole of the insurance sector of the City, and in many ways more integral to international finance and commerce was Lloyd's, which is not included in any of the studies. Lloyd's handled marine insurance, whereas the Royal Exchange concentrated upon life and fire insurance, and was much less successful in the marine business. The Royal Exchange Assurance and London Assurance had a monopoly of corporate marine insurance up to 1824, which in fact served to strengthen the private underwriters in Lloyd's. The monopoly prevented competition from other firms; and, since underwriting by partnerships was also banned, it led to the emergence of an institutional framework where individuals could meet to underwrite separately. The private underwriters came to see the monopoly of the two companies as a protection for themselves. In 1824, the monopoly was overturned, under the onslaught of the Alliance British and Foreign Fire and Life Insurance Co. which was backed by leading City men such as Nathan Rothschild, Moses Montefiore, Samuel Gurney and Francis Baring. However, Lloyd's survived the potential threat, and the marine insurance market continued to have a dual structure: the large, highly capitalized companies on the one hand, which were associated with major banking dynasties, and the individuals who were members of Lloyd's.[28] Clearly, there were two very different avenues of recruitment within the insurance sector of the City, and it is at least plausible to argue that members of Lloyd's were integrated neither with the remainder of the City, nor with the landed aristocracy. The samples analysed by Lisle-Williams and Cassis do not, for that matter, include members of the Stock Exchange, the Baltic Exchange, the Metal Exchange or the whole host of commodity merchants and brokers.

It might be objected that this is to cast the net too wide, extending beyond the reach of finance pure and simple. The line is not, however, easily drawn. A firm such as Dalgety and Co., the Australian wool merchants, did not follow the pattern of other merchants such as Barings in moving from commodity trade to merchant banking, yet was nevertheless heavily involved in the finance market. Dalgety needed to find large sums of money in order to provide trade credit for the wool clip, and increasingly to provide long-term loans to the growers in Australia who were purchasing the freehold of their runs and making improvements. Equally, colonial banks such as the Bank of New South Wales which had made loans to growers moved into the marketing of the clip. It was indeed the competition from colonial banks and finance houses such as the New Zealand Loan and Mercantile Agency, which had access to cheap money from deposits and the sale of debentures, which induced the private partnership of Dalgety to form a public company in 1883 and to tap the market for debentures. The line between 'pure' finance and trade is not easily drawn, and a restrictive definition based upon bankers and merchant bankers might overstate the case for a 'uniform elite'. The example of Dalgety at once suggests that something might have been missed, for here was an example of the loss of dynastic control. When the firm went public in 1883, the involvement of the family in the concern ended, in response to the inability to compete with large public companies.[29] The emphasis upon dynastic continuity might therefore fail to provide the whole story.

This might be true even of the families and firms at the heart of the City who were represented on the court of directors of the Bank of England. There had been a number of disappearances as trade patterns changed. In the early nineteenth century, for example, William Manning (1763–1835) was a long-standing director of the Bank and the president of London Assurance, whose first wife was the daughter of Abel Smith, a member of Cassis's aristocratic group. Nevertheless, he was bankrupted in 1831 when the West Indies trade collapsed.[30] Similarly, Sir John Reid, governor of the Bank in 1839/40, was bankrupted in 1847.[31] Evelyn Hubbard, a partner in a long-established firm of Russian merchants whose father had also been a director of the Bank, resigned from the Bank in 1909 when the gross mismanagement of the firm left him little option.[32] William Lidderdale, a director of the Bank from 1870 until his death in 1902, was governor during the Baring crisis of 1890 and a key figure in the rescue of the firm, for which he was rewarded with a Privy Counsellorship and the freedom of the City. But his own merchant house of Rathbone and Co. made heavy losses in the 1890s, and closed its London office in 1897 when he ceased to be partner. Lidderdale seems to have lost his capital, and to have relied for his livelihood on fees from his directorships of American railroad companies; he left an estate of only £9,338 gross.[33] Failure of current members of the court on such a spectacular scale might be rare; more common was the failure of a firm to provide a representative in the next generation. There was no successor, for example, to the banker Sir August Prevost, a director of the Bank from 1881 to 1913.[34] It is worth reflecting at this point upon the methodology of the various surveys of the City, for a common feature is that they do not measure turnover but rather present snap shots of social characteristics at points in time. This might disguise some important features, for it could be that there was a high level of turnover which makes it essential to consider why some firms and families failed and others succeeded. Survival was less certain and more contingent than some accounts of dynastic continuity might suggest.

Historians of the aristocracy have been concerned to explain how members of the landed elite maintained their position, and part of the answer has been a successful family strategy to handle inheritance, based on the strict settlement.[35] This raises the question of the family strategy of financial families who were faced with the problem of handing over the firm from one generation to the next. This might not be easy, for there had to be a balance between taking money from the firm to provide security for the family, and retaining capital in the business where it was at risk. In many cases, this was not attempted and the firm disappeared after a single generation; or it changed its name as a new partner replaced the retiring member. In some cases, the relationship between family and firm could be muddled, with disastrous consequences for both, such as in Hubbard and Co. where the inheritance of members of the family who were not associated with the firm was used as risk capital. The selection of family members to run the business had to be carefully handled on meritocratic principles if there was not to be disaster: there was a search among a 'recruitment stratum' of kin for the most competent businessmen. Where they were in short supply, non-family members might be offered a partnership, so that the 'recruitment stratum' was widened from the family. This might be by recruitment of men who were partners in their own firms, as in the case of Dalgety, where E. T. Doxat was brought in, with his capital, from the wool-brokers Edenborough, Doxat and Co., and permitted the survival of Dalgety's business in the absence of any competent heir in the family. One possible strategy, therefore, was to search amongst the partners of other firms, so that established elite families might be preserved by the transfusion of blood from other parts of the City. Much less common was the widening of the recruitment stratum beyond the City to, for example, the civil service – a strategy which was adopted more readily in other financial centres. One of the few cases was Clinton Dawkins, who had held high-ranking posts in the Treasury, and in the government of Egypt and India. He became a partner in the London house of J. S. Morgan in 1900, and was not a total success. There might also be promotion of salaried men within the firm from the 'administrative stratum', a strategy which might be treated with caution by family members who feared dilution of control. It was, according to the Barings in 1859, 'the climax of absurdity', but it was adopted by, for example, Antony Gibbs and Son in 1864. Edward Stubbs and Augustus Sillem were two salaried employees who did not bring capital to the firm; they were supplied with shares of one sixty-fourth each by the senior partner, on which they received profits but paid interest. Although they were recruited to the elite from the 'administrative stratum', they were kept socially apart from the family and departed from the elite on their retirement without the appearance of a second generation. The avenues of recruitment were, therefore, by no means standard and require careful analysis before the exact structure of the elite becomes clear.[36]

In view of the problems which were involved in handling the succession of the generations in a world economy in constant flux, it is not surprising that many firms failed. Barings, after all, almost collapsed in 1890 and, although they were rescued, others such as the Spanish house of Murietta were not. The First World War cleared out others, such as Speyer and Wogau, and the slump of the 1930s still more, such as Huths, and Fruhling and Goschen.[37]

These names suggest that one feature of the City was its cosmopolitan character, and one crucial characteristic of London was the absence of government regulations so that it was easy for firms to start business.[38] Rather than stressing the connections with the British aristocracy, it might be more useful to trace international ramifications. A good example is the Seligman network. They emerged from a background in peddling or retailing in the United States, and moved into banking: eight brothers in the 1860s established houses in New York, San Francisco, New Orleans, Frankfurt, Paris and London. Or there is the example of Philip and Gustav Speyer who moved from Frankfurt, where the family was engaged in banking, to New York; Gustav's son Edgar moved to London in 1887, where he was naturalized and became a baronet and Privy Counsellor. The heart of the business, however, was in Frankfurt and New York. These

German–Jewish financiers, based in New York, became a homogeneous elite which intermarried and attended the same synagogue, and it must be wondered how far they were ever really integrated into English society.[39] Much the same point might be made of the Greek houses such as the Rallis and Rodocanachis, who were divided from the 'aristocratic bankers' by religion and who tended to be self-contained.[40] Another group consisted of the 'Yankee financiers' such as Morton, Bliss and Co., or George Peabody, or, most famously, Drexel, Morgan and Co. They built a web of international connections in the same way as the American German–Jewish houses. They did come into contact with London's 'aristocratic bankers': Morgan's London house became Morgan Grenfell in 1910. Edward Grenfell, a member of the long-established merchant banking family, had served an apprenticeship with a merchant bank in London and a domestic bank in the provinces, before he joined J. S. Morgan in 1900 in a salaried capacity, becoming a partner in 1904. He was a capable banker who was in no sense an amateur or passenger. However, the partnership agreements of the Morgan firms in New York, Philadelphia, Paris and London were reorganized to strengthen the ties between them and to give a greater participation by the American partners in the affairs of the London house. The survival of the Grenfell family on the court of the Bank of England for another generation was to be based upon integration into the world of 'Yankee financiers' as much as their connections with the English landed aristocracy.[41]

There was, as Cassis admits, a cleavage between the old merchant banks, even if they were of foreign origin such as Barings, and those such as Speyer and Seligman who exploited the financial resources of London without really integrating into society. However, he does not accept the contention of some historians that the business success of London rested upon the former rather than the latter; he believes that the dominance of the aristocratic group was not seriously challenged, and that it was essentially a matter of time before social acceptance followed from business success.[42] Although he is obviously correct in the case of some families, others did fall by the wayside. Ultimate social acceptance of survivors in any case does not remove the fact that at any one time there was a divide within the City between the old dynasties and newcomers, and it was this tension which helped to maintain the business success of the City.

It is also necessary to take care with the criteria which are used to establish a fusion between finance and the landed aristocracy. The obvious illustration of the alliance of a German–Jewish family with the aristocracy is provided by the Rothschilds, several of whom were ennobled, acquired country seats and married into landed families. Nevertheless, the great house built by Ferdinand Rothschild at Waddesdon should not be read simply as a symbol of adoption of an aristocratic culture: with its French architectural style and furniture it may be seen as a country house which was cosmopolitan rather than English, a symbol of distinctiveness rather than a sign of convergence.[43] It is too easy, and potentially misleading, to assume that land and country houses were acquired as part of a process of acceptance of aristocratic values. The debate over the labour aristocracy provides a corrective, for it is now contended that, far from accepting a middle-class ideology of self-help, the labour aristocrats took the concept and inserted their own meaning.[44] In the same way, the attitude of financiers towards the aristocracy and landed estates might be self-interested and functional, as a means of obtaining crucial information for business decisions, and as an outlet for funds which could provide family stability.[45]

An appreciation of the channels of recruitment into the financial elite does not only require an analysis of cosmopolitan networks and the means by which succession was handled within firms, it also requires an appreciation of the nature of institutions in the City and the way in which membership was obtained. Bodies such as Lloyd's, the Stock Exchange and the Baltic Exchange might be differently constituted, either as proprietary clubs which belonged to investors who made a profit from charging an entrance fee, or clubs which belonged to the members. In the first case, the owner had an interest in a large membership in order to increase income; in the second, the members had an interest in limiting members in order to reduce competition.

Lloyd's had, in the eighteenth century, been a proprietary club based on the coffee house of Edward Lloyd, but in 1771 a new Lloyd's was opened at the Royal Exchange which belonged only to its members. The constitution of Lloyd's was formalized in 1871 by an Act of Parliament which gave it the rights of a corporation. It was regulated by a committee numbering between twelve and twenty, with a term of office of three years, elected by the members. Members fell into two categories, underwriting and non-underwriting, and were elected by the committee who required recommendation from six members. In addition to the members, there were annual subscribers who were mainly insurance companies who used the rooms in order to collect news and gossip. There were also substitutes who were clerks or partners of the members. Underwriting members paid an entrance fee of £105, an annual subscription of £12.12s, and £5.5s for each substitute; non-underwriters paid a £25 entrance fee, £5.5s annual subscription and £5.5s for substitutes. Members also paid £5.5s a year for a seat, that is a fixed place in the room. In 1874/5, there were 710 members, of whom 452 were underwriters; about half the members paid for substitutes; and there were 667 annual subscribers. The result of this system, it was suggested in 1876, was that:

> There is, probably, no society or corporation in existence in which the hereditary element is so strong as in Lloyd's... Besides the recurrence of the same names in the list of members for more than a century, the hereditary element is curiously expressed in the number of individuals of the same family who continue members... But perhaps the most remarkable feature in the element here characterized is the long term during which many members have been associated with Lloyd's.

If these remarks are close to the truth – and it must be admitted that there has been no research on the subject – then it would seem that Lloyd's was relatively closed. However, it was distinct from other aspects of the City: the dynasties which were mentioned at Lloyd's had no connection with the merchant banking dynasties. There were, for example, five members of the Secretan family in 1874/5, seven Burnards, five Duncans – none of them names associated with banking or with the aristocracy.[46] Amongst the list of long-standing members, one name did stand out: John Benjamin Heath (1790–1879), who was a director of the Bank of England from 1823 to 1872. He does, however, serve to support another point which is being stressed. He was born in Genoa, the son of a merchant, and was educated at Harrow; he joined the family firm in Italian trade and foreign banking and was described as 'in the best sense of the word, one of our "merchant princes"'. The firm and the family were, however, to disappear and no dynasty was formed. He did, it is true, become an aristocrat – but as a baron of the kingdom of Italy.[47] Heath provides an excellent example of the turnover which marked the City.

The Stock Exchange was, unlike Lloyd's a proprietary club. There were two distinct interests: the shareholders or proprietors who owned the building, numbering about 500 at the beginning of the period; and the subscribers or members who totalled about 2,000. The proprietors elected nine Managers, who ran the Exchange as a profitable joint-stock company paying a dividend of 20 per cent in the late 1870s. The Managers determined the level of fees for admission, which they clearly did not want to set at a level which would limit the number of members and hence the income. The Committee for General Purposes was elected by the members, with responsibility for admissions and controlling the business of the Exchange. Candidates for membership were not allowed to be engaged in any other business, and had to find three members who were willing to guarantee £750 each in the event of the new member defaulting. The costs of membership were not high, and men who had worked as clerks (the majority of entrants) were admitted on still easier terms. Members who had not served four years as a clerk paid an admission fee of £105, and an annual subscription of £21; members who had worked as a clerk for four years paid £63 for admission and a subscription of £12.12s. The Exchange was, claimed the government enquiry of 1878, 'practically an open market'[48] There was no limit to the numbers of members, which increased from 864 in 1850 to 2,009 in 1878 and 5,400 in 1907; in the ten years between 1900 and 1909, a total of 2,297 new members were elected.[49] The result, it was feared, was 'the very easy admission of a great many young men from the West end of the town ... who go and play at lawn tennis, and tell their friends "I can put you on a good thing"'.[50] Certainly, there was a contrast with New York where the number of 'seats' was strictly limited at 440 between 1865 and the First World War. Seats consequently had to be bought for large sums from retiring members. The price in 1885, for example, ranged from $34,000 to $20,000 and most fell into the hands of large banks – a phenomenon which was not possible in London where members were excluded from other activities.[51]

In London, members faced with competition for business campaigned for a restriction in entry which was at length agreed in 1904, associated with an attempt to end the divide between the proprietors and members. It was agreed that new members who had not been clerks should also own three shares in the Exchange, and new members who had been clerks one share: a share cost between £150 and £250 between 1904 and 1914. New members were also to obtain the nomination of a retiring or deceased member, which cost up to £170. The limits were nevertheless not strict, for the number of shares was increased and the maximum holding of any individual reduced, so that the number of proprietors rose from 1,212 in 1904 to 2,366 in 1914. A quota of clerks could also be admitted without the need for a nomination. The outcome was a slight fall in membership before the war, to 4,855 in 1914. The cost of entry in 1910 was calculated to be £1,315 for someone who had not been a clerk, or £670 for a clerk, which might be reduced to £500 where the nomination was excused. This was higher than the cost of membership in 1870, when it was £63 for a non-clerk or £42 for a clerk, yet the barriers were still not massive.[52]

There was a distinction between members who were brokers and jobbers. In 1908, about 40 per cent of members were jobbers, who took the risks and carried the stock; the brokers dealt with the buyers and sellers of shares which demanded social connections at a time when most clients were private. A partner in a broking firm needed to bring in capital: S. B. Heward brought £10,000 to his uncle's firm in 1886. Jobbers might be able to rise as outsiders, relying on their wits and were less socially exclusive. Brokers were more likely to come from public school backgrounds, utilizing social connections to obtain business at least until the 1930s, and possibly later. Panmure Gordon, for example, was educated at Harrow, Oxford and Bonn; he served in the 10th Hussars; and joined a merchant firm in Shanghai. He became a member of the Exchange in 1865, established his own firm in 1876, and died in 1902. Even so, the Exchange was less prestigious than merchant banking. The first aristocrat to join was Lord Walter Campbell in 1875, the brother-in-law of Princess Louise, and by 1900 there were only three peers and about thirty sons of peers on the Exchange. The first Etonian jobber did not enter until 1891, and a survey of 127 members who died in the First World War indicates that few had a public school or Oxbridge education: eleven went to Eton, six to Harrow, six to Marlborough; fourteen were educated at Oxford and ten at Cambridge. These proportions are lower than among bankers, and members of the Exchange were also less wealthy. A list of seventy-four members who died between mid 1894 and the end of 1896 shows an average estate of £40,042, with one exceptionally large estate of £852,515.[53]

The requirements of brokers started to change in the 1930s, as is suggested by the firm of Phillips and Drew. Until 1936, there were four partners who largely worked for private clients. The senior partner – Reeves – had risen within the firm from office manager, which does suggest some degree of openness; the other partners came from the family. In 1935, a new partner entered: S. J. Perry, who transformed the firm up to his retirement in 1959. He did not have a public school background or social connections, but had trained as an actuary. His connections were professional, and he was responsible for shifting the firm towards links with insurance companies and other large institutional clients, providing advice of a technical nature on 'switching'. This was marked by a change in the method of entry into the firm, and a greater emphasis upon technical skills and meritocratic recruitment. What is not clear is whether this changed the 'recruitment stratum' from which members were recruited, or whether it was a change in the criteria employed in selecting from the same pool.[54]

The social composition of the City of London between 1880 and 1950 was, therefore, more problematic than has been implied by the recent literature. The degrees of openness and closure of parts of the City varied, and the avenues of recruitment differed between various sectors and changed over time. The dominance of the City's business by a tightly knit group associated with the aristocracy is more problematic than is often suggested, and it is doubtful whether this can explain the continued business success of the City. It is possible to stress the openness of the City to newcomers, rather than dynastic closure. Was it perhaps also the case that integration was also less than has been assumed by the proponents of a 'uniform elite'?

III

It has become a common assumption in the history of modern Britain that there was a well-defined City view on questions of economic policy which opposed, or at least neglected, the needs of industry. Such an interpretation is open to dispute: it could plausibly be argued that the City was internally divided, and not necessarily set against the needs of industry. The politics of the City is the subject of another chapter in this collection, and it is not possible to develop this argument at length. It might, however, be illustrated by the debate over bimetallism in the 1880s and 1890s.

The bimetallic controversy has been interpreted as a divide between industry and agriculture on the one hand and the City on the other. Both industry and landowners were suffering from falling prices which could, it was believed by the proponents of bimetallism, be rectified by a more broadly based currency. Furthermore, Indian markets for cotton textiles manufactured in Lancashire were threatened by the devaluation of the silver rupee against the gold-based pound. The City, so it is claimed, believed that its power rested upon the gold standard, and accordingly stood opposed to land and industry.[55] Such an interpretation would in itself challenge the notion of a fusion between land and the City, in which the financial elite could allow aristocratic politicians to speak on its behalf, for a City supporter of gold might not necessarily be able to rely upon a landowner who saw salvation in bimetallism. More crucially, it is wrong to see the City as adopting a uniform position.

The City was divided in its attitudes. Henry Hucks Gibbs, the leading bimetallist, was the senior partner in Antony Gibbs and Son, a leading merchant bank; he was a director of the Bank of England, and for a time one of the MPs for the City. Gibbs drew a distinction between what he called the drones and the worker bees, and he placed the money market amongst the drones who were not interested in production, against the merchants who were. It might also be expected that bankers and merchants who were involved in silver-based countries in South America and the Far East might have supported bimetallism. Gibbs, who was largely concerned with South America, was certainly not isolated within the City. At the Bank, he had the support of H. R. Grenfell. The signatories of the petition of the Bimetallic League in 1895 included some distinguished names: Thomas Baring of Baring Brothers; Sir Robert Jardine and H. M. Matheson of Matheson and Co.; Edward Horsley Palmer of Dent, Palmer and Co.; Sir Albert, Reuben and Edward Sassoon of David Sassoon and Co.; Sir James Mackay and Sir Henry Cunningham of the Chartered Bank of India, Australia and China. The City Committee of the Bimetallic League, comments Cassis, contained 'quelques noms de poids', but he tends to play down the divide in the City: 'ils restent confinés aux transactions commerciales avec une région du monde. Et surtout, ils ne pèsent pas assez lourd, ni en nombre, ni en influence, face à la masse des monometallistes et à leurs leaders qui comprennent tous les grands noms de la banque.'[56] The Bank of England might have been dominated by gold interests, but this begs the question of how far it acted as the spokesman of the City. It has already been suggested that the Court of Directors was recruited in a particular way, which might limit its representativeness and it is as well to remember Ingham's point that the Bank had its own autonomous interests. And the region of the world to which Cassis refers is, of course, India which was integral to British economic and political power before the First World War.

This raises the vexed matter of the empire. The impression which has emerged from recent writings is that the empire benefited the City and the rentiers of the south against the industrialists of the north. This, however, excludes trade and the benefits which flowed in particular to the Lancashire cotton industry. The trade surplus with India was vital to the British system of settlements, for it covered a large part of the deficit with the rest of the world. India in the later nineteenth century was able to increase its exports to other countries (in part because of the depreciation in the rupee), so that its earnings from trade with Europe and America allowed it to run a trade deficit with Britain. The result was that India enabled British industry to overcome increased competition in the world economy. Lancashire interests were adamant that India should not introduce tariffs which would threaten its main market, which collided with the need of the British government in India to raise more taxes to pay the 'home charges' which were mounting because of the devaluation of the rupee. Tariffs were politically more expedient in India, both because they could be justified in nationalist terms as a means of developing Indian industries, and because alternative sources of revenue from internal taxes would generate unrest and give Indians a lever to demand more consultation. But the British government had to face opposition from the Manchester lobby, which generally succeeded up to 1914, in part because of the vital electoral importance of constituencies in the cotton towns. Industry was a beneficiary of empire, and did play a vital role in the debate over policy: it is wrong to see industry as subordinated to a hegemonic fusion of land and finance. In the interwar period, the balance of power swung to India, for tax demands were mounting and the need to placate nationalists became paramount. Fiscal autonomy was granted to India, and tariffs mounted against the Lancashire cotton trade. British industry was to this extent sacrificed, but the key to the shift in policy was not a simple divide between Manchester and the City of London, as a shift in the balance of power between Manchester and Bombay. The Lancashire cotton trade was already in decline, and the role of the cotton constituencies in the winning of elections was reduced. Industry had its voice before 1914 and, as the bimetallic debate suggests, had supporters within the City. Politicians in Westminster had to resolve a complex political equation which cannot be understood in terms of a simple hegemony of the City and land.[57]

The claim can therefore be made that the City did not speak with one voice which dominated the debate over economic policy; it was in any case not so distinct from the needs of industry as some commentators believe. The City might, it is true, not provide long-term finance for industry but this is not to say that there were no links: the role of the City was rather to provide the credit for the marketing of goods by commission agents spread across the world. Landowners might also, for that matter, have a considerable involvement in industry as the owners of docks or mineral rights or as ground landlords in industrial towns. The lines of division were much more complex and confusing than a simple tripartite division into a politically subordinate industry and a dominant alliance of land and finance.[58]

IV

The depiction of the financial elite as closed and integrated which has become a common-place in the analysis of the City seems to obscure many aspects of its social history. The emphasis upon the aristocracy of finance and dynastic continuity has tended to underplay the fact that the City was made up of many niches in which outsiders could establish precarious firms which often failed and rarely succeeded. The vast number of fragile ventures exploited sectors of passing interest, and had a considerable turnover. It has even been suggested, contrary to the Cassis and Lisle-Williams view, that in the Edwardian period the City had *ceased* to be 'an intimate club of familiar people' and had been replaced by 'hordes of specialists'. Many failed, such as Dunn, Fischer and Co. which existed for a brief period between 1906 and the First World War. Here was the reverse of the world of the aristocrats of finance: Charles Fischer, a Swiss Jew, and James Dunn, a Canadian solicitor and stockbroker, who manipulated the market in South American power and traction companies. They were outsiders who never made the establishment – and it might be that they were the dynamic element which allowed the City to survive. 'The world of the Edwardian City of London', Ranald Michie has concluded,

> was not one peopled solely by large, long-established and well-connected firms, whose partners were well integrated into the landed aristocracy of the country...Over time the partners in the older City firms had been able to integrate into the upper echelons of society through generations of contact, education and marriage. A similar process also took place in textiles, brewing, chemicals, steel, coal mining, commerce, law or administration. Time and wealth provided the common denominator in integration, not land and finance. Beyond the select band in the City that possessed such links there existed a continually changing mass of people who enjoyed none of these special relationships and were frequently on

the very edge of society because of their origins, religion and lack of substance.[59]

A concentration on the few families who formed City dynasties is of more significance for the history of the persistence of the aristocracy than it is for the remarkable success of the City of London as a business centre which rested upon fluidity and openness. The acceptance of a 'uniform elite' has served to mask the processes by which members of the financial community were recruited, survived and failed. The next stage in the social history of the City should be to move away from a concern with the relationship between finance and land, to a more detailed awareness of the internal dynamics of the square mile and its denizens.

Notes

1 This chapter is a preliminary report on research which is currently being undertaken on the social history of the City. It is accordingly more in the nature of a commentary on the current state of knowledge, with suggestions for new lines of approach, rather than a presentation of conclusions.

2 The debate on the labour aristocracy dates from the essay by E. J. Hobsbawm, 'The labour aristocracy in nineteenth-century Britain' which was first published in 1954 and reprinted in his *Labouring men. Studies in the history of labour* (London, 1964), pp. 274–315. It has since generated an extensive debate, summarized in R. Gray, *The aristocracy of labour in nineteenth-century Britain, c. 1850–1900* (London, 1981). The tension between production institutions and technology is discussed in, for example, W. Lewchuk, *American technology and the British vehicle industry* (Cambridge, 1987) and W. Lazonick, 'Industrial organization and technological change: the decline of the British cotton industry', *Business History Review*, 48 (1983).

3 The clearest expression of this view is provided by M. J. Wiener, *English culture and the decline of the industrial spirit, 1850–1980* (Cambridge, 1981).

4 For example, M. Edelstein, *Overseas investment in the age of high imperialism: the United Kingdom, 1850–1914* (London, 1982).

5 L. and J. F. C. Stone, *An open elite? England, 1540–1880* (Oxford, 1984); W. D. Rubinstein, *Men of property: the very wealthy in Britain since the industrial revolution* (London, 1981) and 'New men of wealth and the purchase of land in nineteenth-century England', *Past and Present*, 92 (1981), 125–47. For scepticism on the view that new men of wealth did not enter a 'closed' landed class, see F. M. L. Thompson, 'The landed aristocracy and business elites in Victorian Britain', in *Les noblesses européennes au xixe siècle*, Collection de l'École Française de Rome 107 (1988), 267–79, and 'Aristocracy, gentry, and the middle classes in Britain, 1750–1850', in A. M. Birke

and L. Kettenacker (eds.), *Middle classes, aristocracy and monarchy: patterns of change and adaptation in the age of modern nationalism* (Munich, London, New York, Paris, 1989), pp. 15–34.

6 These comments are drawn from A. Giddens, 'Elites in the British class structure', in P. Stanworth and A. Giddens (eds.), *Elites and power in British society* (Cambridge, 1974), pp. 1–21.

7 Giddens, 'Elites', p. 2.

8 T. Lupton and C. S. Wilson, 'The social background and connections of "top decision makers"', *Manchester School*, 27 (1959); see also R. Whitley, 'The City and industry: the directors of large companies, their characteristics and connections', in Stanworth and Giddens (eds.), *Elites and power*, pp. 65–80.

9 M. Lisle-Williams, 'Beyond the market: the survival of family capitalism in the English merchant banks', *British Journal of Sociology*, 35 (1984), 241–71 and 'Merchant banking dynasties in the English class structure: ownership, solidarity and kinship in the City of London, 1850–1960', *British Journal of Sociology*, 35 (1984), 333–62. Figures on concentration in clearing banks are from F. Capie and G. Rodrik-Bali, 'Concentration in British banking, 1870–1920', *Business History*, 24 (1982).

10 Lisle-Williams, 'Merchant banking dynasties', 346–53; Y. Cassis, 'Bankers in English society in the late nineteenth century', *Economic History Review* 2nd ser., 38 (1985), 210–29; L. Davidoff, *The best circles: Society, etiquette and The Season* (1973), chapter 4.

11 Stone, *An open elite*?; Rubinstein, *Men of property*, p. 219, 'New men of wealth', 125–47 and 'The end of 'old corruption' in Britain, 1780–1860', *Past and Present*, 101 (1983), 55–86.

12 D. Cannadine, 'The landowner as millionaire: the finances of the dukes of Devonshire, c. 1800–c. 1926', *Agricultural History Review*, 25 (1977).

13 S. W. Martin, *A great estate at work: the Holkham estate and its inhabitants in the nineteenth century* (Cambridge, 1980).

14 F. M. L. Thompson, *English landed society in the nineteenth century* (London, 1963), pp. 304–6.

15 Cassis, 'Bankers', 213–15 and *Les banquiers de la City à l'époque Edouardienne, 1890–1914* (Geneva, 1984), pp. 121–9.

16 Cassis, 'Bankers', 229 and *Les banquiers*, chapter VII; P. J. Cain and A. G. Hopkins, 'Gentlemanly capitalism and British overseas expansion, I: the old colonial system, 1688–1850', *Economic History Review*, 2nd ser., 39 (1986), 503–10.

17 L. E. Davis and R. E. Huttenback, *Mammon and the pursuit of empire: the political economy of British imperialism, 1860–1912* (Cambridge, 1986), pp. 211–18, 251–2, 313–14; P. K. O'Brien, 'The costs and benefits of British imperialism, 1846–1914', *Past and Present*, 120 (1988), 185, 195.

18 Cassis, 'Bankers', 217–24, 229 and *Les banquiers*, chapter VI.

19 Lisle-Williams, 'Merchant banking dynasties', 353–8.
20 Cassis, *Les banquiers*, pp. 169, 172–3.
21 The phrase is that of P. Anderson, 'The figures of descent', *New Left Review*, 161 (1987), 41.
22 This is true to an extent of Anderson, 'Figures'; see also, for example, E. H. H. Green, 'Rentiers versus producers? The political economy of the bimetallic controversy', *English Historical Review*, 103 (1988), 611 and M. H. Best and J. Humphries. 'The City and industrial decline', in W. Lazonick and B. Elbaum (eds.), *The decline of the British economy* (Oxford, 1986), pp. 223–39.
23 Cassis, 'Bankers', 227–9 and *Les banquiers*, chapter 8.
24 G. Ingham, *Capitalism divided? The City and industry in British social development* (Basingstoke, 1984), pp. 9, 150–1, 224, 226, 228, 230–4.
25 Ibid., p. 6.
26 Wiener, *English culture*.
27 B. E. Supple, *The Royal Exchange Assurance: a history of British insurance, 1720–1970* (Cambridge, 1970), pp. 352–3.
28 Ibid., pp. 186–7, 198, 202.
29 M. J. Daunton, 'Firm and family in the City of London in the nineteenth century: the case of F. G. Dalgety', *Historical Research*, 62 (1989).
30 *History of Parliament, The Commons* 1790–1820, *iv*, *Members G-P*, 540–3.
31 *The Gentleman's Magazine*, 161 (1867), 391.
32 M. J. Daunton, 'Inheritance and succession in the City of London in the nineteenth century', *Business History*, 30 (1988), 272–6.
33 S. Marriner, 'William Lidderdale (1832–1902), central banker and merchant', in D. J. Jeremy (ed.), *Dictionary of business biography iii H-L*, (London, 1985), pp. 786–90.
34 Cassis, *Les banquiers*, p. 54.
35 Stone, *Open elite*?, p. 421.
36 Daunton, 'Inheritance and succession' and 'Family and firm', 168; V. P. Carosso, *The Morgans: private international bankers, 1854–1913* (Cambridge, Mass. and London, 1987), pp. 443–5.
37 S. D. Chapman, 'Aristocracy and meritocracy in merchant banking', *British Journal of Sociology*, 37 (1986), 180–93.
38 See S. D. Chapman, 'The international houses: the continental contribution to British economic development, 1800–69', *Journal of European Economic History*, 6 (1977).
39 B. E. Supple, 'A business elite: German-Jewish financiers in nineteenth-century New York', *Business History Review*, 31 (1957); A. M. Mandeville, *The House of Speyer: a candid criticism of Speyer flotations* (London, 1915?).
40 Chapman, 'Aristocracy and meritocracy'.
41 D. Greenberg, 'Yankee financiers and the establishment of trans-

Atlantic partnerships: a re-examination', *Business History*, 16 (1974), 17–35; Carosso, *The Morgans*, pp. 438–53.

42 Cassis, *Les banquiers*, p. 127; and 'Merchant bankers and the City aristocracy', *British Journal of Sociology*, 39 (1988), pp. 114–20.

43 See R. Davis, *The English Rothschilds* (London, 1983).

44 G. J. Crossick, *An artisan elite in Victorian society: Kentish London, 1840–80* (London, 1978).

45 Daunton, 'Gentlemanly capitalism'.

46 F. Martin, *The history of Lloyd's and of marine insurance in Great Britain* (London, 1876), p. 275, chapter 19.

47 F. Boase, *English biography*, I, col. 1411; *Proceedings of the Society of Antiquaries*, 2nd ser., 8 (1879–81), 101.

48 PP 1878 xix, *London Stock Exchange Commission, Report of the Commissioners*, 267–9; PP 1878 xix, *London Stock Exchange Commission, Minutes of Evidence*, evidence of Francis Levien and W. F. Perowne.

49 R. C. Michie, *The London and New York Stock Exchanges, 1850–1914* (London, 1987), pp. 250–2.

50 *London Stock Exchange Committee, Minutes of Evidence*, Q293.

51 Michie, *London and New York*, p. 253; R. Sobel, *The Big board: a history of the New York stock market* (New York, 1965), p. 129.

52 Michie, *London and New York*, pp. 250–2; D. T. A. Kynaston, 'The London Stock Exchange, 1870–1914: an institutional history', Ph.D. thesis, University of London, 1983, 58–65, 73.

53 Kynaston, 'London Stock Exchange', 86, 89–90, 93–4, 97, 101, 122; Michie, *London and New York*, p. 92.

54 W. J. Reader, 'Phillips and Drew: the making of a modern stock broking firm', unpublished paper delivered at the Institute of Historical Research.

55 Green, 'Rentiers versus producers?'.

56 Daunton, 'Gentlemanly capitalism', 151; Bodleian Library, Ms Harcourt Dept. 163ff. 84–8; Cassis, *Les banquiers*, pp. 349, 355.

57 A. Porter, 'The balance sheet of empire', *Historical Journal*, 31 (1988), 635–99; B. R. Tomlinson, 'The contraction of England: national decline and the loss of empire', *Journal of Imperial and Commonwealth History*, 11 (1982–3); P. Harnetty, 'The Indian cotton duties controversy, 1894–6', *English Historical Review*, 77 (1962); I. Klein, 'English free traders and Indian tariffs, 1874–96', *Modern Asian Studies*, 5 (1973); C. Dewey, 'The end of the imperialism of free trade: the eclipse of the Lancashire lobby and the concession of fiscal autonomy in India', in C. J. Dewey and A. G. Hopkins (eds.), *The imperial impact: studies in the economic history of Africa and India* (London, 1978).

58 This is developed further in Daunton, 'Gentlemanly capitalism'.

59 R. C. Michie, 'Dunn, Fischer and Co. in the City of London, 1906–14', *Business History*, 30 (1988), 195–6, 213.

8 Bankers in French society, 1860s–1960s

ALAIN PLESSIS

For over a century, particularly in France, financiers have been the target of recurrent and impassioned attacks by politicians and journalists seeking to expose their power. With the fall of the Second Empire, Georges Duchêne, a follower of Proudhon, challenged these 'neo-feudalists' who made up the boards of directors of limited companies and thus between them controlling the credit of France. From the crash of the Union Générale in 1882 until the end of the century, anti-Semitism inspired new campaigns: in *Les rois de la République. Histoire de la juiverie* (2 volumes, 1883 and 1886) the propagandist Auguste Chirac gave full reign to a theme which Toussenel, a follower of Fourier, had already exploited in 1847. During the *belle époque*, a polemical work entitled *Contre l'oligarchie financière*, written by a journalist under the pseudonym of Lysis, was reprinted eleven times between 1906 and 1912, while éditions de la Guerre Sociale published *La Démocratie et les financiers* in which Francis Delaisi attempted to show how 'the sovereignty of the people is a myth' since 'financiers rule France'. In 1925, at the height of the franc crisis, Chastenet, a member of parliament, in turn attacked the 'financial oligarchy' and the 'international fraternity of bankers' in *La République des banquiers*. With the economic crisis of the 1930s, the struggle intensified from all sides against these 'two-hundred families' who, the radical leader Daladier inveighed, 'are the masters of the French economy and, in effect, of French politics'. Delaisi renewed his accusations in *La Banque de France aux mains des Deux cent familles*, in March 1936 *Le Crapouillot* devoted a special issue to these two hundred families, the Communist party demanded almost daily that they be fought against, while Bertrand de Jouvenel condemned 'the financial families, the famous Two Hundred Families' who plundered France. In the 1950s, the publicist Henry Coston in turn pilloried *Les financiers qui mènent le monde*, *La*

Haute Banque et les trusts and *Le retour des deux cent familles*, and even today the controversy over the power of money continues.[1]

The uniformity of the criticisms, reiterated for so long, and the vagueness of the terms used as slogans to mobilize public opinion, lead one to ponder on the true social position of the French financial elite and its evolution. But such a study, at least in the present day, has until now been neglected by French economic historians, despite their refusal to separate the economic from the social. The portrayal of a particular financier, whether representative or atypical, cannot in effect replace a true social analysis of the milieu, and such a study would require a statistical basis which has yet to be established.

Moreover, the very meaning of the word 'financier' has been, and is still, open to varied interpretation. Thus in 1926 Octave Homberg, a finance inspector who had been general manager of the Société Générale, auditor of the Banque de France in 1891, director of several companies and even, so it is said, the 'guru' of the Paris Bourse, defined 'the financier worthy of this title' as both 'the creator and the guiding force of wealth', as opposed to the plain banker who was 'a trader in money'. Soon after, Francis Pietri, another finance inspector who became a member of parliament and a minister, viewed 'commercial finance' as the ensemble of 'everything that lives, stirs and moves in the bank and the Bourse', and within it differentiated the world of 'high finance', made up of the Banque de France, the major commercial banks with an open account at the issuing bank, and the stockbrokers.[2]

For lack of adequate research we shall confine ourselves to bankers to the exclusion of other professional categories of financiers such as stockbrokers or the directors of insurance companies. We must also leave out heads of local banks, which were very numerous and active right up until the 1920s, and also, to a large extent, heads of regional banks: these men had long been part of the elite of their towns, for example the Courtois in Toulouse or the Dupont in Valenciennes, but never really made it to the upper echelons of French society. Leaving aside also the directors of mutual credit corporations and specialist semi-limited companies, which increased rapidly particularly after 1945, we shall focus our attention on the world of high finance and the major commercial banks. First we shall consider the position of the men who were actually invested with the management duties and responsibilities in these banks in French society at the end of the last century. Then we shall attempt to trace the path taken by the major developments which affected this milieu, in conjunction with the profound changes that occurred in the French banking system during the first half of the twentieth century (strong concentration, greatly increased role of the state and so on), before finally outlining some of the traits characteristic of bankers at the end of the 1960s.

The French banking system was created in successive and therefore largely heterogeneous layers, just as the world of the influential bankers around 1880 was made up of individuals who entered it a different times. First there was the *haute banque*. This term, in use since the Restoration, describes a restricted elite of about twenty Parisian banks who prided themselves on their honour and their reputation for respectability, reinforced by the very fact of their long-establishment. Some of these firms, for example Mallet or Hottinguer, were founded before the French Revolution, and the others were created between 1800 and 1830. In these family businesses those in charge, who owned the capital, were brothers, brothers-in-law or cousins, and worked together, often tirelessly. Cases of semi-professionalism seem to have been relatively rare. They took on in turn as new partners their own children, previously trained in banking, who in time were called upon to take over. Bankers were thus created from generation to generation. At the beginning of the Third Republic, the most representative members of this high finance, such as Henry Davillier (1813–82), Alphonse Mallet (1819–1906), Alphonse de Rothschild (1827–1905) and Rodolphe Hottinguer (1835–1920), were descended from dynasties already well-established in banking and were heirs to considerable fortunes which they in turn greatly increased. These banking families made up a closed and novel milieu, even if many of the characteristics often attributed to them do not apply to all. In time, those not of French origin, although far from a general rule, became more and more French: the succession in 1868 of James de Rothschild by his son Alphonse, naturalized twenty years earlier, is significant in this respect. The religious differences in this society were great, even if the proportion of Protestant and Jewish families was relatively large. The cohesive nature of these circles, often united one with the other by close ties, was certain, but for all that they were not an exclusively impenetrable group. More frequently than in the past, marriage linked them to families from other spheres of the elite – notably to high-ranking civil servants – and these financial firms would open up when appropriate to those outside the family, to former employees, even occasionally to someone of humble origin who had nevertheless already proved his worth. Although unusual, the case of the Périer bank, which became Périer, Mercet & Cie from 1881–9, is illuminating: the new partner Emile Mercet, a Genevan, was the son of a manservant and a lady's maid. He married a Protestant and joined the Mallet brothers in 1858. Nine years later, at the age of twenty-five, he was engaged by the Crédit Lyonnais to set up a branch in Constantinople, and in 1879 he became manager of the St Petersburg branch. It was on the strength of this international experience that, in 1881, he became a partner in the Périer bank.[3] In short, the list of names that made up the world of high finance was in no way unchangeable, contrary to the impression one gets on finding once again the Vernes,

Rothschild, Mallet and Hottinguer families among the bankers who were directors of the Banque de France in 1934, just as they were during the Second Empire. For banks of equal worth, such as Pillet-Will, Lefebvre and even Périer itself, closed down at the end of the nineteenth century, either for lack of heirs or because the heads of these firms chose to retire from business and enjoy their accumulated wealth. On the other hand, other names, like Mirabaud, Lazard and Camondo, began to appear among the highest ranks. This progressive variations in the constituents of the world of high finance, long, wealthy and ever-changing, was in no way surprising, since it represented after all the ultimate pinnacle formed by a group of private Parisian bankers.

To the public, the important bankers and financiers were represented above all by the Banque de France and its senior management. The very expression the 'two hundred families' was inspired by the General Assembly of the Banque de France, a body reserved for the bank's two hundred largest shareholders of French nationality. Among the members of this Assembly, which met every year at the end of January in the Galerie Dorée of its building in the rue La Vrillière, were a significant number of senior civil servants, some eminent professionals, but above all men of private means from the aristocracy or well-established middle-class families. The practising economic elite represented barely 20 per cent of the total. Thus actual bankers were very much in the minority. And if they participated in this annual meeting, surrounded by members from the most traditional spheres of the elite, it was because it gave them a sense of pride and allowed them to show their place in 'high society', for the actual power of the Assembly was very limited.

The board whose responsibility it was to determine the actual running of the Banque de France and its credit policy was made up of fifteen directors, of whom on average six to eight were influential bankers, four to six were men of commerce, industrialists and directors of various companies, and three were always paymaster-generals. These last were senior civil servants who monitored and discharged public spending for each administrative *département* while also carrying out various banking activities. This board of directors has been considered 'representative of the business elite'.[4] It was in any case a place where influential bankers met representatives of other sections of the economic elite and where both conferred with the top civil servants who usually made up the 'government of the Bank' with its Governor and two Deputy Governors. In its actual running, the Banque de France thus organized regular meetings between the major bankers and other members of the French social élite in order for them to voice their respective points of view.[5]

In the large commercial banks, who from the middle of the nineteenth century became limited companies, the 'bankers' were both the directors who met at regular intervals, and the general manager or managers who were full-time employees. But one may well ask whether these were truly distinct groups with different origins and social status, and which of them actually ran these banks.[6] In around 1880, the recently created credit institutions were headed by a board of directors who met very frequently with every intention of exercising their power, and the membership of these boards reflected in large part that of their founding bodies. Those whose previous professional experience had been in banking had a central place. While the majority of members on the boards of regional banks came from local trade and regional industry (textile industrialists from Lille at the Crédit du Nord, sugar or soap manufacturers and ship-owners at the Société Marseillaise de Crédit and so on), a good half of the directors of the major Parisian institutions came from banking. David Landes has already pointed out that the board of directors of the Pereire brothers' Crédit Mobilier was made up of eminent members of the 'old Bank'.[7] It was the same on the board of the Société Générale, where those in international high finance took up two-thirds of the seats. The three people who had the most influence on this board, together with Denière, its chairman and a director of the Banque de France, were in fact Bischoffsheim, the Genevan Edouard Hentsch and the Scot Edward Blount, whose Parisian banking concern was taken over by the Société Générale in 1870. Edward Blount became Vice-chairman in 1870, before becoming chairman of the Société Générale from 1886 to 1901. The other directors came from railway companies (the PLM above all) and from industry.[8] Although their influence was less great, there were a large number of bankers on the Crédit Industriel et Commercial, where they rubbed shoulders with men of commerce, industrialists and senior civil servants: the Rostand family, an ancient family of businessmen from Marseille who founded the bank Gay, Rostand et Compagnie, held one or two seats on the board for many years. It was the same at the Comptoir d'Escompte de Paris which for a while came under the control of Edouard Hentsch. When this bank was re-formed in 1889 and became the Comptoir National d'Escompte de Paris, among its directors was Edmond Mercet, the one-time partner of the Périers, who became Vice-chairman in 1894 and Chairman in 1912.

The influence of bankers and financiers was also very strong in those institutions which became true investment banks (banques d'affaires) as opposed to deposit banks, especially in the Banque de Paris et des Pays-Bas. This bank was founded by the well-known bankers Bischoffsheim, Schnapper, Haber and the Baron de Soubeyran, who was also at the Crédit Foncier. Its board of directors was then joined by Charles Sautter (a 'banker from the capital' who appeared on the first board of the Crédit Lyonnais), Adrien de Germiny, a former paymaster-general and a director of the Banque de France, and later Charles Demachy, the senior partner of the bank Demachy et Seillière, who later became chairman of

'Paribas' in 1910. There were finally major banks whose directors were originally all, or nearly all, bankers. Hence, at its inception in 1875, the directors of the Banque de l'Indochine fell into two groups, those who came from the Crédit Industriel et Commercial and those who came from the Comptoir d'Escompte de Paris, and the board grew in 1888 with representatives of Paribas and the Société Générale.[9] As for the Banque de l'Union Parisienne, it was run jointly from its foundation by members of the Protestant families of high finance who created it.

The Crédit Lyonnais is a case apart. The exact position in society of its founder, Henri Germain, is difficult to define. The son of a wealthy silk manufacturer, he studied law and became a barrister but never appeared in court. He called himself a 'man of independent means', but in fact he worked for the well-known silk broker of Lyon, Arlès-Dufour, was a director of the Houillères, hauts fourneaux et forges de Chatillon-Commentry, and of various industrial companies. In short, if he had not been in banking before creating the Crédit Lyonnais, he had experience of many businesses. In the group of founders that he surrounded himself with there were mainly silk manufacturers and other industrialists from Lyon, but also some bankers of whom two were Genevan. Perhaps it was because of the great authority of the chairman, Henri Germain, that these last were quickly excluded, giving up their places to newcomers such as the nephew of Eugène Schneider, Desseiligny, the former prefect Bailleux de Marizy, the former stockbroker Léon Masson and later the former banker of Châlon-sur-Saône, Bo, whose bank had been taken over by the Crédit Lyonnais. But, taking the directors of the major credit institutions as a whole, there were more bankers than industrialists among them, although the reverse was true of the boards of banks formed at the beginning of the twentieth century in the second period of industrialization.[10] As for the *notables* – professionals, or more usually top civil servants or 'men of private means' who did not need to work – they remained very much in the minority, even if from time to time banks did offer some directorships to a civil servant from the Quai d'Orsay or to a retiring army officer. Financial management was still in the hands of paymaster-generals rather than finance inspectors. The latter began to be found among the chairmen of the boards of certain banks at the end of the century, for example Collart-Dutilleul at Paribas, Joseph Gay and then Etienne Hély d'Oissel at the Crédit Industriel et Commercial. But they obtained these posts thanks to their economic, social and political connections rather than because of their professional position: the Hély d'Oissel family network was firmly embedded in the Council of State and the Compagnie de Saint-Gobain, and Collart-Dutilleul, who came from a family of financiers who had made its fortune from the time of the Directoire and who numbered many paymaster-generals among its members, was a minister in 1877 before joining the Société Générale.

As for the general managers of these banks, who were only just beginning to be called bankers, a term previously reserved for private bankers, they were mainly active employees who had been recruited from a milieu often more humble than that of the board of directors. In the beginning they had usually been engaged on the recommendation of a director, as was the case with Thors, one of the two general managers of the Société Générale, who was related to one of the bank's founders. At the Crédit Lyonnais, Henri Germain first chose Jacques-François Letourneur as director because of his close links with the Huguenot circles in France, Germany and Switzerland: this son of a Genevan tradesman had worked for the Parisian banker Marcuard from 1846, then for Morel, Fatio & Cie, a firm belonging to the lower echelons of Parisian high finance.[11] His successor as general manager of the Crédit Lyonnais in 1882 was Adrien Mazerat, the son of a small tradesman, who was employed in the offices of the Creusot and became private secretary to Eugène Schneider (whose links with Henri Germain are well-known). He was directly subordinate to the chairman of the Crédit Lyonnais and only took orders from him. At that time, few general managers obtained their position by passing the difficult examination of the finance inspectorate, like Octave Homberg, general manager of the Société Générale from 1880 to 1890. It was rather in the course of a long career in the same bank that such a post was reached. An extreme case would be that of Louis Dorizon: this son of a shoe-maker from Blois joined the Société Générale in 1874 at the age of fourteen as the most junior employee, maybe even as a bellboy. Rising from rung to rung he became secretary general, deputy manager, manager in 1896, general manager in 1909 and finally chairman in 1914.[12]

In conclusion, if banking was a profession open to everyone, then the major bankers (private bankers or directors and general managers of the banks which were limited companies) made up a closed circle comprising mainly those who had inherited a large amount of capital at the beginning of their career. Connections also gave some of them access to such posts, but the true rise of 'self-made men' of humble origin, like Mercet or Dorizon, was exceptional. Both heirs and newcomers acquired their training from rigorous in-house apprenticeships. It was this very practical training that allowed some of these newcomers to succeed on their own merit and realize their ambitions, and justified and prepared the way for the nomination of the heirs to the posts that awaited them. On their marriage, the sons-in-law of Henri Germain, Fabre-Luce, a member of the Marseille middle class, and the baron Georges Brincard, who was descended from a family of wealthy landowners, joined the Crédit Lyonnais to work hard as secretaries to the board of directors. In this way they 'earned their promotion' and proved they were not 'Daddy's boys'. And on the death of their father-in-law in 1905 they quite naturally became joint general managers of the bank while waiting for something better. Higher education rarely played a part in most of these careers, and carried less weight than in-house training and the family legacy.

The position of these major bankers in French high society and their links with other sections of the economic elite seemed to change over time. Because of the very specific nature of their profession they remained separate from the highest pinnacles of commerce and industry, but far form being a closed circle their family alliances with other milieux tended to increase. The positions they held in various industrial or financial companies also caused them to rub shoulders with other businessmen, and some held important posts as employers, as did Henri Davillier, sometime President of the Chambre de Commerce de Paris. They were very wealthy and their wealth tended to overshadow that of other social groups. But at the same time, as fortunes increased and became more transferable, so their owners needed to maintain close links with their bankers: every millionaire now had his own banker just as previously he had had his own lawyer. These same bankers began to adopt a lifestyle that brought them closer to traditional high society. They gradually ceased to live in the Chaussée d'Antin in favour of mansions in areas of high standing, like the place Vendôme, or the areas around the parc Monceau or the place de la Concorde (the *hôtel* Talleyrand, where Alphonse de Rothschild lived in the rue Saint-Florentin, was not far from the home of Henri Germain in the rue du Faubourg Saint-Honoré). Their children, like those of other middle-class families, attended the lycée, and they themselves frequented aristocratic clubs like the Jockey Club or the Nouveau Cercle.

Far more cultured than their predecessors in the July Monarchy or the Second Empire, they mixed with the capital's literary, artistic and fashionable circles, demonstrating their intellectual curiosity and artistic sensibility. Alphonse de Rothschild and Rodolphe Hottinguer, who had a particular taste for Latin, were passionate men of letters with truly cultured minds, and Isaac Camondo was reputed to be a distinguished composer. Louis Dorizon himself, according to Octave Homberg, realized 'how much his lack of culture, the absence of the *humanities* were a handicap to him; so late in life he decided to learn Latin and Greek: in the evenings he would invite to his house those professors who to him made up this store of knowledge he felt he needed...'

The integration of bankers into other spheres of the elites also became more common. There is no doubt that many of the French had long suffered from a persistent 'allergy' (J. Bouvier) to banks, but this allergy was more characteristic of the middle classes and the rural milieux than of high society. There were signs, however, that resistance remained rooted in the heart of French society, to which the picture Zola paints of this milieu in *L'Argent* (1890), and the rise in anti-Semitism at the end of the century – which was not, however, aimed specifically at bankers – bear witness. So too does the following remark made by the aristocrat Le Provost de Launay to Henri Germain in November 1892 during a stormy debate in the *Chambre des Députés*: 'I do not accept that one can be both a member of parliament and a financier...'

From the end of the nineteenth century to the years following the Second World War, the major French banks experienced alternate periods of expansion and stagnation, and even decline. After the economic deceleration of 1865–96, which created serious problems for credit institutions, the recovery that preceded the 1914 war breathed new dynamism into the banks. The First World War and the rise in inflation of 1922–6 weighed heavily on the actual volume of bank resources, and the stabilization effected by Poincaré barely enabled banks to recover their former position. There followed the crisis of the 1930s, which further undermined the strength of the banks, the Second World War, and uncontrolled inflation which accompanied all attempts at reconstruction. Finally, it was only in 1952 that the major French banks regained the volume of resources that had been available to them in 1913 in stable French francs.

Independent of this eventful history, three major trends affected the world of bankers and their position in society, even if they occurred at different times in different credit institutions. First there was the decline in the influence of the major private bankers, which occurred much later than is often thought. Many of the firms in high finance declined, or entered a dormant period between the two world wars, but this was far from a general rule since others, like that of Mirabaud, greatly increased their dealings. Certainly, the decline of these family banks did not automatically lead to a decline in the economic and social influence of those at their head. Many of these banking families, who held considerable fortunes and well-assured positions in numerous industrial and financial companies, retained an important place in French capitalism for a long time. It was primarily nationalization (the semi-nationalization of the Banque de France in 1936, the nationalization of railway companies the following year, the wave of nationalizations of 1944–6) that affected the position of these bankers in the economic elite of France.

A second development, difficult to measure and little studied until now, concerned the relationship between the directors and the general managers within the banks set up as limited companies. From the 'turning-point' of 1914–21, most general managers joined the board of directors at the same time, and had the advantage over the other directors of 'being both party to the actual running and closer to the business through the intermediary of the boards of management'.[13] In addition, these general managers increasingly had the power to become vice-chairmen (like Desvaux at the CIC and Célier at the CNEP) or chairmen of the board of directors of their banks, following the example of Collart-Dutilleul at Paribas at the end of the nineteenth century. It was in this way that Mazerat took over from Henri Germain at the Crédit Lyonnais in 1905, while Germain's sons-in-law shared the general managership of the company between them calling themselves managing directors. In 1922, Georges Brincard in turn became chairman of the board, and Escarra, appointed general manager in 1926, was late called to the chairmanship of the Crédit Lyonnais – by then nationalized – in 1949. Similarly, Henri Ardant, who had started out as general secretary of the Société Générale in 1922, became general manager, Vice-chairman, and finally Chairman at the beginning of the Second World War. This man, whose career in the Société Générale spanned twenty-two years, was the true spokesman of the major Parisian bankers during the 1936–40 debates on the reorganization of French credit policy, and he was chairman of the permanent committee for the organization of banks under the Vichy government.[14]

Thirdly, most of these major bankers, who were now true professionals, had continued in higher education, particularly at the Faculty of Law. And many of these heads of banks came from the finance inspectorate. There are some notable exceptions, for example Finaly, one-time schoolfellow of Proust at the *lycée* Condorcet (this son of a director at the Banque de Paris et des Pays-Bas himself became general manager with full authority in 1919) or Alfred Pose, the director of the new BNCI founded in 1932, a professor at the Faculty of Law. At the Crédit Lyonnais, the continuing influence of Henri Germain's sons-in-law prevented those outside the firm from joining the board of management, even coming from the finance inspectorate. But at the CIC it was the finance inspectors who were in charge, with Guillemin de Montplanet, Desvaux and Charles Georges Picot. François Pietri noted that the Inspectorate thus tended to make up 'the senior management of the country. Nowadays [1931], many credit institutions, like the Société Générale, the Comptoir d'Escompte, the Crédit Industriel et Commercial; chartered banks like the Banque de France, the Banque de l'Indochine, the Crédit Foncier de France; large commercial banks... have finance inspectors as their chairmen or general managers. In some of them, this participation takes the form of an accepted tradition, an unwritten rule.'[15]

Recent studies enable us to chart the rise of the finance inspector in companies, and particularly in banks. This switch to non-governmental employment in banks was for a long time a limited phenomenon, since there were only ten such employees working in banks in 1897, but later their numbers grew steadily to forty-two in 1937 and seventy in 1952.[16] Did this invasion of the top ranks of banking by finance inspectors contribute to the revival of this milieu? Was the passing of this examination a passport giving newcomers right of entry into high finance, or did it simply justify and legitimize the transfer of posts hitherto held by members of the ruling classes? This highlights the essential ambiguity of meritocracy.[17]

Some answers can be found in the calculations of Mme de Malberg who classified those finance inspectors recruited between 1892 and 1946 according to their fathers' socio-professional group. No doubt the results can only be applied to those finance inspectors who moved over into banking:[18] 56 per cent of these inspectors came from the upper middle classes (25 per cent from the moneyed classes including bankers, 25 per cent from the senior civil service and 8 per cent from the professions). For these inspectors, the title they obtained served only to reinforce and confirm their family's social position. But those whose families were already in banking were very much in the minority.

No inspector came from the working classes, and only 4 per cent were from the lower middle classes. But 37 per cent of the total were originally middle class. The inspectorate was thus not a closed body but instead formed a 'bridge' giving certain members of the middle classes access to management posts in banking. In this way it contributed to the renewal of this milieu's structure. The most representative career in this respect was that of Emile Moreau: this son of a magistrate from the provincial lower middle class became in turn Governor of the Banque d'Algérie, Governor of the Banque de France and Chairman of the Banque de Paris et des Pays-Bas.

It is difficult to know whether this new type of banking recruit helped modify the position of bankers in the French elite. The arrival of finance inspectors from the various sections of the middle classes, and the fact that they had passed an examination to prove their general culture and rhetorical skills, should have brought them closer to other spheres of the social elite. But, with the economic crisis and the withdrawal of credit, and the rise of anti-Semitism aimed particularly at Jewish bankers whose possessions were later sequestered during the war, the tendency was to reject bankers, making of them a caste isolated from the rest of the nation. Social conflicts also contributed to this, as witnessed by these remarks made by a former manager of Paribas about his banking contemporaries:[19]

> The top management is made up of men, often distinguished by their culture, their technical skill, the lucidity of their judgment and the depth of their insight. It is one of the smallest of staffs whose very manner of recruitment reduces their number still further. The sons or relations of bankers or defectors from top public administration, they form a veritable caste whose members all demonstrate solidarity in the face of the rest of society, whatever their internal disagreements. They do undoubtedly uphold certain legitimate traditions, but all too often they

> are led, and by an only too natural inclination, to allow their own interests to predominate or to safeguard them by putting intolerable pressure on the State authorities.

After the war, the purging – even if it affected few bankers – and the nationalization of the four major deposit banks, which eliminated the need for private directors, led to a shake-up in management circles and the injection of new blood: the old general managers were very often replaced by their former deputies.[20] The credit boom, linked to the brutal 'bankarization' of the French and the refound dynamism of the economy, and the growing complexity in the organization of banks, created many new management posts in banking institutions. These new positions attracted new generations of finance inspectors and students from the *grandes écoles*. The old-established Rothschild bank itself created for the first time a general managership, entrusted to a former student of the Ecole Normale, Georges Pompidou. It became apparent that earlier trends were becoming more marked, rather than truly new tendencies emerging.

But by the end of the 1960s the position of bankers in French society, and even the very boundaries of this milieu, still had to be determined and raised many questions. A poll carried out in the 1971 *Who's Who in France* provided some answers. Even if this source is in no way an objective one (the names mentioned in it are included according to very specific criteria...) and if it gives some information that is incomplete, if not incorrect, the main characteristics of this milieu take shape on reading the four hundred or so entries concerning bankers or directors of banks. The term 'bank director' began in effect to take over from 'banker' and, although the difference between these two terms is not always obvious, this was a very real change which manifested itself late and far from perfectly. The majority of the major bankers were now bank directors. Half of these men (women made up only 1 per cent of this 'population'...) were born in the provinces, 15 per cent were not born in France and only 35 per cent were of Parisian origin. They came above all from the ruling classes or from the upper middle classes. Thirty-six per cent had fathers in economic professions (12 per cent were the sons of actual bankers), 40 per cent of their fathers were in public administration and 22 per cent were professionals.

They had generally completed further studies, particularly at the Faculty of Law (62 per cent), often at the Ecole Libre des Sciences Politiques (30 per cent), and more rarely at a university for the arts or the sciences (20 per cent) or in an educational establishment abroad (12 per cent). Only 3 per cent had merely passed their school *baccalauréat*, while 1 per cent of these bankers did not mention any specific qualifications. The former students of the *grandes écoles* and those who took the most selective of examinations only made up a third of the whole and were divided essentially between the école Polytechnique (10 per cent), the école des Hautes Etudes Commerciales and the finance inspectorate.

The vast majority of these bankers lived in Paris, which is in no way surprising given the centralization of financial business in France, and their private homes were found in the most sought-after areas of the capital (the sixteenth *arrondissement* above all, then the seventh, eighth and the seventeenth), as well as in the western suburbs. The Chaussée d'Antin, the one-time financial quarter, was inhabited by less than 2 per cent.

Nearly two-thirds of these financiers have all the appearance, in effect, of businessmen who divide their career between banking and other activities, and those who devote their entire career to banking (and rarer still to one single bank ...) feel it necessary explicitly to state this fact that seems almost an eccentricity. These same men move with increasing ease from top posts in government to the head of a major banking firm or the management of an industrial group.

It therefore becomes increasingly difficult to distinguish the major bankers from other spheres of the elite. Even if novels and caricatures reproduce a very traditional image of a banker, which has barely changed for a century, the reality has changed greatly. At the pinnacle of society one often sees the same men become in turn senior civil servants, political leaders, industrialists or bankers. Could this be one of the reasons why the present crisis has not incited against bankers the same specific of exclusion and rejection as during the crisis of the 1930s?

Notes

1 Among the most recent works on this subject see P. Birnbaum, *Le peuple et les gros. Histoire d'un mythe* (Paris, 1979), and R. Sédillot, *Les deux cents familles* (Paris, 1988).

2 O. Homberg, *Le financier dans la cité* (Paris, 1926), p. 231, and F. Pietri, *Le financier* (Paris, 1931). In *F... comme financiers* (Paris, 1981), R. Tendron defines financiers as 'the established class, the *Establishment*'

3 R. Bigo, *Les banques françaises au cours du XIXe siècle* (Paris, 1947), p. 270, and C. Charle, *Les élites de la République, 1880–1900* (Paris, 1987), pp. 167–8.

4 M. Lévy-Leboyer, 'Le patronat français a-t-il été malthusien?', *Mouvement Social* (January 1974).

5 A. Plessis, *La Banque de France et ses deux cents actionnaires sous le Second Empire* (Geneva, 1982), *Régents et gouverneurs de la Banque de France sous le Second Empire* (Geneva, 1985), and *La politique de la Banque de France de 1851 à 1870* (Geneva, 1985).

6 These are the questions Y. Cassis raises regarding London banks in *Les Banquiers de la City à l'époque Edouardienne* (Geneva, 1984), pp. 66ff.

7 D. S. Landes, 'Vieille banque et banque nouvelle: la révolution financière du XIXe siècle', *Revue d'histoire moderne et contemporaine* (1956).

8 *La Société Générale, 1864–1964* (Paris, 1964), *passim.*

9 Yasuo Gonjo, *La Banque de l'Indochine* (*1875–1939*): *l'histoire d'une banque d'outre-mer française* (Tokyo, 1985).

10 Hence at the Banque Nationale de Crédit. Cf. H. Bonin, 'La Banque Nationale de Crédit. Evolution et rôle économique de 1913 à 1932', Ph.D. thesis, University of Paris, X Nanterre, 1978.

11 J. Bouvier, *Le Crédit Lyonnais de 1863 à 1881* (Paris, 1961), pp. 158–9.

12 Homberg, *Les coulisses de l'histoire* (Paris, 1938), p. 109, *Société Générale*, p. 89.

13 E. Chadeau, *Les inspecteurs des Finances au XIXe siècle* (*1850–1914*) (Paris, 1986), p. 257.

14 C. Andrieu, 'L'Etat et les banques commerciales, 1867–1944', Ph.D. thesis, Institut d'Etudes Politiques, 1988, pp. 411ff.

15 Pietri, *Le financier*, p. 87.

16 Chadeau, *Les inspecteurs*, and, by the same author, 'Les inspecteurs des Finances et les entreprises (1869–1968)' in *Le patronat de la seconde industrialisation* (Paris, 1979).

17 On this question cf. Charle, *Les élites.*

18 N. Carré de Malberg, 'Le recrutement des inspecteurs des Finances de 1892 à 1946', *Vingtième siècle* (October-December 1985) 67–92.

19 A. Dauphin-Meunier, *VIe Congrès international de science et de technique bancaires*, Paris, October 1937.

20 On the limited but real nature of this shake-up see F. Bloch-Lainé and J. Bouvier, *La France restaurée* (Paris, 1986). Bloch-Lainé writes, on page 144, of the 'events' of 1944–6: 'To satisfy everyone, the owners of the most important banks were replaced without changing the directors. Apart from a very small number of purgings, scapegoats sacrificed to their rivals or former accomplices, the representatives of ousted shareholders stayed put.'

9 The banker in German society

DOLORES L. AUGUSTINE

I

Two images come to mind when we consider the German banker of the Imperial and Weimar eras.[1] One is that of the patrician, the bourgeois aristocrat. Fritz Stern has done much to create another image, namely that of the 'pariah merchant-prince',[2] the Jewish banker exploited by the aristocratic ruling class of Prussia. Since Jews played a major role in banking, Stern's thesis must be carefully considered, discussing the extent of Jewish over-compensation and feudalization. But were Jewish bankers basically different from non-Jewish bankers? The great economic successes of the German business elite transformed Germany in the late nineteenth century into the most dynamic economic power in Europe and helped the business elite consolidate its wealth, economic power and prestige within German society. Characteristic of the Wilhelmine era were growing business influence on government, engraved in public memory by the Kaiser's meetings with businessmen, the rise of materialistic values and dreams of colonial grandeur, which could (among other things) provide German business with new opportunities for expansion.

Did a unified business elite emerge in this era, or did bankers constitute a distinct economic elite? Did Jewish bankers fully share in this triumphal march of German capitalism? This essay will explore the social barriers and links between banking on the one hand and industry and commerce on the other. It will look at the relationship between the various segments of the business elite and the rest of the upper class – especially the aristocracy, the political elite and state officials.[3] This discussion must take account of the feudalization thesis, which places the social history of the bourgeoisie in nineteenth-century Germany in a political context, especially the new coalition between an important sector of big business and the conservative, agrarian aristocracy. According to this school of thought, the bourgeoisie's (presumed) social capitulation to the traditional, pre-industrial elite went hand-in-hand with its failure to fulfill its 'historic mission' to liberalize and democratize society, political culture and the constitution in Germany. The deficiencies of this interpretation of German history have become apparent in recent years.[4]

The bulk of the quantitative data presented in this paper stem from a study of the wealthiest businessmen in the *Yearbook of Millionaires*. Published in 1912–14 by Rudolf Martin,[5] this is an invaluable primary source for the social historian. In it, the author, a former government official, attempted to list all German millionaires then alive with their addresses and the size of their fortunes and incomes. Using published tax statistics, he assigned the names of persons known to him – not only businessmen, but also landowners, members of the high aristocracy and others – to the anonymous figures. His knowledge of German society is phenomenal, as the economic historian can attest. A comparison with data from actual tax returns[6] reveals a fair degree of accuracy. Considering the rampant tax evasion of the era,[7] Martin's data may in fact be more accurate than the official figures. All entrepreneurs in industry, trade and commerce, and banking[8] who owned a fortune of 6 m. Marks or more were included in the study, making a total of 502 persons. Supplementary information was found in published sources and in public and private papers.[9] These data were processed by computer. In addition, roughly 200 autobiographies and biographies and archive materials on a more loosely defined group of wealthy businessmen were analysed, using non-quantitative methods. Some of these findings will be presented below, in the section on social life.

Of the 502 wealthiest businessmen in Wilhelmine Germany, 27 per cent were bankers. (Fifty per cent were industrialists and 14 per cent merchants.) Three quarters of these bankers were owners or partners of private banks, one-sixth were directors or chairmen of the board of joint-stock companies and the rest were 'entrepreneurs'.[10] According to Manfred Pohl, there were a total of 1,200 private bankers in Germany in 1913. Due primarily to mergers, this figure fell to 700 by 1933.[11] Official government statistics estimate the number of proprietors in banking and finance in 1907 at 4,078.[12] Presumably this figure includes directors and chairmen of the board who were also stockholders, but also a variety of small-scale credit brokers, exchange-booth owners and the like. There were roughly 93,700 small-scale manufacturers and 40,500 middle- to large-scale industrialists in Germany in 1907. In the services sector (trade and commerce, banking and finance, transportation, hotels and restaurants), there were about 42,500 capitalists, 7,200 of which ran middle- or large-scale businesses.[13] In industry and commerce, the elite thus sat at the pinnacle of an entrepreneurial pyramid. Only a small percentage of merchants and manufacturers were part of the upper class. Bankers, on the other hand, constituted an elite in and of themselves. Yet the image of bankers as the highest-status group within the business class is an illusion. Not only bankers, but also large-scale industrialists and merchants throned over the masses of middle- and small-scale businessmen. To form an accurate picture of the bankers' position in society, we must look at their relationship with their peers. A major question to be answered is whether bankers were an integrated part of the business elite.

Another major theme will be the importance of ethnic and regional divisions *within* the financial elite. In 1895, 37 per cent of all bankers in Prussia (including bank directors) were Jewish.[14] According to Werner Mosse, Jews not only played a major role in private banking, but in corporate banking as well.[15] Fifty-four per cent of the bankers in my quantitative study were ethnic Jews.[16] The predominance of Berlin and, to a lesser extent, Frankfurt is also reflected in my data on the wealthiest bankers: fifty-three were active in Berlin, twenty-eight in Hesse (mainly Frankfurt). The next two most important regions were the Hanseatic towns (Hamburg, Bremen and Lübeck) and Rheinland-Westphalia.

The next section focuses on social origins, followed by a section on elevation to the nobility. A discussion of continuity and discontinuity in banking families (the professions of sons) follows. We will then turn our attention to ties by marriage and friendship to other classes. Finally, an attempt will be made to sketch changes that took place in the Weimar era, asking whether 1918 represents a turning point in the social history of the banking elite in Germany.

II

Two-thirds of the bankers in my study were themselves the sons of bankers. Another 23 per cent were sons of middle- to large-scale businessmen in industry or commerce. Only a handful had a non-entrepreneurial background.[17] Eighty-five per cent of the industrialists' fathers and 84 per cent of the merchants' fathers were businessmen. The cases without information pose a problem here,[18] since 'obscure' fathers are more likely not to have been mentioned in the sources than prominent fathers. This is an endemic problem of research on elite recruitment. The conclusions drawn from these data must therefore be tentative. It appears that the largest business fortunes of the late nineteenth and early twentieth centuries were rarely, if ever, formed within one generation. At least some capital base was necessary to set up a business, and most businesses that produced such large fortunes had been built up by the previous generation or generations. This line of argument is only partially applicable to the third of the businessmen who did not run private companies (or to the 23 per cent of the bankers whose fathers were industrialists or merchants). All very wealthy businessmen owned capital. Many of them probably inherited stock or capital with which to purchase stocks. Yet some only became capitalists after working their way up in a company. Here, other factors explain the prevalence of businessmen's sons: the education these men needed to succeed in business was available only to the well-to-do; secondly, the business background was a motivating factor.[19] The – often upper-class – business background of these businessmen[20] contributed to their perception of themselves as part of an elite. Friedrich Zunkel's thesis that the Jewish bankers of Berlin were 'until then of the lower social orders – *deklassiert*, not tied by history and tradition to any social class' is certainly not true of this era.[21]

III

A commonly used indicator of aristocratization[22] is ennoblement. Table 9.1 compares the number of industrialists, bankers and merchants with and without titles of nobility. (Data here and in the following tables refer to the 502 wealthiest businessmen in Wilhelmine Germany.[23]) Bankers and industrialists of older aristocratic lineage (holding titles predating 1870) made up 9 per cent of the total. These blue-blooded industrialists were mainly members of great landowning families which began conducting mining operations on their lands (and which had in some cases expanded into heavy industry). The older banking aristocracy had, on the other hand, generally *started* as banking families. The number of older aristocratic families among the merchants was insignificant. The aristocratic inclination of bankers becomes even more apparent when we look at the granting of titles in the Imperial period (1871–1918). Almost 22 per cent of the bankers were ennobled in this era, as compared with 17 per cent of the industrialists and 15 per cent of the merchants.[24] Nevertheless, a few bankers refused titles of nobility, notably Adolf Salomonsohn, Carl Fürstenberg and Max Warburg. Paul von Schwabach of the Bleichröder Bank did not use his title.[25] All four were Jewish. In fact, the rate of ennoblement among Jewish elite businessmen was not higher than among non-Jewish elite businessmen.[26] In Prussia, Jews were generally only granted a title of nobility if they converted to Christianity, a step many were not willing to take.[27] Nevertheless, more businessmen were raised to the nobility than ever before in the Wilhelmine era, and even in Hamburg – a city with strong bourgeois traditions – a growing number of merchants and bankers were granted (generally Prussian) titles.[28] A somewhat higher proportion of the Rhineland-Westphalian businessmen than of the Berlin businessmen in my study were granted titles of nobility after 1870.[29] This trend doubtlessly reflects elite

Table 9.1 *Titles of nobility among very wealthy businessmen according to sector*[a] *(in %)*

	Sector		
	Industry[b]	Banking	Commerce
No title of nobility	74.3	69.3	81.9
New title (granted 1871–1918)	16.5	21.9	15.3
Older title (predating 1871)	9.2	8.8	2.8
Total	100	100	100
Total (absolute)	249	137	72

Notes: [a] According to the sector in which the businessman was primarily active. Without miscellaneous categories.
[b] Including mining, printing and construction.

businessmen's aristocratic pretentions, which were particularly in evidence among bankers.[30] One conclusion to be drawn from the data is that wealthy bankers were a very high-status group in Wilhelmine Germany. Yet the precise significance of ennoblement remains unclear. Did it represent part of an attempt to assimilate with the aristocracy or did it merely represent a bid for recognition in a society whose traditional symbols of success were associated with the nobility? (It should not be forgotten that titles of nobility were granted by the state, which had won the loyalty of the bourgeoisie by unifying Germany and promoting capitalism.) Thus, we must also look at other indicators as well.

IV

The extent of ties to other classes and the degree of continuity in business is reflected in the sons' selection of a profession. The data show that elite businessmen's sons only rarely strayed into other professions. (Table 9.2) Roughly 70 per cent of industrialists', bankers' and merchants' sons became businessmen. This high degree of continuity is in large part related to the predominance of family enterprises. (70 per cent of the bankers in my study were private bankers, 17 per cent were in corporative banking, and 10 per cent headed a *Kommanditgesellschaft*.) Inheritance was in this age an important form of capital accumulation. As Jürgen Kocka has pointed out, the family also played an important role in motivating and legitimizing the continued role in business for the sake of the children and children's children. Often the son grew into the role expected of him quite

Table 9.2 *Occupations of the businessmen's sons in Wilhelmine Germany (according to sector*[a] *in which businessmen were active*[b], *in %)*

	Sector		
Sons' occupational group	Industry[c]	Banking	Commerce
Traditional pre-industrial elite (without civil servants)	15.0	11.9	8.0
Upper civil servants	3.3	3.7	8.0
Liberal professions, upper teaching[d]	4.9	3.7	8.0
Businessmen in industry or commerce	67.5	22.0	70.5
Bankers	0.8	48.6	1.1
Lower-middle class	6.9	9.2	4.5
Rentiers	1.6	0.9	—
Total	100	100	100
Total (absolute)	246	109	88

Notes: [a] According to the sector in which the businessman was primarily active. Without miscellaneous categories.
[b] Excluding eighteen businessmen who belonged to the aristocracy or whose families had been integrated into the aristocracy. Only cases with information. For occupational classification, see fn. 3. Data were available on the sons of 249 businessmen; data were available on *all* sons of 182 businessmen.
[c] Including mining, printing and construction.
[d] Universities, college preparatory schools and school administration.

naturally. If not, he generally felt obliged to subordinate his personal preferences to the needs of the family. In addition, socialization in a business family imparted skills needed in business, profit-orientation, and a love of power and independence, thus motivating the sons to become businessmen and to succeed.[31]

The data in table 9.2 indicate that, while virtually no industrialists' or merchants' sons went into banking, 22 per cent of the bankers' sons went into industry or commerce. Thus, if the eldest son took over the family bank, younger sons might go into a different line of business. This was also the case with sons of managers who did not own their banks. This figure demonstrates quite dramatically the ties of banking families to the business world (as opposed, for example, to the aristocratic or artistic spheres), and their integration into non-banking business circles.

The rate of assimilation with the aristocracy (measured here in terms of choice of a profession) among elite businessmen's sons was not high, running at about 10 per cent. Somewhat more industrialists' sons than bankers' sons and somewhat few merchants' sons became landowners, officers, diplomats, etc. The number of sons who became university-trained civil servants or members of the liberal professions, teachers or professors was small, though a somewhat larger percentage of sons took up middle-class professions (not counting independent businessmen, who are in the category 'businessmen in industry and commerce').[32]

The sons of the Jewish businessmen in the study were slightly less 'aristocratic' in their professional structure and slightly more tied to business than the sons of non-Jewish businessmen.[33] This finding is surprising in the light of previous research, particularly Hans Dieter Hellige's work on 'Jewish self-hate'. He cites numerous examples of sons of Jewish businessmen in turn-of-the-century Germany and Austria who reacted to anti-Semitism by rebelling against their fathers, turning their backs on business and suppressing their Jewish identity. Some tried to become aristocrats, others became anti-capitalist intellectuals.[34]

Why do we find so little trace of this phenomenon in the data? There are signs of a conflict between the generations in elite business families, but these were apparently better able to reintegrate rebellious sons into the business class than the generally more middle-class families Hellige writes of. We do find an occasional intellectual among Jewish bankers' sons, for example art historian Aby Warburg (1866–1929) and archeologist Max von Oppenheim (born in 1860). (Neither, however, was anti-capitalistic or anti-Semitic.) The case of poet Rudolf Borchardt (born in 1877), whose father was a director of the Berliner Handels-Gesellschaft, corresponds somewhat better to Hellige's thesis.[35] But generally, straying sheep could be induced to return to the fold. A case in point is the Warburg family. Moritz Warburg intended for his son Aby to succeed him, assisted by two other sons, Max and Paul. His fourth son Felix was to become a partner in the grandfather's jewellery business, and his youngest was to become a lawyer. Aby decided at an early age to become an art historian. Moritz Warburg had some difficulty convincing his son Max not to become a chemist. No sooner was this crisis resolved than Max announced that he wanted to become a career officer in the Bavarian army. The father limited his expression of dissatisfaction to a curt letter. Max gave up his plans within a year, and had a very enjoyable time as a bank apprentice in Paris and London, where he became 'more English than an Englishman'. He was made head of the bank. Paul would have preferred a life of scholarship, but his father talked him out of it. He and his brother fell in love with American heiresses and became bankers in New York, thus abandoning the Warburg bank, while providing it with an important connection abroad. Fritz wanted to go into law, which he had studied, but was persuaded by the family to become Max's partner in the running of the bank.[36] Paul Wallich, the son of Hermann Wallich, a director of the Deutsche Bank, went through an aristocratic, anti-Semitic phase in which he toyed with the idea of becoming, not an officer, but a philosopher. His mother was, however, able to convince him without great difficulty that he should go into banking. Paul Wallich writes that the fact that Georg von Siemens (of the Deutsche Bank) was being considered for the post of Finance Minister at the time convinced him that the status of a banker would best satisfy his social ambitions. Wallich overcame his Jewish self-hate and found a place much to his liking in the business world.[37] Examples are also to be found among non-Jewish bankers' sons such as Baron Simon Moritz von Bethmann (1887–1966), of a Frankfurt private banking family. He feared the burden of carrying on the family tradition, and longed for the 'simple life' of an officer, competing with 'farmers' and craftsmen's sons, with good horsemen, gymnasts and riflemen, that is why the world suddenly seemed so simple, natural, healthy and manageable'.[38] His mother convinced him to take over the company, arguing that a career as an officer would be the easy way out, that following in his father's footsteps would be difficult, but that the most difficult things in life are the most worthwhile. There are also examples of a less painful transition from one generation to the next in banking in this period.[39]

Impressionistic evidence from autobiographies and biographies would seem to indicate that the mechanisms of rebellion and succession in banking families were essentially the same in the main banking centres, that aristocratization was moderate in banking families of Frankfurt, Berlin and Hamburg.[40]

Thus, the material on bankers' sons in the Wilhelmine era demonstrates the strong commitment of the younger generation to the family firm. After a late adolescent phase of rebellion, most sons could be persuaded to conform with their parents' wishes. Coercion was not normally necessary. This is partly due to family structures in this era, but also to the high status of bankers in Wilhelmine Germany. Even if there was no room for a son in the bank, or if his father was a bank director in a joint-stock company, the son often went into some other line of business. Thus, banking families were tied into industry and commerce. Only a rather small number of bankers' sons joined other sectors of the middle and bourgeois upper class, despite, for example, the attraction of the life of a scholar. Aristocratization was not prevalent. Jewish over-compensation – if it existed – did not effect the pattern of the sons' choice of a profession.

V

Whereas the question of the sons' choice of a profession was a life-or-death matter for the family firm, spouse selection generally was not. We would expect a greater diversity here. This diversity is to be found in the pattern of intermarriage of elite businessmen's children. Data on bankers'

Table 9.3 *Occupations of the businessmen's fathers-in-law in Wilhelmine Germany (according to sector*[a] *in which businessmen were active*[b], *in %)*

Fathers-in-law's occupational group	Sector	
	Industry[c]	Banking
Traditional pre-industrial elite (without civil servants)	4.7	11.0
Upper civil servants	3.4	4.9
Liberal professions, upper teaching[d]	10.1	7.3
Businessmen in industry or commerce	64.9	52.4
Bankers	5.4	13.4
Lower-middle class	8.1	7.3
Lower class	—	1.2
Lower or lower-middle class	—	1.2
Rentiers	3.4	1.2
Total (in %)	100	99.9
Total (absolute)	148	82

Notes: [a] According to the sector in which the businessman was primarily active. Without commerce and miscellaneous categories.
[b] Excluding eighteen businessmen who belonged to the aristocracy or whose families had been integrated into the aristocracy. Only cases with information. Second and third marriages included. For occupational classification, see fn. 3. Data were available on the sons of 249 businessmen; data were available on *all* sons of 182 businessmen.
[c] Including mining, printing and construction.
[d] Universities, college preparatory schools and school administration.

fathers-in-law (table 9.3) show striking parallels with data on bankers' sons, however. Almost as many fathers-in-law (66 per cent) as sons were businessmen. Most industrialists married businessmen's daughters as well. Probably many of the 502 wealthiest businessmen in Wilhelmine Germany would not have been so successful if they had not married businessmen's daughters. Kocka points to some of the factors that encouraged endogamy in this class: capital accumulation, the ability of a businessman's daughter to socialize the next generation of businessmen, the preferred recruitment of relatives or in-laws (generally seen as more trustworthy than outsiders) to top management, and the usefulness of a network of relatives and in-laws which could serve as business connections, advisers and the basis of pressure groups.[41] The debate on arranged versus love marriages[42] cannot be discussed here, and thus the question cannot be answered as to whether this pattern was the result of a carefully planned strategy or of 'falling in love' with an appropriate partner met in the business circles around which the upcoming businessman's social life revolved. The fact that elite bankers generally married industrialists' or merchants' daughters shows that they were part of a larger entrepreneurial elite.

Somewhat more bankers (11 per cent) married into the traditional pre-industrial elite than industrialists (5 per cent). This is a result of the higher percentage of bankers with titles of nobility. Only a few bankers married daughters of upper civil servants, professionals, teachers, professors or lower middle-class background (not including middle-class business).[43]

Turning to the children's spouse selection, we find a dramatically different pattern (table 9.4). The level of intermarriage among business families is lower here: 35 per cent for industrialists, 37 per cent for bankers, 50 per cent for merchants. Once great wealth was attained, the importance of contracting a marriage for business connections or capital accumulation evidently decreased. Endogamy among bankers' families was very low. Roughly a third of industrialists' and bankers' children, but only a quarter of merchants' children married aristocrats. This is obviously indicative of the prestige the traditional elite enjoyed in the business elite. This is not the only cause. According to Felix Gilbert, the Mendelssohns and Mendelssohn-Bartholdys intermarried with civil servants' and officers' families so as to consolidate connections with the German ruling class.[44] These figures indicate, however, that the rate of intermarriage between very wealthy commoners and the aristocracy was lower than has generally been assumed. Bankers' children were the most strongly aristocratized, merchants' children the least (measured in terms of connubium).

Alliances with the non-business bourgeoisie – upper civil servants, the liberal professions and the lower middle class (without entrepreneurs) – were important, making up a quarter to a third of the totals.[45] Among industrialists' and merchants' children, they held the balance with marriages to aristocrats. Among bankers' offspring, however, connubium with the nobility was more prevalent (at 36 per cent) than connubium with the non-entrepreneurial bourgeoisie (at 26 per cent).

The patterns of intermarriage were very similar in Jewish and non-Jewish elite business families. Intermarriage with the pre-industrial elite was not greater among the Jews in my study. According to Alfred Vagts, business relations based on family ties were more prevalent among Jewish private bankers than among other businessmen in this period.[46] It was particularly common in wealthy Jewish families for relatives to marry.[47]

Table 9.4 *Social structure of families the businessmen's children married into in Wilhelmine Germany (according to sector[a] in which businessmen were active[b], in %)*

Occupational group of sons-in-law and sons' fathers-in-law[c]	Sector		
	Industry[d]	Banking	Commerce
Traditional pre-industrial elite (without civil servants)	30.3	35.8	25.0
Upper civil servants	11.0	5.9	5.6
Liberal professions, upper teaching[e]	10.4	11.2	12.0
Businessmen in industry or commerce	32.7	31.0	42.6
Bankers	2.6	5.9	7.4
Lower-middle class	12.1	9.1	6.5
Rentiers	0.9	1.1	0.9
Total (in %)	100	100	100
Total (absolute)	346	187	108

Notes: [a] According to the sector in which the businessman was primarily active. Without miscellaneous categories.
[b] Excluding eighteen businessmen who belonged to the aristocracy or whose families had been integrated into the aristocracy. Only cases with information. Second and third marriages included. For occupational classification, see fn. 3.
[c] Data on sons-in-law were available for 213 businessmen. Data on sons' fathers-in-law were available for 130 businessmen.
[d] Including mining, printing and construction.
[e] Universities, college preparatory schools and school administration.

Thus, bankers (like industrialists and merchants) were generally married to businessmen's – but not necessarily bankers' – daughters. In this generation, bankers were firmly rooted in the business world. Only a small minority married women of the traditional, pre-industrial elite. In the children's generation, ties to the entrepreneurial class were weaker. Rather than marrying for business connections or money, bankers' children married for social connections or – possibly – for love. A third were drawn to the aristocracy. This represents a fairly moderate rate of aristocratization, especially when one considers that a quarter of the children married into non-entrepreneurial, bourgeois families. Moreover, these aristocratic alliances did not necessarily represent an attempt to become part of the aristocracy, but rather could serve to increase business influence on the ruling class. Wealthy Jewish businessmen's ties to the business class were strong.

VI

The social life of Wilhelmine bankers was largely a function of their business interests. This can be shown both for Berlin and Hamburg, though not in the same sense. This section focuses on these two cities. Berlin bankers socialized mainly, but by no means exclusively, with other members of the business elite. The home of Carl Fürstenberg of the Berliner Handels-Gesellschaft and his wife Aniela, one of the great hostesses of her day, was an important meeting place of bankers, industrialists and great merchants. Bankers predominated among the numerous persons that Carl Fürstenberg called his 'friends'. Among his industrialist friends were Albert Ballin, director of the HAPAG shipline, and the coal merchant and heavy industrialist Fritz von Friedländer-Fuld, with whom he had both a personal and a business relationship.[48] Paul Wallich of the Berlin Handels-Gesellschaft and private banker Weisbach had numerous business friends.[49] Adolf Salomonsohn, co-director of the Disconto-Gesellschaft, and Georg von Siemens, co-director of the Deutsche Bank, had mainly social contacts within their own class, and had an aversion to the aristocracy.[50] There was a high degree of social cohesion in the Jewish haute bourgeoisie, in which bankers predominated.[51] Bankers' mansions were clustered in the Tiergarten district. Bankers and other businessmen met daily at the Club of Berlin or at certain restaurants.[52]

Characteristic of social life in Berlin were the ties between business and government circles. Ever less interested in running for political office and only occasionally socializing with members of the Reichstag,[53] Wilhelmine bankers went to the top when they wanted to influence political decision-making, to secure government support for ventures abroad or to get the kind of inside information that bankers needed to make rational business decisions. A few bankers, notably Max Warburg, Max von Schinckel, Paul Schwabach, Arthur von Gwinner and Carl Fürstenberg, had sporadic personal contact with Kaiser Wilhelm II.[54] Fürstenberg, Schwabach and Friedländer-Fuld were integrated into a loose circle which included Friedrich August von Holstein, the 'Grey Eminence of the Foreign Office,' Helene von Lebbin, a friend of Holstein's and Chancellor Bülow's, Count Bogdan von Hutten-Czapski, a member of the Prussian Upper House, Alfred von Kiderlen-Wächter, State Secretary in the Foreign Office from 1910, and Prussian Finance Minister von Rheinbaben.[55] Diplomatic negotiations were once conducted on Friedländer-Fuld's estate, and Schwabach was entrusted by the Foreign Ministry with small diplomatic missions.[56] Fürstenberg's guests included many more high officials and diplomats representing countries with which his bank did business.[57] Carl von der Heydt, first a representative of his family's Cologne bank and later the owner of an independent firm, also socialized with high officials.[58]

'Junkers' who were not high officials or diplomats generally played a peripheral role in Berlin banking circles. Aristocratic guests occasionally fulfilled a decorative function: 'for some, it is still an especially elevating feeling to surround oneself with military uniforms and noblemen. It flatters one's vanity to have Prince X and Count Y at one's home... Others use officers as filler, as an attractive garnish. They invite them because they are clever and can dance well.'[59] Carl von der Heydt invited many officers to his balls, and he referred in his autobiography to the officer corps as an 'educational force'. If he had higher ambitions, then these were frustrated by the exclusivity of the aristocracy: 'As commoners, we were excluded from the court, which means that we could not be part of court society, by which is meant the exclusive circle of the high nobility which congregated at court, the diplomats, the highest court officials and a few very wealthy noble houses.'[60] Banker Eugen Gutmann often invited officers to parties, as did the stockmarket speculator Max Esser.[61]

The pattern of social life in Berlin banking circles thus reveals few cases of real aristocratization. Ties to the pre-industrial elite were generally sought to pursue business interests. Lamar Cecil, in a well-known article on social contacts between wealthy Jews and Junkers in Berlin,[62] largely misinterprets this relationship. He also overlooks the fact that the social life of Berlin businessmen centred around exclusive business circles. Representatives of intellectual and cultural life were also often present at parties in this milieu.[63] Otherwise, Berlin bankers hardly socialized with the non-business middle class.

The contours of social life in Hamburg provide a contrast in several respects. Hamburg bankers were part of a patrician upper class which included the great ruling senatorial families and members of the liberal professions. According to Richard Evans, the ties between the legal profession and business interests were particularly close. Divisions between bankers and other elite businessmen had virtually ceased to exist: 'merchants and merchant bankers were often virtually indistinguishable; and in the second half of the century there was a further merging of interests between merchants, bankers, shipowners and industrialists'.[64] The most important social barrier, as far as businessmen were concerned, was between the patrician upper class and the middle class. The term 'society' played a predominant role in social life up until the First World War. One person could be part of it and another not, though the former had recently moved to Hamburg while the latter was of an old (Hamburg) family.[65] Banker Max von Schinckel, the son of a wealthy merchant, was not accepted in high society until he married Olga Berckemeyer, of an old patrician family.[66] Jews were generally accepted in professional and political, but not social contexts.[67]

According to Evans, it was customary for wealthy merchants to invite politically influential people to stag dinners. Guests included heads of the administration, leading officials, members of the Citizens' Assembly, great merchants, a few clergymen, members of the university-educated bourgeoisie (the liberal professions and teaching) and artists. According to Senate Syndic Buehl, 'An advantage of this institution was that it often afforded the opportunity to deal with difficult official or political problems. These were much easier to decide at the dinner-table than they were at the committee table.'[68]

Unlike in Berlin, in Hamburg the influential personalities bankers associated with were generally not of the aristocracy. And otherwise, there was little contact with the pre-industrial elite. Schramm writes that officers were seldom invited to parties in bourgeois circles.[69] Max von Schinckel was a rarity – an 'aristocratized' Hamburg banker. He cultivated friendships with the nobility, including the high nobility. Rohrmann writes that a characteristic of his was 'the overly eager enumeration of noble acquaintances, especially in recollections in his memoires, in which he wrote that he was "personally acquainted," "on intimate terms," or "good friends" with a number of barons and counts, princes and dukes'.[70] This quest for social recognition outside Hamburg society doubtless has a great deal to do with the fact that he was a newcomer.

The social life of bankers in Berlin and Hamburg was more similar than may appear on the surface. In Hamburg, there was a patrician upper class, consisting of bankers and merchants, lawyers and some other members of the liberal professions, and the political and administrative elite. However, not even a wealthy banker could be certain of admittance to this lofty sphere. This uncertainty was especially great if he was *nouveau riche* or Jewish. In Berlin, bankers and other members of big business courted the favour of the political and administrative elite, but were not integrated into it because of the very different nature of the political structures in Berlin. Contacts with diplomats and the Foreign Office are a result of the international interests of Berlin banks. In both cities, there were isolated cases of aristocratization. The impression that Berlin businessmen were more 'aristocratized' results from a misunderstanding of their relationship with high officials and diplomats. Because of the power structures in Berlin, the non-business bourgeoisie was of less interest to the business elite than in Hamburg. In both Hamburg and Berlin, bankers socialized mainly with other big businessmen. Wealth was generally newer in Berlin. Nevertheless, the business wealth elite was quite exclusive, though class lines were probably not as clearly delineated as in Hamburg. Due to the prominent role of Jews in Berlin, there existed an exclusive Jewish haute bourgeoisie that had no real counterpart in Hamburg. As in Hamburg, Berlin bankers socialized with merchants and industrialists. Friendships with the latter were often based on business relationships between the banks and the enterprises they helped finance.

VII

How did the social world of bankers change in the Weimar era? Mosse points to structural changes in the German economy that had a major impact on the role of bankers. First, the importance of banks in the financing of industry declined after the First World War, leading to the weakening of the 'special relationships' between industrial enterprises and their banks. On the other hand, the role of banks in importing capital from abroad took on new significance. The international connections of Jewish private banks proved particularly useful here. Third, a number of bankers – among whom Jews figures prominently – were used as advisors and negotiators abroad by the German government. Fourth, bankers played a central role in the concentration and amalgamation of industrial enterprises. However, the economic crises of the Weimar era contributed to the rise of anti-Semitism and anti-capitalism, paving the way for National Socialism.[71] Sixth, the relative decline of private banking opened the way for new men. However, a continuous process of concentration in the banking sector[72] led to a gradual concentration of entrepreneurial power in the hands of an ever more exclusive group of persons. On the whole, economic factors contributed to the growing prominence of bankers before the onset of the Great Depression.

For lack of quantitative data, we can only formulate hypotheses on the social origins, sons' professions and patterns of intermarriage of Weimar bankers. While a number of old dynasties survived into the Weimar era, a growing number of 'self-made men' of the commercial lower middle and middle classes were – according to Mosse – to be found among Jewish bankers. Jewish prominence in corporative banking did not reach its peak until after 1918.[73] On the other hand, the downfall of the nobility and the powerful position of bankers in the German economy contributed to a very high rate of intergenerational continuity in private banking. Siegmund Warburg, whose father – living as an invalid on a landed estate – had discouraged him from becoming a banker, was recruited into the Warburg bank by his uncle, Max Warburg, just after the war. Though Siegmund had originally aspired to a career in academics and politics, he soon came to realize that as a banker he occupied a position of greater influence and prominence which afforded him the opportunity to work politically with Walther Rathenau, Gustav Stresemann and Hjalmar Schacht. Bankers' sons did occasionally rebel. Max's son Eric went off to work for $100 a month in Oregon, but then came back and became Max's right-hand man, travelling back and forth between New York and Hamburg for fifteen years.[74] While many members of the older banking elite such as Hans Fürstenberg and Siegmund Warburg married bankers' daughters,[75] newcomers such as Hjalmar Schacht or Jakob Goldschmidt were more likely to be married to women of lower-middle-class origins.[76]

Similarly, the social circles of the exclusive older banking patriciate and of the more middle-class newcomers apparently showed considerable differences. Franz von Mendelssohn's home was a focal point of Berlin society as early as the years of the hyper-inflation. While the remnants of Wilhelmine court society met at the home of Willibald Dirksen and the new republican circles congregated at Paul Schwabach's home, the Mendelssohns were careful to commit themselves neither to monarchist nor to republican society. Cultivating the bourgeois style of the Wilhelmine era, they represented the faction of old wealth.[77] The ageing Carl Fürstenberg's sarcastic anecdotes concerning Berlin parvenus reflect the social barriers within wealthy business circles of this period.[78] These barriers were not impenetrable, however. Hans Fürstenberg was not ashamed of his friendship with Jakob Goldschmidt, though he wrote of him: 'He enjoyed the company of close relatives, who revealed his lower-middle-class origins.'[79]

Like his father, Hans Fürstenberg considered a large number of men with whom he conducted business to be friends. These business friends were, however, almost exclusively bankers. The same is true of Siegmund Warburg's social ties within the business world. This perhaps reflects the declining importance of 'special relationships' with industrial firms. Fürstenberg and Warburg also had social connections with the government. Warburg's friends included Rathenau, Stresemann and Baron Konstantin Neurath, who was Foreign Minister under Papen. Fürstenberg socialized with diplomats and a state secretary.[80] By 1933, bankers had become 'virtually the apex of Berlin society', according to Fürstenberg.[81] Then the entire framework of Weimar society collapsed.

VIII

The banker of the Wilhemine era was part of a socially exclusive business elite. Generally he was himself a banker's son. The wealthiest industrialists and merchants were also businessmen's sons. Thus, the social origins of this group contributed to their perception of themselves as part of an elite. A slightly higher percentage of very wealthy bankers were ennobled in this era than were very wealthy industrialists or merchants. This does not reflect a higher propensity of Jewish businessmen to seek or accept honours, but is rather indicative of a characteristic of wealthy bankers as a group.

A higher percentage, not only of bankers, but also of elite industrialists' and merchants' sons became businessmen. Almost a quarter of bankers' sons went into industry or commerce, demonstrating that banking families were part of a larger business elite. Data on fathers-in-law revealed a similar pattern, while data on the sons-in-law and sons' fathers-in-law presented a different picture. Only a third of industrialists' and bankers' children and half of great merchants' children married into business families, evidently because such connections were of lesser importance in very successful business families, which often did not need new capital and business connections to stay in business. Ties of marriage between bankers' families and industry and commerce were strong in the generation of the children. The rate of aristocratization was low as far as the sons' and fathers-in-law's professions go. A third of bankers' and industrialists' children, but only a fourth of merchants' children married into families of the pre-industrial elite. This represents a significant, but not overwhelming, rate of aristocratization. It must also be stressed that connubium with the aristocracy is not necessarily indicative of a desire to move out of the business world. These could be useful connections. The tendency to contract aristocratic alliances was not higher among Jewish businessmen. A sixth of the bankers' sons, a fifth of the bankers' fathers-in-law, and a fourth of the bankers' children's spouses were of the non-business bourgeoisie (upper civil servants, the liberal professions, teaching and the lower middle class without capitalists). Thus, bankers were not really well integrated into the bourgeoisie as a whole, but neither were they cut off from it. (The same is true of very wealthy industrialists and merchants.) Ties with the administrative elite were not, taken alone, very significant.

In Hamburg and Berlin, the banker's social life was generally shaped by his business interests. Only an occasional banker really seems to have sought integration with the aristocracy. In Hamburg, bankers were generally part of the haute bourgeoisie, which included the liberal professions and the political and administrative elite. This was not the case in Berlin, where bankers sought the favour of the non-bourgeois ruling class, but normally without fusing with it or subordinating business interests. In both Berlin and Hamburg, social ties bound businessmen together. Here again we find that bankers were part of a larger business elite. The results of this empirical study on very wealthy bankers indicates that they were part of an exclusive business elite with few ties to the middle class per se. Socially this elite pursued links with the ruling class – in

Prussia the pre-industrial Junker class, in Hamburg the bourgeois patriciate.

In the Weimar era, the banking elite became more diverse in terms of its patterns of recruitment and social life. Bankers played a central political and economic role. However, as anti-Semitism and anti-capitalism became linked in the crisis of the Weimar Republic, Jewish bankers increasingly became the 'social pariahs' that they had not been in Wilhelmine Germany.

Notes

1 This chapter draws material from a larger project, which has been submitted as a doctoral dissertation at the Free University of Berlin. Research for this article was supported in part by a grant from the International Research & Exchanges Board (IREX), with funds provided by the National Endowment for the Humanities and the United States Information Agency. None of these organizations is responsible for the views expressed.

2 In his double biography of Bismarck and banker Gerson Bleichröder, *Gold and Iron* (New York, 1977). Term used on p. 465.

3 A word must be said on the class model used here. In my analysis below, I distinguish between the pre-industrial, traditional elite (consisting of big landowners, members of the high nobility, those holding court posts, officers, diplomats and civil servants holding the office of *Landrat*), upper (university-educated) civil servants (without *landräte*, teachers and professors) and the rest of the non-business bourgeois upper middle class (the upper echelons of the professions, teaching, political offices and the ministry). Where it was not possible to distinguish between upper- and middle-class businessmen (due to the ambiguity of the terminology in the sources) these are together in the category 'businessmen'. Small-scale businessmen (including master craftsmen and the petty bourgeoisie) are in the category 'lower middle class'. The lower middle class also includes farmers, middle-grade civil servants (who had no university education), white-collar workers, factory foremen, non-commissioned officers and professions in the arts and literature. See Peter Lundgreen, Margret Kraul and Karl Ditt, *Bildungschancen und soziale Mobilität in der städtischen Gesellschaft des 19. Jahrhunderts* (Göttingen, 1988), vol. II, pp. 319–64. I have modified this model for my purposes.

4 See David Blackbourn, 'The discreet charm of the bourgeoisie: reappraising German history in the nineteenth century', in David Blackbourn and Geoff Eley, *The peculiarities of German history* (Oxford and New York, 1984), pp. 230–7; Hartmut Kaelble, 'Wie feudal waren die deutschen Unternehmer im Kaiserreich? Ein Zwischenbericht', in Richard Tilly (ed.), *Beiträge zur quantitativen vergleichenden Unternehmensgeschichte* (Stuttgart, 1985), pp. 148–71. See also my article, Dolores L. Augustine-Pérez, 'Very wealthy

businessmen in Wilhelmine Germany', *Journal of Social History*, 22 (1988), 299–321.

5 Rudolf Martin, *Jahrbuch der Millionäre Deutschlands* (18 vols., Berlin, 1912–14). Volumes appeared on all German states aside from Baden, the Grand Duchy of Hesse (the Prussian province of Hesse-Nassau was included), Alsace-Lorraine (then part of Germany, now in France), the Thuringian states and a few minor principalities.

6 StA Potsdam (State Archives, Potsdam), Polizeipräsidium Berlin, Pr.Br.Rep. 30 Berlin C Tit. 94 *passim* and Zentrales Staatsarchiv, Dienststelle Merseburg, Ministerium für Handel und Gewerbe, 2.2.1. Nr. 1018–2536 and Rep. 120 A IV *passim*. Data were found in fifty-seven cases.

7 See Kurt Nitschke, *Einkommen und Vermögen in Preußen und ihre Entwicklung seit Einführung der neuen Steuern mit Nutzanwendung auf die Theorie der Einkommensentwicklung* (Jena, 1902), pp. 24–6; Polizeipräsident Berlin an Handelsministerium, 1912, StA Potsdam, Pr.Br.Rep. 30 Berlin C Tit. 94 Nr. 9650.

8 The definition of who was an entrepreneur was not based on his function, but rather on his position (owner, member or chairman of the board, etc.).

9 Reference works such as the *Neue Deutsche Biographie* (13 vols., Berlin, 1953–82) were used, as well as autobiographies and biographies. The most important archive for the quantitative study was the 'Institut zur Erforschung historischer Führungsschichten' in Bensheim, West Germany. The state archives of the G.D.R. in Potsdam, Merseburg, Leipzig and Dresden also yielded a considerable body of data. Further material was gained through correspondence with descendants of the persons under study, genealogists and public archives in West Germany.

10 Private banks as defined here include the following legal forms: the G.m.b.H. (Gesellschaft mit beschränkter Haftung) and the Kommanditgesellschaft. 'Entrepreneurs' are defined as directors or chairmen-of-the-board of joint-stock companies under the control of a family. See A. D. Chandler and H. Daems, 'Introduction' to Chandler and Daems (eds.), *The Rise of Managerial Capitalism* (The Hague, 1974), pp. 5f.

11 See Manfred Pohl, *Konzentration im deutschen Bankwesen. 1848–1980* (Frankfurt am Main, 1982), p. 464.

12 See *Statistik des deutschen Reichs*, Neue Folge vol. 202: *Berufs- und Betriebszählung vom 12. Juni 1907, Gewerbliche Betriebsstatistik* (Berlin, 1909; reprint Osnabrück, 1972), table 1, p. 120.

13 Based on official statistics: ibid., Neue Folge vol. 214, Abt. II, Heft 2 (Berlin, 1910), table 12, p. 14. Small-scale capitalists were defined as those owning businesses with eleven to fifty employees. Thus this figure excludes craftsmen and the petty bourgeoisie. Medium- and large-scale entrepreneurs were those employing over fifty persons.

These categories were taken from Helga Nussbaum, *Unternehmer gegen Monopole* (Berlin, G.D.R., 1966), p. 33.

14 According to Monika Richarz, introduction to Richarz (ed.), *Jüdisches Leben in Deutschland*, vol. 2: *Selbstzeugnisse zur Sozialgeschichte im Kaiserreich* (Stuttgart, 1979), p. 30. In this paper, Jews are defined ethnically. Ideally, an ethnic definition of Jewishness would include converted Jews and Christians, whose family was Jewish a couple of generations back – such as the Mendelssohns – to the extent that these individuals considered themselves to be Jewish or who demonstrated solidarity with the Jewish community. In actual practice, it is very difficult to use self-definition as a criterium in a quantitative study. Thus, converted Jews and Christians of Jewish descent were considered to be Jews for the purposes of the present study. For a similar definition of Jewishness, see Werner E. Mosse, *Jews in the German economy. The German-Jewish economic elite 1820–1935* (Oxford, 1987), pp. 1–2. Mosse points out that the Judaic religion constituted just one element of Jewish identity in this era, along with social origins, endogamy, family and business networks, and traditions.

15 See ibid., pp. 218–36.

16 Fifty-nine per cent of the 121 Jewish businessmen, but only 17 per cent of the 361 non-Jewish businessmen were bankers. Werner Mosse's figures are very similar. See ibid., p. 205. On the causes of Jewish predominance in banking, see esp. pp. 380–3.

17 The fathers' occupations fell into the following categories: 1 per cent traditional elite, 4 per cent upper civil servants, 2 per cent liberal professions or teaching, 5 per cent non-entrepreneurial middle class (including master craftsmen), 1 per cent middle or lower class and 1 per cent rentiers.

18 The percentages were calculated *without* the cases without information. Cases without information make up the following percentages of the *totals*: 17 per cent for industrialists, 28 per cent for bankers, 15 per cent for merchants.

19 On the recruitment of German businessmen, see Jürgen Kocka, *Unternehmer in der deutschen Industrialisierung* (Göttingen, 1975), pp. 38–9, 47–50, 115, 122–3; Hartmut Kaelble, 'Long-term changes in the recruitment of the business elite', *Journal of Social History*, 13 (1980), 404–23.

20 Half the industrialists and over two-thirds of the bankers are known to have been the sons of upper-class businessmen. In the rest of the cases, it is unknown if the father was of the middle or upper class.

21 *Der Rheinisch-Westfälische Unternehmer, 1834–1879* (Cologne and Opladen, 1962), p. 122. Zunkel is writing of the pre-1870 period. He makes unfortunate use of stereotypes, describing these bankers as 'particularly purposeful, ambitious, egotistical and strong-willed'. Thus, his thesis on their social origins probably simply derives from a

preconception that Jews are 'rootless'. For Peter Gay's comments on this passage, see *Freud, Jews and Other Germans* (New York, 1978), p. viii.

22 'Aristocratization' is a better term than 'feudalization', because the phenomena described by it has nothing to do with feudalism as it developed in medieval Europe. See Hartmut Kaelble's comments in 'Wie feudal waren die deutschen Unternehmer im Kaiserreich? Ein Zwischenbericht', in Richard Tilly (ed.), *Beiträge zur quantitativen vergleichenden Unternehmensgeschichte* (Stuttgart, 1985), pp. 148 and 150.

23 For the sources, see fn. 5 and 9.

24 If we exclude those born into the nobility (titles predating 1871) and look only at those born as commoners, then the percentages for industrialists, bankers and merchants are 18 per cent, 24 per cent and 16 per cent respectively.

25 Georg Solmssen, *Gedenkblatt für Adolf und Sara Salomonsohn zum 19. März 1931* (Berlin, 1931), p. 20; Carl Fürstenberg, *Die Lebensgeschichte eines deutschen Bankiers, 1870–1914*, ed. Hans Fürstenberg (Berlin, 1931), pp. 198–199; Alfred Vagts, 'M. M. Warburg & Co. Ein Bankhaus in der deutschen Weltpolitik 1905–1933', *Vierteljahrschrift für Sozial- und Wirtschaftsgeschichte*, 45 (1958), 294; Hans-Konrad Stein, 'Der preußische Geldadel des 19. Jahrhunderts. Untersuchungen zur Nobilitierungspolitik der preußischen Regierung und zur Anpassung der oberen Schichten des Bürgertums an den Adel', 2 vols., unpublished Dissertation, University of Hamburg, 1982, pp. 61–3, 68.

26 Data to be presented in my dissertation.

27 Baron Max von Goldschmidt-Rothschild was the only non-converted Jew in Prussia to be granted a title of nobility. See Martin, *Jahrbuch*, vol. 12, p. 65. Jews could, however, seek ennoblement in one of the smaller territories which did grant titles to Jews; these titles then had to be recognized by the Prussian government.

28 See Elsabea Rohrmann, 'Max von Schinckel, hanseatischer Bankmann im wilhelminischen Deutschland', Dissertation, Hamburg, 1971, p. 289. According to my data, new titles of nobility were hardly less prevalent among elite businessmen (all sectors) in Hamburg (11 per cent) than among elite businessmen in Berlin (15 per cent). Throughout the nineteenth century, wealth was the determinant of social status in Hamburg, and titles of all sorts, but particularly titles of nobility, were rejected. Richard Evans writes, 'the wealthy of nineteenth-century Hamburg were for the most part stern republicans, abhorring titles, refusing to accord any deference to the Prussian nobility, and determinedly loyal to their urban background and mercantile heritage'. Richard J. Evans, *Death in Hamburg. Society and politics in the cholera years 1830–1910* (Oxford, 1987), p. 560; see also pp. 33–5, 559–62. Hamburg gradually became part of the Reich, and a process

of assimilation took place which, Evans argues, did not go very far. However, the growing number of new titles of nobility among the very wealthiest citizens of Hamburg is striking. In a petition directed at the Ministry of Trade and Commerce, Baron John von Berenberg-Gossler asked that his son, who was to take over the family's bank, be allowed to inherit the baronage without establishing a landed entail, arguing that his son should have the title because the heads of two other Hamburg banks were also barons. Source: Zentrales Staatsarchiv, Diensstelle Merseburg, Geheimes Zivilkabinett, 2.2.1. Nr. 1048, Bl. 5–9.

29 All sectors. According to Friedrich Zunkel, titles of nobility were more prevalent among Berlin businessmen – Jewish bankers in particular – than among the entrepreneurs of the Rhineland and Westphalia before 1870. See Zunkel, *Unternehmer*, p. 122.

30 Ennoblement was far rarer among the masses of non-elite businessmen. Only about 5 per cent of the eighteenth- and nineteenth-century entrepreneurs of German-speaking areas listed in the *Neue Deutsche Biographie* were nobles. See Wilhelm Stahl, *Der Elitenkreislauf in der Unternehmerschaft. Eine empirische Untersuchung für den deutschsprachigen Raum* (Frankfurt am Main and Zurich, 1973), p. 247. The rate was even lower among Westphalian textile manufacturers and heavy industrialists. See Hans-Jürgen Teuteberg, *Westfälische Textilunternehmer in der Industrialisierung. Sozialer Status und betriebliches Verhalten im 19. Jh.* (Dortmund, 1980), p. 38 and Toni Pierenkemper, *Die westfäfischen Schwerindustriellen 1852–1913. Soziale Struktur und unternehmerischer Erfolg* (Göttingen, 1979), p. 73. For an English summary of the Pierenkemper book, see 'Entrepreneurs in heavy industry: Upper Silesia and the Westphalian Ruhr Region, 1852 to 1913', *Business History Review*, 53 (1979), 65–78.

31 This is an adaptation of Kocka's theses, which refer to an earlier period. See 'Familie, Unternehmer und Kapitalismus', *Zeitschrift für Unternehmergeschichte*, 24 (1979), 99–135. For an English summary of this article, see 'The entrepreneur, the family and capitalism', *German Yearbook on Business History*, 1981, pp. 53–82. See also Augustine-Pérez, 'Very Wealthy', esp. 308, 311–14.

32 The number of sons in middle-class professions may in reality have been somewhat higher. See section II.

33 Cross-sectoral data. To be presented in detail in my dissertation. Percentages for professions other than those in the 'feudal' and business sectors revealed no real differences between Jews and non-Jews.

34 Hans Dieter Hellige, 'Generationskonflikt, Selbsthaß und die Entstehung antikapitalistischer Positionen im Judentum', *Geschichte und Gesellschaft*, 5 (1979), 476–518.

35 On Warburg, see Max M. Warburg, *Aus meinen Aufzeichnungen*

(private print, New York, 1952), p. 6; Jacques Attali, *Siegmund G. Warburg*, trans. Hermann Kusterer (Düsseldorf and Vienna, 1986), pp. 63–4, 84. On Oppenheim, see Wilhelm Treue, 'Max Freiherr von Oppenheim – Der Archäologe und die Politik', *Historische Zeitschrift*, 209 (1969), p. 37–74. Walther Rathenau – not a banker's son – expressed anti-capitalist and anti-Semitic sentiments in his early writings and in private. See Hans Dieter Hellige, 'Rathenau und Harden in der Gesellschaft des Deutschen Kaiserreichs', in *Walther Rathenau. Maximilian Harden. Briefwechsel 1897–1920* (Munich and Heidelberg, 1983), p. 15–299. On Borchardt, see Werner Kraft, *Rudolf Borchardt. Welt aus Poesie und Geschichte* (Hamburg, 1961).

36 See Attali, *Siegmund G. Warburg*, pp. 62–85; Warburg, *Aus meinen Aufzeichnungen*, pp. 6–10.

37 See Paul Wallich, *Lehr- und Wanderjahre eines Bankiers* in *Zwei Generationen im deutschen Bankwesen 1833–1914* (Frankfurt am Main, 1978), pp. 160–87.

38 Quotation out of Bethmann's unpublished memoirs, in Baron Johann von Bethmann (ed.), *Bankiers sind auch Menschen* (Frankfurt am Main, 1973), pp. 260–1; see also pp. 258–9. My translations here and below.

39 A particularly detailed account is that of Hans Fürstenberg: *Erinnerungen. Mein Weg als Bankier und Carl Fürstenbergs Altersjahre* (Düsseldorf and Vienna, 1968), pp. 15–19.

40 *Cross-sectoral* data for these three cities on the sons' professions reveal a similar rate of aristocratization (around 10 per cent).

41 See Kocka, 'Familie', 101–17.

42 See Marion A. Kaplan, 'For Love or Money', *Leo Baeck Institute Year Book*, 28 (1983), 263–300; Werner E. Mosse, 'Jewish Marriage Strategies', *Studia Rosenthaliana*, 19 (1985), 188–202.

43 The percentage for the middle class may in reality have been somewhat higher. See section II.

44 See Felix Gilbert (ed.), *Bankiers, Künstler und Gelehrte* (Tübingen, 1975), p. XXXIV. Gilbert's mother was a Mendelssohn.

45 The percentage for the middle class may in reality have been somewhat higher. See section II.

46 See Vagts, 'M. M. Warburg', 291. Friedrich W. Euler comes to a similar conclusion in 'Bankerherren und Großbankleiter nach Herkunft und Heiratskreis', in Hanns Hubert Hofmann (ed.), *Bankherren und Bankiers* (Limburg an der Lahn, 1978), p. 135.

47 See Gilbert, *Bankiers*, p. XXXIV.

48 C. Fürstenberg, *Lebensgeschichte*, *passim*.

49 See Paul Wallich, *Lehr- und Wanderjahre eines Bankiers* in *Zwei Generationen im deutschen Bankwesen 1833–1914* (Frankfurt am Main, 1978), pp. 343–5; Werner Weisbach, '*Und alles ist zerstoben.*' *Erinnerungen aus der Jahrhundertwende* (Vienna, Leipzig and Zurich, 1937), p. 109.

50 See Georg Solmssen, *Gedenkblatt für Adolf und Sara Salomonsohn zum 19. März 1931* (private print, Berlin, 1931), pp. 10–12, 19; Karl Helfferich, *Georg von Siemens. Ein Lebensbild aus Deutschlands grosser Zeit*, vol. III (3 vols., Berlin, 1923), p. 240.

51 See for example Willy Ritter Liebermann von Wahlendorf, *Erinnerung eines deutschen Juden 1863–1936*, ed. Ernst Reinhard Piper (Munich and Zurich, 1988), esp. pp. 49, 67, 83–4.

52 On the Tiergarten, see Erich Achterberg, *Berliner Hochfinanz. Kaiser, Fürsten, Millionäre um 1900* (Frankfurt am Main, 1965), pp. 43–6. On the Club of Berlin, see Gwinner, *Lebenserinnerungen* pp. 54–6; Max I. Wolff, *Club von Berlin. 1864–1924* (Berlin, 1926), esp. pp. 20–9, 89, 99; P. Wallich, *Lehr- und Wanderjahre*, pp. 352–3. On a restaurant where businessmen met, see C. Fürstenberg, *Lebensgeschichte*, p. 397.

53 On dwindling interest in political office-seeking among businessmen, see Hans Jaeger, *Unternehmer in der deutschen Politik (1890–1918)* (Bonn, 1967), pp. 25–106.

54 See ibid., pp. 172–8; Attali, *Siegmund G. Warburg*, p. 83; Rohrmann, *Max von Schinckel*, p. 190; Fritz Stern, *Gold and Iron. Bismarck, Bleichröder and the Building of the German Empire* (New York, 1977), p. 544; C. Fürstenberg, *Lebensgeschichte*, p. 439.

55 See Rudolf Vierhaus (ed.), *Das Tagebuch der Baronin Spitzemberg* (3rd edn., Göttingen, 1963), esp. p. 475; Count Bogdan von Hutten-Czapski, *Sechzig Jahre Politik und Gesellschaft*, vol. II (Berlin, 1936), p. 63; Baron Werner von Rheinbaben, *Viermal Deutschland. Aus dem Erleben eines Seemanns, Diplomaten, Politikers* (Berlin, 1954), p. 76; Fürstenberg, *Lebensgeschichte*, pp. 333, 550.

56 See von Hutten-Czapski, *Sechzig Jahre*, p. 63; Jaeger, *Unternehmer*, p. 181.

57 See C. Fürstenberg, *Lebensgeschichte*, *passim*.

58 See Carl von der Heydt, *Unser Haus* (private print, place of publication unknown, 1919), p. 33.

59 Fedor von Zobeltitz, *Chronik der Gesellschaft unter dem letzten Kaiserreich*, vol. II (Hamburg, 1922), p. 210.

60 Von der Heydt, *Haus*, pp. 30–1; see also pp. 29, 35–7.

61 On Gutmann, see Polizeipräsident Berlin to Handelsministerium, 1898, StA Potsdam, Pr.Br.Rep. 30 Berlin C Tit. 94 Nr. 10239. On Esser, see Polizeipräsident Berlin to Handelsministerium, 1896, StA Potsdam, Pr.Br.Rep. 30 Berlin C Tit. 94 Nr. 9748.

62 See Lamar A. Cecil, 'Jew and Junker in Imperial Berlin', *Leo Baeck Institute Year Book*, 10 (1975), 47–58.

63 See for example Fürstenberg, *Lebensgeschichte*, esp. pp. 95, 99–100, 142, 216–17, 317, 334, 398–9; Wilhelm Treue, 'Das Bankhaus Mendelssohn als Beispiel einer Privatbank im 19. und 20. Jahrhundert', *Mendelssohn-Studien*, 1 (1972), 54–5, 57–8; Cécile Lowenthal-Hensel, 'Franz von Mendelssohn', *Mendelssohn-Studien*, 6 (1986), 259; Felix Gilbert (ed.), *Bankiers, Künstler und Gelehrte.*

Unveröffentlichte Briefe der Familie Mendelssohn aus dem 19. Jahrhundert (Tübingen, 1975), p. 229.
64 Evans, *Death*, p. 559.
65 Percy Ernst Schramm, *Neun Generationen*, vol. II (Göttingen, 1964), p. 417.
66 Rohrmann, *Max von Schinckel*, p. 75.
67 See Evans, *Death*, pp. 392–3; P. Wallich, *Lehr- und Wanderjahre*, p. 227; Lamar Cecil, *Albert Ballin* (Princeton, 1967), p. 37. For examples of growing social acceptance, see Schramm, *Neun Generationen*, p. 417; Cecil, *Albert Ballin*, p. 37 (on Ballin's friends among the Protestant patriciate).
68 Quoted in Evans, *Death*, p. 21; see Evans on these dinners. Presumably, bankers were also among the hosts and guests.
69 See Schramm, *Neun Generationen*, pp. 425, 426. Max Warburg did extend invitations to officers. See Gertrud Wenzel-Burchard, *Granny. Gerta Warburg und die Ihren* (Hamburg, 1975), pp. 20–1.
70 Rohrmann, *Max von Schinckel*, p. 289.
71 See Mosse, *Jews*, pp. 324–8.
72 See Pohl, *Konzentration*, pp. 285–388, 464.
73 See Mosse, *Jews*, pp. 330–50, 364–5.
74 See Attali, *Siegmund G. Warburg*, pp. 123–4, 138, 144.
75 Fürstenberg's father-in-law was actually a legal consultant to Moscow banks in the czarist era. See H. Fürstenberg, *Erinnerungen*, p. 194. On Warburg, see Attali, *Siegmund G. Warburg*, p. 149.
76 See H. Fürstenberg, *Erinnerungen*, pp. 157, 161.
77 See Treue, 'Bankhaus Mendelssohn', 58.
78 See H. Fürstenberg, *Erinnerungen*, p. 171. See also Hans Fürstenberg's remarks on new wealth, pp. 145, 170.
79 Ibid., p. 161.
80 See Attali, *Siegmund G. Warburg*, pp. 125, 161–72; H. Fürstenberg, *Erinnerungen*, pp. 151–62, 180–94.
81 Ibid., p. 105. See also Attali's comments on Warburg's reception in Berlin in 1930 in *Siegmund G. Warburg*, p. 162.

10 Financial elites and society: comments

JOSÉ HARRIS

These chapters – as well as the relevant sections in G. Kurgan's and Cassis and Tanner's ones – offer us a classic example of the polar attractions of 'splitting' and 'lumping' in social and institutional history. All the contributors either implicitly or explicitly see financial institutions and their members as occupying some kind of special, salient position in modern socio-economic and political structures. Yet all suggest that this salience differs in characters, not merely between different periods and different national contexts, but between different types of financial institution within the same national culture, and even between different examples of the same kind of finance house. Thus, as Martin Daunton's paper helpfully reminds us, by no means all persons engaged in financial practices can be seen as part of a single homogeneous group. In terms of social status, recruitment patterns, financial rewards and access to government, merchants banks in the City of London differed from each other and from the joint-stock banks, which in turn differed from the Stock Exchange, Lloyds and other financial groupings. Similarly, Dolores Augustine's study of German bankers demonstrates that the social character of a financial elite in a bourgeois and patrician city like Hamburg might be quite different from that of its counterpart in administrative and aristocratic Berlin. The study of Cassis and Tanner shows that the economic and cultural milieu of financial groups in Switzerland was dependent upon highly localized cultural and political traditions of the different cantons. A. Plessis' study reminds us that even a virtually hereditary banking caste might allow for a great deal of idiosyncrasy and occasionally replenish itself with recruitment from the sons of grooms, chambermaids and shoe-makers. G. Kurgan's analysis of Belgian finance points to a very high degree of overlap and integration between bankers and other sections of the Belgian industrial and professional bourgeoisie.

If bankers and financiers constituted a 'type' they were therefore an 'ideal type' rather than a class of people with common and unvarying social characteristics. Does the variety and variability of the profiles presented in these chapters suggest that, when rooted in concrete historical circumstance and in detailed archival research, our impulse towards a general sociology of financial elites simply founders in a sea of idiosyncratic detail? For all their emphasis on diversity, all these five studies engage with certain common themes and suggest certain lines of general enquiry along which historical research into financial elites might move forward. These may be summarized as follows:

1 There is the question of just how far financiers and financial interests of various kinds do in fact form distinct social and economic groupings; or whether, as is suggested by several of these papers, they are often functionally interlocking with and sometimes socially indistinguishable from the rest of the business community.[1]

2 When financial groups do form a discrete and identifiable elite, does their distinctiveness stem from the fact that they are engaged in something which is functionally separate from other parts of the economy, or is it simply because they are richer than other men of business? Is it because they have personal ties with some supposedly superior group like the landed aristocracy, the diplomatic service or public administration, or is it because they have some kind of privileged access to political power arising from the services that they perform for government?

3 There is the question of whether financial groups form a single elite or, as is suggested by several of these papers, a hierarchy of status groups, within which the norms, customs and levels of social acceptability prevailing in the old-established layers may not extend to newcomers. (There is also the possibility, most clearly spelt out in A. Plessis' chapter, that financiers may indeed form a distinct and economically privileged group, but that this may not necessarily confer social status. On the contrary they may be perceived as a contemptible and marginal group, lacking both personal honour and collective civic virtue – a view recurrent in French society throughout the nineteenth century and during the interwar years.)

4 If financiers are definitely perceived as a distinct and coherent group, what are their relationships with wider society, and what are the mechanisms (religious, educational, matrimonial or other) by which they are either integrated with or excluded from other parts of the social structure?

In answering these questions all chapters appear to indicate that, although the elite status and degree of integration enjoyed by financiers varied widely, it did not do so randomly. Daunton's paper makes use here of the four-part typology of elites set out by the sociologist Anthony Giddens; suggesting that we need to look both at the 'open' or 'closed' nature of the old-established elites to which financiers sought entry, and at the character of the 'secondary stratum' from whom new elites are recruited. Several of the studies underline the fact that large-scale cosmopolitan societies offer different opportunities for and exhibit different patterns of integration from small cohesive ones. The aspirations of financial groups varied according to circumstance. As Dolores Augustine points out, the motives for integration on the part of financiers might be functional and pragmatic rather than snobbish and status-seeking; German bankers, for example, often wanted to be introduced to aristocrats, not because they were nervously ambitious to improve their social standing, but because they sought useful contacts and political information. (The same ambiguous and instrumental approach to social climbing was also evident in the attitudes of the British Rothschilds, who wines, dined and did business with the aristocracy, but were horrified when a Scots aristocrat sought the hand of a Rothschild daughter in marriage.[2]) Several of the chapters touch upon the role of education and ideology in the process of furthering or hindering integration, and there seems to be scope here for much more detailed inquiry, particularly into the sphere of religion. We appear to lack detailed knowledge, for example, about the role of Anglicanism in fostering *common* cultural links between certain old established banking families and the British aristocracy; and about the role of judaism, quakerism, English dissent and continental protestantism in fostering the opposite phenomenon, namely a sense of separate and distinct identity. We need also perhaps to think a little more about the role of churches of all complexions in providing a kind of free masonry for financial elites and their clients (a role which may well have declined as banks became less local and more cosmopolitan).

These studies also give us information about intermarriage with other elite groups and about sources and patterns of recruitment. In all the societies under review the dynastic and hereditary element in finance houses was strong, but the practice of family recruitment by no means precluded the absorption of new talent (which was then frequently grafted into the old stock by judicious marriage). Moreover, although single-generational ascent to the top of a banking house was rare, many hereditary bankers began their careers by working out an apprenticeship on the counting-house floor. One point that must be very striking to British readers is the relatively high degree of migration and mobility between different sectors and occupations that appears to have prevailed for more than a century in French, German and Belgian business circles. The frequency with which continental banking communities drew upon lawyers, bureaucrats and engineers is something that even in the 1990s appears unusual to the student of British financial institutions.

Another point touched upon by several authors was the question of professional and interest group organization; and it appeared that in all countries the formal organization of banking and finance groups had been casual and amorphous, by comparison with the formal structures and high public profile often adopted by comparable groups of industrial employers. This lack of organization may have been an indicator of strength rather than of weakness. It may imply that bankers have been able to exert much closer and more effective *informal* influence upon government and administration than has typically been the case with the industrial sector. It leads finally into the elusive issue of the role of bankers in politics, and of how far financial groups have been able to exert either legitimate or illegitimate influence over the course of public policy. This question exists at many levels. There is the demonology of high finance, which perceives financiers as using their economic and social power to impose their will on the body politic; a demonology that seems to be more or less endemic in the political rhetoric of all countries, occasionally surfacing as a major element in real politics. There is the less dramatic but more demonstrable influence that stems not from crude corruption but from a common ideology and mentalité that are shared with those actively engaged in government. And there is the political influence that comes from sheer technical virtuosity; from the fact that bankers and financiers have command over a species of arcane knowledge, deemed rightly or wrongly to be indispensable to the exercise of power and the making of policy in modern states.

Notes

1 A salutary warning against simplistic assumptions on this point may be derived from Roland Quinault's recent study of Joseph Chamberlain, which reveals that Chamberlain – often cited as the champion of provincial industrial capitalism against cosmopolitan finance – from 1870 onwards had all his business interests in the City of London. See R. Quinault, 'Joseph Chamberlain: a reassessment', in T. R. Gourvish and A. O'Day (eds.), *Later Victorian Britain, 1867–1900* (Basingstoke and London, 1988), pp. 71–2.

2 Even though the aristocrat in question was Lord Rosebery, shortly to become prime minister. When Rosebery married Hannah Rothschild her male relatives stayed away from the wedding (Robert Rhodes James, *Rosebery*, (London, 1963), pp. 83–6; Cecil Roth, *The Magnificent Rothschilds* (London, 1939), p. 87).

III FINANCIAL INTERESTS AND POLITICS

11 The influence of the City over British economic policy *c.* 1880–1960

E. H. H. GREEN

The historiography of the British financial sector's resilience and success in the midst of Britain's 'one hundred year decline' is one of Britain's few growth industries. To do full justice here to the range and complexity of the work which has been produced on this subject is not possible, but at the risk of over-simplifying some of the analyses which have been developed it is perhaps worth outlining the central contentions which have emerged from some of the more important contributions in the field. The first is that the City's survival and prosperity has not simply been the product of happenstance or the financial sector's own market capabilities. Rather it has been contended that the City owes a great deal of its success to the fact that British economic policy has, over the long-term consistently supported and fostered its interests. Perhaps the most pungent statement of this argument can be found in the work of Sidney Pollard. In his essay on the decision to return to gold in 1925, and in his more recent indictment of British economic policies between 1945 and the 1980s, Pollard has argued convincingly that the policy outlooks of successive British governments have favoured City interests.[1] Pollard's central concern throughout, however, has been to analyse the *effects* of policy rather than to explain how policies were arrived at, and thus although the notion of City influence is implicit in much of his work it has not been Pollard's concern to show how, if at all, the City has exercised influence. Those analysts who have addressed this last issue have produced two basic postulates concerning the ability of the City to influence policy-making. On the one had it has been argued, most notably by Geoffrey Ingham and Robert Boyce,[2] that historically the City has been by far the most coherent of Britain's economic interest lobbies. As a consequence the articulation and advocacy of City interests is seen to have been relatively unproblematic, thereby endowing the financial sector with a great advantage in presenting a case to the government.[3] It has also been contended that the

City has obtained privileged access to the highest levels of decision-making through the Bank of England and the Treasury. This contention is central to the thesis developed by Frank Longstreth who, in describing the financial sector as the dominant 'fraction of capital' within the broader structures of British capitalism, argues that the City has 'penetrated' the British state through the 'media' of the Bank and the Treasury and has thus institutionalized a position of influence within the policy-making apparatus.[4] Likewise Geoffrey Ingham has seen the 'City–Bank–Treasury' nexus as a key explanandum of the City's influence and success.[5] Ingham, however, has rejected the 'instrumentalism' of Longstreth's description of the relationship between these institutions. In Ingham's analysis the interests of the City, the Bank and the Treasury have indeed shown an historical elision, but not because the Bank and the Treasury have acted as the City's cat's-paws. The Bank and the Treasury, Ingham argues, have cooperated in 'the continued reproduction of pro-City policies' over the long run, but they have done so, he contends, for their own reasons – the Bank in order to retain control over the money supply and thus its authority within the financial structure, the Treasury because of its need to fund public debt and to retain its authority over the rest of the state apparatus.[6] Where Ingham and Longstreth are closer together, and where their analyses overlap to some degree with that of Peter Hall,[7] is on the issue of how and why this close relationship between the City, the Bank and the Treasury has been sustained. Here primary importance has been attached to what Hall and Ingham have described as Britain's historical-structural integration with the international economy. In particular Britain's long-term imbalance on visible trade is thought to have enhanced the importance of Britain's invisible sector and privileged its needs: Britain's extreme vulnerability to capital flight and movements against sterling has, it is argued, given the City a strategic importance in the governance of the economy and, by dint of this, allowed it to exercise an effective 'veto' over policies which run counter to its interests.[8] In this scenario successive governments, and the Treasury and the Bank in particular, have had to listen to the voice of the City or risk currency instability and monetary disorder. In short a set of institutional links between the City and the British state, and the straightforward economic clout of the financial sector, have been established as the key factors inducing a long-term bias towards City interests in British economic policy.

The aim of this paper will be to assess the historical viability of this description of the City's ability to influence policy. Intentions rather than outcomes form the focus of this paper, for the simple reason that the outcome of a policy need not necessarily reflect its intentions, and intentions are clearly of primary historical importance in assessing the influences that have shaped a particular set of decisions. In terms of issues, the primary focus of this paper will be the areas of interest established in the existing literature, namely the nature and power of the City as a lobby and the relationship between the City, the Bank of England and the Treasury. In addition there will also be some discussion of the City's direct engagement in British party politics which will also draw to some extent on existing treatments of the subject. This essay will, however, depart from the established framework of analysis in two ways. The first is a matter of approach. Whilst the present author would not pretend that the source base of this essay is in any sense comprehensive it is hoped that the archival material deployed here will make some contribution to rectifying a scholarly imbalance in the treatment of the subject, for thus far the City's influence has been much theorized but largely unstudied in terms of genuinely historical sources.[9] Ironically, this concentration on archival sources contributes to this paper's second mild innovation, which is one of interpretation – ironically, because, unlike most archivally based studies, this paper will stress the role of ideas and ideology in its assessment of the City's influence.

The City as an interest group

At first glance the idea of categorizing 'the City' or 'the financial sector' as a single interest group is in itself dubious. Arguably the City has been as historically fractured as any other sector of the British economy, with merchant banks, private banks, joint-stock and clearing banks, insurance companies, stock brokers and, latterly, building societies engaging in distinctive market practices. But even when one allows for a significant degree of disparity between the various elements which have made up Britain's financial sector it is still possible to detect a number of factors which, since the late nineteenth century at least, have contributed to the emergence of a fundamental homogeneity of interest and outlook in the City. To begin with there is the fact of centralization. The merchant banks, the aristocracy of British finance, have always centred their activities on London, and although some of the larger houses had provincial branches in the early to mid nineteenth century most of these had closed by the 1890s.[10] Likewise, Britain's major private banks were also very much London-based concerns. In the nineteenth century the only forms of banking which were not centred on London were Britain's 'country' and joint-stock banks. However, as the result of an almost continuous process of amalgamation, merger and take-over Britain's local banks had, by the early twentieth century, been absorbed into a highly concentrated group of clearing houses. This group – the so-called 'Big Five' – all had their headquarters in London; outside of Scotland only some Lancashire and Yorkshire banks retained their provincial character, and by the end of the 1920s most of these had merged with London concerns.[11]

The simple geographical concentration of Britain's banking institutions should not be underestimated as a factor in creating a close collective identity, but there were other influences at work as well. Of particular importance was the authority of the Bank of England. In the context of Britain's international banking role the Bank of England exercised enormous influence. The Bank's management of the gold standard mechanism protected the value of sterling and secured its position as the medium of international trade, thereby providing the base upon which Britain's acceptance and discounting houses built their reputations and fortunes. In this respect the Bank established the rules of the game by which Britain's international financiers played. With regard to Britain's domestic financial structure the Bank of England's authority was also very pronounced. From the mid eighteenth century the Bank of England had acted as a *de facto* lender of last resort to other banks, and this position had been established *de jure* by the 1844 Bank Charter Act. Designed as a means of stabilizing the British banking system in the face of recurrent crises the 1844 Act gave the Bank of England control over the supply of money and thus immense power over Britain's financial system. What is more the Bank did not simply exercise formal control over note issue, it also controlled access to London's bill market and rediscounting facilities, which meant that the Bank had effective power over the credit facilities and basic liquidity of other banks and financial institutions. The Bank's authority was undoubtedly resented in some banking circles, especially in the clearing banks, but by the end of the nineteenth century the Bank's position had largely been accepted even in these quarters, for the simple reason that the Bank did in fact serve their interests. By taking on the role of lender of last resort the Bank had absolved all other banks and financial institutions of the responsibility of carrying inordinately large reserves, thereby allowing them to make maximum profitable use of the funds at their disposal. Hence, even when pressure was brought to bear on Britain's major clearing houses to increase deposits at the Bank to supplement its reserves they acquiesced – the only alternative would have been for the clearing banks to establish their own central reserve, an action which would have brought them greater autonomy but no obvious economic gains. Such a scheme was canvassed in the early twentieth century by Edward Holden, the Chairman of the Midland Bank, but the idea collapsed and the clearing banks thus implicitly accepted the Bank's authority.[12] By the early twentieth century, therefore, Britain's banking structure was not only highly concentrated but had at its centre a governing institution with real authority.

Whilst it was certainly the case that the Bank wielded great power, its working relationship with the rest of the banking system was not based solely on authority, a point which emerged very clearly in what was perhaps the first detailed investigation of Britain's modern financial system. Giving evidence to the Macmillan Committee in late 1929 Sir Ernest Harvey, the Deputy Governor, pointed out that the Bank had a close *consultative* relationship with other financial institutions. In part, Harvey argued, this was due to the fact that the bulk of the corporate Stock Exchange membership, the clearing banks, and a large number of issuing and discount houses, were all customers of the Bank in its capacity as a bank.[13] However, Harvey went on to state that, when it came to matters of policy rather than strict business, the Bank was 'in frequent informal intercourse with the representatives of all the important banks' and in particular that there was 'an arrangement... by which once a quarter the meeting of the clearing banks is held at the Bank of England with the Governor'.[14] There was no direct reference in Harvey's evidence to relations between the Bank and the merchant banking sector, but then this was hardly necessary, for in a passage of questioning which, for once, embarrassed Harvey a number of the Committee pressed him about the representative dominance of merchant bankers on the Bank's Court of Directors and Committee of Treasury.[15] Harvey's attempt to play down the significance of this phenomenon rang a little hollow at the time, and this prime example of the Bank's close connection with the aristocracy of finance has since been confirmed by a number of historical surveys.[16] In brief, the picture which Harvey painted was essentially one of a close network of informal contact, information exchange and general consultation, with the Bank acting as a sounding board and coordinator for the banking community. However, it should also be stressed that the informal structures of contact to which Harvey attached so much importance were supplemented by formal institutional arrangements that facilitated and coordinated close relations within and between the various elements of the banking community. Two of these were of particular importance. On the one hand there was the Accepting Houses Committee, formed in August 1914, which stood at the apex of the merchant banking sector. Membership of this Committee, which was drawn exclusively from the major merchant banking houses, was controlled by the Committee itself, but Bank of England approval was also necessary to confirm new admissions. The equivalent body for the clearing houses was the Committee of London Clearing Banks (CLCB), dominated by the 'Big Five'. Although it was only in 1911 that the Bank inaugurated regular meetings with the CLCB, by 1932 it had been established by the Bank's Committee of Treasury that the CLCB was to be the only formal means of communication with the clearing houses,[17] and this, coupled with the fact that Britain's clearing banks were so concentrated, ensured that the CLCB was both genuinely authoritative and representative. One other institution, of lesser importance but worthy of note was the London Chamber of Commerce. This was a far more amorphous body and carried far less weight than the AHC or the CLCB, but it did provide a link between the somewhat exclusive banking sector and other elements of London's business community, and its contribution to the fostering of a distinctive 'City interest' should not be ignored.[18] In terms of its institutional structure it is thus difficult to escape the conclusion that Britain's banking community did indeed possess a cohesion that set it apart from other sectors of the British economy.

It is not surprising that British bankers should have developed such a tight-knit institutional framework for the exchange of views and information and to coordinate the banking response to particular issues. In many respects these institutional arrangements were themselves a reflection of the way in which the market activities of the various sectors of Britain's financial community had converged towards the end of the nineteenth century. Britain's merchant, overseas and to a lesser extent, private banks were from the outset very cosmopolitan animals, but in the late nineteenth century their commitment to international activities grew ever more pronounced. At the same time, however, competition in the international markets intensified, something which posed problems for Britain's international finance houses because of their relatively small capital base.[19] The response of the international houses to this problem was simple enough. To begin with syndication became an increasingly frequent practice, something which forged even closer links between the firms which dominated British haute finance. In addition the international houses began to tap external funds, especially the abundant resources of Britain's increasingly large clearing banks and insurance companies. This last development had a two-fold significance: the first was that it became very common for merchant bankers in particular to secure directorships with other financial institutions:[20] the second was that the clearing houses and larger insurance business accelerated their already fast-developing engagement in overseas activities.[21] It may have been the case that the division of labour between domestic and international finance houses had been broken down, but the important thing was that competition took place in the same international market, and the fundamental interest of all was the preservation and development of that market and Britain's dominant position within it.

The City's policy priorities

In general three things were deemed central to the well-being of British banking interests in the period circa 1880–1960. The first was that, as far as was possible, the government should not attempt to regulate the market activities of the banking sector. Before 1946 this was an area of policy relatively free from controversy. The only issue which caused the banking community any concern was the move to regulate bank amalgamations in the early 1920s, when the banks waged a successful campaign against statutory controls and defended the practice of self-regulation.[22] In 1946, however, the nationalization of the Bank of England provoked the fear that 'the Bank ... might be obliged to transmit any direction which the Government thought fit to impose',[23] and that governments would use the Bank's authority to control or at least supervise more closely banking activities. Once again, and this is an issue which will be dealt with in more detail later in this paper, the banks gained reassurance on this point, but they remained on the alert against the possibility of government intervention, and sought to protect themselves again in 1951, when Hugh Gaitskell considered compulsory registration of bank liquidity, and in 1958–9, when the Radcliffe Committee was established to examine possible shortcomings in Britain's monetary system.

If freedom from restraint was one leitmotif for bankers, then another was the desire to maintain Britain's pivotal role in a liberal world trading order. This broad desire was linked to two aspects of policy in particular – the maintenance of sterling's international role and free trade – both of which were seen as essential prerequisites for London's banking supremacy. With regard to sterling's role the focus of concern in the period 1880–1931 was the gold standard. Giving evidence to the Royal Commission on Currency in July 1887, Bertram Currie, the Chairman of one of London's largest private banks,[24] stated a central City assumption when he declared that:

> The United Kingdom, and more particularly London is and has been for many years, the financial centre of the world ... [and] this supremacy arise[es] ... from the knowledge that a debt payable in London will be discharged in a definite quantity of a certain metal.[25]

That Currie should have felt obliged to state what to him and many others seemed obvious was a result of the bimetallic assault on the gold standard which reached its peak in the years 1886–98. The details of this debate are too tortuous to be dealt with at length here:[26] it is simply worth noting that in a controversy which revolved around the merits of retaining Britain's integration with the international economy the bulk of City opinion demonstrated an overwhelming commitment to the gold standard and Britain's international role.[27] This commitment, as is well known, was still very much in evidence in the years after the First World War. The issue of the return to gold, and the defence of the gold standard, are topics which have been studied exhaustively, and there is little to be gained from any further detailed analysis here; suffice it to say that the reestablishment and defence of the gold standard at pre-war parity took on a totemic significance in the attempt to reassert London's international dominance.[28] The abandonment of the gold standard, resisted to the last, brought a forced restriction on sterling's international role and was seen as a major threat to the City's position. However, the strong support which the City gave to the creation of the 'Sterling Area' in the 1930s and its continuation in the 1950s were an indication of the City's continued commitment to the maintenance of London's international status.[29] In spite of the disruptions of two major wars, and the collapse of the classical gold standard system, Britain's banking community remained wedded to a cosmopolitan vision of their role and interests.

The City's international orientation was also very clear in the marked commitment of Britain's bankers to free trade. The rationale of banking support for free trade was straightforward. Much of the City's income came from servicing world trade, and thus the greater the volume of world trade the greater the City's income. Hence any move away from free trade was deemed inimical to London's interests. Such a view found clear expression in the response of leading City lights to the most determined effort that was made to reverse Britain's commitment to free trade – Joseph Chamberlain's tariff reform campaign. In an address to the Institute of Bankers in December 1903 Felix Schuster, who was later to become Chairman of the Committee of London Clearing Banks, spoke out strongly against tariff reform, declaring that: 'if our trade, for any reason whatsoever were to be restricted, were to be confined within narrower channels ... others ... would oust us from our supreme position in the International Money Market'.[30] City disapproval of the tariff campaign was further evinced by the general refusal of bankers to involve themselves in Chamberlain's Tariff Commission, and an investigation into City attitudes towards tariff reform, carried out at Chamberlain's behest by the journalist H. A. Gwynne, confirmed a solid banking commitment to free trade.[31] The tariff campaign of the early twentieth century certainly witnessed the clearest expression of pro free trade sentiment in the City, but in the 1920s the City remained in the van of those opposed to any extension of tariff protection for Britain's beleaguered industries.[32] In the wake of the 1931 crisis, and the almost complete collapse of the international trading order, *force majeure* compelled the British government and the City to accept imperial preferences and a modicum of protection. After the Second World War, however, the City embraced the liberal trading order established under United States auspices, and reaffirmed its traditional commitment to the free flow of goods and, in even more uncertain terms, capital.

Freedom from restraint and the preservation of London's pivotal position in the world's financial markets – these were the constant priorities of the City in the period from 1880 to 1960, and there could be few complaints about their being fulfilled. What still needs to be explained, however, is how the City obtained such general satisfaction, and it is to this issue that this paper will now turn its attention.

The structures of City influence

Political influence

The formation of economic policy is a matter for elected governments and any account of City influence cannot, therefore, ignore the question of the City's role in party politics. Until the last quarter of the nineteenth century the bulk of City opinion undoubtedly saw its natural allegiance as lying with the Liberal party. However, as the nineteenth century drew to a close Britain's bankers, along with the Whig aristocracy and the urban middle classes, gravitated to the political right. In part this was a response to uncomfortable political developments within the Liberal party, but the alliance between finance and the Conservative party was cemented at a deeper social level by the increasing propensity of the Conservative aristocracy to rescue their ailing fortunes by diversifying their marriages and their investments away from land and towards finance.[33] From the turn of the century the loyalty of the City to the Conservative party did not waver, even during the period of the tariff reform campaign, and, particularly after the First World War, City funds provided a crucial source of income for Conservative party coffers.[34] Clearly the City's links with the Conservative party cannot be overlooked in any analysis of City influence, especially as between 1880 and 1960 the Conservative party were in office for forty-six of the seventy peace-time years.[35] But there are clear limits to the weight one can place on the City's ability to sway Conservative opinion. To begin with the simple fact that between 1903 and 1913, and again in 1923, the Conservative party advocated policies which ran counter to City priorities places an important question mark against the notion of an overriding City voice in Conservative circles. Furthermore, although it is the case that the City has paid the Conservative piper a great deal, this does not necessarily mean that it has always called the tune. Other business groups, notably brewing, construction and major manufacturers, have also been large contributors to Conservative party funds, and their demands and interests have not necessarily intersected and have often conflicted with those of the City. A further weakness in the argument for City influence over the Conservatives is that in terms of votes and seats the City cannot deliver a direct electoral pay-off. The City of London itself has only returned a maximum of two MPs, and although a large number of seats in suburban London and the south-east have been made up of constituents largely dependent on City employment and activities, they have never represented a majority of the Conservatives' Parliamentary cohorts.

'Knowledge is power'

To most observers outside the profession the activities of bankers have always seemed somewhat arcane. Even now activities such as market-making, arbitrage, currency hedging and bond-dealing are surrounded by a mystique which bankers have done little to dispel and much to encourage. By itself this conceit may not appear to have much significance, except for the fact that historically it has been used to support the assertion that matters like monetary and credit policy, exchange rates and currency issues are best left to those that understand them. In August 1895, commenting on the way in which bimetallists had been campaigning for support in agricultural districts, the *Banker's Magazine* declared itself appalled that such subjects should be presented to people 'who know as much about legal tender as about lunar geology'.[36] Had such views been confined only to banking circles their historical significance would be minimal, but the evidence suggests that politicians and civil servants frequently accepted the argument that bankers know best. For example, Sir Richard Hopkins, giving evidence to the Macmillan Committee, claimed ignorance of matters of high finance and stated that Treasury relied on the Bank's advice for all decisions with regard to exchange rate and credit policy. Likewise Hopkins' political master during the 1931 crisis, Ramsay MacDonald, told Montagu Norman in the July of that year that as he knew nothing of monetary matters he was forced to rely implicitly on the advice of financiers such as Norman himself.[37] Nor was such 'ignorance' dispelled in the post-war years – Sir Edward Bridges, Hopkins' successor as head of the Treasury deferred to the Bank's advice on most matters of monetary policy because: 'The high officials of the Bank of England have long and intense training and experience in their particular field. They are specialists ... [whereas] officers of the Treasury are laymen.'[38] In the light of this evidence it is difficult to disagree with Sayers' conclusion that financiers 'deliberately cultivated a mystique that at best befuddled and at worst intimidated those who had to take political responsibility'.[39] Furthermore, it is difficult to escape the conclusion that the cultivation of the 'mystique' of the banking expert ensured that, over the years, financiers dominated many of the most important government advisory committees which dealt with issues of financial and monetary policy.[40] As a result of the claim to a monopoly of expertise in certain fields of policy, the City was able to secure a crucial input into the formulation of policies which affected its most cherished interests.

The Treasury, the Bank and the City: an overlap of institutions

The claim to expertise in a field of policy is one thing, but a policy-making apparatus which is receptive to that claim is another, and it is here that the City enjoyed its most important advantage in securing an input into government economic decision-making. The key relationship in this context throughout the period 1880–1960 was that between the Bank and the Treasury. The Bank of England stood at the apex of Britain's banking structure, acting as a coordinating and supervisory agency for other banking institutions. In this role it functioned as a sounding-board of City opinions. However, the Bank also had another function as a quasi-state institution in the period before 1946 and as a formal state institution thereafter, its main task being to act as the government's banker and to arrange the marketing of Treasury bills. In this dual role the Bank functioned as a go-between, mediating relations between the government and the City. As a consequence the Bank developed a particularly close relationship with the Treasury.[41]

The implications of the Treasury–Bank relationship were very far-reaching given the self-defined roles of the co-respondents. In the period between 1880 and 1939 the Treasury saw its function as that of 'national housekeeper...not breadwinner' in that its central concern was with funding government debt and managing the government's finances.[42] This strict limitation of the scope of government economic policy to the realm of finance ensured that the Treasury's main, almost sole, contact with the British economy was with the financial sector as represented by the Bank. As a quasi-state institution the Bank's role was to ease the Treasury's task of managing the state's finances, but as the leading voice of the City the Bank's overriding concern was to protect the stability and indeed prosperity of Britain's banking sector. Insofar as the government's financial position impinged directly on the London money market, and insofar as the London money market was essential to the stability of the government's financial position there was only one possible outcome – the 'real' economy was relegated to a side-show and the Treasury and the Bank defined the function of government policy in terms of assisting the financial sector to create the correct climate for 'sound' economic activity. The result of this, however, was that the definition of 'sound' economic activity effectively lay with the City.

That this should have been the case in the years before 1946 is perhaps no surprise. With the Treasury constrained by its narrow definition of economic policy and dependent on the Bank to negotiate its position in the City, it was almost impossible to avoid the City exercising a strategic influence over government policy. But surely the post-1945 situation witnessed a fundamental change, in that governments accepted a broader definition of economic management whilst the Bank, through nationalization, was brought under formal state control and relieved of its hybrid status. Superficially this seems to be the case, but in actual practice very little changed. Although the 1944 commitment to full employment entailed as a necessary corollary a commitment on the part of post-war governments to 'economic management' the techniques of management adopted were very limited in their scope. Here the crucial development was the retreat from physical economic controls and the substitution of monetary and fiscal techniques of management which occurred after 1947. This development had a two-fold significance. To begin with it ensured that the Treasury, sidelined during the wartime years, re-emerged as the government department with overall responsibility for economic policy. This was of great benefit to the City. As Keith Middlemass has argued, the wartime years had seen the conscious fostering of a 'sponsoring' relationship between various government departments and the sectors of the economy which came within their sphere of influence: the trade unions fed into the Ministry of Labour, industry dealt primarily with the Board of Trade and the City dealt with the Treasury.[43] The reestablishment of 'Treasury control' thus carried with it implicitly the reestablishment of the City's privileged access to the hub of economic decision-making. Even more important, however, the decision to rely almost exclusively on monetary and fiscal levers to manage the economy necessarily foregrounded the role of the financial sector in the actual implementation of government policy. As one Treasury official summed up the situation in January 1958, 'the abolition of physical controls in the [immediate post-war] period meant that greater reliance was placed on purely monetary controls' with the result that 'successive Governments have found it necessary to make requests to the banks, through the Bank of England, with a view to restraining [or increasing] the provision of bank credit'.[44] In this respect Britain's much-vaunted 'Keynesian Revolution' begins to look far less of a radical break from pre-war practice than has generally been assumed.[45]

However, surely it was the case that the nationalization of the Bank had adjusted the authority relationship between the City–Bank–Treasury triangle. It was certainly assumed at the time of the Bank's nationalization that its authority had effectively been transferred to the government; this was not the case. Of course many analysts have stressed that in practice successive post-war governments 'chose' not to exercise the new authority over the City with which the state was endowed, and that they preferred to keep an 'arm's length' relationship with the Bank and to rely on voluntary cooperation from the banks in matters of monetary and credit policy. This is in large part true, but to lay stress on what governments *chose* to do is to underestimate the legal constraints on any alternative course of action, for in fact the government's powers over the Bank of England, and thus over the rest of the banking structure, were severely limited even after 1946. On two occasions in the 1950s the Treasury had reason to take the advice of the Treasury Solicitor on the question of governmental authority over the Bank, and the results came as somewhat of a surprise, namely that the government's authority was strictly limited.[46] In order to make their fiscal and monetary management effective, successive governments were forced to rely on 'the voluntary response of the bankers to official requests.'[47]

The emphasis on monetary policy in post-war economic management, and the fact that the institutional arrangements for the control of monetary policy remained fundamentally unchanged, leads almost inexorably to the conclusion that for the most part post-war economic management was simply 'a modification of the art of central banking'.[48] The stated goals of government economic policy in the 1950s were indeed different to those of the 1930s, but the economic and institutional instruments used to achieve these new goals retained their pre-war shape. This became very clear in the discussions between the Bank and the Treasury in the build-up to the Radcliffe Committee of Enquiry into the working of Britain's monetary system in the late 1950s. The close relationship between the Bank and the Treasury was confirmed by Sir Roger Makins prepared statement to the Committee, which is perhaps worth quoting at length:

> the relationship between the Treasury and the Bank is necessarily very closely knit. From one point of view it is that of customer and banker. The Bank of England holds the Government accounts and acts as the agent of the Treasury in a great many operations, and gives it advice on monetary policy ... the Treasury looks after the public debt and the Bank the money market. In most matters, the final authority rest with the Treasury,[49] though this is not formally the case with the movements of the bank rate. This is the Bank's decision.[50]

With Treasury and Bank officials dominating the Economic Steering Committee and its various subcommittees, the Bank and the Treasury, as Makins' pointed out, were very much in command of economic policy-making. Nor was this close collaboration confined simply to the process of policy development, the Treasury and the Bank also sought to ensure that their *articulation* of policy was closely aligned. With the Radcliffe enquiry looming Treasury and Bank officials went into a huddle, and a series of high-level discussions took place in order that the two institutions could get their story straight.[51] The upshot of all this was that the Treasury and the Bank collaborated very closely in the preparation of evidence for the Committee, but also decided not to make this collaboration too obvious. Thus Makins wrote to the Governor of the Bank in May 1957 to confirm that 'we will help each other to collect and present the facts, working through the normal channels of Treasury/Bank consultation', and although he argued that 'we should not attempt... to arrive at anything like a "party line"' he went on to stress that 'as we shall be testifying on the same subjects, I hope each of us will keep in touch with the other's thinking while we prepare our positions'.[52]

If the manner in which the Treasury and the Bank prepared for the Radcliffe Committee demonstrated that the intimacy of these two institutions was unchanged by post-war developments, it was also the case that the policy arguments which they drew up for presentation to the Committee also reflected long-established concerns. The basic problem which the Radcliffe Committee was set up to investigate was the working of Britain's monetary system and the issue of whether the government, reliant as it was on monetary devices for economic management, had adequate control of the system and if not what improvements could be made. Naturally this called to the fore the government's relationship with the banking sector, and in particular raised the question of whether the government needed to establish greater controls over banking activities. The far-reaching implications of this question for Britain's banking interest were brought to the fore in a Bank of England discussion paper circulated in the Treasury in late 1957. In this paper the Bank outlined what it saw as the central problem for Britain's monetary system and the government's ability to control it, which was that simple moves of interest rate could not prevent government debt from gravitating to the banking system and bringing about a rise in banking liquidity and private sector credit. This in turn was seen to result in inflationary pressures which the government sought to control through 'informal arrangements with the banks... to limit this increase in private credit'.[53] Such a situation was, according to the Bank, non-optimum, firstly because it was difficult to make such a policy fully effective, and secondly because it had an adverse effect on services rendered to the banks' private customers. In order to gain more effective control over the monetary system, the Bank argued, the government would have to adopt one or more of a number of alternative techniques, all of which, as the Bank pointed out, had 'one feature in common – namely a measure of compulsion'.[54] The alternatives the Bank outlined were a Liquidity Ratio, an Advances Ratio, and Advances Limit, an Investment Ratio, a Cash Ratio, Ways and Means Advances, Treasury Deposit Accounts, and Special Bank Deposits with the Treasury. However, the Bank deemed all of these to be undesirable. According to the Bank all of them meant an external definition and determination of banking liquidity, which meant the 'imposition of a standard of conduct not founded upon [the banks'] experience of their own business', and that as it would be 'evident that the object of the change was not to secure a sounder position of individual banks... the economic policies of Government might be brought into question and Government credit suffer'.[55] Equally important the Bank contended that the introduction of such compulsory mechanisms would introduce 'rigidity into a banking system doing a large volume of international business' and that as it was impossible to limit such measures 'to banks whose business is primarily in the United Kingdom' because 'the UK business of British and other banks operating...overseas is highly interrelated' this would 'prejudice the standing and operations overseas of British banks'.[56] The picture which emerges from the Bank's presentation of the problem of monetary control is clearly one of an overriding desire to protect the banking structure from government interference, which serves to reinforce a central contention of this paper that the Bank's vision of its function and its policy priorities were not altered by post-war developments.

The Treasury's response to the Bank's paper reinforces the notion of further significant continuities of outlook in that department. On the one hand the Treasury fully accepted the Bank's argument that the essence of the problem was that excess liquidity resulting from the government debt had led to a loss of control over the monetary system and in particular the supply of money.[57] Given that the Treasury, like the Bank, regarded the loss of control over the money supply as a very great evil, they were prepared to countenance the 'lesser evil' of some compulsory restriction of banking liquidity, but on the understanding that 'the Treasury...agree that if the choice has to be made, a technique should be selected that disturbs [the banking system] as little as possible'.[58] In the end this led to the introduction of the very inoffensive 'Special Deposits' system, but the real 'alternative technique' of monetary control which the Treasury advocated and began to work towards lay outside the realm of the alternatives put forward by the Bank. In fact the Treasury argued that the correct strategy was 'not limiting the access of the Treasury to the money market' but limiting things like public investment in the nationalized industries.[59] That the Treasury felt impelled to take such a line was without doubt a result of the continuing priority they accorded to their role as 'national housekeeper'. It is interesting to note that the Treasury's 'Brief' for its witnesses to the Radcliffe Committee stressed the fact that the Treasury had been steadily attempting to reduce the market in Treasury bills during the 1950s, but that it was not going to be possible to make rapid further progress on this reduction because 'we are faced with a very heavy succession of debt maturations over the next few years'.[60] Given this situation, and given the Treasury's self-defined priorities, they were very reluctant to pursue a strategy which in any way (and the Bank had warned them that any measure of compulsory controls might have this effect) jeopardize the government's position in the money market.

One conclusion of this paper is thus that the institutional structure of

British economic policy-making, and the basic tools of domestic economic management, have, over the long run, ensured that banking sector priorities have been translated into governmental priorities. In this respect this paper's findings are largely in accord with the central assertion of Geoffrey Ingham's study of the City's role in British economic policy-making. However, this paper would also suggest that the structural links between the City and the British state, important as they are, cannot stand alone as an explanation of the long-run primacy which has been accorded to the financial sector by the state.

The Treasury and the City: an overlap of economic ideology

Economic debate in Britain since the late nineteenth century has revolved around one central issue in particular: the question of Britain's relative decline as a manufacturing power and the parallel decline of Britain's share of world trade. Between 1880 and 1960 a number of official investigations examined the problem, but throughout the attitude of the Treasury remained remarkably consistent. In the period 1880–1931 the Treasury's economic outlook was fundamentally that of Gladstonian Liberalism, based on the familiar triptych of free trade, the gold standard and balanced budgets, all of which were historically and logically linked in a supposedly self-acting mechanism binding an open British economy to the international economy – according to Robert Chalmers, a Treasury Permanent Secretary in the late nineteenth and early twentieth century, it was self-evident that 'free trade and sound finance are really two sides of the same coin'.[61] The implications of this 'model' for the domestic 'management' of the economy have been dealt with very fully by Peter Clarke and Geoffrey Ingham, and this paper does not seek to add anything to their complementary treatments of the subject.[62] What this paper would seek to suggest, however, is that this Treasury 'model' of the economy also had immensely important implications in terms of 'external' economic policy; implications which ensured that the Treasury consistently supported and fostered the City's economic activities.

The issue which best demonstrates the workings and implications of the Gladstonian Treasury 'model' is that of invisible exports, the level of which was, of course, a bench-mark of the level of City prosperity. In the late nineteenth and early twentieth century a large number of commentators became alarmed at the degree to which Britain's visible trade balance had deteriorated, but the Treasury remained remarkably sanguine. The reason for the lack of alarm in official circles was explained by Edward Hamilton's notes on the question in 1898. Estimating Britain's visible trade gap at £194,000,000 Hamilton argued that there was no cause for concern because:

> In the first place, we supply foreigners every year with a huge amount of capital... the aggregate amount may be put at £2,000,000,000. The interest on this at 4.5% would be £90,000,000, which is being paid in the form of imports without any corresponding exports. In the second place there are also 'invisible' exports to be taken into account in the shape of freights and profits on our vast shipping trade... [which] may be put at £90,000,000. When therefore the excess [of imports over exports] goes on increasing, there is no reason to suppose that it is due to other causes than interest due on the increased capital invested abroad and an augmented carrying trade.[63]

For Hamilton there was no problem – Britain's trade imbalance was simply the 'natural' outcome of Britain's position as the mercantile and financial hub of the international trading community. This analysis, and the same set of assumptions, reappeared in an even clearer form in Treasury discussion of the Tariff Reform issue, a Treasury memorandum on 'The Fiscal Problem' defending free trade on the grounds that any drastic change in fiscal policy was bound to have adverse effects on the London money market and disrupt Britain's invisible income.[64]

In the interwar years the Treasury's emphasis on the importance of Britain's invisible earnings became even more pronounced. At no time was this more clearly demonstrated than in the internal government discussions which led up to the return to the gold standard. For example Ralph Hawtrey, whose important role in shaping Treasury ideas has recently been acknowledged,[65] argued in July 1924 that, as a result of fluctuations in the value of sterling, London's forward exchange market and the number of bills drawn on London were falling away. Hawtrey went on to state that:

> The shrinkage of business is a serious evil... London loses the direct profit on the business. But that is not all, for mercantile business tends to be transacted at the centre from which it is financed. The greatest factor in the material prosperity of this country is not manufacturing but *commerce*... [and] the diversion of commerce to other countries is the severest economic loss to which we could be exposed.[66]

In order to prevent this 'severe loss' and to 'reestablish the business of London as a world clearing centre' it was necessary, Hawtrey argued, to create the conditions in which 'a sufficient number of foreign currencies... [were] fixed in value in relation to sterling',[67] that is to say it was essential to restore the gold standard.

The Treasury's rationale for the return to gold in terms of Britain's economic development was very clear, the emphasis throughout being the absolute necessity of regaining London's pivotal position in the international economy. This priority was also clear in the Treasury's 'cosmopolitan attitude towards capital flows'.[68] Throughout the interwar period the Treasury remained very hostile to the idea of diverting capital from foreign to home investment. According to the Treasury 'model' it was the case that 'what we invest in foreign loans must, sooner or later, be exported',[69] that is to say the Treasury regarded it as axiomatic that capital export was an important engine for later visible exports. Whether or not this argument, as was far more clearly the case with the gold standard, was consciously designed to defend the City's international investment activities is a moot point. Intentional or not, however, the Treasury's insistence that foreign loans were a thing to be encouraged was yet another example of the 'cosmopolitan' assumptions which underpinned the Treasury approach to the functioning of the British economy, an approach which ensured that the most cosmopolitan interests within the economy were always guaranteed priority.

The classical Treasury model of the economy came tumbling down in 1931, a development which evidently caused great traumas – one senior Treasury official described it as the end of the civilized world.[70] The gold standard and free trade were abandoned and balanced budgets became a thing of subterfuge rather than fiscal reality. However, the destruction of the Treasury's cosmopolitan economy in the 1930s was by no means permanent, for as the shape of Britain's post-war economic structure evolved the links with the international economy, and the City's primacy, were once again foregrounded in the Treasury's plans.

In summing up the post-war Treasury's outlook Peter Hall has argued that 'Gladstone coexisted uneasily with Keynes'.[71] In fact one might go further than this, for it is possible to argue that Keynes coexisted uneasily with Keynes. In the interwar years Keynes had been the scourge of the bankers, arguing in the General Theory that investment was far too important to be left to people with the attitudes of casino gamblers, and calling, in less temperate fashion, for the 'euthenasia of the rentier'. However, as one of the main architects of Britain's post-war economic system, Keynes emerged as an unexpected champion of Britain's banking interests. The full range of Keynes' activities in the key period 1944–6 is a subject which this paper cannot deal with comprehensively, but even a brief examination of his more important contributions to the development of post-war reconstruction indicate how far Keynes helped to reestablish what was, in many respects, a very traditional conception of Britain's economic structure. In a Memorandum to the Cabinet in May 1945 Keynes set out his basic principle for 'Overseas Financial Policy' in the post-war period. His thrust throughout was the necessity of a liberal, multilateral trading order. This, Keynes argued, was partly necessary because the USA would not accept anything else, but he also stressed that: 'The international system is, on its merits, in our interests.'[72] Keynes' reasoning for this was two-fold. On the one hand he argued that 'what suits our exporters is to have the whole world as their playground', but in addition Keynes saw multilateralism as essential because of Britain's position as 'the financial centre of the greater part of the British Commonwealth and also of a number of countries outside it': indeed Keynes went so far as to argue that his proposals were 'intended to be, the means to recover for London its ancient prestige and its hegemony'.[73] This theme ran through all of Keynes' arguments for the Bretton Woods system, his proposals for an International Clearing Union and his campaign for a rapid transition to sterling convertibility. Keynes' efforts in this direction drew a somewhat scathing response from one of his old Treasury adversaries, who spoke of 'the ironical but pathetic ... thought of Keynes at Bretton Woods taking a leading part in producing a scheme for getting as near as he dared to an International Gold Standard';[74] but, leaving the bitterness of this comment aside, there was undoubtedly something to this argument. Writing to Montagu Norman in December 1941 Keynes, in outlining his thoughts on post-war financial arrangements, told his old *bête noire* that 'the essence of the scheme [for an international bank in this case] is very simple ... It is the extension to the international field of the essential principles of central banking', and he went on to add that the multilateral clearing system he envisaged would be a return to the pre-1914 system and 'something similar to the gold standard in its best nineteenth century days'.[75] Moreover, just as the gold standard had been unequivocally associated with London's paramount position, so Keynes argued that his proposals were 'an essential condition of the continued maintenance of London as the banking centre of the Sterling Area' and that they would protect 'the traditional advantages of banking in London'.[76]

Clearly it would be reductionist in the extreme simply to collapse Keynes' proposals into a mere retread of classical Gladstonian Treasury thinking, but equally it would be a mistake to underestimate the degree of overlap that existed in terms of the priorities of the two systems. Indeed developments in the 1950s appear to demonstrate that, whilst Keynes had succeeded in giving fresh impetus to the Treasury's cosmopolitan leanings, he had failed to fuse those leanings to anything but traditional concerns. To illustrate this point one only need refer to the Treasury's attitude to Britain's trade balance. As had been the case since the late nineteenth century, Britain's visible trade deficit in the late 1940s and 1950s was a source of perennial concern. As opposed to the situation in the 1890s post-war Treasury officials were willing to accept that this represented a significant problem, but whereas the late nineteenth-century Treasury had seen Britain's invisible earnings as a reason to discount the idea of the problem, the post-war Treasury saw invisible earnings as the actual solution to the problem. Thus one Treasury adviser at the Overseas

Finance Division wrote in January 1950 that concern over the balance of payments was a product of a failure

> to bring out sufficiently clearly the continued importance of the United Kingdom's position ... as a banker for the Sterling Area and as a hub of a great multilateral system of trade and payment ... varying from investments in long-term projects ... to the transitory migrations of 'hot money'.[77]

The solution to the balance of payments problem advocated by this particular official was simply to do the sums differently and give more weight to invisibles! Although this solution was not broadly countenanced the idea of using invisible earnings to off-set the visible gap certainly was, and throughout the 1950s the Treasury worked assiduously with the Bank of England to foster the development of London's international role. The net result was that the Treasury reestablished its pre-war, cosmopolitan attitude towards capital flows, even to the point of relaxing Exchange Control rules – it being noted in September 1955 that:

> one hundred per cent insistence ... would hamper ... trade practices involving arbitrage, forward buying, hedging etc and might well mean a considerable reduction of potential invisible earnings ... [and that] the Treasury and the Bank have, therefore, made every effort to allow a variety of suitable special arrangements and have been keen to re-open ... many of the international commodity markets which have been traditionally situated in London even when ... the transactions have involved a certain degree of convertibility.[78]

What emerges from this brief survey of the Treasury's conception of Britain's economic structure is a constant emphasis on the importance of Britain's international economic role. The emphasis of the Treasury's argument has shifted over time, but the basic tenet of the Treasury's position has been that the City's earnings have been either a mark of underlying prosperity or the means to achieve prosperity. In this respect the Treasury's definition of what actually constitutes a healthy economy, has, over the long run, constantly foregrounded the role of Britain's financial sector.

Concluding remarks

The influence of the City over British economic policy is a complex issue, frequently made more controversial than need be the case by the fact that the notion of a 'bankers' ramp' has for so long been part of the demonology of British politics. This paper does not pretend to have dealt with the issue in anything like a comprehensive or definitive fashion, but some tentative conclusions are worth presenting. To begin with there is a strong prima facie case in support of the notion that the City has benefited from conscious efforts to sustain its functions and prosperity. Arguably the City was damaged more than any other sector of the British economy by the dislocations of war, but during both periods of reconstruction the City's needs were accorded primacy by government. That this should have been the case can in part be attributed to the effectiveness of the City as an organized 'lobby' – the highly concentrated structure of Britain's financial institutions, especially the banks, and their common market practices have given the City a greater homogeneity of interest than any 'rival' group canvassing for government support. But an 'interest group' analysis of the City's influence is inadequate by itself as an explanation of their privileged position. The structural link, both institutional and functional, between the City and the British state has also been of central importance, in that successive governments have perforce been dependent on City finance and hence City confidence in the pursuit of their policies and the day to day funding of government activities. In addition, however, there has also been a crucial ideological dimension to the City's influence. Between 1880 and 1960, and indeed beyond, debates on the evolving structure of the British economy have tended to revolve around the issue of whether Britain should remain an open economy with structural links to the international economy, or whether a more 'autarkic' approach should be adopted. The perpetual bias within the British state, and in particular within its key economic department, has been to perpetuate the open, internationally orientated strategy. In this respect the influence of the City need not necessarily been seen as direct, but a product of the fact that the City's earnings have served to justify and perpetuate a set of assumptions about the optimum path for British economic development.

Notes

1 S. Pollard, 'Introduction' to S. Pollard (ed.), *The gold standard and employment policies between the wars* (London, 1970), and S. Pollard, *The wasting of the British economy* (London, 1982).
2 G. Ingham, *Capitalism divided* (London, 1984), R. W. D. Boyce, *British capitalism at the crossroads* (Cambridge, 1987).
3 The City's advantage here is seen as particularly important given the difficulties experienced by agriculture, industry and labour in shaping a strategy to satisfy their more stratified constituents.
4 F. Longstreth, 'The City, industry and the state' in C. Crouch (ed.), *State and economy in contemporary capitalism* (London, 1979).
5 Ingham, *Capitalism divided.*
6 Ibid., p. 232.
7 P. Hall, *Governing the economy* (Oxford, 1986).
8 See Longstreth, 'The City', passim, Ingham, *Capitalism divided,*

pp. 128–50 and Hall, *Governing the economy*, pp.77–9. The emphasis in each case is different, but the core of the argument is essentially similar.

9 The outstanding exceptions are Boyce, *British capitalism*, which deploys an impressive array of evidence regarding City leverage over government, and Y. Cassis, *Les Banquiers Anglais, 1890–1914* (Geneva, 1982) which, although dealing with the issue less directly, offers some important suggestions as to social, economic and political power of the City.

10 See S. Chapman, *The rise of merchant banking* (London, 1984), pp. 150–68.

11 In the case of the Lancashire banks this was the result of many of them having over-extended their cotton accounts during the 'flotation boom' of 1919–21 – their vulnerability being exploited by Montagu Norman in order to bring them under London control. For this development see J. H. Bamberg, 'The government, the banks and the Lancashire cotton industry 1919–35', unpublished Ph.D. thesis, Cambridge University, 1984.

12 For this episode and its significance see M. de Cecco, *Money and empire* (Oxford, 1974), pp. 99–100.

13 Royal Commission on Finance and Industry (hereafter Macmillan Committee): Evidence of Sir Ernest Harvey, 28 November 1929, Q.52, in R. S. Sayers, *The history of the Bank of England*, vol. III (Cambridge 1976), pp. 121–2.

14 Ibid., Q.408, p. 153.

15 Ibid., QQ.96–114.

16 See in particular Cassis, *Les banquiers*. It is, of course, a connection which has survived to the present day. It is, for example, interesting to note that the present Governor, Sir Robin Leigh-Pemberton, was the first to come from a clearing bank.

17 Sayers, *Bank of England*, vol. II, p. 553.

18 For an interesting discussion of the London Chamber's input into the City's life and issues affecting various City interests see S. R. B. Smith, 'British nationalism, imperialism & The City of London', unpublished Ph.D. thesis, London University, 1985.

19 See Chapman, *Merchant banking*, pp. 39–56.

20 Ibid., pp. 150–68, and also appendix 2.

21 Amongst Britain's clearing houses Lloyds and Barclays were already engaged in extensive international operations by the early twentieth century, whilst the larger insurance groups, and here the Phoenix is a good example, were also expanding their overseas business.

22 For this controversy see Sayers, *Bank of England*, vol. I, pp. 235–52.

23 E. G. Compton to Sir E. Bridges, 23 January 1947, PRO, T233/52. I have as yet been unable to unearth the 'voluminous' correspondence between the banks and the Treasury on the subject of the Bank's

nationalization which Compton refers to in this memorandum, but Compton used this correspondence to prepare his memorandum.

24 Currie was Chairman of Glyn, Mills and Currie, London's largest private bank. In the 1890s he was also to be the first president of the Gold Standard Defence Association.

25 Royal Commission on Currency, *Second Report*: evidence of Bertram Currie, 8 July 1887, QQ.6644–6716.

26 For an initial survey of the bimetallic question see E. H. H. Green, 'Rentiers versus producers? The political economy of the bimetallic controversy c. 1880–98', *EHR*, 103 (1988), 588–612, and also the forthcoming debate between Green and A. C. Howe, 'The bimetallic controversy re-opened', *EHR*, 105 (1990).

27 Even the very mild sop thrown to the bimetallists in 1897, whereby the Bank of England agreed in principle to holding one-fifth of the Issue Department's reserves in silver, attracted vehement opposition, the London clearing banks declaring that they 'entirely disapproved', see Committee of London Clearing Banks to Bank of England, 22 September 1897, reproduced in full in Bank of England, Minutes of The Court of Directors Meeting, 23 September 1897, 8 April 1897–4 April 1898, fos. 121–2, Bank of England papers.

28 Donald Moggridge's, *British monetary policy* (Cambridge, 1972), is still the most authoritative treatment of the controversy over the return to gold, although Boyce, *British capitalism* contains the most detailed analysis of the City's support for the policy.

29 As Keynes was to note in 1944, 'the Sterling Area was a brave attempt on our part to maintain the advantages of multilateral clearing to the utmost possible extent', J. M. Keynes to Lord Catto, 6 November 1944, in J. M. Keynes, *Collected works, vol. XXIV: Activities* 1944–6*: the transition to peace* (London, 1979), pp. 162–4.

30 F. Schuster, address to the Institute of Bankers, 16 December 1903, published as 'Foreign trade and the money market', *Monthly Review*, January 1904.

31 H. A. Gwynne to J. Chamberlain, n.d. December 1903, J. Chamberlain papers, Birmingham University Library.

32 See Boyce, *British capitalism*, pp. 214–58.

33 For this development see in particular Cassis, *Les banquiers*, and W. D. Rubinstein, *Men of property* (London, 1981).

34 See Boyce, *British capitalism*, pp. 24–5.

35 I have included in this total the periods 1918–22 and 1931–9 on the basis that the ostensibly coalition governments during those years were dominated by the Conservatives.

36 'Politics and finance', *The Banker's Magazine*, 60, 617 (August 1895), 139–40.

37 J. R. MacDonald to M. Norman, July 1931, cited in P. Williamson, 'A bankers' ramp? Financiers and the British political crisis of August 1931', *EHR*, 99 (1984), 770–806. Williamson's work

demonstrates in exhaustive detail how far it was the control of the flow of information which provided financiers with their ability to persuade the government as to the 'correct' policy course.

38 *Committee of Enquiry on the Working of the Monetary System: Principle Memoranda of Evidence*, vol. III, p. 47: evidence of Sir Edward Bridges.

39 Sayers, *Bank of England*, vol. II, p. 387.

40 For example the British delegation to the 1892 Brussels International Monetary Conference was packed with 'sound' City men. Likewise the City raised a very strong protest when it felt that the Committee appointed to investigate the Indian Currency question in 1898 was 'insufficiently expert', Petition of the 'London Bankers' to the Chancellor, the First Lord of the Treasury, and the Secretary of State for India, n.d. May 1898, Bank of England papers, Misc. Committee of Treasury papers, G 20/4. Further important examples of advisory committees upon which the voice of finance was dominant were the Cunliffe Committee, which recommended the return to gold, the Colwyn Committee, which made recommendations on bank amalgamations in the early 1920s, and the post-1945 Capital Issues Committee.

41 For a description of this relationship from the horse's mouth see especially, Macmillan Committee: evidence of Sir Ernest Harvey, 12 December 1929, QQ. 454–67, in Sayers, *Bank of England*, vol. III, appendix 21 and Grigg, *Prejudice*, p. 56.

42 For a full discussion of the Treasury's self-defined role see P. F. Clarke, 'The Treasury's analytical model of the British economy between the wars', unpublished paper presented to the Washington Economic History Conference, Summer 1988.

43 K. Middlemass, *Power, competition and the state*, vol. I: *Britain in Search of Balance 1940–61*, (London, 1986), pp. 28–9.

44 M. Widdup to F. Lees, 13 January 1958, PRO T233/1410.

45 For confirmation of this point see Clarke, 'Treasury model'.

46 See R. J. B. Anderson (Treasury Solicitor) to W. Armstrong, 5 September 1957, referring to T. Barnes to Sir W. Eady, 15 June 1951, PRO T233/1664.

47 E. G. Compton, Memorandum on control over credit policy, 4 February 1958, PRO T233/58.

48 Clarke, 'Treasury model'.

49 Given the advice which the Treasury had just received from its solicitors this comment was slightly economical with the truth, but the Treasury was very cagey about anyone learning the full fact about the Treasury–Bank relationship. In 1955 the Treasury had refused to assist a Conservative MP, hoping to address the Institute of Bankers about this relationship, on the grounds that 'the whole subject...contains vast stretches of thin ice', I. P. Bancroft to H. Ashton, 21 September 1955, PRO T233/1205. See also Compton's

view that 'it would be inexpedient to reveal the existence of these...opinions to the Radcliffe Committee and so to the Bank and to the public', E. G. Compton to Makins, 10 December 1957, PRO T233/1410.

50 Sir R. Makins, prepared statement for the Radcliffe Committee, September 1957, PRO T233/1407.

51 In early April 1957 Makins saw the Deputy Governor and stressed that the Treasury and the Bank 'should...start from the same base line, using the same geography and history books'. At the same time Makins suggested to Robert Hall and Edmund Compton that they get together with the commercial banks. Makins, memorandum on 'The Monetary Enquiry', 5 April 1957, PRO T233/1407. Later in the same month Hall and Compton went to see the Bank's Chief Cashier, with the result that it was decided that 'our general line is that we should agree with the Bank in our accounts, either in papers for the committee or in evidence to the committee, of what has happened, and in our descriptions of the mechanism', Sir E. Compton, memorandum on 'The Monetary Enquiry', 18 April 1957, PRO T233/1407. There are very interesting parallels between the Treasury–Bank preparations for this enquiry and their collaboration in 1929–30 over the Macmillan Committee, for a detailed description of the Treasury–Bank strategy on that occasion see P. F. Clarke, *The Keynesian revolution in the making* (Oxford, 1988).

52 Sir R. Makins to Lord Cobbold, 17 May 1957, PRO T233/1407.

53 Bank of England, memorandum on 'Some possible modifications in technique', November 1957, PRO T233/1410.

54 Ibid.

55 Ibid.

56 Ibid.

57 See unsigned Treasury memorandum on 'Alternative techniques' (sent to R. Hall and Sir R. Makins), 12 December 1957, PRO T233/1410. Also Sir E. Compton to Sir R. Makins, 13 December 1957, ibid and the Treasury memorandum on 'Alternative techniques: brief for Treasury witnesses to the Radcliffe Committee', 13 January 1958, ibid, all of which accepted the Bank's analysis.

58 Compton to Makins, 13 December 1957, ibid.

59 Unsigned Treasury memorandum on 'Alternative techniques' (sent to R. Hall and Sir E. Compton), 12 December 1957, PRO T233/1410.

60 Treasury memorandum on 'Alternative techniques'.

61 R. Chalmers to T. H. Farrer, 19 November 1898, Farrer papers, London School of economics, vol. 1, fo. 28.

62 Clarke, 'Treasury model', Ingham, *Capitalism divided*.

63 E. W. Hamilton, notes on 'Excess of imports over exports', 28 November 1898, E. W. Hamilton, Private Office paper, PRO T168/39.

64 'The fiscal problem', Unsigned Treasury memorandum (sent to E. W.

Hamilton), 8 August 1903, copy in Steel–Maitland papers, Scottish Record Office, GD 193/88/1/147.

65 See in particular Clarke, 'Treasury model' and Clark, *Keynesian revolution.*

66 R. Hawtrey, notes on 'Sterling and gold', n.d. July 1924, Hawtrey papers, Churchill College, Cambridge, HTRY 1/26.

67 Ibid.

68 Clarke, 'Treasury model'.

69 F. Leith-Ross, Memorandum, 9 August 1928, T172/2095, cited in ibid.

70 Grigg, *Prejudice and judgement*, p. 259.

71 Hall, *Governing the economy*, p. 61.

72 J. M. Keynes, 'Overseas financial policy in stage III' 15 May 1945, in Keynes, *Collected works, vol. XXIV: Activities 1944–6: the transition to peace* (London, 1980), pp. 256–95.

73 Ibid.

74 Grigg, *Prejudice and judgement*, p. 260.

75 J. M. Keynes to Lord Norman, 19 December 1941, in Keynes, *Collected works, vol. XXV: Activities 1940–4: shaping the post-war world: the clearing union* (London, 1980), pp. 98–100.

76 J. M. Keynes, 'Plan for an international clearing union', paras. 64–134 of Treasury memorandum on external monetary and economic problems, 31 March 1942, ibid., pp. 108–39, 123.

77 S. Goldman to R. W. B. Clarke, 3 January 1950, PRO T235/3291.

78 Unsigned Treasury memorandum on 'Exchange control' (sent to J. McKean), 30 September 1955, PRO T233/1205.

12 The political influence of bankers and financiers in France in the years, 1850–1960

HUBERT BONIN

The myth of the omnipresence of the controllers of wealth is ineradicable in France, so evident appears to be the strength of capital: the autonomy of decisions made by politicians seems restricted by a 'wall of money', and major choices in economic policy seem to be imposed by the prime movers of financial capitalism. Civil liberties seem compromised, so great is the influence of the world of finance as it creeps insidiously into a venal press, into the heart of a corrupt parliament, and even into the very core of governments whose ministers maintain too close links with financial spheres. Thus 'crises' break out repeatedly, substantiating these myths as half-political, half-financial scandals reveal the interpenetration of the networks of influence and decision-making.[1] Fact thus confirms belief[2] as 'hidden money' (J. N. Jeanneney) is brought to light. Faced with such an assumption of guilt, historical analysis must pursue its course with care. Research into the world of finance remains fragmentary, the controllers of wealth remain in charge of the preservation of archives,[3] of their accessibility, of selecting which files should be made public and to which readers.

A financial community

It is difficult to isolate the major paths of influence of the world of finance, for it remains an undefined community. If, in the case of industrialists, centres of power and cores of pressure groups have long been identified, in the case of bankers and financiers, structures of collective organization are difficult to uncover. For a long time the profession did not have recourse to organs of the press, to specialized journals, the 'voice' of banking and finance. The Chambre syndicale des banquiers de Paris et de province, the Union syndicale des banquiers (established in 1821), even the Association Professionnelle des Banques, founded at the time of the

Liberation, appeared unwilling to represent their profession, being primarily the administrative organs of those various 'alliances' which ensured the cohesion of the Parisian and provincial markets, particularly by defining the many scales of charges and conditions of banking. The Association Française des Banques was responsible for the negotiations surrounding collective agreements in that field. It was only at the beginning of the 1980s that the Association Française des Banques claimed to be a 'pressure group', with a communications department holding many press conferences and giving out press releases, while the Fédération française des sociétés d'assurances acted in parallel.

Frequenting banking archives and reading about the employers' sphere leads one to think that the world of finance played a minimal role in employers' organizations – the CGPF (Confédération Générale de la Production Française) between the wars, then the CNPF[4] (Confédération Générale du Patronal Français) – even if Roger Lehideux, a partner in the family bank Lehideux, was a member of the committee of the CGPF in the 1930s. But specific groups were established – such as the Association nationale des sociétés par actions, created in 1930 to obtain tax concessions, or from 1950–60, the various associations of credit institutions or investment companies – without, however, calling themselves 'pressure groups' or conducting publicity campaigns.

Even if the world of finance rejected out of prudence the cumbersome system of explicit instruments of representation, the reality of a 'Marketplace' can be recreated. The several hundred decision-makers in financial institutions had many opportunities of discussing different politico-financial points of view amongst themselves, and of defining common positions which each would then undertake to reproduce within his own sphere of operation. This sociability was easily maintained, since the majority of those active in the world of finance came from the same sociological milieu.[5] They had often studied the same subjects and formed links of friendship which the very unfolding of their subsequent careers reinforced: they frequented the same financial administrations, shared the same public or private career profile which, in this case, within the major banks, was the classic 'bank round', or passed through the prestigious finance inspectorate – in short, moved over from government administration to public or private financial companies.

A form of community thinking explains the certain cohesion found in collective mentalities, a relative convergence in the way realities are perceived and in politico-financial reactions which goes beyond differences of temperament and opinion. The training of finance inspectors, before and after their entrance examination, made this easier for them. This immediacy in conveying reactions and opinions was facilitated by the intimacy that existed between the Civil Service and companies: a single generation of decision-makers worked both in the public and the private sectors, increasing the opportunities for official or informal discussions. The younger generation, still confined to the Civil Service, waited for promotion from the older generation to private or, since 1945, nationalized financial concerns.

Through these forms of sociability, its sociology and collective mentalities, the world of finance seemed a relative community, apt to express solidarity and mobilize its networks of influence without needing to endow itself with bodies of representation or to appear a 'pressure group' or even to put pressure on the authorities. However, this relative proximity, indeed this intimacy, did not necessarily lead to unequivocal positions. 'In order to understand the balance of power, it would be a mistake to assume that automatic solidarity from institutional neighbours or family ties is a certainty.'[6]

Does the 'wall of money' exist?

The controllers of wealth had enormous potential for promoting their interests. They claimed to be the holders of stocks of money essential to the life of the country, to be the driving force behind the collecting of money from savers and investors – private, banking or institutional – thus to be tools indispensable to the smooth running of national financial affairs. They could be tempted to set themselves up as counter-powers, indeed almost as the power, by giving posts if not to 'men of straw' then at least to politicians – 'sure and faithful friends' – who had spent part of their careers in business.

The exercise of political power?

The world of finance occasionally intervened directly in the management of the country's affairs, or played a key role in it. Even the new republics opened their management to directors from business. In this way the banker Goudchaux became Minister of Finance in 1848. J. Bouvier[7] examines the essential influence of the business world in the support given to the Republic by numerous members of the centre parties of parliament, oscillating between their taste for the established order and their wish for democratic reforms, heirs to the liberal Orleanism of 1830–60. Among them were men of finance like Say, Germain, the head of the Crédit Lyonnais, or Casimir-Périer: the move to the left of these centrists from June 1874 was a mark of the fear of unrest that the restoration of a reactionary monarchy would incite. The winning over of some Orleanists to the Constitution in 1875 laid the institutional foundations of the regime before these moderates established the right wing of the republican left which came to power in 1876–9. From this fringe of the reformist business milieux came the ironmaster Magnin, promoted to Minister of Finance under Ferry in 1879–81, then Governor of the Banque de France from 1881 to 1897. Thus some of the interests of the financial world were taken into account in defining the Republic's economic policy in the same way as those of industrialists and agriculturalists. Moreover, Say, one of the managers of the Compagnie du Nord in the Rothschild group, was more than once Minister of Finance (in 1877–8 and 1882–3). The opportunist Republic seduced a large proportion of the business world, anxious to find the institutional solution the most propitious to maintaining civil order and thus the tranquility of the business climate.

Thus a lasting tradition was established according to which politicians close to the world of finance, indeed financiers engaged in political life, took up their position on the moderate fringe of the majorities in order to exert a moderating influence and insist on the preservation of the general interest by listening to certain private economic interests. Say's refusal to join Gambetta's 'great ministry' in 1881–2 sealed Gambetta's downfall and, especially, the downfall of the project to nationalize railway companies launched by the republican left. On several occasions the Republic included high-level decision-makers close to the world of finance. The best known is Rouvier, Minister of Finance in 1889–92 and 1902–5, Prime Minister in 1887 and 1905–6, who was also linked to the Marseilles bank at the start of his career before founding the Banque Française pour le Commerce et l'Industrie in 1901. An expert in financial matters, because of his talent and business links, he was employed, like Caillaux, at the heart of the networks of influence which advocated the opening up of France to the tide of international finance. But for Rouvier, this opening up should not be making them dependent on the diplomatic or industrial requirements made by the partisans of a diplomatic and financial policy in keeping with nationalist interests, symbolized by Poincaré.[8] Between the two world wars as well, men close to the world of finance were to be found in the moderate parties, namely the Fédération républicaine, the Union républicaine démocratique and the Alliance démocratique. They welcomed François de Wendel, an industrialist but also Director of the Banque de France, Flandin, a business lawyer, and Rothschild. But no leading politician was again to be found as close to the world of finance, nor indeed to the world of business, as Rouvier or Say, until bankers and financiers reappeared at the forefront of executive power in 1940–4 with the 'Vichy technocrats'.

On many occasions, the political world publicized its proximity to the world of finance. Must we conclude then that there was collusion, that capital triumphed, and that Rouvier, Baudouin or Monnet carried out their duties as financiers in order to conduct a policy expressing particular interests? We could on the other hand conclude that their occupation as men of finance furnished them with contacts useful to their rise and then with experience beneficial to their new tasks, but that these tasks invested them with a public service mission different from their previous or subsequent private responsibilities, as happened to Pompidou when, from running the Rothschild bank, he rose to lead the Cabinet of the Prime Minister, de Gaulle, in 1958, then to the post of Prime Minister in 1962–8. In fact, these were two sections of the 'Establishment' that met and interlinked in the mutual knowledge of having both reached the level of the country's elite, which allowed for a certain toing and froing between them. It was the fact of belonging to a common *bonne bourgeoisie* (A. Daumard) of ability that united these men and facilitated the exchange of responsibilities between the two spheres of finance and politics, without the necessary interference of interests, as integrity and a sense of the general interest prevailed over the ties of friendship and loyalty. One can in no way conclude from this that, even in those specific periods full of the rise of men of finance to top ministerial posts, politicians were subordinate to financiers, that financiers had succeeded in posting 'Trojan horses' within the walls of the regime, be it democratic or Vichyste.

The exercise of monetary and budgetary power?

The proximity of the world of finance in relation to the political apparatus, or the direct role it could have played in it, was an effective influencing factor on certain state economic and financial choices. This was particularly apparent in monetary policy since, until 1936, it could have been claimed that the world of finance exerted a substantial influence in the Banque de France, in particular the 'Haute Banque', many representatives of which were members of the board of directors (*Régents*) of the Central Bank: among the fifteen directors in 1935 there were still six bankers alongside the nine industrialist directors.

It is difficult to assess the balance of power between the wishes of the state or the Governor it appointed and the wishes of the directors, more or less representative of the world of business and finance. The vision of a 'public service' upheld by governors, often expert in law and public finance, coming particularly from the Council of State – in the case of the four governors of 1834–79 – might have been counterbalanced by attitudes closer to the immediate needs of the business world. Would there then have been a 'wall of money' at the heart of the Banque de France, hampering the freedom of the state's monetary actions? It is easy to pinpoint tensions between the two factions during the Second Empire[9]; a Civil Service concerned with an increase in branches, with an increase in the volume of rediscount, was often confronted by directors more interested in discount in the single Parisian market and alert to the risks run by the Central Bank.

The press campaign mounted in 1860–1 by a large proportion of the world of finance, pressure from moderate members of parliament worried by the budget deficit, and the demands of the banker Fould for his return to the Ministry of Finance – with his 'memory of Tarbes' – proving that he had no wish to be a 'senior civil servant charged with facing the consequences of the major decisions of Napoleon III', outlined the establishment of a true pressure group. Fould 'is in a situation largely "independent" of the sovereign's will, and he is assured of the backing of major groups of interests, particularly the Rothschilds. Strengthened by their support, he does not accept that he is simply a servant or an instrument of the State; he is the representative of high finance who claims the right to exert a major influence at the very summit of the State.'[10]

However, the contradictions within the two 'camps' were great. Certainly, the Empire was expansionist, favoured the breakthrough of the Pereire bank and new banks and wished to push back credit limits, and in that it came up against the sensitivity of more traditional bankers. A. Plessis notes the tension in the 1850s between the state's aspirations and the directors' reservations, and, on many occasions, their rigidity. But the state obtained the necessary concessions from them by playing on the threat of the non-renewal of privilege of the issuing bank, or by making use of the directors' wish to prevent the Pereire bank from competing with it. The world of finance had at its disposal means of influence; sometimes it made use of men at the centre of monetary and budgetary power, but it was itself divided, and the state, next to which it claimed to be a pressure group, was in turn far from a solid 'block': hence the delicate equilibrium between tendencies which resulted less in a balance of power than in repeated compromise whereby each accepted modifications in policy. It was less in the name of private interest that the various interveners acted than in the service of their interpretation of the general interest – not conceived of by them as the sum of their private interests – which explains the wide margin of negotiation and reciprocal concessions within the framework of what was basically the same notion of business management. There is nothing to indicate that a 'wall of money' was to encircle the politicians of the Third Republic, as far as it is possible to reconstruct the process of financial decision-making of 1870–1914.

A right of inspection in financial and monetary policy?

The fear of the world of finance's excessive power of influence was reborn in the 1920s. While the left experienced a recovery which reinforced those elements within it more or less in favour of an extension of the state-controlled economy, some sections of the world of finance maintained their adherence to traditional ideas: private enterprise economy and a return to the moderate disequilibrium of pre-1914. The wall of money was to gain ground in the years 1922–8 in the monetary and financial sphere. When pinpointing those speculating against the franc,[11] it must be noted that French interests were added to the banks and foreign markets that were implicated in a diplomatic and financial struggle against France: firms reduced their francs and inflated their currency stocks while banks managed their assets and their clients' investments as best they could. But this speculation began from the second term of 1922 when the right of the 'Bloc national' was in power because of the risk of military tension, and continued until January–March 1924. If this speculation then recovered under the left in 1925–6, it was primarily out of mistrust in the fact of the incompetence, hesitations and divisions of public management: 'International finance' was particularly concerned with preserving the value of its stocks of money. Banks could not be accused of setting themselves up as a threat to the left since they continued to hold and sign large quantities of national defence bonds – which they could present at a discount to the Central Bank – and even protested when, from the second term of 1926, the consolidation of bonds was introduced since this removed liquid funds. The 'wall of money' which then established itself corresponded to the 'wool-stocking plebiscite' concerned about the drift of the Cartel's management and, perhaps, the risk of a majority slide to the left towards the socialists ready for a fiscal increase.

A wall of money against the left?

Opportunities for pressure from groups of interest arose in the very definition of monetary policy. The plurality of centres of decision-making – the Treasury, the Banque de France, the government, influential members of parliament within a fluctuating majority and on the Financial Commission, and ministers – opened the way for diverging points of view and thus for the establishment of a balance of power, however informal. The world of finance did not so much make up a homogeneous pressure group: instead the 'wall of money' was a labyrinth of smaller walls. At the Banque de France, the directors and the Governor were unanimous in denouncing the laxity of the ministerial management, whether the banker François-Marsal, who became Minister of Finance in 1920–1, or the left of 1924–6. Acting against François-Marsal they raised discount and pleaded with Millerand for stringency and his agreement to public borrowing in an attempt to reduce part of the floating debt.

From 1920 to 1926 a number of the directors tolerated Treasury loans out of a wish to keep on good terms or out of an awareness that the only alternative solution would be an austerity impossible to achieve given the diplomatic and financial climate of the time. It was only belatedly that they demanded that the Treasury stand firm: in March 1925, Wendel – at the same time steel industrialist, senator and director of the Banque de France – managed to establish a hesitant majority to ask for the cessation of hidden loans and an increase in the ceiling of official loans, which contributed to the downfall of the Herriot government, already well-worn. In this single case a 'wall of money' could well have arisen. However, parliament voted in favour of raising the ceiling and the world of finance had little to do with the internal dissolution of a Cartel rent by its divisions. However, J. N. Jeanneney points out the upsurge in Wendel's influence, who campaigned within the right wing for a national union run by the centre-right, in the face of similar proposals put forward by the centre-left (Caillaux and Briand): 'It is most evident that the general public is beginning to realize that my position in the URD and the Bank, my friendship with Marin and some other influential people, allow me to cause a certain disruption in the equilibrium. This will not make my developments easy', noted Wendel[12] in June 1926. One must remember, despite the impression given by Wendel's role and that of an informal group of Bank directors, that when, on his return to power, Poincaré asked the Banque de France to rediscount a new package of Treasury bonds, the Governor himself refused on 26 July 1926, while his predecessor Robineau had agreed to a similar request by Poincaré in 1923–4.

Henceforth, Moreau intended to state the autonomy of the Central Bank even if, two days later, he agreed to discount to banks the bonds of a loan which they had made to the Treasury. But was this to raise a wall of money or merely to put the Bank, until then somewhat servile, back within its own walls? 'The discount portfolio leaves a lot to be desired. More than half is made up of bills of liability which goes against the Statute. Political intervention was all-powerful in this matter, as indeed in the recruitment and promotion of staff', noted Moreau[13] on 1 July 1926. Caillaux's promotion of Moreau gave rise to a counter-power, this time stripped of all political implication, contrary to Wendel's action. It cannot then be claimed that Wendel carved out for himself a fief in the board of directors; the directors, concerned with stringency, joined ranks with the Governor, and Wendel no longer seemed to be the leader among them, as the debates on the future of the franc demonstrate.

The gold franc and the wall of money

While the debate on the level at which to fix the franc gathered momentum in 1926–8, a split arose between revaluators – in favour of a return to the gold franc of 1914 – and stabilizers who, with the Central Bank's

economists, wished that having checked the franc's drift, its too strong recovery could be prevented. Thus revalued, it would be as harmful to the economy, through deflation, as to the public debt. The priority was to support economic activity. The market was strongly divided: the classicism of its ideas led it to follow 1925 Anglo-Saxon policy; but realism grew, in particular under the influence of Raymond Philippe, the then driving force behind the Lazard bank. J. C. Debeir suggests that investment banks understood the interests of industrial groups, who were great exporters and thus happy with the depreciation of the franc, better than High Finance, too limited in its activities of managing funds. The stabilizers, influential among the bankers and management of the Banque de France, pressed for a financial agreement with the Anglo-Saxons, as in 1924 when France had been supported by a loan from the Morgan bank. The revaluators benefited from their relations with the stars of the market-place, like Wendel or Rothschild, supported by the press read by economic decision-makers. But, however powerful their influence, each had to recognize the primacy of political power: Poincaré was convinced by the Treasury not to turn to Anglo-Saxon aid, but to attempt a gradual monetary revaluation by buying currency, supported by the repatriation of floating capital. Then, after much hesitation, he decided to reject revaluation: 'Those speculating on the rise of the franc hope to wear down our defence and force us to give up our price of 1924. Their press campaign is intended to move the public and make them believe in the revaluation of the franc. They think they play all the more surely by basing themselves on the personal feeling of the Prime Minister. But we will resist', answered Moreau[14] on 6 May 1927. It was not until 8 June 1928 that Poincaré, the sole ultimate decision-maker, came round to the solution of stabilization.

The groups of influence that weighed heavily on the political and financial life of 1920–8 could at times have checked an evolution and helped determine a political change. However, the groupings of established interests were always changing. Most importantly, they were not in charge of decisions: Caillaux replaced the directors of the Central Bank and the Cartel could raise the ceiling of its loans. The directors themselves were primarily legitimists and, although it pained them to do so, supported the state, except in March 1925. It must be noted, however, that the change in the majority only really occurred in July 1926 and cannot be seen as a direct result of this rejection. The government retained control of its choices, as shown by Poincaré in 1926–8. Certainly, the world of finance circulated much information, advice, even demands; but it was itself divided without a stable majority opinion. Pressure was undeniably applied, even by industrialists. It was, however, the uncertainties and the divisions in government that facilitated the infiltration of the business world's influence. As soon as a majority was established, this infiltration weakened.

The controllers of wealth and industrial policy

From the time when banks were linked to large companies, through their credit or their interests, it has often been imagined that they were in a position to direct the reconstruction of the industrial apparatus, to have control, according to a coherent strategy, over the effort of concentration and rationalization capable of reinforcing the power of the French economy; which calls to mind the relation between 'financial power and industry in France'.[15] Bankers were well placed to compare the changes in their client firms, their balance sheets, their investments, the structure of their capital and their profitability. The links they maintained in the provincial and foreign markets allowed them to sustain comparisons between the companies within a particular field, from one field to another and one country to another. Does this mean they gave in to the temptation to direct 'industrial politics'? Their thoughts on the future of firms are revealed by reading the archives, since the search for solutions that would lead to an improvement in their financial situation often ended in a global reflection on the future of the field, particularly in periods of tension or recession, when bank credit and the financial market laboured to satisfy companies' financial needs.

In the 1920s, the experts, the engineers of studies on banks, indulged at times in ambitious syntheses. E. Bussière has demonstrated the Paribas' capacity to imagine the rationalization of the European iron and steel industry during or after reconstruction, in parallel with the ideas of the Société Générale de Belgique:

> An agreement should exist between banks to stop loans and establish a central company of metallurgical industries whose aim would be to finance those metallurgical companies who accepted the merger and its conditions of financial and technical restructuring. These changes are indispensable, as much to reduce industrial disasters as to equip factories to produce at lower cost... Banks, and in particular investment banks, would play an important role in the reconstruction of firms and the utilisation of available economic means. To this end they would have to follow the running of these firms very closely... There would have to be an agreement between the banks only to finance those companies who accepted the merger and its conditions of a financial and technical restructuring...

dreamed this director of the Paribas.[16]

However, bankers remained dependent on the goodwill of contractors, the 'captains of industry'. E. Bussière[17] pertinently described the attempts of some bank directors to imagine a bringing together of French and Belgian companies in the iron, steel and metallurgical industries, oil and electromechanics. If Paribas, like the Société Générale de Belgique, at times caused a merger between firms, it could not claim to be their guide. It was the strongest companies that instituted trends which the banks cooperated with, from within the shareholders' 'round tables'. Moreover, Paribas, not wishing to increase share-taking, reduced a number of its fixed assets in the 1930s. Its deep roots in the iron and steel industry prevented it from becoming the spearhead of the necessary rallying of French forces, whether between the wars or in the years 1950–60. Its rival, the BUP (Banque de l'Union Parisienne), also found itself at the centre of several fields (the car industry, public works) from 1920–30, through strong lending or high interest, but did not claim to be the spur behind restructuring.[18]

An investment bank could offer opportunities for debates, research and meetings between eventual partners, as Paribas did in the electrochemical industry in 1960–70. It could be the keystone of these alliances, heading, as arbiter, the 'round tables' established between the co-investors when firms merged. It could strike its fist on the table to underline the financial risk presented by an industrial solution, as Paribas was to do at the beginning of the 1960s faced with the fall in the computing firm Bull's accounts.[19] But, for investment banks to set themselves up as the driving force behind industrial rationalization, this rationalization would have to occur. Bankers did not attempt to take the place of public authorities in defending industrial plans; the power of money did not take the place of political power, despite the latter's recurrent paralysis.[20] The initiative remained in the hands of the contractors, whose taste for fiefs maintained the dispersal of the means of production: the 'wall of money' could not vanquish the Vauban-style fortifications of the 'captains of industry'.

A 'wall of money' against the indiscreet

On the other hand, for a long time the 'wall of money' managed to preserve the daily life of bankers from the indiscreet gaze of politicians. These bankers benefited from a totally liberal environment in which to conduct their business right up until the 1940s! If commercial and fiscal legislation imposed banal rules, the banking profession avoided all specific legislative framework. A sub-committee on credit organization was set up in 1936 but came to nothing in 1940. The Occupation led to the creation of the *Comité d'organisation des banques* in September 1940, presided over by the head of the Société Générale. Then, in June 1941, the *Commission de contrôle des banques* was born, with the Governor of the Banque de

France, the Director of the Treasury, the President of the financial department of the Council of State, bankers and trade-unionists. From 1945 the *Commission*, the Conseil National de Crédit, the Banque de France, the Treasury and a large number of by-laws brought down the wall of banking secrecy. Liberalism which was won in the years 1860–80 – with the gradual liberalization of the general statutes of companies (the law of 1867 amended in 1893) and of the particular statutes of certain new major banks – triumphed so long as banks experienced a period of serene expansion, even if the debts from overdue payments in 1914–18 and the ban on the export of capital in 1918–28 hampered their activity. Members of parliament and ministers called for banking regulations, private bills were put forward in the Chamber, extra-parliamentary committees or committees of enquiry proposed suggestions for reform, and in 1925–9 the socialists nurtured the idea of a higher council of banks, exchanges and companies. Freedom triumphed, as Poincaré said:

> If fiscal control is possible – the current one is stringent – a technical control, a general control, a banking control would be singularly more complicated. It would have to adapt to extremely varied situations, given the considerable differences that exist between the operations of a deposit bank and those of an investment bank. Moreover, a control enforced by civil servants could lead the public and bankers to fear a kind of stranglehold of agents of the State over private commerce.[21]

However, during the crisis of the 1930s, it was worries over the future of the market and the fate of investment, rather than polemics on the 'wall of money', that threw members of parliament and certain financial and professional specialists into panic. Ideas were broached to institute a control over bank accounts, a parliamentary commission on banks was established in 1936 to study the development of the banking crisis of 1931–5.[22] But it was the conjunction of the collapse of their field and their political reputation that forced bankers to resign themselves to the dismantling of the wall of financial secrecy that had existed for six or seven decades.[23]

The wall of money, a paper tiger?

The first breaches

The capacity that the controllers of wealth had for resistance should have expressed itself forcibly at those key moments in the state-controlled offensive to hinder the plans of the public authorities. However, the 'wall of money' crumpled like a piece of paper: the world of finance did not intervene as such in the movement that rebelled in reaction against the Popular Front, except by making allusive criticisms in the reports of the boards of directors to the general assemblies of 1937. Despite the Liberals' appeals to parliament, Wendel's in the Senate and those of large shareholders during the final General Assembly, the Banque de France saw its statutes toppled by the left in July 1936. Certainly, the replacement of some of the directors by the state (Banque de France and Banque de l'Indochine) in 1936 was answered in 1937 by the dismissal of the Director General of the Paribas, Horace Finaly, by its board of directors on which the former Governor of the Central Bank, Moreau, had recently become President; yet I. Kolboom reveals no action on the part of the bankers in his *Revanche des patrons.*[24]

The double momentum created by nationalizations did not seem to break up against the barbicans constructed by the world of finance. Admittedly, the representatives of the owners of railway companies negotiated step by step the terms of their depossession, which occurred in 1937; but divisions were rife, particularly among the members of the nationalizing camp, according to the conditions each envisaged.[25] The influence of men of finance was then essential since the Compagnie du Nord, with Rothschild and Mayer, appeared to be the leader of the railway firms. 'Nationalisation... was accepted and even to a certain extent desired by the management, who had no wish to continue to bear, for very little profit, the burden of responsibility for a company whose costs depended on decisions which escaped them totally. Politically, it was in the interests of the ensemble of French employers that its opponents should no longer have at their disposal a target for their attacks', underlined F. Caron.[26] The controllers of wealth lost one of their prize possessions but preserved the 'private sector', their financial interests and their shares, not reclaimed by the SNCF. In the final analysis, under the Popular Front, they only lost supreme power within the Banque de France – but they kept their shares – as well as their power and their 51 per cent in the railways. The 'wall of money' was not high, but was this not because its assailants made few demands?

Walled-in money (1945)

On the other hand, faced with the virulence of its assailants at the Liberation, the response of the controllers of wealth should have been severe. However, the political circumstances of the nationalizations of 1945–6 were such that the world of finance, as indeed did the body of employers, felt somewhat 'in a corner'.[27] Faced with the line of social and political forces that had been drawn up, it could only give in. Despite everything, it did have a margin of manoeuvre, through the bias of a number of administrators at the Ministry of Finance open to moderate solutions that would avoid shocking their own liberal attitudes and damaging the credit of France with savers and, more importantly, the international markets. The sociological and ideological proximity of the directors of banks and those of the Ministry of Finance could then have been an asset for the former. At the very heart of the 'enemy' camp were many influential political figures linked to the world of finance. This was the case among the 'moderates' of the majority with Pleven, a former banker, Minister of Finance, follower of de Gaulle and member of the centre-left UDSR (Union Démocratique et Socialiste de la Résistance); also Burlot, an MRP (Mouvement Républicain Populaire) member of parliament, Treasurer of his party but also President of an important insurance company, the Paternelle, who was close to Louvel, Director of a public works company, President of the *Commission de la production et de l'équipement* and a colleague in the MRP of Schuman, President of the *Commission des Finances*. However, the MRP had not put forward a nationalization bill; it was content to hope for an increase in state control and the state's approval of the nomination of banking chiefs.

No influential group could establish itself, particularly since the private reactions of the world of finance were difficult to grasp. J. N. Jeanneney only indicates the employers' concern with 'gaining time' in their calls for preparatory studies. Would it have been possible to mobilize the mass of shareholders in the name of 'popular capitalism', since the four major nationalized deposit banks attracted 400,000 shareholders? In December 1946, the Banque de France, the Banque d'Algérie, deposit banks and, in April 1946, thirty-four insurance companies were nationalized without meeting any resistance. Striking only one bargain would have allowed Burlot to have his Paternelle excluded from the list by the socialists.

The conditions of maintaining the two investment banks Paribas and the BUP (Banque de l'Union Parisienne) in the private sector remained vague, all the more so because Pineau, secretary of the Fédération des employés de banque, had been dismissed by Paribas in November 1938 and was the socialist spokesman of the bill proposed in November 1945. As early as November–December, the government rallied behind investment banks, under the leadership of Pleven, whose position was described in the statement of the law's aims: 'On national territory itself, merchant banks can only assume their duties if they preserve the spirit of initiative and the drive necessary to renew an ageing and exhausted economy. Nationalisation, whatever its form, would certainly not leave them with the power to fulfil this role.' The pro-nationalization *Commission des Finances* came round to this position since it decided against modifying the bill and thus rejected constraining the government to confrontation by calling for a second reading of the bill by members of parliament.

With neither pressure from an influential group nor the complicit action of some 'Trojan horses' within the majority, the non-nationalization of investment banks was inscribed in a clear philosophy: the state wanted to put an end to the power of money by controlling credit; but it did not want to become the sole investor in the country and, therefore, had to let financial companies, investment banks and other investment companies live. The state nationalized 'circulating capital', deposit banks and insurance companies, but not 'fixed capital'. Far from submitting to the 'wall of money', it trimmed with its own hands the hedges of this French financial garden of mixed economy designed at the time of the Liberation. The 'wall of money' thus turned out to be a paper tiger: it found no influential group to defend the world of finance; political will had been enough to defeat the controllers of wealth and, indeed, to reject the moderate projects proposed by the directors of the Ministry of Finance regarding the nationalization of insurance companies.

A mixed management of the financial market

The unearthing of indications of collusion between finance and politics, of the successful use of pressure and of networks of influence led by the controllers of wealth, thus remained deceptive since no connection seemed to appear. On the one hand was expressed rather a wish for independence from the state; on the other a wish that demonstrated, when necessary, the primacy of politics. It would, however, be naive to think that the power of influence of the world of finance was non-existent. However, it would seem fallacious to discern it within a balance a power that sought to establish a relationship in which politics was dependent on money, and the general interest was dependent on private interest. In effect, it was in the common management of the general interest that the political or the administrative interest and private interests often met, to manage the interests of the market.

Financiers wanted reforms that would broaden their market and clientele, increase their profits, diversify and improve financial techniques – in other words the 'practices' of the market. The state wanted to enlarge the basis of its collection of resources, to benefit from the advances in financial techniques which would contribute to economic development and increase its fiscal revenue. Both sides were concerned with maintaining confidence, with the market's credit, with whether the market had to be saved from the threat of collapse and crash; or whether financial innovations would cause uncertainty detrimental to the tranquility of the market and of savers. The government's fear was that 'public faith' would be compromised, that money would no longer make good the budgetary deficit and service the national debt. The two parties sought less confrontation and the victory of the one over the other, than shared success. The balance of influence played a part within the framework of this conception since the debate then turned to the technical means of implementing a common project.

The dependence of the state on the financial world: the expertise of the financial world

This approach did not ignore the possibility of the ascendency of the world of finance. The public authorities had long needed the expertise of specialists in financial affairs to complement the talents of top civil servants and academics. Was the general interest then only explained by the opinions of representatives of the private interests? The government thus established a Committee of Experts in 1926 on which there were several bankers. Were the abilities of the Treasury then inadequate, requiring experts to assess a new situation? Or did the state simply require the caution of experts to convince political bodies and the electorate of the need for a solution which each group sensed was called for? In fact, there was as yet no solution, and the Committee's report was submitted in July 1926, only just in time to outline the policy of the new Poincaré government.

The influence of experts seemed paramount. Banking archives show that, particularly between the two world wars, bank directors often held discussions with the Minister of Finance over financial issues that went beyond the simple framework of immediate private interest, for the banks remained invested with a prestigious power of expertise, which explains the nominations of Fould, Say and François-Marsal as Minister of Finance, even if this practice disappeared from 1924 to 1960. The same recourse to banking 'grey matter' inspired the market reformers in the 1960s: a number of expert committees were established in which bankers played a key role, as on the *Commission de financement du Plan* and particularly the *Comité Lorain* – the head of the Société Générale – which in 1963 suggested reforming the banking system and inspired the Debré-Haberer reforms of 1966–8. Bankers, insurers, the Banque de France and top civil servants thus formed a community of thought which aimed at the common promotion of private interests and expansion.

The affirmation of state autonomy in relation to the world of finance

A 'public world of money' affirmed its autonomy in relation to the private world of money as much by its financial strength as by its capital of expertise. In the 1920s, the technical teams of the Banque de France expanded, a movement that increased in momentum after the nationalizations of 1945 and the attribution to the Central Bank of the role of guardian of the market. From then onwards, the duo of the Treasury and the Banque de France became the key to monetary policy and credit.[28] At its centre was the gradual implementation between 1934–8 and the period following the war of a 'Treasury circuit' which allowed the state to dispose of essential resources without depending too much on the goodwill of savers, bankers and the market. From February 1936, the Banque de France, moving from commercial rediscount to financial rediscount, officially discounted banks their Treasury bonds. After the war, the issue of bonds by the Caisse des Dépôts, the mobilization of its equivalents by the Treasury, the placing of state assets with insurance companies who had to maintain a ceiling for their assets in bonds, the fixing of ceilings for Treasury bonds for banks in 1948, the close relations between nationalized banks and the Treasury which facilitated short-term loans, all contributed to encourage the flow of the money supply into public coffers.

The Treasury, similarly provided with missions to breathe new life into the economy and investment, became a controller of wealth, 'a power machine',[29] and an efficient counter-power to the Banque de France, in a duality better balanced than that of the nineteenth century. Their collaboration at times reduced the banks' margin of manoeuvre, particularly during periods of control or limiting of credit; the dismissal of the President of the Crédit Lyonnais in 1974 appearing perhaps as sanctioning a disregard for monetary orders.[30] The controllers of wealth no longer formed the traditional triangle of High Finance, the major banks and the Banque de France; instead they formed a square: private banks, public banks, the Banque de France, and the Treasury and Caisse des Dépôts. This complexity tended to diminish further the notion of a 'balance of power' in the framework of a common and stable management of the market.

The co-management of the market: the protection of the market

> At the government's request, we have, in conjunction with Messres Lazard Frères, carried out a study of the reorganization of A. Citroën Ltd. This study has served as the basis for establishing a plan for whose realization Messres Lazard Frères and ourselves have been happy to hand over our examination to the Maison Michelin.[31]

This commission by the Paribas in 1935 indicated the first area open to the joint action of different financial powers: what was important was to guarantee the smooth running of the market, to check any crisis of confidence among depositors, savers and investors, particularly in the crisis years favourable to a crash. This caused the Banque de France to support the Comptoir d'Escompte de Paris in collapse in 1889, with the guarantee of other banks, and it intervened a second time in 1914 to support the unsteady Société Générale. If, in these two cases, the motivating force behind these decisions is little known, by contrast, between the world wars, the links that led to collective attempts to keep threatened institutions afloat were rebuilt. The executive authority, the Banque de France – who initiated the action in January 1921 – and a consortium of fifty-five banks thus mobilized to keep the Société centrale des banques de province, a Parisian manifestation of numerous regional institutions, afloat. At the time of the crash of the Banque Nationale de Crédit, the fourth largest deposit bank,[32] the Banque de France rediscounted the commercial bills with the guarantee of banks and the state in September 1931. However, it was at the highest level on 25 and 26 September, during meetings between Flandin, Minister of Finance, the Director of the Movement général des fonds (the Treasurer), the heads of the major banks and the Governor of the Central Bank, that the state's guarantee was decided after an interministerial meeting with Laval. The continuing run on deposits and the hesitations of banks conferred a key role on the Treasury in safeguarding a market made gangrenous by the succession of major bank crises, more especially as the panic-struck ministers feared that the government would be put in an embarrassing position in front of the Chamber with elections only a few months away. It reimbursed depositors 2,075 million francs (5,075 million francs at present value) at the end of September and beginning of October 1931, then organized in January 1932 the replacement of the Banque Nationale de Crédit by the Banque Nationale pour le Commerce et l'Industrie. From then on a 'Market solidarity' was defined whose implementation involved bankers, the Central Bank, the Treasury and often the Minister of Finance's Cabinet.

The modernization of the market

This market community blossomed under its common definition of the 'products' and techniques which would enable the modernization of financial markets. At the end of the 1920s, the acuteness of the European economic war explained the reflections on financial instruments proposed to firms. It was thus, in response to the wishes of the Minister of Trade and of Poincaré in 1926–7 and to the aspirations of exporting firms, that insurers, bankers and top civil servants perfected legislation for credit insurance of exports (with the guarantee of the state in 1928) and the creation of the Société Française d'Assurance-Crédit in 1927, the perfect expression of this convergence between the public and private sectors around a project of general interest.[33] The same modernizing spirit inspired the work which led to the formation of the Banque Nationale Française du Commerce Extérieur in 1920, the Banque Française d'Acceptations in 1929 and, at the end of the 1920s, to establishments specializing purely in medium-term credit, through companies common to several banks wishing to share the risks since the Central Bank did not rediscount claims made in this way.

It was to the ancestors of the 'market institutions' created since the war that the market entrusted the tasks of increasing specialized credit, either because it was less costly to concentrate the training of competent teams with them, or because public money – the state, the Banque de France, the nationalized banks – had to have a share in the capital or in the contributions of interest bonuses, or finally because banks wished to share their risks. Thus the Banque Française du Commerce Extérieur was created in 1946, the Crédit National evolved, first founded in 1919 but reconstituted during the second period of Reconstruction, and the Caisse Nationale des Marchés de l'Etat was set up in 1936. In the same way the groups of J. Francès (the future Compagnie La Hénin) and J. de Fouchier (Compagnie Bancaire)[34] were launched, in which the market's banks met in types of 'clubs' to support the setting up of 'specialized credit' (housing, consumer spending, capital investment).

This co-management of the market's 'mixed financial economy' was emphasized in the establishment of techniques that would enlarge the money markets. Each time, the market worked out a common legislative and statutory framework that would allow the 'product' to be born, to develop in healthy conditions, respectful of the interests of the Inland Revenue and of investment, and then to be improved. It was the era of continuous bargaining, of increased working hours within the committees of experts representing each profession and within public–private committees. Private interest groups and ministers discussed together the legal and legislative position of each technique. Was this 'administration by milieu' merely an outgrowth of financial companies (public or private)? Sometimes it was the government that wished to stimulate a sector of the market and solicited it, as with financial companies destined to finance oil exploration or overseas development; sometimes a market establishment felt a need for or sensed the usefulness of a technique, as did M. Lauré, President of the Crédit National, when he argued in favour of credit-leasing; sometimes inventive teams created 'products' that they presented to the authorities for their approval and which the whole market would later often improve, as did J. de Fouchier with bonds convertible into shares.

Can one believe, moreover, that the state could allow itself to be 'colonized' by financial specialists while its own services were often the breeding ground for those institutions with which it was negotiating? The state's concern was to inflate the money market, to attract savers and investors in order for them to take over from the Treasury – the 'banker of the economy' – of the period of Reconstruction and to be able to respond to the explosion in financial needs as they appeared during the preparatory work on the Fourth, Fifth and Sixth Plans. The state had a formidable weapon at its disposal in the Treasury's 'approval', often indispensable for the launch of financial companies, and in the omnipotence of the Inland Revenue, the ultimate sovereign of accounting rules. This incessant legal and financial negotiation explains the increase in specific articles of financial law and regulations which, every year, the money markets refined. Their implementation at the end of the 1960s and the beginning of the 1970s opened the way for many partnerships and the whole market became one great 'planning office'.

An all-powerful septet?

A capitalism of mixed financial economy flourished where, rather than a balance of power between private interests and the general interest, the search for a common economic interest dominated, within the framework of a quasi-financial 'neo-corporatism', what P. L. Birnbaum called 'the technocratic directing space'. The risk then arose of this system's domination over political power which, freed from the influence of the controllers of wealth, would be subjugated to the guardianship of technostructures set up with control of public or parapublic money; a septet of finance inspectors – the Director of the Treasury, the Governor of the Banque de France, the Director of the Caisse des Dépôts, the Presidents of the four major private deposit banks, later nationalized in 1945 – would become the master of the market.

Directing his socialist observations at the world of money in the 1930s, Auriol feared that the constraints of the struggle against a market crash would lead to domination by the controllers of wealth, set up as a final recourse. The safeguarding of several banking firms, industrial or tertiary, revealed the key role played by the Caisse des Dépôts,[35] solicited to bring in capital, the Banque de France and some bankers. The duo of the Banque de France and the Caisse des Dépôts appeared to Auriol as the affirmation of an original financial capitalism with the birth of a financial world on the fringe of the public and the private, creating a centre of financial power likely to disrupt the government's decision-making ability. This change was symbolized by Tannery, all the more so because he was promoted to the head of the Banque de France in 1934–5. The financial indecision or incompetence of politicians led to the increase of this centre's responsibilities in 1931–6 – which explains Auriol's vigilance in 1936 and the immediate replacement of the Governor of the Banque de France.

The setting up of this 'technostructure' led by a virtuous 'septet' seemed irreversible. The world of finance consisted from then on of several spheres of power: to the dual power of politics and private finance was added the pole of public finance with, at its core, a Treasury that was both the source of executive power and the breeding ground for directors of parapublic financial power. The problem of the political influence of the financial world was overturned since, from then on, it was politics, or at least its outgrowth, the financial public sector, that became a financial world in itself with strong periods when a representative of this public financial technostructure rose to the Ministry of Finance, like Baumgartner who passed from the Treasury to the Banque de France, then to the Ministry in 1960–2, or J. P. Fourcade in 1974–6. From then on, analyses of the games of influence and balances of power between the players of the market came within the framework of reflections on the decision-making within the economic apparatus of the state.

Conclusion

At the risk of appearing naive, it could be claimed that the power of the financial world is illusory. Its means of influence can easily be contained; what is important is its power of expertise and its ability to raise resources for the state. But the former has not prevented political power from preserving its autonomy of decision, and the state has not lacked the latter, even if the Banque de France has often shown its reservations; and, little by little, a stable 'Treasury circuit' has been established. What is truly at stake is the management of the market, its constant supply of money, its expansion in the face of other markets and the needs of the economy and the state, the upkeep of its credit and the confidence of savers and investors. However, in the recurrent negotiations linked to the crises or demands of modernization and the adaptation of techniques and practices, numerous parties are involved: the world of private finance experienced divisions; the Banque de France was a dual institution for a long time with its directors, themselves without a net majority, and its Governor; and finally, the trend for public money increased little by little, diversifying opportunities for divergence. Politics' margin of manoeuvre was preserved, indeed heightened, when the range of proposed solutions increased. Private interests showed themselves to be strangely malleable and submissive when, in the name of the general interest, public authorities appropriated for themselves a proportion of the controllers of wealth's inheritance. The bustle of the market has most often united in a common task the representatives of private interests and those responsible for the 'general interest', since the former can only exist if the latter is satisfied.

Notes

1 See chapter 14, 'L'argent mythique', pp. 225–39 (with selective bibliography), in Hubert Bonin, *L'argent en France depuis 1880, Banquiers, financiers et épargnants dans la vie économique et politique* (Paris, 1989).
2 Pierre Birnbaum, *Le peuple et les gros. Histoire d'un mythe* (Paris, 1979); René Sédillot, *Les deux cents familles* (Paris, 1989); Anatole France, *L'Ile aux Pingouins* (Paris, 1908).
3 Bonin, 'L'histoire et les historiens face aux archives de la banque', in Maurice Hamon and Félix Torres (eds.), *Mémoire d'avenir. L'Histoire dans l'entreprise* (Paris, 1987).
4 Henri Weber, *Le parti des patrons. Le CNPF (1946–1986)* (Paris, 1986); Bernard Brizay, *Le patronat, Histoire, structure, stratégie du CNPF* (Paris, 1975); Henry Ehrmann, *La politique du patronat français, 1936–1955* (Paris, 1959); Jean Maynaud, *Les groupes de pression en France* (Paris, 1958).
5 Birnbaum, *La classe dirigeante française* (Paris, 1978), and *Les sommets de l'Etat* (Paris, 1977); Nathalie Carré de Malberg, 'Le recrutement des inspecteurs des Finances de 1892 à 1946', *Vingtième siècle. Revue d'histoire*, 8, October 1985, pp. 67–91.
6 Jean-Noël Jeanneney, *L'argent caché. Milieux d'affaires et pouvoirs politiques dans la France du vingtième siècle* (Paris, 1981).
7 J. Bouvier, 'Aux origines de la IIIe République: les réflexes sociaux des milieux d'affaires', *Revue historique*, 1953, reprinted in Bouvier, *Histoire économique et histoire sociale* (Geneva, 1968); Bouvier, *Le Crédit Lyonnais (1863–1882)* (Paris, 1961).
8 Bonin, *L'argent en France*, pp. 111–15.
9 A. Plessis, *La politique de la Banque de France de 1851 à 1870* (Geneva, 1985).
10 See Plessis, *La politique de la Banque de France, passim.*
11 Jean-Claude Debeir, 'La crise du franc de 1924', *Relations internationales*, 13, Spring 1978, and 'Inflation et stabilisation en France (1919–1928)', *Revue économique*, 13, July 1980; Jeanneney, 'La spéculation sur les changes comme arme diplomatique (1924)', *Relations internationales*, 13, Spring 1978, reprinted in *L'argent caché*, 'La première bataille du franc (novembre 1923-mars 1924)', *Relations internationales*, 13, Spring 1978, and *François de Wendel en République. L'argent et le pouvoir, 1914–1940* (Paris, 1976).
12 Cited by Jeanneney, *François de Wendel.*
13 E. Moreau, *Souvenirs d'un Gouverneur de la Banque de France. Histoire de la stabilisation du franc, 1926–1928* (Paris, 1954).
14 Ibid.
15 Bertrand Bellon, *Le pouvoir financier et l'industrie en France* (Paris, 1980); François Morin, *La structure financière du capitalisme français*

(Paris, 1975), and *La banque et les groupes industriels à l'heure des nationalisations* (Paris, 1977); Mahmed Sagou, *Paribas. Anatomie d'une puissance* (Paris, 1981).

16 Eric Bussière, 'Les banquiers ont-ils voulu assumer le contrôle de l'économie au lendemain de la première guerre mondiale?', working paper, University of Paris 4, 1988.

17 Bussière, 'Les relations entre la France et la Belgique dans les rivalités économiques et financières en Europe (novembre 1918-mars 1935)', Ph.D. thesis, University of Paris 4, 1988.

18 Bonin, 'Les banques face au cas Citroën (1919–1930). Essai d'appréciation de la puissance bancaire', *Revue d'histoire moderne et contemporaine*, 32, January–March 1985, and 'Les banques ont-elles sauvé Citroën (1933–1935)? Réflexions sur la marge d'initiative bancaire', *Histoire, Economie, Société*, 3, 1984; Michel Bauer and Elie Cohen, *Qui gouverne les groupes industriels? Essai sur l'exercice du pouvoir du et dans le groupe industriel* (Paris, 1981); Jean Padioleau, *Quand la France s'enferre. La politique sidérurgique de la France depuis 1945* (Paris, 1981).

19 Bonin, 'L'informatique française en quête d'entrepreneurs et de marchés (1963–1983)', *Revue historique*, 280/1, 567, 1988.

20 E. Cohen, *L'Etat brancardier. Politiques du déclin industriel (1974–1984)* (Paris, 1989).

21 R. Poincaré, Prime Minister, in the journal *Banque*, August 1929.

22 Maurice Ansiau, 'Evolution du crédit et contrôle des banques', *Revue d'économie politique*, November 1934; Pierre Cauboué, *Philosophie de la banque* (Paris, 1931).

23 Claire Andrieu, 'Genèse de la loi du 13 juin 1941, première loi bancaire française (septembre 1940–septembre 1941)', *Revue historique*, April–June 1983, and *Les banques sous l'Occupation. Paradoxes de l'histoire d'une profession* (Paris, 1990).

24 Ingo Kolboom, *La revanche des patrons. Le patronat français face au Front populaire* (Paris, 1986).

25 François Caron, *Histoire de l'exploitation d'un grand réseau. La Compagnie du chemin de fer du Nord (1846–1937)* (Paris-La Haye, 1973), pp. 542–55; Georges Ribeill, 'Y a-t-il eu des nationalisations avant la Guerre? La nationalisation des chemins de fer (1937): rupture et continuité', in C. Andrieu, Lucette Levan-Lemesle and Antoine Prost (eds.), *Les nationalisations de la Libération. De l'utopie au compromis* (Paris, 1987).

26 Caron, *Histoire de l'exploitation d'un grand réseau.*

27 Jeanneney, 'Le patronat au piquet (septembre 1944–janvier 1946)', *Revue historique*, 1980, reprinted in *L'argent caché.*

28 Andrieu, 'A la recherche de la politique du crédit 1946–1973', *Revue historique*, March 1984; Henri Koch, *Histoire de la Banque de France et de la monnaie sous la IVe République* (Paris, 1983).

29 Yves Mamou, *Une machine de pouvoir. La Direction du Trésor* (Paris, 1988).

30 Jean Saint-Geours, *Pouvoir et finance* (Paris, 1979).

31 Annual report of the board of directors of the Paribas, 21 April 1936.

32 Bonin, 'La Banque Nationale de Crédit. Evolution et rôle économique (1913–1932)', Ph.D. thesis, University of Paris 10, 1978.

33 Bonin, *SFAC (Société Française d'Assurance-Crédit). Soixante ans au service des entreprises (1927–1987)*, internal document of the SFAC (Paris, 1987).

34 Bonin, *Suez Du Canal à la Finance (1858–1987)* (Paris, 1987) (for the J. Francès group included in *Suez*); J. de Fouchier, *La banque et la vie* (Paris, 1989).

35 Jean-Marie Thiveaud, *Caisse des Dépôts et consignations, 1816–1986*, Dossiers CDC (Paris, 1988); Roger Priouret, *La Caisse des Dépôts, 150 ans d'histoire financière* (Paris, 1966).

13 Banks and banking in Germany after the First World War: strategies of defence

GERALD D. FELDMAN

Well before historians interested in the economic growth of late-developing nations celebrated the contributions of German banks to German industrial development and other historians raised questions about how long the universal banks of the German type played the key role ascribed to them by Hilferding, Lenin and Gerschenkron, German economic commentators cast a very sober look at the historical course being taken by Germany's bankers and banking system. Not perchance, some of the most significant observations were made at the end of 1923, when a near decade of profound economic instability brought on by war, revolution and inflation was coming to its tumultuous end and the time for an effort at genuine accounting had begun.

Thus, the editor of *Plutus*, Georg Bernhard, in an article of December 1923, had no doubt about the fact that Germany's extraordinary economic development in the past century had:

> firstly to be ascribed to the fruitful activity of the great German universal banks.... This achievement of the German banks, to have created a rich capitalistic cultural nation out of an unfruitful, barren soil in a surprisingly short period must be repeatedly emphasized in the face of the many attacks which have been made against the German banking system for decades.

And yet, he also felt obligated to say that 'the majority of German banks, since they had grown beyond a certain extent, have distanced themselves further and further from the pioneering activity of their first decades'. Enterprising bankers of the old stamp had given way to administrators, and, even before the war, the initiative had been seized by 'flexible industrialists'. Especially after the war, the banks had ceased to 'place their stamp on industrial and economic life'. Bernhard was particularly critical of their failures in the inflation. They had refused to recognize

Germany's severe capital shortage and, in their unpreparedness and unwillingness to deal with it, had promoted the inflationary discounting of commercial bills when the credit crisis hit, and had then resisted sensible and timely reform of the currency. The most that could be said for them is that they had profited as best they could from the various speculative practices of the inflation and had thereby functioned as participants in rather than determiners of events.[1]

Alfred Lansburgh, writing from a rather different perspective at the same time, also sharply criticized the banks, not only for going along with the inflationary policies of the Reichsbank and government, but also for 'betraying' their customers by failing to assist them in efforts to protect themselves against the currency depreciation. Instead, according to Lansburgh, the banks placed their resources at the disposal of the government's abrogation of the confidentiality of bank accounts in its efforts to get information for revenue purposes and participated in implementing onerous foreign exchange regulations that deprived customers of resources needed for legitimate economic purposes. As a result, according to Lansburgh, these customers turned away from the banks, hoarded their money and sought the services of dubious new banks set up to deal in foreign exchange. Bernhard did not share this anti-statist posture, but the two writers did agree and sharply criticized the banks for seeking to make up for lost capital and deposits through excessively high interest rates and charges on credits and very low rates on deposits. Once stabilization came, the true loss of capital compared with the pre-war period was evident, and Lansburgh saw the future of German banking quite bleakly:

> Thus the position of the banks in the economy has been fundamentally transformed. They are no longer, as before the war, the rulers of a great, united, and tightly organized money market... but nothing more than the administrators of that portion of the national surpluses which others, in the steaming hot house of the organizations created in the war and inflation, have left over for them.[2]

These are dismal and somewhat confusing pictures of the condition of Germany's banking industry on the brink of Weimar Germany's brief stabilization, a period during which most historians would agree that the banks regained a substantial amount of influence because of the capital shortage and would even go so far as to designate it as an 'era of the bankers'.[3] Neither Bernhard nor Lansburgh really offer any viable alternatives for the past behaviour of the banks, let alone suggest that one was on the brink of a restoration of banker power and influence. For the historian dealing with the interwar period, this nascent 'era of the bankers' raises the question of how the banks and bankers positioned themselves and/or became positioned to play the powerful – and unsuccessful – role that ended in the banking crisis of 1931, and it is the argument of the discussion which follows that this was achieved by the strategies of defence they adopted between 1918 and 1923 as well as the condition in which this left them when the inflation ended.

In attempting to present a picture of German banking and bankers during this period, it is useful to begin with a number of caveats. First, research on German banking is still in its infancy, and much remains to be done by way of discovering and exploiting primary source materials. Second, what we know beyond official bank publications and statistics of often limited value is very much determined by the prominence of the banks and bankers, that is, those who spoke out most frequently and chose to 'represent' the banking community. Even here, the most widely quoted and cited bankers were anything but united in their views and opinions on important subjects. Third, 1918–23 was a very chaotic period, in which a burst of inflation in the fall and winter of 1919–20 was followed by a relative stabilization from the spring of 1920 to the spring of 1921. This was in turn followed by a year of galloping inflation before the hyperinflation began in the summer of 1922. While, with the benefit of hindsight, one may detect certain long-term tendencies at work in the entire period, and especially in the period of relative stabilization, much decision-making was short-term response to developments for which there had been no past experience and guesses about the future.

Only in this way, for example, is the behaviour of many of Germany's eminent bankers intelligible. Thanks to the government induced inflation, severe reduction in the amount of goods available for purchase, and price controls on many items, their liquidity increased enormously during the war and the immediate post-war period. As shall be shown, they claimed that they were 'swimming in money' and rejected all claims that Germany was suffering from a capital shortage. The war had significantly reduced the amount of credit the banks needed to supply to industry. Since the government was industry's chief customer and paid its bills promptly, industry had little cause to borrow or discount commercial bills. The banks, deprived of their usual business in commercial bills and in regular stock-market transactions, were reduced to the function of 'deposit banks lending chiefly to public authorities'.[4] This disproportionate involvement with the affairs of the Reich continued after the war, for, while the banks disengaged themselves from their war bond holdings fairly rapidly, they quickly became large-scale holders of the treasury bills the Reichsbank was ceaselessly discounting for the government. While the bankers certainly were not enthused about the 'Socialist' governments in Berlin, they did seem to hold fast to the faith that European governments did not go bankrupt. Thus, when Director Klaproth of the Hannover'sche Bank inquired what the Deutsche Bank director Mankiewitz thought of investment in long-term treasury bills that would reach maturity in 1924 Director Wassermann of the Deutsche Bank replied on Mankiewitz's behalf with measured optimism:

> While Herr Mankiewitz sees extraordinarily hard times coming for the private economy, he inclines to the view that the credit of the state cannot be shaken in its foundations and that the possibility of a state bankruptcy is barred for internal reasons. At the same time, Herr Mankiewitz limits himself to saying that this view of future developments, which is so favorable for the credit of the state... is so personal that he would not want to be bound by it as the giving of actual advice.[5]

Bankers, at least respectable ones, do after all have a reputation for caution and conservatism, and one of the grave difficulties Mankiewitz and his colleagues faced in the post-war inflation was making intelligent judgements and decisions in what had become veritable madhouses by the turn of 1919–20. Thanks to the spiralling public debt with its accompanying monetary and treasury note emissions, the restarting of international trade along with the reopening of the stock market, and the accompanying feverish speculation in currencies and industrial shares, the beginning of a spectacular – at least in nominal terms – process of capital increases and industrial consolidations, and the government use of the banks to impose its requirements for the deposit of securities and the providing of information relevant to tax assessments, the banks were not only 'swimming in money', but drowning in work. As Mankiewitz plaintively reported to Klaproth in January 1920, 'there exist conditions in our offices which I never would have imagined possible in so orderly a concern as the Deutsche Bank', and that his stockbrokers were 'dropping from exhaustion'.[6]

The banks soon became used to these conditions, however, and once spring and relative stabilization came, the great banks were in a position to return to the expansionary process begun before the war and accelerated during the war in which massive capital stock increases were combined with the take-over of provincial banks. The way began to be paved for the greatest bank merger of the inflation, that of the two great banks, the Nationalbank and the Darmstädter Bank, which finally took place in July 1922 after the Nationalbank had taken over the Deutsche Nationalbank Bremen in 1920 and then formed a fifty-year community of interest with the Darmstädter in 1921. In June 1920, the Commerz- and Discontobank fused with a major provincial bank, the Mitteldeutsche Privatbank to become the Commerz- und Privatbank, increasing its capital and reserves between 1919 and 1920 from 104.5 to 270.7 million marks. Although the Mitteldeutsche Privatbank had once been reputed to have a loose connection with the Deutsche Bank, Director Wassermann unconcernedly welcomed reports of the merger: 'If the Commerz-Bank has now really become a great bank, then I would be extraordinarily happy. We have a national interest in strong banks, but the meal was rather large and will produce digestive complaints.'[7]

The Deutsche Bank, having been compelled to disgorge many of its important holdings abroad because of the loss of the war, had a particularly hearty appetite and, in November 1920, finally took over the Hannover'sche Bank, the Braunschweiger Privatbank and the Privatbank zu Gotha, all of which had a combined share capital of 79 million marks and 15 million in reserves. This fusion with major provincial banks required the Deutsche Bank to raise its share capital from 275 to 408 million marks, 74.8 million of which were underwritten by a consortium led by one of the Deutsche Bank's affiliates, the Essener Credit-Anstalt. The new shares were kept in friendly hands by being offered either as an attractive option for old sharesholders of the Deutsche Bank or used in exchange for the stocks of the banks involved in the merger. Furthermore, by its takeover of the Hannover'sche Bank, the Deutsche Bank was able to increase its interest in two other major provincial banks, the Württembergische Vereinsbank and the Hildesheimer Bank, which it eventually was to take over, respectively, in 1924 and 1928. By their policy of fusion, the great Berlin banks, whose role had been magnified since the war because of their government debt holdings and engagement in foreign exchange transactions, thus became truly national banks with vastly increased responsibility and large networks of branches under their control. In 1913, the Deutsche Bank had fifteen branches; by 1924, it had 142. The Commerz- und Privatbank increased the number of its branches from eight to 246 during the same period.[8]

This imperialism was not always welcome in the provinces. The Deutsche Bank's efforts to take over the Elberfeld Bankverein in 1919 ran into such opposition that it was compelled to beat a retreat, and its attempt to take over the Siegener Bank for Commerce and Industry in 1921 was also temporarily frustrated. In fact, there was much public hostility to the Hannover'sche Bank takeover, since it was 'simply not understood for what reasons so intrinsically well-constructed and distinguished an institution could give up its independence'.[9]

Some of the larger provincial banks sought to protect themselves against this envelopment by Berlin. Thus, the Allgemeine Deutsche Credit-Anstalt, Leipzig (ADAC), which had been conducting a very successful expansionist policy of its own in Saxony and Thuringia, joined in a 'close friendly alliance' with the Bayerische Hypotheken- und Wechsel-bank and the Barmer Bankverein as well as with the private banking house of Hardy & Co. in 1921, while a similar relationship was established between the private Berlin Bank, Mendelssohn & Co. and the Bayerische Vereinsbank. Although the Leipzig and Bavarian banks were allied with the Disconto-Gesellschaft, these other friendly relationships had the specific purpose of providing a counterweight to the great 'D' banks by establishing agreements on a regional division of their markets, facilitating expansion into Austria, as in the case of the Bavarian banks, and conducting business in Holland – all without involving the Disconto-Gesellschaft.[10]

There was nothing very mysterious about the motives of the great banks. They wished to expand, eliminate competition and control and centralize the banking business throughout the country by gaining access to the capital and silent reserves of the prestigious provincial banks. This was necessary if they were to meet the challenge created by the development of large-scale industrial enterprises with increasingly large capital reserves as well as capital requirements. The role of the inflation in this concentration process was important. The high liquidity at once made possible and encouraged this development, and certainly one of the best inflation hedges available to the banks at this time was the acquisition of the buildings, facilities, personnel and shares of other banks. That this could be done on the cheap only added to its attractiveness. The great discrepancy between the value of the shares of the great banks and that of the provincial banks meant that provincial bank shares could be bought up at low cost even when rumours of an impending fusion suddenly increased their market value. Furthermore, the difference between the internal and external value of the mark enhanced the advantages of the great banks because, although share prices tended to rise whenever the exchange rate declined, the real value of the rise of shares was in no way equal to the depreciation of the mark. The tendency of fusions to occur when the mark fell may have been related to this phenomenon.[11]

While the power and advantages enjoyed by the large enterprises certainly played their role in the inflationary concentration process, especially in the industrial sphere where ruthless take-overs with scant regard for the wishes of smaller enterprises often took place, the use of persuasion remained in good form when dealing with established and respected businesses and seems to have been particularly important in the courtship of fusion-shy provincial banks. Concentration was not only a policy of expansion by the strong against the weak. It was also a strategy of consolidation and defence in a very uncertain economic situation, and this line of argument figured prominently in the persuasive efforts of the great bankers. As Oscar Schlitter of the Deutsche Bank pointed out to a recalcitrant supervisory board member of the Siegener Bank, the concentration movement had the 'explicit purpose of gathering together the forces that lie scattered about at those junctures where they can find the best support in the competitive economic struggle'. Germany's dangerous political situation and her dependence on raw materials along with the depreciation of the mark could create demands which 'the financial strength of the individual enterprise is incapable of meeting'. For this reason, 'economically weak enterprises must seek support more than before from the stronger'. This was as true for banking as it was for industry in Schlitter's view:

> At the present time many industries are still living on a certain excess of cash, so that the banks have increasing means which they can place to some measure at the disposal of other enterprises in need of money. How long this will last, however, cannot be foreseen, and perhaps the Siegerland industry will one day, instead of having the money which it is keeping in the banks at the present time, once again be in need of money. The existing provincial banks are not today any longer in a position to meet such demands on their own. The monetary depreciation today requires sums on short notice that previously were viewed as gigantic.

When industries were suddenly compelled to pay the costs of raw materials or wages without having immediate buyers or found it necessary to grant customers longer periods to meet their bills, Schlitter argued, their demands would prove more than the provincial banks could handle and 'only the inner strength of a great bank can do for the nation's industry what is necessary in order to hold out in the great economic struggle'.[12]

These arguments not only revealed why the great banks promoted and many provincial banks sought fusion at this time, but also some of the peculiarities of the banking 'boom' of 1920–1. As the most direct beneficiary of the state's inflationary policies, the banking sector had 'partially emancipated itself from the conditions of the German business world'.[13] It made huge paper profits from its interest and provision charges on loans, stock exchange and money market transactions. Dividends to the great bank shareholders ranged between 7 per cent and 12 per cent in 1919, 10 per cent and 18 per cent in 1920, and 12.52 per cent and 24 per cent in 1921. Large silent reserves were being set aside. It must, of course, always be emphasized that these increased profits, dividends and reserves were on nominal rather than real values.[14]

What all this meant for the structure of the economy, however, was less certain. In the past, the banks had played a leading role in stabilizing the economy and pointing the way towards concentration and rationalization, but now critics were charging that the banks were catering to the speculative fever that had gripped the masses of Germans, accepting and indeed participating in the tendencies to water stocks by granting generous options on new capital emissions, and doing nothing to prevent the practice of senselessly creating majority blocks of stock in order to take over companies behind the backs of their directors for no apparently sound economic reason. The banks, however generous with their credits, were enjoying a boom 'insured by the increasing impoverishment of the Reich'.[15]

It could also be argued, however, that, if the inflation had 'emancipated' the banks from the condition of industry, it had also promoted the further emancipation of important segments of industry from the control of the banks. As Klaproth tersely put the matter, 'the great industrial corporations in general rule the banks and not the reverse'.[16] Some of the bankers spent a good deal of time pandering to and chasing after the industrial leaders. If, for example, Arthur Salomonsohn of the Disconto-Gesellschaft got on well with Hugo Stinnes, one of whose great goals in life was to emancipate himself fully from the control of the banks, it was because Salomonsohn was supportive of everything Stinnes did to the point of nodding approval when Stinnes declared that it would be the task of the industrialists to restore the health of the currency while the men of finance handled the details.[17] Who would have imagined such passivity from a man who stood at the head of the German bank which historically was most famous for its influence on industrial development? Stinnes' relationship with the ageing but intractable head of the Berliner Handelsgesellschaft, Carl Fürstenberg, was less satisfactory. Fürstenberg resigned in protest from the supervisory board of one of the enterprises controlled by Stinnes because of opposition to the latter's policies. The relationship went from bad to worse when Stinnes managed to get an interest, albeit nothing resembling a controlling interest, in the BHG by purchasing 40,000 shares of its stock in March 1922 from a notorious Hungarian–Rumanian speculator, Emil Cyprut. Stinnes was also reported to have expressed the intention of buying a controlling interest in the Deutsche Bank, which certainly intensified that bank's watchfulness over what was happening to its shares, and he did get control over the Barmer Bankverein in 1923. In the last analysis, however, it was less Stinnes' interest in taking over banks than the use of them made by himself and his fellow industrialists as well as by speculators like Cyprut and the no-less notorious Hugo J. Herzfeld, as well as the relative voicelessness of bankers during this period that was significant. Herzfeld, for example, employed the mediation of Jakob Goldschmidt of the Nationalbank who, like Salomonsohn, seemed to have worked well with Stinnes in the sale of the controlling interest in the Bochumer Verein to Stinnes in 1920.[18]

It was indicative of the change in the balance of power between banking and industry that a powerful and respected banker like Goldschmidt should effusively court Stinnes, and complain that Salomonsohn was being undeservedly favoured with supervisory board positions in firms in whose acquisition he, Goldschmidt, had played a role. He literally ran after Stinnes' business and his favour:

> As you know, I have in every respect the great desire to do more than conduct business for your concern from time to time. You have given me your confidence in such an open, and for me, gratifying way, that I entertained the hope not to be entirely forgotten by you in such matters as Böhler, Braunschweiger Kohle, Alpine, etc.'

Stinnes, however, knew how to keep bankers in their place, and, while pointing out how he was happy to fulfil Goldschmidt's wishes 'in general', the circumstances made it impossible for him to use Goldschmidt in these transactions.[19]

A classic illustration of the incapacity of the great banks to guide or effectively influence the processes of concentration and fusion then underway was provided by the struggle between the Stinnes and Haniel interests for the control of the greatest South German machine-builder, the Maschinenfabrik Augsburg-Nürnberg (M.A.N.) in the fall of 1920, a struggle in which Paul Reusch of the GHH, representing the Haniel group, won by playing upon the fears and eccentricities of the M.A.N.'s chief stockholder, the Baron von Cramer-Klett. Although two eminent bankers on the M.A.N. Supervisory Board, Oscar Schlitter of the Deutsche Bank and Franz Urbig of the Disconto-Gesellschaft, favoured Stinnes and were scandalized by Reusch's victory, all they could do was protest and adjust to the results.[20]

Nevertheless, Reusch was a great general director, an aggressive manager-entrepreneur with the money of a great old industrial family behind him and fully worthy of competing with Stinnes for the jewel of South German industry. For the scion of an old banking family like Baron S. Alfred von Oppenheim of the famous Cologne banking house, who sat on many industrial supervisory boards, some of the people who were gaining control of old industrial enterprises irritated him no end. He expressed satisfaction that the iron merchant firm of Ottenheimer, which had bought stock in the Witten Cast Steel Company in the hope of forcing it to give Ottenheimer its marketing operations, was being rejected by Witten. The latter dealt in speciality products and did not need the services of Ottenheimer, 'which has become big during the war'. Oppenheim drew a parallel between Ottenheimer and the Cologne iron merchant, Otto Wolff, who had also become a major industrial figure during the war, and angrily pointed out to General Director von Schaewen of the Phoenix concern that: '[O]ne sees everywhere the bad consequences of the war and revolution profiteers, who are insatiable and seek to extend their interests further everywhere.'[21] They would, however, have to hold their noses, for, in the course of 1920, Wolff not only became a major stockholder in Phoenix, but also its chief marketing agent.

This is not to say that the assistance and advice of bankers were not welcomed or cherished by many industrial firms. Franz von Mendelssohn contributed mightily to keeping Krupp above water during these years by securing Dutch loans. The service of German banking house branches in Holland proved extraordinarily helpful in providing an asylum for the flight of German capital. Max Steinthal's constant advice to Mannesmann on the disposition of its foreign currency resources was both welcomed and heeded.[22] Yet, those who were unable to escape the control of bankers on their supervisory boards could not but envy those who had. Thus, a paper manufacturer testifying after the stabilization was most grateful for the support his firm had received from the banks during the war, when it had huge debts and inadequate markets, but had cause to resent their influence afterwards:

> We have an old factory that should be expanded. The management takes the position that it should be expanded during the inflation. The bank says: that can bring us into hot water and lead to a bankruptcy. The expansion is thus delayed due to the influence of the banks. But now it is being carried out and naturally costs gold marks; it will be very expensive. The bank takes the view today that it is unquestionably correct that it is done today because one did not know earlier how things would be. The management takes the view that it should have been done earlier, for then it would have cost nothing.[23]

As has been shown, the banks could not treat major firms and concerns this way any longer, and war and inflation had reduced some of their leverage on others. Nevertheless, they made a great and largely successful effort to protect what leverage they still had for the time when the economy would stabilize and their more traditional services and influence might once again be needed. The greatest threat to a recovery of their position came in the winter and spring of 1920, when important members of the Reichsverband der Deutschen Industrie and the Economics Ministry proposed the establishment of an Economic Bank (*Wirtschaftsbank*) to secure credit for industry, above all foreign credit, by founding a bank that would pool the credit and resources of industry needed to provide guarantees for such credit. On the industrial side, this constituted one of a number of attempts to liberate industry from the state and its finances, while on the governmental side, the proposal was viewed as a mechanism for the direction of investment in the process of reconstruction and rationalization. What triggered the entire effort, however, was a common perception of immediate and long-term problems. On the one hand, small and medium sized industry were complaining bitterly about the exorbitant interest rates charged by the banks for operating credit. On the other hand, there was general anxiety about what was perceived to be a nascent credit crisis that was bound to hit once the printing presses were halted. The plan to thus mobilize industrial credit and investment funds in a new way combined with proposals to change the laws governing savings banks and permit them to buy and sell industrial shares and thereby mobilize their funds and those of their customers provoked massive opposition from the banks that received lengthy expression in hearings in the Reich Economic Council in 1920 and early 1921.[24]

The basic argument of the bankers was that they were 'swimming in money' and quite ready to meet any and all legitimate credit demands placed upon them. Of course, no one claimed that there was a credit shortage because of insufficient liquidity but rather that many businesses could not afford interest rates of 9–10 per cent, especially when there was only a 1.5 per cent interest rate given to depositors. The interest rates, which were to become much higher in the course of the inflation, were disguised in a variety of commissions for various real and imagined services. The businessmen compelled to accept these conditions complained that the banks had formed a condition cartel which monopolized the credit market, hampered production and kept prices high.[25]

The answer to these complaints by the illustrious bankers called to testify before the committee was that it was as non-sensical to compare pre-war and post-war interest rates as it was to compare the pre-war and post-war price of butter. Like everything else, banking had become more expensive. The inflation itself had vastly increased the need for more personnel in the banks, as well as for expansion of facilities, so that wage and material costs in the banking industry were higher than ever. To the great irritation of the banks, they were particularly burdened by being forced to perform new services for the tax authorities because of the requirement that all paper assets be placed on deposit and the termination of the privacy of bank accounts. Under these circumstances, it was impossible to give higher interest on deposits or demand less for credit, the bankers argued. While the eminent Hamburg private banker Max Warburg admitted that the banks had been overly inventive in concocting commissions, he pointed out that 'if you see the costs and burdens which the banks have today and how through a strike of bank employees they shoot up by millions, then one cannot think ill of the banks and bankers if they create a certain reserve through the invention of commissions'.[26]

The hearings laboured particularly under the difficulty of confusion between the problem of credit for long-term capital investment and the long-run and short-run availability of operating capital. The proponents of the economic bank were constantly trying to focus on the danger that the credit structure was too vulnerable, that the future could bring a severe credit crisis, and that something had to be done to prepare for the emergency. They foresaw a time when there would be neither enough operating capital nor enough long-term capital to renew and rebuild the German economic plant. They felt it was erroneous for the representatives of the banks to continue to deny that there was a problem and simply to claim that they were in a position to provide all the credit that was needed.

Warburg sought to allay such fears. He pointed out that the banks actually wanted to give industry credit since their investment in treasury bills and other forms of government paper could only be viewed as 'second class'. He knew of no deserving firm that had been denied money and suggested that the banks had found a solution to the great sums needed as a result of the inflation by forming credit consortia to help out firms where necessary. As he colourfully explained:

> When today a great industrial enterprise, which earlier needed 3 million now needs 30 million and the individual bank is unwilling to give this credit..., then a credit consortium is formed.... With the help of this credit consortium and with the help of our greatest helper, the Reichsbank, which ceaselessly prints notes, we will always be in a position to give every credit that is demanded. (Laughter) The credit shortage will only start at that moment when the Reich and the currency becomes solid and we no longer, as before, have inflation.[27]

Warburg seems to have maintained a measured optimism that Germany could pull through her credit difficulties if she were smart and lucky and warned against presenting foreigners with Germanic schemes requiring 'complicated brainwork'. Furthermore, he thought it important to recognize that Germany was living on 'the credit of earlier decades', that is, the huge speculative engagement of foreigners in the mark in the belief that German productivity and sound financial practices would be restored. Indeed, it was estimated that two-thirds of the 40 billion in bank deposits belonged to foreigners whose intentions were largely speculative.[28] It certainly was more agreeable to listen to Warburg than to Jakob Goldschmidt, who relentlessly stressed that Germany's failure to undergo a major economic crisis was a sign of her misery rather than her health, who pointed out that England and America, by not trying to prevent this crisis with 'brute force and bureaucratic organization' were insuring that it would be shorter, who prayed that the crisis would finally come so that 'we can slowly return to a healthy state', and who boldly asserted that the high interest rates for credit were beneficial and could go even higher. Goldschmidt, like Salomonsohn, did not think the banks should be in the business of providing credit for long-term plant expansion and renewal. This had to come through the traditional means of incorporation and capital stock issues, and, while many private firms were reluctant to surrender their independence or family character by becoming corporations, there were important tax inducements for doing so and it was, in any case, unfair to ask either the banks or the taxpayers to bear risks that could be properly distributed by such readily available and traditional means. The bankers insisted that the banks only had a responsibility to provide operating capital, and then only to firms which were good credit risks, and even then not for the production of goods for which there was no market and that would make things worse.[29]

The dilemma, of course, was that many of the good credit risks were those who had benefited from war profits and were themselves operating as bankers for the firms they were absorbing. George Bernhard, for example, rejected the simple equation between good banking practice and the general welfare of the economy. He argued for an economic bank because 'such a bank would be in a position to supply the difference between the credit that is privately possible economically and that which is necessary from a [national – GDF] point of view'.[30]

The bankers and other critics of the economic bank program, however, were unswerving in their opposition to deviations from traditional banking practices. They particularly resisted every suggestion that the reserves of the savings banks be tapped for capital investment in industry, although the savings banks had in fact become increasingly engaged in a variety of municipal and private commercial activities, and the industrialists were especially anxious to have this capital serve industry.[31]

If the effort to keep the savings banks to their traditional functions was a losing battle for the credit banks, the struggle against the Economic Bank was successful thanks to the support given to them by the Reichsbank and the Finance Ministry, the former because it also wished to avoid a powerful competitor, the latter for fiscal reasons. At the same time, the bankers were greatly enthused about the Reichsbank's proposal for relieving the need for working capital through the reintroduction of commercial bills. Because of the wartime government payments in cash, high liquidity, and the demand by industrial trade associations for immediate payment in cash in the post-war inflation, commercial bills had virtually disappeared from use. The Reichsbank viewed the reintroduction of 'solid commercial bills' in the amount of about 20 billion marks an excellent means of relieving operating credit difficulties in a 'safe' manner. In the Reichsbank's view, commercial bills had a host of advantages. They permitted a three month delay in cash payment; a portfolio of such bills, if solid, could be used to procure further credit. They also reduced cash requirements in the economy and thereby would make it possible for the Reich to reduce liquidity through taxation and long-term loans from the domestic economy without bringing the economy to a standstill because of a credit shortage. The Reich would then be in a position to purchase back its treasury bills, while the Reichsbank and other banks would once again have reliable portfolios of commercial bills instead of dubious treasury bills. That this vision of the pre-war order of things, where credit for operating capital was given with solid bills based on real production and sales proved so palatable to everyone was not very surprising. When someone warned that the reintroduction of commercial bills might produce a fantastic credit demand by industry beyond the banking system's capacity, the bankers assured him that such worries were unfounded.[32]

The test of this proposition came with the severe credit shortage that manifested itself with the onset of the hyperinflation in the summer of 1922. The hyperinflation came in the wake of repeated reparations and domestic political crises and a loss of foreign confidence in the future of the German mark. Once the allegedly non-existent credit crisis struck, the cry for the reintroduction of commercial bills became universal, and it was the bank's 'great helper', the Reichsbank, that felt compelled to come to the rescue by discounting and rediscounting commercial bills, many of which were really nothing more than 'financial bills', and doing so at negative real interest rates. This service of providing free loans whose principle was repaid in increasingly worthless paper to a favoured group of leading industrial firms certainly assisted the banks, who could rediscount their own bills at the Reichsbank. Nevertheless, they still found themselves unable to serve the credit needs of their customers because of the serious decline in their capital and long-term deposits, especially in real terms. The banks, supported by the Reichsbank, argued that much of the fault lay in the abrogation of the privacy of bank accounts for tax reasons, and claimed that this was why deposits were so low. They claimed that the relationship between bankers and their customers was analogous to that between doctors and their patients or lawyers and their clients. Most importantly, however, the reluctance to use banks was leading to an uneconomic use of capital, depriving the economy of liquidity, and encouraging rather than discouraging tax evasion and flight of capital.[33]

This was an argument which might have had some cogency in 1920–1 but which made little sense in 1922–3 because of the domestic flight from the mark into goods. The practical response of the banks was to sell their holdings of treasury bills back to the Reichsbank, thus helping to make them increasingly unmarketable, terminate forward exchange transactions on foreign currencies in order to reduce risks, raise their interest rates to unheard of levels, urge the Reichsbank to discount commercial bills so as to reduce the heat on themselves, and cut their own lending every time the Reichsbank exercised a modicum of restraint. All this, of course, made industry, big and small, very angry at the banks, but big industry could at least turn to the Reichsbank. Thus, in the fall of 1922, Stinnes fumed at the banks for closing down their forward exchange transactions so suddenly, condemned the 67 per cent interest they were demanding as 'such a misfortune, that it cannot be borne', and argued that 'a serious word' with the bankers was necessary. In the end, however, he admitted that 'the only salvation' was a 'proper discount policy by the Reichsbank', and that 'the credit and money shortage can only be set aside if the Reichsbank can be brought to perform the great deed it had performed at the outbreak of the war, when it accepted every form of bill presented to it.... The other banks can do as good as nothing. If the Reichsbank does not print more notes, they [the other banks] also can be of no use.'[34]

In 1923, the Reichsbank printed the German currency right out of existence, and one of the central accomplishments of its policy, and the policy advocated by Stinnes, was to promote an exfoliation of special banks in a position to provide bills with the two 'discount-capable signatures' required by the Reichsbank and to give commercial bills so bad a name. This played no small role in making it possible to undermine traditional German banking practice in the stabilization and promote that policy of Reichsbank restrictiveness in the discounting of commercial bills that was to have such fatal effects in 1931.[35] The point here is not to break a lance for the real bills doctrine, but rather to suggest how very much the inflation experience and the strategies of defence chosen or imposed upon the bankers by circumstances limited their capacities to play a more effective and positive role in the subsequent period.

This perspective is also important in assessing the differing roles of bankers and industrialists in the negotiations on the reparations issues and in the stabilization of the currency in 1923. While banking and industry were at one in their opposition to the Versailles Treaty and highly critical of fulfilment and while divisions can be found in both groups between hardliners and compromisers, it may generally be said that the bankers, especially Max Warburg and Carl Melchior, were more sympathetic to a solution that emphasized compromise and a financial arrangement among the leading industrial nations, while the industrialists were above all concerned with a settlement that would make a continuation of Germany's economic reconstruction possible through limitations on reparations and a rollback of social reforms within Germany. Stinnes, in particular, sought a solution that would permit Germany to stabilize her currency below pre-war parities so as to make a continued export offensive possible. The bankers, in contrast, seemed to accept the return to the gold standard and pre-war parities as dogma. For Stinnes, at least, the distinction between the two approaches was very clear. When asked in late 1922 about bringing bankers into negotiations with the French, one of his leading directors reported:

> I clearly emphasized the primary [significance] of the productive economy against the secondary significance of the financial side and showed on the basis of previous developments... what kinds of dangers arise when finance is granted a dominant influence on questions which in the first instance involve production.[36]

How different from England, where the power of the City and the Cunliffe Committee Report of 1919 insured that England's post-First World War reconstruction would be defined in terms of the priority of a return to the gold standard and pre-war parities! If the City could assert the primacy of financial over industrial interests at home and win the support of international financial interests at the Brussels international economic conference of 1920, it could not dictate to German industry, and neither could the German bankers. Indeed, from this perspective, the pre-war power and prestige of German banking, such as it was, lay in its enthusiastic participation in the adventure of German industrialization, an adventure which post-war German industrialists were unwilling to terminate in the name of financial virtue. Berlin was not London, and the great Ruhr industrialists were in a position to use their regional power base to exert national influence through vertical expansion into manufacturing as well as through industrial peak associations. They could test and, where necessary, defy the will of the bankers and the bureaucrats in Berlin. If Germany could be said to have an economic ideology, then that ideology was productivist and nationalist, and both the bankers and the capital city in which their leadership was increasingly concentrated, could easily be charged with 'internationalism' and 'unproductive' finance capitalism. The hostility towards finance capital was primarily a middle-class and lower middle-class phenomenon. Big industry itself seldom levelled such charges publicly, and there was little open conflict between industry and banking, especially since the bankers tended to follow the industrialist lead in opposing 'Socialist' policies. The important point is that the economic values of Germany were defined by the productivist dynamism of industry, above all its leadership on the Rhine and Ruhr, rather than by finance. The hard line and dominant role of industry in the early years of the reparations question must be understood in these terms as must industry's inflationary policies as well as its insistence on the creation of valorized currencies of rather unorthodox character once the hyperinflation had gotten out of hand.[37]

It was industry which took and promoted many of the initiatives leading to stabilization in 1923, while the banks and bankers followed. The major bankers and banks exhibited a rather conservative and unimaginative spirit in dealing with proposals for valorized accounts and for the establishment of the Rentenbank and Rentenmark in 1923. The point again was not that their arguments were neither technically competent nor cogent in resisting anything but a return to solid gold currencies and disapproving measures that would finish the destruction of the existing paper mark. They were certainly correct in warning that repudiation of the mark would hurt Germany's credit in the future and make it possible to lend only at very high interest rates. This resistance, however, meant that events would necessarily pass them by and that the measures would be taken despite their opposition.[38]

Nevertheless, however severely weakened, their strategies of defence insured that they would remain in a position to play a crucial role in the attempt to pick up the pieces once stabilization came and also in a position, through their collaboration with one another and through their intermediation of foreign loans, to continue to exercise a powerful influence on industry. Indeed, even Stinnes feared the banks, and in his will instructed that 'after my decease care must in general be taken to conduct business without bank credits as soon as possible even if on a smaller scale'.[39] Apparently, it was not advice that was followed, and in 1925, a year after Stinnes death, Jakob Goldschmidt, no longer chasing after Stinnes' business but instead the member of a consortium organized by the Reichsbank to liquidate it, was insisting that Hugo Stinnes, Jr 'had no right any longer to dispose of his assets since they are mortgaged to the banks in return for their credits'.[40] Undoubtedly, there was a measure of *Schadenfreude* in this liquidation as well as in the efforts of the banks to organize the liquidation of numerous other concerns during the stabilization crisis 'in a form bearable for the general public'. In its report for 1925, Goldschmidt's Danat Bank expressed considerable satisfaction not only at the success in cleaning up industry but also at the bank's own success in firing large numbers of employees hired during the inflation and cutting down on superfluous branches. To its distress, the banks still had to suffer constant complaints about their interest rates and conditions that lacked 'objectivity'. One could not expect that

> in a capital-starved land like Germany, in which the rebuilding of capital can only proceed very slowly, normal interest rates will obtain.... The earning capacity of the banks must be such that, aside from an appropriate return on their capital, it will also allow a gathering of resources that will make it possible for them to solve the great tasks of a national and general nature which press upon the attention of the banks.[41]

Such strategies of defence, however, had their limits, as the Danat Bank was to discover in the liquidations of 1931.

Notes

1 Georg Bernhard, 'Bankbedingungen', *Plutus. Kritische Zeitschrift für Volkswirtschaft und Finanzwesen* (15 December 1923), pp. 389–92.
2 Alfred Lansburgh, 'Bankwende', *Die Bank* (1923/II), p. 375.
3 See the contribution of Harold James to this book.
4 P. Barrett Whale, *Joint stock banking in Germany. A study of the German credit banks before and after the war* (London, 1930), p. 196.
5 Wassermann to Klaproth, 18 May 1920, Hannover'sche Bank, Deutsche Bank Archiv.
6 Mankiewitz to Klaproth, 30 January 1920, ibid.
7 Wassermann to Klaproth, 15 May 1920, Deutsche Bank Archiv. More generally, see Whale, *Joint stock banking*, pp. 227f.
8 Karl Erich Born, 'Deutsche Bank during Germany's Great Inflation

after the First World War', *Studies on economic and monetary problems and banking history*, No. 17 (Frankfurt, 1979), pp. 22f.; Manfred Pohl, *Konzentration im deutschen Bankwesen (1848–1980)* (Frankfurt/Main, 1982), pp. 308–10.

9 Klaproth to Mankiewitz, 2 October 1920, Deutsche Bank Archiv. See also, Born, *Studies on economic and monetary problems*, p. 22.

10 Willi Strauss, *Die Konzentrationsbewegung im deutschen Bankgewerbe. Ein Beitrag zur Organisationsentwicklung der Wirtschaft unter dem Einfluß der Konzentration des Kapitals. Mit besonderer Berücksichtigung der Nachkriegszeit* (Berlin and Leipzig, 1928), pp. 31f, 85f.

11 This is evident from the Hannover'sche Bank correspondence in the Deutsche Bank Archiv, but see also Strauss, *Konzentrationsbewegung*, pp. 65–7 and Costantino Bresciani-Turroni, *The economics of inflation. A study of currency depreciation in post-war Germany* (London, 1937, reprinted 1968), pp. 256ff.

12 Schlitter to Schleifenbaum, 30 April 1921, Deutsche Bank Archiv.

13 Fritz Reisser, 'Bankpolitik von 1920', *Plutus*, 20 July 1921, pp. 238–40, quote on p. 239.

14 Whale, *Joint stock banking*, p. 238.

15 *Plutus*, 20 July 1921, p. 240.

16 Klaproth to Wassermann, 11 May 1920, Deutsche Bank Archiv.

17 Felix Pinner, *Deutsche Wirtschaftsführer* (Berlin, 1924), p. 188.

18 See Enquete Ausschuss, *Wandlungen in den wirtschaftlichen Organisationsformen. 1. Teil: Wandlungen in den Rechtsformen der Einzelunternehmungen und Konzerne* (Berlin, 1928), p. 187; Pinner, *Deutsche Wirtschaftsführer*, pp. 192–4; Paul Uffermann, *Könige der Inflation* (Berlin, 1924), pp. 91–6; Paul Uffermann and Otto Hüglin, *Stinnes und Seine Konzerne* (Berlin, 1924), p. 75; Arnold Tross, *Der Aufbau der eisenerzeugenden und eisenverarbeitenden Industrie-Konzerne Deutschlands* (Berlin, 1923), pp. 67, 73.

19 Goldschmidt to Stinnes, 10 May 1921, Archiv für Christlich-Demokratische Politik der Konrad-Adenauer-Stiftung (ACDP), Nachlass Stinnes, I-220, Nr. 270/1.

20 See Gerald D. Feldman, *Iron and steel in the German inflation, 1916–1923* (Princeton, 1977), p. 237.

21 Oppenheim to Schaewen, 8 April 1920, Mannesmann-Archiv, P/1/25/38.

22 On the role of Mendelssohn credits in enabling Krupp to stay out of foreign hands, see Feldman, *Iron and steel*, pp. 263f. The extraordinary correspondence between Steinthal and General Director Bierweis of Mannesmann is to be found in the Mannesmann Archiv MM 091. For the German banks in Holland, see Johannes Houwink ten Cate, 'Amsterdam als Finanzplatz Deutschlands', in Gerald D. Feldman,Carl-Ludwig Holtfrerich, Gerhard A. Ritter, Peter-Christian Witt (eds.), *Consequences of inflation* (Berlin, 1989), pp. 149–80.

23 Ausschuss zur Untersuchung der Erzeugungs- und Absatzbedingungen der deutschen Wirtschaft, *Verhandlungen und Berichte des Unterauschusses für allgemeine Wirtschaftsstruktur. 3. Arbeitsgruppe. Wandlungen in den wirtschaftliche Organisationsformen. Vierter Teil. Kartellpolitik. Erster Abschnitt* (Berlin, 1930), p. 330.

24 These plans are briefly discussed in Gerald D. Feldman, 'The political economy of Germany's relative stabilization during the 1920/21 Depression', in Gerald D. Feldman, Carl-Ludwig Holtfrerich, Gerhard A. Ritter, Peter-Christian Witt (eds.), *The German inflation. A preliminary balance* (Berlin and New York, 1982), pp. 180–206, esp. 196–202. The record of the meetings of the 'Ausschuss zur Prüfung von Maßnahmen gegen die finanzielle Not der produktiven Städe' is to be found in Zentrales Staatsarchiv Potsdam (ZSAP), RWR, Bd. 459–60.

25 Testimony of a Berlin clothing manufacturer, 28 October 1920, ibid., Nr. 459, Bd. 1, B1. 82f.

26 Meeting of 11 February 1921, ibid. Nr. 460, Bd. 2, B1. 185.

27 Meeting of 29 January 1921, ibid., B1. 130f.

28 For Warburg's remarks, see the meeting of 11 February 1921, ibid., B1. 179. For the estimate on foreign deposits, see the meeting of 20 October 1920, ibid., Bd. 459, B1. 9. More generally on this speculative engagement, largely but not solely American, see Carl-Ludwig Holtfrerich, 'Americanische Kapitalexport und Wiederaufbau der deutschen Wirtschaft 1919–23 im Vergleich zu 1924–29', *Vierteljahrschrift für Sozial- und Wirtschaftsgeschichte*, 64 (1977), pp. 497–529.

29 Meeting of 11 February 1921, ZSAP, RWR, Nr. 460, Ibid., B1. 186–93.

30 Meeting of 16 November 1920, ibid., B1. 152ff.

31 *Ausschuss zur Untersuchung der Erzeugungs- und Absatzbedingungen der deutschen Wirtschaft. Der Bankkredit* (Berlin, 1930), p. 40. See also Richard H. Tilly, 'Gemeindefinanzen und Sparkassen in Westfalen in der Inflation, 1918–1923,' in Kurt Düwell and Wolfgang Kollmann (eds.), *Rheinland und Westfalen im Industriezeitalter, Bd. 2. Von der Reichsgründung bis zur Weimarer Republik* (Wuppertal, 1984), pp. 398–411, and Carl-Ludwig Holtfrerich, 'Auswirkungen der Inflation auf die Struktur des deutschen Kreditgewerbes', in Gerald D. Feldman (ed.), *Die Nachwirkungen der Inflation auf die deutsche Geschichte 1924–1933* (Munich, 1985), pp. 187–209.

32 Meetings of 29 January and 11 February 1921, ibid. Nr. 460, Bd. 2, B1. 98ff., 272ff.

33 See the reprinted version of Arthur Salomonsohn's speech to the RWR in *Bank-Archiv*, 22 (1 November 1922), pp. 29–32 and the statement of the various banking organizations and editorial comments in ibid. (15 January 1923), pp. 111f.

34 For these quotes, see the meeting of the directors of the

Reichsverband der deutschen Industrie reprinted in Gerald D. Feldman, *Industrie und Inflation. Studien und Dokumente zur Politik der deutschen Unternehmer 1916–1923* (Hamburg, 1977), pp. 315–24, quotes on p. 318. More generally, see also Reichsbank to RFM, 9 October 1922, ZStA Merseburg, Rep. 120 A XI 1, Nr. 35, Bd. 2, Bl. 103–15. Holtfrerich, *The German inflation 1914–1923. Causes and effects in international perspective* (Berlin and New York, 1986), pp. 66ff.

35 See Alfred Lansburgh in *Die Bank* (1923/II), p. 372 and Harold James, 'Did the Reichsbank draw the right conclusions from the great inflation?', in Gerald D. Feldman and Elisabeth Müller-Luckner (eds.), *Die Nachwirkungen der Inflation auf die deutsche Geschichte 1924–1933* (Munich, 1985), pp. 187–209.

36 Aktennotiz Osius, 27 November 1922, ACDP, Nachlass Stinnes, I-220, Nr. 046/3. These issues will be dealt with in greater detail in my forthcoming study, *The great disorder. Politics and society in the German inflation, 1914–1924* (Oxford, 1992). See also, Hermann J. Rupieper, *The Cuno government and reparations 1922–1923. Politics and economics* (The Hague, 1979), pp. 50ff.

37 On the triumph of financial orthodoxy after the war and England's role, see Dan P. Silverman, *Reconstructing Europe after the Great War* (Cambridge, Mass. and London, 1982) and Fred Hirsch and Peter Oppenheimer, 'The trial of managed money: currency, credit and prices 1920–1970', in Carlo M. Cipolla (ed.), *The Fontana economic history of Europe. The twentieth century. Part two* (Glasgow, 1976), pp. 603–97, esp. pp. 610–21. For a more detailed analysis, see my forthcoming, *The great disorder*.

38 For banking resistance to the currency reform, see Paul Beusch, *Währungszerfall und Währungsstabilisierung* (Berlin, 1928), pp. 166–9. Max Warburg praised Helfferich for having a completed plan, but attributed its success to Helfferich's popularity in right wing circles so that the new money found 'more acceptance than the project itself deserved'. See Warburg Papers, unpublished memoirs, 1923, p. 64.

39 Testament of March 1920, ACDP, Nachlass Stinnes, I-220, Nr. 300/7.

40 Report to Silverberg, 10 June 1925, Bundesarchiv Koblenz, Nachlass Paul Silverberg, Nr. 554, Bl. 87.

41 Danat report, ibid., Bd. 552, Bl. 148f.

14 Banks and bankers in the German interwar depression

HAROLD JAMES

How far economic development is shaped by non-economic, and specifically by institutional, factors has been one of the perennial questions in economic history. It arises particularly acutely in the case of banking history. What peculiarities in economic structure are generated by the particular institutional features of a system of financial intermediation? Does the way banks are organized affect their ability to deal with the rest of the economy? Some analysts attempt to go beyond an institutional examination, and examine the broader issue of how the social circumstances and the intellectual horizons of a banking community affect the rationality of its collective decisions.

Issues such as these have always been at the heart of investigations of Germany's banking system. This paper considers how and why the impact of economic institutions changed in the aftermath of the First World War.

Alexander Gerschenkron famously related the institutional position of banks to relative economic backwardness and particularly to capital scarcity.[1] The Gerschenkronian tradition accords to credit banks the central role in Germany's economic development, since after the mid nineteenth century they mobilized large sums for industrialization that would otherwise have been unforthcoming. They took a sustained interest in companies by means of the *Kontokorrent* (loans through overdrafts on current account). When the capital market appeared receptive, they managed the issuing of shares and flotation of companies on the Stock Exchange; and they used their influence on Supervisory Boards (*Aufsichtsräte*) to influence firms' policies and especially to regulate competition and promote cartels and mergers.

But this creative role did not last for ever. By the turn of the century as cartelization and merger fever grew hotter, most commentators agreed that the power of the bankers was curtailed. The capital shortage was less acute; and the new large industrial undertakings developed their own substantial financial resources. Often they appeared as creditors rather than as debtors; and, in some industries, notably chemicals, the dependence on banks had never really existed. 'In the generation immediately preceding the War... leaders of outstanding ability were more often found in the ranks of industrialists than in those of bankers', wrote a British commentator. The economist Adolf Weber pointed out that, by the first decade of the century, the major steel and engineering concerns had relations with several bankers – whom they played off against one other. In 1925 Oscar Wassermann of the Deutsche Bank explained that bankers' influence had declined over the past twenty-five years, 'with the growth of our economy in general and the internal strengthening of individual enterprises the opportunity to develop power becomes ever rarer; and with the emergence of a general prosperity that makes raising money ever easier, the banks lost influence'. More recently, Jürgen Kocka concluded that Hilferding's account of the dominant position of *Finance Capital* (1910) appeared too late, at the moment when it was ceasing to be an accurate description of bank-industry relations.[2]

It is tempting to believe that this description of the reduced power of banks after the turn of the century itself soon became out-dated, as a result of the First World War. The massive destruction of capital restored one of the characteristics of economic backwardness – capital scarcity – and offered banks at least an opportunity to resume their central role in German development.

Banks and power

The power of banks rested on their range of economic contacts, as well as on bankers' position within German society. Economic linkages became more and more associated with the assumption of a social role by bankers.

In dealing with the power of banks, it is helpful to break the financial sector into subdivisions. There are the major Berlin credit banks or great banks (*Grossbanken*), also sometimes called the D-banks, which played a central role in industrial finance, in issuing and on the bourse, as well as in overseas trade. Private bankers (numbering almost 1,200 before 1914, 1,400 by 1925 but only 700 in 1933)[3] financed trade on a more regional or local basis, and usually concentrated on particular lines of business. Publicly owned banks, and in particular the *Sparkassen* (savings banks) drew their deposits from a much wider and therefore poorer social group, and also lent much smaller sums. They gradually extended their activities to include cheque-accounts by 1907; and after 1926 they could give *Kontokorrent* credit. More prosperous savers resorted to the mortgage banks. If we concentrate only on one banking group – for instance the great banks – we are apt to ignore the wide range of financial services offered in Germany and to believe, as many contemporaries as well as some subsequent analysts have done, that the great banks distorted Germany's industrial development by only dealing with large companies.[4] The reality was that big horses rode big courses, but also that Germany had plenty of smaller horses and smaller courses.

Social status accompanied economic prominence: from the influence of a small-town banker in a community of local notables to the Berlin bankers who played *Weltpolitik*. Bankers had emerged as a major social force in Germany by this time. In making any international comparison of the position of financiers, political and social ideas as well as economic opportunities play a crucial role. In England a financial oligarchy, associated with the ancien regime values of an older landed aristocracy and indisposed towards the claims of domestic manufacturing industry, developed an interest in imperialism and overseas expansion. How different was the role of the City in Germany? Did German bankers constitute a more or less independent power elite than their British equivalents?

In the popular imagination, the linking of finance with the old order had been established at least since the trauma of the speculative mania of the early 1870s *Gründerjahre* (the first years following the German unification in 1870). Aristocratic backing had enabled the railway promotion schemes of Bethel Strousberg to advance so successfully. Strousberg himself wrote after his bankruptcy that 'the halo which surrounds the word "banquier" is the Golden Calf before which everyone in this age genuflects'.[5] Berlin bankers formed a quite well-defined *Geldaristokratie* (financial – or banking – aristocracy) which refused to think of itself as a *Mittelstand* (middle class) and instead chose aristocratic values and living styles. By the reign of Wilhelm II leading private bankers and same directors of great banks moved with relative ease in court circles, were frequently given titles of nobility and spoke freely with the Kaiser. Such an association of *haute banque* and court was not at that time particularly German: Lord Revelstoke and Sir Ernest Cassel consorted with the Prince of Wales (later Edward VII) on the turf at Newmarket in much the same way as Max Warburg and the Kaiser on yachts in the North Sea.

In addition, careers in the Civil Service and in the increasingly bureaucratized great banks were frequently intertwined. The intimacy of this connection did constitute a German peculiarity, and the bureaucratic synthesis of ancien regime court and haute finance took place to a quite unique extent. Karl Helfferich's career is a fine example, exceptional only in the extent of its rapidity and success. He began as an academic economist, then went into the Colonial Office and became a Director of the Deutsche Bank before returning to public service as Treasury

Secretary and then as Interior Secretary and Deputy Chancellor. Wilhelm Regendanz was in the Colonial Office before taking a Prokura (power of attorney) with M. M. Warburg & Co., and continued to play a highly adventurous role in pushing German interests in Morocco and Nyassaland before the First World War, and after 1918 in promoting Ukrainian anti-bolshevik nationalist movements.[6]

The orientation of the great banks towards foreign trade, and with it a political task, had developed under the Kaiserreich. Jakob Riesser's classic textbook on German banking opened with a statement of banks' national responsibility:

> They had to strengthen our financial, and with it our political influence abroad; nor was this done without many a bitter experience. For in this field they met the competition of the majority of the great powers in the underwriting of foreign loans, the promoting of foreign undertakings, and the opening of international business relations, with the disadvantage that their rivals had entered the field long before them. By assisting the German navigation, and establishing German banks abroad, they imparted to the German name a renown previously undreamed of, thus extending by their activity the sphere of German business and political influence.[7]

Of the leading Weimar bankers a substantial number had been involved in the promotion of Germany's overseas interests: Franz Urbig (Disconto Gesellschaft) in the Far East; Arthur von Gwinner (Deutsche Bank) in Anatolian railways, for which his father was given a hereditary noble title by the Kaiser; Emil Georg von Stauss (Deutsche) in the Balkans and Rumania; Paul Millington-Herrmann in Chile; and Henry Nathan (Dresdner Bank) in the Deutsch-Südamerikanische Bank in Latin America.

Apart from informal activity expanding German influence, there were well-developed links of banks to the civil service, which persisted after 1918. Georg von Simson (Darmstädter-und Nationalbank, or Danat Bank) came from a family with a long and distinguished tradition in the Prussian bureaucracy; Adolf von Dombois on the Supervisory Board of the bank had been President of the Prussian State Bank (Seehandlung), and Josef Koeth an economic planner in war and demobilization, as well as Reich Minister of Economics in the second Stresemann cabinet. Carl Michalowsky, a Director of the Deutsche Bank, had been a judge and a civil servant in Prussia. On the executive of the Dresdner Bank, Georg Mosler and Walter Frisch had both been civil servants: Frisch in the Interior Ministry, the Economics Ministry and the Auswärtiges Amt. Paul von Koerner on the Supervisory Board had been the director of the trade political department of the Auswärtiges Amt.

Moreover banks had to adopt some of the values of society at large. The big Berlin banks, with the exception of the more self-consciously bourgeois (but also smaller) Berliner Handelsgesellschaft, tried to maintain an aristocratic element at least on their supervisory boards. This remained as true after the war as it had been in the Kaiserreich. Some of these men were industrialist–nobles, such as the two Henckel von Donnersmarcks on the Supervisory Board of the Darmstädter-und Nationalbank in 1925, or the Bavarian industrialist Theodor von Cramer-Klett (Dresdner Bank). Others just leant a social cachet and contacts in the beau monde, such as Adolf Fürst von Schaumburg-Lippe (Dresdner Bank), or Hermann Fürst von Hatzfeld Herzog zu Trachenberg (Deutsche Bank). In 1925 the Darmstädter-und Nationalbank had four aristocrats on a Supervisory Board of fifty-seven, the Deutsche four out of fifty-six, the Dresdner three out of forty-nine and the Commerzbank four out of forty-six; and even the Berliner Handelsgesellschaft had one Hamburg and one Austrian nobleman.

Military preparation in the Kaiserreich completes the picture of the etatist orientation of bankers. It was in the First World War that the synthesis of *haute banque* and autocratic-aristocratic state reached its apogee, with the inclusion of bank officials in the military government and the creation of what was often called a 'financial general staff'. The social and political role of bankers grew more powerful even as their purely economic significance was reduced.

The capital market in the 1920s

How far was this order disturbed by the political revolution of 1918–19 and democratization, and also by the turbulent economic development of Weimar? The most obvious impact was economic. The war and the post-war inflation severely weakened the capital position of German banks. The total assets of the Berlin great banks fell from 8,391 million marks in 1913 to 1,750 million Reichsmarks at the end of 1923, and only recovered in 1924 to 4,439 million Reichsmarks. Savings banks were even more savagely hit: their assets fell from 20,802 million marks in 1913 to 1,534 million Reichsmarks at the end of 1924. Worst affected of all were the mortgage banks as the depository of savings by the well-off (11,369 million marks in 1913 and 566 million Reichsmarks in 1924). For all banks the figures are 66,388 million marks and 13,741 million Reichsmarks respectively.[8] Since bankers' power depends substantially on their financial strength, they have suffered a heavy blow. At first sight, it appeared that German banking had been literally decimated and bank influence in the German economy ended completely.

On the other hand, the generally prevailing capital scarcity in the aftermath of the inflation, the consequence of the wiping out of savings as well as of changed income distributions, meant that banks occupied what was potentially a position of immense importance. The capital shortage was reflected immediately in the high level of interest rates. In addition, all studies of credit in the later 1920s show not only higher interest, but also wider risk spreads.[9] Carl Melchior said immediately after the stabilization of the mark, in March 1924: 'Interest rates and bank fees are today at a level that is dangerous for the economy. This is the consequence of the enormous reduction, reckoned in gold currency, of business for banks, and the increase in costs of each transaction.'[10] The high rates, and the risk premia, persisted even when bank lending had expanded. In 1925 Oscar Wassermann offered the following analysis: 'If bank interest plays a much greater role in the cost calculation of industry and commerce than previously, that is less the consequence of the level of interest rates than of the amount of credit needed.'[11]

Bankers' leverage over the rest of the economy in addition increased because of the mergers in banking which produced a considerably higher concentration. Between the war and the 1930s, the large Berlin banks swallowed up numerous smaller banks; and in 1929 two spectacular mergers occurred. The Commerz- und Privatbank took over the Mitteldeutsche Kredit-Bank; and the Deutsche Bank joined the Disconto Gesellschaft, taking in some smaller houses – the Norddeutsche Bank, A. Schaaffhausen'scher Bankverein and the Süddeutsche Disconto-Gesellschaft. The creation of the giant Deutsche Bank und Disconto Gesellschaft was explicitly justified by the need to create a larger capital basis to strengthen the power of banking in the light of the emergence of the vast industrial concerns IG Farben AG and Vereinigte Stahlwerke. As a 1926 memorandum of the Disconto Gesellschaft put the case: 'In order to be able to keep pace with industry, it is necessary to create a bank bloc of such size that its issuing power dominates the domestic capital market, and that unreasonable competition by alternative groups would be pointless.'[12]

Supervisory boards provided a means for bankers to exercise power over their clients. In 1932/3, bank directors and private bankers had 5,759 seats on company boards (or 19 per cent of the total in Germany), and one banker had thirty-seven positions.[13] It is notoriously hard to be precise about what power a member of a supervisory board could exercise in practice: the relation could be purely formal or, on the other hand, the external symbol of an intimate liaison. Anecdotal evidence at least suggests that supervisory boards in the 1920s played a much more prominent role and established a closer relationship than was the case subsequently, in the 1930s, or after the Second World War.[14]

Some very large firms escaped from bank hegemony by creating, Japanese style, their own financial companies. IG Farben scored the biggest success here, with its house bank the Deutsche Länderbank; but even before the war the firms that later joined the IG had been substantially independent of bank control. Vereinigte Stahlwerke can be viewed as an attempt to escape the financial dependence that such historic steel firms as Fried. Krupp AG had been forced into it in the aftermath of the inflation. On the other hand, even some of the largest firms became or remained firmly under bank tutelage. Mannesmann for instance had always been closely associated with the Deutsche Bank; and AEG, which had previously worked with the Berliner Handelsgesellschaft, in the late 1920s became heavily dependent on the Dresdner Bank.

The plight of small firms was even more acute. Their access to the capital market had always been harder, and they complained that they found it difficult to obtain loans from the great banks. Previously the savings banks and local private bankers had been their major source of credit; but these institutions recovered only very slowly after the inflation. As a result Ernst Walb was able to refer to the 'generally recognized gap in credit supply for small and medium size industry', analogous to the 'Macmillan gap' commented on simultaneously in Britain.[15]

Not only did the small firms incur substantial costs; they had also become very vulnerable to crisis. Thus von Brasch writing in a survey of the textile industry: 'War and inflation robbed the wholesale trade of its economic basis, capital power. The consequence is that the task of keeping inventories, which requires a large amount of capital, and the assumption of the risks of cyclical, seasonal or fashion fluctuation is passed on to industry.'[16] C. Brückner blamed the predicament of Saxon industry on its inability to raise credit: 'Both domestic and foreign creditors have operated very cautiously because of the sharp reduction in business morality as a result of the inflation and the widespread practice of delayed payment.' Or there is the case of the Berlin pencil industry, where investments had to be made using short-term credits from local banks.[17]

The long-run price paid for dependence on short-term bank credit proved devastating. In 1931, after the outbreak of the German banking crisis the combination of bank withdrawals of short-term funds and extraordinarily high interest rates forced a dramatic destocking, and also pushed many firms into illiquidity. Firms such as Krupp, which had borrowed heavily, had to reduce their inventories quickly.[18] Widespread dependence on banks meant that a financial crisis could be quickly transmitted to the rest of the economy. The pressure to reduce inventories, which already existed from 1930, provided a powerful push to price-deflation; and this in turn led to the reduction of the *values* of inventories and the erosion of bankers' securities against loans. In short it produced that process characterized by Irving Fisher as debt-deflation. This debt-deflation represents the pathology of a highly leveraged economy.

The rapid rise in financial intermediation in the second half of the 1920s and the resulting prominence of banks and bankers reminded those contemporaries with a sense of history of the gigantic speculative expansion of the early 1870s. Thus Hans Fürstenberg of the Berliner Handelsgesellschaft retrospectively: 'The morals and practices of the inflation and the multitude of new rich produced relapses into the circumstances of nineteenth-century high capitalism. One simply had to howl with the wolves.'[19] Banking in the later 1920s was an intensely competitive business, although the market shares of the major Berlin banks remained surprisingly constant. Banks competed by paying large dividends, even when they could not justify them, in order to maintain their share price. They tried to take over other institutions in order to extend their deposit base and their credits. Above all they competed by lending.

The banks' immediate response to the capital scarcity of business and agriculture was to expand lending, despite an adequate capital basis and despite reserve ratios well below those prevailing before 1914. This response depended on Germany's reintegration into international financial markets in the aftermath of the Dawes plan (1924): a substantial part of bank lending was financed by foreign loans to German banks. Sixty-six per cent of the loans to the Berliner Handelsgesellschaft in June 1929 came from abroad, 35 per cent for the Deutsche Bank and between 40 per cent and 45 per cent for all the other major banks.[20] The consequence is that, looking at lending alone, it appears that banks rapidly recovered after the shock of the inflation. Loans of the great banks already exceeded the 1913 level by 1926. By 1929 they stood at 9,595m. RM (198 per cent of the 1913 level); for all banks the corresponding figures are 26,794m. RM and 174 per cent of 1913 levels.[21] Loans from private bankers are not included in these figures; but all the evidence suggests that large numbers of private bankers disappeared in the later 1920s, or were taken over and became branches of the great banks.[22] The small banks, which had played so essential a role in the financial system of pre-war Germany were thus disappearing, while the savings and mortgage banks were struggling to make good their inflation losses.

A changed banking system led to a weakness in the structure of industry, which became apparent even before the 1931 crisis. In 1930 a commission of inquiry complained about the results of excessive competition in banking: the result, it argued, was to channel too much credit into particular branches of industry. It also commented on the concentration of bank credits with very large customers and the neglect of smaller firms. Though the commission was (wrongly) prepared to concede that each bank insisted on the provision of proper securities, 'the origin of the illiquidity of enterprises is to be seen in the way in which the competing banks proceed to offer credit independently of each other [to

Table 14.1 *Liquidity ratios of German banks, 1905–1932*

	Great banks		All banks	
	Cash liq.	1st deg. liq.	Cash liq.	1st deg. liq.
Year end				
1905	9.5	53.6	8.6	—
1913	7.4	50.7	6.7	50.0
1924	6.1	52.8	6.2	50.9
1929	3.5	39.6	3.2	35.7
1930	3.9	36.0	3.4	34.9
30 April				
1929	2.2	37.8	1.9	35.7
1930	1.9	37.0	1.7	36.4
1931	2.0	34.9	1.7	36.2
1932	2.6	27.6	1.9	29.1

Notes: Cash liquidity = cash and assets at central bank.
First degree liquidity = cash liquidity + bills + assets with other banks.
Source: Untersuchung des Bankwesens 1933.

the same borrowers]'.[23] The full extent of this weakness, however, was only exposed after 1931, when it emerged that some companies, notably the major Berlin brewers Schultheiss-Patzenhofer, had borrowed from different banks against the same securities.

For the banks, the expansion of lending occurred on a very unstable base. The precariousness of this position is evident in the falling liquidity ratios for all banks in the course of the 1920s (see table 14.1).

Some explanation should be given for these extremely low levels. They may even give too rosy a picture: the year-end figures clearly include some window-dressing, but so albeit to a lesser extent do the month-end figures.[24] The figures seem bizarre – indeed incredible – to any Anglo-Saxon observer, and it is tempting to think that the cash liquidity figures are so low as to be useless as a guide to day-to-day bank operations, and that the first degree figures represent the true level. Bankers appear to have treated bills as a reserve in the belief that they could at any time be discounted by the central bank. Many of these bills were not genuinely commercial in that they were related to an underlying trade transaction, but represented an easy way of creating credits between banks (*Finanzwechsel*). Apart from doubts about quality, there should also have been a hesitation about the circumstances in which the Reichsbank would buy bills from bank portfolios. The Reichsbank had no legal obligation to buy bills, and its ability to do so was constrained by the international limitations on the system – in particular the requirement of a 40 per cent gold and foreign currency reserve against the note issue. The inflow of foreign money meant that this constraint was likely to be a particular difficulty at any time that the banks were under pressure: and such a linking of external and internal crisis occurred in the spring of 1929, and again in the summer of 1931. In July 1931 the combination destroyed the German market: as Wassermann of the Deutsche Bank complained at the time, the Reichsbank was simply not willing to take the one billion Reichmark in bills needed to allow German banks to continue to make payments. 'The only way to fight the run is to pay', he said in the familiar terminology of Bagehot, the classic of the English, but unfortunately not of the German banking tradition. Riesser's classic in fact had made exactly the opposite point about crisis management: 'The "Great Banks" should cooperate in all these directions, not only by word or through influencing their clients, but by their own example, especially by exercising the greatest reserve in withdrawing their credit balances from the Reichsbank, and in presenting bills for rediscounting.'[25]

In addition to the decreased liquidity reserves, the banks were also vulnerable in that their capital base was small and their reserves against loss inadequate. The accumulation of hidden provisions against losses, 'stille Reserven' had been destroyed in the inflation; and after 1924 banks attempted to build them up once more. The 1927 accounts of the great banks for instance understated earnings from interest income in order to make such accumulations. After this time, however, they declined:[26] in other words, the highly competitive situation – forcing high dividends to be declared – weakened the banking structure already before the onset of any other symptoms of economic depression. Banking problems thus predate the world economic crisis: German industrial production reached its pre-crisis peak only as late as 1929.

Shrinking liquidity reserves, and falling hidden reserves after 1927, expanding credit, and merger mania – these were the product of Germany's highly competitive environment. Banks, it appears, were ill-placed to take advantage of the opportunities presented them by competition. The great banks had become highly bureaucratized: their personnel had swollen in size during the inflation, and then needed to be pruned back severely. The Deutsche Bank's staff had been 9,587 at the end of 1913; it reached 37,000 in 1923 and was cut to 18,699 at the end of 1924 and 16,000 by 1925. The Danat Bank's fell from 29,000 in October 1923 to 7,500 in 1926; the Dresdner's from 22,853 in 1923 to 9,484 in 1925. The number of branches had expanded as small banks and private bankers were absorbed; but the branch managers had little flexibility, and were not compensated in line with the profitability of their branch. Rewards for success at the basic level of the banking industry, where the day to day decisions on matters such as credit allocation were actually taken, were absent.

After the 1931 crisis, bankers tried to explain that their mistakes had arisen out of a result of pressure from 'public opinion and government' to take large quantities of foreign loans and pass them on to domestic borrowers.[27] What is this but a polite obfuscation of the fact that they acted under the pressure of market forces and of a struggle to retain market shares?

Banks and public policy

Before the war, one of the sources of banks' political influence had been the increased demand of the state for funds – partly for the financing of military and naval expenditure, but most crucially for foreign investment as part of a broad conception of Weltpolitik. In the 1920s, the public demand for funds was at least as great. The German capital shortage and the consequent new prominence of bankers in economic life were blamed on a changed income distribution which had reduced the propensity to save;[28] but also on the crowding out effects (*Ausstechen*) of the rapid growth of public debt.[29] It is important to note that these effects did not depend on the absolute size of public debt (which in 1920s Germany was low in comparison with Britain or France), but on its rate of growth, and on the share of new government borrowing in total new borrowing.

What kind of a grip did the mounting public deficits give to the financial community? Is it reasonable to argue that the state was imprisoned by the bankers? The state was certainly a very large debtor, though in the eyes of some hardly a secure or trustworthy one after the experience of the great inflation. There are instances of foreign creditors asking for *bank* guarantees of bank to government loans in the aftermath of the inflation, a bizarre perversion of normal business practice. But in general, until the outbreak of the Great Depression, big public borrowers could dominate the market, and play-off the variety of competing lenders against each other: foreign banks, German domestic banks and publicly owned banks. In 1929, after an attempt to fund the floating Reich debt failed, the German state turned to non-bank lenders, and in particular industrial corporations, for short-term loans. But, by 1929, such a move was interpreted as a sign of the government's weakness, and forced a budget-balancing campaign of economies and tax increases. German governments were imprisoned by the attitude or the sentiment of the capital market; and this increasingly sceptical and even hostile mood represented a major limitation on Germany's 'room for manoeuvre' (to use Knut Borchardt's phrase). In order to escape these limitations and the monthly fear that there would not be sufficient funds to pay civil servants, a rigorously orthodox deflationary policy was pursued: the change took place already in the last months of Hermann Müller's Great Coalition, and then deflation was pushed with particularly devastating consequences by Chancellor Heinrich Brüning.

Did the bankers manage to translate the market power that followed from the 1920s capital shortage into political influence? Or were they restrained by the competitive pressure? The idea of a political connection of bankers played a prominent role in the historiography of the GDR. In Kurt Gossweiler's account, the Dresdner Bank and the Danat (together with Hjalmar Schacht) took a pro-American position, while the Deutsche and the Disconto remained faithful to the 'pan-German tradition of world dominance'.[30] Such a schematic presentation demands a considerable amount of intellectual hocus-pocus. As an example, when Georg Solmssen in 1931 demanded the replacement of Luther by Schacht the attempt must have been hypocritical, since Schacht and Solmssen belonged to different blocs; in addition, the idea of the greater dependence of the Danat and the Dresdner on American money is incorrect. In the summer of 1929, when thanks to a secret Reichsbank survey we have a statement as to the extent of the major banks' dependence on foreign loans, the Disconto Gesellschaft was in fact slightly more proportionately indebted abroad than the Dresdner or the Danat.[31]

There is no doubt that some German bankers in the 1920s had positions of great political significance. As before the war, foreign policy required expert financial assistance. The Versailles Treaty put financial issues at the centre of the diplomatic stage. Max Warburg had already been offered the post of Imperial Treasury Secretary in the last Imperial government of Prince Max of Baden, and his partner Carl Melchior played a critical part at the Versailles conference, and continued to represent Germany's interests through the Weimar Republic.

In domestic politics, Jacob Goldschmidt played a central part in the appointment of Hjalmar Schacht in 1923, first as Currency Commissioner and then as Reichsbank President. Goldschmidt's competitors complained subsequently that he had unfair advantages because of his excellent contacts with 'influential circles in government'.[32] In municipal politics, he and other bankers – such as Louis Hagen and Robert Pferdmenges in Cologne – could play a major role. But, on the national scene, the influence of the bankers weakened. When the lending crisis reached an initial climax in 1929, it was not the private bank directors who tried to exploit the government's situation for their own political ends. The Reichsbank President, Schacht, wanted to use the financial embarrassment of the state as an opportunity to bring down the socialist-liberal coalition government. He was opposed by the world of private finance. In

December 1929, Goldschmidt and Max Warburg intervened again in an attempt to persuade Schacht not to sabotage loans for the city of Berlin and for the central government, but they had no success.

During the depression and the Brüning years, despite the constraint imposed on government action by market sentiment, there are few concrete examples where bankers used their powerful financial position specifically to formulate and push political goals. Where they did – as with the attempt led by George Solmssen to secure the dismissal of Reichsbank President Luther after the banking crisis and his replacement by Schacht – they were unsuccessful. Most bankers were reluctant to rock the boat or to cause a political crisis: again and again in the People's Party (DVP) they tried to bring the party to support Brüning. Mendelssohn and Goldschmidt defended the Chancellor,[33] for the quite simple reason that they recognized the strong interest banks had in the continuation of the political order. They had brought vast foreign sums into Germany; and they would be threatened if the foreign capital dried up, or if government authorities could not or would not repay loans. In this sense by the early 1930s, the bankers had become just as imprisoned by the state of the capital market as the government itself. In consequence, they could not exercise much leverage.

The idea that bankers could determine policies, veto decisions of which they disapproved, and force on reluctant governments unpopular policies however belongs to the standard rhetorical armoury of interwar politics. Politicians often seek villains when they try to explain their impotence in the face of large events. Such conspiracy theories about bankers were not a uniquely German phenomenon: in Britain it was widely believed that a 'bankers' ramp' had brought down Ramsay MacDonald's second Labour government. In France the 'deux cents familles' of the Regents of the Banque de France were thought to have frustrated Edouard Herriot's socialist-radical coalition in 1926. Germany during the depression had its fair share of near paranoid theories about bankers' behaviour. Brüning, with the suspicious mind of a Catholic bachelor, believed many of them.

At two critical moments, in his opinion, bank intrigues had harmed German developments. The main culprit was the Deutsche Bank, the motive a misplaced and exaggerated competitive spirit. Oscar Wassermann had, Brüning believed, supported the NSDAP before the 1930 elections in the belief that a major Nazi success would prompt a large capital flight and a financial crisis; and that the weakest German banks would be so vulnerable that the Deutsche Bank could emerge strengthened from the cataclysm.[34] There is in reality no foundation for this fantasy of Brüning's, and it is not repeated in his posthumous memoirs. On the second occasion the charge seems more seriously founded, however. Brüning, as well as others, attribute the initial reluctance in the first days of July 1931 of the Deutsche Bank to help solve the emerging banking crisis to a renewed wish to hurt the weaker banking houses. It is just as likely that Wassermann was reluctant to help in July 1931 because it was impossible at the time to see what sort of commitment would be required on the part of his bank. Brüning believed also that he could identify the source of the panic of 1931: the Deutsche Bank had spread rumours about the Dresdner in Switzerland.[35] There is little evidence to support this claim.

The combination of the 1931 banking crisis with a highly developed paranoia in the official mind about the role of bankers, a widespread popular anti-capitalism which saw in banks the cruel and exploitative weapons of a 'system', and less or more open anti-semitism produced between 1931 and 1933 a series of bank reforms and restructurings. The policy-makers were not sympathetic to banks: Brüning's Finance Minister Hermann Dietrich for instance told his State Secretary, 'The trading jew, who has taken so much in interest from us, should now be really made to cough up.'[36] In the first place, many directors were purged. Brüning insisted that the bank directors responsible for the mistaken policies should be removed as far 'as this might be compatible with the continuity of the technical leadership'. One third of the Deutsche Bank's directors, one half in the Commerzbank, and all but two of the former directors of the Danat and the Dresdner lost their positions. Goldschmidt, who was associated with the Nordwolle failure, and Stauss of the Deutsche Bank, who was linked with Schultheiss, disappeared. Some of the replacements for the departed directors came from smaller banks, but most often they were taken from the public sector. Carl Bergmann, who had been in the Deutsche Bank before the war, and from 1919–21 had been State Secretary in the Reich Finance Ministry before returning to private banking and then retiring, moved to the Dresdner Bank. Together with him went Samuel Ritscher, who had been a director of the state-owned Reichskreditgesellschaft. The extensive personnel changes at the top of German banking did not demolish, but rather helped to strengthen the statist tradition of German banking.

The rescue package implemented after July 1931 involved state aid for banks and exchange control, linked with a foreign creditors' agreement to leave short-term loans in Germany (the so-called Standstill Agreement, in force for six months and renewed in January 1932 as the German Credit Agreement of 1932). But the bank rescue also involved a formal structure to regulate and control banking and accounting practice. In September 1931 the government established a Curatorium for Banking, which was to produce general guidelines and supervise the activities of a Banking Commissar charged with examining banks' books, and in particular their foreign assets and liabilities.

Schemes for a much more radical alteration of German banking practice also flourished after the banking crisis. The close German connection between industry and banking had long been a source of comment and envy outside Germany. As recently as July 1931 the British Committee on Finance and Industry (Macmillan Committee) had reported – partly under the influence of the eloquent testimony of Dr Goldschmidt about the superiority of the German system – that:

> We believe that our [British] financial machinery is definitely weak in that it fails to give clear guidance to the investor when appeals are made to him on behalf of home industry... We believe it not unfair to say that certainly in Germany and America, and possibly in France also, there would be found many more men with an intimate knowledge of the problems of industry than in England.[37]

After the failure of the Danat Bank, the analysis was not turned around: the long-term lending of German banks and their close ties with industry had been a source of instability and not of strength. It would thus be desirable to separate commercial short-term banking from investment banking, as in England (or as was done in the US with the Glass-Steagall Act). Such a proposal formed one element in the Wagemann proposal of January 1932 for tackling the economic crisis (the part that attracted more attention concerned credit expansion). Ernst Wagemann, the Director of the Reich Statistical Office, recommended separating out short-term deposits, that could be lent out only short-term, from long-term investments protected and locked in by fixed terms of notice.

Other proposals for a radical bank reform involved splitting up one or more of the major banks into regional banks that might ensure a more even distribution of credit across the country, and end the centralization of the market around Berlin. The usual candidate for this treatment was the Dresdner Bank, which had taken over the failed Darmstädter. Finance Minister Dietrich was a strong exponent of this plan; and it was revived by Nazi economic 'experts' during the 1933 Bank Inquiry. Others wished to go further – to nationalize the banking system altogether. Yet a third group thought that the English-style Wagemann proposals might be appropriate. The savings banks could be barred from giving short-term credits, while banks should be prevented from entering the capital market. The actual outcome of the Bank Inquiry was much more modest. The radical proposals were simply ignored by Schacht, now reinstated by Hitler as President of the Reichsbank. As Schacht explained:

> the whole object of the Inquiry in his view was to let all the people with new theories talk themselves out, and to bring them face to face with competent experts, who would give the real answers to their theories. Dr. Schacht would confine himself in the main to asking questions. The

> Chancellor [Hitler] seemed to him absolutely sound and was always prepared to take good advice. Dr. Schacht believed in fact the parity theorists would have no great influence in this affair.[38]

An important part of this defensive action was the argument that the 'mistakes' of the 1920s could not be due to any structural problems. Instead, the problems concerned politics and leadership and morality. As one Nazi legal commentator explained the development of policy since 1933: 'The flaws in the German credit structure are not to be found in its construction or in its form but lie in the first place in the incorrect behaviour of the leaders of credit institutions in an economic system that is dying before our eyes, and in the political system.'[39]

The results of the Inquiry's deliberations were embodied in the new Bank Law of 5 December 1934, which extended and tightened the legal supervision already established in 1931, and in addition provided for a limitation of large credits to single borrowers, legal reserve requirements, and the restriction of long-term deposits, as well as limiting the number of supervisory board seats occupied by any individual banker.[40]

The relative autonomy given under the December 1934 Law, and the later privatization of the partly state-owned banks, mattered little as their control of credit had already been broken by the events of the world economic crisis, and by the foreign withdrawals and the flight of German capital. Additional legislation made the capital market less central to the operation of German business. In particular the limitation of dividends to 6 per cent or less (29 March 1934 and 4 December 1934) promoted self-financing, and with it greater autonomy from bank influence.

Regulation replaces competition

It is much easier to describe briefly the development of banking and credit after 1933 than it is to give an accurate summary of the chaotic competitive circumstances of Weimar. Businesses financed their expansion either from their own accumulated reserves (aided by the restriction on dividend payment) or with state assistance. Bank credit played a relatively minor role. Taking the ratio of bank assets to GNP as a proxy for the extent of financial intermediation, there was actually a fall between 1932 and 1939 (from 99.1 per cent to 82.7 per cent). (For comparison, the 1925 ratio was 32.6 per cent and that in 1929 68.0 per cent.)

The savings banks (*Sparkassen*) increased their deposits and their general level of activity, and the Berlin great banks fell back. From 1932 to 1939 the total assets of all banks increased from 56,193m. RM to 95,033m. RM (+69 per cent); those of the Berlin great banks rose only by 15 per cent, however, while those of the savings banks shot up by 102 per cent.[41] The new deposits flowed indirectly to the state, which had become unambiguously the dominant borrower. Budget deficits as a proportion of GNP rose from 1.1 per cent in 1931/2 to 6.7 per cent for 1936/7; and until the end of 1938 these increasingly large sums were financed smoothly and unproblematically through bank lending.

In the relationship of state and banking world, all the power now lay on the side of the state; and bankers were acutely aware of their helplessness.

The interwar period in Germany can be divided into two eras: first of all an era of capital shortage, a highly competitive banking system, and great power being exercised by financial intermediators. There followed a period of regulation, little competition, and little power for bankers. The 1920s in retrospect appeared as the 'era of the bankers'. But the explanation for the uniquely important position of banks in this decade lies not with the traditions of German banking, or with the social pre-occupations of the bankers, or with their political involvement. It is a result most immediately of the post-war capital shortage. The institutional framework of German banking as established before the First World War was actually torn apart in the 1920s by market pressures; then in the 1930s by state action. By the end of the 1920s, German banks and the way of life they represented had become highly vulnerable to crisis; but the statist tradition remained, and the banking system of the 1930s was especially open to a new and highly radicalized form of state intervention.

Notes

1 A. Gerschenkron, *Economic backwardness in historical perspective* (Cambridge Mass., 1962).

2 P. Barrett Whale, *Joint Stock Banking in Germany: a study of the German credit banks before and after the war* (London, 1930), p. 55; *Verhandlungen des VI Allgemeinen Deutschen Bankiertages in Berlin* (Berlin, 1925), p. 25; J. Kocka, 'Entrepreneurs and managers in German industrialization', in P. Mathias and M. M. Postan (eds.), *Cambridge economic history of Europe*, VII, Part 1, (Cambridge, 1978), p. 570.

3 *Deutsches Geld- und Bankwesen in Zahlen 1876–1975* (Frankfurt, 1976), p. 122.

4 See the contemporary criticism of Alfred Lansburgh in *Die Bank*. This sort of attack was revived by H. Neuburger and H. Stokes, 'German banks and German growth 1883–1913: an empirical view', *Journal of Economic History*, 34 (1974); see the reply of R. Fremdling and R. Tilly, 'German banks, German growth and econometric history', *Journal of Economic History*, 36 (1976).

5 B. H. Strousberg, *Dr. Strousberg und sein Wirken von ihm selbst geschildert* (Berlin, 1876), p. 38.

6 J. G. Williamson, *Karl Helfferich 1872–1924: economist, financier, politician* (Princeton, 1971). E. Rosenbaum and A. J. Sherman,

M.M. Warburg & Co. 1798–1938: merchant bankers of Hamburg (London, 1979), p. 106.

7 J. Riesser, *The German great banks and their concentration in connection with the economic development of Germany* (Washington, 1911), pp. 11–12.

8 *Deutsches Geld- und Bankwesen*, pp. 74–5, 78–9, 102–3.

9 For instance, Leopold Merzbach's comments in *Verhandlungen des Deutschen Bankiertages 1925*, pp. 87–8.

10 Melchior papers, Warburg bank archive, 8 March 1924 memorandum.

11 *Verhandlungen des Deutschen Bankiertages 1925*, p. 40.

12 M. Pohl, *Konzentration im Deutschen Bankwesen 1848–1980* (Frankfurt 1980), p. 353. The quotation is from a memorandum by A. Solmssen (Disconto Gesellschaft) of 16 September 1926, and is cited in F. Seidenzahl, *Hundert Jahre Deutsche Bank* (Frankfurt, 1970), p. 313.

13 Figures from *Untersuchung des Bankwesens 1933* (Berlin, 1933). II.

14 See for instance H. Fürstenberg, *Mein Weg als Bankier und Carl Fürstenbergs Altersjahre* (Wiesbaden, 1966), pp. 187–8.

15 E. Walb, 'Uebersetzung und Konkurrenz im deutschen Kreditapparat', *Untersuchung*, p. 145.

16 A. v. Brasch, *Das Rohstoffproblem der deutschen Woll- und Baumwollindustrie* (Berlin, 1935), p. 36.

17 K. Diehl (ed.), *Wirkungen und Ursachen des hohen Zinsfusses in Deutschland* (Jena, 1932), pp. 198, 223.

18 See *Wirtschaft und Statistik*, 12 (1932), 596.

19 Fürstenberg, *Mein Weg*, p. 141.

20 H. James, *The Reichsbank and public finance in Germany 1924–1933* (Frankfurt 1985), p. 179.

21 *Deutsches Geld- und Bankwesen*, pp. 74–9.

22 See for local examples from Halle and Stuttgart, Enquete-Ausschuss, *Der Bankkredit* (Berlin, 1930), pp. 30–5.

23 Enquete-Ausschuss, *Der Bankkredit* (Berlin, 1930), p. 173.

24 See on this Reichsbank Director Karl Nordhoff's terrifying comments for the 1933 Inquiry, 'Ueber die Liquiditätsfrage', *Untersuchung*, p. 481.

25 Institut für Zeitgeschichte, Schäffer diaries 11, 11 July 1931. Riesser, *German great banks*, p. 24. See also Otto Hütner's 'Golden Law' of 1854, quoted by J. Blatz, *Die Bankenliquidität im Run 1931* (Cologne, 1971).

26 See A. Lansburgh in *Die Bank* (November 1928), p. 207; and *Untersuchung* (1933), I, p. 65.

27 Thus Otto Christian Fischer in 1933, *Untersuchung*, p. 526.

28 Diehl, *Wirkungen und Ursachen*, p. 870. Recently, C.-L. Holtfrerich, 'Auswirkungen der Inflation auf die Struktur des Kreditgewerbes', in G. D. Feldman (ed.), *Die Nachwirkungen der Inflation auf die deutsche Geschichte 1924–1933* (Munich, 1985), pp. 196–7.

29 Diehl, *Wirkungen und Ursachen*, especially pp. 575, 870.

30 K. Gossweiler, *Grossbanken, Industriemonopole und Staat. Oekonomie und Politik des staatsmonopolistischen Kapitalismus in Deutschland 1914–1932* (Berlin, 1972).

31 James, *Reichsbank and public finance*, p. 179.

32 O. C. Fischer, 'Die fehlerhafte Kreditpolitik', *Untersuchung*, p. 526.

33 See M. Grübler, *Die Spitzenverbände der Wirtschaft und das erste Kabinett Brüning* (Düsseldorf, 1982), pp. 416–18.

34 Schäffer diaries 15, 20 November 1931.

35 H. Brüning, *Memoiren 1918–1934* (Stuttgart, 1970), pp. 313–19.

36 Schäffer diaries 15, 17 November 1931.

37 *Committee on Finance and Industry*, Reports and Minutes of Evidence, 1931 (CMnd 3897) pp. 166, 168.

38 Bank of England, OV34/5, 6 October 1933 G. H. Pinsent notes on interview with Schacht.

39 H. Pröhl, *Reichsgesetz über das Kreditwesen* (Berlin, 1939), p. 2.

40 See O. C. Fischer, *Die Funktionen des Kredits und das Reichsgesetz über das Kreditwesen* (Berlin, 1935).

41 *Deutsches Geld- und Bankwesen*, pp. 74–5; 78–9; 102–3.

15 Finance and politics: comments

M. J. DAUNTON

Financiers, it was once commonly believed on both the left and the extreme right, controlled or at least colluded with politicians. This particular demonology has been largely exorcized by recent research which has pried into the records, rather than relying upon prejudice and ideology. The greater subtlety of analysis is clearly shown in the paper by Hubert Bonin. Bankers might be divided, which gave politicians the opportunity for autonomy in decision-making; they might even go against the majority view. Where politicians *did* follow the advice of bankers, it cannot simply be assumed that it was the result of dependence: it might be a consensus based on a commonsense solution. After all, the protection of financial stability is not only in the interests of bankers but also of small traders and savers.

The two papers on Germany provide detailed substantiation of the complex and shifting balance between different interest groups. In Germany, the power of the banks seems to have been curtailed after the First World War, which marked the peak of the synthesis of the great banks and an autocratic-aristocratic state. Industry was emancipated from the banks which were obliged to mount a partially successful defensive strategy against the state. In the case of reparations and stabilization, it was the interests of industry rather than bankers which were dominant. After 1924, the power of the banks did increase in a situation of capital shortage but there is little sign that this was translated into political influence. In fact, the banks were in a precarious position because of their lending policy which was exposed in the depression, and they were susceptible to state regulation and intervention.

The political leverage of the banks in both France and Germany would appear to be strictly limited. The interpretation of Ewan Green would suggest that Britain was an exception, and that the bankers were much more powerful than in continental Europe. Green emphasizes the greater cohesion of bankers than industrialists, and their ability to secure policies through the use of technical expertise, and by means of the institutional and ideological overlap between the Treasury, Bank of England and City. The result, he claims, was to relegate the productive sector to the sidelines, and to emphasize the open, international character of the economy.[1] But is this altogether convincing, and might it not be possible to argue that the power of British bankers was similarly constrained and contingent? Whether a policy issue is defined as 'technical' is part of what was at stake: if the bankers can insist that a particular problem is technical, then they have won the debate; if the government can maintain that it is a political question, then the bankers have lost. The circumstances in which technical expertise could be used was the outcome of a political tussle which needs to be analysed with due attention to the existence of ambiguities. A government might wish to define an issue as 'technical' in order to avoid odium for an unpopular decision. Neither do bankers have a monopoly of technical expertise, and the civil servants of the Treasury had a sense of ineffable superiority in relation to the narrow, self-interested advice of City men.

The 'Treasury view' was more than the City view in another guise, which neglected the needs of production. The position which was adopted by the Treasury was that British industry was uncompetitive because of its high costs, and that the correct solution to its difficulties was to tackle this issue by making industry more efficient through deflation-induced rationalization. Domestic reflation on the lines advocated by Keynes would, it was believed, blunt the drive to increase efficiency. The Treasury was not ignoring industry: on the contrary, it gave more weight to industrial efficiency than to unemployment. Perhaps it was mistaken, but that is a different matter from saying that industry was ignored and the City obeyed.[2] A similar point might be made in respect of the return to gold in 1925, where it is too easy to stress the difference in attitude between the City and the rest of the economy. It was, after all, not only the City which had an international or cosmopolitan dimension, but also the Lancashire cotton industry, South Wales coal exporters, and Clydeside ship-builders.[3] It might therefore be that a better way to characterize the debate over British economic policy is in terms of the number of competing interests upon the government, and cross-currents between finance and industry, which gave politicians room for manoeuvre and autonomy.[4] Many British historians would be inclined to accept the general tenor of Bonin's analysis, and to urge the abandonment of the notion that the City had a peculiarly strong leverage over political decisions and policies. The emphasis has, therefore, switched to the autonomy of the state and away from a reductionist view of the state as the creature of a dominant economic elite.

Although the demonology of the power of bankers has been largely exorcized, it nevertheless continues to define the problematic for most historical research on the subject of finance and politics. The time has come to move beyond this definition of the problem, and one way in which it could be extended is by asking why it is that at some points in time the demonology did inspire mobilization against bankers and financiers. Most of the historical literature deals with the ability of the bankers to mobilize, rather than the circumstances which determined whether the demonology became an active political force resulting in mobilization against them. One possible explanation is suggested by Harold James, that politicians seek villains in order to explain their own impotence in the face of phenomena which escape their control. This was clear in Germany in the early 1930s, when the paranoid belief of politicians such as Brüning that the banks had harmed German interests complemented popular, often anti-semitic, hostility to financiers. It was also very convenient for the Labour party in the 1930s to blame a 'bankers ramp' for bringing down the government in 1931.[5] The difference was that this perception did not find any purchase in popular sentiments; neither did it have any great impact on the policies pursued by the Labour government of 1945–51 despite the discussion in the 1930s of the creation of a national investment bank. The question of what determined the emergence of popular anti-banking sentiment and the willingness of politicians to mobilize against the banks deserves further consideration.

The United States provides two periods in which there was mobilization against the banks, in the 'bank war' over the recharter of the Second Bank of the United States in the 1830s, and the populist campaign of the 1880s and 1890s. These episodes arose in part from a debate over the nature of American society, and the extent to which it should survive as a 'farmers' republic' or be transformed into a capitalist society. The veto of the recharter of the Second Bank of the United States by President Jackson in 1832 formed the basis of the two-party system of pro-banking Whigs and anti-banking Democrats. Two vital issues were involved: the nature of social mobility and the power of the rich, of which the Bank was a symbol; and of the power of the Federal government, which chartered the Bank, against the states. The debate over banking was part of a fundamental divide over the nature of American society, which was to reemerge in the later nineteenth century in the ideology of the populists. Clearly such ideas as those of the Jacksonian Democrats and populists were more likely to have a purchase in a society in which there were a large number of indebted small owner-occupying farmers; it was less likely to be the case in England where farmers were usually tenants who did not have mortgages. The problems were also likely to be intense in periods of falling prices, when the real burden of debts was increasing, which helps to explain the hostility to banks in the United States in the 1880s and 1890s. Such hostility might, however, also be used by one group of bankers against its rivals. The failure to recharter the Philadelphia-based Second Bank of the United States did not come amiss to the bankers of New York, and the hostility of farmers to large national banks could benefit locally based or cooperative banks.[6]

The discussion of the United States does raise another point: the role of regulations. The political campaigns of the 1830s did mean that there was a lack of a central bank in the United States, which had the consequence that the financial system was susceptible to panics. When a national banking system was introduced during the civil war, it still did not have a single lender of the last resort, and operated alongside the state-chartered banks so that the system remained prone to crisis. It was also biased against the needs of the south which had not been party to the formulation of the legislation. A high threshold of entry was established, and land could not be used as security which effectively limited the development of national banks in the south, with the consequence that interest rates remained high. Banking regulations might, therefore, be a weapon in a battle between non-banking interest groups, rather than simply an outcome of a tussle between politicians seeking to control banks and bankers eager for privileged status.[7]

The political process which leads to the formulation of regulatory systems is complex, and deserves more attention. This entails a consideration not only of the formulation of regulations but also of their implementation, for they might be something of a sham designed to restore confidence without impinging upon the banks. The Swedish regulations of 1934, for example, might at first sight appear to be strict, yet they were in fact full of loop-holes. Regulations might, however, have a practical impact which affected the success of financial centres. It might be argued that there are two potentially contradictory requirements for a successful financial centre: political stability and a permissive regulatory regime. The development of Tokyo as a financial centre has been limited by the existence of a tight regulatory system, despite the stability of post-war politics and the economic power of Japan. Regulations might act to drive business away from one centre and attract it to another, a process which is illustrated by the Federal Reserve's Regulation Q which fixed the interest paid by US banks on time-deposits, without restricting dollar deposits in foreign banks. This led to the development of the Eurodollar market in London in the 1950s, assisting the City to recover an international role which was in danger of erosion. The coincidence of political stability and permissive regulations has been achieved most obviously in the case of London, and the explanation of why this state of affairs emerged, and with what practical consequences, requires careful analysis. Whatever the explanation, the emergence of regulatory systems is worthy of much greater analysis by historians of financial centres.

The chapters concentrate upon the great banks, and it should be remembered that there were also savings banks and mortgage banks and trustee savings banks and post office banks and agricultural banks. This might give the state the ability to use one layer of the financial system against another in order to increase its autonomy, so that, to take one example, the creation of the Postsparkasse (PSK) in Austria in 1883 was a means by which the Feudal-Conservative government of Taafe could attempt to free itself from the hold of the Liberal Rothschilds over imperial debt management. This strategy was reinforced by the creation of *Landerbank* answerable to the Treasurer. In Britain, by contrast, the creation of the Post Office Savings Bank (POSB) in 1861 (which acted as the inspiration for the PSK) was not designed as an attack upon commercial bankers, and the aim was rather to replace the small, local trustee savings banks which were run by members of the middle class in order to receive the savings of the workers. These banks were a drain upon the Exchequer because deposits were placed with the state which paid above the market rate of return; and they were also resistant to government supervision. The savings placed with the POSB were transferred to the National Debt Commission for the purchase of government bonds, which gave the Chancellor a useful source of funds while reducing the subsidy to the trustee savings banks. Unlike Austria, where the PSK moved into the provision of cheque accounts in order to reduce the role of the Liberal bankers, in Britain a firm line was drawn against any competition with the commercial banks.[8] The same type of institution could therefore have different political motivations, and might also be used in divergent ways. The deposits of the savings banks in Britain were used in order to finance the national debt; in France, they could be used from 1894 to attempt to solve another political problem, by being loaned on favourable terms for the construction of workers' housing.[9] English banks have only become involved in the housing market in the last few years, whereas in Germany public mortgage banks were heavily involved in lending to the *Terraingesellschaften* which speculated in land and constructed tenement buildings.[10] Whether the banks were connected with housing, and whether the housing issue became a point of political conflict, might help to explain popular attitudes towards bankers. In England, housing finance was largely left to the building societies which, certainly from the interwar period, had large assets. Was the policy of the government in any sense to give these financial institutions favourable tax treatment in order to encourage owner-occupation as a 'rampart' to protect property?[11] The concentration upon the concept of finance capital and the relationship between the great banks and industry has obscured other possible connections and conflicts.

The agenda for debate over the political ramifications of finance was set not only by Hilferding's study of *Finance capital*, but also by Hobson's *Imperialism*. The conclusion which has emerged from the analysis of German history is that Hilferding was writing at the very point when the power of the banks had peaked, so that he was not charting the course of the future. What about imperialism? This theme was absent from the discussion at the conference, yet recent work on Britain has tended to substantiate some of Hobson's interpretations. One synthesis on the development of the British empire emphasizes that it was not the outcome of the dynamics of industrial capitalism, but of the needs of 'gentlemanly capitalists', the financiers and aristocrats who stood against the provincial industrialists. The British empire, it has been argued, benefited the gentlemanly capitalists, but was largely paid for by the industrialists and working classes through higher taxes.[12] This largely confirms the perceptions of Hobson. The analysis has not convinced everyone,[13] and some of the issues are discussed in my own paper on the social structure of the City of London, where it is argued that there was a complex interplay between the needs of industry, finance and the British government in India in which it cannot be assumed that finance was in the ascendant. There might be a divide within the British state, between the Secretary of State for India who was a member of the British cabinet concerned with the need to win elections at home, and the Viceroy of India who was more concerned with harmony in the subcontinent. The situation was probably different in other imperial powers, for in France there was no clear divide between the metropolitan area of France and the colonies, which allowed the concerns of the colonists to be introduced into the mainstream of domestic politics in a way which did not happen in Britain.[14] The analysis of the politics of finance should therefore move beyond the boundaries of the nation state.

The argument of Hobson's *Imperialism* has received massive attention, yet it is not always appreciated that his case against financiers as the motor of imperialism was not accepted by most members of the Liberal government before the First World War. David Lloyd George had considerable sympathy for Hobson's view that income was maldistributed, and that land was a parasitical fraction of capital. However, he did not follow Hobson to argue that the export of capital was a cause of domestic poverty; rather, Lloyd George believed that capital exports would increase the supply of food through the development of the infrastructure in producing countries, so reducing prices and leading to a recovery in the standard of living of the British workforce. This interpretation confirms the lack of political mobilization in Britain against bankers. It does not mean, however, that the export of capital was without political problems. The popularity of capital exports led to unpopularity for government securities, which constrained government borrowing and so frustrated the schemes of social reform which Lloyd George wished to expand in order to contain the rise of the Labour party.[15] Many political historians have an inclination to neglect the importance of financial issues in shaping government policy, whether it be defence or social security; what is needed is for historians of the financial sector to explain to the non-specialist the problems which faced governments in funding their activities, and how this might affect political decision-making. This is a point to which eighteenth-century historians are more sensitive, especially in comparing the structure of British and French government finance, and their perception needs to be extended to the nineteenth and twentieth centuries.[16] The rejection of the old demonology should lead to a more interesting and helpful analysis of the differing structures of tax regimes, and of the social and political considerations which determined their nature; the need for the government to turn to capital markets, and the contrasts in the attraction of government bonds in comparison with other securities; and the ability of the state to draw upon the deposits of savings banks or insurance funds for its purposes. A comparative history of taxation and government finance would be a useful extension to the debates started by this collection of essays.

Notes

1 The point is developed in the account of the bimetallic debate in E. H. H. Green, 'Rentiers versus producers? The political economy of the bimetallic controversy', *English Historical Review*, 103 (1988).

2 G. C. Peden, 'The "Treasury view" on public works and employment in the interwar period', *Economic History Review*, 2nd. ser., 37 (1984), especially pp. 175–6.

3 P. Williamson, 'Financiers, the gold standard and British politics, 1925–31', in J. Turner (ed.), *Businessmen and politics: studies in British politics, 1900–45* (London, 1984), pp. 105–29; R. S. Sayers, 'The return to gold, 1925', in L. S. Pressnell (ed.), *Studies in the Industrial Revolution* (London, 1960).

4 This is the conclusion of P. Thane, 'Financiers and the British state: the case of Sir Ernest Cassel', *Business History*, 28 (1986), 94–5.

5 See P. Williamson, 'A "bankers' ramp"? Financiers and the British political crisis of August 1931', *English Historical Review*, 99 (1984) argues that Labour ministers had an independent belief in the need for balanced budgets, and welcomed pressure from the City and the Bank of England which for its part was careful not to dictate how spending cuts should be made or to threaten the Labour government.

6 L. Goodwyn, *The populist moment: a short history of the agrarian revolt in America* (Oxford, 1978); B. Hammond, *Banks and politics in America from the Revolution to the Civil War* (Princeton, 1957); R. V. Remini, *Andrew Jackson and the bank war* (New York, 1967);

J. M. McFaul, *The politics of Jacksonian finance* (Ithaca, 1972); R. H. Timberlake, *The origins of central banking in the United States* (Cambridge, Mass., 1978); J. R. Sharp, *The Jacksonians versus the banks: politics in the states after the panic of 1837* (New York, 1970); W. G. Shade, *Banks or no banks: the money issue in western politics, 1832–65* (Detroit, 1972).

7 J. A. James, *Money and capital markets in postbellum America* (Princeton, 1978); R. Sylla, 'Federal policy, banking market structure, and capital mobilization in the United States, 1863–1913', *Journal of Economic History*, 36 (1976).

8 For Austria, see M. Wagner and P. Tomasek, *Bankiers und Beamte: Hundert Jahre Osterreichische Postsparkasse* (Vienna, 1983); and for Britain, H. O. Horne, *A history of savings banks* (Oxford, 1947).

9 N. Bullock and J. Read, *The movement for housing reform in Germany and France, 1840–1914* (Cambridge, 1985), p. 480.

10 N. Bullock, 'Berlin', in M. J. Daunton (ed.), *Housing the workers, 1850–1914: a comparative perspective* (Leicester, 1990).

11 See A. Offer, *Property and politics, 1870–1914: landownership, law, ideology and urban development in England* (Cambridge, 1981), chapter 9 and pp. 405–6.

12 P. J. Cain and A. G. Hopkins, 'Gentlemanly capitalism and British overseas expansion, I: the old colonial system, 1688–1850', *Economic History Review*, 2nd ser., 39 (1986); L. E. Davis and R. E. Huttenback, *Mammon and the pursuit of empire: the political economy of British imperialism, 1860–1912* (Cambridge, 1986); P. K. O'Brien, 'The costs and benefits of British imperialism, 1846–1914', *Past and Present*, 120 (1980).

13 M. J. Daunton, '"Gentlemanly capitalism" and British industry, 1820–1914', *Past and Present*, 122 (1989); A. Porter, 'The balance sheet of empire', *Historical Journal*, 31 (1988); P. Kennedy, 'The costs and benefits of British imperialism, 1846–1914', *Past and Present*, 125 (1989).

14 J. G. Darwin, 'The fear of falling: British politics and imperial decline since 1900', *Transactions of the Royal Historical Society*, 5th series, 36 (1986), p. 40.

15 A. Offer, 'Empire and social reform: British overseas investment and domestic politics, 1908–14', *Historical Journal*, 26 (1983).

16 See especially J. Brewer, *The sinews of power: war, money and the English state, 1688–1783* (London, 1989). An exception for the later period is the work of H. G. C. Matthew, 'Disraeli, Gladstone and the politics of mid-Victorian budgets', *Historical Journal*, 22 (1979), who points out that the income tax in Britain was more readily accepted than in Germany, France and the United States where it was a source of tension.

IV FINANCE AND FINANCIERS IN SMALLER EUROPEAN COUNTRIES

16 Finance and financiers in Switzerland, 1880–1960

YOUSSEF CASSIS AND JAKOB TANNER (WITH FABIENNE DEBRUNNER)[1]

In the course of their history, Swiss banks have become a myth, an integral part of the image of a 'small, wealthy and clean country'. The so-called 'Gnomes of Zurich' represent in the eyes of international public opinion a financial centre, which plays a prominent role in the worldwide capital market, gold business and the global currency system: a role that transcends the capacities of a small state in the field of foreign policy. In spite of an unparalleled series of scandals which have erupted since the 1970s, the growth potential of the financial sector seems to be undiminished.

The international role of the Swiss banks, in comparison with the size of the country, must be the starting point in any analysis of the position of finance and financiers in the Swiss economy, society and politics. Has this international impact been translated into a position of overwhelming power within the domestic economy? Is the power of the banks a genuine one or is it merely a reflection of a more original predominance of the industrial capital, of the large industrial firms which are the backbone of the export-orientated Swiss economy? What are the repercussions of the strength of the financial sector on the position of the financial elites in Swiss society? How can we define and measure the power of banks?

This chapter examines these questions. The first section deals with the tradition of Swiss banking and the genesis of the modern financial sector up to 1880. The second section is concerned with the development and the structure of the financial sector between 1880 and 1960: in particular its contribution to the employed workforce and to GNP, the problem of the concentration in the banking sector and of relationships between banks and industry. The third section examines the financial elites and considers whether they can be marked off from the leading groups in the economy and society. The question of the weight of the financial interests in Swiss politics is examined in section four.

Tradition and genesis of the financial sector

Apart from a few exceptions, the cities which dominated the territory of the so-called *Confoederatio Helvetica* (CH) were characterized by a strong capital-formation, a large volume of capital exports and a relatively low level of interest rates.[2] 'In the 18th century, Switzerland was reputed to be one of the richest countries in Europe, a country with great capital liquidity', writes F. Ritzmann in a pioneering study of the Swiss credit and banking system.[3] These characteristics strongly influenced the institutional shaping and commercial orientation of the financial sector and were an important factor in agricultural modernization and the industrial revolution. The commercial and financial centres of the Ancien Regime were dominated from the beginning of the eighteenth century by private bankers who specialized in long-term foreign investment and the foundation for the legendary standing of Switzerland as a financial centre. As Julius Landmann pointed out in 1916: 'To the north of the Alps, Switzerland is the oldest capital-exporting area and the oldest banking place in the international capital market.'[4] However, because of a lack of demand and low interest margins, a short-term credit business failed to emerge.

The combination of a propensity for saving with a high degree of industrial self-financing maintained the liquidity of the capital market during the industrial revolution. According to J.-F. Bergier, until the 1820s successful entrepreneurs achieved such big profits that they could accumulate fortunes in bank accounts.[5] Even later, the capability of the Swiss industry for self-financing remained relatively high.[6]

New types of banks emerged in the 1830s, during the transitional period from the restoration to the era of political regeneration: the cantonal banks, which were publicly owned, and the savings banks. These new banks were able to collect deposits from broader strata of the population and direct them into land and mortgage business, which was experiencing a 'powerful development'[7] as a result of the modernization of agriculture and the rise of tourism. These newly founded banks, to which one should add the mortgage banks, were above all local and regional institutions[8] and have been seen, especially the cantonal banks, as a political instrument in the hands of the 'Ständeeliten'. Until the mid nineteenth century, up to the foundation of the Swiss Confederation in 1848, the Swiss banking system was therefore characterized by the coexistence of two separate credit systems. One was essentially a country banking system, based on a regional network of relationships where debtors and creditors knew each other and agreed on expectations about the gains and risks of an investment.[9] The other was international orientated and consisted of larger banks which concentrated on the long-term investment requirements of their customers. This system was in the hands of urban elites of private bankers who were able to deal with global financial problems and to run a circumspect investment policy all over the world.

From the 1850s, this combination of regional and international banking proved inadequate to face the new challenge of an increased capital formation on a national scale. Only joint-stock companies could provide the capital for large investment projects, and this to an extent hitherto undreamt of. Stimulated by the example of the French Crédit Mobilier, newly created credit and trade banks acted as real 'steam engines of credits' and mobilized deposits for the financing of railway construction and manufacturing industry. Within half a decade, the integration of the Swiss credit market increased significantly, and by the turn of the century, the nationwide equalization of interest rates was completed.[10]

Thus, in the second half of the nineteenth century, a series of modern Swiss 'Grossbanken' (big banks) came into being: in 1856 the Crédit Suisse in Zürich; in 1862 the Bank of Winterthur, which merged in 1912 with the Toggenburger Bank giving birth to the Union Bank of Switzerland whose head office was soon to be transferred to Zürich; in 1869 the Popular Bank (Schweizerische Volksbank) in Bern; and in 1872 the Basler Bankverein which, after several amalgamations, changed its name to Schweizerischer Bankverein – Swiss Bank Corporation – in 1898. With the addition of Bank Leu, also of Zürich, these banks form today the group of the so-called 'big banks'. Until 1945, this group was clearly dominated by two banks: the Crédit Suisse of Zürich and the Swiss Bank Corporation of Basel. The Union Bank of Switzerland caught up in the 1950s and 1960s and eventually became the largest bank in the country.

These new universal banks have been described as a 'strange mixture of commercial banks, holding companies, central banks and investment trusts'.[11] They offered a wide range of financial services and were not afraid of risky experiments and speculative practices. The emergence of the 'universal banks' gave a new shape to the banking system. From the outset, the level of capital concentration was extremely high. The modern Swiss credit apparatus took form in the period of general prosperity of the third quarter of the nineteenth century, with the foundation of the great banks, the definitive use of banknotes, the foundation of stock exchanges in the principal cities and the formation of a series of life insurance companies.[12]

The process, however, did not go unchallenged. In the 1860s railway and banking interests became embroiled with state power, at the expense of indebted peasants, small trade and handicraft, creating a highly explosive political issue. In the face of rising interest rates, the 'democratic movement' of the late 1860s launched the slogan 'popular banks against aristocratic banks', with the aim of freeing the capital market from its

Table 16.1 *Changes in the numbers of banks, bank offices and total assets and liabilities, Switzerland, 1910–1960*

	1910	1920	1930	1940	1950	1960
Banks	449	378	362	335	325	319
Bank offices				1,051	1,311	1,519
Total assets (billion Sw. francs)	7.9	13.5	21.2	17.2	25.8	50.8
Total assets/bank (billion Sw. francs)	18	36	60	51	79	159

Source: Statistisches Jahrbuch der Schweiz, 1910ff.

domination by big business interests. The second wave of foundation of the cantonal and local banks took place in this political climate. Nevertheless, the newly created big banks became the dynamic element of the Swiss banking system, as they not only worked as agencies of domestic capital accumulation, but also participated successfully, by the end of the nineteenth century, in international financial transactions and adapted the structure of their assets to the growth pattern of the large industrial undertakings.

Development and structure of the banking system, 1880–1960

As in the European countries, the number of banks decreased in Switzerland during the period under review (table 16.1).[13] An important factor was the foundation of the National Bank in 1907: the concentration of banknote issue in its hands rendered the functions of many other banks redundant and lead to a so-called '*Bankensterben*', that is the disappearance of a great number of banks through merger or liquidation. This accelerated the concentration process as the remaining banks opened new branches and started moving outside their native city, mainly by taking over local banks. The density of the banking network increased after the turn of the century and the number of bank offices tripled between 1900 and 1950.

In periods of inflationary expansion (1924–9 and 1950–73), the growth of banks' assets and liabilities exceeded that of national income, whereas in periods of stagflation such as the two world wars, or in the deflationary periods accompanying economic crisis, it fell behind it, as can be seen from table 16.2. The sensitivity of banking to the business cycle was relatively high, as the big banks were greatly vulnerable to depressions, but were in turn able to generate inordinately large profits in periods of boom. However, during the period 1913–73 taken as a whole, national

Table 16.2 *Compared growth of national income and total bank assets, 1913–1973 (in %)*

	Annual growth rates	
	National income	Total bank assets
1913–24	5.6	3.8
1924–29	4.1	7.8
1929–38	−1.5	−1.3
1938–45	6.8	1.9
1945–50	5.4	5.5
1950–60	6.0	7.4
1960–73	10.3	12.5

Source: Statistisches Jahrbuch des Schweiz, 1959/60; F. Ritzmann, *Die Schweizer Banken* (Bern, 1973).

Table 16.3 *Employment in the financial sector in Switerland, 1888–1955*

	Population census[a]		Business census[b]	
		%		%
1888	6,429	0.6		
1905			9,915	1.0
1910	12,296	0.7		
1920	22,957	1.2		
1929			25,816	2.2
1930	29,542	1.5		
1939			29,502	2.4
1941	31,969	1.6		
1950	40,040	1.7		
1955			42,128	2.3

Notes: [a] Banks, stock exchanges, insurance companies, auxiliary workforce.

[b] Banks, finance companies, insurance companies, estate agents.

Source: Statistisches Jahrbuch der Schweiz, 1932ff.

income grew at an annual rate of 6 per cent whereas the aggregate bank assets increased at a rate of 5.7 per cent. Over the long term, Ritzmann's diagnosis that 'the growth of total bank assets was similar to that of the national income and the position of the banking sector in the Swiss economy appears to have been relatively stable'[14] seems correct.

The figures given in table 16.3 show that, in terms of employment, the relative weight of the financial sector more than doubled in the first half

Table 16.4 *Swiss Banking: percentage of employment and contribution to national income, 1929–1955 (in %)*

	1929	1939	1955
Employment	1.6	1.5	1.3
National Income	3.3	2.3	1.9

Source: Statistisches Jahrbuch der Schweiz, 1932ff.

Table 16.5 *Share of total assets by categories of banks, Switzerland, 1880–1965 (in %)*

	1880	1913	1929	1935	1945	1955	1965
Big banks	12	27	41	21	28	31	40
Cantonal banks	28	38	36	40	45	40	36
All other banks	60	35	23	39	27	29	24

Source: Statistisches Jahrbuch der Schweiz, 1910ff.; Ritzmann, *Schweizer Banken*.

of the twentieth century and has now become comparable to the chemical industry. The percentage of women employed increased from 19 per cent to 29 per cent between 1930 and 1960.

The contribution of the financial sector is difficult to estimate because of a lack of statistics relating to financial matters. Table 16.4 gives some approximate results which make clear, however, that the banking business contributed relatively highly to the national income.

Concentration

The level of concentration in the banking system can be considered from different points of view. The official banking statistics distinguish between eight categories of banks: (1) cantonal banks, (2) big banks, (3) regional and savings banks, (4) loan banks, (5) other banks, (6) financial companies, (7) branches of foreign banks, (8) private banks.[15] Table 16.5. indicates that the big banks were able to enhance their relative importance in comparison with all other categories of banks. However, it also gives the impression of a temporarily interrupted secular concentration trend. Only in the mid 1960s did the position revert to what it had been at the end of the 'golden twenties'. The cantonal banks and the big banks developed in opposite directions in periods of boom and crisis.[16] From the 1880s, however, both categories expanded at the expense of the local and savings banks.

F. Ritzmann has argued that the degree of concentration in the banking system remained remarkably stable during the period under review.[17] Although the aggregate assets increased more than 44 times between 1880 and 1965, their relative distribution hardly changed. So Ritzmann's hypothesis that 'the present uneven size distribution is built into the Swiss banking system from its origins'[18] appears at first sight plausible. Two questions, however, have to be considered in order not to underestimate the trend towards concentration in the twentieth century. Firstly, should informal cooperation between banks not be considered as another form of concentration, in particular credit cartels, pressure groups, personal networks and gentlemen's agreements? And secondly, is the role of the big banks, and therefore the degree of concentration in the banking system not underestimated in view of their part in what was the increasingly important sphere of international financial operations?[19]

One can have an indication of the importance of these operations by looking at the proportion of gross profits originating from retail banking: the difference between interests received and interests paid was 38 per cent for all the Swiss banks in 1938 and 28 per cent for the big banks only; in 1947 it was respectively 41 per cent and 35 per cent.[20] The big banks earned therefore a greater part of their profits through commissions and other 'extra-ordinary' operations. Since the 1950s, for example, the business of investing abroad foreign funds deposited with Swiss financial institutions, without any intermediate stage in the Swiss economy, has mainly been undertaken by the 'big three' banks and these assets do not appear in their balance sheet.

Because of the limited business radius of the cantonal and local banks and the 'universal' character of the big banks, the Swiss banking system was not very specialized, being in that respect closer to the German than to the English model. This 'decentralized character'[21] of the financial sector created serious problems in the nineteenth century, particularly as far as the regulation of the money supply and the introduction of a national currency were concerned. It should be noted, however, that despite this the international reputation of the Swiss banks was built on the very specialized services they were able to offer.

Banks and industry

The year 1885 marks a turning point in the curve of the Kuznets cycle of the Swiss economy. The prosperity which then began was based on investments and exports and coincided with an accelerated population growth and process of urbanization. The spread of mechanization and the beginning of mass production brought about increased capital investments. The 'secret' of the Swiss success, that is the combination of 'high quality work and capital intensity',[22] started to reveal its effectiveness. In addition the newly formed modern enterprises were increasingly dependent on the international market. This had repercussions on the business cycle, which tended to be affected by variations of demand in foreign economies rather than by domestic factors.[23]

The newly created big banks moved from railway finance to industrial finance. This was made possible by the *Kontokorrent* credit which was dove-tailed for the financial needs of trade and industry and therefore reflected the close links between finance and industry. A *Kontokorrent* is a bank account used for running expenditures and incomes and ensures the equalization of demand for money between regions and branches. Short-term loans often took the form of overdrafts. These credits, however, were frequently used to finance investments. At the same time, the rapid increase of loans and deposits activated the money multiplier, thereby supplying the economy with a purchase power far in excess of banknotes put into circulation by the 36 note-issuing banks.[24] In 1915 the share of deposits on current account already amounted to 56 per cent of total money supply; it slowly decreased during the interwar years and regained this level in 1962.[25] The discount of bills of exchange had been essential as a means of credit and payment in the mid nineteenth century; after the First World War, however, it lost most of its significance. According to E. Schneider, this long-term decline of the bill of exchange was mainly due to the increased capacity of trade and industry for self-finance.[26]

The relationship between banks and industry is clearly emphasized in the words of Heinrich Schmidt (1912), professor at the St Gallen business school and secretary of the cantonal federation of industrialists:

> The development of the Swiss industry owes a great deal to the commercial banks. Without their help, they could have achieved neither the rate of growth of the last twenty years nor their current expansion, and large corporations would not have been able to emerge.... Commercial banks have also been instrumental in converting many of the most dynamic Swiss industrial firms into joint stock companies.[27]... By taking over local banks and setting up a network of branches in every business centre of the country, these banks have succeeded in concentrating a large part of the national capital, thereby preventing it from dispersal and exodus.[28]

In the early twentieth century, a direct presence in the foreign markets became a strategic factor for business expansion. Schmidt also emphasized the 'unusually expansive character of Swiss industry' and noted that:

> by financing the setting up of factories abroad, the commercial banks maintained a close relationship between Swiss multinational companies

> and Swiss capital and therefore with the Swiss economy. In addition, the concentration of capital in the hands of the big commercial banks has ensured the independence of Swiss capital abroad and protected it from the risks of being taken over by foreign money powers.

In the eyes of the author, this strength had been decisive against the 'financial imperialism' of other industrialized countries.[29]

In his study of the Swiss big banks, E. Schneider reaches the conclusion that in 1933 they could 'exercise an influence' on 469 corporations (3 per cent of the total) which had a combined capital of 2.86 billion francs (33 per cent of the total)[30] The finance companies – also called loan banks, trust banks or investment trusts – acted as an important link between large banks and industrial concerns, particularly in the development of the 'new' industries such as machinery and electricity. According to a study by J. Landmann in 1916, these two branches benefited the most from the export of Swiss capital.[31] As a rule the finance companies were founded by the big banks and remained under their patronage and control.[32] The 'intimate interaction between capital concentration and industrial development' diagnosed by Schmidt in 1912 manifested itself in the fact that capital exports were translated into commercial orders.[33]

Accelerated internationalization after the Second World War

The adjustment of the Swiss economy to international demand suffered a mere temporary backlash during the Great Depression. During the war the preconditions for the internationalization of the Swiss financial sector in the late 1950s and 1960s were created. In the first place the Swiss banks succeeded in financing the public debt between 1939 and 1945, contrary to what had happened during the First World War when the government had to resort to printing money, thus creating inflation. Secondly, although banks concentrated their activities on the domestic market after 1939,[34] they were also engaged in a profitable foreign exchange and gold trade, first with the Axis powers and then with the western allies. In the case of Germany, the banks converted 1.7 billion francs worth of gold in free convertible currency;[35] it has been established that out of this sum more than one billion was money stolen by the Nazis. In the post-war period, the tradition of 'money laundering' was a useful starting point for the resumption of international activities.

A look at different growth rates illustrates the degree of internationalization of the Swiss financial sector and the rapidity with which it occurred. Between 1950 and 1973, the national income grew at an annual rate of 8.4 per cent, whereas the growth of bank foreign assets and liabilities was twice as large, respectively 17 per cent and 16 per cent. The so-called *Treuhandgeschäft* (trustee deposits) reached a growth rate of 26.6

per cent, increasing their share of the deposits of all Swiss banks from 0.5 to 15.7 per cent during the same period.[36] Foreign exchange, portfolio management and trade in precious metals also expanded proportionately.[37] With the exception of the London branch of the Swiss Bank Corporation, already opened in 1898, the big banks opened their first branches abroad during the war period; but this movement did not really expand before the 1960s.[38]

In the interwar years, Switzerland became greatly involved in short-term capital transactions;[39] these had developed in a more autonomous way as a result of the currency crisis, having hitherto mainly been generated by the need for settling balance of payments deficits. In the post-war era of growth, Switzerland as a financial centre played a central role in these short-term credits, becoming a turn-table for these transactions. It should be noted that, in contrast to traditional credit operations, this type of capital movement has little to do with trade, industry, agriculture, transport or urban infrastructure. Despite these developments, however, the backbone of Switzerland's financial strength has remained the issue of medium- and long-term securities on behalf of Swiss and, mostly, foreign borrowers and placed by the Swiss banks with local and, mostly, foreign investors. It is mainly in these activities that Swiss bankers have acquired worldwide prominence and stature.

Another feature of the post-war era is the growing tendency by the large corporations to integrate banking functions, thus blurring previous distinctions between the two sectors. Today an analysis of the financial sector has to take into account the cash management and investment policy of multi-nationals. The uncoupling of banking from its domestic base, the involvement of banks in the rapidly expanding 'grey and black markets' (capital flight, drugs, weapons) and the fact that the larger enterprises employ a greater proportion of their workforce abroad than at home (in the case of Nestlé this proportion is as high as 95 per cent)[40] have led to a hidden antagonism between the big banks and the multi-national companies on the one hand and the rest of the national economy on the other. In the late 1970s this conflict assumed a political dimension and was debated in terms of an incompatibility between 'financial centre' and 'industrial economy';[41] and the risks involved by the banks' strategy were clearly perceived.[42] The banking community has on the whole opposed attempts to regulate financial activities or to impose excessive taxation; and the big banks especially have threatened to move important parts of their business to other locations if Switzerland as a financial centre were to lose its attractiveness.

Financial elites

Because of the decentralized character of the Swiss banking system, in particular with the existence of the cantonal banks, a definition of the Swiss financial elite is difficult. There was in a sense a financial elite in each canton, linked with other cantonal elite groups, which could be considered as a first stratum of the Swiss financial elite. This is however too wide a group, which might reflect the Swiss consensus but not the internal cleavages within the banking world, in particular the hierarchies of financial centres.[43] The criteria of definition chosen for this analysis are that the members of the financial elite must have, at least potentially, a national or even an international stature. This excludes the cantonal and local banks and means that this elite was concentrated in the big banks, finance companies and major private banks, not only of Zürich, which had become by the late nineteenth century the predominant financial centre of Switzerland, but also of Basel and Geneva, which retained a not insignificant part of the international banking business.[44]

During the period 1880–1960, the Swiss financial elite appears to have been affected by three major transformations. Firstly, the replacement of private family interests by corporate interests on the boards of the big banks. Secondly, a growing professionalization of the banking elite, in particular through the increased power of the salaried managers at the expense of the directors. And thirdly, a more diversified recruitment, especially at the geographical level. These transformations mostly took place at the end of the period under review.

From private to corporate interests

In the mid nineteenth century, banking traditions greatly differed between Zürich, Basel and Geneva. As is well known, Zürich, which was to emerge as the leading financial centre of the country, lay behind the two other cities. A consequence of this situation was that Zürich had only a handful of private banks and from an early stage merchants and industrialists established joint-stock banks in order to support their expanding activities. The Bank in Zürich, established in 1837, was the first joint-stock bank in Switzerland, but the Crédit Suisse, founded in 1856 on the model of the French Crédit Mobilier, was the most spectacular and most successful case.[45] In Basel and Geneva, the domination of powerful private bankers' dynasties hampered the development of joint-stock banks, at least until the private bankers decided to establish themselves such institutions: thus the Basler Handelsbank was formed in 1863 and, on a larger scale, the Basler Bankverein in 1872. The latter was to become the Swiss Bank Corporation after the merger with the Zürcher Bankverein in 1896 and the

Schweizerische Union Bank of St Gallen in 1897.[46] In Geneva, the private bankers limited their cooperation to the issuing business by creating the Union Financière de Genève. Only in the interwar period did the Geneva private bankers support the development of a joint-stock bank, the Comptoir d'Escompte de Genève, established in 1855 but until then only linked with small local firms. It grew rapidly after the First World War and ranked during the twenties and early thirties among the 'big banks'.[47] However, it ran into difficulties in the 1930s, was merged with the Union Financière under the name of Banque d'Escompte Suisse in an attempt to rescue it and finally collapsed in 1934.[48]

Despite these differences in banking traditions, there does not appear to have been, at the sociological level, any fundamental differences in the composition of the financial elites of Zürich, Basel and Geneva, in the sense that they remained for a long time composed of members of the traditional economic elites. This appears very clearly by comparing the boards of the Crédit Suisse and of the Swiss Bank Corporation. Until 1914, the board of the Swiss Bank Corporation comprised a majority of bankers: on the one hand the members of the founding families, such as the Laroche, Burckhardt, Ehinger, Passavant and others, on the other hand representatives of the German banks involved in the foundation of the bank, but who disappeared after the First World War. It was not until 1940 that the Basel private bankers lost the majority on the board of the Swiss Bank Corporation, being by then about a third. In 1960, they had almost completely disappeared, being replaced by representatives of various economic interests, in particular senior executives of major industrial companies – in the first place of course CIBA, the chemical enterprise based in Basel, but also firms such as Von Roll or Georg Fischer in mechanical engineering, Holderbank in the cement industry – and of insurance companies such as 'La Suisse' or 'Helvetia'. From being almost a negligible percentage before 1940, these corporate interests formed that year about a third of the board and two thirds in 1960, the remainder, including a few professional bankers, usually former general managers promoted to the board, and a handful of politicians and professionals, in other words the typical composition of the board of a modern Swiss bank.

As far as the board of the Crédit Suisse was concerned, it was dominated in its first phase by economic interests linked to the first industrial revolution, that is textile merchants and industrialists. Once again, until 1940, 80 per cent of the businessmen with a seat on the board of the Crédit Suisse belonged to this group; from then on, their number declined in the same proportion as that of the private bankers in the Swiss Bank Corporation. This massive presence of textile interests long outlived the importance of this industrial branch for the Swiss economy and until further investigation must be attributed to vested interests in the bank. There were for example representatives of the Abegg family on the board of the Crédit Suisse between 1868 and 1953. They were all partners in the firm of Abegg & Cie, silk merchants, with a capital of 2 million francs and forty-seven employees in 1923.[49] Carl Abegg, the founder of the firm, was chairman of the Crédit Suisse between 1883 and 1911, the longest serving chairman of the bank; he was succeeded on the board by his son and his grandson. Another dynasty was that of the Jenny, cotton spinners and weavers from Ziegelbrücke, in the canton of Glaris, with a three generations presence extending from 1869 to 1961. Caspar Jenny was vice-chairman of the bank between 1953 and his death in 1961. The family firm, with 625 workers in 1880, ranked among the largest firms in the country; with 600 workers in 1964, it had become a comparatively small firm, but its head still counted among the *notables* of the bank.[50] Other such dynasties included the Syz, the Schwarzenbach, the Keller, the Schmidheiny. As in the case of the Swiss Bank Corporation, the presence of representatives of the machine-building or electrical industries on the board of the Crédit Suisse is hardly noticeable before 1940 and even later. This did not prevent the Crédit Suisse from being actively involved in the financing of the electrical industry, in particular through the Bank für elektrische Unternehmungen – also known as Elektrobank – the major finance company in this field, in which it had from the outset an important stake.[51]

The situation was of course different in Geneva where the private banks remained entirely under family control. But this could only be achieved by opting for a specialization in a certain type of banking activity – private portfolio management – compatible with a small-sized family firm.

Professionalization

The other component of the financial elite consisted of the general managers of the big banks. They played a central role from the beginning in a bank like the Crédit Suisse, where no professional banker sat on the board, but only at a later stage in the Swiss Bank Corporation, where the position of managing-director was not created before 1900; in 1937, however, following an internal reorganization, the responsibilities of the directors were delegated to the newly created general management.[52] From 1920 on, the number of general managers oscillated between four and six in both banks. The position of the managers of the Swiss banks is certainly more comparable to that of the members of the executive board (*Vorstand*) of a German bank than to that of the general managers of an English bank[53] as far as both their professional and social positions were concerned. Apart from their responsibility over the management of the bank, in terms of strategic decisions as well as day-to-day running, it was the managers rather than the directors who represented their bank's interests on the board of other companies. Virtually all the general managers became directors of their banks, usually at the end of their career. Moreover, respectively since 1911 and 1920, all the chairmen of the Crédit Suisse and the Swiss Bank Corporation were former general managers, with one exception in each bank. Although there is a lack of information about their social origins, education and marriages, general managers appear to have been drawn from a similar background to the directors, that is middle to upper middle class, with perhaps an emphasis on the professions rather than business. Some of them, particularly those who reached the very top, had been university educated, usually with a law degree, but a simple banking apprenticeship was by no means an obstacle on the way to a successful banking career. Careers were often, but not always, spent in the same bank. Some managers were recruited in other banks, while some others were former senior civil servants, for instance Peter Vieli, a merchant's son, who had been in the diplomatic service and then at the Ministry of Public Economy before becoming general manager of the Crédit Suisse between 1937 and 1952. Adolf Jöhr had headed one of the three departments of the Swiss National Bank before becoming general manager of the Crédit Suisse between 1918 and 1939 and chairman from 1940 to 1953. Another future chairman, Rudolf Speich, of the Swiss Bank Corporation, had also spent some time at the Ministry of Public Economy before being recruited by the bank in 1920, at the age of thirty. Born in Beyrouth, the son of a businessman from Glaris, he married the daughter of an industrialist from the same canton, Fritz Jenny, from the firm Fritz and Caspar Jenny mentioned above, and a director of the Crédit Suisse. Speich was chairman of the Swiss Bank Corporation between 1944 and 1961.

Recruitment

The financial elite undoubtedly belonged to the Swiss upper classes. In a country with no landed aristocracy, the urban patricians mainly consisted of merchants and bankers and members of their families who could include lawyers, doctors, scientists and so on. Social origins are an indication of this status. During the period under review, a majority of members of the financial elite came from business families, as can be seen from table 16.6. This is an indication of a limited degree of circulation between the business and other elite groups. The high proportion of bankers' sons is in large part due to the Geneva private bankers who were almost exclusively members of old established banking families. A change is once again noticeable around 1940. Not so much in terms of social as

Table 16.6 *Social origins of the Swiss banking elite, 1880–1965*

Father's occupation	1880		1900[a]		1920[b]		1940		1960	
		(%)		(%)		(%)		(%)		(%)
Banker	7	(18)	8	(13)	17	(18)	13	(15)	12	(12)
Banking family	8	(21)	7	(12)	8	(8)	5	(6)	—	—
Other business	6	(15)	8	(13)	7	(7)	19	(21)	29	(29)
Politician, senior civil servant, professional	3	(8)	4	(7)	11	(12)	10	(11)	12	(12)
Lower middle class, working class	1	(2)	0	(0)	4	(4)	4	(4)	4	(4)
No information	14	(36)	33	(55)	49	(51)	38	(43)	43	(43)
Total	39	(100)	60	(100)	96	(100)	89	(100)	100	(100)

Notes: [a] Swiss National Bank: 1906.
[b] Union Bank of Switzerland included from 1920.
Source: Authors' calculations from a sample of bank directors and managers.

in terms of professional recruitment, the increasing number of sons of lawyers, doctors, professors, politicians and so on reflecting the rise of the corporate interests on the boards of the banks. Bankers with a lower middle-class or working-class background remained exceptional cases. However, they did exist – for example Leopold Dubois, who was born into a working-class family of La Chaux-de-Fonds, in the canton of Neuchâtel. After a few years as a school master, he became general manager of the Cantonal Bank of Neuchâtel and then of the Federal Railways before joining the Swiss Bank Corporation as managing director in 1906, becoming its chairman between 1920 and 1928. Or Fritz Richner, the son of a railway employee, who climbed step by step to the top of the ladder of the Union Bank of Switzerland to become general manager in 1941 and chairman in 1953.

Education is not in itself an indicator of social status. In particular in private banking, there existed a long and persistent tradition of a banking apprenticeship followed by practical experience abroad in an allied firm before being admitted as a partner. As can be seen from table 16.7, two trends clearly emerge about the education of Swiss bankers. The first one is the persistence of the practical formation through an apprenticeship without any higher education. Up to 1960, it was possible to reach the top position of a major bank after having started as an apprentice and usually having spent some time abroad. This was for example the case of Ernst Gamper, general manager and then chairman of the Crédit Suisse. The second and stronger trend is the increased number of university educated cases at each generation. A first progression is noticeable for those active

Table 16.7 *Education of the Swiss banking elite, 1880–1960*

	1880		1900[a]		1920[b]		1940		1960[c]	
		(%)		(%)		(%)		(%)		(%)
Apprenticeship	8	(21)	11	(18)	11	(11)	14	(16)	9	(10)
Commercial or technical school	2	(5)	6	(10)	10	(10)	10	(11)	5	(6)
University	5	(13)	7	(12)	23	(24)	33	(37)	47	(52)
No information	24	(61)	36	(60)	52	(55)	32	(36)	29	(32)
	39	(100)	60	(100)	96	(100)	89	(100)	90	(100)

Notes: [a] Swiss National Bank: 1906.
[b] Union Bank of Switzerland included from 1920.
[c] Geneva private bankers not included.
Source: Authors' calculations from a sample of bank directors and managers.

after the First World War, but the decisive step is made with the generation active in 1960 with 55 per cent of all cases, but 77 per cent of those about which details of education are known, having gone to university. Law studies was the most common choice, followed by the Federal Technical High School in Zürich.

Little is known about other aspects of social integration. Social life, marriages and networks of relationships outside the officers corps, boards of directors and trade associations remain to be thoroughly investigated. Considering the federal structure of Switzerland, these networks are likely to have been stronger at the cantonal level, for neither the political capital, Bern, nor the most dynamic economic centre, Zürich, superseded the economic, social and political roles of other centres. In that respect, it is significant that, despite their growth and their gradual expansion over the whole country, the Swiss big banks did not entirely lose their original cantonal character. Until 1960 the members of the board of the Crédit Suisse were in a majority from the canton of Zürich, and this proportion was as high as 70 per cent before 1914. In the Swiss Bank Corporation, the natives of Basel lost the absolute majority after the First World War, but continued to form a significant, and by far the single largest, minority – between 30 and 45 per cent. In the Union Bank of Switzerland, the proportion of members from Zürich hardly fell under 50 per cent before 1960.

Distinctive characters of the Swiss banking elite

To what extent did the Swiss financial elite constitute a distinct business elite and can we speak in its case of an aristocratic bourgeoisie?[54] The notion of 'aristocratic bourgeoisie', since first employed by Stendhal, has primarily been used to describe private bankers, preferably international bankers belonging to the 'Haute banque'. This type of banking aristocracy undoubtedly existed in Switzerland, particularly in cities like Basel and Geneva. The Genevan private bankers could in many respects be seen as epitomizing the banking aristocracy: wealth, maintenance of family control over old-established firms, international connections, aristocratic way of life, social exclusiveness, patronage. In addition, their longevity makes them more comparable to the English merchant banks than to their more natural counterparts, the French 'Haute banque'. There is, however, an important difference in comparison with London or Paris, which can be dated back to the beginning of the period under review: the Genevan private bankers constituted an 'aristocratic bourgeoisie', but only within the boundaries of the canton of Geneva. With the expansion of the 'big banks', with the growing role of Zürich as the main financial centre, their economic power and political influence, although by no means negligible, were bound to decline, the more so as their interests, especially as far as insurance and finance companies were concerned, were mostly centred in companies registered in Geneva. A comparison with a city like Hamburg seems more appropriate. Like Geneva, Hamburg is a city of old merchant and banking traditions, for a long time dominated by a number of patrician families with a deeply rooted self-esteem.[55] And, although Hamburg was successful in maintaining its position as an international financial centre, it has been relegated into second place, first by Berlin and then by Frankfurt. The same applies to an even greater extent to private bankers in Basel, who gradually lost control over the joint-stock banks they had founded.

Since the interwar years, the dominant position in the world of Swiss banking has been held by the senior bank managers. Although extremely powerful and enjoying a position at the top of the social hierarchy, they do not appear to have constituted a distinct business elite, as for example did the 'City men'. They appear on the contrary to have been full members of an elite of senior officials of major companies, whether financial or industrial, and of the state bureaucracy.

Rather than the existence of an aristocratic bourgeoisie before 1914 or of a distinct business elite for the twentieth century, what is more striking in the case of Switzerland is the strong integration of bankers and industrialists and indeed of the various elite groups, an integration which was probably stronger than in the other European countries. Until the Second World War this strong integration appears, once again, to have been primarily due to the federal structure of Switzerland. The networks of relationships between the financial elite and the other elite groups were similar to that existing at the regional level in other European countries, which were characterized by a greater density than at the national level. However, from the late nineteenth century, the big financial institutions were no more part of these networks in the larger European countries. The Midland Bank was founded in 1836 by industrialists from Birmingham and the Crédit Lyonnais in 1863 under the leadership of businessmen from Lyon. The Crédit Lyonnais moved to Paris in 1865 and the Midland Bank to London in 1891 and both rapidly became truly national banks.[56] In Switzerland, a couple of banks of European size emerged after the First World War, but they remained in the hands of a local elite. The fact that Zürich, which had no strong banking traditions, became simultaneously the leading financial and industrial centre of the country must have also reinforced this tendency. But the close links of the Swiss Bank Corporation with the Basel chemical industry cannot be solely attributed to mutually fruitful business relationships. After the Second World War, however, with the stronger interactions between the state, the major financial institutions and the multi-national industrial companies, the Swiss example becomes more familiar.

Political influence

Liberal corporatism

As in other European countries, the era of 'organized capitalism'[57] started in Switzerland at the turn of the twentieth century. The specific international orientation of the Swiss case, however, suggests the relevance of the notion of 'liberal corporatism'. Three main characteristics can be outlined. Firstly, a higher degree of cartelization and concentration in the economy, with a wave of mergers and the emergence of new large corporations in the years preceding the First World War. The degree of banking interlocking also increased, as evidenced by the growth of the inter-bank credit transactions.[58] Secondly, the establishment of a system of mediation between the state apparatus and the various interest groups and classes of the population; this was concomitant with the formation of several professional associations organized at the national level: in 1897 the cartel of note-issuing banks, in 1907 the Association of cantonal banks, and in 1912 the Swiss Bankers' Association, the most encompassing and powerful organization in the banking sector. Thirdly, the increased level of state intervention: in 1897, for example, the Basel Stock Exchange was nationalized. The insurance business was provided with a legal framework. The banking world opposed to state intervention a strategy of self-regulation. In the interwar period, this mainly took the form of 'gentlemen's agreements'. This strategy proved successful as it was only in 1934, amidst a banking crisis requiring life-saving measures by the state, that a banking law came into being. By introducing banking secrecy, however, this law was a state protection of Swiss international banking rather than a tightening of political control.

Members of the financial elite were themselves little engaged in parliamentary activities, and indeed a decline in the number of businessmen in parliament can be observed throughout Europe from the late nineteenth century. Each bank permanently had one or two national councillors (MPs) and one or two cantonal councillors on its board, the two mandates being often combined in the same person. Future federal councillors (Cabinet Ministers) did on some occasions have a seat on the board of a big bank, the most notable cases being Arthur Hoffmann in 1900 and Nelo Celio in 1960, both at the Crédit Suisse.

The Swiss National Bank

The question of a national currency became more acute with the development and internationalization of Swiss banking and industry.[59] As is well known, political unification and monetary union did not coincide in Switzerland. After the foundation of the Federal State in 1848, Switzerland was still 'reduced to no more than a money province of her western neighbour' (France). The vulnerability of the monetary system was blatantly exposed during the Franco–Prussian War in1870–71, when the 'whole credit machinery of the country came to a standstill'.[60] Because of the free competition between a great number of note-issuing banks and a general dependence on foreign currency, the money supply remained not only inelastic but also unreliable. The absence of a central bank with a monopoly for issuing banknotes was seen by contemporary observers as a 'deficiency which, if continued, would cause serious economic damage to the country'.[61]

The Swiss National Bank was finally created in 1905 and opened its doors in 1907. It was a joint-stock company with public and private shareholders, the majority of the shares being held by the cantonal governments. The Swiss National Bank enjoyed a great autonomy from internal politics, especially the organized socio-economic interests, and only had at its disposal relatively modest instruments of intervention in the domestic economy. It was intended to be immune from the political conflicts arising from the high indebtedness of agriculture. For the foundation of the National Bank did not serve everyone in the same way; it was obviously harmful to the existing note-issuing banks, but it perfectly suited the needs of the big banks and the large exporting industrial companies. Five years after its inauguration, H. Schmidt pointed out: 'One can understand that the Swiss industrial magnates, with their extensive payment transactions abroad, have been pleased with the beneficial effects that the foundation of the National Bank has had on these transactions.'[62] As for the big banks, which were also interested in the acquisition of foreign assets through the finance companies, they also benefited from a central bank ensuring internal liquidity and supporting the money market.

Capital exports and strong currency

The alliance between international finance and multi-national industry dominated Switzerland's monetary policy.[63] In the years of monetary instability following the First World War, the Swiss franc acquired the reputation of an internationally accepted medium of payment and refuge currency. This was achieved by a sharp control of the money supply after 1918, which had a negative impact on domestic growth. Henceforth capital exports were carried out on the basis of a strong home currency. The franc now embodied the values perceived as specifically 'Swiss' by the whole country: security and stability. Capital exports could continue to act as an incentive for the export of industrial products based on high technology, ensuring a strong international position for the Swiss economy. There existed therefore a link between rationalization of the industrial structure and increased involvement in foreign capital markets.

The chronically deflationary tendency of Swiss financial policy must be judged in this context. The strengthening of the currency's purchasing power on the foreign markets remained the priority of the economic elites, even though the constant pressures for re-evaluation drove the small export industries into a profit-squeeze; this was undoubtedly the case in the 1930s. The propensity of the overwhelming majority of the innumerable savers to favour a strong budget policy perfectly coincided with the interests of high finance. During the Great Depression the Federal Council (the Swiss government) could enforce wage-cuts through arguing that these would be compensated by lower prices. This deflationary policy was a natural consequence of the government's refusal to devalue the currency until the autumn of 1936. It had harmful effects on small peasants, craftsmen and small- and medium-sized exporting industries, and was unsuccessfully fought by the labour movement. The strength of the Swiss franc had to be demonstrated in order to maintain international confidence in the currency of a small state. Many Swiss economists developed the cult of capital exports. Eduard Kellenberger, for example, coined the dictum: 'From the Swiss point of view, capital exports mean the pursuit of strength, capital imports the decay of power.'[64]

Conclusion

The world of banking in Switzerland, its weight in the country's economy and society, present a contrasted picture. A very powerful group of big banks, whose domination over the banking system increased considerably in the course of the twentieth century, was able to emerge in a comparatively unconcentrated banking system where the cantonal banks, partly for constitutional and legal reasons, have been able to retain a fair share of the domestic banking business. In the same way, a powerful national banking lobby has coexisted with a socially divided banking elite whose roots, even within the big banks themselves, have remained cantonal rather than national. These contrasts can be explained by the federal structure of the Swiss state and by the existence in the country of at least three financial centres of international significance. In the end, however, the defence of financial interests at the national level has proved to be the strongest factor. Capital exports carried out by the banks and financial companies had an unmistakable impact on the foreign policy of Switzerland, which continued to be dependent on the economic internationalization process. The maxim of 'armed neutrality' strengthened internal social and ideological cohesion and acted as an integration factor, thus counterbalancing the centrifugal effects of regionalism in the financial sector. Since the late 1930s, a collective defence against extraneous influences and immigrants was promoted, legitimated through the so-called '*Geistige Landesverteidigung*' ('spiritual defence'). This attitude of socio-cultural self-sufficiency embodied in the mentality of the Swiss people developed simultaneously, in a complementary way, with the economic cooperation of the Swiss financial and industrial elites with their foreign counterparts, therefore supporting each other, especially during the crucial period of the Second World War when the conditions for the rapid growth of the following decades were laid.

Notes

1 The authors should like to thank David Kynaston for his corrections on an earlier draft of this chapter.

2 *Handbuch des schweizerischen Volkwirtschaft* (HSV), 1939, vol. II, p. 11.

3 F. Ritzmann, 'Die Entwicklung des schweizerischen Geld-und Kreditsystems', *Schweizerische Zeitschrift für Volkwirtschaft und Statistik*, 100 (1964), 237. (All quotations translated by the authors.)

4 J. Landmann, 'Der schweizerische Kapitalexport', *Zeitschrift für schweizerische Statistik und Volkwirtschaft*, 52 (1916), 390.

5 J.-F. Bergier, *Die Wirtschaftsgeschichte der Schweiz* (Zürich-Cologne, 1983), p. 33.

6 F. Ritzmann, *Die Schweizer Banken* (Bern, 1973), p. 58, Max Iklé, *Die Schweiz als internationaler Bank-und Finanzplatz* (Zürich, 1970), p. 131.
7 HSV 1939/I, p. 606.
8 Ritzmann, 'Entwicklung', 239.
9 See H.-J. Siegenthaler, Introduction to *Raumordnung der Wirtschaft*, edited by Schweizerische Gesellschaft für Wirtschafts-und Sozialgeschichte, (Lausanne, 1983), pp. 1ff.
10 Ritzmann, *Schweizer Banken*, pp. 243, 246.
11 Ibid., pp. 61ff.
12 Ritzmann, 'Entwicklung', 242–3.
13 For the time series see Ritzmann, *Schweizer Banken*, Statistical appendix, pp. 261ff.
14 Ritzmann, 'Entwicklung', 247.
15 See P. Stauffer and U. Emch (eds.), *Das Schweizerische Bankgeschäft* (Thun, 1972), pp. 23ff.; Swiss National Bank, *Das schweizerische Bankwesen* (annually).
16 See A. Hartmann, *Der Konkurrenzkampf zwischen Grossbanken und Kantonalbanken* (Zürich, 1947).
17 Ritzmann, 'Entwicklung', 252.
18 Ibid., 254.
19 E. Schneider, *Die schweizerischen Grossbanken im Zweiten Weltkrieg 1939–1945* (Zürich, 1959), pp. 210ff.
20 Ibid., p. 250; *Stat. Jahrbuch der Schweiz* (1939) 222; (1949) 224.
21 N. Reichesberg, *Handwörterbuch der schweizerischen Volkwirtschaft* (Bern, ca. 1907), vol. I, p. 408.
22 Landmann, 'Kapitalexport', 389.
23 See E. Gruner (ed.), *Arbeitershaft und Wirtschaft in der Schweiz 1880–1914*, vol. I (Zürich, 1988), pp. 91ff. See also M. Benegger, 'Die Schweizerische Wirtschaft 1850–1913. Wachstum, Strukturwandel und Konjunkturzyklen', Zürich, 1983 (Ms).
24 See Ernst Dürr (ed.), *Geld-und Bankpolitik* (Cologne-Berlin, 1971).
25 Ritzmann, 'Entwicklung', 262; Ch. Grüebler, *Die Geldmenge der Schweiz 1907–1954* (Zürich, 1958).
26 Schneider, *Schweizerischen Grossbanken*, p. 119; R. Kunz, *Die Gewinn und Verlustrechnung der schweizerischen Banken in den Jahren 1914–1944* (Munich, 1952), p. 73; M. W. Hess, *Strukturwandlungen im schweizerischen Bankwesen* (Winterthur, 1963), p. 122.
27 P. H. Schmidt, *Die schweizerischen Industrien im internationalen Konkurrenzkampf* (Zürich, 1912), p. 125.
28 Ibid., pp. 124, 122.
29 Ibid., pp. 133, 135.
30 Schneider, *Schweizerischen Grossbanken*, p. 194; *Stat. Jahrbuch der Schweiz* (1934), 329.
31 Landmann, 'Kapitalexport', 397; Landmann, *Die Schweizerische Volkwirtschaft* (Einsielden, 1925), p. 348.

32 R. J. Kaderli and E. Zimmermann, *Handbuch des Bank–, Geld– und Börsenwesens der Schweiz* (eds.) (Thun, 1947), p. 517.

33 Schmidt, *Schweizerischen Industrien*, p. 121.

34 Schneider, *Schweizerischen Grossbanken*, pp. 190, 205–6.

35 W. Rings, *Raubgold aus Deutschland* (Zürich-Munich, 1985).

36 Swiss National Bank, *Das schweizerische Bankwesen im Jahre 1976* (Zürich, 1977), pp. 26, 36.

37 There are no precise data available on that particular point.

38 Schneider, *Schweizerischen Grossbanken*, pp. 51–2. See also Y. Cassis, 'Swiss international banking 1900–1950' in G. Jones (ed.), *Banks as multinationals* (London, 1990) and Cassis, 'La place financière suisse et la City de Londres, 1890–1990', in P. Bairoch & M. Körner (eds.), *La Suisse dans l'économie mondiale* (Geneva-Zürich, 1990).

39 HSV 1939, vol. II, p. 6.

40 S. Borner and F. Wehrle, *Die Sechste Schweiz. Überleben auf dem Weltmarkt* (Zürich, 1984).

41 See *Finanzplatz gegen Werkplatz*, Dossier SPS (Bern, 1978).

42 H. Kleinewefers, *Das Auslandgeschäft der Schweizer Banken* (Zürich, 1972).

43 For a discussion of the hierarchy of financial centres in Switzerland in an international perspective, see C. P. Kindleberger, 'The formation of financial centres', in *Economic response. Comparative studies in trade, finance and growth* (Cambridge, Mass., 1978), pp. 100–5, who argues that there is one major financial centre in each country, Zürich in the case of Switzerland.

44 The following analysis is based on a sample of bankers established for the years 1880, 1900, 1920, 1940 and 1960. The directors and general managers of the Crédit Suisse and the Swiss Bank Corporation have been considered for each of the selected years, those of the Union Bank of Switzerland and the Banking Committee of the Swiss National Bank from 1920 on. For Geneva, the directors of the Association Financière/Union Financière have been studied for the years 1880, 1900 and 1920 and the two senior partners of the major private banks Bordier & Cie, Darier & Cie, Ferrier, Lullin & Cie, Hentsch & Cie, Lombard, Odier & Cie, Mirabaud & Cie, Pictet & Cie thereafter. Unless otherwise indicated, all information originates from this sample.

45 See W. A. Jöhr, *Schweizerische Kreditanstalt 1856–1956* (Zürich, 1956).

46 See H. Bauer, *Société de Banque Suisse 1872–1972* (Basel, 1972).

47 See J. Seitz, *Histoire de la Banque à Genève* (Geneva, 1931).

48 On the Geneva banking crisis, see A. Spielmann, *L'aventure socialiste genevoise* (Lausanne, 1981).

49 Archives fédérales, Berne, Fabriken-Verzeichnis E 7172 (A1) 1923.

50 Ibid., 1895 and E 7172 (B 1967/142) 1960.

51 See P. Hertner, 'Les sociétés financières suisses et le développement de

l'industrie électrique jusqu'à la Première Guerre Mondiale', in F. Cardot (ed.), *1880–1980. Un siècle d'électricité dans le monde* (Paris, 1987) pp. 341–55.

52 Bauer, *Société de Banque Suisse*, pp. 266–7.

53 For some interesting international comparisons, see N. Horn 'Aktienrechtliche Unternehmensorganisation in der Hochindustrialisierung (1860–1920). Deutschland, England, Frankreich und die USA im Vergleich', in N. Horn and J. Kocka (eds.), *Recht und Entwicklung des Grossunternehmen im 19. und frühen 20. Hahrhundert* (Göttingen, 1979), pp. 123–89.

54 For a recent use of this concept in a European comparative perspective, see J. Harris and P. Thane, 'British and European bankers 1880–1914: an aristocratic bourgeoisie?', in P. Thane, G. Crossick and R. Floud (eds.), *The power of the past. Essays for Eric Hobsbawm* (Cambridge, 1984).

55 See Dolores Augustine's chapter in this volume.

56 See J. Bouvier, *Le Crédit Lyonnais de 1863 à 1882. Les années de formation d'une banque de dépôts*, 2 vols (Paris, 1961); A. R. Holmes and E. Green, *Midland. 150 years of banking business* (London, 1986).

57 H. A. Winkler (ed.) *Organisierter Kapitalismus. Voraussetzungen und Anfänge* (Göttingen, 1974); Winkler, 'Organisierter Kapitalismus? Versuch eines Fazits', in Winkler, *Liberalismus und Antiliberalismus* (Göttingen, 1979) pp. 264ff.

58 Ritzmann, 'Entwicklung', 258–9.

59 See R. Zimmermann, *Volksbank oder Aktienbank? Parlamentsdebatten, Referendum und zunehmende Verbandsmacht beim Streit um die Nationalbankgründung 1891–1905* (Zürich, 1987).

60 Reichesberg, *Handwörterbuch*, vol. III, p. 1488; vol. I, p. 416.

61 Ibid., vol. I, p. 409.

62 Schmidt, *Schweizerischen Industrien*, p. 130.

63 See G. Arlettaz, 'Crise et déflation. Le primat des intérêts financiers en Suisse au début des années 1930', *Relations internationales*, 30 (1982), 159–75.

64 E. Kellenberger, *Kapitalexport und Zahlungsbilans*, vol. 3 (Bern, 1942), p. 372.

17 Finance and financiers in Belgium, 1880–1940

G. KURGAN-VAN HENTENRYK

I

The rise of industrial Belgium at the beginning of the nineteenth century was closely connected with the establishment of a banking system which, well before the French *Crédit Mobilier* or the German banks, channelled into key sectors of heavy industry the capital which was vitally necessary to modernize and expand it.

At the beginning of the 1880s, in an economic climate which had been generally unfavourable since 1873, the banking system was going through a period of rapid change. For some forty years the financial market had been dominated by two rival banks, the Société Générale and the Banque de Belgique. The financial crises of 1876 and 1885 swept away the Banque de Belgique and several less important institutions, with the result that the Société Générale found itself in a dominant position in a banking system whose universal character had been becoming more pronounced since 1870.[1]

From 1880 onwards the country's chief banks lost their character as investment banks or holding companies and began to combine these activities with those of deposit banks. At this time, deposits already outstripped shareholders' funds in the eight existing mixed banks – they were respectively 227 and 144 million francs – while their investments reached some 184 million. Some fifty lesser institutions served as deposit banks, while a growing number of foreign banks and bankers were beginning to settle on Belgian soil.

Until 1895, Belgian banks were extremely cautious in their dealings with traditional industries, that is to say coal and steel. Over and above their part in the issue of public funds – Belgian and foreign – they also showed a keen interest in transport concerns – railways and trams – both in Belgium and abroad.

Alongside its developing activities as a deposit bank, the Société Générale founded a specialized subsidiary, the Société Belge des Chemins de Fer, which, either in isolation or in association with foreign groups, obtained railway concessions in France, Germany, Austria and Italy. While this company's foreign interests were concentrated almost entirely in standard-gauge railways, other banks became involved in companies constructing narrow-gauge lines and tramways. From 1880 onwards genuine specialized holdings were being formed, from amongst which three groups emerged: the Société Générale des Chemins de Fer Economiques (the Banque de Bruxelles in association with the Banque de Paris et des Pays-Bas and with the private banks of Brugmann and Cassel); the Compagnie Générale des Chemins de Fer Secondaires (the Banque Centrale Anversoise and the Philippson-Horwitz bank); and the Empain group. Characteristically, Edouard Empain founded his own bank in 1880 so as to underpin his industrial concerns.

The period of rapid expansion of the Belgian economy which began in 1895 went hand in hand with a spectacular development of the financial markets. Since the mid nineteenth century the joint-stock company had been instrumental in the transformation of capitalism and the concentration of industrial enterprises. Half a century later, finance capitalism took off thanks to an ever closer link between banks and industry, and a growing dissociation between the ownership of capital and its management. The part played by the banks in new enterprises was unprecedentedly large.

In 1892, stocks issued by the joint-stock companies were valued at 99 million francs, while the stocks of the companies in which the banks took a hand were valued at only 14 million, or 14 per cent, to which they contributed 12 million francs of new money. Some twenty years later, in 1911, of the 603 million francs' worth of stocks issued, the companies in which the banks had a stake represented 245 million, or 41 per cent. By then the banks' share of new money had risen to 134 million francs. Their contribution in terms of new capital had grown to a lesser extent, but still rose from 12 per cent to 22 per cent. This increased participation in industrial enterprises was connected both with the growing number of universal banks, which numbered about thirty in 1914, and the rapid rise of the finance companies, a kind of proto-holding company. A few examples will give a meaningful illustration of this development.

In the Liège region, one of the focal points of industrial growth, there were close links between the Crédit Général Liégeois and the local industrialists. Altogether its directors had mandates in about twenty metallurgical and coal-mining companies. This was also the time when the Banque de Bruxelles began the ascent which was to put it in second place among Belgian institutions after the war. It was founded after 1870, and so arrived on the scene rather late to gain a foothold in the traditional sectors of industry; therefore it flung itself actively into the tram companies and into a new industry, electricity. In April 1914 it entered into an alliance with the industrialists Coppée and Warocqué with the aim of getting a firm foothold in the coal industry.

The development of the electricity industry clearly shows the urgent need felt at the dawn of this century to create an association of industrial and banking interests. Although it was the initiative of industrialists and some big cities which first introduced electricity in the 1880s, the kernel of the big holdings in the industry was created at the turn of the century, with the foundation of the Société Belge d'Entreprises Electriques by the Banque de Bruxelles, the Banque de Paris et des Pays-Bas and certain private bankers (1895), and also of the Société Financière de Transport et d'Entreprises Industriels, better known as SOFINA (1898), as a result of an association between some private bankers, the Banque Liégeoise, and a group of German bankers and industrialists. It was, in fact, the danger from German competition in this sector which prompted the Empain group's takeover, in 1904, of an electrical construction firm (Ateliers de Constructions Electriques de Charleroi, or ACEC), and the creation of the Compagnie Générale de Railways et d'Electricité which was designed to take charge of the group's network of transport and electrical companies.

In spite of this expansion, the Belgian banking system was still dominated by the Société Générale group and its subsidiaries, as is shown in table 17.1 which details the resources of the chief institutions on the eve of the First World War. However, the position of the Société Générale had been modified by the transformations it had undergone between 1880 and 1913.

The development of the Société Générale was characterized by its activities as a deposit bank, the diversification of its financial and industrial interests both in Belgium and abroad, and a tendency to leave the exploration of new sectors to others, though it was quite ready to move in on them once they had showed themselves to be profitable.

There were three facets to the expansion of the Société Générale's banking activities. The first was the structuring of its resources. From 1871 to 1913, the growth in its shareholders' funds and long-term loans was in fact modest: the former grew from 75 million francs to 100 million, the latter from 31 million to 57 million. By contrast, deposits increased to a very remarkable extent, from 18 million in 1871 to 52 million in 1880, reaching 288 million in 1918. Grafted on to this direct collection of deposits was the second facet, the take-over of provincial banks and the creation of a network of eighteen sponsored banks, which together had sixty-one branches by just before the war. Finally, from 1890 the Société Générale embarked on an expansion of its foreign banking interests with

Table 17.1 *The Belgium banking system in 1913 and in 1930*

1913	Resources (million francs)	1930	Resources (million francs)
Société Générale group		*Société Générale group*	
Société Générale	482	Société Générale	6,515
Banque d'Anvers	157	Banque d'Anvers	927
Subsidiaries of the Société Générale	535	Subsidiaries of the Société Générale	6,212
Banque Belge pour l'Etranger	166	Banque Italo-Belge	3,029
Banque Italo-Belge	89	Total	20,731
Total	1,429	*Banque de Bruxelles group*	
Universal banks		Banque de Bruxelles	3,301
Crédit Général Liégeois†	149	Subsidiaries of the Banque de Bruxelles	2,712
Banque Générale Belge	104	Banque Belge d'Afrique	261
Banque de Bruxelles	101	Total	6,274
Banque Internationale de Bruxelles†	100	*Flemish banks group*	
Banque d'Outremer*	100	Algemene Bank-vereniging	1,463
Banque Liégeoise†	56	Middenkredietkas	1,875
Comptoir d'Escompte de Bruxelles*	22	Crédit Général	495
Crédit Général de Belgique	20	Total	3,833
Crédit National Industriel	17	*Solvay group*	
Total	669	Banque Générale Belge	1,470
Antwerp commercial and universal banks		Mutuelle Solvay	931
Banque de Reports, de Fonds publics et de Dépôts*	199	Total	2,401
Crédit Anversois	140	*Other universal banks*	
Banque Centrale Anversoise†	110	Banque Belge du Travail	316
Banque de Crédit Commercial	66	Banque Industrielle Belge	242
Banque de Commerce	47	Banque des Colonies	201
Total	563	Total	759
Deposit Bank		*Antwerp banks*	
Caisse Générale de Reports et de Dépóts	423	Crédit Anversois	1,032
Grand Total	3084	Banque de Crédit Commercial	454
		Banque de Commerce	422
		Total	1,908
		Deposit bank	
		Caisse Générale de Reports et de Dépôts	1,902
		Grand Total	37,808

Notes: * Taken over by Société Générale group.
† Taken over by Banque de Bruxelles group.

the acquisition of the Banque Parisienne, which, together with the protestant 'Haute banque', became in 1904 a major French investment bank, the Banque de l'Union Parisienne, in which the Société Générale kept a large stake. But the real take-off came in 1902 with the foundation of the Banque Sino-Belge, whose activities opened with the receipt of the indemnity exacted from China after the Boxer Rebellion. After its launch into exchange and arbitrage, the bank became involved in credit for international commerce, opened an agency in London, and created a presence in Egypt. In 1913, having bought up the Anglo-Foreign Banking Corporation which gave it a foothold in the City, it took the name of Banque Belge pour l'Etranger, under which it was to become the fulcrum of the Société Générale's foreign banking interests. In 1911, the Société Générale took a hand in the founding of the Banque Italo-Belge, which was designed to support Belgian undertakings in South America.

At the beginning of the 1880s, the Société Générale still ranked as an investment bank specializing in the coal and metallurgical industries. By 1913 it had become a finance group of international importance whose industrial and financial ramifications extended throughout the world, though it did not cease to be the lynch-pin of domestic industry. Its investment portfolio more than doubled between 1880 and 1913, rising from 81 million francs to 202 million. That it was becoming a more markedly universal bank is shown by the change in the proportion of its investments to that of its shareholders' funds (98 in 1880, 202 in 1913) and to shareholders' funds plus loan capital (67 in 1880, 128 in 1913). Leaving the fostering of commercial credit to its sponsored banks and to the Banque d'Anvers, the Société Générale concentrated rather on financing and on the search for outlets for the companies under its control. Thus much of its energy was devoted to acquiring a stake in firms which might place equipment orders in its factories, whether in transport or in coal and metal industries abroad. Only at the turn of the century did it gain a foothold in two sectors which were to become the basis of its prosperity between the wars: electricity and colonial enterprise.

Despite its prominence in the financial markets, on the eve of the First World War the Société Générale no longer stood as the sole and undisputed leader in industrial finance. At the beginning of the 1880s it had indeed been the only banking institution to supply large amounts of new money to joint-stock companies. Thirty years later it was sharing this task with several universal banks, the most energetic being the Banque d'Outremer and the Banque de Paris et des Pays-Bas, whose Brussels branch had become an integral part of the Belgian financial market.[2]

On the other hand, one cannot fail to notice that even in those industrial sectors in which it had, or was acquiring, a dominating interest, it rarely functioned as a trail-blazer. Thus, although at the beginning of the 1880s it had a dominating influence over two out of the three biggest Belgian metallurgical concerns, it was not until the height of the crisis, in the 1890s, that it resolved to modernize its factories and convert them into steelworks, long after the Cockerill Company which played the leading role in the development of the Belgian steel industry. Similarly, in 1895 it sought to imitate Cockerill's brilliant Russian success of ten years earlier by creating the Métallurgie Russo-Belge, which was to become one of the most prosperous Belgian concerns ever created in Russia.

Though several tramway holdings were set up from the 1880s onwards, it was not until 1911 that the Société Générale gained a foothold in one of the most dynamic concerns of that period, the Compagnie Mutuelle des Tramways. Similarly, it was not until 1905 that it entered the electricity sector, ten years behind the Banque de Bruxelles.

Finally, the Société Générale entrance on the colonial scene is a perfect illustration of its caution and its ability to profit from the experience of the pioneers who had gone before. It actually took King Leopold II twenty years to persuade it to commit itself in the Congo by creating the so-called '1906 companies' for the development of the Katanga and the exploitation of the mineral resources of the Congo. By that time, some Antwerp financiers, along with the group headed by Albert Thys, the founder of the Banque d'Outremer, were already firmly established, at the King's instigation, in Africa.

While the influence of Belgian private bankers was in decline, the penetration of foreign banks in Belgium had grown to an unprecedented extent. Between 1888 and 1911 their proportion of the new money supplied by banks for new share issues rose from 6 per cent to 37 per cent.[3] To this must be added the contribution of foreign banks registered under Belgian law such as the Banque Internationale de Bruxelles and the Banque Centrale Anversoise, founded with German capital, whose principal directors belonged to the German communities in Brussels and Antwerp. This German dynamism was a counterweight to the older influence of the French and the long-established importance of the Banque de Paris et des Pays-Bas. Moreover, it was because of their close links with France that Belgian financial interests were able to draw amply on the French capital market for the funds they needed to finance their undertakings.

The First World War wrought a profound disruption in the Belgian economy. Not only was the industrial base in large measure pillaged or destroyed, but the state's need for money caused a transfer of banking activity from the industrial and commercial sector to the financing of state enterprises. Inflation, penury and lack of investment swelled bank deposits while the country became poorer in real terms.

During the war, the German occupation, hostile to the Banque

Nationale, entrusted the issuing of banknotes on behalf of the latter to the Société Générale. The Société Générale had played a key part in the organization of the Comité National de Secours et d'Alimentation (which distributed food and general aid), whose lynch-pin had been one of the Société Générale's directors, Emile Francqui. Thanks to the support of the USA, this organization became largely responsible for feeding the Belgian people. By reason of the wide-ranging responsibilities which it had undertaken during the Occupation, the directors of the Société Générale were convinced that Belgian industry must be reorganized, and made more specialized, and thus better able to stand up to foreign competition on overseas markets after the war.

Thus at the beginning of 1919 the governor, Jean Jadot, faced with a devastated steel industry, recommended that all its factories be brought into a single trust and specialize each in one product, with only one rolling mill being rebuilt for each unit. But the Société Générale had not enough weight in the steel industry at that time to impose its will on big firms like Cockerill and Ougrée-Marihaye which were intent on preserving their independence.[4] In spite of this failure, the episode shows us something of the changing role of the banks in the interwar Belgian economy. It was marked by a reintegration of banking activities into the national economy; a concentration of banking and industrial undertakings into powerful finance groups, with a fresh rivalry emerging between the Société Générale and the Banque de Bruxelles; and the replacement of exports of capital abroad by an interest in colonial enterprise.

The immediate post-war period saw the foundation of numerous new banks amidst the euphoria of economic revival and in a spirit of speculation. Most of them were to prove ephemeral. By contrast, the universal banks, whose pre-war expansion had been based on foreign investment, became definitively involved in the rebuilding of the domestic industry. In fact, the losses from foreign investments (especially in Russia), the slackening of external commercial contacts and the instability of the exchanges completely transformed their process of development. The requirement of capital for reconstruction gave them numerous outlets at a time when the accumulation of savings during the war and the redistribution of fortunes had increased their supply of current and deposit accounts. Thus in the decade from 1920 to 1930 banks increased their aid to industry both by augmenting their current-account credits and by direct participation in industrial companies.

The corollary of this massive intervention in industry was to give the banks a policy of acquiring a stranglehold on the economy, but also to prompt various groups to resist the hegemony of the universal banks by creating new banking institutions as counter-weights. Even before the war, the banks had been creating holding companies to manage their interests in transport firms. After the war this practice became much more widespread, especially between 1925 and 1930. It had the advantage of relieving the bank of the management of part of its industrial activities by entrusting it to specialist managers; it reduced the lock-up of capital, while extending the bank's control by means of indirect intervention. In this way it could stimulate the development of a sector of industry by forcing it to modernize its techniques and concentrate its enterprises.

In certain sectors, it was the mixed banks alone which initiated the modernization. A clear case of this is the glass industry: the traditional manufacturing in the Charleroi region was swept away in a few years by the introduction, by the banks, of the mechanized production of glass panes, and by the 1930 restructuring of the industry under the auspices of the Société Générale.[5] Similarly, the Société Générale was assured of a monopoly in the Belgian copper industry through the mining activities of its subsidiary, the Union Minière, in the Katanga.

However, other sectors were modernized and concentrated, on the joint initiative of banks and industry. Thus the Société Générale managed its interests in the coal industry directly by beginning the concentration of its mining activities in Wallonia, whereas the Banque de Bruxelles entrusted the management of its coal interests to the industrial group Coppée. By forming the industrial coal producers into a cartel at the end of the twenties, the Société Générale and Coppée acquired a dominant position in this sector.[6]

It was without doubt in the electricity industry that the interwar tendency towards concentration was most strongly felt, and it gave rise to the keenest competition. Without lingering over details of the organization of this sector – scene of rivalry between the public authorities, industrialists who produced electricity for their own use, and private firms (producers and distributors) – we should point out that those private firms themselves experienced a technical and financial concentration. As regards finance, an enormous restructuring took place between 1928 and 1935 with the creation of big specialized holdings, including Sofina (reorganized in 1928), Electrobel and Tractionel (set up in 1929) and Electrorail (1930).

While Electrobel was the result of an amalgamation of firms originally launched by the Banque de Bruxelles, and of a redistribution of the interests of five groups involved in the electricity industry (the Banque de Bruxelles, the Banque de Paris et des Pays-Bas, the Société Générale, the Mutuelle Solvay and Sofina), Tractionel was a subsidiary of the Société Générale, which was regrouping all its interests in tramways and electricity. Electrorail, however, was the outcome of the Empain group's desire to unify the management of its companies' financial services.

By the end of the thirties, these four holdings were in control of the private producers and suppliers of electricity, with 95 per cent of the available power capacity and 85 per cent of the assets of the suppliers. By reason of their complex and multiple connections with gas, tramway, electrical equipment manufacturing and foreign electricity companies, they exercised a *de facto* monopoly, focusing on Tractionel.[7]

This industrial concentration on the initiative of the universal banks demanded the deployment of ever-increasing resources. In order to augment them, the universal banks went in for the collection of long-term deposits in preference to bond issues. Apart from the Société Générale, which had set up a network of agencies via its sponsored banks, the collection of deposits was exceedingly haphazard in Belgium. After the war the universal banks undertook it more systematically, not only by extending their own networks, but also by acquiring and incorporating other institutions. From the competition between the Société Générale, the Banque de Bruxelles and the Banque d'Outremer, the Société Générale was to emerge as victor.

While the Société Générale was strengthening its network by promoting the amalgamation of several of its subsidiaries, in 1916 the Banque de Bruxelles embarked on an expansion of its banking interests with the take-over of the Banque Internationale de Bruxelles and the acquisition of an interest in the Banque Liégeoise, one of the oldest Belgian banks. After the armistice it set up a network of subsidiaries in Belgium and in the Congo, either by acquiring substantial interests in provincial banks or by setting up new institutions in various places.

The Banque d'Outremer had likewise expanded its banking interests when in 1919 it took over the Comptoir d'Escompte de Bruxelles. Feeling the threat from its acquisitive competitors, some of its directors tried to consolidate it by a vain attempt at a rapprochement with the Crédit Général Liégeois.

Early in 1928 the rivalry between the Société Générale and the Banque de Bruxelles came to a head. In January the Société Générale announced a take-over of the Banque d'Outremer which gave it an 80 per cent controlling interest in the Congo economy. Anxious to hold its ground, the Banque de Bruxelles took over the Crédit Général Liégeois, with a dowry of interests in numerous industrial concerns in the Liège region, and in tramway and electrical enterprises. The struggle between the two banks was pursued in other sectors of the economy. The Banque de Bruxelles, in search of fresh resources, founded the Compagnie Belge pour l'Industrie, regrouping its chief industrial interests and appealing to the capital market. The Société Générale reacted by raising its capital to a billion francs, making it one of the leading institutions on the European continent. But the banks found it progressively more difficult to find fresh capital on the Belgian market by reason of the successive issues of company stocks which had been offered to the public.

While in 1911 the banks' input of new money amounted to 22 per cent of the total value of company share issues, in 1928 it reached 42 per cent. Moreover, 68 per cent of this new capital came from the joint-stock banks and 19 per cent from the holding companies which depended on them; the part played by foreign banks was negligible. According to Chlepner, who reckons the total value of issues made between 1919 and 1929 at 46 billion francs, 15 billion – a little less than a third – came from banks and financial institutions, 5 billion from colonial securities, and slightly more than 3 billion was issued as company shares in transport, gas and electricity, and metal manufacturing.[8]

Table 17.1 clearly reveals the concentration of banking interests which took place between 1913 and 1930, and the consolidation of the power of the Société Générale, which held 55 per cent of the resources of the principal Belgian banks and groups.[9] The competition forced the Banque de Bruxelles to jettison some of its ballast, and it was in electricity that the decline in its influence was most apparent: after the struggles of 1928–9 it was obliged to give up its interest in Sofina and accept an equal one-fifth share in Electrobel. In 1930 the Société Générale pursued the neutralization of Electrobel by making a secret agreement with Sofina to demarcate their respective zones of influence.[10]

In spite of the importance of the universal banks to the economy, attempts were made in the internal period to cut back the spreading tentacles of their influence. But – to show just how important the universal banks were in the economy – the promoters of new banks, whatever the origin of their resources, also went in for the acquisition of industrial interests.

We have already remarked on the desire of some industrial groups to preserve their independence from the banks, even while they felt the need for a banking service for their own interests. Thus the Solvay group, which had created a holding company in 1913 and acquired interests in the Banque Générale Belge, amalgamated its financial interests from1931 by creating a new universal bank, the Société Belge de Banque. Similarly, the Empain group set up the Banque Industrielle Belge as a financial service for its undertakings in Belgium.

But the most striking innovation of this period was incontestably the formation of a banking group out of the credit cooperatives in rural areas and set up by the Flemish Catholic agricultural organization Boerenbond on the model of Raffeisen; also the acquisition by that group of a Brussels bank, the Crédit Général de Belgique. In spite of its cooperative nature and its role as a savings bank, the group committed its resources to the acquisition of industrial interests via the Algemene Bankvereniging in which the Boerenbond had an 85 per cent stake.

On the socialist side, the Banque Belge du Travail, founded in 1913, with resources chiefly made up of deposits from working-men's organizations, cooperatives, mutual benefit societies, trade unions and the party, had also begun to engage in the financing of industry and the take-over of other banking institutions.

In 1932 Belgium felt the full fury of the world economic crisis. For several months the banks had been unable to realize their investments except with heavy losses, and had been trying to recover their debts from industrialists. While the older banks had enough reserves to ride out the crisis, the smaller ones born in the boom years could not, and, having a smaller number of depositors, they quietly disappeared. On the other hand, the banks backed by the Belgian Workers' party and the Flemish Christian Democrats found themselves in difficulties. Because of their links with political parties, the problem of saving them and ensuring proper management became a subject of furious polemic, and when the Belgian Workers' party and the Flemish Christian Democrats suspended payments in 1934 the entire banking system was put under threat. The Banque Belge du Travail was left to its fate after the Catholic and Liberal parties refused to come to its assistance, while the Boerenbond crash hastened the downfall of the Catholic-Liberal cabinet and was central to negotiations for the formation of the next cabinet, nicknamed 'the government of the bankers', at the end of November 1934.[11]

From 22 August 1934, the mixed banks were compelled by royal decree to exercise their functions as deposit banks separately from those as investment banks. On 5 December 1934 the Société Générale amalgamated all its sponsored banks and concentrated all its deposit activities in a new bank, the Banque de la Société Générale, subscribing half of its capital (500 million francs), which it released in cash.

In 1931 the Banque de Bruxelles, which had been severely tested by the financial battles of 1928 and 1929, had amalgamated with its subsidiaries, becoming more of a deposit bank. Without giving the details of the severance, suffice it to say that it led to the creation of two new companies, a deposit bank which retained the name 'Banque de Bruxelles' and a holding company called the Société de Bruxelles pour la Finance ('Brufina').

Under pressure from the Catholic church and from Flemish Christian Democratic circles reluctant to lose a banking network which supported the development of Flemish enterprise, the Boerenbond banking system was reorganized under the auspices of several public credit institutions. Its various constituents were amalgamated into a new deposit bank, the Kredietbank voor Handel en Nijverheid, set up on 9 February 1935. All the former directors were removed, and certain Flemish public figures deemed worthy of trust were called upon to constitute the board of directors. From the start this new bank pursued an independent policy and promoted the development of the economy of Flanders.

The banking reform of 1935, of which more below, was the sequel to measures taken in August 1934. It wrought a transformation in the system by limiting the banks' activities to short-term operations. But, as they were forbidden to acquire interests in industry, and, as the demand for short-term credit from industrial firms was not very great, they were compelled to channel their resources into state borrowing. Even before the war, Belgian banks had taken on the characteristics of deposit banks: a smaller element of shareholders' funds in their resources, a drop in advances to private enterprise, a growth in short-term loans to the state, and the development of investments made up of government stocks.

II

Up to now, there has been no social study of the Belgian banking world. While it is true that the Brussels institutions early acquired a dominant position, it is nonetheless also true that in the nineteenth century there were still private banking houses outside the capital. The wealth of their owners ensured them a prominent position in the best local circles, and, thanks to the property qualification system, provided them with seats in Parliament.[12]

In the early 1880s the boards of joint-stock banks were for the most part made up of prominent members of society. Both the Société Générale and the Banque de Bruxelles called on persons who had attained eminence in some other field, or on relatives of existing directors.[13] Professional jurists, advocates, magistrates and senior civil servants figured largely. Four out of the seven directors of the Société Générale were of this class at that period. Meanwhile, the Jewish 'haute banque' of German origin were making their way into Belgian high finance and society and were involved, along with the private bankers, in the foundation of joint-stock banks.[14] The Liège region was covered by a dense web of family relationships uniting industrialists and private bankers in dynasties which dominated the boards of the local joint-stock banks. The Liège financiers were to guard their independence jealously up to the First World War.

While in most banks it was social class – the upper ranks of the bourgeoisie – and family influence which gave access to a seat on the board, the end of the nineteenth century saw a move towards the professionalizing of the director's role in the Société Générale. But the professionalization – and this is a peculiarity of the Belgian universal banks – developed along two lines simultaneously: first, the recruitment of engineers who had demonstrated their ability within industries controlled by the bank, and second, the promotion from the ranks of employees who had begun as book-keepers in their early youth and climbed slowly up the career ladder within the bank or within one of its banking subsidiaries. In other words, there was a dichotomy between those who had made their careers in industrial firms and had an advanced technical training, and those few employees of the bank itself who had fought their way up to the point where they could aspire to the highest echelons.

An outstanding example of the latter progression is supplied by the governor Ferdinand Baeyens, who entered the bank at sixteen as book keeper, became the lynch pin of its developing activities as a deposit bank, joined the board in 1875, and became a governor in 1893, leaving the Société Générale twenty years later. This remarkable rise was further marked when he joined the ranks of the nobility with the title of baron. It undeniably encouraged the speedy development of professionalization, though considerable weight was still carried by leading public figures. At the beginning of the twentieth century there were three engineers on the board, and one officer. Two of them came from families of industrialists. The officer, Léon Barbanson, came from a prominent bourgeois family in Luxemburg. He was not less than the son of a former deputy governor and the son-in-law of Victor Tesch, an influential liberal politician who was governor of the Société Générale from 1878 to 1892. The fourth man, Victor Stoclet, was the son of an advocate who sat on the boards of several railway companies controlled by the bank. However, in the first ten years of the twentieth-century engineers from more humble social backgrounds, like Jean Jadot and Léon Janssen, were able to grasp the reins of power along with politicians and other public figures.

It is nonetheless the case that, although there was incontestably some social mobility in pre-1914 Belgium, a man like Edouard Empain, whose brilliant career had been crowned by a peerage conferred by King Leopold II, could complain at the end of his life that he had never really been accepted by the establishment. 'High finance and the leading industries are a closed world where no-one can enter who has not at least twenty-four quarterings', as he wrote to a friend in 1918.[15]

The upheaval of the war and the growing influence of the Société Générale in industry altered the conditions of recruitment to the board. On the one hand, professional qualifications became more important than social or political eminence. In 1924, the board was enlarged to nine and its average age reduced by the accession of three engineers aged about forty who had won their spurs in the war and in the companies belonging to the group. A fellow-feeling among those who had had experience of overseas companies also had some part to play. It was thus that at the end of 1912 Jean Jadot brought Emile Francqui (then managing director of the Banque d'Outremer), whom he had got to know in China, on to the board of the Société Générale, in spite of their former rivalry.[16] His deputy, Firmin Van Bree of the colonial companies, was to be one of a batch of new directors in 1924, while Emile Sengier, who had begun his career under Francqui in China, was to become one of the Société Générale's key men in the Congo. On the banking side, the appeal was to the bank's own men who had imbibed the spirit of the firm since their earliest youth.

The emergence of this meritocracy did not prevent the reforming of networks of family relationships in Belgian banking circles, despite the broadening of their recruiting base. The effects of the banking reform of 1934–5 were not felt immediately. It was only after the Second World War that people began to perceive a distinction between the directorship of the deposit banks and that of the holding companies.

Concluding this survey of the bankers' social importance, we should mention the remarkable contribution made by some of them to the development of scientific research, and in patronage of the arts, in the Belgium of the 1920s.

III

Moving now to the political importance of the Belgian bankers, we cannot fail to be struck by the abrupt change after the First World War. It must be remembered, in this connection, that under the property qualification for voting rights which was in force until 1893, the Parliament was a centre of power disputed by liberals and catholics, in which the commercial world was determined to gain a foothold. The adoption of universal suffrage (mitigated by the plural vote) in 1893 did little to alter the situation, insofar as the catholics were able to keep an absolute majority and remain in power from 1884 up to the First World War. The adoption of universal suffrage in 1918 changed the political balance by bringing a massive influx of socialists into Parliament. As proportional representation had been the rule since 1899, Belgium entered a period of political instability, with a succession of coalition governments. At the same time, the bankers' sphere of influence shifted from Parliament to the government itself.

The relationship between the worlds of banking and politics can be analysed on two levels. On the one hand, the private bankers, though few in number, were getting themselves elected. A seat in Parliament was an important constituent of social eminence, especially in the provinces. Most of them were liberals. On the other hand, the joint-stock banks automatically reserved several seats on the board for members of Parliament – influential ones if possible – or, even better, for former ministers. While the Banque de Bruxelles had been a liberal preserve since its foundation, the Société Générale paid more attention to the ebb and flow of political power. Since its foundation, the Palace had always advised on the choice of the governor and kept a representative on the board or in the college of commissioners; moreover, the bank had always been careful to keep the right political balance among its directors.

Thus, in 1880, the board was made up of both Catholics and Liberals

– at a time when the government in power, with an absolute majority, was Liberal – but three of the directors were members of Parliament, all liberals; one of them was Victor Tesch, a former minister who had joined the Société Générale in 1868 after a conflict with the progressive wing of his own party. When the Catholics regained a majority in 1884, the interest shifted to former Catholic ministers who were also close to King Leopold II: Joseph Devolder in 1891, Count Paul Smet de Naeyer in 1908. The circumstances in which Emile Francqui acceded to the board show the Société Générale's anxiety to maintain the right political complexion. Believed to be a Liberal and a freemason, he was prevented from succeeding Joseph Devolder in 1910 in favour of Edmond Carton de Wiart, a former secretary to Leopold II, and had to wait two more years before succeeding the liberal Léon Barbanson.

In the interwar period, the make-up of the board became distinctly less political. The general shake-out of 1924 was in the interests of greater professionalism; no director held a parliamentary seat. However, as far as ideology went, the Catholics were in the majority. But this cessation in the active involvement of members of parliament, far from denoting an estrangement from the political sphere, actually evidences the shift of power relationships from the Parliament to the government which had already been under way before the war.

There can be no doubt that the influence which certain eminent financiers, like Georges Theunis and Emile Francqui, had gained through their wartime activities led to their being called upon to take part in government during the economic and financial crisis.[17] Thus Georges Theunis, of the Empain group, was to be prime minister from 1921 to 1925.

Because of their network of overseas contacts, and especially because of the prestige of Emile Francqui, the private bankers supplanted the Banque Nationale in the negotiations over German reparations. They torpedoed the attempt at stabilizing the franc made by the minister Albert-Edouard Janssen, a product of the Banque Nationale. This failure contributed to the collapse of the first Christian-Democrat/Socialist coalition cabinet in 1926.

The cabinet of National Unity headed by Henri Jaspar called upon the man who had inspired it, Emile Francqui, the deputy governor of the Société Générale; he managed to stabilize the situation thanks to his special relationships with English and American banks. He took advantage of his sojourn in government to reduce the Banque Nationale's function as a source of credit and to extend the influence over it of the private banks.

We have already spoken of the government of the bankers set up in November 1934 to deal with the Boerenbond crisis. The failure of its deflationary policies, which had been intended to keep the Belgian franc on the gold standard, forced it to give way to the cabinet of National Unity headed by Paul Van Zeeland. He implemented a ruthless devaluation which gave a boost to the economy. Using its special powers, this cabinet instituted the royal decree of 9 July 1935 which reformed the banking system. Not only did this confirm the cleavage of functions of the universal banks, it also submitted all institutions with the status of banks to the control of a new body, the *Commission bancaire*.

The banking reform was seen at the time as a victory for the proponents of state intervention in the economy. A closer examination of the creation and content of the royal decree reveals the close collaboration between the Liberal Finance Minister, Max-Léo Gérard, and the bankers. What is more, it was the banks themselves, anxious to restore public confidence, who were the main force behind the reform, and if they accepted a regulation of banking activities it was with a close eye on the preservation of their own interests.[18] Thus it is not surprising to find Max-Léo Gérard being called to the presidency of the Banque de Bruxelles in 1937. Another episode, controversial as it may be, is equally revealing of the importance of the big banks in Belgium at this period: on 15 May 1940 P.-H. Spaak, Minister for Foreign Affairs, entrusted their leading directors, A. Galopin (Société Générale), Max-Léo Gérard (Banque de Bruxelles) and F. Collin (Kredietbank), with the task of guiding the Belgian people as best they could in the eventuality of a German occupation.[19]

IV

To conclude: the period 1880 to 1940 saw the apogee of the universal banks in Belgium and their suppression after the crisis of the 1930s. On the social level, the professionalization which had been begun at the end of the nineteenth century reached its zenith in the 1920s, especially in the Société Générale, though the links between banking and industrial elites remained close. As for the bankers' political importance, the fifteen years after the First World War were a golden age. The strong characters and widespread influence of men like Georges Theunis and, in particular, Emile Francqui certainly had a lot to do with this success.

Notes

1 The history of the Belgian financial market in the first half of the nineteenth century has been exhaustively studied; not so the period examined in the present article. Two older works are still indispensable for the role of the banks in the economy: S. Chlepner, *Le marché financier belge depuis cent ans* (Brussels, 1930) and R. Durviaux, *La banque mixte, origine et soutien de l'expansion*

économique de la Belgique (Brussels, 1947), from which the figures presented here were taken. For a more extensive bibliography see G. Kurgan-van Hentenryk, 'Banque et entreprises', in *La Wallonie. Le pays et les hommes* (Brussels, 1976), II, pp. 25–52; and J. Rassel-Lebrun, 'L'emprise de la Société Générale et de la Banque de Bruxelles', ibid., pp. 231–45; 'La Banque en Belgique 1830–1980', *Revue de la Banque* 8/9 (September 1980); H. van der Wee and M. Verbeyt, *Mensen maken Geschiednis. De Kredietbank en de Economische Opgang van Vlaanderen 1935–1985* (Brussels, 1985). (An abridged French translation with no bibliography appeared under the title *Les hommes font l'histoire. La Kredietbank et l'essor économique de la Flandre 1935–1985*.)

2 Of the 18 million francs' worth of new money invested by the banks in share issues from limited companies in 1882, 5 million (28 per cent) came from the Société Générale; the contribution of the other banks was negligible. In 1911, by contrast, of the 134 million francs of new money invested by the banks, the Société Générale contributed 8.5 million (only 6 per cent), the Banque d'Outremer 9.4 per cent, the Banque de Bruxelles 4.9 million, the Crédit Anversois 5 million, the Banque Internationale de Bruxelles 2 million, and the Banque de Paris et des Pays-Bas 9 million (Durviaux, *Banque mixte*, pp. 88, 97, 102).

3 The following data will demonstrate the respective roles of the Belgian joint-stock banks, finance companies, private banks and foreign banks and bankers in the investment of new money in the share issues of joint-stock companies (figures in thousands of francs):

	Total	Joint-stock banks	Finance companies	Belgian private banks	Foreign banks and bankers
1874	23,821	11,643		11,000	1,178
1882	18,166	7,533	8,879	567	1,187
1911	134,306	47,766	27,528	8,723	50,289

Durviaux calculates the contribution of the universal banks by adding the investments of the joint-stock banks to those of the finance companies which they controlled (Durviaux, *Banque mixte*, p. 90).

4 E. Bussière, 'La sidérurgie belge durant l'Entre-Deux-Guerres: le cas d'Ougrée-Marihaye (1919–1939)', *Revue Belge d'Histoire Contemporaine* (hereafter *RBHC*) 15 (1984), pp. 307–9.

5 J. L. Delaet, 'La mécanisation de la verrerie à vitres à Charleroi dans la première moitié du XXe siècle', in G. Kurgan-van Hentenryk and J. Stengers (eds.), *L'innovation technologique, facteur de changement (XIXe-XXe siècles)* (Brussels, 1986), pp. 135ff.

6 G. Kurgan-van Hentenryk and J. Puissant, 'Die industriellen Beziehungen im belgischen Kohlenbergbau seit dem Ende des 19.

Jahrhunderts', in G. D. Feldman and K. Tenfelde (ed.), *Arbeiter, Unternehmer und Staat im Bergbau. Industriellen Beziehungen im internationalen Vergleich* (Munich, 1989), pp. 163–219 and 365–71. (English translation, Berg, New York/London, 1990).

7 G. Kurgan-van Hentenryk, 'Le régime économique de l'industrie électrique depuis la fin du XIXe siècle'in F. Cardot (ed.), *1880–1980. Un Siècle d'électricité dans le monde* (Paris, 1987), pp. 121ff.

8 Chlepner, *Marché financier*, p. 124.

9 H. van der Valk, *De betrekkingen tusschen banken en industrie in België* (Haarlem, 1932). p. 123 (cited in Durviaux, *Banque mixte*, p. 133) gives the following percentage stakes for the Société Générale in Belgian industry: coal, 25–30; metallurgical, 48; zinc, 60–75; copper, 100; railways and tramways, 20; maritime, 40; electricity, 15; glass, 40; chemical, 30; artificial silk, 40; sugar, 90; tobacco, 50; colonial enterprise, 80–90.

10 E. Bussière, 'Les relations entre la France et la Belgique dans les rivalités économiques et financières en Europe: novembre 1918–mars 1935', unpublished dissertation, University of Paris IV (1988), II, pp. 524ff.

11 H. Schoeters, 'Les interventions de crise et les collusions politico-financières en Belgique entre 1930 et 1940', *RBHC* 7 (1976), 3/4, pp. 426ff; M. R. Thielemans, *La grande crise et le gouvernement des banquiers. Essai.* (Brussels, Institut de Science Politique, 1980).

12 See J. Stengers (ed.), *Index des éligibles au Sénat (1831–1893)*. Examples might be F. Legrelle (Antwerp), E. Balisaux (Charleroi), G. de Lhoneux (Huy), E. Nagelmaekers-Pastor (Liège), V. Tercelin-Monjot (Mons).

13 The board of directors of the Société Générale de Belgique since 1830 was the subject of a seminar of the History department of the Université Libre de Bruxelles. The first results are presented here. For the Banque de Bruxelles, see the study by A. M. Dutrieue, 'La Banque de Bruxelles au miroir de son conseil d'administration de 1871 à 1914', memoir, Catholic University of Louvain, Louvain-la-Neuve, 1987–8, to be published shortly.

14 Thus Jonathan Bisschoffsheim and his son Ferdinand sat in the Senate in succession from 1862 to 1888. Léon Lambert, son of Samuel Lambert, a correspondent and ally of Rothschild, was ennobled by Leopold II. Jacques Cassel, Franz Philippson, and Raphaël de Bauer, managing director of the Banque de Paris et des Pays-Bas, acquired Belgian citizenship and became eligible for election to the Senate.

15 Empain to Charles de Broqueville, 16 September 1918 (Archives Générales du Royaume, de Broqueville papers, no. 98).

16 G. Kurgan-van Hentenryk, 'Emile Francqui au service de l'expansion belge en Chine (1896–1903)', *Académie Royale des Sciences d'Outremer, Bulletin des séances* (1971–3), pp. 417ff.

17 On the influence of the bankers between the wars see Thielemans,

Grande crise; H. van der Wee and K. Tavernier, *La Banque Nationale de Belgique et l'histoire monétaire entre les deux guerres mondiales* (Brussels, 1975); L. Ranieri, *Emile Francqui ou l'intelligence créatrice, 1863–1935* (Brussels, 1985); G. Vantemsche, 'De val van de regering Poullet-Vandervelde: "en samenzwering der bankiers"?', *RBHC* 9 (1978), 1/2, pp. 165–214; 'Preciseringen omtrent het verloop van de politiek-financiele krisis van 1926', *RBHC* 16 (1985), 1/2, pp. 107–28; R. Depoortere, 'La Banque Nationale 1918–1932', *Relations Internationales*, 56, hiver 1988, pp. 457–73.

18 G. Vantemsche, 'L'élaboration de l'arrêté royal sur le contrôle bancaire (1935)', *RBHC* 11 (1980), 3, pp. 389ff.

19 J. Gérard-Libois and J. Gotovitch, *L'an 40* (Brussels, 1971), pp. 171ff.

18 The political economy of banking: retail banking and corporate finance in Sweden, 1850–1939

MATS LARSSON AND HÅKAN LINDGREN

The problem to be discussed in this chapter is how the specific structure of the Swedish banking system was shaped in the late nineteenth century, and how it developed in the first half of the twentieth century. Above all, however, we will try to explain the oscillations between two abstract constructions of banking 'systems', the extremes of retail and investment banking. Our approach is basically institutional, analysing the different influences on the banking system as constraints and possibilities for economic behaviour. In explaining specific banking behaviour, three main spheres of influence will be stressed, all formed and specified by the picture of reality held by the economic actors: (1) ideas and prototypes of banking systems imported from economically more advanced countries abroad, (2) mutual bonds and relations to the commodity sector of the economy and (3) mutual dependence on and relations to the state and the gradual change of governmental control within the banking system.

Traditionally, finance activities are characterized by two extremes, retail or consumer banking and investment banking. Retail banking is based on credit mediation, and it is carried out by 'banking' agents or institutions accepting deposits and providing loans for both consumption and investment requirements. To attract savings deposits it is necessary to pay interest, and often one has to pay a rate even for cash deposits. The income of a retail banking institution consists mainly of what is called net interest, that is the difference between lending and deposit rates. Another way of financing lending, which preceded and for a long period of time competed with banking based on deposits, was to issue banknotes for circulation. Thus, in the long run, the most important function of the early banks was to create markets for paper money, a new and effective instrument of exchange, which tremendously reduced society's transaction costs.

For purposes of analytical convenience, the UK banking system can be termed an ideal type (in a Weberian sense) of retail banking. The joint-stock banks which appeared in England and Wales in the 1820s and 1830s are generally referred to as archetypes of a banking system, concentrating on short-term lending and cash deposits, being the administrators of the mobile cash surpluses of business. Even if modern research has moderated this view, and even if there were important differences between the Scottish and the English systems of banking at that time, it is quite clear that British deposit banks stressed short-term operations, relying to a great extent on cash deposits and preferring self-liquidating discount credits and overdrafts rather than loans. In England international banking and industrial investment were dominated by institutions outside the banking system. The international banking business, which included foreign state loan issues, international bill brokerage and the credit-financing of the British import trade, was carried out by the so-called merchant bankers, originating from private banking houses. Industrial investment operations were effected by private investment companies and investment trusts, and the market for long-term venture capital was far more developed in England than in any other country.[1]

Investment banking refers to activities where financial and consultative service is given to business in all possible ways. It includes long-term lending and long-term capital mobilization. Moreover, it includes what is now known as corporate finance, i.e. participation in new share issues and in restructuring and structuralizing operations. The origins were the private, family-owned banking houses such as the Rothschilds, which in the late eighteenth century and during the Napoleonic wars earned large amounts of money by intermediary operations in the fast-growing market for state loans. The investment bankers specialized in issuing and underwriting activities, both in bonds and shares. In this way they helped to create secondary markets for two financial instruments, the bond and the share, which were to become of great importance for financing the industrial growth of the twentieth century. Further the investment bankers acted as middle-men in all sorts of transactions. They became professionals in initiating and realizing mergers and industrial transformation, and their income derived mainly from commissions and fees.

A prerequisite for successful investment banking was the existence of legal possibilities to deal with stocks and shares, not only as a broker but also as an owner. Trade cycles made investment banking extremely risky, in particular when issuing activities and merger operations were combined with a policy of helping infant industries stand on their own two feet. The considerable risks to which investment bankers were exposed required special demands for liquidity and solvency.

The historical stage is crowded with investment bank failures, the most spectacular being the Crédit Mobilier bankruptcy in France 1867. Crédit Mobilier was a systematic attempt to organize, with support from the public authorities of the second empire (Napoleon III), venture capital mobilization to new and growing industrial enterprises. The venture capital was raised by bond issues of the Crédit Mobilier institution. Established in 1852 its operations were successful for some years but the combined effect of inadequate liquidity and the 1866 crisis forced the bank into bankruptcy in 1867 and liquidation in 1871.

Posterity has regarded the Crédit Mobilier as a model for banking institutions as intermediaries to promote industrial development and growth, and for a long time the name of the French institution has been used as a concept describing investment banking activities in general. In fact, however, the Crédit Mobilier was a very special, and even late, type of bank concentrating on long-term industrial finance. To contemporaries, the Belgian Big Banks – the Société Générale (1822) and the Banque de Belgique (1835) – seemed just as important as the Crédit Mobilier as models for establishing investment and share-issuing banks.[2]

Transferred to Germany, corporate financing was combined with retail banking into a mixed banking system, often referred to as German or Continental universal banking. The German universal banking system was deeply rooted in the private banking traditions of the country. In the last quarter of the nineteenth century, the German joint-stock banks developed into big universal banks. They combined regular retail banking with corporate finance, including share acquisitions and issuing activities on a large scale. The German banks became known as initiators and promoters of industrial change, cooperating quite intimately with industry, initiating mergers and collaborating with each other in the creation of cartels and syndicates.[3]

The choice of a banking system in nineteenth-century Sweden

Compared with western European countries such as Britain, France, Belgium and the Netherlands, the financial sector in Sweden was not very well developed in the middle of the nineteenth century. The principal duty of the national bank of Sweden (*the Riksbank*) was to preserve the domestic currency and the exchange rates; otherwise, it did not function as a central bank. The Riksbank was established as the commercial bank of Stockholm. In a conservative and bureaucratic manner it distributed cheap credits to trade and industry, being the most important instrument in implementing the economic policy resolutions of the Parliament, *the Riksdag*.

In rural areas, and with public support, a number of local savings banks were established from the 1820s onwards. The savings banks stayed small but, established in great numbers, they became important as market-makers for deposits by introducing institutional saving to the general public. The idea of the savings-banks movement was mainly philanthropic, to reduce the costs of poor-relief for the local governments by stimulating family saving.

Regional commercial banks started to develop in Sweden in the 1830s, but it was not until the late 1850s that they worked together in a system for national clearing and payments service. Still, in 1855, the number of so-called 'enskilda' (private) joint-stock banks was only eight. They were small and their activities limited to the administrative centres where they had their head offices. The motive for establishing new commercial banks was mainly political, and an effect of the struggle for power between the government and the Riksdag. The government had no influence on the Riksbank, which was the bank of the Swedish Parliament. By establishing new commercial banks, provided with rights of issuing banknotes, the government could extend its sphere of influence in monetary policy, and the privilege of the Riksbank of controlling the supply of money was curtailed.

The first private joint-stock bank, *Skånska Privatbanken* (later Skånes Enskilda Bank), got its royal charter in 1830 and started operations during the following year in Ystad in southern Sweden. As with all other private banks up to 1864, Skånes Enskilda Bank was a joint-stock bank, with the owners being jointly liable for the bank's obligations. It financed its lending mainly by note issues, which made it possible to have external funds at one's disposal at the cost of 2 per cent. Owing to competition all the early private banks had problems in attracting deposits, as the rate of interest was regulated by charter and practice to a maximum of 5.25 per cent. In the traditional, 'non-institutionalized' credit market, where a lot of merchants, brokers and money-lenders were long established, the maximum rate of interest was easily (and frequently) circumvented by special commissions and brokerages, or simply by making a difference between the sum total written on the promissory note and the amount of money paid.[4]

With new industries, growing grain and timber exports, and higher business activities due to the Crimean war, the need for a more effective credit market increased. In Stockholm, the capital of Sweden and the very centre of Swedish commercial life in those days, the resistance to new bank foundations was intense both from the Riksbank and the influential private money-lenders. Finally, in 1856, *Stockholms Enskilda Bank* was established, being innovative in two important operational respects. Though the new commercial bank was an ordinary '*enskild*' bank chartered with the privilege of note issues, it managed to capture a large part of the Stockholm deposits market by introducing new instruments of depositing. For the first time the operations of a Swedish commercial bank were largely based on the stockholders' equity and deposits from the general public.

Moreover, the new bank introduced new possibilities for an effective transfer of payments within the country. Free of charge, the regional commercial banks were allowed to open transfer accounts in Stockholms Enskilda Bank. A national network of commercial banks was built up, which brought together the distant regions into a national system for clearing and payments, and made possible the transfer of capital from surplus to deficit regions. Quite naturally financial intermediation, the transfer of payments and credits, appeared as the main function of the new banking institutions: at the threshold of the industrial revolution the Swedish economy was characterized both by an undeveloped infrastructure and a growing need for transactions.

In this it is not difficult to recognize foreign influences. The prototype of the Swedish banking system was the Scottish one, although 'developed and adapted to the requirements of the country into which it has been adopted'.[5] The Swedish commercial banks concentrated on bill discounting and short-term lending, attracting mainly liquid and short-term deposits. In both Scotland and Sweden they were organized as joint-stock banks with unlimited liability for all shareholders. In both countries they worked with note issues as well as with deposits acquisition as the basis for their lending. And, as the most important contrast to what characterized the specifically English system, the functions pursued by both the Scottish and Swedish banks were much more extensive. The financial markets in these countries were less developed and specialized. Thus quite diverse banking functions were concentrated in the commercial banks. These banks came to dominate the entire credit market, and they did this in a financial system characterized by extensive cooperation and unification.[6]

In the 1860s institutionalized banking in Sweden developed quickly, promoted by a liberal wave in economic policy. In 1863, following the British example of 1862, joint-stock banks which had their liability limited to company assets, but without any privilege to issue notes, were allowed. In the next year, 1864, full freedom of trade was introduced, and the fixing of the interest rate at 6 per cent as a maximum was abolished. A number of new banks were established, and there were forty-four commercial banks in operation in 1865, compared to only eight private banks ten years earlier.

The first non-issuing joint-stock bank, *Skandinaviska Kredit AB* (later Skandinaviska Banken), was established in Sweden in 1864. A new continental influence began to appear. From the very outset, the new joint-stock bank was meant to be a Scandinavian crédit mobilier with a strong element of Danish and Dutch ownership, and its ultimate purpose was to prevent branches of new British banks from being established in Sweden. Owing to the sudden international crisis of 1863, Skandinaviska Banken became a purely Swedish business matter, and in general its operations did not differ from those of Stockholms Enskilda Bank. In fact the two banks, originally intended to be complementary, became intense competitors: the central clearing function for the regional commercial banks, for example, which had been kept by Stockholms Enskilda Bank, was in some years transferred to Skandinaviska Banken.[7]

German universal banking gaining ground

Three important trends can be observed in Swedish banking practices during the second half of the nineteenth century. First, the commercial banks gradually took over the role in financing industry played earlier by the old merchant and trading houses. This process accelerated during the financial crises of 1863 and 1866 when some of the most respectable money-lenders and banking firms were liquidated, but was not completed until the 1890s, when the commercial banks finally took over the financing role of the old merchant houses.

Secondly, Swedish commercial banks gradually inserted new activities within their banking functions. The underwriting of industrial bond issues for subsequent public offer, for example, became a recognized banking function. Thirdly, and largely as a consequence of the expansion of the banking functions, the operations of the commercial banks were subject to increasing legislative regulation, and the public supervision of the banks' activities grew.

The fundamental cause explaining these processes is to be found in the rapid industrial transformation of the Swedish economy, first in the beginning of the 1870s and again during the prolonged boom 1895–1913. The relative backwardness of Sweden at that time and the desire for industrial development gave rise to more demand for long-term rather than short-term credits. Due to this demand, Swedish banks became involved to an increasing degree in industrial medium- and long-term finance, although venture capital provisions were still formally closed to the banks. By organizational innovations, however, German universal banking was implemented into the Swedish system.

Modern research has shown that both the influence of German banks, their entrepreneurial role and their dominance of big industry have been greatly exaggerated.[8] To contemporary debaters on economic-political questions, however, it was quite real. The rapid process of industrialization in Germany during the last quarter of the nineteenth century, and the successful participation of banks in that process, became an ideal for those in Sweden who wanted to increase the growth and transformation of society by using 'idle' bank capital as venture capital.

A mixture of short- and long-term activities, and of credit intermediation and corporate finance had turned out to be profitable for both the banks and industry. Just as other late-comers on the industrial scene with ambitions to catch up with those who were ahead – influential people in Sweden, both businessmen and politicians – felt the need to use bank capital as a spear-head in the industrialization process. A causal relationship was assumed between bank capital operating intimately with industrial capital, together initiating mergers and creating cartels and syndicates, and economic growth.

In Sweden the introduction of corporate finance in commercial banking was by no means undisputed. Share trading and new share issues were becoming increasingly commonplace in the 1890s, a trend that necessitated a reorganization of the Stockholm Stock Exchange in 1901, which, in turn, further stimulated share trading. During the first decades of this century, there was an intense public debate on the question if, how and to what extent bank capital should be used as venture capital to increase the pace of economic transformation.[9]

The main arguments in this debate were as follows. Opponents of the German system maintained that deposit business was fundamental to Swedish commercial banking. An increased exposure to risks could put the safety of deposits into question. Mere suspicions about insolvency could be devastating, both to the single bank and to the whole banking and monetary system. Advocates for investment banking as part of the regular business for commercial banks argued that even lending on share collateral, a recognized commercial banking function, was risky as stock prices show great flexibility. Even in lending it is up to the bank not to get involved in too risky operations by, for example, accepting as collateral shares of venturesome companies with uncertain prospects.

An interesting argument raised by the advocates for a universal banking system, was the advantage of including the market for venture capital under the domain of public control. If banks are allowed to deal with shares, or if they are allowed to run special investment/issuing banks, this would in fact introduce sound bank practices and have a stabilizing effect on markets for venture capital, as the commercial banks were controlled by a government office, the Bank Inspectorate.

From the very beginning, the commercial banking institutions had developed in close cooperation with the state and its government authorities. The '*enskilda*' private banks were instruments for the monetary policy of the government in opposition to the Parliament. They were privileged with the right of note-issuing and the right of receiving the deposits of the general public. On the other hand, their operations were regulated by banking law, and they were dependent for their existence on royal charters, reviewed every tenth year. In short, the banks were privately owned, but publicly regulated.

But the government regulations should not only be considered as checks on bank behaviour: the restraints and the supervision of the state also opened prospects. The close links to the state were a competitive advantage in relation to the traditional money-lenders and merchant houses, and, by increasing the confidence of the general public, they were essential for making the success story of the new banking institutions possible. The connections to the state and the government can even be seen in the status of bank clerks. Compared to the rest of the private sector, the terms of employment in banking – as in the insurance business – were extraordinary, imitating those of civil servants.[10]

Depositor security was given high priority in Swedish banking legislation, which was clearly shown in the 1874 law applicable to '*enskilda*' private banks which were allowed to issue banknotes. The traumatic crises of 1878–9 – when a lot of prominent banking firms went bankrupt and one of the big banks, Stockholms Enskilda Bank, was badly hit – clearly demonstrated the dangers of a banking system that was too closely tied to the fluctuating industrial and real estate sectors. In 1886 the first banking law affecting joint-stock banks with limited liability to be passed in the Riksdag contained a prohibition, which already applied to private, note-issuing banks, to trade or acquire shares and real property for their own account.

The right for '*enskilda*' private banks to issue their own banknotes was successively curtailed at the end of the nineteenth century. As a consequence, these banks too became increasingly dependent on deposits for their operations. A note-issuing monopoly for the Swedish Riksbank was accepted in principle in the 1880s, but it was not until 1904 that the private note-issuing right was totally abolished. The '*enskilda*' private banks, their liability not being limited to company assets, were then supposed to reorganize into banks with limited liability, but only two of them did so. The other banks kept their unlimited liability ownership, because it was regarded as easier to obtain foreign credits for banks with unlimited liability. This special institutional form of banking was not abolished until 1934, when all commercial banks were transformed into limited liability companies.[11]

In practice the legislative ban on the owning of shares did not close the market for corporate finance to the commercial banks. To avoid the prohibition on share dealing and share ownership, the Swedish banks engaged themselves in supplying venture capital to industry through channels which were formally unimpeachable, and embryonic forms of modern financial concerns developed. Executives, leading managers and members of the bank boards organized themselves into private consortia or syndicates, to which the bank made the necessary advances to make share underwriting and industrial restructuring operations possible. Investment and issuing companies were formed, legally separated from, but totally financed by and working in close collaboration with their parent-banks.

The consortia were usually dissolved when a particular operation or project had been completed. The formation of affiliated issuing companies meant, however, that more permanent banking groups were established, in many ways working as a modern financial concern and offering a complete program of investment banking to industry. Close contacts developed between the commercial banks and their industrial clients, and, not least important, expert knowledge on industry and corporate finance was incorporated in the banking organization.

Around the outbreak of the First World War the importance of industry to the Swedish commercial banks grew as a base for their activities. Owing to the war, but also to the long-term change in capital imports, the volume of international finance decreased heavily. The intermediation of foreign loans had been the main source of revenue and an important base for deposits for the banks. When capital imports ceased, industrial clients, and developed client relationships to industry, became a most valuable and well-charged asset for the banks.[12]

The expansion of banking operations into more risky fields had to be balanced to keep stability and to protect the deposits of the general public, and the need for making supervision of the banks' activities more effective was urgently felt. In 1907 the Bank Inspection Board was created as an independent government office, and the number of civil servants increased substantially. This made it possible to centralize the control of banks. As an independent civil service department, the Bank Inspection Board had the right to render binding decisions on the banks, without working through the different Country Administrations, as the Bank Inspector had previously been obliged to do.[13]

A bill submitted to the Swedish Riksdag in 1907 supported the idea that special share-issuing banks – investment banks – should be established. These would not only counteract speculation in share-issuing activities, but also promote the development of industry. The law, passed in 1909, permitted commercial banks, in cooperation with each other, to establish such investment banks. Exceptional safety standards were imposed however, and the new banks were to operate under the same public and banking regulations that applied to the ordinary commercial banks. The 1909 law proved to be of no significance, and the entire question of share purchasing rights for ordinary commercial banks was reviewed during the following years.[14]

In search of a bank identity, 1912–1939

By the introduction of the 1911 Banking Law in 1912, a certain freedom to purchase shares was granted to the Swedish commercial banks. The right to acquire shares was restricted and related to the size of the bank. But increased freedom in this area was met by countervailing powers, and the public control of the commercial banks was extended. The free entry to the market, which had applied for joint-stock banks with limited liability, was now abolished. All commercial banks had to be chartered by the government, and the right to operate a bank had to be confirmed by the state for a maximum of ten years. The public control of the establishment of banks was supported by the bankers, who wanted to reduce the intense competition in banking business: in 1908 the growth of commercial banks had culminated when eighty-four commercial banks had been registered.[15]

The supervision of the Bank Inspection Board was extended and specified in the new banking law. The regulations gave public officials the potential for direct intervention, and the commercial banks were not only forced to send detailed accounts on their financial position on a monthly basis, but had to open their banks and archives for inspection by the Board on request. Such inspections were done irregularly, mostly every second to fourth year, and huge reports were written, being a most valuable source of information for later bank historians. The most important effect of the increasing role of the Bank Inspection Board was probably to make bank practices more homogeneous and to develop the internal control function within the banks themselves.

The right to acquire shares given to the commercial banks in the 1911 Banking Law was restricted and related to the size of the banks' equity. For the larger banks in particular, possibilities now opened for direct participation in the process of supplying venture capital to industry. Moreover, the legal restrictions on the volume of share ownership by the banks were no real impediment to enlarging the share business. Subsidiary companies to the banks were formed, in some cases provided with surprisingly small bases of equities though their total operations were extensive. The operations were financed by loans from their parent banks, and the shares acquired with pledged for the loans, often at high collateral values.

The economic upswing in Sweden generated by the First World War had considerable bearings on future developments. It was a hectic boom, characterized not only by business optimism, fast rising stock prices and increasing volumes of new issues and mergers, but also by a huge redistribution of income and wealth, followed by increased social and political tensions. The financial markets were quite liquid and totally

Table 18.1 *Money capital held by financial institutions in Sweden, 1918–1938*
(Millions of Sw. Crowns and share in percent, 31 December)

	1918		1926		1938	
	Crowns	%	Crowns	%	Crowns	%
Commercial banks	4,502	62	3,431	41	4,260	33
Private savings banks	1,624	22	2,793	34	3,685	29
Post office savings bank*	75	1	261	3	807	6
Rural credit societies	1	—	6	—	61	1
Private insurance companies	1,000	14	1,417	17	3,256	25
State pension funds	93	1	423	5	840	6
Total	7,295	100	8,331	100	12,909	100

Notes: * Incl. postal giro service (credit balance).
Source: H. Lindgren, *Bank, investmentbolag, bankirfirma*, p. 202.

dominated by the commercial banks: the financial system can be described as an extremely bank-oriented system (table 18.1). A violent credit expansion financed the operations of the fast-growing issuing companies. The operations opened new placement opportunities for securities, supporting the wave of new share issues on the market. In 1917–18, in particular, there was a tremendous increase in the volume of share issues on the Swedish stock market, and, in constant prices, the sales volume of the Stockholm Stock Exchange in 1918 was not to be exceeded until 1980.[16]

The boom of the 1910s stimulated the establishment of new banks, and fifteen new commercial banks were chartered in 1917–19. The merger movement was however much stronger, the total net number of banks decreasing from eighty-one in 1910 to only forty-one ten years later. The competition for deposits was an important factor behind the mergers, as well as explaining the vast investments made in new branches during these years (table 18.2). But other competitive forces within the banking system also contributed to the merger behaviour of banks in those days, the most important being competition between banks for regular industrial clients. By a merger with another bank, attractive industrial customers could be incorporated into the acquiring bank's sphere of interest.

Government policy and the extension of public control also favoured in different ways a development towards larger banks. Larger banks with many clients and diversified credits meant reduced risks, which increased depositor security and made the whole system more stable. There is a lot of empirical evidence supporting the view that the Bank Inspection Board

Table 18.2 *Concentration of commercial banks in Sweden, 1910–40*

	No. of bank companies	No. of branch offices	No. of inhabitants per office
1910	81	545	10,133
1915	66	721	7,923
1920	41	1,410	4,187
1925	31	1,091	5,548
1930	30	1,045	5,877
1935	28	1,024	6,060
1940	28	1,030	6,180

Source: SOS. Uppgifter om bankerna.

at this time regarded small banks as a danger to the stability of the banking system. The 1911 Banking Law increased the minimum requirements for equity in commercial banks, and in some cases small banks were even officially encouraged to merge with larger banks. Moreover, control was more effective if the number of banks was reduced.

Swedish banking thus experienced a far-reaching transformation during the 1910s. These changes were affected by the new bank legislation as well as the turbulent economic boom during the war. In relation to commercial banking the developments can be summarized in three major tendencies, which also had a bearing on the development of the banking system during the 1920s and 1930s:

1 a growing concentration of the banking industry, meaning a sharp reduction of the number of commercial banks;
2 extension of the public control of commercial banks by the Bank Inspection Board;
3 deeper bank involvement in industrial companies, both by increasing credit facilities, corporate finance activities and share ownership, stimulated by inflation and the substantial growth of deposits.

The fundamental problem was that bank involvement in investment activities eased the availability of credits, increased inflation and added fuel to speculation. When the post-war slump arrived to Sweden in the autumn of 1920, the consequences were catastrophic. Suspended dividend payments, bankruptcies, deflation and heavy share value losses placed the issuing companies in an untenable situation. By the middle of the 1920s most of them had gone into liquidation.

The value of both shares and property fell sharply. This meant that banks, when the industrial companies could no longer pay the interest rates or instalments, had to take over securities to protect their claims. The huge amounts of credits given to bank owned or affiliated share-issuing companies, which had been borrowing against shares as collateral, made the situation worse. The interests and direct share holdings of commercial banks thus increased, and suddenly the banks found themselves as owners of a substantial part of Swedish industry. But since the market prices of the shares taken over by the banks as claims against default continuously decreased, many banks were forced to depreciate the value of their assets or even reorganize their business.[17]

Thus the commercial banks themselves were badly hit. The largest of them, Svenska Handelsbanken, was financially reconstructed in 1922. The amalgamation movement in the banking sector hit a new peak, as mergers became a solution to the problem of how to avoid liquidations (table 18.2). Many banks found it necessary to do such heavy writing-offs that the only alternative to bankruptcy was to merge with another bank. The second largest of the commercial banks, Skandinaviska banken, could escape formal reconstruction only by carrying overvalued assets forward and putting off the necessary writing-offs. In 1932, when the Kreuger crash made the financial problems of Skandinaviska banken acute, a far-reaching reconstruction eventually took place with huge support loans from the Swedish government, totalling SEK 200 million.

During the post-war crisis in the early 1920s, the Swedish government intervened to support and reconstruct the banking system. A new body was established, *AB Kreditkassan*, in which the government cooperated with a consortium of private banks in organizing a public financial support for banks facing severe problems. Quantitatively the support given by the state to reconstruct the banking system was not very impressive: public costs have been estimated at SEK 95 million, whereas the openly made depreciations (irrespective of the use of hidden reserves) made by the banks totalled SEK 570 million. Qualitatively, however, public support was quite important, both helping individual banks to avoid liquidation and eliminating domino-effects throughout the system.[18]

The government emergency support to avoid depositor losses was however combined with a radical criticism from the left, which questioned the whole bank-industrial symbiosis. When in 1920 the Social-democrats for the first time formed a government of their own, the nationalization issue was brought into the political limelight. To form a public commercial bank was one of the long-term goals of the Social-democratic party, either through a new establishment or by taking over an existing bank. Proposals concerning a public partnership were put forward to the two largest banks, Svenska Handelsbanken in October 1922 and Skandinaviska Banken in January 1923, but were turned down by the board of directors of both banks.[19]

The take-over of *Jordbrukarbanken* in April 1923 was hardly any substitute for ownership influence in the two largest banks, despite a nearly 100 per cent public ownership. AB Jordbrukarbanken was scarcely involved in industrial financing, but was a medium-sized commercial bank working within the agricultural sector. In 1925 public ownership was extended to a second bank, *Göteborgs Handelsbank*, in which the government got half the shares. When the financial problems of the banking sector stabilized in the middle of the 20s, it was more difficult for the left-wing parties to gain political support for further banking nationalizations. In 1928, however, the Social-democratic party introduced a bill in the Riksdag to investigate how the public ownership in Jordbrukarbanken and Göteborgs Handelsbank should be used to establish a large publicly owned bank. The bill was rejected by the Riksdag, and not until the Social-democratic so-called 'harvest time' after the Second World War were these plans realized.[20]

The political tensions are clearly reflected in a protracted public debate on relations between the banks and industry in the interwar years, partly inspired by the Rudolf Hilferding theories of finance capital and the dominance of banks over industry as a necessary result of capitalist development.[21] The delicate question in public debate was, whether the increased integration was to be seen as a conscious attempt by banks to strengthen their hold on industry, or if the growing industrial ownership was 'the banks' burden' and an undesired effect of over-speculation and crisis. During the boom years at the end of the 1920s, however, a large portion of the stocks held by the banks were sold, forming the base of the rapid build-up of Ivar Kreuger's empire. The Kreuger collapse of 1932 returned these stocks to the banks, also producing a redistribution of industrial ownership between the leading commercial banks.

The Kreuger *débacle* also made the Swedish government suspend all share purchase rights of the commercial banks, and the swing of the pendulum was now back where it had been before 1912. When suggesting this ban on stock operations, the Banking Commission stated that 'the right to acquire shares means quite simply that the banks become industrialists, not only sources of credit... the risks associated with loan operations are so substantial that the banks should not assume the additional risks of entrepreneurship'.[22] The Swedish banks should give priority to retail banking, and corporate finance activities were excluded from the functions of commercial banks.

The prohibition to purchase shares came into force from 1934. As a matter of fact, however, industrial assets could be found in the portfolios of the Swedish commercial banks even in the late 1950s.[23] First of all, a general four year period of grace was granted for the disposal of shares held by the banks in 1934. Moreover, and this is the real reason, the banks were allowed to hold old shares even after 1938, if these shares could not be sold without losses to the bank.

Among the larger banks, Göteborgsbanken was alone in disposing of its industrial interests on a really large scale. The reason for this was the shaky standing of the bank after the Kreuger collapse and the crises of the 1930s. The three other large commercial banks, Svenska Handelsbanken, Skandinaviska Banken and Stockholms Enskilda Bank, did not actually dispose of their shareholdings, but transferred them in the 1930s and 1940s to affiliated investment companies, indirectly controlled by the banks. In this way the stable client relationships between the banks and their industrial customers were protected. The banking group ownership in Sweden was consolidated for a long time, and clearly defined industrial spheres of bank interests were institutionalised.[24]

Conclusions

That the Swedish banking system developed by vacillating between the two model extremes of retail and investment banking seems to be an empirically well-founded conclusion. It is also quite obvious, and in fact somewhat more interesting as well, that the banking system developed by balancing between, on the one hand, influences from structural changes in the sphere of production and in demand from industry, and on the other from foreign models showing how to organize the system as well as from political ideas and economic policy objectives. More difficult, however, is the question *to what extent* different factors affect the oscillations, and how the causal factors are related to each other.

Originally organized as a system of deposit banks giving priority to retail banking, the banking system responded to the needs of an economy at the threshold of industrialization: to satisfy the demand for new and more effective means of exchange, to create a national system of clearing and payments service and to complement the traditional merchants' houses in the short-term financing of (above all) export trade. The political tensions between the government and the Riksdag, which explains the specific institutional forms of banking introduced in Sweden up to the 1860s, are essential in explaining the shaping of the system; but they can only be understood in the larger economic context.

The profound structural changes in the economy of late nineteenth-century Sweden were fundamental to the introduction of investment banking and corporate finance into the banking function. The demand for long-term credits increased heavily when the transport and industrial sectors grew, and the commercial banks, successful in their competition with smaller banking firms and trading houses, quickly seized the new opportunities for business. Underwriting business in industrial bonds became a recognized banking function, and with impulses from German universal banking the involvement of Swedish commercial banks in industry increased. Share-trading on their own account was forbidden to the banks up to 1912, but the bankers were innovative, finding new organizational instruments for their corporate finance activities.

In these developments two features, both related to the political and ideological field, are of special interest. One is the Swedish fear of lagging behind and not keeping up with industrially more advanced economies, which was a crucial argument when looking at the fast growth and the banks' industrial performance in Germany. The second is that the increased freedom granted to the commercial banks in corporate finance was exchange – and countervailed – by increased public control of the banking sector. The Bank Inspection Board was created in 1907 as an independent government office, but had as its forerunner a special section within the ministry of finance. The importance of the increased control was firstly to settle, by law, the general rules of the game. Secondly, and probably the essential point, bank practices were made more homogeneous by public control and the banks had to make their own internal control more effective. Thirdly, the bank legislation and the control system had a direct bearing on the structure of banking, supporting the merger movement in Swedish banking during the 1910s and early 1920s.

The economic upswing in Sweden during the First World War, and the following deep depression in the early 1920s, are crucial in explaining the return back to more pronounced retail banking in the 1930s. The new political situation after the war, characterized by the rise of left-wing parties, calling the whole of capitalist society into question, paved the way for a *renaissance* of deposit banking. With the new legislation in 1934, share-holding and share-purchasing were prohibited to commercial banks. At this time, however, the personal and economic bonds between the larger banks and their industrial customers were firmly established and could not be dissolved by political will. Corporate finance disappeared in regular commercial banking, it is true, but survived in affiliated investment companies, being important instruments of consolidated banking group ownership in Swedish industry after the Second World War.

Notes

1 In a balanced and well-documented analysis, *Industrial finance 1830–1914* (London, 1979), pp. 210–44, P. L. Cottrell presents a number of arguments for his view that British commercial banks were involved in industrial financing, in both medium- and long-term investment projects. The reason for the, by and large, small importance of bank credits was the lack of demand from industry, which continued its traditional reliance on internally generated funds. Cf. the more orthodox view in a general survey such as K. E. Born,

International banking in the 19th and 20th centuries (Leamington Spa, 1983), pp. 46–72, 160–4.

2 G. B. Nilsson, *Banker i brytningstid* (Stockholm, 1981), pp. 369–84; cf. B. Gille, 'Banking and Industrialization in Europe 1730–1914', *The Fontana economic history of Europe 3* (London, 1978), pp. 255–74.

3 R. Tilly, *Financial institutions and industrialization in the Rhineland, 1815–1870* (Madison-London, 1966), pp. 81–109.
The picture of an early 'continental' system of industrial banking is modified in a recent study by R. Rudolph, *Banking and industrialization in Austro-Hungary. The role of the banks in the industrialization of the Czech crownland, 1873–1914* (Cambridge, 1976). Rudolph's results show interesting similarities between Swedish and Austrian-Hungarian development. In the latter part of the nineteenth century, the Austrian banks were clearly averse to taking risks and did not get involved in providing venture capital. 'It was not', he states as a general conclusion, 'until after the turn of the century that serious connections had developed, until the marriage between banks and industry could be said to have been consummated' (p. 185).

4 G. B. Nilsson, 'Kreditens jättekraft. Svenskt bankväsende i brytningstid och genombrottstid vid 1800-talets mitt', *Uppsala papers in economic history*, Research Report No. 18 (1988); I Nygren, *Fràn Stockholms Banco till Citibank. Svensk kreditmarknad under 325 àr* (Stockholm, 1985), pp. 38–57.

5 R. H. Inglis Palgrave, *Notes on banking in Great Britain and Ireland. Sweden, Denmark and Hamburg* (1873), cited in G. B. Nilsson, *Banker i brytningstid*, p. 384. The distinctions made between the English, Scottish and Swedish systems of banking are also referred to in G. B. Nilsson's research, *Banker i brytningstid*, pp. 337–44, 381–3.

6 There were, however, significant differences between the Scottish and the Swedish systems of commercial banking. Owing to a less developed deposits market, for example, note-issuing became much more important to the Swedish '*enskilda*' banks than to their Scottish counterparts.

7 In fact, the coming existence of Skandinaviska Kredit AB was an immediate response to The English and Swedish Bank Ltd, founded in late 1863 according to the new Companies Act of 1862, with its head office in London and branches in Gothenburg and Stockholm (G. B. Nilsson, *André Oscar Wallenberg. II. Gyllene tider 1856–1866* (Stockholm, 1989), pp. 170–208; E. Söderlund, *Skandinaviska Banken i det svenska bankväsendets historia 1864–1914* (Stockholm, 1964), pp. 1–29, 115–20.

8 B. Gille, 'Banking and industrialization', pp. 296–7; H. Pohl, 'Forms and phases of industry finance up to the Second World War', in W. Engels and H. Pohl (eds.), *German yearbook on business history* (Berlin/New York, 1985); R. Rudolph, *Banking and industrialization*

in Austro-Hungary; V. Wellhöner, 'Zur Frage einer Herrschaft der Grossbanken uber die Industrie. Eine Kapitaltheoretische Untersuchung mit historischem Bezug auf die Schwer-und Elektroindustrie im Deutschen Reich von 1880 bis 1914' (Diss. Universität Bielefeld, 1988).

9 As a matter of fact, the principal arguments can still be recognized in the Swedish public debate of the 1980s. The fundamental issue investigated by the present Commission on Capital Markets (set up by the Swedish government in 1985) is how far-reaching banking regulations should actually be in order to protect the rights of the depositors and the system of payments, but still make it possible for banks to operate on the risk capital markets. See further M. Larsson and H. Lindgren, 'Risktagandets gränser. Utvecklingen av det svenska bankväsendet 1850–1980', *Uppsala papers in economic history*, Basic Reading No. 6, (1989).

10 This relates both to hours of work, possibilities for holidays and pensions, and an employment security scheme taken over from the public sector (H. Lindgren, *Bank, Investmentbolag, bankirfirma. Stockholms Enskilda Bank 1924–1945* (Stockholm, 1988), pp. 90–141).

11 E. Söderlund. *Skandinaviska Banken 1864–1914.*, pp. 178–82; L. E. Thunholm *Svenskt kreditväsen* (Stockholm 1989), pp. 23, 37–9.

12 R. Lundström, 'Banks and early Swedish multinationals,' in A. Teichova, M. Lévy-Leboyer and H. Nussbaum (eds.), *Multinational enterprise in historical perspective* (Cambridge, 1986), pp. 209. The long-term relationships between Swedish commercial banks and their industrial clients is discussed, from a perspective of contractual arrangements, in H. Lindgren, 'Long-term contracts in financial markets: bank-industry connections in Sweden, 1900–1970', in M. Aoki, B. Gustafsson and O. E. Williamson (eds.), *The Firm as a Nexus of Treaties* (London, 1990), pp. 263–88.

13 E. Söderlund, *Skandinaviska banken i det svenska bankväsendets historia 1914–1939* (Stockholm, 1978), pp. 3–27.

14 S. Fritz, 'Frågan om affärsbankernas aktieförvärvsrätt under 1900-talets första decennium', in: *Från vida fält. Festskrift till Rolf Adamson 25.10.1987* (Stockholm, 1987), pp. 59–85. No share-issuing banks according to the law of 1909 were ever founded.

15 M. Larsson, 'Public control of commercial banks and their activities – the Swedish example, 1910–1970, in S. Fritz, W. Kastner and M. Larsson, 'Banking and bank legislation in Europe, 1880–1970', *Uppsala Papers in Economic History*, Working Paper No. 2 (1989), pp. 41–9.

16 H. Althaimer. 'Börsen och företagens nyemissioner', in I. Hägg (ed.), *Stockholms Fondbörs. Riskkapitalmarknad i omvandling* (Stockholm, 1988), pp. 39–56.

17 M. Larsson and H. Lindgren, *Risktagandets gränser*, pp. 11–20.

18 A. Östlind, *Svensk samhällsekonomi 1914–1922* (Stockholm 1945), pp. 612–17.

19 M. Larsson, 'Government subsidies or internal restructuring – Swedish commercial banks during the crisis of the 1920s', in P. L. Cottrell, H. Lindgren and A. Teichova, *European industry and banking 1920–1939: review of bank-industry relations* (Leicester, forthcoming).

20 E. Söderlund, *Skandinaviska Banken 1914–1939*, pp. 44, 364–8.

21 R. Hilferding, *Finance capital. A study of the latest phase of capitalist development* (London, 1981), pp. 191–235.

22 *SOU* 1932:30, p. 49.

23 U. Olsson gives an expressive example of continuous share holding in his *Bank, familj och företagande. Stockholms Enskilda Bank 1946–1971* (Stockholm, 1986), pp. 202–3: not until 1956 did Stockholms Enskilda Bank dispose of its majority share-holding in AB Scania Vabis, the motor company which nowadays has merged with SAAB. Still up to 1962, the bank held a substantial minority block in Scania Vabis, one fifth of the shares.

24 H. Lindgren, 'Banking group investments in Swedish industry', *Uppsala Papers in Economic History*, Research Report No. 15 (1987), pp. 13–28.

V THE RISE OF EXTRA EUROPEAN FINANCIAL CENTRES

19 Money and power: the shift from Great Britain to the United States

KATHLEEN BURK

In 1900 Great Britain held sway as the predominant financial power in the world, a position which both supported and symbolized her international political and strategic power. In 1980 the United States held sway as the predominant financial power, a position which likewise supported and symbolized her super-power status. In both cases, however, an ultimately successful financial competitor was close behind. For Britain the First World War accelerated the process of comparative financial decline, while the Second World War consolidated and confirmed it; for the US, the causes of decline in her turn were more diverse and probably more controllable, but the outcome threatens to be similar as, slowly but ineluctably, the US is superseded by Japan as the predominant financial power. Few would object to this bare summary: confusion only arises when attempting to ascertain what it all means. It is necessary, for example, to distinguish between public and private money: does the term 'financial power' refer to private money controlled by bankers and private investors, or public money controlled by governments? Does 'financial power' exist if abundant private money cannot be directed according to government policy? Both resources *and* will are required to exercise effective power, and therefore it can be argued that during certain periods, such as the 1920s, the US was a potential rather than actual financial power, willing to act negatively but not positively. Secondly, both ability and will varied between wartime and peacetime. Until 1945, both the American and the British governments largely restricted the utilization of public money as a weapon to wartime; only thereafter was indicative guidance of bankers replaced by direct flows of public money to other countries.

With the benefit of hindsight, it can be argued that the symbolic beginning of this shift took place in January 1900. Britain was locked in combat with the two Boer republics in South Africa, the Transvaal and the Orange Free State, and the government needed to raise funds. The usual method was to issue the irredeemable stock, Consols, or a dated stock, repayable in, for example, five to ten years. But the London money market was tight and interest rates would therefore be high; besides this, the government preferred not to add to the permanent debt, and this ruled out Consols. Furthermore, the Treasury wanted to replace its gold stock – supplies of gold from the Rand had virtually ceased with the onset of war – and this meant going outside London. For all of these reasons, the Chancellor of the Exchequer, Sir Michael Hicks Beach, decided that he must turn to the New York money market. This was, in fact, the first time since the Seven Years War (1756–63) that the British government had looked abroad for funds, and the City of London was not pleased. Nevertheless, part of the £30 million National War Loan of 1900 was placed in New York, as were portions of three of the subsequent four Boer War loans[1] – a harbinger of the future. Indeed, 'the assertion began to be heard [in the US] that New York was destined to oust London as the central market of the world'.[2]

It should not be thought that Britain was the only foreign government which turned to the US in the early years of the century: there were many foreign issues floated from 1899 to 1905, when the London and Continental money markets were tight and there was an abundance of floating capital in New York. As *The Commercial and Financial Chronicle* noted in January 1901, 'Our bankers were able to make a departure and began to take part in the floating of European government loans, thus reversing the old-time position, where we had to seek rather than furnish capital abroad.' Mexico and Canada were even more important borrowers, and Japan as well turned to the US. Overall, between 1900 and 1913, nearly 250 foreign loans, with a par value of almost $1.1 billion, were placed in the US. One measure of why this was possible was the growth in American banking assets: between 1900 and 1910 they more than doubled, from $10.7 billion to $22.4 billion, while the assets of life insurance companies also expanded, from $1.7 billion to $3.8 billion. The latter numbers are of particular interest as denoting the rise of the institutional investor, although no inference can be drawn as to investment preferences between home and abroad. Finally, the numbers of individual investors also increased, from about 4.4 million in 1900 to about 7.4 million in 1910, or from nearly 6 per cent to over 8 per cent of the American population.[3]

But, as the British government discovered during the First World War, this great investment community had definite ideas about the types of issues in which it would invest. During the war, Britain found it necessary to turn to the US for munitions, food and supplies of various sorts: by October 1916 fully 40 per cent of British war expenditure was being disbursed in North America, and Britain had somehow to find the dollars necessary to pay for the goods. She (and France) attempted in 1915 to tap the American investing public by issuing a $500 million non-secured loan with an interest rate of 5 per cent, but it was a failure, with $187 million of the bonds being left with the underwriters, and only $33 million of the bonds being bought by the ordinary, non-institutional, investor. While there were political reasons for the failure of the 1915 Anglo–French loan, such as the disinclination of German-Americans, Irish-Americans and Jewish-Americans, and banks in the regions where they had influence, to buy the bonds, there were also primarily investor-orientated reasons for its failure: Americans still were not overly familiar with foreign issues and many distrusted them, and they were used to bonds providing 5½–6 per cent interest and secured with unimpeachable collateral.[4] Consequently, for the remainder of the war, Britain found it necessary to rely on collateral loans with increasing rates of interest.[5]

Britain's need to raise ever more dollars in order to pay for war supplies for herself and her allies nearly bankrupted her: by April 1917 she had only three weeks' supply of dollars in hand or anticipated to pay for goods ordered in the US, and by July 1917, but for American aid, the rate of exchange of the pound against the dollar would probably have plummeted. Indeed, only American financial support averaging $100 million a month kept the pound formally on the gold standard – and the withdrawal of such American aid by March 1919 meant the abandonment by Britain of the pre-war parity of £1 = $4.86. In short, the July 1917 exchange crisis was a turning point: thereafter the relationship of the pound to the dollar was virtually as important as its relationship to gold.[6] The weakness of the British financial position encouraged elements in the American government to consider how to exploit this.

The idea that the US might at last be in a position to challenge the British on their own ground – i.e. international trade and finance – was one that had gained increasing currency since the beginning of the new century. However, it was manifestly obvious that the US suffered a crucial weakness at the very centre of the financial system, and this was the lack of a central bank. The Federal Reserve Act of 1913, which established the Federal Reserve System, was intended to remedy that lack,but the Act had a secondary purpose as well: in order to promote foreign trade, the Act was meant to establish conditions which would enable a duplicate of the London discount market to grow up in the US. First of all, it permitted national (rather than state-chartered) banks with more than $1 million in capital to open branches abroad; and secondly, linked to this power to open foreign branches was the power to create trade acceptances based on the importing or exporting of goods, and these acceptances would be eligible for discount at Federal Reserve Banks.[7] It was the power to finance trade through the bill of exchange or acceptance eligible for discount, thereby creating a liquid market, which was intended to be a direct challenge to the position of the City of London.

This power came none too soon, since access to sterling credits was strictly limited during the First World War by British exchange controls. The result was that the dollar largely replaced the pound as the means of paying not only for American exports and imports – a source of commissions which the City never really recovered[8] – but also for more of Europe's trade with Latin America and the Far East. Trade, indeed, was as important a factor in the American government's interest in this development as financial power *per se*; for example, the Secretary of the Treasury, William Gibbs McAdoo, saw the war as the chance for the US 'to become the dominant financial power of the world and to extend our trade to every part of the world'.[9] Many in Britain feared just that, since the expansion of American financial and trading interests could only be at the cost of Britain's, but while the war raged there was very little Britain could do about it, since her own resources had to be concentrated on war-related requirements.

During the 1920s, however, the City attempted to recover its former position, while Wall Street strove to consolidate, and to improve, its lead. London laboured under a number of handicaps. Britain had been forced off gold in March 1919, and this had at least two important effects. First of all, the foundation of Britain's traditional dominance in trade finance was the convertibility of the pound into gold, and this had now ceased; traders might well prefer to invoice their goods in a currency which was both convertible and widely acceptable, such as the dollar. Secondly, it was the primary goal of both the British Treasury and the Bank of England to return to the pound to the gold standard and to keep it there, and this required limitations on the outflow of capital. From 1920 to 1925 Montagu Norman, the Governor of the Bank of England, imposed an 'embargo' of sorts on foreign loans. He asked bankers in early 1920 to refrain from issuing short-term foreign loans, 'short-term' being defined as having a maturity of less than twenty years. Nevertheless, by April 1924 Norman believed that, in spite of his requests, too many issues were taking place, and he decided that foreign lending should be limited to reconstruction loans, which he defined as those guaranteed by the Treasury or supported by the League of Nations.

In April 1925 Britain returned to the gold standard, but the Bank of England still thought that it would be necessary to 'discourage foreign issues and investments by all possible means'.[10] In October of that year the Chancellor of the Exchequer, Winston Churchill, told Norman that he hoped that no loan would be floated on behalf of any country which had not settled its war debts with Britain, and an embargo in this form remained until October 1928. For other foreign borrowers, however, the

Chancellor removed the prohibition on 3 November 1925, and foreign lending took off. But, in 1930, Norman and the Chancellor agreed that Norman should approve all foreign loans, and in 1933 a strict embargo on overseas loans was imposed, although loans to the Empire were still allowed.[11]

In addition to the official restrictions, London was at a particular disadvantage compared with New York in the amount of capital available for loans. For one thing, she had been forced during the war to liquidate about 15 per cent of her overseas investments, primarily through the sale of American investments,[12] and thus lost the income generated by them, including dividend receipts. For another, a stream of gold had flowed from east to west during the war: from August 1914 to July 1917 Britain alone had sent £305 million (just under $1,500 million) in gold to the US.[13] By 1925 the position compared with 1913 was stark: in 1913 Europe had held 63 per cent of the world's total stock of gold and North America 24 per cent, while by 1925 Europe held 35 per cent and North America 45 per cent.[14] The US had benefited greatly from supplying the allies during the war, and the increase in banking assets over the 1920s demonstrated that the industrial and exporting boom continued: in 1920 assets of all reporting banks stood at $53 billion, while by 1929 they had climbed to $72 billion, an increase of nearly 36 per cent.[15]

Indeed there was so much spare capital floating around New York that in certain cases, according to a contemporary writer, foreign borrowers 'had not to beg' for advances – 'they [were] actually besieged ... until they had accepted loans'.[16] Foreign loans earned large commissions, and, until the last stages of the bull market lured capital back into the New York stock market, a great deal of it was loaned abroad. The size of commission demanded, of course, could influence a borrower towards one market or another, and historians have differed as to whether London or New York was the cheaper market.[17] (Of course, it is necessary to know the date of an issue, since rates varied over time.) Short-term rates were often higher in London to support the rate of exchange; on the other hand, long-term money rates were usually cheaper in London because brokerage rates were lower. If the occasion warranted it, however, this disadvantage might be overcome:

> The American banker is at a disadvantage in international competition in the margin of profit he requires: overhead charges are higher in New York than in any other centre and banks there are accustomed to substantial profits on domestic banking business. They are reluctant to work for the same narrow margin as their European rivals. This does not mean that it is an easy task to defeat American bankers in a rate-cutting contest. If it comes to that, they are prepared to work without any profit or even at a loss in the field of international business, and to make up for their losses in the field of domestic business.[18]

New York did have one big disadvantage compared with London, and that was in the lack of a sizeable investing public for foreign issues. American firms frequently attempted to get around this by issuing a foreign loan in New York and then placing a substantial amount of it in London. Certainly a half-dozen New York firms maintained branches in London for the express purpose of distributing the issues for which they had taken responsibility with British insurance companies and other big investors. New York would then receive the commission income and the US the trading contracts, while Britain received neither. The British position was further damaged because these American issues absorbed funds which would otherwise have been available for lending by British banks on their own account; instead, they had to decline proposals and send the rejected customers to New York.[19]

For all of these reasons, then, New York emerged by the end of the decade of the 1920s as the more important international financial centre. London had the experience and the expertise, and could exploit traditional relationships, and certainly after the return to gold in 1925 the pound to a great extent recaptured its place as the primary trading currency. But, in the end, capital told. Comparing foreign capital issues publicly offered in New York (excluding refunding issues) with the overseas issues on the London market, in 1924 the values were $969 million versus £134 million, in 1927 $1,337 million versus £139 million, and in 1929 $671 million versus £94 million.[20] And with the abandonment of the gold standard in September 1931 and sterling's eventual fall in value from $4.86 to $3.49, the pound again resigned its former position as a trading currency.

During the decade of the 1920s, officials in both countries attempted, within the constraints of law and custom, to utilize the power of their financial centres to further general policy objectives, such as European reconstruction, stabilization of currencies and the financing of war debts and reparations. Reference has been made to the activities of the Governor of the Bank of England and the Chancellor with regard to the exchange rate of the pound, but Bank and Treasury officials also encouraged private bankers in their financial activities in, for example, Austria, in a bid to recapture pre-war influence.[21] As for the US, certain officials, such as the Secretary of Commerce, Herbert Hoover, strove to gain the power to guide private American overseas lending, and it was eventually decided that the US State Department should be apprised of all foreign bond issues prior to flotation in the US to see if they accorded with the national interest, although the American government denied all responsibility for the quality of the loans. Both governments, in short, wanted private money to come forward and fulfil needs which, after 1945, would be seen as the duty of governments themselves to meet. But, in the 1920s, and indeed in the 1930s, it was still unacceptable to both the British and American governments either to use public money to foster foreign economic policy objectives in peacetime or to force unwilling private banks and investors to provide the funds.

The collapse of economies worldwide and the onset of depression thoroughly discouraged foreign lending for a time, although the City of London wished to resume lending as soon as possible – New York, on the other hand, preferred to bring the money back home and keep it there.[22] The options were soon foreclosed with the onset of war, and, indeed, during the Second World War the question of activity in financial centres was irrelevant. Both were wholly controlled as far as foreign lending of any sort was concerned, and the relative positions of the City and Wall Street were effectively frozen for the duration. After the war, the fact that the pound was inconvertible (except for a six-week period during July–August 1947) until 1 January 1959, effectively directed overseas requests for finance largely to New York. Certainly during this period there was no question as to New York's overwhelming predominance.

Even more overwhelming was American predominance in the use of public funds for foreign policy objectives, a complete reversal of matters in comparison with the post First World War period. During the early stages of the Second World War Britain had become an international bankrupt even more quickly than had been the case during the First World War, and thus the US entered the war as paymaster of the alliance, a position only partially achieved during the First World War. She determined to exact agreement from the UK to various external economic policies such as convertibility and free trade,[23] in exchange for financial support, and thus the UK was forced to agree to full convertibility for the pound, with baleful effects in 1947, as well as to certain unpalatable elements in the Bretton Woods system. By means of Marshall aid, the US helped the European economies to rebuild themselves, and the growth thereby stimulated enabled them to return to convertibility and modified free trade by the early 1960s. Public rather than private money was now the fuel.

It is notable that it was during the 1960s, the period of overwhelming American financial predominance, that decisions were taken by the American government for domestic political and economic purposes which were to foster the regrowth of London as a financial centre. The American balance of payments position was weakening; a primary cause of this was a deficit on capital account as US multi-national corporations invested abroad, but dollars were also moving abroad because of American foreign aid and military expenditure (especially in Vietnam). The response of the US government was to try and reduce private capital outflows. The Interest Equalization Tax of 1964 taxed the purchase by Americans of foreign securities from foreigners, while in January 1968, under the Foreign Direct Investment Program, net transfers of capital by US investors for direct investment in advanced European countries and

South Africa were subject to a moratorium. Both of these measures greatly stimulated the growth of the Eurodollar market, but it must be said that probably the most important stimulus of Eurodollars (i.e. dollar deposits held in Europe rather than in the US) was the Federal Reserve's Regulation 'Q', dating in fact from the 1930s, which stipulated that interest paid by US banks on time-deposits was fixed, whereas dollar deposits in foreign banks were not subject to a ceiling. As a result, London banks bid for US dollar deposits which they then lent back to the US. Other contributory factors were the dollar's position as the main reserve currency, and the preference, for geopolitical reasons, of countries such as the USSR for holding their dollar deposits outside of the US.[24]

Over the 1960s, dollars flowed to and around Europe, with the Eurodollar market growing from $1,500 million at the end of 1959 to over $50,000 million in 1970.[25] There grew up in London, groups of both lenders and borrowers of dollars, both of whom could deal with much more flexibility about rates and conditions than they could in New York. The growth of the market was particularly stimulated by the activities of the British merchant and overseas banks, whose foreign exchange departments arranged many of the deals.

The growth of the Eurodollar market, the resumption of convertibility starting on 1 January 1959 and the steady increase in its self-confidence over the 1960s and 1970s enabled the City to exploit traditional expertise and contacts and thereby slowly to regain a position of importance as a financial centre. If it was no longer predominant, nor for very long was New York: rather, they were both important for different reasons. If the sole measure is the amount of capital available for loans, New York until the mid 1980s was clearly the most important centre; on the other hand, if the value of foreign exchange transactions is considered, London in the late 1980s transacted more business than New York.[26] At certain times of the day London is more important because it is awake and New York is asleep. During periods when relationship banking is strong, London can have an edge; when transaction banking is the fashion, the US banks, having more capital, can dominate. What frequently happens, of course, is that issues are joint issues. In the 1920s, both centres preferred Anglo-American issues because they combined the expertise of London and the capital of New York;[27] in the 1970s and 1980s multi-bank and multi-centre loans became the norm because of their size and the need to spread risk. What gave London its edge was experience and the fact that it was comparatively lightly regulated.

If London has in some sense recovered its former position and joined the US (and latterly Tokyo) as one of the world's most important financial centres, the same comparison cannot be made between the British and American governments as financial powers. The First World War saw the shift between Great Britain and the US as dominant and subordinate financial powers, and the US emerged from that war as a creditor nation. She refused actively to exploit this position in the interwar period, but this reticence was overcome by the requirements of war and reconstruction from 1939, and she openly and aggressively used her financial might to force various unpalatable decisions upon Britain and, to a lesser extent, other European nations. The US, in fact, emerged in 1945 as hegemonic, and spent the subsequent forty years acting as one, taking financial decisions on domestic political grounds which frequently adversely affected other countries. She inflated, and then exported her inflation, expecting other countries to take painful decisions which she herself avoided taking. But suddenly, in 1985, the US discovered that she was no longer the supreme financial world power, but was instead a debtor rather than a creditor nation,[28] precisely the position of 1914. Japan now wears the crown, and, although reticent about using its financial power for political purposes, it will in due course come to it as the US did.

But the position at the end of the century will most likely differ in structure from that at its beginning. In 1900 Britain was the dominant financial and geographical power, and the one supported the other. In 1945 the US held this position, in an even more lop-sided manner, since there was absolutely no competition. By the end of the century, even though Japan may be the strongest power financially, neither it nor Tokyo as a financial centre will dominate. Rather, it is more likely that there will be three centres – the US, Europe and Japan – with Japan drawing part of its strength from being the leader in the rapidly growing Far Eastern economy. If the UK government takes sensible decisions and refrains from overly heavy regulation, London will thrive as the European financial centre and the UK will benefit. For the foreseeable future the financial world, along with the geopolitical world, will be multi-polar.

Notes

1 For a brief description of the four loans which drew on American funds see Kathleen Burk, 'Finance, foreign policy and the Anglo-American Bank: The House of Morgan 1900–1931', *Historical Journal*, 61, 145 (June 1988), 199–201. For more details plus extensive references see Kathleen Burk, *Morgan Grenfell 1838–1988: the biography of a merchant bank* (Oxford, 1989), pp. 111–23.

2 Alexander Dana Noyes, *The market place: reminiscences of a financial editor* (New York, 1938), p. 175. 'In 1900 and 1901, New York banking houses had taken $128,000,000 newly issued British government bonds direct from the Exchequer, something never previously dreamed of.' Ibid., p. 192.

3 Vincent P. Carosso, *Investment banking in America: a history* (Cambridge, Mass., 1970), pp. 80–5.

4 Lord Reading, 'Memorandum', 29 October 1915, Cab. 37/136/39;

Cabinet Committee on the Co-Ordination of Military and Financial Effort, 'Memorandum', 31 January 1916, Cab. 37/141/38, both Public Record Office, London. Kathleen Burk, *Britain, America and the sinews of war 1914–1918* (London, 1985), pp. 72–5.

5 Burk, *Sinews of war*, chapter 5.

6 Ibid., pp. 203–6. Kathleen Burk, 'J. M. Keynes and the exchange rate crisis of July 1917', *Economic History Review*, 2nd ser., 32, 3 (August 1979), 405–16.

7 John J. Broesamle, *William Gibbs McAdoo: a passion for change, 1867–1917* (Port Washington, 1973), p. 129. Harold van B. Cleveland and Thomas F. Huertas, *Citibank 1812–1970* (Cambridge, Mass., 1985), pp. 73–7.

8 Cleveland and Huertas, *Citibank*, p. 124.

9 Quoted in Broesamle, *McAdoo*, p. 129.

10 Sir Henry Clay, 'Embargo on foreign capital issues', 15 June 1930, Box 34, Clay Papers, Nuffield College, Oxford.

11 Sir Henry Clay, *Lord Norman* (London, 1957), pp. 239, 368, 416–17.

12 Derek H. Aldcroft, *From Versailles to Wall Street, 1919–1929* (London, 1977), pp. 240–1. It is estimated that, during the war, US investment banks arranged the resale of more than $3 billion of American securities held in Europe. Carosso, *Investment banking in America*, p. 216.

13 Elizabeth Johnson (ed.), *The collected writings of John Maynard Keynes, vol. XVI: Activities 1914–1919* (London, 1971), p. 249.

14 Committee on Finance and Industry, *Report*, Session 1930–1. vol. 13, Cmd. 3897, June 1931. par. 141. Total gold stock in 1913 was £1,803 million and in 1925 £2,102 million. Ibid.

15 US Bureau of the Census, *Historical statistics of the United States, colonial times to 1957* (Washington, 1960), p. 624.

16 Quoted in Carosso, *Investment banking in America*, p. 262.

17 Aldcroft, *Versailles to Wall Street*, p. 242 and Cleveland and Huertas, *Citibank*, p. 386 fn 19, argue that it was cheaper to borrow in New York than in London; D. E. Moggridge, *British monetary policy 1924–1931: the Norman conquest of $4.86* (Cambridge, 1972), p. 200, states the opposite.

18 Paul Einzig, *The fight for financial supremacy* (London, 1931), p. 52.

19 Ibid., pp. 73–5.

20 Committee on Finance and Industry, appendix IV, tables 2 and 3.

21 Michael J. Hogan, *Informal entente: the private structure of cooperation in Anglo-American economic diplomacy, 1918–1928* (Columbia, 1977), pp. 60–2; Eduard März, *Austrian banking and financial policy: Creditanstalt at a turning point, 1913–1923*, trans. Charles Kessler (London, 1984), part 5, chapter 2; T. Lamont to D. W. Morrow, 15 May 1921, file 1, Bundle 156 (Austria. Reconstruction. 1923/24 Loan), Morgan Grenfell Papers, Morgan Grenfell Group, London.

22 R. H. Brand, 'Memorandum', 1931, File Acceptance Houses Committee, 1A, Documents and Memoranda, Morgan Grenfell Papers.

23 L. S. Pressnell, *External economic policy since the war, volume I: the postwar financial settlement* (London, 1987), *passim.*; Donald Moggridge (ed.), *The collected writings of John Maynard Keynes, vol. XXVI: Activities 1941–1946: shaping the post-war world. Bretton Woods and reparations* (Cambridge, 1980), pp. 1–238; Sir Hugh Ellis-Rees, 'The convertibility crisis of 1947', Treasury Historical Memorandum No. 4 (December 1962), T.267/3, PRO; Kathleen Burk, 'Britain and the Marshall Plan', in Chris Wrigley (ed.), *Warfare, diplomacy and politics: essays in honour of A. J. P. Taylor* (London, 1986), pp. 210–30; Michael J. Hogan, *The Marshall Plan* (Cambridge, 1987); and Alan S. Milward, *The reconstruction of western Europe 1945–51* (London 1984), who places less emphasis than others on the responsibility of Marshall aid in stimulating European economic recovery.

24 Kathleen Burk, 'The international environment', in Andrew Graham (ed.), *Government and economies in the postwar world* (London, 1990), chapter 1.

25 A. Dequae, *Report on the Eurodollar market* for the Council of Europe, Doc. 2939, 28 April 1971, 6.

26 In April 1989 London foreign exchange trading averaged $187 billion per day, with Tokyo trading averaging $115 billion a day and New York trading $129 billion. Figures issued by the Bank of England on 13 September 1989. *The Guardian*, 14 September 1989. For details see 'The market in foreign exchange in London', Bank of England Quarterly Bulletin, vol. 29, no. 4 (November 1989), 531–5.

27 'Our experience...showed that evidence of cooperation with Great Britain particularly was of great influence with the investors throughout this Country...' J. P. Morgan & Co. to Morgan Grenfell & Co., 23 January 1924, no. 2050, file 31, Box Hist. 5, Morgan Grenfell Papers.

28 Robert Gilpin, *The political economy of international relations* (Princeton, 1987), pp. 328–34.

20 The Yokohama Specie Bank during the period of the restored gold standard in Japan (January 1930–December 1931)

HIROAKI YAMAZAKI

1 Introduction

According to *The preeminence of international financial centers* by Howard Curtis Reed, Yokohama ranked fourth, Tokyo ninth and Osaka tenth as international banking centres in 1930.[1] Three centres in Japan were among the second group after the two financial centres of London and New York in 1930. What factors enabled these three centres to reach such a level by that time? In answering this question, the Yokohama Specie Bank (Y.S.B.) must become the first object of observation. The bank occupied a dominant position in financing Japan's foreign trade, and during the 1920s it accounted for nearly 50 per cent of foreign exchange transactions for Japanese exports and imports.[2] In addition, it was the largest in scale except for the Bank of Japan and was the most profitable among the large banks in 1929.

Two sets of its histories trace the development of the Y.S.B., 'A history of the Yokohama Specie Bank' and 'A complete history of the Yokohama Specie Bank'.[3] But the former only covers the period before 1920, and the latter chronologically describes the activities of the bank and is not a scholarly work. There are some other valuable scholarly works on the Y.S.B., but most of them are mainly concerned with its foreign exchange transactions and lack a composite analysis of the bank.[4] The aim of this paper is to sketch broadly its activities during the period of the restored gold standard in Japan and outline its characteristics. The reason why we confine our observation to only two years (January 1930 to December 1931) is (1) we can not give a complete analysis of the bank for a longer period because of the lack of documents and (2) this period was the final stage of the Japanese gold standard and in this sense it occupies a significant position in modern Japanese economic history.

Section 2 deals with the business trends of the Y.S.B., in particular its total assets and liabilities at the end of 1929, and changes from 1929 to 1931. Such an examination allows us to know the contents of each account in its balance sheet for the first time. Section 3 deals with the foreign exchange transactions of the Y.S.B., especially with regard to its response to aggressive 'dollar buying' by banks and companies in various fields and by individuals (domestic and foreign). By utilizing internal documents of the bank, the bank's response to 'dollar buying' and its effects will be examined in more detail than in other works. Section 4 deals with the activities of its branches* in London, New York and Asian financial centres in order to observe the relationship between the Y.S.B. and the two largest international financial centres and the position of its Asian branches within its worldwide network. In the concluding remarks, two characteristics – the government relationship and entrepreneurship – will emerge from the foregoing observations, and the relationship between these characteristics and the rise of the 'Tokyo' market will be considered.

2 Business trends of the Yokohama Specie Bank: from 1929 to 1931

A comparison of total assets and liabilities of the Yokohama Specie Bank with that of Mitsui Bank at the end of 1929

Japan returned to the gold standard in January 1930 and abandoned it in December 1931. This part deals with the business trends of the Y.S.B. during this period by analysing its total assets and the liabilities.

Before proceeding to the main subject of this section I will compare the total assets and liabilities of the Y.S.B. with that of Mitsui Bank at the end of 1929 (table 20.1), just before Japan's return to the gold standard. This will be in order to draw out its characteristics as a special bank that specialized in foreign exchange business. Mitsui Bank was a representative bank among private banks in pre-war Japan and was affiliated with Mitsui zaibatsu, the largest zaibatsu at the time.

For the Y.S.B., in terms of liabilities, loans from bankers and bills rediscounted were about equal and together comprised a quarter of the total. By contrast, Mitsui Bank had no such accounts. It is clear from this that the Y.S.B. specialized in foreign exchange business and relied heavily on the Bank of Japan and foreign financial centres for raising funds necessary for its business.

On the other hand, the percentage of deposits were smaller in the case

* The word 'branch' when used in connection with the New York business of the Yokohama Specie Bank is applied in a general manner. This was actually an 'agency', licensed under New York branch state banking law, which forbade foreign branch banks.

Table 20.1 *A comparison of balance sheets between the Yokohama Specie Bank and Mitsui Bank, end of* 1929 ('000 *yen*, %)

	Y.S.B.		Mitsui Bank	
Assets				
Cash and deposits with bankers account	112,817	(8.6)	45,591	(5.0)
Cash	24,910	(1.9)	24,305	(2.7)
Deposit with bankers	87,387	(6.7)	19,752	(2.2)
Bullion and foreign currency	520	(0.0)	1,534	(0.2)
Call loans	—	—	18,480	(2.0)
Securities account	282,906	(21.6)	234,169	(25.8)
Various public loan bonds	277,404	(21.2)	—	—
Various debentures	5,503	(0.4)	—	—
Bills discounted account	157,873	(12.1)	40,010	(4.4)
Advance account	186,751	(14.3)	414,378	(45.7)
Advance to government	243	(0.0)	—	—
Advance	100,807	(7.7)	389,920	(43.0)
Current account overdrawn	41,361	(3.2)	24,457	(2.7)
Advance against exchange contracts	40,679	(3.1)	—	—
Bad and doubtful debts	3,661	(0.3)	—	—
Securities lent	—		3,038	(0.3)
Foreign exchange account	515,703	(39.4)	82,645	(9.1)
Bills bought	379,419	(29.0)	61,604	(6.8)
Interest bills	136,284	(10.4)	14,405	(1.6)
Foreign correspondents	—		6,634	(0.7)
Correspondents	1,171	(0.1)	230	(0.0)
Liabilities of customers against acceptance and guaranty	26,954	(2.1)	19,292	(2.1)
Bank properties	23,018	(1.8)	7,943	(0.9)
Miscellaneous account	992	(0.1)	1,160	(0.1)
Temporary payment	992	(0.1)	46	(0.0)
Uncalled capital	—	—	40,000	(4.4)
Total	1,308,185	(100.0)	906,940	(100.0)
Liabilities				
Notes account	6,182	(0.5)	—	—
Notes in circulation	5,938	(0.5)	—	—
War notes taken over from government	243	(0.0)	—	—
Deposit account	646,610	(49.4)	660,373	(72.8)
Public bonds and coupons redemption fund	8,944	(0.7)	—	—
War notes redemption fund	80	(0.0)	—	—
Fixed deposit	270,590	(20.7)	437,277	(48.2)
Current account	83,196	(6.4)	52,762	(5.8)
Special current account	—		98,163	(10.8)
Deposit at notice	81,196	(6.2)	67,869	(7.5)
Special deposit	202,030	(15.4)	—	—
Foreign drafts in home currency	599	(0.0)	—	—
Miscellaneous deposits	—	—	4,400	(0.5)

Table 20.1 (*cont.*)

	Y.S.B.		Mitsui Bank	
Loan account	344,398	(26.3)	—	—
Loan from bankers and others	174,328	(13.3)	—	—
Bills rediscounted	170,070	(13.0)	—	—
Foreign exchange account	15,747	(1.2)	42,131	(4.6)
Drafts sold	15,747	(1.2)	696	(0.1)
Foreign correspondents	—	—	41,434	(4.6)
Correspondents	1,177	(0.1)	630	(0.1)
Acceptance and guaranty	26,954	(2.1)	19,292	(2.1)
Bills payable	—		272	(0.0)
Miscellaneous account	37,341	(2.9)	10,192	(1.1)
Unpaid dividend	39	(0.0)	—	—
Unpaid interest	5,087	(0.4)	—	—
Partial payment for bills	6,773	(0.5)	—	—
Rebate on undue bills	9,949	(0.8)	—	—
Suspense	11,403	(0.9)	—	—
Exchange conversion margin	4,090	(0.3)	—	—
Shareholders account	229,778	(17.6)	174,044	(19.2)
Capital	100,000	(7.6)	100,000	(11.0)
Statutory reserve fund	—	—	28,700	(3.2)
Reserve fund	106,000	(8.1)	38,952	(4.3)
Special reserve fund	2,500	(0.2)		
Reserve for bad and doubtful debts	3,546	(0.3)	—	—
Profit for present account	17,732	(1.4)	6,391	(0.7)
Total	1,308,185	(100.0)	906,940	(100.0)

Notes: Figures in parentheses show percentages to total.
Source: The annual reports of the Y.S.B. and Mitsui Bank for the latter half of 1929.

of the Y.S.B. (49 per cent) than for Mitsui (73 per cent). There was also a difference between the two in the type of deposits. The Y.S.B. was smaller than Mitsui in terms of the percentage of fixed deposits and was larger than Mitsui in terms of the percentage of special deposits. The difference in the position of deposits in total liabilities was a reflection of the fact that it received both loans from bankers and bills rediscounted.

The difference in the position of special deposits was mainly based on the Y.S.B.'s character as a national policy-oriented financial institution. Details concerning the special deposits of the Y.S.B. will be explained later.

As for assets, the foreign exchange account constitutes nearly 40 per cent in the case of the Y.S.B. but only 9 per cent for Mitsui. In this we can clearly see the Y.S.B.'s character as a foreign exchange bank. On the other hand, both loans and bill discounting account for 26 per cent in the case of the Y.S.B., whereas Mitsui's share is 50 per cent. Bill discounting alone, however, amounts to 12 per cent in the case of the Y.S.B., significantly larger than Mitsui's 4 per cent. The higher position of the Y.S.B. in terms of bill discounting reflects the fact that its main customers were foreign trading companies that used discount bills more often than others.

The percentage of deposits with the banks of the Y.S.B. amount to 7 per cent, as compared to 2 per cent for Mitsui. Moreover, there is a difference in the specifics of this. Mitsui Bank deposited all non-working money with the Bank of Japan, whereas the percentage of deposits with the Bank of Japan in the case of the Y.S.B. comes to only 23.3 per cent of its total deposits with banks. This was because the Y.S.B. constantly had to deposit a certain amount of money with banks, both domestically and abroad in order to meet the need for funds to settle foreign exchange sold in Japan or other countries.

In sum, in contrast to Mitsui Bank, the Y.S.B.'s character as both a foreign exchange bank and a national policy-oriented bank appears in its composition of assets and liabilities. The Y.S.B.'s position as a national policy-oriented bank will become clear later when we examine the details of each account.

Details of each account among total assets and liabilities of the Yokohama Specie Bank at the end of 1929[5]

Assets

1 Deposit with Banks

Current accounts with bankers constituted 99.9 per cent of the total deposits with banks. A breakdown by branch reveals that Tokyo's share amounted to 64.6 per cent of the total, New York's 8.9 per cent, and London's 8.8 per cent. The Y.S.B. deposited funds with large banks in New York and London. In Tokyo it deposited funds with the Bank of Japan and Yasuda Bank. Deposits with the Bank of Japan correspond to loans from that bank. It is natural for banks to deposit a certain amount of money with the banks from which they borrow money. Deposits with Yasuda Bank, on the other hand, were not ordinary deposits but substantial advances to that bank. Yasuda Bank was one of the five largest private banks, but it suffered from repayment delay from enterprises affiliated with Asano zaibatsu which had a close tie with Yasuda zaibatsu. This caused a decrease in Yasuda Bank's deposits, which went from 722 million yen in 1928 to 590 million yen in 1930, while the amount of deposits in the other largest banks increased. In this sense, advances to Yasuda Bank by the Y.S.B. helped to relieve Yasuda

Bank from the danger that its deposits would be withdrawn on a large scale by small depositors.

2 Securities

About 90 per cent of securities were held by the head office and 10 per cent by the New York branch. The bank held securities to operate non-working funds and they were often utilized as collateral for loans from bankers.

3 Bill discounting

Details of outstanding bill discounting by borrowers and by branches show that 'banks and companies' occupy 92.9 per cent by borrowers. Tokyo 42.8 per cent, and Osaka 37.2 per cent by branches. Although I have no data that show details of 'banks and companies' for 1929, data for 1935 show the following interesting facts. With regard to the Osaka branch, trading companies, such as the Nikon Menka (Raw Cotton) Co. and the Gosho Co., both dealing in raw cotton, almost monopolistically together with the Toyo Menka, occupied a dominant position. With regard to the Tokyo branch, by contrast, bill discounting to relieve enterprises and important persons from difficulty and bill discounting based on national policy comprise 75.4 per cent of the total. Examples of the former are bill discounting to Fusanosuke Kuhara and enterprises affiliated with Kuhara zaibatsu which became almost bankrupt around the mid 1920s, bill discounting to Ensuiko Seito (sugar refining) which almost went bankrupt during the financial crisis of 1927. Examples of the latter are bill discounting to the South Manchurian Railway Co. and to the Manchurian government.

4 Advances

About 40 per cent of advances comprised advances to Hanyehping Coal and Iron Co., The China-Japan Industrial Development Co. and the Bank of Taiwan. The Y.S.B. borrowed money from the Ministry of Finance and then advanced it to these institutions. These advances were part of national policy at the time. The Y.S.B. also engaged in activities in Shanghai. Its branch there advanced money to Hanyehping Coal and Iron Co., the China-Japan Industrial Development Co. and Russia-Asia Bank. It also advanced money to Kawasaki-Zosen (ship-building), Yokohama Koshin Ginko (bank) and Doshi Boeki (trading) in order to relieve them from bankruptcy. As a whole, it is estimated that national policy-oriented advances occupied at least half of its total advances and that relief-based advances also occupied a considerable proportion.

5 Advances against exchange contracts
These are advances to exporters until the export bill is bought by a foreign exchange bank. Borrowers of these advances were thus exporters, that is foreign trading companies.

6 Current accounts overdrawn
It is estimated that the main borrowers of this account were the same as those receiving advances against exchange contracts.

Liabilities

1 Fixed deposits
About 40 per cent of fixed deposits comprised deposits by Japanese immigrants in the United States. Also deposits by trading companies and large enterprises connected with foreign trade occupied a significant position, followed by deposits by diplomats, export cooperative unions, foreign foundations and Japanese firms abroad.

2 Special deposits
Deposits by the old Imperial Russian government and an agent for the Bank of Japan occupied 94 per cent of this account. The latter came from the Deposit Bureau of the Ministry of Finance.

3 Deposits at notice
Deposits by the Imperial Russian government, the Bank of Japan in London, and the Japanese government at Shanghai occupied about 90 per cent of this account.

4 Current accounts
China and Manchuria (by regions) and foreigners (by borrowers) occupied a more important position than other deposits. In this sense this account functioned as a channel to absorb local money in the form of deposits in districts where silver currency was circulated. Also, Mitsui Bussan, Tokyo Kaijo Kasai Hoken (Marine and Fire Insurance) and the Rockefeller Foundation were the prime users of this account in Tokyo and/or London. The government account and government officials occupied a somewhat lesser position in London.

5 Loans from bankers
About 40 per cent of the loans comprised loans from the Bank of Japan and the Ministry of Finance, and funds raised by these loans were advanced to Hanyehping Coal and Iron Co., The China-Japan Industrial Development Co. and the Bank of Taiwan, as stated earlier. The Y.S.B.

Table 20.2 *Details of loans from bankers of the London branch and the New York branch of the Yokohama Specie Bank, end of 1929*

Lenders	Amount
London branch ('000 *pounds*)	
Lloyds Bank	1,300
Midland Bank	2,000
Westminster Bank	1,250
National Provincial Bank	1,000
Total	5,550
New York branch ('000 *dollars*)	
Guaranty Trust Company	2,000
French American Banking Corp.	1,000
National Shawmut Bank of Boston	1,000
First National Bank of Boston	2,000
Chatham Phoenix National Bank and Trust Company	1,000
Lee Higginson and Company	500
Commercial National Bank and Trust Company	1,000
International Acceptance Trust Company	1,000
J. P. Morgan Company	1,000
Total	10,500

Source: The Y.S.B., The Report by the Auditor's Room for the latter half of 1929.

also borrowed money from the four largest banks in London and large commercial banks and investment banks in New York (table 20.2).

6 Bills rediscounted

Bill rediscounting was mainly done in New York and London, but the former was three times the size of the latter. The Y.S.B. dealt with established bill brokers and large banks in New York and with well-known discount houses and large banks in London.

To sum up, the composition of assets and liabilities of the Y.S.B. clearly reflects its character as a foreign exchange bank. The foreign exchange account occupied an important position (39.4 per cent) among assets.

Among liabilities, on the other hand, bills rediscounted, all of which was done in New York and London, accounted for 13.0 per cent. Loans from bankers, excluding loans from the Bank of Japan and the Ministry of Finance, occupied 7.3 per cent. Foreign exchange accounts occupied 1.2 per cent. The total of these thus comes to 21.5 per cent. In addition, there were deposits, advances and bills rediscounted by or to foreigners, and deposits with foreign banks. The amounts of each are not trivial and should not be overlooked.

But this is not the only characteristic of the Y.S.B. The composition of assets and liabilities of the Y.S.B. also reflects its activities as a national policy-oriented bank. The accounts which were closely related with its function as a national policy-oriented bank, their amounts and their percentage of the total are as described in table 20.3.

In total, 30.3 per cent of the total assets and 26.3 per cent of the total liabilities were closely related with its activity as a national policy-oriented bank. In a word, the Y.S.B. occupied a unique position in the international money market as a national policy-oriented and multi-national foreign exchange bank.

The change of details of each account among total assets and liabilities of the Yokohama Specie Bank during 1929–1931[6]

In this section, I will only point out the changes in its main accounts which are closely related to its characteristics as both a bank specializing in foreign exchange transactions and a government policy-oriented one.

Assets

1 Deposits with banks
Current accounts with Yasuda Bank increased from 36,000 thousand yen to 50,000 thousand yen. As explained previously, these were actual advances to that bank for the purpose of relieving it from the danger that deposits there would be withdrawn on a large scale by small depositors who were anxious about the bank's deteriorating performance.

2 Bill discounting
Broken down by branch, the amount of the home office increased from 8,570 thousand yen to 50,660 thousand yen. This increase was mainly determined by security backed by merchandise collateral and miscellaneous borrowers, including individuals. During this period, the head office in Yokohama advanced money to silk-reelers; this was based on a law designed to compensate losses when banks advanced money to silk-reelers to stabilize the price of raw silk. From these facts, we can assume that the increase in the amount of bill discounting was mainly caused by these advances to silk-reelers.

3 Advances
The amount of advances by the Tokyo branch increased from 5,690 thousand yen to 32,640 thousand yen. Advances to banks and corporations and advances secured by bonds mainly brought about this

Table 20.3 *Assets and liabilities of the Yokohama Specie Bank related to its activity as national policy-oriented bank, end of* 1929

	Thousands of yen
Liabilities	
Notes in circulation	6,182 (0.5%)
Public loans and coupon redemption fund	8,944 (0.7%)
Public deposits among deposits at notice	69,809 (5.3%)
Public deposits among special deposits	189,764 (14.5%)
Loans from the Bank of Japan and the Ministry of Finance	78,292 (6.0%)
The part in shareholders' accounts which corresponds to the ratio occupied by the government in the capital stock (20.0%)	45,956 (3.5%)
Assets	
Deposits with bankers (Bank of Japan and Yasuda Bank)	56,362 (4.3%)
Half of advances	50,400 (3.9%)
A part of bill discounting in Tokyo branch	15,607 (1.2%)
Government bonds among securities	221,379 (16.9%)

increase. During this period the Y.S.B. advanced 10,000 thousand yen to the Japan Industrial Bank and more than 60,000 thousand yen to Yasuda Bank in Tokyo. Among advances to Yasuda Bank, as mentioned before, 50,000 thousand yen took the form of deposits. Therefore, about 10,000 thousand yen was formally advanced to Yasuda Bank. The total of both the 10,000 thousand yen to the J.I.B. and the approximately 10,000 thousand yen to Yasuda Bank constituted about three quarters of the increase in advances by the Tokyo branch.

4 Advances against exchange contracts: foreign exchange accounts

The amount of advances against exchange contracts greatly decreased, from about 40,000 thousand yen to 27,000 thousand yen. Also the amount of foreign exchange accounts considerably decreased, from 480,000 thousand yen to 396,162 thousand yen. Both changes were basically determined by a decrease in Japanese foreign trade during this period. The amount of Japanese exports decreased from 1,863,860 thousand yen in 1929 to 1,119,320 thousand yen in 1931, and the amount of Japanese imports also decreased from 1,872,948 thousand yen in 1929 to 1,354,357 thousand yen in 1931. The decrease-ratio was 40 per cent in the case of exports and 28 per cent in the case of imports.

Liabilities

1 Special deposits

Special deposits sharply decreased from 220,000 thousand yen to 105,000 thousand yen. A decrease in the deposits by an agent for the Bank of Japan was especially great, falling from 172,369 thousand yen to 71,698 thousand yen. This drop was mainly brought about by a change in the deposits of the Bank of Japan and by the Deposit Bureau of the Ministry of Finance.

2 Loans from bankers

Loans from bankers showed a marked increase, rising from 170,000 thousand yen to 358,000 thousand yen. The percentage of this account of total liabilities also increased from 13.3 per cent to 27.6 per cent. Broken down by branch, the increase of both the chief accountant and the New York branch were especially great. As for the chief accountant, the Y.S.B. sold a large amount of dollars to speculators who expected a future decline in the yen and bought a large amount of dollars in futures. The Y.S.B. was in an over-sold dollar position as a result of this operation. It thus received a considerable amount of yen when these futures contracts were completed. But it also converted a large amount of yen into gold and shipped gold mainly to the United States in order to offset its over-sold dollars and to carry out dollar selling contracts in the New York market. For this operation, the Y.S.B. required a large amount of yen to buy gold from the Bank of Japan.

The Y.S.B.'s need for yen was thus determined by two factors: the extent of completion of dollar-selling contracts and the amount of gold shipments. From September 1931, when Britain abandoned the gold standard, to November 27, 1931, the amount of gold shipments actually surpassed the amount of completion of dollar-selling contracts by 139,000 thousand yen. This increased the Y.S.B.'s need for yen. In addition, as mentioned before, the Y.S.B. advanced a large amount of money to the Japan Industrial Bank and Yasuda Bank during this period. These factors led to a considerable increase in loans from the Bank of Japan by the chief accountant of this bank. As for the New York branch, it had to increase loans from American bankers in order to complete the Y.S.B.'s dollar-selling contracts.

3 Bills rediscounted

Bills rediscounted significantly decreased in both New York and London. The decrease in Japanese foreign trade caused a decrease in the amount of bills receivable, and this in turn led to a decline in the amount of bills rediscounted.

The Y.S.B. had two distinguishing features: it was a bank specializing in foreign exchange transactions and a government policy-oriented bank. As for the former, the percentage of foreign exchange accounts of total assets decreased from 39.4 per cent to 30.6 per cent. The percentage of loans from bankers in foreign countries of total liabilities slightly increased from 7.3 per cent to 9.3 per cent, while the percentage of bills rediscounted of total liabilities considerably decreased from 13.0 per cent to 5.9 per cent. If we combine these two accounts in the liabilities category, the percentage decreased from 20.3 per cent to 15.2 per cent. The weight of these accounts, which is closely related to the Y.S.B.'s activity as a foreign exchange bank, decreased, and this stemmed from a significant decrease in Japanese foreign trade during the so-called Showa Crisis period. As for those parts of the bank's operations which were closely related to its activity as a government policy-oriented bank, changes in these categories are shown in table 20.4 below. The percentage increased from 30.3 per cent to 34.4 per cent in terms of assets, and also increased from 26.3 per cent to 30.5 per cent in terms of liabilities. The Y.S.B. strengthened its character as a government policy-oriented bank during this period. Moreover, in foreign exchange transactions, the Y.S.B. sold a large quantity of dollars aggressively with the support of the government and the Bank of Japan. In calculating the above figures, we have not taken into account the relationship with the government in terms of foreign exchange accounts. If we include this into the above figures, the percentage becomes higher. The foreign exchange transactions of the Y.S.B. during this period will be discussed later.

3 'Controlled selling of dollars' by the Y.S.B.[7]

The most consipicuous activity of the Y.S.B.'s foreign exchange transactions during this period was the 'controlled selling of dollars' (a direct translation of the Japanese 'Tosei Uri'). In this section I will analyse this operation.

Speculative 'dollar buying' and 'controlled selling of dollars' by the Y.S.B.

Japan returned to the gold standard on 11 January 1930, but many banks and companies, both foreign and domestic, felt uneasy about its stability. The National City Bank sold yen just after Japan's return to the gold standard, and several foreign banks and Japanese banks followed suit. As a result, the yen exchange rate often dropped under the gold export point and a large amount of gold was shipped abroad, leading to a rapid drop in the gold reserve held by the Bank of Japan. The Bank of Japan let the

Table 20.4 *Changes in the Yokohama Specie Bank's operations related to its activity as a government policy-oriented bank, 1929–1931*

	thousands of yen			thousands of yen	
Liabilities					
Notes in circulation	6,182	(0.5%)	→	11,330	(0.9%)
Public loans and coupon redemption fund	8,944	(0.7%)	→	8,704	(0.7%)
Public deposits among deposits at notice	69,809	(5.3%)	→	68,424	(5.3%)
Public deposits among special deposits	189,764	(14.5%)	→	93,529	(7.2%)
Loans from the Bank of Japan and the Ministry of Finance	78,292	(6.0%)	→	216,679	(16.7%)
The part in shareholders' accounts which corresponds to the ratio occupied by the government in the capital stock (20.0%)	45,956	(3.5%)	→	46,138	(3.6%)
Assets					
Deposits with bankers (Bank of Japan and Yasuda Bank)	56,362	(4.3%)	→	57,554	(4.4%)
A part of advances	50,400	(3.9%)	→	70,400	(5.4%)
A part of bill discounting in Tokyo branch and the head office	15,607	(1.2%)	→	56,607	(4.4%)
Government bonds among securities	221,379	(16.9%)	→	211,500	(16.3%)

Y.S.B. sell dollars aggressively against dollar buying which they judged speculative. This operation was called 'controlled selling of dollars' and started at the end of July 1930. The Bank of Japan allowed the Y.S.B. to convert yen which the Y.S.B. acquired in this operation into gold at par and ship it abroad. The Y.S.B. could then complete future dollar selling contracts by utilizing this gold in the United States. At the same time the Y.S.B. was expected by both the government and the Bank of Japan to complete a part of the dollar selling by buying dollars at suitable times and suitable places.

The amount of 'controlled selling of dollars' by the Y.S.B. is shown in table 20.5. The amount increased several times and it was especially large in September 1931, when Britain abandoned the gold standard. The right-hand column in this table shows the daily changes in the amount in September. After 21 September uneasiness about the Japanese gold standard rapidly mounted and the amount of 'controlled selling of dollars' by the Y.S.B. greatly increased. In response to the aggressive dollar buying which caused this large increase in the 'controlled selling of dollars', the Bank of Japan raised the official bank-rate to the highest level

Table 20.5 *The amount of 'controlled selling of dollars' by the Yokohama Specie Bank, 1930–1931*

Amount by month		During Sept. 1931	
Month	Amount	Day	Amount
11 July 1930–		Sept. 1	260
31 Aug.	20,300	5	200
Sept.	54,059	10	850
Oct.	800	11	100
Nov.	—	14	313
Dec.	100	16	50
Total, 1930	75,289	19	1,720
Jan. 1931	2,850	21	38,743
Feb.	350	22	28,703
Mar.	30,555	23	3,750
Apr.	13,900	25	13,735
May	5,515	26	20,347
June.	18,099	28	7,560
Jul.	41,208	29	6,962
Aug.	14,825	30	2,320
Sept.	125,613	Sept. 21–30	122,120
Oct.	48,958		
Nov.	◁ 500		
Dec.	◁ 380		
Total, 1931	301,489		
Grand Total	376,778		
31 July 1930– 31 Aug. 1931	202,640		

Notes: 1 Yen converted into dollar at the rate of $1 = Y2.
2 ◁ designates buying by the Y.S.B.
Source: The Bank of Japan, *The 100 year history of the Bank of Japan*, vol. 3 (Tokyo, 1983).

and tightened the financial market in order to compel buyers of dollars to sell them and to offset their future dollar buying contracts. The buyers contracted with the bank to buy dollar futures and had to pay in yen to acquire spot dollars at the future delivery date. The buyers had to prepare the necessary amount of yen to execute this transaction, but the tightening of the financial market made it difficult for them to do so. The Bank of Japan expected that buyers would sell the dollar, but there was a sudden political change. The Seiyukai took over the Minseito and changed the cabinet and the Finance Minister changed from Junnosuke Inoue to Korekiyo Takahashi. The Seiyukai and Takahashi had insisted that Japan immediately abandon the gold standard and this took place on 13 December 1931. The total volume of 'controlled selling of dollars' by the Y.S.B. amounted to 376,778 thousand dollars.

Buyers of dollars

Table 20.6 shows the top ten buyers of dollars under the Y.S.B.'s 'controlled selling' program. The National City Bank accounted for 40 per cent of the total, followed by foreign banks, such as The Hongkong and Shanghai Bank, The Netherland Trading Society and The Chartered Bank. Among Japanese banks and companies, Mitsubishi Bank ranked second, Sumitomo Bank third, the Bank of Chosen fifth, Mitsui Bank seventh, and Mitsui Bussan eighth.

The right-hand column of the table also shows the amount of 'controlled selling' of dollar futures contracts that were not yet completed as of 10 December 1931, broken down by buyers. The National City Bank still ranked first but its share decreased to 32.2 per cent, the position of Mitsui Bank and Mitsui Bussan rose, and the share of Mitsui Bank rose to 17.3 per cent and that of Mitsui Bussan also rose to 14.8 per cent. After Japan's abandonment of the gold standard, the yen exchange rate fell by almost 50 per cent and the value of the dollar almost doubled. If dollar buyers were in an overbought position after Japan's abandonment of the gold standard, they could thus earn a profit from dollar-buying operations.

Of course, foreign exchange banks maintained tight secrecy with regard to the real position of the foreign exchange and we do not have accurate data on this. But the fact that The National City Bank, Mitsui Bank and Mitsui Bussan occupied the top positions in the amount of 'controlled selling' contracts of future dollars which were not yet completed on 10 December 1931, just before Japan's abandonment of the gold standard, suggests the possibility that it was very possible to earn profits from dollar buying operations.

'Controlled selling of dollars' and the Yokohama Specie Bank

The Y.S.B. was in a dollar over-sold position as a result of 'controlled selling of dollars' when Japan abandoned the gold standard. Table 20.7 shows that the Y.S.B. sold dollars amounting to 754 million yen in this operation, shipped gold abroad amounting to 415 million yen, and bought dollars to the amount of 134 million yen in the market. It was thus able to cover a part of its dollar selling operation. It could cover 55 per cent of its dollar 'controlled selling' by gold shipments and 18 per cent by buying dollars in the market. As a result, the bank stood in an over-sold dollar position amounting to 206 million yen as of 10 December 1931.

Table 20.8 shows the procedure by which the Y.S.B. dealt with this and

Table 20.6 *Ten largest customers in the Yokohama Specie Bank's 'controlled selling of dollars' 1930–1932 ('000 dollars)*

	Aug. 1930–Aug. 1931			Sept. 1931–March 1932			Uncompleted forward contracts as of 10 December 1931	
	Name of enterprise	Amount		Name of enterprise	Amount		Name of enterprise	Amount
1	National City Bank	142,510 (40.2)	1	National City Bank	130,642 (32.7)	1	National City Bank	22,103 (32.2)
2	Mitsubishi Bank	34,300 (9.7)	2	Mitsui Bank	46,550 (11.6)	2	Mitsui Bank	11,850 (17.3)
3	Sumitomo Bank	33,000 (9.3)	3	Sumitomo Bank	31,700 (7.9)	3	Mitsui Bussan	10,133 (14.8)
4	Hongkong and Shanghai Bank	21,450 (6.1)	4	Mitsui Bussan	30,054 (7.5)	4	Sumitomo Bank	3,700 (5.4)
5	Bank of Chosen	18,700 (5.3)	5	Mitsubishi Bank	19,550 (4.9)	5	Hongkong and Shanghai Bank	3,500 (5.1)
6	Netherland Trading Society	15,085 (4.3)	6	Hongkong and Shanghai Bank	19,200 (4.8)	6	Mitsubishi Bank	2,600 (3.8)
7	Mitsui Bank	12,200 (3.4)	7	Bank of Chosen	15,430 (3.9)	7	Chartered Bank	2,400 (3.5)
8	Mitsui Bussan	11,731 (3.3)	8	Toyo Menka	8,888 (2.2)	8	Bank of Chosen	2,065 (3.0)
9	Chartered Bank	8,700 (2.5)	9	Chartered Bank	8,700 (2.2)	9	Nichizui Boeki	1,340 (2.0)
10	Nomura Securities	6,399 (1.81)	10	Bank of Taiwan	8,250 (2.1)	10	Handels Bank	1,085 (1.6)
	Total including others	354,420		Total including others	399,995		Total including others	68,654

Notes: Figures in parentheses show percentages.
Source: Documents possessed by the Bank of Tokyo.

Table 20.7 *Details of 'controlled selling of dollars' by the Yokohama Specie Bank, 1930–1932*

1 *Details of 'controlled selling' (yen)*

31 July 1930–10 December 1931	Total of 'controlled selling'	754,415,400
	Amount of specie shipped	414,881,000
		339,534,400
	Covered by the market	133,522,000
	Difference	206,012,400

2 *Details of the amount covered by the market (thousands of yen)*

	New York	Shanghai	London	Japan	Others	Total
31 July 1930–18 September 1931	41,633	3,911	17,740	10,800	11,652	85,736
18 September 1931–10 December 1931	23,450	800	—	23,536	—	47,786
Total	65,083	4,711	17,740	34,336	11,652	133,522

Source: Documents possessed by the Bank of Tokyo.

the losses which arose from the final over-sold position of dollars. The Y.S.B. was allowed to ship gold abroad in the amount of 89 million yen even after Japan's abandonment of the gold standard. The Y.S.B. could buy dollars amounting to 56 million yen at the exchange rate of 49.375 dollars at par from the Bank of Japan. Thus, 60.8 million yen remained as the amount of over-sold dollars by the Y.S.B. The Y.S.B. carried forward this amount of dollar future selling contracts at the end of the latter half of 1931 to the next period and finally dealt with this as follows. The Y.S.B. had sold dollars at the rate of 49.375 dollars, so the total over-sold dollars amounting to 60.8 million yen equalled 30 million dollars. The dollar exchange rate rose to 33 dollars per 100 yen on 15 February 1932 when this calculation was made. Thirty million dollars thus had equalled 91 million yen. The Y.S.B. had sold dollars amounting to 30 million dollars and had acquired 60.8 million yen before but this 30 million dollars equalled 91 million yen at the time. The Y.S.B. suffered a loss of 30 million yen. How did the Y.S.B. deal with this loss?

At the time Y.S.B. held deposits from the old Imperial Russian government amounting to 74.6 million yen, including interest. On the other hand, the Y.S.B. lent 70.3 million yen to the Japanese government at 2 per cent interest. The Y.S.B. took the view that the depositor's right to withdraw the deposit had been extinguished by the lapse of time and earned profits of 74.6 million yen. On the other hand, the government

Table 20.8 *The disposal of losses accompanying the 'controlled selling of dollars' by the Yokohama Specie Bank, 1930–1932*

Deposit from the old Imperial Russian government	YY58,499,725.67	
Interest fund for the deposit	YY16,103,189.49	
Total	YY74,602,915.16 (A)	
Loan (2% interest)	YY70,288,225 @ 96	YY67,489,645,60
Government bonds (5% interest)	YY26,190,000 @ 87.05	YY22,798,395.00
Difference	YY44,098,225	YY44,691,250.60 (B)
(A)–(B)	YY29,911,664.56	
Interest of loan for the latter half of 1931	YY702,882.25	
Total	YY30,614,546.81	
YY60,800,000 (X) @ 49 3/8	$30,020,000.00	
YY85,771,428.57 (Y) @ 35	$30,020,000.00	
YY90,969,696.96 (Z) @ 33	$30,020,000.00	
(Y)–(X)	YY24,971,428.57	
(Z)–(X)	YY30,169,696.96	
Uncompleted Forward Contracts	YY206,000,000.00	
Amount of shipping gold among the above	89,000,000.00	
Outstanding balance	YY117,000,000.00	
Amount of Dollar Buying from the Bank of Japan at the Rate of $49 3/8	YY56,200,000.00	
Outstanding Balance	YY60,800,000.00 (X)	

Source: The Bank of Tokyo, *A complete history of the Yokohama Specie Bank* vol. 3, p. 562.

converted the 2 per cent loan, whose term was to expire in June 1931, into 5 per cent bonds to mature in fifty-five years. According to the government official's explanation, the total principal and interest of the 5 per cent bonds, amounting to 26.2 million yen, was equal to that of the 2 per cent loan, amounting to 70.3 million yen for the same years. But the Y.S.B. suffered a loss amounting to the difference between 70.3 million yen and 26.2 million yen, or a loss of 44.1 million yen. Strictly speaking the loss accompanied by this conversion was 44.7 million yen because of the difference between the nominal value and the market price of the loan and the bond. As a result of this operation, the Y.S.B. earned profits of 74.6 million yen on the one hand and suffered a loss of 44.7 million yen on the other, earning a net profit of 30 million yen. By utilizing net profits from the above-mentioned special operation the Y.S.B. thus could completely

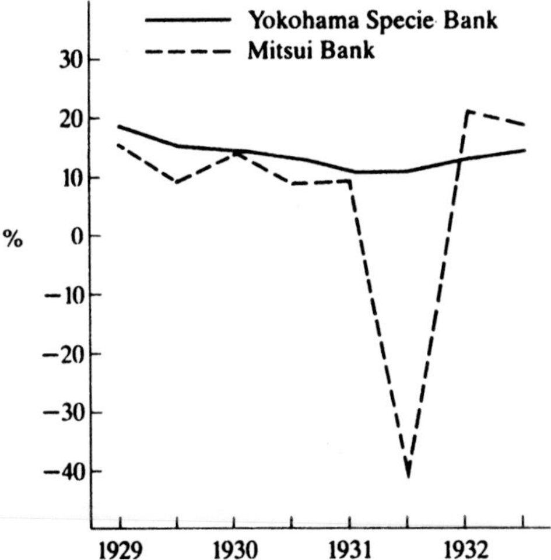

Figure 20.1 Changes in the rate of profit of the Yokohama Specie Bank and the Mitsui Bank, 1929–1932. *Source*: The annual reports, 1929–32 of Y.S.B. and Mitsui Bank.

offset the losses from the 'controlled selling of dollars' and a sharp decline in the yen after Japan's abandonment of the gold standard.

As is clear from the above, the 'controlled selling of dollars' was in the end neutral to the Y.S.B.'s calculation of profits and losses. Concerning its statement of profits and losses in the latter half of 1931, an internal document of the Y.S.B. tells another interesting story. According to a document titled 'An examination of each branch's business record the latter half of 1931', all branches except the chief accountant section recorded deficits totalling 1,047 thousand yen. The chief accountant section recorded profits of 6,387 thousand yen. The latter derived from 'the disposition of foreign exchange funds' amounting to 4,997 thousand yen, the transfer of 'special rebates' to a profit and loss account of 2,750 thousand yen, and profits from foreign exchange transactions amounting to 9,000 thousand yen. On the other hand, this section suffered losses of 9,960 thousand yen as a result of a decline in the value of securities. 'The disposition of foreign exchange funds' entailed the transfer of profits which arose as a result of an increase in the value of foreign exchange funds in several foreign branches. 'Special rebates' were a kind of secret reserve and had been accumulated almost yearly. The Y.S.B. transferred a part of it to the published statement of profits and losses. There is no concrete data for the profits from the foreign exchange transactions but a document from an auditors' meeting indicates that the bank could oversell the pound before Britain abandoned the gold standard and earn a profit from this operation. This was in sharp contrast to Mitsui Bank, which suffered a large loss because of a decline in the value of the pound at the time. The Y.S.B.'s loss as a result of the decline in the value of securities was also true for other Japanese banks. But the Y.S.B. differed from Mitsui and Mitsubishi in that it earned rather stable profits even in the latter half of 1931 in spite of the large losses in securities holdings. The stability of the Y.S.B.'s profit-rate is shown in figure 20.1.

4 The activities of the London, New York and Asian branches

The activities of the London branch

As shown in table 20.9 which shows the balance sheet of the London branch of the Y.S.B., a characteristic of this branch was that it raised money mainly from loans from bankers and bills rediscounted on the one hand and operated money primarily in bills receivable and the chief accountant account on the other. Moreover, following the above main account, there were deposits on the liabilities side, and deposits with bankers, loans, government and company bonds on the assets side. The London branch's main activities were to pay T.T. (Telegraphic Transfer) which the other branches sold and sent to London and to collect money for bills receivable which the other branches sent to London. The collected money was deposited with bankers and utilized as funds for paying T.T. In order to pay T.T. the branch often had bills rediscounted in the market and borrowed money from bankers. Bonds which the branch held were often utilized as security for borrowing. The government and the Bank of Japan frequently deposited money with the branch as a special deposit and deposits at notice. The branch sometimes lent money to Japanese banks and companies as well as British banks. The above accounts thus became the primary components of the balance sheet of the London branch. The chief accountant account appeared on the asset side when the branch paid T.T. which other branches sold and on the liabilities side when the postal time necessary for sending the bills which the other branches bought lapsed as a counterpart to the bills receivable account.

According to table 20.9 the percentages of the above accounts of the total at the end of January 1930 were as detailed in table 20.10.

Concerning the position of the London branch of the Y.S.B. in the London money market, we have the following information. The amount of bills rediscounted at the end of January 1930 came to £3,810. The total bills discounted by the five largest banks in Britain was 215,081 thousand pounds at the end of December 1930 or the end of June 1931.[8] The bills discounted account included treasury bills discounted but a report by the Y.S.B. estimated that the ratio between bills and treasury bills was 2:1 at the end of 1933.[9] If we use this ratio and estimate the amount of ordinary bills discounted by the five largest banks in December 1930/June 1931, the amount comes to 143,387 thousand pounds. The Y.S.B. accounted for

Table 20.9 *Details of the balance sheets of the London branch, 1930–1931* ('000 *pounds*)

Liabilities

	Public loans and coupon. redemption fund	Fixed deposits	Current account	Deposits at notice	Special deposits	Loans from bankers	Bills rediscounted	Correspondents	Others	Total
Jan. 1930	346	77	404	1,036	1,727	4,350	3,810	—	1,719	13,469
Jan. 1931	1,070	81	317	3	1,728	—	2,113	3	647	6,815
Feb.	901	85	298	4	1,705	1,000	2,770	3	736	7,502
Mar.	346	83	328	5	1,704	750	2,519	3	752	6,490
Apr.	284	133	329	7	1,702	1,100	2,544	3	727	6,829
May	411	125	309	8	1,741	700	2,462	3	885	6,644
Jun.	741	77	423	10	1,612	3,100	2,504	3	917	9,405
Jul.	399	82	392	12	1,708	3,200	1,975	3	814	8,585
Aug.	768	83	334	13	1,625	1,060	1,572	3	725	6,173
Sept.	252	81	440	1,015	1,699	5,800	1,793	—	737	11,817
Oct.	181	82	473	1,008	1,629	4,000	1,600	—	686	9,659
Nov.	389	81	440	1,005	1,659	3,400	976	—	642	8,592
Dec.	740	84	494	1,019	1,576	5,100	1,345	—	872	11,330

Assets

	Advances	Bad and doubtful debt	Advances against exchange contracts	Interest bills	Interest bills receivable	Bills bought	Bills receivable	Current account with bankers	Corre-spon-dents	Public loans and debenture accounts	Chief accountant account	Profit and loss account	Other
Jan. 1930	1,412	46	2,334	2,896	1,504	3,946	59,238	5,048	63	10,076	53,785	158	8,516
Jan. 1931	1,512	—	671	590	590	1,976	46,354	8,129	43	24,584	22,851	—	1,177
Feb.	1,539	—	1,282	490	490	1,858	41,465	3,905	490	25,378	20,628	4	346
Mar.	1,405	—	670	818	818	2,154	31,894	2,645	36	24,789	45,691	138	579
Apr.	1,355	—	358	813	813	757	26,702	3,811	37	23,654	49,640	2	342
May	1,277	—	240	556	556	946	24,612	1,774	58	25,132	50,173	—	363
Jun.	1,226	—	149	397	397	831	23,066	1,501	88	21,375	21,498	—	346
Jul.	1,205	—	510	587	587	821	24,055	5,644	82	28,793	23,620	42	409
Aug.	1,303	—	1,351	418	418	854	24,325	1,744	123	29,468	19,466	63	478
Sept.	1,272	—	2,868	429	429	4,364	26,880	1,627	40	28,723	10,430	170	692
Oct.	514	—	3,729	2,436	2,436	4,725	30,357	2,892	46	29,307	30,999	138	396
Nov.	531	—	4,125	1,312	1,312	6,249	32,206	1,037	66	29,339	10,201	229	377
Dec.	528	—	2,921	2,471	2,471	5,076	32,934	4,874	90	25,653	6,677	194	246

Source: The Y.S.B., *Jissai Hokoku Cho* (General Balance Sheet).

Table 20.10 *Distribution of the Yokohama Specie Bank's operations at the London branch, January 1930*

	%
Liabilities	
Loans from bankers	32.3
Bills rediscounted	28.3
Special deposit	12.8
Deposits at notice	7.7
Assets	
Chief accountant account	41.9
Bills receivable	34.8
Loans	9.6
Current accounts with bankers	3.7

about 2.7 per cent of the total amount of bills (except treasury bills) discounted by the five largest banks.

The Y.S.B.'s loans from bankers at the end of January 1930 amounted to 4,350 thousand pounds. The total amount of money at call and short notice of the five largest banks in Britain was 228,230 thousand pounds at the end of December 1930 or the end of June 1931. The Y.S.B. accounted for about 1.9 per cent of the total money at call or short notice supplied by the five largest banks.

The amount of loans from bankers greatly decreased in the latter half of 1930 and reached zero at the end of September and November 1930 because the surplus money was sent to London. But the London branch's fund position became tight with the increase in the 'controlled selling' of foreign exchange. In response to this situation, the Deposit Bureau of the Ministry of Finance deposited 1.2 million pounds with the London branch and sold British treasury bills amounting to 1 million pounds which was to be utilized as security for loans from bankers to the Y.S.B. In addition, the Y.S.B. adopted the policy that it would decrease the amount of overbought pounds because uneasiness about the pound was mounting. As a result, the outstanding amount of bills receivable at the London branch decreased from the 3 million pound level during the period from January to July 1931 to the 2 million pound level after July 1931. The outstanding amount of bills rediscounted also decreased from the 2 million pound level during the period from January to June 1931 to the 1 million pound level or less after June 1931. Furthermore, the bank tried to borrow pounds to the utmost of its borrowing potential amounting to 5 million pounds, in order to decrease the risks accompanied by its over-

Table 20.11 *Distribution of the Yokohama Specie Bank's operations at the New York branch, January 1930*

	%
Liabilities	
Bills rediscounted	39.7
Special deposits	37.7
Loans from bankers	13.4
Assets	
Bills receivable	39.8
Chief accountant account	36.1
Government and company bonds	6.8
Deposits with bankers	3.4

bought position of the pound. The British treasury bills mentioned above were utilized as security for this borrowing from bankers. After Britain's abandonment of the gold standard, borrowing from bankers became difficult and the London branch could barely borrow 5.1 million pounds, nearly equivalent to the above facility limit for the branch, at the end of 1931.[10]

Table 20.9 shows that the amount of deposits at notice increased from 13 thousand pounds to 1,019 thousand pounds and the amount of loans from bankers increased from 1,050 thousand pounds to 5,100 thousand pounds from August to December 1931. The former was based on the deposits by the Deposit Bureau of the Ministry of Finance and the latter was partly supported by the Y.S.B.'s acquisition of British treasury bills from this Bureau. In sum, the support by the government enabled the London branch to borrow pounds to its limit of borrowing which London bankers allowed it during the difficult stage after Britain had left the gold standard.

The activities of the New York branch

The activities of the New York branch were very similar to those of the London branch. The percentages of the main accounts in the balance sheet at the end of January 1930 were as indicated in table 20.11.

The New York branch's percentage of bills rediscounted and special deposits was much higher than that of the London branch. The export of raw silk, the largest export product in pre-war Japan, was mostly directed to the United States. Therefore, the amount of bills rediscounted was much larger than in the case of the London branch. Special deposits came primarily from the Bank of Japan, which assisted the Y.S.B. in responding to the dollar buying operations of speculators just after Japan's return to the gold standard. On the assets side, bills receivable was larger than the chief accountant account and this was a result of Japan's export structure as explained above.

The New York branch was such that the branch raised dollars mainly from bills rediscounted, special deposits and loans from bankers and operated mainly in bills receivable and the chief accountant account. This structure was basically the same as that of the London branch, despite some differences, as explained above. Table 20.12 shows the position of the New York branch of the Y.S.B. in the New York money market. The New York branch accounted for 3.2 per cent of the total outstanding bank acceptances in the New York money market and also accounted for 1.4 per cent of the total outstanding commercial paper there at the end of 1928. The percentage was especially high (8 per cent) for bank acceptances of import bills. It is clear that the Y.S.B. occupied an important position in the New York money market around the end of the 1920s. Table 20.13, which records changes in the main accounts of the New York branch in 1931, shows that the amount of special deposits largely decreased from 47,576 thousand dollars in May to 22,515 thousand dollars in June and the amount in the chief accountant account on the assets side also decreased from 50,173 thousand dollars to 21,498 thousand dollars during the same period. The decrease in the special deposit was due to drawing by the deposit bureau, causing a decrease in the supply of credit from the branch to the chief accountant and other branches. The amount of bills rediscounted and that of bills receivable also decreased during January to August. This was caused by a decrease in the amount of Japan's exports during the Showa Crisis period. On the other hand, loans from bankers increased from 14,000 thousand dollars in January to the 30,000 thousand dollar level in August as a result of an increase in the 'controlled selling' of dollars by the Y.S.B.

After Britain left the gold standard, most of the drawing (the selling of foreign exchange in order to raise money) by other branches came to be done in dollars and the branch's fund position became very stringent.[11] Early in October its borrowing potential was almost exhausted and it negotiated with J. P. Morgan & Co. and Guaranty Trust Co. about borrowing on the security of en-route gold. In addition, the Y.S.B. acquired permission to borrow US treasury bills amounting to 4.1 million dollars from the Bank of Japan. Also it would buy United States bonds amounting to 26.56 million dollars from the Deposit Bureau, on condition that it resold them in the near future, preparing for the worst.

After Japan's abandonment of the gold standard, the supply of credit was restricted all the more. The New York branch asked the Bank of Japan to permit the Y.S.B. to ship gold amounting to 20 million yen on

Table 20.12 *The position of the Yokohama Specie Bank in the New York money market, 1924–1928* (thousands of dollars %)

	Imports	Exports	Domestic shipment credit	Domestic warehouse credit	Dollar exchange	Based on goods stored in or shipped between foreign countries	Total	Commercial paper outstanding (total)
Bankers acceptances outstanding (total)								
1924	292	305	37	162	23	—	821	797
1925	311	296	25	103	19	16	773	621
1926	283	260	28	115	26	40	755	525
1927	312	390	20	196	28	130	1,080	555
1928	315	496	16	173	39	243	1,284	383
Outstanding bills or papers handled by the New York branch								
	(4.3)	(0.4)					(1.7)	(1.2)
1924	12.6	1.25					14.0	9.6
	(7.1)	(2.75)					(3.2)	(1.0)
1925	22.0	2.75					24.8	6.5
	(7.4)	(1.7)					(3.3)	(1.3)
1926	20.9	4.3					25.2	6.9
	(6.7)	(2.2)					(2.7)	(1.7)
1927	20.8	8.55					29.4	9.6
	(8.0)	(2.7)				(0.8)	(3.2)	(1.4)
1928	25.2	13.3				2.0	40.5	5.5

Source: The New York branch of the Y.S.B., *New York Waribiki Shijo ni okeru New York Shiten Toriatsukai Tegata ni tsuite* (on the bills and papers handled by the New York in the New York Money Market), 1929.

Table 20.13 *Details of the balance sheets of the New York branch, 1930–1931 ('000 dollars)*

	Public loans and coupon redemption fund	Special deposits	Loans from bankers	Bills rediscounted	Correspondents	Profit and loss account	Others	Total
Liabilities								
Jan. 1930	4,916	56,236	20,000	59,115	2	—	8,753	149,022
Jan. 1931	8,031	46,353	14,000	37,300	826	75	1,315	107,900
Feb.	3,734	46,945	14,500	30,349	830	—	1,057	97,415
Mar.	2,483	47,501	33,350	25,993	858	—	678	110,863
Apr.	3,750	46,964	35,000	20,504	610	—	670	107,498
May	1,611	47,576	36,450	18,113	510	115	782	105,157
Jun.	1,236	22,515	26,050	19,076	716	90	815	70,498
Jul.	5,390	21,272	37,650	19,490	1,074	—	915	85,792
Aug.	1,063	21,955	34,500	20,131	1,078	—	923	79,650
Sept.	958	22,164	32,000	20,060	1,225	—	1,151	77,558
Oct.	2,747	22,618	54,800	23,363	1,377	—	690	105,595
Nov.	782	24,425	36,800	21,539	1,537	—	676	85,759
Dec.	632	26,349	27,800	25,751	632	—	598	81,762

Assets

	Advances	Current accounts over-drawn	Advances against exchange contracts	Bills dis-counted	Interest bills	Interest bills receivable	Bills bought	Bills receivable	Current account with bankers	Corre-spon-dents	Public loans and debenture accounts	Chief accountant account	Profit and loss account	Others
Jan. 1930	1,297	—	51	—	311	4,683	18	4,683	495	41	140	5,649	44	703
Jan. 1931	271	40	—	15	200	3,638	16	3,638	1,164	11	962	—	6	485
Feb.	246	35	—	17	166	3,482	8	3,482	1,148	38	1,870	7	12	464
Mar.	321	37	—	16	136	3,297	17	3,297	474	35	913	699	17	518
Apr.	396	9	—	10	141	3,106	16	3,108	437	26	980	1,199	13	486
May	396	1	—	7	204	3,145	9	3,145	602	28	917	615	1	708
Jun.	496	—	—	10	209	3,246	14	3,246	1,107	12	701	2,801	—	797
Jul.	421	—	—	14	206	3,248	14	3,248	597	6	488	2,866	13	703
Aug.	471	—	—	17	155	2,861	20	2,861	906	6	843	337	17	532
Sept.	396	—	—	16	181	2,741	10	2,741	424	9	2,301	5,177	34	523
Oct.	296	—	—	9	314	2,382	41	2,382	400	24	2,111	3,656	60	359
Nov.	296	1	—	5	233	2,305	57	2,305	563	19	2,340	2,176	81	408
Dec.	276	1	—	5	341	2,522	48	2,522	1,000	7	2,459	3,853	15	677

Source: The Y.S.B., *Jissal Hokoku Cho* (General Balance Sheet).

Table 20.14 *The scale of each branch of the Yokohama Specie Bank in terms of the amount of in-flow money in* 1927 ('000 *yen*)

Ranking	Name of branch	Amount
1	London	6,643,593
2	New York	5,804,654
3	Shanghai	2,502,956
4	Dairen	2,381,543
5	Bombay	1,646,795
6	Calcutta	768,053
7	San Fransisco	614,579
8	Tsingtau	600,077
9	Sourabaya	568,463
10	Tientsin	564,854
11	Hamburg	509,824
12	Hong Kong	483,384
13	Seattle	453,354
14	Singapore	424,170
15	Rangoon	381,911

Source: The Ministry of Finance, *Ginko Kyoku Henpo Syowa 2 Nen Ban* (An Annual Report of the Bureau of Banking, 1927).

18 December and asked again on 22 December that the Bank of Japan would permit the Y.S.B. to ship gold amounting to 20 million yen early next year and another 30 million yen later. The first request was immediately approved. Concerning the latter, the government refused to permit the Y.S.B. to ship gold but instead recommended that the government let the Deposit Bureau sell foreign bonds to the Y.S.B., subject to rebuying by the Bureau in future, and that the New York branch borrow money from the bankers in New York on the security of those bonds. In addition, the government promised the Y.S.B. that it would send a certificate issued from a financial commissioner of the Ministry of Finance to New York banks when they refused to give loans to the New York branch. The certificate would promise that the Japanese government would allow the Y.S.B. to ship gold when the bank could not pay the debts at the fixed dates.

Meanwhile, the amount of loans from bankers increased rapidly from the 30 million dollar level for the period March to September to 54.8 million dollars in October, then decreased to 36.8 million dollars in November and 27.8 million dollars in December 1931. The amount of loans from bankers in December was supposed nearly to reach the limit of its borrowing which the branch was allowed by New York banks, although it nominally decreased from the end of October to the end of

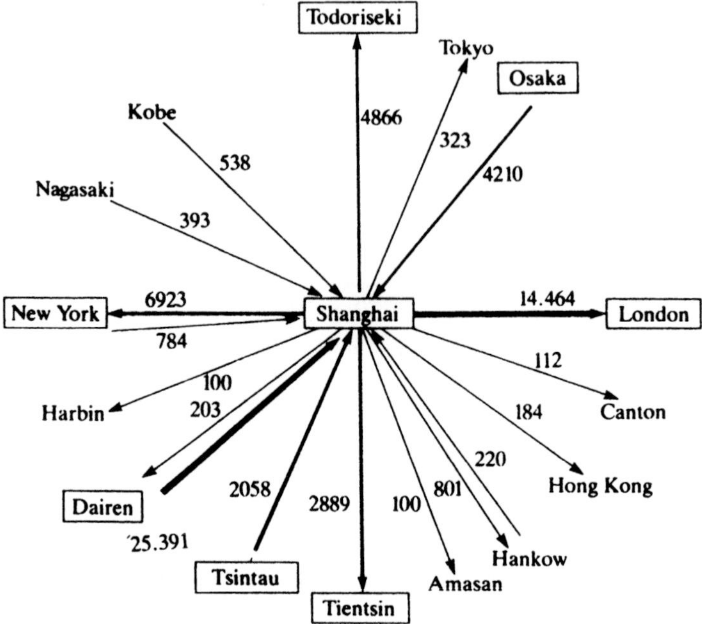

Figure 20.2 Money-flow between the Shanghai branch and other branches of the Yokohama Specie Bank in July 1932. *Source*: The Y.S.B., *Todoriseki Keisankakanjo Uchivakehyo* (Specification of balance of chief accountant account), July 1932.

December. According to volume 3 of *A complete history of the Yokohama Specie Bank*, 'the Y.S.B. borrowed money to its utmost limit' and loans from bankers reached 22.5 million dollars on 11 December.[12] The amount on 31 December somewhat exceeded this limit.

Thus, the New York branch succeeded in borrowing money to the utmost limit of its potential and the support given by the government and the Bank of Japan enabled the branch to tide over difficulties in its financial management. Moreover, the Bank of Japan gave support to the Y.S.B. in Japan as well. The decrease in the limit of its borrowing potential caused a decrease in the chief accountant account on the asset side of the New York branch and the latter caused financial difficulties for the chief accountant in Japan. Loans from bankers, mainly from the Bank of Japan, increased rapidly from 9.7 million yen in June 1931 to 154 million yen in December 1931.[13] The support given by the Bank of Japan relieved the Y.S.B. from the difficulties it faced in its financial management in Japan at a critical stage just after Japan abandoned the gold standard.

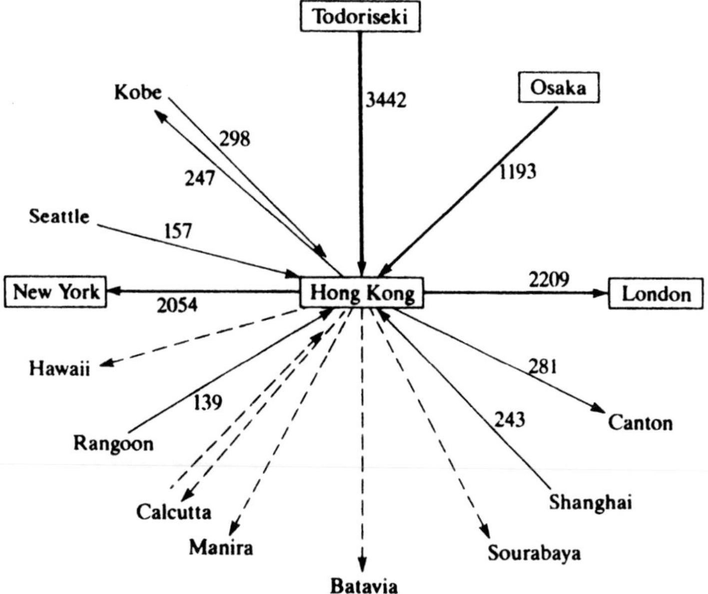

Figure 20.3 Money-flow between the Hong Kong branch and other branches of the Yokohama Specie Bank in July 1932. *Source*: The Y.S.B., *Todoriseki Keisankakanjo Uchivakehyo* (Specification of balance of chief accountant account), July 1932.

The activities of the Asian branches

This section deals briefly with the activities of its branches in the Asian financial centres that Geoffrey Jones describes in chapter 21. According to table 20.14, which shows the scale of each branch in terms of total money-flows in each branch, Shanghai ranked third, Hong Kong twelfth, and Singapore fourteenth, Shanghai ranked next behind the London branch and the New York agency; the Hong Kong and Singapore branches had about one-fifth or one sixth of the money flows in Shanghai.

Figures 20.2, 20.3 and 20.4 show the network of credit among the headquarters and branches of the Y.S.B.. These charts are derived from the data presented in the 'Specification of the balance of the chief accountant account in July 1932'. In all three cases the largest amount of credit was between each branch and the London branch, the New York agency and branches in Japan. In addition, the Shanghai branch had a close relationship with the Dairen branch, branches in North and Middle China, and the Hong Kong branch. The Hong Kong branch did business with branches in South China, the South Seas and Shanghai. The Singapore branch did business with branches in the South Seas. Of these relationships, the one between Dairen and Shanghai and that between

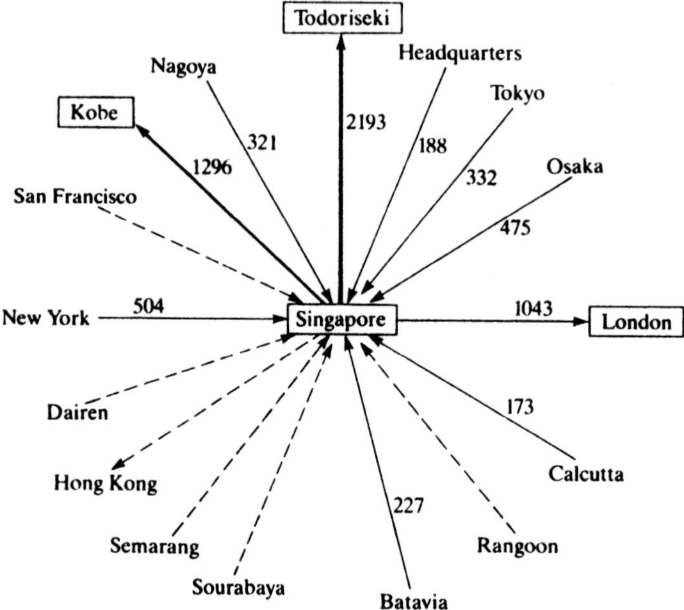

Figure 20.4 Money-flow between the Singapore branch and other branches of the Yokohama Specie Bank in July 1932. *Source*: The Y.S.B., *Todoriseki Keisankakanjo Uchivakehyo* (Specification of balance of chief accountant account), July 1932.

Shanghai and Hong Kong were mainly based on a silver exchange operation which sought to utilize differences in the price of silver between these markets.[14] Therefore, apart from the flow of credit between each of the three branches and the London branch, the New York agency and branches in Japan, and also the flow of credit as a result of the above silver exchange operation, there was a kind of division of labour among these three branches in the region where they were primarily involved. The Shanghai, Hong Kong and Singapore branches acted as regional centres and supplied and absorbed money to and from neighbouring branches in each region and at the same time had close relationships with branches in the two major international financial centres, as well as Japan.

5 Conclusion

According to Shigeo Horie, a former president of the Bank of Tokyo, the successor to the Y.S.B., a distinguishing feature of the Y.S.B. was its foreign exchange transactions, which aggressively launched it into the international money market as part of government policy at that time.

This is very suggestive. The Y.S.B.'s activities had two aspects: one as a national policy-oriented bank and the other as a private bank. As for the former, I emphasized that the transactions related to government policy occupied a large part of the total assets and liabilities of the bank. We can also find this character in its 'controlled selling of dollars operation'. It sold dollars unlimitedly against the speculative and aggressive dollar buying by banks and private citizens, both foreign and domestic, with the support of the Bank of Japan and the Ministry of Finance. As a result of the failure of their attempt to keep Japan's gold standard, the Y.S.B. suffered a large loss due to its oversold position of dollars. In spite of this, the bank completely covered this loss through a special operation approved by the Ministry of Finance.

But this is only one side of the story. We should not overlook the fact that the bank rebought about 18 per cent of the total amount of 'controlled selling of dollars' in the market. A governmental institution alone would probably not have been able to do this. Also, we should observe that the bank earned profits by timely pound-selling when Britain abandoned the gold standard and that the bank was able to accumulate a large amount of secret reserves during normal periods of operation. These enabled the bank to make up for many of its losses suffered in its bond holdings in the latter half of 1931. These activities are related to the private aspect of the bank. Despite limitations imposed by the government, the bank sought large profits and higher salaries for its personnel and behaved as a private foreign exchange bank in the market. In a word, the characteristic of the bank was that it combined a government policy-oriented character with a kind of entrepreneurship.

How did these characteristics contribute to the development of the Tokyo, Yokohama and Kobe markets as shown in Curtis' book?

A tentative answer to this is as follows. First, the government gave support to the Y.S.B. in many ways in exchange for the restrictions it imposed on the bank. This enabled it to compensate for the disadvantage it faced with regard to higher interest rates in Japan as a result of her backwardness and to cover a part of its risks as well, and thus to grow amidst severe competition from foreign banks. Through this process of growth, the employees gradually accumulated the know-how to handle foreign exchange transactions, allowing the bank to obtain creditworthiness in the London market.

Second, in this process the bank closely cooperated with Mitsui Bussan, the famous general trading company which occupied a dominant position in Japanese foreign trade, especially before the First World War. The close cooperation between the two made them more competitive towards foreign banks and foreign trading companies in various fields.

Third, as for staff recruiting and training, the bank mainly recruited graduates from famous universities, such as the University of Tokyo and

Tokyo Commercial College (the predecessor to Hitotsubashi University), and trained them on the job. A typical course of promotion was to move employees regularly (normally every two or three years) from one branch to another in the following way: headquarters → Shanghai → Bombay → New York → London → headquarters. At first new graduates learned the practical business of foreign exchange in general at the headquarters and moved to Shanghai and/or Bombay, there learning the silver exchange business. After that they moved to New York and/or London and became experienced in international money-flows and the mechanisms of the two largest international financial centres. Through this process of training and promotion in the important financial centres, they accumulated experience in foreign exchange transactions and became competent foreign exchange experts. The worldwide network of branches enabled the bank to collect more information than other banks, contributing greatly to the fostering of many specialists.

Fourth, during the First World War, when Japanese foreign trade developed rapidly, the Y.S.B. earned enormous profits and accumulated a large amount of secret reserves which stabilized its business record. During and after the First World War, large zaibatsu banks, such as Mitsui, Mitsubishi, and Sumitomo, and two special banks, the Bank of Taiwan (Formosa) and the Bank of Chosen (Korea), entered the foreign exchange business. The diffusion of information about foreign exchange transactions accumulated by the Y.S.B. assisted their development and fostered the rise of the Tokyo, Yokohama, Kobe markets as major international financial centres.

Notes

1 Howard Curtis Reed, *The preeminence of international financial centers* (New York), 1981), p. 20.

2 The average market share of the Y.S.B. in foreign exchange transactions relating to merchandise trading in Japan amounted to 42.3 per cent for 1924–31 and 47.5 per cent for 1932–6. The Bank of Tokyo, *Yokohama Shokin Ginko Zenshi Dai Ikkan* (A complete history of the Y.S.B., vol. 1) (Tokyo, 1980), p. 599.

3 The Yokohama Specie Bank, *Yokohama Shokin Ginko Shi* (A history of the Yokohama Specie Bank (Yokohama, 1920); The Bank of Tokyo, *Yokohama Shokin*, vol. 1–6 (Tokyo, 1980–4).

4 The representatives of this kind of article are Tomokazu Mizunuma, 'Yokohama Shokin Ginko no Gaikoku Kawase Boeki Kinyu' (Foreign exchange and financing the foreign trade of the Yokohama Specie Bank) in Yokohama City, *Yokohama Shishi Dai Yon Kan Ge* (A history of Yokohama city, vol. 4, No. 2) (Yokohama, 1968); Kayoko Miyoshi, 'Nihon no Boeki to Yokohama Shokin Ginko' (Japan's foreign trade and the Yokohama Specie Bank), *The Journal of Economic Studies* (The University of Tokyo), 17 (1974); Hisahiko

Saito, 'Nisshin Senso Igo ni okeru Yokohama Shokin Ginko no Gaikoku Kawase Gyomu no Hatten to Shinyo' (The development of the foreign exchange business of the Yokohama Specie Bank and credit since the Sino-Japanese war), *Mita Business Review*, 28, 6 (1986). Toshihiko Kato's article, 'Yokohama Shokin Ginko no Kenkyu Shi' (A research history of the Yokohama Specie Bank), in Kazuo Yamaguchi and Toshihiko Kato, *Ryo Taisenkan no Yokohama Shokin Ginko* (The Yokohama Specie Bank during the interwar period) (Tokyo, 1988) gives a birds-eye view on its research history in Japan.

5 The description in this section is based on my paper 'Kinkaikinki no Yokohama Shokin Ginko – Shisan Fusai Kosei to Naibuteki Shinyo Netto Waaku-' (The Yokohama Specie Bank during the period of Japan's restored gold standard – its structure of assets and liabilities and its internal network of credits) in Kazuo Yamaguchi and Toshihiko Kato, *Ryo Taisenkan*, pp. 64–90.

6 The description in this section is based on ibid., pp. 101–22.

7 The description in this chapter is based on my paper 'Doru Gai to Yokohama Shokin Ginko' (Dollar buying and the Yokohama Specie Bank), in Kazuo Yamaguchi and Toshihiko Kato, *Ryo Taisenkan*, pp. 354–93.

8 These figures are computed from the balance sheets listed in The Bankers' Almanac and Year Book for 1930–1.

9 Yokohama Shokin Ginko Todoriseki Chosa Ka (Research section of the chief accountant of the Yokohama Specie Bank), *Rondon Manee Maaketto* (London money market) (Tokyo, 1934) p. 147.

10 The Bank of Tokyo, *Yokohama Shokin Ginko Zen Shi Dai San Kan* (A complete history of the Yokohama Specie Bank, vol. 3) (Tokyo, 1981) pp. 447–74, 485–90.

11 Ibid., p. 555.

12 Ibid., pp. 476–9, 492.

13 The Yokohama Specie Bank, *Todoriseki Oyobi Honten Sokanjo Motocho Zandaka Kinyu Cho* (General balance book for chief accountant and headquarters).

14 Hiroshi Rinoie and Yoshitoshi Shimobayashi, 'Dairen o Chushin to suru Shanhai Nihon Kan Kawase Sankaku kankei' ('A triangle relationship of foreign exchange transactions among Dairen, Shanghai and Japan'), in Kesasuke Tsuchiya (ed.), *Shina Keizai Kenkyu Dai San Pen* (A study of Chinese economy, vol. 3) (Shanghai, 1930), pp. 1–67; Minetro Hamada, *Chugoku Saikin Kinyu Shi* (A recent financial history of China) (Tokyo, 1936) pp. 432, 433.

21 International financial centres in Asia, the Middle East and Australia: a historical perspective[1]

GEOFFREY JONES

Emergence and growth

Financial centres are much discussed but rarely defined. A major difficulty is that the products of the financial sector are diverse, and include markets for capital, money, debt, insurance and other financial services, and gold, silver and other precious metals. A 'financial centre' might include some or all of these markets. The twentieth-century financial services industry has also seen very rapid product innovation, especially since the emergence of a global capital market from the late 1950s. The upshot is that the identification – and ranking – of financial centres is a subjective matter, and a 'financial centre' in one time period may look very different from one in another period.

There are also marked differences in the geographical areas served by financial centres. Almost every modern economy has some kind of 'centre' where there is a clustering of financial services serving the requirements of the rest of the country. Bangkok has served this role in Thailand over the last one hundred years. Such 'national financial centres' are beyond the concern of this chapter however which focuses on centres which provide financial services for an area outside their own political boundaries: a location where there is a concentration of activity engaged in the international trade of capital and financial services.[2]

There is general agreement that there has usually existed a hierarchy of international financial centres. Howard Curtis Reed's pioneering attempt to rank financial centres over time both surveys the variety of names given to different types of centre and develops a hierarchy of his own.[3] In the present context, a simpler typology seems more appropriate, in which centres can be divided into three types. Type A are *sub-regional* – international financial activities are clustered in such places, but often their focus is on bilateral trade between the centre's host economy and other economies. Type B are *regional* – these centres supply financial services to an entire region, which might be very large ('Asia' or the 'Pacific Rim'). Finally, type C are *global centres* – supplying a broad range of financial services to the entire world, a role London pioneered in the nineteenth century, and which it shares with New York and Tokyo in the contemporary period.[4]

Table 21.1 attempts to identify the leading international financial centres of the Middle East, Asia and Australasia from the First World War onwards, dividing the centres into types A, B and C. Japan is not included in this analysis. Tokyo, Osaka and Yokohama were all international financial centres of sorts in the 1920s, but the era of nationalism and war in the 1930s and 1940s greatly curbed this role. By the time the Japanese economic miracle was underway in the 1960s, Tokyo had sufficient international banking activity to qualify as an international financial centre (probably type B), but regulation and other factors constrained its role until the 1980s, when a full-blown global centre emerged.

This identification of international financial centres is crude and subjective compared to Reed's statistical analysis, which investigates the role, as financial centres, of seventy-six cities between 1900 and 1975 (and eighty cities in 1980) using a large number of variables. However, there is probably little fundamental conflict between the identification and hierarchical positions suggested here and the Reed analysis. In Reed's ranking of 'international banking centres' for five yearly intervals between 1900 and 1980, Hong Kong appears in the 'top ten' every year except 1970 and 1980, and Shanghai was also ranked highly before the Revolution. Hong Kong also featured in Reed's lists of 'international financial centres' between 1955 and 1980. Singapore appears less important than suggested in this paper, but Reed himself cites evidence that he might have underestimated its significance. Reed does not identify a Middle Eastern centre that was more important than Beirut until 1980, when he adds Bahrain to his sample of cities. Reed also places these centres in about the same position in the hierarchy of financial centres as suggested here.[5]

Reverting to the typology suggested here, during the interwar years Shanghai, Singapore and Hong Kong have the greatest claims to be type A international financial centres. The number of banks with representation in a city provides one proxy of financial activity. In 1919 Shanghai had twenty-three modern banks represented there, Hong Kong fourteen, and Singapore twelve: in all cases these were largely foreign institutions. As civil disorder spread through China in the 1920s, Shanghai developed as the Republic's monetary and banking centre. The city experienced a trebling of population between 1914 and 1936, leaving it nearly four times

Table 21.1 *Financial centres in Asia, the Middle East and Australasia since 1919*

1919–39			1945–65			1965–75			1975–present		
A	B	C	A	B	C	A	B	C	A	B	C
Shanghai			Hong Kong	Beirut			Beirut			Bahrain	
Singapore			Singapore				Singapore			Singapore	
Hong Kong							Hong Kong			Hong Kong	
										Sydney	

as large as the British Colony of Hong Kong in that year, which was essentially a smaller version of Shanghai throughout the interwar years. By 1936, thirty-three foreign banks had branches in Shanghai, including British, American, German, Belgian, Dutch, Portuguese and Japanese institutions, all of which were actively engaged in foreign trade finance and exchange operations, utilizing the free exchange market existing at Shanghai. There were seventy-four Chinese commercial banks in the City, linking Shanghai with the rest of China. In addition there were branches of the major banks established by the Overseas Chinese community, including four from Hong Kong, three from the Straits Settlements and one from the Philippines, which specialized in handling the remittances flowing between the various Chinese settlements in Asia.[6]

Other financial activities were also well-represented in Shanghai. The city had a Stock Exchange, on occasion which, for example, companies developing Malaya tin or rubber were floated.[7] Shanghai was 'the pivot of British business in China'.[8] British merchant houses which operated in Shanghai, such as Dodwell's, Gibb Livingston's and Gilman's, provided a range of trading, shipping and insurances services.[9]

Singapore, the major city of the British Colony of the Straits Settlements, had grown over the nineteenth century as a major regional trading centre. Western traders and bankers flourished in a complementary relationship with their Chinese and other Asian counterparts.[10] Between the late nineteenth century and the interwar years, for example, most of south-east Asia's rice trade was organized and financed through Singapore by means of a system of barter conducted by Singaporean Chinese merchants, in turn linked to European merchants trading in tin and tropical produce.[11] International banking activity developed early: the rulers of Thailand and other neighbouring states kept their accounts in Singapore banks in the second half of the nineteenth century, before their own states had modern banks. Modern banking grew in interwar Singapore (there were twenty-two banks represented there by 1941) and the Singapore branch often acted as a regional head office overseeing other branches in neighbouring Malaya and sometimes elsewhere, a role still very common in the 1980s. Traditional Asian credit institutions were well represented in Singapore, not only Chinese but also Indian, such as Chetty bankers, and these were all engaged in interregional trade and exchange operations. In 1932 a powerful modern Chinese bank, the Overseas Chinese Banking Corporation, was established at Singapore. Singapore, like Shanghai, had its own Stock Exchange, on which many Malayan tin and rubber companies were quoted, and a substantial number of diversified western trading companies, such as Borneo Company performing shipping, trading and insurance functions. The slump in the prices of commodities such as tin, rubber and palm oil from the late 1920s left south-east Asia in a depressed economic condition before the Second World War, but Singapore retained its position as the leading financial centre.

The limitation of type A status to Shanghai, Singapore and Hong Kong is arbitrary. There were other cities where financial services were clustered, though their 'sub-regional' roles were less extensive. In British India, Bombay and Calcutta had large numbers of banks (many foreign owned) and their own Stock Exchanges. However, the Indian capital and money markets were severely fragmented, and primarily focused in British India, especially in the 1930s as India entered its 'relative disengagement from the international economy'.[12] It would be extremely difficult to identify any sub-regional financial centres in the interwar Middle East. Cairo came closest. It had a number of branches of banks, and other financial institutions, and a Stock Exchange established in 1903, but even in the interwar years most of this activity was built around the finance of Egypt's cotton trade with the rest of the world.

In the two decades after the Second World War, the most significant event was the advent of Beirut as a regional financial centre. Beirut had been a centre of banking activity in the old Ottoman Empire. During the interwar years, under French control, the city had supplied financial services to its Syrian hinterland. After the war, and now the capital of an independent Lebanon, Beirut became a leading banking centre, overwhelmingly concerned with short-term capital. By 1965 nearly ninety banks were active in Beirut, many of them foreign. Aided by a banking secrecy law in 1956 (modelled on that of Switzerland), Beirut became a depository for flight capital from all over the Middle East, much of which was channelled via Beirut to Europe and the United States.[13] An early feature of the Beirut money market was the large percentage of deposits in foreign currency. As early as 1953 a branch of a British bank in Beirut had 40 per cent of its deposits in foreign currency, mostly US dollars: this was some years before the conventional starting date for the Eurodollar market.[14] From the late 1950s foreign currency deposits in Lebanon grew very rapidly: in 1964 they comprised 35 per cent of total commercial bank deposits, and ten years later 68 per cent.[15] Despite Beirut's very important role as a short-term money market between the 1940s and the mid 1970s, its other financial activities were minimal. The Beirut Stock Exchange, for example, was established in 1920, but never grew to any significance.[16]

The advent and growth of the Euro-currency loan and bond markets at the end of the 1950s and in the 1960s, already pre-figured by developments in Beirut, brought fundamental changes to international banking and finance, and an enormous stimulus to their growth. These supranational markets, outside national regulatory control, also provided new opportunities for places such as Beirut, Hong Kong and Singapore, for they enabled international banks to settle 'offshore' to raise and supply capital on a world-wide basis.[17]

After 1965 the availability of IMF statistics on the foreign assets held by banks enables a more quantitative picture to be presented of the location of international financial activity, although it must be stressed that these statistics measure only one type of business conducted at financial centres.[18] Table 21.2 gives this measure of international banking activity by country between 1965 and 1987.

As table 21.2 suggests, until the mid 1960s Lebanon was the leading centre for international banking activity in Asia, the Middle East and Australasia, once again excluding Japan. Singapore continued to function as a 'centre' of sorts, but probably less so than in the interwar years because it suffered from political and other uncertainties until the mid 1960s, when it withdrew from Malaysia, and abandoned its attempt at import substitution in favour of an export-oriented industrialization strategy. As part of this new strategy the government established an Asian currency market. The development of the Euro-currency markets found no echo in Asia until 1968, when the Singapore government permitted the Bank of America to establish an operation dealing in foreign currency (an Asian currency unit as such institutions became known), designed to collect dollars circulating in Asia for on-lending to their Asian customers. The interest earned from non-resident deposits was made tax-exempt. Singapore thus acquired first-mover advantages in the new Asia dollar market, and it was well-placed to take advantage of the flood of petrodollars following the 1973–4 crisis. The number of Asian currency units in Singapore grew from one in 1968 to fifty in 1974 to 115 in 1980. Over the same period, the total assets of these Asian Currency Units expanded from US$ 30.5 million to US$ 199.9 million to US$2,438 million. In addition to this development, the Singapore government encouraged the

Table 21.2 *International banking activity 1965–1987; percentage share by leading countries*

	1965	1970	1975	1980	1985	1987
UK	17.1	25.0	22.2	19.6	19.9	18.5
US	23.7	8.6	9.7	11.2	15.1	11.6
Japan	5.7	4.4	3.6	3.6	6.6	12.2
France	4.3	6.8	7.3	8.1	5.8	5.6
Germany	7.7	9.5	6.8	4.7	3.8	4.9
Switzerland	8.3	9.4	8.4	7.7	6.9	7.0
Luxembourg	0.9	2.5	5.3	5.7	4.4	4.8
Bahamas	—	4.8	9.7	6.9	4.8	3.3
Lebanon	1.3	0.4	0.4	0.2	0.1	n.a.
Bahrain	—	0.04	0.4	1.7	1.7	1.3
Singapore	—	0.3	1.9	2.4	4.1	4.4
Hong Kong	1.1	0.8	1.6	2.1	3.4	5.6
Australia	—	—	0.05	0.02	0.04	n.a.
Others	29.9	27.46	22.65	28.08	23.36	20.8
Total amount of all countries (US $ billion)	44.8	149.4	565.9	1,821.4	2,964	4,725.3

Source: IMF, *International Financial Statistics Yearbook*, 1981 and 1988. The data give the foreign assets held by deposit banks in each country at year end.

growth of an Asian bond market through the issue of loans in the early 1970s, and this market took off around 1976.[19]

By 1975 Singapore was well-established as the leading Asian centre for short-term loans and borrowings in a range of convertible currencies, and also as an international market for the issue of medium- and long-term bonds in convertible currencies. By that year there were seventy commercial banks with banking operations in Singapore (and another thirty-eight representative offices), twenty-one merchant banks, four discount houses, thirty-six finance companies, sixty-nine insurance companies and five 'international money brokers'.[20] However, Singapore had comparatively little expertise in certain areas of financial activity, such as fund management and loan syndication.

The Communist Revolution in China in 1949 ended Shanghai's role as an international financial centre. Hong Kong was the direct inheritor of the mantle: indeed, many of the Colony's industries of the 1950s were founded and prospered under Shanghaese entrepreneurs. It had a growing number of banks and was the headquarters of a major regional bank, the Hong Kong and Shanghai Banking Corporation. Hong Kong attracted substantial 'hot' or 'funk' money in the 1950s, especially from the Overseas Chinese community in south-east Asia. Table 21.2 suggests that international banking activity there in 1965 nearly approached the level of Lebanon. However in the decade after 1965 Hong Kong allowed Singapore to take advantage of the new opportunities offered by the global capital markets. The Bank of America expressed an interest in establishing an Asian Currency Unit in Hong Kong rather than Singapore, but the colonial government declined to grant exemption from a 15 per cent withholding tax on offshore currency transactions, a policy which was not changed until 1982. Hong Kong also failed to develop as a centre for the Asian Bond Market to rival Singapore. One handicap was that the Hong Kong government traditionally worked on the basis of balanced budgets and rarely needed to issue debt.

Hong Kong's 'take off' as a type B financial centre came several years later than that of Singapore, and all through the 1970s it was Singapore, rather than Hong Kong, which had a greater claim to be Asia's leading financial centre. The 1970s, however, saw growing internationalization of Hong Kong's financial activities. Between 1969 and 1979 total bank credit rose six fold, while the relative share of offshore loans in total bank credit rose from 2.6 per cent to 26 per cent. There was a similar trend towards internationalization in the financial markets. Short-term money market activities ceased to be confined to inter-bank dealings in Hong Kong dollars. After 1974, when a ban on import and export of gold was removed, Hong Kong developed a large gold market, and in 1977 a Commodities Exchange was established. Hong Kong developed expertise in areas such as fund management and loan syndication, in which Singapore lagged.[21]

Hong Kong and Singapore functioned, to some extent, as complementary financial centres in the 1970s and early 1980s, each specializing in various activities. There was little duplication and funds flowed between the two centres to take maximum advantage of their respective regulatory, fiscal and other advantages. As one writer described the process,

> shrewd bankers and businessmen find it most advantageous to have investment operations at Hong Kong and to collect ADM deposits at Singapore... Singapore is primarily a funding centre, whilst Hong Kong is a 'booking' centre for lending. Funds are banked together in Singapore and this is rechannelled to Hong Kong for on-lending to non-bank borrowers.[22]

The period after 1975 saw the rapid emergence of Bahrain as a regional (type B) financial centre. Bahrain had a tradition of acting as a banking centre to the economically backward Gulf. The first modern bank on the Arab side of the Gulf was established there in 1920 by the Eastern Bank, a British-owned bank.[23] During the 1950s and 1960s it began to serve as a regional base for British banks and other companies.[24] Yet Bahrain's role as a financial centre remained modest – the country even used the Indian Rupee as its currency until 1965 – until shortly after the 1973–4 oil crises. The catalyst was the Bahrain government's decision in 1975 to allow Offshore Banking Units (OBUs – modelled on Singapore's Asian Currency Unit's) to be established, which were exempted from all corporate profits tax.

After 1975 Bahrain's offshore banking units grew very rapidly. There were two OBUs in 1975, fifty-eight in 1980 and seventy-five in 1983. Their total assets expanded over the same period from US$ 1,687 million to US$ 37,466 million to US$ 62,741 million. Bahrain's function, at least initially, was as a collecting centre for the surplus savings of oil-rich Saudi Arabia and Kuwait, which were recycled to the outside world. Business transactions were largely of a short-term nature. Between 1976 and 1986 87 per cent of OBU assets and 97 per cent of OBU liabilities had a maturity of one year or less, with some tendency for borrowing to be on a shorter-term basis than lending. Most of the currency dealings in Bahrain were in US dollars, although there was some use of regional currencies. In 1980 22 per cent of assets were denominated in regional currencies such as Saudi riyals, Kuwaiti dinars, UAE dirhams and Qatar riyals, although this percentage tended to fall in the 1980s. It was 14.4 per cent in 1986.[25]

Bahrain replaced Beirut as the regional financial centre of the Middle East. The Lebanese financial system began to show signs of strain in the mid 1960s, notably with the collapse of the largest bank in the country, Intra Bank, in 1966. The Arab-Israeli War in 1967 caused further difficulties for the financial system.[26] Nevertheless Lebanese banking proved very resilient until the outbreak of the Civil War in 1975, when funds began to by-pass Beirut and banks began to withdraw or reduce their operations. Beirut's role as a regional financial centre was further damaged by the Israeli invasion of 1982, which caused enormous physical destruction and the withdrawal of practically all remaining foreign personnel. The Israeli's completed the elimination of any remaining confidence in Beirut's ability to act as a financial centre by overriding Lebanese banking secrecy laws by forcing banks to reveal the accounts of wealthy Palestinians.[27]

The post-1975 period saw the advent of Sydney as a fledgling regional financial centre. Twentieth-century Australia had a well-developed financial system and capital markets. Before 1939, however, the Australian economy was heavily tied to that of Britain and the country had little international activity. 'Melbourne and London were then Australia's financial centres', as one writer has recently observed.[28] Links with Britain weakened after the Second World War, but the Australian financial system was highly cartelized and regulated within a framework of exchange controls. Foreign institutions were not allowed to undertake commercial banking in the country, apart from the descendants of British banks established in the nineteenth century. The last of these, the ANZ Group, migrated from Britain in 1976 and became an entirely Australian institution.[29] There was, however, substantial foreign activity in merchant banks and a variety of non-banking financial intermediaries, usually in the form of joint-ventures with Australian interests.[30]

Australia, therefore, offered unpromising soil for an international financial centre until the late 1970s, when a process of liberalization began. The big change came in 1983 when the newly elected Labour government lifted exchange controls and floated the Australian dollar. In 1985, fifteen foreign banks were granted full banking licences. The full consequences of Australia's extremely fast and comprehensive financial and banking deregulation for the development of Sydney's role as a financial centre remain to be seen.

Apart from the entry of Sydney and the exit of Beirut as regional financial centres, the fifteen years after 1975 showed some diversification of functions by the centres and also a tendency towards instability. After 1975 Singapore developed more business in fund management and loan syndication, while Hong Kong sought to expand its role in Asia currency and Asia bonds by, for example, abolishing the 15 per cent withholding tax on foreign currency deposits in 1982. Both developed markets in financial futures. Hong Kong's growth was particularly spectacular; by October 1987 Hong Kong claimed to have the second largest stock index market in the world, with as many as 30,000 contracts changing hands each day. Unfortunately the collapse of world stock markets in that month revealed the growth to have been based on reckless and corrupt speculation, and the Hong Kong futures market collapsed. A year later, in October 1988, daily turnover rarely exceeded 600 contracts.[31] Bahrain, in the 1980s, suffered from the decline of oil revenues from the oil-exporting Gulf states, the Iran/Iraq war and the Third World debt crisis, for many of Bahrain's offshore banks had been heavy lenders to developing countries. The assets of Bahrain's OBUs fell continuously from US$ 62,741 million in 1983 to US$ 55,680 in 1986.[32] One consequence of this trend was a growth in the regional dimension of Bahrain's offshore banking sector. In 1980 36 per cent of OBUs in Bahrain originated from western Europe, 17 per cent from North America and 21 per cent from the Arab world. In 1986 the proportions were 32 per cent, 12 per cent and 32 per cent.[33]

In the late 1980s it remained a hazardous exercise to rank financial centres in any more than the most general terms. Using the proxy of the amount of foreign assets held by deposit banks, it can be seen from Table 21.2 that the international banking activity of Hong Kong grew substantially in the 1980s, and by 1987 the volume of foreign assets there was greater than in Singapore, which grew rather more slowly between 1980 and 1987. International banking activity in Lebanon has been in absolute decline since 1980, while Bahrain has failed to maintain its rapid growth of the 1970s. Australia's share of international banking activity remained, in 1987, very small. Singapore and Hong Kong rivalled in size the international financial centres of Continental Europe, but remain far less important than 'the three key financial centres of the world' – London, New York and Tokyo.[34] Other measures confirm such a view. In 1988 probably around 85 per cent of all equity trading took place in the United States, London and Tokyo.[35]

A number of features emerge from this brief survey of the emergence of financial centres in Asia (outside Japan), the Middle East and Australasia since the First World War. First, financial centres come and go. Shanghai went in 1949. Beirut came after 1945 and went after 1975. Sydney began to emerge as a financial centre in the 1980s. Only Singapore and Hong Kong showed continuity over the whole period, with a considerable rise in their importance from the late 1960s.

Secondly, while the financial centres of London, New York and – later – Tokyo developed within large advanced industrialized economies, the centres that grew in Asia and the Middle East were often located in small economies and indeed, physically small countries. Shanghai and Sydney provide exceptions, though it is arguable if interwar Shanghai can be regarded as an integrated part of the national Chinese economy, while Australia is an extremely thinly populated country compared to ASEAN neighbours such as Indonesia. Within the general problem of why international financial activity is not randomly scattered around the world, there is a more specific problem of why financial centres have tended to flourish – especially over the last thirty years – in these small economies.

Thirdly, no Asian, Australian or Middle Eastern financial centre – once more apart from Japan in the 1980s – has achieved global status. By 1990 London, New York and Tokyo offered capital markets, money markets and a range of financial services on a world-wide basis. The centres discussed have remained regional financial centres, integrated into global financial markets (as the rapid fallout from the October 1987 stock market crash indicated) but not primary centres. None of the centres have offered the full range of financial markets available in London or New York, and indeed centres have tended to specialize, and to operate in niches in the markets.

An explanatory framework

This section offers some reasons for the growth of the Asian, Middle Eastern and Australasian financial centres. Why did Beirut, Bahrain, Singapore and Hong Kong emerge as centres, rather than (say) Damascus, Kuwait, Seoul and Taipai? Unfortunately, there is no theory of financial centres, or even of international service centres, which can be readily applied to answer such a question. 'It is a curious fact', Charles Kindleberger observed in a seminal study in 1974, 'that the formation of financial centres is no longer studied in economics'.[36] Urban and regional economists focused on the location of commerce and industry rather than financial services, while the literature on the money and capital markets showed little interest in the physical location of these markets. Since 1974 there have been more studies of financial centres, but this work has resulted in the accumulation of valuable data and insights rather than the formulation of any rigorous model.[37]

A straight application of traditional models of comparative advantage is unhelpful. Such a factor endowments approach might suggest that international financial centres developed in economies with abundant or 'surplus' capital. This helps to explain the growth of London in the nineteenth century, and the subsequent emergence of New York and Tokyo. However, this model does not explain London's continued primacy when Britain ceased to be a capital exporter, nor New York's when the United States became a net debtor. Although Bahrain's geographical and cultural proximity to the major Arab Gulf oil producers was an important permissive determinant of its development, along with Singapore and Hong Kong it grew and functioned essentially as an entrepôt. The rapid growth of Tokyo in the 1980s does indicate, however, that capital abundance enables barriers to entry to becoming an international financial centre to be rapidly overcome.

It is helpful to make a preliminary distinction between the original and the subsequent growth of financial centres, although this will need to be qualified subsequently. In explaining the origins of our particular financial centres, three general factors seem to be important:– reputation, willingness to act as a haven, and accessibility.

A variety of features make up the reputation of a financial centre. In general, it can be suggested that bankers, financiers and investors will be attracted to a location which has a reputation for stability, integrity, impartiality and confidentiality. Different types of financial activity will weigh certain of these features more heavily than other types. Depositors, for example, might put heavy emphasis on the integrity and business ethics of a financial centre, while certain firms of speculative trading might flourish if the integrity level is somewhat lower.

Confidence in political stability was an essential pre-requisite for the emergence – and maintenance – of a financial centre. Investors seek an assurance that their funds will be safe and, at all times, accessible and mobile. It is significant that the majority of financial centres in Asia and the Middle East often developed in areas which had a legacy of British political institutions. Twentieth-century Britain, although lacking in many business management and entrepreneurial skills, excelled at creating stable governance structures with due respect for the process of law. Hong Kong has been a British colony throughout the century. Australia inherited the political structures of its British colonists. Singapore was a British colony until 1959, and Bahrain was under British 'protection' until 1971. The British inheritance gave these places stable administrative structures, and familiar legal systems for British and American financial institutions. Shanghai and Beirut lacked a British political inheritance, but at both there were special factors which enhanced political confidence in them. Shanghai was one of China's nineteenth-century Treaty Ports and home of a large international settlement: a foreign community which was self-governing. Beirut flourished as a rare instance of stability in the Arab World in the 1950s and 1960s. Its unique constitution, which shared power between assorted religious groups, apparently guaranteed political stability, providing a contrast with the revolutionary and anti-western governments which took power in Egypt, Iraq and Syria in the 1950s, and in Libya in 1969. With the Communist victory in China and the outbreak of the Lebanese civil war, political confidence evaporated and with it Shanghai and Beirut's role as financial centres. Hong Kong's future as a financial centre rests heavily on the maintenance of political confidence in the post-1997 situation, as evidenced by the fluctuations in the Hong Kong markets because of political events within the People's Republic of China. In the 1984 Joint Declaration on the future of Hong Kong, the British and Chinese governments emphasized their commitment that Hong Kong 'shall retain the status of an international financial centre'.[38]

It is widely agreed that regulatory activities of governments have played an important part in the emergence of financial centres. They are crucial to the integrity, impartiality and confidentiality elements of a centre's reputation. A variety of government-imposed barriers to trade in financial services have influenced the location of financial activity, probably more than trade barriers have influenced the location of foreign direct investment in manufacturing. Regulatory measures and exchange controls in western Europe and the United States after the Second World War provided a major stimulus to the development of offshore financial centres. The role of the Federal Reserve's Regulation Q, which imposed a ceiling on the level of interest paid on bank deposits, in the development of the Eurodollar, and later Asiadollar, markets is perhaps the most dramatic example of this point.[39]

Conversely, regulatory regimes in host economies attracted – or hindered – the emergence of financial centres. Extensive regulation can substantially raise costs, and, if the regulatory authorities are unpredictable or corrupt, generate an unacceptable degree of concern about integrity and impartiality. However some regulation to provide consumer protection can stimulate the growth of a financial centre by, for example, reducing the cost of funds. Some regulation, but not too much, appears to provide the ideal institutional structure.

A fully fledged central bank was certainly not essential for the emergence of a financial centre.[40] European commercial banks often performed quasi-central banking functions in the initial stages of a centre's development, and, indeed, the absence of a central bank could make a location attractive. 'Whilst I realise what a great boon Central Banks are to Commercial Banks generally', the General Manager of one British exchange bank wrote to his manager in Singapore in 1949, 'it would certainly not suit any of the British Banks at the moment for a Central Bank to be established in Malaya. You would find it would cut into your business very considerably.'[41] Singapore had no central bank before the establishment of the Monetary Authority of Singapore in 1971, and Bahrain before the formation of the Bahrain Monetary Authority in 1973 (although the Bahrain Currency Authority created in the mid 1960s performed some central bank functions). In Lebanon there was no central bank until 1964: some central banking functions were performed by the French-owned Banque de Syrie et du Liban, which also acted as a commercial bank.[42] Hong Kong remains (in 1990) without a central bank. The British-managed Hongkong and Shanghai Banking Corporation (Hongkong Bank for short) performed some regulatory and central bank roles in addition to its position as the Colony's largest commercial bank. It shared with another British overseas bank the issue of bank notes in the Colony, acted as the banking system's clearing bank, and, sometimes, served as banker of last resort at times of banking crisis.[43]

While the initial growth of a financial centre benefits from little regulation and, perhaps, the absence of a central bank, as the centre grows in complexity more regulation may be required to maintain a desirable reputation. Hong Kong has been the most reluctant of the centres discussed here to move in this direction. The Colony's First Banking Ordinance was passed in 1948, but this had almost no regulatory content. A banking crisis in 1961 finally led to the establishment of a Banking Commissioner's Office in 1964 to enforce minimum capital and liquidity requirements. A major stock-market collapse in 1973–4 led to regulatory controls on deposit-taking companies. The 1980s saw further regulatory measures. Stock-market scandals in 1987, which threatened the Colony's reputation, led to much greater regulation of financial markets, with banks in Hong Kong being obliged to meet the capital adequacy rules set by the Basle agreement two years ahead of the agreed international timetable. Before 1987, however, the general pattern had been that the government responded to a crisis with more controls, rather than tried to pre-empt problems. 'Hong Kong's financial liberalism', Lee and Yao observed in 1982, 'has tended at times to border on permissiveness'.[44]

Permissiveness was a visibly more potent stimulus to the emergence of financial centres than prudence. Excessive regulation has provided infertile ground for the growth of international financial centres. Tokyo was hindered from becoming such a centre until its highly regulated financial markets began to be de-regulated in the 1980s. Post-independence India provided an even more unpromising regulatory framework for the emergence of a financial centre. During the 1950s and 1960s, the central bank, the Reserve Bank of India, was highly interventionist, enforced strict controls of banking ratios, sought to influence bank lending portfolios and pressured foreign financial institutions to hire Indian staff. In 1969 the government nationalized most of the domestic banking system, creating uncertainty about future intentions towards foreign institutions.[45] The impact of these policies on the British-owned Grindlays Bank was evident in 1971 when that bank began planning its world-wide business strategies: 'In the sub-continent, high tax rates and uncertain attitudes of governments towards foreign banks will make it necessary to scrutinise very carefully the likely earnings of any new investment. Our guiding principle must again be rationalisation and consolidation of existing business.'[46]

If reputation was one important factor in the emergence of these financial centres, the willingness to act as a haven for foreign enterprise and capital was another crucial factor. Shanghai, Beirut, Hong Kong, Singapore and Bahrain (and perhaps even Sydney since the mid 1980s) developed as financial centres not because of indigenous strengths in their capital markets or in their systems of management education, but through their willingness to permit foreign financial institutions to operate with considerable freedom in their territories, Like reputation, the haven dimension had several aspects.

At the most basic level, international financial centres did not develop in countries such as India, Australia and Japan while they excluded or very closely regulated foreign banks. Beirut, Bahrain, Singapore and Hong Kong were all characterized by a great willingness to allow foreign financial institutions to operate, just as nineteenth-century London had been willing to let foreign 'merchant bankers' locate and flourish there. After 1950 oil-rich Kuwait provided a more obvious home for an international financial centre than neighbouring Bahrain, but only one foreign institution – the British Bank of the Middle East – was ever allowed to operate in the country, and this bank was localized at the expiry of its concession in 1971.[47] 'There is little doubt', Rodney Wilson concludes, 'that the absence of nationalistic pressures has aided Bahrain's emergence as a leading banking centre, as foreign banks which were unable to establish themselves in Saudi Arabia or Kuwait found Bahrain the most conveniently placed alternative'.[48]

The degree of international 'openness' was always an important factor encouraging international banks to locate at a particular site. In 1971, for example, a director of Grindlays Bank isolated the Pacific Basin as an area of major economic development in the future, and his discussion of the 'four contenders' for the Basin's 'financial centres' – Tokyo, Sydney, Singapore and Hong Kong – provides a valuable insight on the factors which made a centre attractive to the western banking community:

> The first two (i.e. Tokyo and Sydney) should dominate the area, yet may not do so. The latter two (i.e. Singapore and Hong Kong) show all the signs of doing so and I believe they will. Tokyo will be a necessary base for most international banks, but their freedom will remain controlled. Sydney, too, remains remarkably insular. As for Hong Kong and Singapore, both benefit from Chinese commercial acumen, both have an international outlook, both are dependent on international trade, and both have competent monetary authorities guiding them.[49]

A willingness to let foreign firms operate provided financial centres with required skills. Hong Kong's liberal employment rules and willingness to let international law and accounting firms operate in the Colony provided the legal and accounting skills which facilitated the development of the loan syndication business there.[50]

Fiscal regimes were an element of the haven factor. None of the financial centres discussed here can be regarded as 'tax havens' in the strictest sense. They should be distinguished from the 'tax havens' which flourished in the western Hemisphere from the late 1960s, such as the Bahamas (whose importance can be seen in table 21.2), Cayman Islands, Anguilla, the New Hebrides and the Netherlands Antilles. Financial institutions usually established a token presence at those places through which business could be recorded as a device to avoid tax.[51] In Lebanon, Bahrain, Singapore and Hong Kong taxes were usually light rather than non-existent. Yao stresses the simplicity of Hong Kong's tax structure as a favourable factor in its growth as a financial centre.[52]

Variations in tax laws often explain why particular activities developed at one place rather than another. As already noted, it was Singapore's exemption from tax on interest earned from non-resident deposits which gave it the advantage over Hong Kong in the Asia Dollar Market. Conversely, international banks favoured Hong Kong as a 'lending' centre because of a tax system which – before 1978 – did not subject income generated outside the Colony to tax, while in Singapore offshore income earned by banks was still subject to income tax.[53]

An absence of exchange controls was an important part of the haven element in the growth of financial centres. London did flourish as a centre despite the existence of British exchange controls before 1979, although it functioned as an entrepôt in non-sterling currencies. Certainly, given the development of the Asian and Middle Eastern centres as financial entrepôts, the absence of free convertibility would have been a formidable handicap. Arguably the existence of exchange controls was one factor hindering the development of financial centres in South Korea and Taiwan, the two Asian NICs apart from Hong Kong and Singapore. Post-war Lebanon was distinguished from all its Arab neighbours by free convertibility and a liberal foreign exchange policy.[54] Singapore began reducing its exchange controls from the mid 1960s and in 1978 all remaining controls were abolished.[55] Although post-war Hong Kong was in the sterling area, the colonial authorities tolerated in the 1950s and 1960s an open market in foreign exchange to coexist alongside a market dealing with foreign exchange at official rates subject to sterling area constraints. Formal exchange controls ended altogether when Hong Kong left the sterling area in 1972. Singapore and the Arab Gulf States were also allowed open exchange markets within the sterling area.[56]

Accessibility was the third factor which stimulated the emergence of financial centres. International financial centres require good communications. Beirut in the 1950s and 1960s was distinguished by efficient post and telephone systems. It was the first centre in the Middle East to have telex equipment installed, and Lebanon even had its own airline, Middle Eastern Airlines.[57] In the era of jet airlines, the correlation between excellent air communications and status as an international financial centre was striking. Bahrain was the headquarters for Gulf Air, which it partly owned. Singapore and Hong Kong were the homes of Singapore Airlines and Cathay Pacific respectively, two of the most dynamic Asian airlines in the 1970s and 1980s.

The widespread use of English among the local labour force was another dimension of accessibility, certainly from the 1950s. The high level of international activity by American and British banks meant that a centre where English was little spoken would have problems in attracting a large foreign bank presence. British colonial rule or protection in Singapore, Hong Kong and Bahrain left a legacy of an English speaking labour force, while the British banks which were active in those places provided training (usually 'on the job') for nationals in English and basic banking principles.[58]

Accessibility to business customers was also important. Singapore began growing as a banking centre in the late nineteenth century because it was there that the heads of the British agency houses and trading firms operating in south-east Asia were usually found. Hong Kong in the second half of the nineteenth century was the headquarters of important expatriate merchant houses, such as Jardine Matheson. Bahrain performed a similar role, on a greatly reduced scale, in the Arabian Gulf.

Advantages of accessibility were also derived from time zone positions. 'Singapore's offshore currency market owes its existence in part', Arndt observes, 'to Singapore's time zone advantage, the fact that its business hours overlap with those on the US West Coast and Tokyo and for an hour or two with London'.[59] Beirut and later Bahrain had time zone advantages which enabled them to operate after Singapore closed but before the western European centres opened. Technological advantages in the 1980s, however, reduced such advantages in certain markets because it became possible to conduct financial operations without the physical presence of people.

Reputation, accessibility and willingness to act as a haven for foreign enterprise, therefore, stimulated the emergence of particular financial centres in Asia, the Middle East and Australasia. The retention or loss of this status is, naturally, also explained in part by such factors. However the subsequent growth of such centres also raises the matter of economies of agglomeration.

As Kindleberger observed in his 1974 article, the concentration of banking and financial activities at a given point leads to positive externalities and economies of scale.[60] Firms become linked in organized markets where liquidity and efficiency increases with the number of participants. Unless there is a regular flow of business, prices will be uncertain. There are advantages of having a number of markets in close proximity to one another, including the development of specialized ancillary services and the creation of a pool of skills. Professional services such as lawyers and accountants accumulate at centres. A supply of skilled labour is available for new entrants. Networks of personal contacts develop. The result is a momentum towards further growth and a reluctance to exit from such a centre unless there is a major change of circumstances, such as the Communist Revolution in China or the outbreak of Civil War in Lebanon. It follows that departure on a large scale – as with Beirut in 1975 – will produce a rapid downward spiral of activity at a financial centre, as external economies fall.[61]

The European connection

Many of the links between Europe and the financial centres discussed in this chapter will already be apparent. It is immediately evident that they have not played a large role in the loss of Europe's position as a 'world banker'. New York from the late nineteenth century, and Tokyo in the 1980s, challenged London and other European financial centres. Hong

Kong, Singapore and Bahrain have competed with London for certain types of business, but only in specialized areas. Bahrain in the 1980s, for example, was said to be 'competing with any major financial centre in Europe not only in the recycling of petrodollars but also in all international banking business relating to trade and industrial links with the Middle East'.[62] However, in the typology developed in the first section, no Asian (apart from Japan), Australasian and Middle Eastern country has developed a type C, or global financial centre. Only regional financial centres have emerged and these have not offered the wide range of markets available in London, New York or Tokyo.

Any threat posed by the Asian and Middle Eastern centres to these centres, including London, was reduced by their volatility, in contrast to the longevity (despite the changing circumstances of their domestic economies) of London and New York. Shanghai and Beirut disappeared as financial centres. In the 1980s Bahrain's future was clouded by warfare and political upheavals in its proximity, and by the world debt crisis. After 1982, when the 1997 handover of sovereignty to China first became an issue, Hong Kong's markets fluctuated violently with political events in China. The reasons for the volatility of these financial centres is evident. The Asian and Middle Eastern centres were not located in large economies with (at least originally) surplus capital and domestic currencies used widely in international transactions. They developed as entrepôts, dealing in others' currencies, and their attractiveness as havens and locations with a desirable reputation was vulnerable to – for example – political changes outside their control. Shanghai, Hong Kong, Beirut, Bahrain were points of stability in unstable and changing regions; safe havens for money to flow through, if not linger.

The origins of the Asian and Middle Eastern financial centres were closely tied to European business and trading enterprise. The initial clustering of western banks and other financial institutions at Shanghai, Singapore and Hong Kong was the result of flows of trade, capital and people between Europe, especially Britain, and east and south-east Asia. Foreign trade finance and the related exchange business were the principle concerns of the western banks which established branches at these places. Many of the companies initially quoted on the Stock Exchanges of Shanghai, Singapore and Hong Kong were established by Europeans to exploit regional trading and commodity opportunities.[63]

Over time, these trading and financial links between Europe and Asia declined, but the rise of global capital markets provided new links. The Eurodollar and Asian dollar markets were in essence the same market, and funds moved between the European, Asian and Middle Eastern financial centres. Table 21.3, which provides a snapshot of the geographical distribution of assets and liabilities of Offshore Banking

Table 21.3 *Assets and liabilities of Bahrain OBUs and Singapore ACUs in 1979 (per cent)*

	Assets				Liabilities			
	Europe	Asia	Arab	Other	Europe	Asia	Arab	Other
Bahrain	25	n.a.	53	22	28	n.a.	58	14
Singapore	15	73	n.a.	12	29	52	n.a.	19

Source: G. Germidis and Charles-Albert Michalet, *International Banks and Financial Markets* (Development Centre Studies, OECD, Paris, 1984) pp. 71, 77.

Units in Bahrain and the Asian Currency Units (ACUs) in Singapore for the single year of 1979 brings out this point.

As Table 21.3 shows, in 1979 Europe provided virtually 30 per cent of the funds in both the Singapore and Bahrain offshore banking sectors, while a quarter of the Bahrain funds, and 15 per cent of the Singapore funds, were employed in Europe in that year.

The European role in the emergence of these non-western financial centres was considerable. Shanghai flourished as an international settlement of the western powers. Singapore, Hong Kong, Bahrain and Sydney all had British colonial or settler pasts, as did many tax havens elsewhere in the world, such as the Bahamas, Cayman Islands, Gibraltar and the Channel Islands. Stable government structures and legal systems and the English language were among the more important British legacies. European trading companies and banks played a leading role in the initial accumulation of financial institutions and skills at these centres. In Beirut until the mid 1960s, and in Hong Kong until the present day, French and British managed commercial banks performed quasi-central banking functions. Western financial institutions provided training which created a pool of skills.

It would be misleading, of course, to imply that the Asian and Middle Eastern financial centres were entirely the legacy of European colonialism or business. India experienced both British imperial rule and considerable activity by British banks without developing a major financial centre. Interaction between western enterprise and a dynamic local business community was important. In Shanghai, Hong Kong and Singapore, British and other western bankers were joined with Chinese business communities with their own powerful commercial and financial traditions and institutions. In the Middle East, the Lebanese had a strong mercantile tradition in the Arabian Gulf, while Bahraini's were noted for their trading and outward-looking perspective compared to their neighbours. It was as sovereign states in the 1960s and 1970s that Singapore and Bahrain took decisions about tax and regulations which led to their growth as regional financial centres.

Conclusion

This chapter has examined international financial centres in the Middle East, Australasia and Asia, excluding Japan, from the First World War to the present day, adopting a crude typology which distinguishes a hierarchy of such centres by their geographical activity. Type A are sub-regional international centres, type B are regional and type C are global. In the interwar years, Shanghai, Hong Kong and Singapore were identified as type A centres. In the two decades after the Second World War, Shanghai disappeared as a financial centre because of the Communist Revolution in China, Hong Kong and Singapore retained their type A status, and Beirut emerged as a type B centre. Between 1965 and 1975 Singapore and Hong Kong joined Beirut in this category, a development related to the growth of the Euro-currency markets. After 1975 political problems destroyed Beirut's role as an international financial centre, but Bahrain and, later and to a much lesser extent, Sydney became type B centres.

We have suggested an explanatory framework for the emergence and growth of type A and type B financial centres (this framework may also apply to global, type C, centres but other factors are also involved). Their emergence rested on reputations for stability, integrity, impartiality and confidentiality, on their haven status, and on accessibility. It is thus highly appropriate that, of the three leading Asian and Middle Eastern financial centres at the end of the 1980s, two (Singapore and Bahrain) are islands while the third (Hong Kong) has most of its international financial activities located on Hong Kong island rather than its small foothold on mainland China. These financial centres grew as islands of hospitality to western banks and business. They are, as Shanghai and Beirut were, places where the financial transactions of western capitalism can be safely, efficiently and profitably conducted, in English. Once started, further growth was encouraged by economies of scale and agglomeration. Such was the size of these economies, that only a major change in a centre's reputation, haven status or accessibility could, by prompting a large number of exits, lead to its decline and disappearance.

Notes

1 This chapter has benefited enormously from comments on an earlier draft by Mark Casson, Paul Campayne, Frances Moss and Brian Quinn, and from comments by Mira Wilkins and other participants at the Geneva Conference. I would like to thank Grindlays Bank and

the Hongkong Bank Group for permission to cite material from their confidential archives.

2 Many economists are critical of, or dubious about, the concept of international trade in services. See, for example, H. G. Grubel, 'There is no direct international trade in services', *American Economic Review*, Papers and Proceedings (1987). For a contrary view, which defines trade in financial services 'in terms of value added created using the factors of production of one country and then sold to residents of another country', see Ingo Walter, *Global competition in financial services* (Cambridge, Mass, 1988), especially chapter 5.

3 Howard Curtis Reed, *The preeminence of international financial centers* (New York, 1981), pp. 3–7.

4 Paul Campayne suggests that, using this typology, a type D should be introduced, consisting of specialized global centres, such as Chicago (futures markets) and Zurich (fund management).

5 Reed, *Preeminence*, *passim*. For contradictory evidence on Singapore's importance, see p. 41. Reed sees five types of international and financial centres by 1980: host international financial centres, international financial centres (including Bahrain, Beirut, Singapore and Sydney in 1980), supranational financial centres of the second order (including Hong Kong in 1980), supranational financial centres of the first order (New York and Tokyo in 1980); and the supranational financial centre (London).

6 F. H. H. King, *The history of the Hong Kong and Shanghai Banking Corporation* (Cambridge, 1988) III, pp. 368–71.

7 F. H. H. King, *The History of the Hong Kong and Shanghai Banking Corporation* (Cambridge, 1988), II, pp. 457–8.

8 Jurgen Osterhammel, 'British business in China, 1860–1950s', in R. P. T. Davenport-Hines and Geoffrey Jones (eds.), *British business in Asia since 1860* (Cambridge, 1989), p. 202.

9 Stephanie Jones, *Two centuries of overseas trading* (London, 1986), chapter 6.

10 Wong Lin Ken, 'Singapore: its growth as an entrepot port, 1819–1941', *Journal of Southeast Asian Studies*, 26 (1978); J. J. van Helten and Geoffrey Jones, 'British business in Malaysia and Singapore since the 1870s', in Davenport-Hines and Jones, *British business*, pp. 160–1.

11 W. G. Huff, 'Book keeping barter, money, credit and Singapore's international rice trade, 1870–1939', *Explorations in Economic History* (1989).

12 B. R. Tomlinson, *The political economy of the Raj* (London, 1979), p. 44; A. G. Chandavarkar, 'Money and credit', in D. Kumar (ed.), *The Cambridge economic history of India* (Cambridge, 1983); Reed, *Preeminence*, includes Bombay and Calcutta as one of his top ten 'international banking centres' in 1925, but they subsequently disappear from his lists until after the Second World War.

13 Rodney Wilson, *Banking and finance in the Arab Middle East* (London, 1983), pp. 57–60; Abdul-Amir Badrud-Din, *The Bank of Lebanon. Central banking in a financial centre and entrepôt* (London, 1984), pp. 141ff.
14 Geoffrey Jones, *Banking and oil* (Cambridge, 1987), pp. 190–1.
15 Wilson, *Banking*, p. 59.
16 Badrun-Din, *Bank of Lebanon*, 161–2.
17 There is an enormous literature on the growth of the Euromarkets. For links between this and the growth of 'offshore' centres, see J. Sengupta, 'Internationalization of banking and the relationship between foreign and domestic banks in the developing countries', *International Journal of Development Banking*, 16 (1988); Sarah Bartlett, 'Transnational banking: A case of transfer parking with money', in R. Murray (ed.), *Multinationals beyond the market* (Brighton, 1981); Reed, *Preeminence*, p. 53.
18 S. R. Choi, A. E. Tschoegl and C. M. Yu, 'Banks and the world's major financial centers, 1970–1980', *Weltwirtschaftliches Archiv* (1986) ranks financial centres on the basis of the number of the world's Top 300 banks with an office in the centre in question. Singapore was ranked the eleventh largest international financial centre in 1970 and sixth in 1980. Hong Kong eighth in 1970 and fifth in 1980.
19 S. Y. Lee, 'The Asian dollar market, Asian bond market, and the Hongkong Bank Group', in F. H. H. King (ed.), *Eastern banking* (London, 1983); S. Y. Lee and Y. C. Yao, *Financial structures and monetary policies in Southeast Asia* (London, 1982).
20 Hafiz Mirza, *Multinationals and the growth of the Singapore economy* (London, 1986), p. 127.
21 Y. C. Yao, 'The rise of Hong Kong as a financial centre', *Asian Survey*, 19 (July 1979).
22 Lee, 'Asian dollar market', p. 578.
23 R. Wilson, 'Financial development in the Arab Gulf: The Eastern Bank experience 1917–50', *Business History*, 29 (1987).
24 Jones, *Banking and oil*, p. 172.
25 Wilson, *Banking*, pp. 110–19; Talal Shoker, 'Offshore financial centres in the Middle East', Institute of European Finance, Research Papers in Banking and Finance RP 88/21 (1988), University College of North Wales, Bangor; Arab Banking Survey, *Financial Times*, 25 November 1987.
26 Jones, *Banking and oil*, pp. 198–204.
27 Shoker, 'Offshore financial centres', pp. 3–4.
28 Michael T. Skully, 'Financial institutions and markets in Australia', in M. T. Skully (ed.), *Financial institutions and markets in the South-west Pacific* (London, 1985), p. 4.
29 D. T. Merrett, *ANZ Bank* (Sydney, 1985), pp. 295–301.
30 There was a surge of foreign investment in Australian financial institutions in the late 1960s and early 1970s. 'Overseas participation

in Australian investment banking and financial institutions', *Financial Review* (1970); 'Big London banks forge links with Australia', *The Australian*, 9 July 1971.

31 'Hong Kong as a Financial Centre', *Financial Times*, 26 October 1988.

32 Arab Banking Survey, *Financial Times*, 15 November 1987.

33 Shoker, 'Offshore financial centres', p. 13.

34 Derek F. Channon, *Global banking strategy* (Chichester, 1988), p. 56.

35 *Far Eastern Economic Review*, 14 April 1988, p. 65.

36 C. P. Kindleberger, 'The formation of financial centers; A study in comparative economic history', *Princeton Studies in International Finance*, No. 36 (1974) p. 1.

37 Reed, *Preeminence*; H. W. Arndt, 'Comparative advantage in trade in financial services', *Banca nazionale del lavoro* (1988). In addition to the empirical literature cited above, see also D. Germidis and Charles-Albert Michalet, *International banks and financial markets in developing countries* (Development Centre Studies, OECD, Paris, 1984), chapter 3 on offshore financial centres.

38 'Hong Kong as a Financial Centre', *Financial Times*, 26 October 1988; 'Hong Kong shows political nature', *Financial Times*, 26 May 1989.

39 Channon, *Global banking strategy*, p. 4.

40 For the theoretical debate on the merits of 'free banking' versus having a central bank, see B. Klein, 'The competitive supply of money', *Journal of Money, Credit and Banking*, 6 (1974); R. G. King, 'On the economics of private money', *Journal of Monetary Economies*, 12 (1983); Charles Goodhart, *The evolution of central banks* (Cambridge, Mass. 1988).

41 R. N. Drake to C. R. Wardle, 14 April 1949, Mercantile Bank Archives MB 970, Hongkong Bank Group Archives.

42 Badrun-Din, *Bank of Lebanon*, pp. 27–35.

43 Lee and Yao, *Financial structures*, pp. 224–5.

44 Ibid., p. 47; Yao, 'Rise', pp. 690–1. 'Hong Kong as a business and trading centre' *Financial Times*, 8 November 1989.

45 Jones, *Banking and oil*, pp. 243–9; information on the Indian business of Mercantile Bank of India and National and Grindlays Bank from Hongkong Bank Group Archives, and Grindlays Bank Archives respectively.

46 Draft Strategic Concept, 14 December 1971, Office of the Chairman, Grindlays Bank Archives.

47 Jones, *Banking and oil*, pp. 135–149.

48 Wilson, *Banking*, p. 111.

49 'Economic Prospects. The Next Five to Ten Years', report by William M. Clarke, July 1971, Office of the Chairman, Grindlays Bank Archives.

50 Yao, *Rise*, p. 686.

51 Germidis and Michalet, *International banks*, p. 78 dub such havens as 'fictitious offshore financial centres'. Walter, *Global competition*, p. 161, distinguishes places such as Hong Kong and Singapore from countries 'like the Bahamas and the Cayman Islands, which represent "booking" rather than "functional" centers (the actual transactions are done elsewhere)'. For information on the Caribbean tax havens, see *Euromoney* (May 1989) supplement on 'Treasure Islands'.
52 Yao, *Rise*, p. 685.
53 Lee and Yao, *Financial structures*, p. 225.
54 Wilson, *Banking*, p. 57.
55 Mirza, *Multinationals*, p. 125.
56 F. H. H. King, 'The Hong Kong open market, 1954', in F. H. H. King (ed.), *Asian policy, history and development* (Hong Kong, 1979): F. H. H. King, *The history of the Hong Kong and Shanghai Banking Corporation*, IV (Cambridge 1991), pp. 345–7. On the 'Kuwait Gap', see Jones, *Banking and oil*, pp. 137–8.
57 Wilson, *Banking*, p. 58.
58 For the case of the Middle East, see Jones, *Banking and oil*, p. 288.
59 Arndt, 'Comparative advantage', p. 72; Channon, *Global banking strategy*, p. 72; Mirza, *Multinationals*, p. 123.
60 Kindleberger, 'Formation', p. 11.
61 The importance of external economies of scale is stressed in an unpublished Bank of England report on London's position as a financial centre cited in 'The City finds its head start under attack', *Financial Times*, 1 June 1989. See also Economists Advisory Group, *City 2000, The future of London as an international financial centre* (London, 1984), chapter 2.
62 Sengupta, 'Internationalization of banking', p. 42.
63 R. P. T. Davenport-Hines and Geoffrey Jones, 'British business in Asia since 1860', in Davenport-Hines and Jones, *British business*, p. 10.

22 Extra-European financial centres: comments

MIRA WILKINS

The last three chapters are very different and excellent. I will consider each in turn. Apropos the introduction to Dr K. Burk's essay, I am not yet prepared to write off the United States as being necessarily superseded by Japan – challenged yes, but the dollar remains a far more significant currency than the yen. True, America is now a debtor nation in international accounts – by official reports.[1] And, true, Japan appears to be the world's leading creditor nation. Yet, as ultimately Dr Burk concludes, Tokyo is still far from being *the* global financial hub.

Dr Burk documents the rise of New York as a financial centre. Before the First World War, the United States was a debtor nation in international accounts, attracting more foreign capital than it invested abroad. At the eve of the First World War, it was the world's premier debtor nation.[2] At the same time, it was starting to serve as a lender, and even more important, its companies were beginning – in fact on quite a substantial scale – to make foreign *direct* investments.[3] The United States by the turn of the century was already the world's largest manufacturing country, an industrial colossus. The United States Steel Corporation had a capital of over $1 billion.

In the financial sphere superiority came later, with the First World War (1914–1918) the transition period; after 1918, the United States emerged as a creditor nation. The change was dramatic.[4] The US economy was stimulated by the war; by contrast, the British economy was disrupted. Charles Kindleberger has argued that, in the aftermath of the First World War, and through the interwar years, there was no global financial leadership – either by New York or London.[5] New York was not prepared to assume leadership, while London was not able to resume leadership. Earlier James Nordyke had written that the existence of New York and London as financial centres in the interwar period created 'a kind of external diseconomy or social cost ... and this multi-centred system appeared to contain inherent instabilities'.[6] Clearly, in the 1920s, however, many transactions that once went through London moved through New York. The New York Stock Exchange, before the First World War a purely domestic market,[7] now dealt on a regular basis with foreign securities.

After the Second World War, the United States achieved undisputed global financial (and industrial) hegemony.[8] Yet, I find Dr Burk's point on how the United Kingdom 'was forced' to cooperate with the United States in Bretton Woods very curious. After all, it was John Maynard Keynes, along with Harry Dexter White, who worked closely in the establishment of this post-war system.

Throughout her paper, Dr Burk treats the financial sector as separate from the underlying economic conditions in Britain and the United States. America's financial prowess and New York's ascent as a financial centre was based on the growth of the *nation's* absolute and relative economic strength. Yet, the re-emergence of London as a financial emporium in the 1970s and 1980s seems more linked with the heritage of experience than predicated on Britain's economic prowess. Like Amsterdam in the nineteenth century, London has retained its position as a financial centre long after its relative industrial (and more general economic) status has diminished.

Dr Burk writes of the United States, Europe, and Japan as financial centres, but her historical exposition is on New York, London, and peripherally Tokyo. Financial centres are still in *cities*. They emerge – or so it seems to me – more through the dynamics of the market place than through public policies *per se*. Dr Burk's conclusion, 'if the UK government takes sensible decisions' implies conscious acts of state in relationship to the viability of financial centres. But her narrative has shown that the two *state* actions most affecting the course of London as a financial centre were the decisions to declare war in 1914 and 1939 – decisions that surely must be evaluated as 'sensible' or 'not sensible' by criteria distinct from any relevant to the role of London as a financial centre. In sum, Dr Burk's paper demonstrates that, in the case of the United Kingdom, *political* decisions (to participate in the two world wars) – decisions made with little or no regard for the *financial* consequences – most profoundly affected the viability of England as an economic power and, more particularly, London as a financial centre.

Professor Yamazaki's essay, by contrast with Dr Burk's, is one that deals with a single, highly significant bank in a short, but very important period of Japanese economic history. Professor Yamazaki gives us hitherto unpublished – at least in English – details on the characteristics of the assets and liabilities of the Yokohama Specie Bank in late 1929, just before Japan removed the embargo on gold exports (imposed in 1917). He shows how the bank's accounts changed 1929–31. In doing so, he provides a rare glimpse into the internal functionings of the major Japanese overseas bank.

In my comments I will consider this paper in connection with our theme of finance and financiers in Europe. The first item that stands out for me is the problem of how one defines an international financial centre? Clearly, the Yokohama Specie Bank, headquartered in Yokohama from its origin in 1879 to the time of the Second World War, was engaged in international trade and international finance. It was a multi-national bank which very early in its history established itself in London and New York and indeed worldwide. But, do the connections of this one bank – albeit a very significant bank – make Yokohama a financial centre? Did *foreign* financial institutions set up a base in Yokohama? Was Yokohama a truly cosmopolitan city? That is not evident. The yen in 1929–31 was far from being an 'international currency'. I believe it is probably far-fetched (and ahistorical) to call Yokohama a major financial centre in 1930, the year Japan was able to return to the gold standard.

Second, do the transactions of the Yokohama Specie Bank in world markets help us define and clarify the relative position of London and New York as financial centres? Here the answers seem more positive. Professor Yamazaki's table 20.14 (on 1927) suggests the importance of London. In 1929, the Yokohama Specie Bank's borrowings in London were greater than in New York (see table 20.2). Yet, during 1929–31, New York seems in most ways the more significant centre (Compare tables 20.9 and 20.13).

Despite Professor Yamazaki's discussion of the important *dollar* transactions in these years, it is *after* England abandons the gold standard (September 1931) that Japan follows in December. One can assume a connection and if so, clearly, British leadership would seem of paramount importance. All of this goes to confirm the notion of an ill-defined (or shifting) centre in the interwar years.

As further confirmation of the ambiguities, when I viewed Professor Yamazaki's table 20.6 on the Yokohama Specie Bank's controlled selling of dollars between August 1930 and March 1932, I was impressed by how incidental Europeans seemed. In this period, among the ten largest buyers of dollars from the Yokohama Specie Bank, the *only* London incorporated bank involved was the Chartered Bank, an eastern exchange bank. On the other hand, the listing of the Netherland Trading Society, which bought 4.3 per cent of the dollars in the first period (August 1930 to August 1931), came as a surprise. Amsterdam as a financial centre has not been discussed in the previous chapters; were these Dutch transactions an anomaly?

New York was, as noted, a relatively new international financial centre in 1929. In October 1929 the famous New York Stock Market crash took place, with worldwide ramifications. Obviously the Japanese, when they resumed the gold standard in January 1930 – like many Americans in January 1930 – did not understand the implications of the crash. I would have liked to have seen Professor Yamazaki discuss the effects on the Yokohama Specie Bank during 1930 and 1931 of the economic downturn in the United States – and more specifically how the crash affected the relative position of financial centres (as reflected in the strategies of Yokohama Specie Bank).

Professor Yamazaki attributes the abandonment by Japan of the gold standard in December 1931 not to what was happening in the world economy but to the change in political circumstances in Japan, a new government and a new finance minister. If one argues that this abandonment related to political conditions, surely Professor Yamazaki should mention and discuss the implications of the Japanese invasion of Manchuria in September 1931 and the new conditions created by the military action. Professor Yamazaki's paper is, however, for the most part apolitical. The Yokohama Specie Bank, he writes, had borrowed from New York banks to the 'limit' by December 1931. What was the impact of the Manchurian incident?[9]

The Yokohama Specie Bank continued as a major overseas bank until the US entry into the Second World War. Its post-war successor, the Bank of Tokyo, has played a prominent role in the emergence of today's Japan as a financial power. Much of the human capital from the Yokohama Specie Bank remained in the successor organization; indeed, that knowhow certainly contributed after the Second World War to transforming Tokyo into a truly formidable global financial centre.

The third paper in this group is of yet a different nature. It is a stimulating discussion of financial centres on the periphery. Unlike in the late nineteenth, early twentieth century, when we had a worldwide diffusion of capital, in the post First World War years and particularly in the post Second World War ones, we have had a diffusion beyond Europe's boundaries of *financial centres*, New York, Tokyo and many others. Some of these 'many others' are the subject of Geoffrey Jones's essay. The diffusion has in recent times moved very far afield – virtually always influenced from the European core. None of the centres that Jones deals with has yet become 'global'. Each remains limited in many respects.

Jones's article contains a wealth of new material and is a most thoughtful presentation. Here again *political* considerations seem highly relevant in the emergence and persistence of the international financial entrepôts. Shanghai disappears as a financial centre with the advent of a communist China; Hong Kong rises to more than fill the gap. Beirut becomes a political nightmare; Bahrain replaces Lebanon as a middle-eastern regional financial hub. I like what Dr Jones has written on regulation, although New York City became an international financial centre despite US and New York state heavy regulation of foreign banking institutions. Likewise, regulation of foreign banks in Tokyo is still far from slight. Perhaps stability – predictability – is more important for a major financial centre than the absence of government intervention.

What is the relationship between stock markets and international financial centres? For European ones, the stock market usually seemed a necessary adjunct. So, too, New York had a significant, active domestic Stock Exchange, indeed, Stock Exchanges, long before New York City became a global financial centre. How does one integrate this with an analysis of the periphery?

Note that the small economies, Taiwan and South Korea, former Japanese colonies and always included as newly industrializing nations, are *not* among Jones's financial centres. Is it that their heritage was Japanese rather than European – and Japan's post Second World War triumph was first and foremost industrial, and only very recently has Japan, because of its capital riches, become a world-class financial power?

Great Britain and the United States (and Japan) became industrial giants first and then financial leaders; some of the countries where the new financial centres are located do not seem to have taken the industrial step first, although others seem to follow that pattern. How important today, and yesterday, is industrialization to regional and global financial centres?

These three contributions are linked with the substance of this conference in various ways. First, while the theme of the conference is finance and financiers in Europe, essentially what emerges from both the Burk and Jones papers is that the inspiration for financial centres worldwide is not really Europe, but England – and not really England but London. Where is the overseas financial centre inspired by Berlin, Brussels, Zurich or Stockholm? Paris undoubtedly influenced Beirut and Amsterdam the centres in Curaçao and Aruba, but these are exceptions. The nineteenth- and twentieth-century story is overwhelmingly about the impact of London. This is not merely a matter of empire: Jakarta did not become a financial centre, nor did Saigon. There was something very special about London.

There is a second point in this context related to Latin America and Africa, the two continents not covered in the three papers considered in this section. In Central and South America there was (at least until the late 1980s) one financial centre of great significance: Panama. In its heyday, it fit all of Jones's criteria: the city was within a small economy, with a reputation for financial secrecy and safety, with a willingness to act as a haven, and it was easily accessible. Here there was little or no British influence. There was, however, the Panama Canal and sizeable US influence. The US dollar was legal currency. As for Africa, Johannesburg remains a provincial rather than an international centre; no other financial emporium has emerged.

A third point deals with the problem of national treatment. Financial centres are by their very nature cosmopolitan. All of us have difficulty in handling the melange of nationalities in a single centre. London is not simply British; it has within its boundaries institutions from many countries. For the preeminent centres, it is not so much comparative history that is important but rather the study over time of cross-border institutions that operate within the financial centres and engage in complex intrafirm transactions on a global basis.

Certainly from the late nineteenth century onwards (and perhaps even earlier), financial centres on the European continent have been and continue to be subordinate in stature to London. And, in concluding this closing synthesis, we should end on a note of wonderment. Why is it with the triumph of continental western Europe that London remains *the* global financial centre, re-emerging after an era of being temporarily eclipsed by New York? Why when we talk of periphery centres in extra-European areas is New York as the influence generally subordinate to London? Is London triumphant because of the English language, as Jones has suggested? (New York also has the English language.) Why is it that the extra-European centres tend to be regional or specialized, while the continental European city centres likewise tend to be regional and specialized? In the nineteenth and twentieth centuries only London and in the twentieth century, to a lesser extent, New York – and potentially perhaps Tokyo – seem to take first rank.

Notes

1 A number of American economists (including Raymond Vernon and Robert Eisner) believe that the 'official' figures misrepresent the actuality, that US direct investment abroad is at book value and thus underestimated; as a consequence of this, America now is in fact a creditor rather than a debtor in world accounts.

2 Mira Wilkins, *The history of foreign investment in the United States to 1914* (Cambridge, Mass., 1989).

3 Mira Wilkins, *The emergence of multinational enterprise: American business abroad from the colonial era to 1914* (Cambridge, Mass., 1970).

4 Mira Wilkins, *The maturing of multinational enterprise: American business abroad from 1914 to 1970* (Cambridge, Mass., 1974), chapter 1.

5 Charles P. Kindleberger, *The world in depression, 1929–1939* (Berkeley, Calif. 1973).

6 James W. Nordyke, International finance and New York: the role of the outflow of private financial capital from the United States in the determination of the significance of New York as a center of international finance, 1958 Princeton University dissertation, published New York, 1976, pp. 15, 245–6.

7 R. C. Michie, *The London and New York stock exchanges 1850–1914* (London, 1987), p. 271.

8 At least, by the 1950s, everyone was convinced of this. It is interesting to read in Nordyke's 1958 dissertation that 'The failure of United States institutions to participate in financing non-United States trade is connected with what is generally thought to be a deficiency in the amount of capital exported from the United States, a deficiency which official policy has sought to remedy by encouraging private credit extension to foreigners.' See Nordyke, *International finance*, p. 247.

9 I am asking a rhetorical question, since I have discussed the impact at length in Mira Wilkins, 'The role of US business' in Dorothy Borg and Shumpei Okamoto (eds.), *Pearl Harbor as history: Japanese-American relations 1931–1941* (New York and London, 1973), pp. 353ff.

INDEX